3 9153 00939648 4

P9-BXV-226

THE SOCIAL AND ECONOMIC HISTORY OF THE HELLENISTIC WORLD

I. Portrait of Alexander the Great

The 'Azara' herm of the Louvre. Poor Roman copy of an excellent Greek original. The style is that of Lysippus. Inscription: *'Αλέξανδρος | Φιλίππου | Μακεδών.*

Photograph supplied by Archives Photographiques

THE SOCIAL & ECONOMIC HISTORY OF THE HELLENISTIC WORLD

By

M. ROSTOVTZEFF

Hon. D.Litt., Hon. Litt.D. (Cambridge)
Hon. Litt.D. (Harvard), Hon. Litt.D. (Wisconsin)
Professor of Ancient History in Yale University

VOLUME I

OXFORD
AT THE CLARENDON PRESS

Oxford University Press, Amen House, London E.C.4
GLASGOW NEW YORK TORONTO MELBOURNE WELLINGTON
BOMBAY CALCUTTA MADRAS KARACHI LAHORE DACCA
CAPE TOWN SALISBURY NAIROBI IBADAN ACCRA
KUALA LUMPUR HONG KONG

FIRST EDITION 1941
REPRINTED LITHOGRAPHICALLY IN GREAT BRITAIN
AT THE UNIVERSITY PRESS, OXFORD
FROM CORRECTED SHEETS OF THE FIRST EDITION
1953, 1959, 1964

PREFACE

It is hardly necessary to insist upon the importance of the so-called 'Hellenistic' age in the history of mankind. As every student of ancient history knows, the old-fashioned conception of this age as a time of decay of Greek civilization and of a pitiful collapse of Greek political life is unfounded or at least one-sided and misleading. Without doubt the Greeks of the Hellenistic period developed great creative activity in all departments of their life and were responsible for many, sometimes fundamental, novelties in the political, social, economic, and cultural development of the ancient world. Under their beneficent influence other nations remodelled their own institutions and in consequence achieved brilliant results in many directions.

This book is devoted to the study of one aspect of the Hellenistic world. A few words to define what I mean by the term 'Hellenistic world' will not be out of place. The history of the modern word 'Hellenistic' and the various meanings assigned to it cannot be discussed here. Suffice it to say that the term, as I use it, has definite implications in respect of chronology, geography, politics, and civilization. By 'Hellenistic world' I mean the world created by Alexander's conquest of the East, which existed as long as the States into which it disintegrated retained their political independence, and the Greeks in those States held the leading role in all spheres of life; that is to say, approximately from the time of Alexander to that of Augustus. It covered the area of the former empire of Alexander with some slight additions such as the Bosporan kingdom, certain parts of Asia Minor, the Sicilian kingdom of Hiero II, and some Greek city-states. Though these last never formed part of Alexander's Empire, they were Greek in their structure and civilization, and did not differ in this respect from the rest of the Hellenistic world.

My study is therefore not a social and economic history of the ancient world in the Hellenistic period. I have excluded from my special treatment various important parts of it, such as, on the one hand, the so-called 'Barbarians' of Europe, Africa, and Asia—Scythians, Sarmatians, Thracians, Illyrians,

Celts, Iberians; and, on the other, two groups of highly civilized and well-organized States, one in the West—Italy, most of Sicily, and Carthage—and another in the East and South—China, India, Parthia, south Arabia, Nubia, and Meroe.

This geographical limitation of my field of investigation requires some words of explanation, especially as regards the two groups of highly civilized States and nations just mentioned, which stood in varying degrees under Greek influence and some of which included several Greek States and other organized groups of Greek settlers. The exclusion of the western group from my study was dictated by several considerations, of which the most important may be formulated as follows. Although the relations between Rome and Carthage, the two leading States of the West, on the one hand, and the eastern section of the Mediterranean world on the other were very close and the Greek element was strongly represented in their population, the former were not in fact Greek States, nor was the character of their social and economic structure and of their civilization Greek in its essential features. In Italy the 'Italians' gradually built up their own peculiar political, social, economic, and cultural life and extended it in course of time to Sicily, Gaul, and Spain; in Africa the Phoenicians did the same. These regions can therefore hardly be included in the notion of the 'Hellenistic world', however close they may stand to it. To study their peculiar social and economic structure in the Hellenistic period in the light of their own past and with due attention to the influence exerted on them by the eastern section of the ancient world would certainly be a fascinating and highly important undertaking. But it would require much space and much special research. If such a study had been included in this book, as I had originally contemplated, it would have doubled its size while contributing little to a correct understanding of the Greek and Hellenistic East. The subject requires treatment in a separate work, which would centre on the West, a task which I am too old to undertake. I know that my point of view in regard to this geographical limitation is not shared by the majority of modern historians of the ancient world. I anticipate their criticism.

The situation is similar as regards the second, the eastern

and southern group of civilized States more or less closely connected with the Hellenistic world. Most of them stood, in varying degrees, under the influence of Hellenistic civilization and absorbed some of its features, which affected to a certain extent their social and economic evolution. But they never became constituent parts of the Hellenistic world, even to such an extent as did Italy and north Africa. They retained in full their national and political identity, and their social and economic life in the Hellenistic period was practically a continuation of their past, only slightly affected by foreign, that is to say, Hellenistic influences.

An examination of their social and economic development in the Hellenistic period, of the foreign elements which contributed thereto, and of the part played therein by the changes of a general character which Alexander's conquests effected in the ancient world, is one of the important tasks which face an historian of antiquity. But, as in the case of the West, it is a separate undertaking which could not be carried out within the framework of the present book. Moreover it requires special competence and knowledge (in the first place acquaintance with several Oriental languages) which I do not possess. The social and economic evolution of the Hellenistic world was not, in my opinion, fundamentally affected by the trend which this evolution took on its eastern and southern periphery.

Nevertheless, when and where the contact with these two groups of States and with the so-called 'Barbarians' appeared to me an important and in some cases a decisive factor in the evolution of the Hellenistic world, I have paid, in the measure of my capacity, due attention to it. This is the reason why both the western and eastern extremities of the Hellenistic world play a larger part in the second volume of this work than in the first.

In dealing with the Hellenistic world I have confined myself to its social and economic aspect, but not because this aspect of Hellenistic life had been neglected by modern scholars. Several eminent historians of the ancient world have included in general surveys of the Hellenistic period or in special monographs on certain parts of it excellent chapters concerned with its social and economic features. Nor have I thus limited the scope of my book because I regarded these features as more important for an understanding of Hellenistic life than those which belong to the political, constitutional, cultural, or religious spheres. While appreciating the importance of the social and economic aspect of human life in general, I do not overestimate it, in the Marxian fashion. My reason for restricting the field of my investigation is purely personal: I imagine that I am more competent in this field than in others. I have, however, kept before me as a guiding principle, in this as in the other historical works which I have written, the maxim that the complexity of life should never be forgotten and that no single feature should ever be regarded as basic and decisive.

To the material relating to the Hellenistic world I have applied the same method as I adopted in my previous study of the Roman Empire. The present work, that is to say, is not intended to be a social and economic survey of the Hellenistic world or an essay on ancient economics and sociology. I have sought to present some pages of history. In the title I have chosen for it the emphasis lies not so much on 'social' and 'economic' as on 'history'. This aim explains the structure of the book. I was obliged to set out the material in historical sequence, to follow the trend of evolution, to deal with the social and economic phenomena in the light of the general political, constitutional, and cultural development of the time. This method is, of course, not free from objection. It requires much space. Moreover it disperses to some extent the attention of the reader and makes repetition at times unavoidable. But it has the advantage of presenting the social and economic features of human life not as dry abstractions, in the form of statistics and tabulations, but as living dynamic phenomena, indivisible from and closely correlated with other equally important features of that life. To enable the reader to sum up the results of my historical study, I have added to the seven historical chapters an eighth chapter in which I have endeavoured to enumerate and to discuss, sometimes at greater length than in the historical chapters, certain basic elements in the Hellenistic economy which we may regard as creations of that period.

Planned originally as a short survey, the book has in course of elaboration become intolerably long, more than twice as long as my volume on the Roman Empire. This I very greatly regret. There is much truth in the witty remark of one of the greatest Hellenistic writers: μέγα βιβλίον, μέγα κακόν. But its length could not have been much reduced. It is in part explained by the method of treatment referred to above; but it is mainly due to the character of our evidence, which is scanty and hopelessly scattered, very difficult to date, to arrange, to understand, and to interpret. The problems present themselves in long series, and very few can be solved with a fair degree of probability. In these conditions it was impossible to put forward mere statements unsupported by the production and discussion of the relative evidence. I fully realize the irritation that such discussions may cause and the interruptions they unfortunately introduce in the flow of my narrative. But they were inevitable, since I had no intention of setting forth as facts what are, in general, no more than more or less probable conjectures.

To this general explanation I may add some remarks concerning the composition of the book and the material that I have used. In discussing the economic and social evolution of the Hellenistic world I have endeavoured to treat it as a unit, in spite of its growing political, social, and economic differentiation. But since its constituent parts present far-reaching peculiarities, which became ever more accentuated as time went on, it was necessary to subdivide Chapters IV, V, and VI into sections, each dealing with one part of the Hellenistic world. In this subdivision I have not followed a rigid scheme. Since the centre of gravity shifted gradually from one part of that world to another, certain regions have, in some periods, been given greater prominence, attention, and space than in others, and the order of their treatment has varied in each chapter.[1] I have, however, in proceeding thus, endeavoured to

[1] For example, in the case of Rhodes and Delos. In Ch. IV these important centres of economic life are discussed in the section devoted to the cities of the mainland of Greece and of the Greek islands, while in Ch. V they are dealt with in connexion with the Oriental monarchies, and in Ch. VI a special section is allotted to them.

keep a certain balance. It was difficult to avoid being led astray by the abundance of evidence relating to one locality and the scarcity relating to another; to avoid over-emphasizing, for example, Delos and Athens at the expense of Rhodes and the other leading cities of the Hellenistic world, or Egypt at the expense of Syria, Macedonia, and Pergamon. And yet a somewhat larger space had inevitably to be assigned to the better-known regions, regardless of their importance at a given period, in order to make as full use as possible of the available evidence.

As regards the material used in the treatment of my subject, I have tried not to confine myself to written sources, but also to utilize to the utmost the archaeological and numismatic testimony. I am fully aware how difficult the enterprise was and how imperfect are the results. Much has been done in the field of archaeology and numismatics in the last century, an enormous mass of information has accumulated. But in this brilliant development the share of the Hellenistic period has been rather meagre. Not that little material has been discovered. The material is overwhelmingly abundant. But very little attention has been paid to its systematic collection, dating, and study, especially from the economic standpoint. In these conditions it is probable that errors will be even more numerous in the part of my book which is based on this evidence than in that which rests on written sources. But an endeavour in this direction was imperative, and I was not to be deterred by the fear of reprimands from critics more expert in archaeology and numismatics than myself.

It is fortunate that I have been able not only to refer to and to make use of the archaeological and numismatic material but also, thanks to the liberality of the Clarendon Press, to present some of it to the reader in reproductions on separate plates and in line-drawings in the text. The illustrations are not intended to amuse the reader and to console him for the dryness of the text and notes. They form an important constituent part of my work. It was no easy task to select from the thousands of objects stored in museums and from the hundreds of extant ruins of ancient buildings and towns the most typical and instructive. The choice was large and the methods of selection many. I have endeavoured to keep a fair balance between two groups of monuments: the sculptures, paintings, mosaics, and ruins of ancient settlements which reflect ancient life, and those which illustrate the economic activity of the Hellenistic world, especially in the field of industry.

If I have been more or less successful in the illustration of my book, I owe it in large part to those institutions and individuals who have helped me by liberally supplying me with photographs and casts, and by their competent assistance in selecting, dating, and interpreting the various objects reproduced. The list of these is very long and their names will be recorded at the end of this Preface. I will here limit myself to mentioning the names of my chief advisers and extending to them my thanks: Prof. J. D. Beazley of Oxford, Miss Gisela M. A. Richter of the Metropolitan Museum of New York, and Prof. Dr. R. Zahn, formerly Director of the Classical Collection of the State Museums of Berlin, in the field of archaeology; and Mr. E. T. Newell, President of the American Numismatic Society, and Prof. A. R. Bellinger of Yale, in that of numismatics.

A few words will suffice as regards my rather copious notes, more copious than those in my *Social and Economic History of the Roman Empire*. In them the reader will find cited the most important ancient sources (literary, epigraphical, papyrological, numismatic, and archaeological) and references to modern works dealing with the problems discussed. In recording the most important epigraphical, papyrological, archaeological, and numismatic material I have endeavoured to keep pace with the feverish activity of modern scholars engaged in the publication of new texts and monuments, and in the restoration and more accurate dating and interpretation of old ones. This has proved no easy task, for modern efforts in this direction produce an uninterrupted flow of articles, notes, and reviews scattered over scores of periodicals and hundreds of books, and I am not confident of complete success. Nor has it been easy to make use of all the major and minor modern contributions to the study of the subjects treated in this book. The number of these contributions is overwhelmingly large and every day increases it. If I have overlooked some, I must ask the indulgence of the authors and of my readers.

In this connexion I must add that the endeavour to make due use of new material and modern contributions has delayed the publication of the book considerably. It was ready in manuscript in 1936. Since that time I have revised it twice. But I could not do so a third time. I have, therefore, to my great regret, not taken systematically into consideration the material and modern studies published in the second half of 1938 and in 1939 and 1940, though I have made such casual references to some of these as could be inserted in the proofs. My evidence, both for source material and for modern works, is naturally more up to date in the last than in the first chapters. Some additions will be found in the few *addenda* and *corrigenda* at the end of the work.

In conclusion a few remarks about certain details in the matter of spelling and citations. I am afraid that in the spelling of Greek and Oriental personal and geographical names I have not been entirely consistent. As regards the latter, the names of countries and cities appear, as a rule, in the latinized form more familiar to my readers. But there are some exceptions to this rule: I have retained, for example, the Greek spelling of the names of the islands and of some cities such as Pergamon and Corupedion, this being more familiar to the reader than the latinized form. As for the personal names I have used the traditional spelling for the most common. For those less common I have done the best I could, especially in spelling Oriental names. In citing periodicals and the most common modern books I have endeavoured to follow in the main the system of abbreviations used in the *Cambridge Ancient History*. But complete uniformity and consistency were unattainable. Everyone who has written a book of considerable length including thousands of references knows how difficult it is to keep in this respect to one and the same uniform standard.

At the end of his Preface an author usually gives himself the pleasure and the privilege of mentioning those who have been kind enough to help him in his work. The list is a long one. My first thanks are due to my dear friend Prof. J. G. C. Anderson and to Sir Paul Harvey. They have not only revised my manuscript and made my English readable—an arduous and tedious task—but have also read all the proofs. Mr. Anderson in addition—in order not to delay unduly the publication of the book in the difficult times in which it was printed—took on himself the task of reading alone the last revision of the proofs and giving the final *imprimatur*. My debt to these two gentlemen is immense.

In the next place I have to express my gratitude to the Clarendon Press. I fully realize that my book does not deserve the care and attention given to it by this famous, broad-minded, and thoroughly scientific institution. And I shall never forget that this care and attention remained the same in the dark days of war as they had been in the brighter days of peace.

The proofs of the book have been read by two of my younger friends: Prof. E. Bikerman, of the École des Hautes Études, Paris, and Prof. C. B. Welles of Yale. They have saved me from many errors and have made interesting and valuable suggestions of which I have made due use. I am much indebted and very grateful to them.

I must also mention that my still younger friends and students, Dr. Leroy Campbell, Dr. R. Fink, and Dr. F. Gilliam, have helped me to verify the thousands of references in the text and notes. If, nevertheless, many errors remain, it is not their fault.

Several of my learned friends have been kind enough to supply me with statements relating to obscure and controversial problems, or have given me first-hand information on monuments with which they are especially familiar. Some of these statements (those of J. G. Milne, Oxford, Prof. R. P. Blake, Harvard, E. S. G. Robinson, British Museum, and F. O. Waagé, Cornell University) are printed as separate Excursuses. Others are incorporated in the text, notes, and descriptions of the plates. Such are the contributions of A. R. Boak concerning Karanis, of F. E. Brown concerning Dura, of A. von Gerkan concerning Miletus, of C. Hopkins concerning Seleuceia on the Tigris, of J. Keil concerning the monument of Belevi, of F. Krischen concerning Cnidus, of the late Prof. J. H. Rogers of Yale concerning the problem of inflation, of H. Seyrig, Director of the Service of Antiquities in Syria, concerning various monuments of Syria, and of P. R. Mouterde concerning the royal weights of Syria.

I have mentioned above that in collecting the material for my illustrations I have had repeated recourse to the help and support of various learned institutions and of private individuals who happened to be in possession of interesting objects. Their response to my appeal was always cordial and their help liberal. It is a special pleasure to me to name them here and to extend to them my sincerest thanks. As regards private scholars and collectors, I remember with gratitude the assistance of Dr. Chr. Blinkenberg, Dr. O. Brendel, Count Chandon des Briailles, Prof. F. Krischen, Mrs. William H. Moore, Mr. R. W. Smith, Sir Aurel Stein, Sir Leonard Woolley. Much longer is the list of museums and other learned institutions which have never refused me their help and assistance. Let me record, in the U.S.A., the Metropolitan Museum of Arts in New York, the Boston Museum of Fine Arts, the Chicago Oriental Institute, the Yale Gallery of Fine Arts, the Princeton Expedition to Antioch, the Michigan Seleuceia Expedition, the Yale Dura Expedition; in France, the Louvre and the Cabinet des Médailles; in England, the British Museum; in Germany, the German Archaeological Institute and the Museums of Berlin, Munich, Gotha, and the Pelizaeus Museum of Hildesheim; in Denmark, the Ny Carlsberg Glyptothek; in Holland, the Allard Pierson Museum of Amsterdam; in Rumania, the Museum of Bucharest; in Bulgaria, the Museums of Sofia and Plovdiv; in Italy, the Mostra Augustea di Romanità in Rome, the German Archaeological Institute in the same city, and the Museum of Naples; in Egypt, the Museums of Alexandria and Cairo; in Cyrenaica, the Archaeological Service of that country; in Tunisia, the Archaeological Service and the Museum of Bardo; in Greece, the National Museum of Athens and the French School at Athens; in Rhodes, His Excellency the Governor and the Service of Antiquities; in Turkey, the Ottoman Museum; in Iraq, the Bagdad Museum; in Iran, the Museum of Teheran; in Syria, the Service of Antiquities and the Museums of Beirût and Damascus. The authorities of these museums and institutions have liberally supplied me with photographs, drawings, coloured copies, &c., but first and foremost have never refused me their valuable advice. I am deeply indebted to them for it.

The index has been compiled with great care and attention by my wife, Sophie Rostovtzeff.

The book is dedicated to my wife and to my friend Franz Cumont. Without their encouragement and their warm support in dark moments of doubt it would never have been written.

M. R.

August, 1940

Note to Second Impression

PROFESSOR ROSTOVTZEFF was, for reasons of health, unable to co-operate in the preparation of this impression, which had already gone to press before his death on 20 October 1952. I therefore bear sole responsibility for the changes which have been made. These are limited to those which could be made without resetting the book. The first and second volumes stand unchanged save for the correction of a few material errors. In the third volume I have indicated where material to which Rostovtzeff had access before publication has since been published, and where he quoted documents published in periodicals, &c., which have since been republished in standard collections, I have added the reference to the latter. New references to corpora, &c., have been inserted either in the body of Index II or in the Addenda to it. Similarly I have inserted references to new editions of works which have appeared since 1940 in fresh editions. I have added no new material inaccessible to Rostovtzeff. Bibliographical citations have not been checked systematically throughout, but I have corrected all errors I came across.

This is not the place to assess Rostovtzeff's contribution to the study of antiquity, but it may be said without fear of contradiction that it was unique, and that he dominated the historical and archaeological studies of the ancient world in the first half of the twentieth century, no less than, in a slightly different way, Thommsen dominated those of the preceding half century. In a dozen spheres, each demanding its own discipline and technique, he was a pioneer, and to each he brought not only immense learning and prodigious power of research, but also a full awareness of the wider historical issues involved. His main theses always aroused, and will continue to arouse, controversy; but his place among that very small band of scholars whose work marks an epoch in many fields is assured.

P. M. FRASER

November, 1952

CONTENTS

VOLUME III. NOTES

LIST OF PLATES

FIGURES IN THE TEXT

I

POLITICAL DEVELOPMENT

A. THE WAR OF SUCCESSION AND THE FORMATION OF THE LEADING HELLENISTIC MONARCHIES

It may be thought superfluous to begin a book treating chiefly of social and economic questions with a survey of political events. Many excellent surveys of this kind exist, and I might have referred my readers to one of the more recent of these.[1] But I have found it advisable to undertake the tedious task of repeating some well-known facts to the interpretation of which I can add very little. Political events are so closely connected with social and economic phenomena, and in discussing these so many names and circumstances of a political character have to be mentioned, that I have felt it incumbent on me to spare the reader, who may wish to refresh his memory on various points in the complicated political history of the Hellenistic period, the necessity of constant reference to other books, or at least to facilitate recourse to them.

To write a short survey of the political events that followed the death of Alexander is no easy task. Our information is very unevenly distributed over the various portions of this period, some being amply illustrated by reliable literary sources, while others are left in almost complete obscurity by our literary tradition. It will therefore be expedient to begin each section of my survey of political events by describing briefly the character, and estimating the trustworthiness, of the ancient sources bearing on the period. It must be remembered that sometimes the sources which bear on political history also furnish information on economic and social history.

We are fortunate in having abundant and reliable information regarding the earliest period of Hellenistic history, that between the death of Alexander and the battle of Ipsus (323–301 B.C.). Our chief authority is the short account given by Diodorus in Books XVIII–XX of his general history of the ancient world. A far more detailed narrative was that of another writer of Roman times, Arrian, but his history of the Successors ended with the return of Antipater to Europe (321 B.C.), and is known to us only from brief extracts by Photius and from fragments preserved in a Vatican palimpsest and by Suidas. Still shorter than the survey of Diodorus is that furnished by the epitome by Justin of the *Historiae Philippicae* of Pompeius Trogus. We have biographies by Plutarch—vivid and substantial, though not always entirely reliable—of Phocion, Eumenes, Demetrius, and Pyrrhus. Also some biographical essays, shorter and drier, by Cornelius Nepos on Phocion and Eumenes. Pausanias has excellent excursuses dealing with some of the protagonists of our period: Ptolemy, Lysimachus, Seleucus, Pyrrhus; while some of the *Stratagems* of Polyaenus and Frontinus afford useful information. A very interesting fragment of local history is contained in Memnon's historical sketch of Heraclea Pontica. Important chronological data will be found in a fragment of the Chronicle of Paros (336/5–302/1 B.C.) and in some fragments of a Babylonian Chronicle in cuneiform recently found and published.

The bulk of our literary information, at least the most trustworthy part of it, goes back to the detailed history of the early Hellenistic age written by Hieronymus of Cardia, a friend of Eumenes and later a member of the staff of Antigonus. To the groundwork that he provided some supplementary facts were added by later historians of the Hellenistic period and were borrowed from them by the above-named and other writers of Roman times.

It is not surprising to find such an abundance of literary sources for the earliest years of the Hellenistic period, whereas, for those which followed Ipsus, as will be shown later, the extant literary record is almost completely silent. The protagonists of the two decades that followed the death of Alexander, the picturesque figures of Antipater, Craterus, Perdiccas, Eumenes, Antigonus, Demetrius, Ptolemy, Lysimachus, and Seleucus left a deep impression on the ancient world and greatly interested the educated public of Roman times. These decades were the heroic age of the Hellenistic world, and hundreds of stories and anecdotes, centring round its leading men, were current in the literary tradition of the Roman period. Every cultured man of that time was therefore supposed to know something about the early Hellenistic kings.

The literary evidence is supplemented by many important documents. Though few papyri bearing on these years have been found in Egypt, we possess many first-rate inscriptions filling up gaps or illustrating little-known episodes. The abundant series of coins at our disposal are, as usual, very helpful in elucidating certain important chronological and other problems of this period.

So much for the sources of our knowledge about the political events that followed the death of Alexander the Great.[2] His sudden decease created great and widespread confusion throughout the ancient world, but especially in Babylon, where Alexander had been residing, and in the camp of his enormous army. We must not forget that this army had just been reorganized and was ready to start on another great expedition. We must realize also that it was almost exclusively on the army that the power of Alexander rested and that the army knew this and felt itself one with its great leader. It was therefore naturally this army in the field at Babylon, and not the army at home in Macedonia, that regarded itself as entitled, according to Macedonian tradition, to settle the question of the succession on the death of the king. The choice of the army was limited. Alexander had left no children and there remained no adult males of the house of Philip except a half-brother of Alexander, a youth named Arrhidaeus. Since, however, Roxane, the wife of Alexander, was expecting a child, the chiliarch Perdiccas, commander-in-chief of the army, and with him the higher aristocracy and gentry of Macedonia, the officers and the horsemen, who were loyal to Alexander and ready to carry on his policy of creating an Irano-Macedonian Empire, advised the army to await her delivery. But the Macedonian phalanx, which never shared the Irano-Macedonian ideas of Alexander, much preferred a scion of Philip's house, about whom they knew little, but who represented in their eyes the Macedonian tradition of Philip. An acute conflict arose, which was ultimately settled by a compromise. Philip Arrhidaeus was to be proclaimed king on the understanding that if the child of Roxane should be a boy (and it was a boy) he, under the name of Alexander, should be a kind of minor co-ruler with Philip.[3]

By this compromise the unity of the empire was preserved, but only nominally. In fact it was divided among the generals of Alexander (by the redistribution among them of the satrapies), and it was evident that most of these generals were not prepared to obey the orders of those who would act in the name of the king, if they were strong enough to support by force of arms their claim to practical independence. Moreover, though the problem of the succession was settled, the problem of the regency was not. It was decided in Babylon that Perdiccas should be chiliarch, a title which meant commander-in-chief of the army and grand vizir of the empire, but that Craterus should be *προστάτης* of the king, a sort of guardian and prime minister, superior in rank to Perdiccas. Which was to have the decisive voice? The question was settled by an accident. While events were developing in the East, the Macedonian and Greek portion of the empire was in great danger. Here the ruler was old Antipater, the most respected man in the realm, the associate of both Philip and Alexander. He held the command in Macedonia and Greece and in this way controlled the supply both of armed men and of brains, without which Alexander's empire could not exist. He was now engaged in a serious struggle with a powerful and active coalition of Greek States headed by Athens, which soon after the death of Alexander had begun what is known as the Hellenic or Lamian war with the object of restoring the liberty of Greece. The situation of Antipater was difficult. He was besieged (after a defeat) in Lamia, and the prestige, nay the domination, of Macedonia in Greece was at stake. No wonder that Craterus, instead of returning to Babylonia with the 10,000 veterans whom he was leading to Macedonia by Alexander's order, getting control of the kings, and settling the question of the regency, decided to sacrifice his own ambition to the urgent needs of the Macedonian Empire and to leave the question of the regency in suspense. He therefore left the kings in the hands of Perdiccas and continued his march to the West, where he helped Antipater to bring the Hellenic war to a successful conclusion.

This did not mean, however, that Antipater and Craterus recognized Perdiccas as their superior who had the right to give them orders. In fact Perdiccas never dared to do so. And it was only natural that, as soon as Perdiccas was appointed prime minister in place of Craterus and by assuming this office showed unmistakably that he took his position seriously and expected to be obeyed when he gave orders in the name of the kings, not only Antigonus and Ptolemy* among those who received such orders, but also Antipater and Craterus, resolved to oppose Perdiccas by force, as if he were a usurper and not the more or less legitimate head of the empire of Alexander.

Such were the circumstances in which the leading generals of Alexander began the long and exciting struggle for the succession. Some of them earnestly endeavoured to maintain the unity of the empire. This was the policy of Perdiccas and his chief assistant Eumenes, and still more of Antipater and Craterus. The struggle of the last two with Perdiccas was a struggle for the regency and nothing else. Some wanted to have a free hand in their own satrapies, in other words to be recognized as practically independent rulers. This was the attitude of Ptolemy, and many others would certainly have adopted it had they only been as strong and as confident of their strength as he. Whether they all realized that this meant the end of the unity of Alexander's empire, we have no means of knowing. Ptolemy, at any rate, never showed any desire to make Egypt the centre of a world-empire of his own. And finally some, like Leonnatus and Antigonus the One-eyed, would have liked to preserve the unity of the empire provided that they were its rulers and masters. The majority of the satraps, however, had, at least at the beginning of the struggle, no definite ideas regarding their relations with the empire as a whole. They tried to keep their satrapies in their own hands, to increase their territories and their revenues, and to share their power and their resources as little as possible with any one else.

All the satraps, and first and foremost Perdiccas, Antipater,

* Ptolemy had been appointed satrap of Egypt by decision taken at Babylon.

and Craterus, had larger or smaller bodies of Macedonian soldiers under their command. The largest and the most experienced force was, of course, that in the hands of Perdiccas, and this fact, more than his office or the presence of the kings in his camp, gave him the greatest power in the empire. But the superiority of Perdiccas was not so overwhelming as to suppress all opposition to his rule. He was soon challenged by Antigonus and Ptolemy, who refused to obey his orders; and the rebels were supported, at first tacitly, then openly, by Antipater and Craterus. An appeal to arms was therefore the only way open to Perdiccas of settling the problem of supreme power. The military operations that ensued were conducted by Eumenes against Craterus and Antipater in Asia Minor, and by Perdiccas himself against Ptolemy in Ptolemy's satrapy. Craterus was defeated by Eumenes and fell on the battle-field; while Perdiccas, unsuccessful in his attempt to cross the Nile, was killed by his own officers—a striking illustration of the weakness of the centripetal forces even in the central camp of the Macedonian army itself.

The disappearance from the stage of the two former representatives of the central power, Perdiccas and Craterus, was followed by a temporary arrangement which resulted in an almost successful attempt by Eurydice, the newly wedded wife of Philip Arrhidaeus, to abolish the regency altogether. Then the army at a conference at Triparadeisos in north Syria (321 B.C.) appointed Antipater, the oldest and ablest general of Alexander, ἐπιμελητὴς αὐτοκράτωρ (administrator with full powers) of the State. Antipater accepted the appointment and reorganized the State. The satrapies were again redistributed, and Antigonus was appointed commander of a part of Perdiccas' army and guardian of the kings; he was commissioned to rid Asia of the rest of the army of Perdiccas, which remained under the control of Eumenes and Perdiccas' own brother Alcetas. Cassander was appointed chiliarch under Antigonus. This organization was, however, shortlived. Antigonus would not share his power with Cassander and showed little loyalty to the kings. This was the reason why Antipater took the kings with him to Macedonia and transferred the centre of the empire to the West. From here he intended to rule over the rest of it. The East, however, was left in the hands of the satraps, under the control of a kind of over-satrap in the person of Antigonus, who was still supposed to carry on in the name of the empire the commission referred to above. It was certainly not from love of Antigonus that Antipater left him in so powerful a position. Antigonus was without doubt allowed to remain commander-in-chief in Asia in order to prevent another war, which Antigonus would certainly have started as soon as Antipater had settled in Macedonia, had he not been given the chance of becoming supreme ruler in Asia. It was a similar consideration that forced Antipater tacitly to recognize the claims of Ptolemy to be master in his own satrapy. It seems therefore that the unity of the empire was rather a formula than a fact, and that, had Antipater lived longer, even he would not have been able to maintain the formula.

The arrangement concluded at Triparadeisos and the withdrawal of Antipater to Macedonia kept Greece quiet for a time. The country had suffered severely during the Lamian war. The greatest disaster was the final loss by Athens of her sea-power; her large fleet was destroyed by the navy of the central government in two or three battles. War, however, went on in Asia Minor, where Eumenes and Alcetas opposed Antigonus and anarchy reigned until the latter destroyed the army of Alcetas with its leader and forced Eumenes to shut himself up in Nora, an impregnable Cappadocian fortress.

Two years after Triparadeisos (319) Antipater died and the army, in accordance with his wish, appointed Polyperchon, one of the older generals of Alexander, as his successor. It was known to every one, and more particularly to Antipater himself, that Polyperchon was not a man of outstanding ability. He was much inferior to any of the leading satraps of Alexander's empire, to Antigonus, Ptolemy, Lysimachus, and Seleucus. And yet Antipater appointed him, preferring him even to his own son Cassander. There is no doubt that his intention was to select a man, not of genius, but of honest and reliable character, who would actively support the kings and remain loyal to them. None of the more important leaders inspired him with confidence in their trustworthiness. It was evident that any of them, if appointed, would promote his own interests and not those of the kings. Whether Polyperchon would succeed depended mainly, not so much on his own ability, as on the faithful support of the army. Antipater probably believed that the army would remain loyal. In this he was mistaken. The Macedonian army was no longer guided by devotion to the royal house. Selfish interests predominated. The army was still the most powerful factor in the political history of the time, but it was ready to serve anyone whom it could trust and who knew how to handle it.

The death of Antipater meant a fresh outbreak of war both in the West and in the East. Though Polyperchon's appointment was perfectly regular, it was not recognized as such by the leading rulers of the various parts of Alexander's empire. It was plain that they would not recognize any central authority, if it were not their own. In the East Antigonus at once started a systematic conquest of Asiatic satrapies whose governors would not obey his orders, and Ptolemy rushed to occupy Syria. In the West Cassander, the chiliarch under Polyperchon, who some time previously had been unwilling to co-operate with Antigonus in the same capacity, now refused to act as second to Polyperchon, escaped to Antigonus, and with his help and the support of Ptolemy, and before long of Lysimachus also, started a war in Greece.

In the West, Polyperchon retorted by proclaiming, in the name of the king, Greek freedom and autonomy, which meant for most of the Greek cities internal revolutions and small local wars—revolutions of the *demoi* against the pro-Macedonian oligarchs and wars of the cities against the Macedonian garrisons. He, moreover, opened a prospect of internal war in Macedonia, where Cassander had many supporters, by inviting Olympias to come and act as guardian of her grandson. This ultimately meant a deep rift between the two kings, or, more precisely, between the two women who were acting respectively on their behalf. Everybody knew that Olympias, now the guardian of Alexander, bitterly hated Eurydice, the wife and guide of Philip.

In the East, Polyperchon and Olympias appointed Eumenes, who had succeeded by clever diplomacy in escaping from Nora, chief commander of the king's army in Asia with instructions to wrest that country from Antigonus. We must remember that at Triparadeisos Eumenes had been outlawed by the Macedonian army. This verdict, so far as we know, had never been reversed.

The war which ensued was bitter, bloody, and cruel. In the East, Antigonus succeeded in conquering Eumenes and those Oriental satraps who had given him half-hearted support. Eumenes, betrayed by his allies and by the Macedonian soldiers, was executed in Antigonus' camp (316). But the victory of Antigonus was not complete, for Seleucus, who had been appointed at Triparadeisos satrap of Babylonia, fled to Egypt and made it clear to Ptolemy that the success of Antigonus meant the ruin of Ptolemy.

Nor were the kings successful in Greece and in Macedonia. Athens, after a shortlived attempt to recover her democratic constitution, was forced by Cassander into submission, and another oligarchy or tyranny—the régime of Demetrius of Phaleron—replaced in 317 the government of Phocion, who was executed (318). In Macedonia, Polyperchon was driven out by Cassander, but, while the latter was absent fighting in the Peloponnese, he succeeded in bringing Olympias back to Macedonia and in handing over to her Alexander and Roxane (317). There Olympias, though opposed by Eurydice and Philip, found at first general support. But her cruel execution of Philip and Eurydice, whom she captured, and of all who supported them alienated the sympathies of the army and of the population and turned them in favour of Cassander. Cassander came back from Greece with a strong force and besieged Olympias in Pydna. Hunger forced her to surrender, and surrender meant death. She was killed, at the order of Cassander, by the relatives of her numerous victims (316). Cassander was now master of Macedonia—for Polyperchon was immobilized in Thessaly and finally fled to Aetolia—and Alexander (with Roxane) was in his hands, as a prisoner of war, and not as king. Cassander wished to be recognized as the legitimate successor of the last legitimate king of Philip's line.

Central government and the right of Philip's dynasty to rule Alexander's empire ceased after these events to be factors in the political development of the Hellenistic world. The

PLATE II

1. The head of a marble statue here represented (at one time in Heidelberg, now somewhere in Switzerland) has been identified with great probability as that of Lysimachus, by minute comparison with the rare coin portraits of that able general of Alexander, then King of Thrace and for a time successor of Antigonus the One-eyed in Asia Minor and of Demetrius in Macedonia. The statue is a Roman copy of a Greek original of the school of Lysippus. (Photograph supplied by Dr. O. Brendel.)

First published and identified by O. Brendel, 'Ein Bildnis des Königs Lysimachos von Thrakien', *Die Antike*, iv (1928), pp. 314 ff.; cf. the judicious remarks of E. Pfuhl, *J.D.A.I.* xlv (1930), p. 8 f., fig. 4. (For the coins of Lysimachus bearing the portrait of the king, see O. Brendel, loc. cit., and E. Pfuhl, loc. cit., pl. iv, 5—coins of Lysimacheia. Cf. my pl. xviii, 7 and 8: two specimens of the splendid coinage of Lysimachus issued after 297 B.C. with the idealized portrait of Alexander, which shows a slight resemblance to the features of Lysimachus; on these coins see E. T. Newell, *Royal Greek Portrait Coins*, 1937, p. 19).

2. Marble mask of a portrait statue of Ptolemy Soter found in Egypt. The practice of making only certain parts of a statue in marble (which, being imported, was expensive, see the works quoted in Ch. IV, n. 180) was peculiar to Egypt. The mask shows a striking resemblance to some coins of Soter which represent him as not yet an old man, probably before he assumed the title of king (see my pl. iii, fig. 2, cf. pl. xxviii, fig. 4, and pl. xxix, fig. 2). The portrait of Soter shows no trace of the idealization so prominent in the portraits of Alexander and Lysimachus. On the coins and in the various sculptures it is always treated in a realistic manner with emphasis on the leading traits of Soter's character: iron power of will and determination guided by prudence and intelligence. (Photograph supplied by Dr. F. Poulsen).

The mask of Soter has been several times published and discussed. A full bibliography and sound remarks on style and workmanship, together with a full enumeration of other plastic portraits of Soter, will be found in F. Poulsen, 'Gab es eine alexandrinische Kunst?' *Collections of the Ny Carlsberg Glyptothek*, ii (1938), pp. 14 ff. Cf. the beautiful plaster model (see description of my pls. xlv and xlviii) of a silver *emblema* showing the superimposed profile portraits of Soter and his wife Berenice (cf. my pl. xxix, 2) recently published and illustrated by A. Adriani, *Bull. Soc. Arch. Alex.* xxxii (N.S. x. 1) (1938), pp. 77 ff., and pl. vi. For the position that the royal portraits occupy in the history of Alexandrian sculpture in general I may quote here once for all the two short surveys of Alexandrian sculpture (including the portraits) by A. W. Lawrence, 'Greek sculpture in Ptolemaic Egypt', *J.E.A.* xi (1925), pp. 179 ff., and I. Noshy, *The Arts in Ptolemaic Egypt*, 1937, pp. 82 ff. (who closely follows Lawrence).

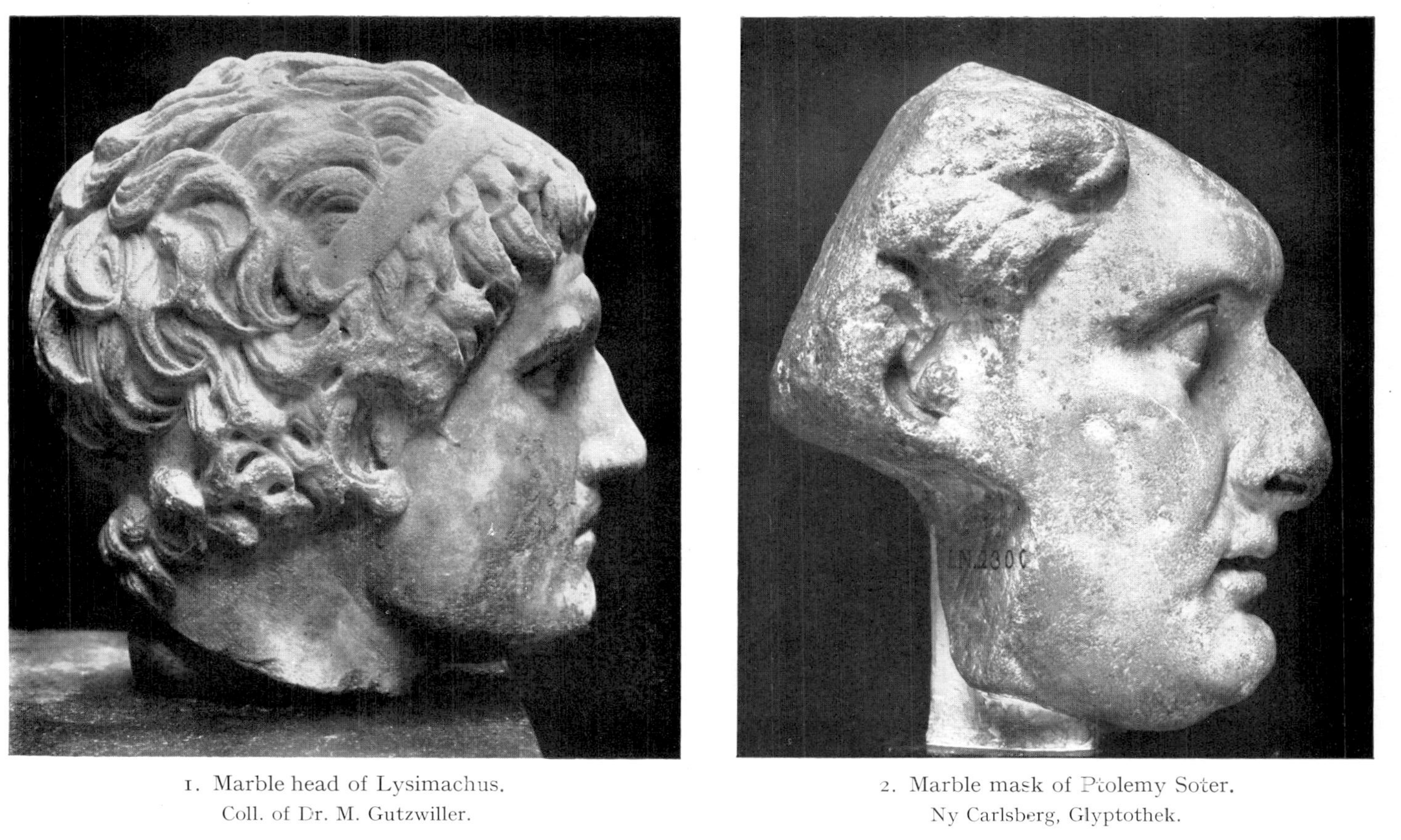

1. Marble head of Lysimachus.
Coll. of Dr. M. Gutzwiller.

2. Marble mask of Ptolemy Soter.
Ny Carlsberg, Glyptothek.

question at issue now was whether among the rulers of the satrapies there was one willing and strong enough to come forward as candidate for Alexander's succession and to restore his world-empire. It was evident to everybody at that time that there was one man who quite openly aimed at the succession, Antigonus the One-eyed, assisted by his son Demetrius. He assumed the position of overlord in Asia after his great victories over Eumenes, and this position he intended to retain after his return to Asia Minor. It was natural that the other strong rulers of this time, who never looked upon themselves as satraps of a central government, Cassander, Lysimachus, and Ptolemy, should at once take diplomatic action designed to show Antigonus that they regarded themselves as his equals and as his associates in the war against Eumenes and therefore entitled to their share in the profits of this war. Both Antigonus and his opponents were ready for war, and war began immediately after Antigonus had given his—of course negative—answer to the embassies of his former friends.

The war began in 315. In Greece, Antigonus was able to enlist for himself the services of Polyperchon and of Polyperchon's son Alexander (the latter soon betrayed him); in Asia he drove Ptolemy out of Syria. After these first successes he was ready for military operations on a still larger scale. He built a strong fleet in Phoenicia and later strengthened it by an alliance with Rhodes, and thus became master of the Mediterranean. In Greece he opened a diplomatic attack on Cassander, whom he denounced as a public enemy on account of his treatment of Roxane and Alexander, and declared himself regent and guardian of the king in place of Polyperchon, who was now his subordinate. To obtain the support of Greece he repeated, in modified form, Polyperchon's proclamation of Greek liberty. Some of the Greek cities of Asia Minor and the cities of the Cyclades he formed into free leagues, which he treated as his allies. Ptolemy tried to counter by having recourse to the same political device, but as his move was not supported by military operations, his proclamation of liberty had very little effect in Greece. The struggle in Greece, carried on by the naval and land forces of Antigonus under the command of his generals, was difficult and complicated. No decisive success was gained by Antigonus, and Cassander remained strong and full of energy. In 314/13 Antigonus designed to bring the war in Greece and Macedonia to an end by simultaneous attacks on Cassander in both countries. In Greece his lieutenant Polemaeus was active. He intended himself to lead the attack in Macedonia by crossing the Dardanelles. But the plan failed. Lysimachus prevented him from crossing the Dardanelles and thus rendered the successes of Polemaeus in Greece almost nugatory.

The course of events in the East had an even more decisive influence on the outcome of the great war. After driving Ptolemy out of Syria, Antigonus had left his son Demetrius at Gaza. Ptolemy, in order to make a diversion which would relieve his European allies and at the same time eliminate the danger of an invasion of Egypt by Demetrius, now himself appeared in Palestine (312) and inflicted a crushing defeat on Demetrius and his army at Gaza. His success was necessarily of short duration. Demetrius soon got a partial revenge and the return of Antigonus himself to Syria forced Ptolemy finally to retire to Egypt. Nevertheless the diversion of Ptolemy was not without permanent results. During his short occupation of Syria he had helped Seleucus to reoccupy his own former satrapy of Babylonia, and the skill and energy of Seleucus allowed him to consolidate and to extend his power in the farther East. The return of Seleucus to Babylon was at once recognized by Antigonus as a new factor which might ruin all his plans, and he quickly sent Demetrius to Babylonia at a moment when Seleucus was occupied in the eastern satrapies. The expedition of Demetrius (311) was not a success. He was forced to retire from Babylonia and to make peace with Seleucus. What he learnt of the situation in Babylonia probably convinced him that a long campaign rather than a raid would be required to crush Seleucus.

Antigonus therefore decided to suspend the military operations and to come to an understanding with his opponents (311). It is probable that he realized the necessity of first re-establishing his authority in the East by crushing Seleucus before proceeding with his struggle against Cassander, Lysimachus, and Ptolemy. Threatened by Seleucus in the rear and deprived of the resources in men, horses, elephants, and money which the farther East might supply, he probably regarded himself as inferior to his enemies.

Why the enemies of Antigonus consented to make peace with him and betray Seleucus is more difficult to understand. They were probably not ready for a decisive struggle. Cassander still had the young Alexander, the legitimate king in whose name Antigonus pretended to act, near him in Macedonia, and unrest was widespread in Greece. Ptolemy and Lysimachus were no doubt influenced by reasons unknown to us. At any rate a peace was made, from which Seleucus was excluded, whereby Antigonus was acknowledged as ruler over the whole of the East including Syria and the satrapies of Seleucus, and the liberty of the Greek cities was confirmed. Cassander was recognized as ruler of Macedonia until Alexander should be of age to assume the position himself. Lysimachus obtained no increase of territory. Ptolemy lost Syria but retained Cyprus. The peace was a great diplomatic victory for Antigonus.[4]

As was to be expected, Antigonus used the armistice to attempt to reconquer the eastern satrapies, while his opponents were getting ready for a renewal of military operations. A typical illustration of the incompleteness of our information even on this period of Hellenistic political history, not as regards details but as regards basic events, is the fact that before the discovery of a mutilated Babylonian chronicle which was first published by S. Smith in 1924 we had not the slightest idea of the real character of Demetrius' expedition to Babylonia and of the long and eventful war between Antigonus and Seleucus in the same region immediately after the peace of 311. The chronicle shows that this last war continued from 310 to the end of 308, and that peace was made at the beginning of 307/6 B.C. The prolonged absence of Antigonus in the East gives an acceptable explanation of the development of affairs in the West, and his failure to conquer Seleucus is now seen to have been the decisive factor in the vicissitudes of the war in the West during the second struggle of Antigonus for power and in his final defeat at Ipsus. There would have been no Ipsus if Seleucus had not remained strong and independent and if he had not had time and opportunity to consolidate his power in the East, to organize and increase his army, and to attach this army to himself by strong ties of discipline and devotion. The years of the abortive raid of Demetrius and of Antigonus' expedition against Seleucus were truly epochal years, and not only in the history of the Seleucid Empire.[5]

While Antigonus was busy in the East, his enemies, without engaging in another regular war, disposed of some of the difficulties that had forced them in 311 to accept his conditions of peace. Cassander removed King Alexander by murdering him (310), and was able in the following year to lure Polyperchon, who, for the benefit of Antigonus, had provoked a war in Greece by putting forward Heracles, a real or pretended son of Alexander, and proclaiming him king of Macedonia, into betraying his tool and entering Cassander's service. Meanwhile Ptolemy took steps in Greece ostensibly directed against Cassander by freeing Corinth and Sicyon (308), occupying these cities with his garrisons, and substituting himself for Antigonus in the Island League which the latter had created. It was these events which made Antigonus abandon his operations against Seleucus and hurry to the West. With Greece in the hands of Ptolemy and Cassander, and with the islands under the protectorate of Ptolemy, Antigonus was open to attack on his western front, the coast of Asia Minor, and his rule in Asia was imperilled. His main efforts were directed against his most dangerous enemies: Cassander in Greece, and Ptolemy. The two operations had a brilliant but not a lasting success. Demetrius succeeded in restoring liberty to Athens (307) and to a large part of Greece. With his splendid fleet he was able to defeat the fleet of Ptolemy off Salamis in Cyprus (306) and re-establish the authority of Antigonus in the island. This spectacular victory gave Antigonus a pretext for proclaiming himself king and for acting accordingly.

His first step was an attempt to suppress Ptolemy by invading Egypt. In this enterprise, however, he failed. Ptolemy retorted by proclaiming himself king (304), in order to make it clear that he was not prepared to admit the claims of Antigonus. Lysimachus and Cassander, and after them Seleucus, made a similar demonstration by assuming the royal title. Another attempt of Antigonus to undermine the power of Ptolemy is to be seen in the great siege of Rhodes (305/4), the principal emporium of Egyptian trade. The siege was famous in the annals of the ancient world: the struggle between liberty on one side and royal power on the other, between *hybris* and reverence for the gods, between citizens and subjects, between spirit and material power, presented contrasts which struck the Greek imagination. While Antigonus was vainly trying to conquer Ptolemy, his other enemy, Cassander, was increasing his strength. The work of liberation done by Demetrius in Greece was jeopardized. Cassander was threatening Athens and was steadily gaining ground in Greece. Demetrius with his great fleet returned to Greece. Athens was saved. Sicyon and Corinth and the majority of the cities of the Peloponnese recovered their liberty. The Hellenic league of Philip and Alexander was restored (302).[6] Cassander was prepared to make a separate peace.

But the successes of Antigonus and Demetrius were more spectacular than real. Lysimachus and Seleucus, the strongest members of the coalition against Antigonus, had not yet said their word. It was a great success for Cassander that he was able to persuade Lysimachus and after him Ptolemy and Seleucus to start vigorous operations against Antigonus. The united armies of Lysimachus and Seleucus, even without the support of Ptolemy, would evidently be a match for the forces of Antigonus. The only problem was to effect their junction. This was done by the unusual military skill of Lysimachus. The result was the battle of Ipsus, which brought the empire of Antigonus to an end (301).

The battle of Ipsus itself and the course of history after this battle are much less well known than the events discussed above. We have only excerpts of Diodorus after Book XX and are consequently deprived of his continuous and more or less substantial narrative for the period subsequent to 301, for which the summary of Justin is but a poor substitute. Plutarch, however, in his lives of Demetrius and Pyrrhus, still followed (at least partly) Hieronymus of Cardia, whose work dealt with events up to the death of Pyrrhus (272); and the other scattered references bearing on this period are also in all probability derived chiefly from Hieronymus. We are therefore somewhat better informed about the years between Ipsus and the death of Pyrrhus than about the following period, for which Phylarchus' dramatic but not fully reliable history was the main source for those who later dealt with it. I will return later to the literary sources for this period. More abundant, although less abundant than for the preceding and the following periods, is our documentary (especially epigraphic) evidence. The proceedings of Demetrius and Lysimachus, particularly those of Demetrius in Greece and of Lysimachus in Asia Minor, are well illustrated by many substantial inscriptions.

The battle of Ipsus was of great importance for the future. The empire of Antigonus was destroyed by a coalition of his leading rivals, first and foremost Lysimachus and Seleucus, in the second line Cassander and Ptolemy. But none of the victors was satisfied with his share of the spoils. They all had their own designs, and Lysimachus and Seleucus in particular never regarded the settlement after Ipsus as final. They certainly contemplated the creation of empires similar to that of Antigonus, Lysimachus from his own kingdom, to which, after Ipsus, he had added a large part of Asia Minor (including Cappadocia, but without Pontus and Bithynia) and to which he planned also to add Macedonia and Greece sooner or later, Seleucus from his powerful and opulent Eastern monarchy. Ptolemy had no such plans; his policy was only to enlarge his own kingdom by annexing to it regions which were indispensable if he was to make Egypt an impregnable stronghold—the Syrian coast, which he invaded at once, Cyprus, and perhaps some parts of southern Asia Minor.[7] He intended, further, to acquire a hegemony over the great commercial routes and the leading commercial cities of the Aegean. Cassander, in view of the exhaustion of Macedonia, was prepared to be satisfied with an undisturbed control over Macedonia and Greece.

However, though Antigonus was dead, his son Demetrius, who had been his strong right hand, the conqueror of Ptolemy at Salamis and besieger of Rhodes, was alive and full of energy.[8] He was not prepared to give up his aspirations, and confidently hoped to restore his father's empire. He was still in possession of the strongest fleet in the Aegean, still the president of the powerful Hellenic League, still in control of the Island League;

he also held Cyprus and many Greek cities in Greece (especially Athens), in Asia Minor (Ionia and Caria), and even on the Phoenician coast. He was still a dangerous rival to the victors of Ipsus. His policy is branded by most modern scholars as adventurous, haphazard, and inconsistent. But one must realize the difficulty of his position, that of a great king without an empire, and his dependence on various contingencies which kept arising alike in Greece and Macedonia and in Asia as a result of the changing relations between the leading powers. His chief aim was (as it always continued to be) to recover his lost empire, either in its former vast extent or on a reduced scale.

After Ipsus he first tried to mobilize Greece against the victors and thus to restore at least his prestige. But he found Athens unwilling to open her gates to him, and the Hellenic League broken up. To take action in Greece meant a long war with Cassander, with little prospect of success. Being in possession of an excellent navy and of many strongholds in Cyprus and in Asia Minor, he preferred to try his fortune in Asia to begin with. His first operations against Lysimachus were successful. He was also successful in his diplomacy. The united front of the victors was far from solid. Seleucus was angry because Ptolemy was holding south Syria; Cassander was anxious about the Asiatic kingdom of his brother Pleistarchus; Lysimachus, now the neighbour of Seleucus, felt insecure and feared the latter's ambitious projects. Thus a league was formed against Seleucus (299) and he was almost isolated. It is not surprising that Seleucus concluded an alliance with Demetrius, who apparently at the same time entered into diplomatic relations with Ptolemy and sent him Pyrrhus of Epirus as a hostage.* The solidarity of the anti-Demetrian triumvirate was evidently unstable. The relations of Ptolemy and Cassander were far from cordial, and Ptolemy accordingly took advantage of the detention of the king of Epirus in Alexandria to do Cassander a bad turn. He sent Pyrrhus back to Epirus and restored him to his ancestral throne.

In Greece Cassander was supreme. Even Athens preferred a policy of neutrality friendly to Cassander to a new political experiment. The principal supporters of this policy

* See note 7 to this chapter.

PLATE III

1. SELEUCUS I issued very few coins displaying his likeness. But his portraits appear on the coins of his son Antiochus I minted while his father was still alive (between 293–281 B.C.), and after his death on those of Philetaerus of Pergamon. It is the obverse of one of the latter coins which is reproduced here (description pl. XXIX, 4). Statues of Seleucus (see next plate) certainly existed in large numbers. It was these statues which inspired the die-cutters of the Seleucid kingdom and of Pergamon. The portrait shows some Lysippian traits, but is much more realistic than the Lysippian portraits. It shows the king as an old man and stresses his individual features.

2. PTOLEMY SOTER (tetradrachm from the coll. of E. T. Newell, unpublished). The portrait was probably derived from portrait statues of the king.

3. DEMETRIUS POLIORCETES (drachm from the coll. of E. T. Newell, mint of Ephesus, cf. pl. XXVIII, 6). The portrait (note the horn, the symbol of royal strength and power) is slightly idealized though it renders forcibly the individual characteristics of the king. E. T. Newell, *The Coinages of Demetrius Poliorcetes*, 1927, p. 65, no. 54 f.

4. ANTIOCHUS I (see pl. XXVIII, 8). An absolutely realistic portrait of the successor of Seleucus I in his advanced age.

5. PHILADELPHUS and ARSINOE (from *B.M.C.*, pl. VII, 7, cf. my pl. XXIX, 2). Posthumous coin struck by Philopator and showing the deified brother and sister (*ἀδελφοί*).

A more detailed analysis of the coin-portraits of the Hellenistic kings in connexion with the existing plastic portraits will be found in the admirable article by E. Pfuhl, 'Ikonographische Beiträge zur Stilgeschichte der hellenistischen Kunst', *J.D.A.I.* xlv (1930), pp. 1 ff. The historical setting is emphasized in the excellent monograph by E. T. Newell, *Royal Greek Portrait Coins*, 1937.

1

2

3

4 5

Enlarged coin portraits of 1. Seleucus Nicator, 2. Ptolemy Soter, 3. Demetrius Poliorcetes, 4. Antiochus I, 5. Philadelphus and Arsinoe

were Phaedrus, Philippides, and especially Lachares. The situation changed when Cassander died in 297. By his death Demetrius gained a fresh opportunity. As his situation in Asia Minor was far from promising and he had quarrelled with his ally Seleucus over his Phoenician possessions—which practically meant war and in fact did lead to military operations (296)—Demetrius decided to evacuate Asia Minor altogether and to seek success in Greece. His energy was unbroken, his resources in men, ships, and money were abundant, and he expected to find in Greece no dangerous rivals. He therefore abandoned his possessions in Asia Minor to his enemies and sailed for Greece. With Greece under his control his prospects of conquering Macedonia and of then taking revenge on his enemies were good. His rivals understood this, and at once formed an alliance against him.[9]

In Greece the coalition against Demetrius did nothing to prevent him from carrying out his plan. He first restored his power in the Peloponnese and then took Athens, which resisted him for some time under the leadership of Lachares,[10] who in 295 by a *coup de main* concentrated all power in his own hands (294). Then he placed his garrisons in Piraeus and Munychia, and from Athens continued the reconquest of Greece. While he was fighting with Sparta a new prospect was opened to him in Macedonia. Antipater and Alexander, Cassander's sons by Thessalonice, the last survivors of Philip's house, shared for a while the rule over Macedonia. But Antipater, probably supported by Lysimachus, killed his mother and attacked Alexander, who appealed to Pyrrhus and Demetrius for assistance. Demetrius hastened to Macedonia, to find that Alexander had already been established there by Pyrrhus as sole ruler. Demetrius treacherously murdered Alexander at Larissa and was elected king by the Macedonian army.

From 293 onwards Demetrius was once more the strongest ruler in the Aegean world. His rivals did not dare to attack him openly, especially as they probably all had affairs at home to settle first. Demetrius thus had time and opportunity to subdue as much of Greece as he could. Of his proceedings in Greece we know little. His principal enemies were Epirus, Aetolia, and Sparta. His chief source of trouble in Greece was

Boeotia, which rose repeatedly against him, and he never felt quite comfortable at Athens. But the weakest point in his position was the situation in Macedonia. He had grown up and been educated in the East, in the atmosphere of a semi-Oriental monarchy. His father's Macedonian army in that part of the world was no longer the Macedonian army of Philip. It had become used to the manners and customs of its orientalized leaders. The Macedonian army at home was a very different body. Most of the men were born and educated in Macedonia and were not familiar with the East. For them the conduct of Demetrius, who behaved in Macedonia just he had behaved —with general approval—in Asia, was an insult and an outrage. It was natural that Demetrius should very soon lose his prestige among the Macedonians. They were prepared to abandon him at the first opportunity. Such an opportunity presented itself when it became clear to his enemies that Demetrius considered himself ready to launch an expedition on a large scale to reconquer his lost possessions in Asia (289).

This Lysimachus regarded as his last chance to prevent Demetrius from carrying out his plans. He was constantly in touch with the enemies of Demetrius in Greece—Pyrrhus and the Aetolians; he knew the real difficulty of his position there, for it was solely by force that Greece was kept more or less quiet; and above all he realized that in Macedonia Demetrius was not master of his own soldiers. The situation would be altered at once if he were allowed to cross to Asia.

Combined operations were begun by Lysimachus and Pyrrhus. They invaded Macedonia in the spring of 288 and found Demetrius unprepared. When Demetrius and his Macedonians faced Pyrrhus and his army near Beroea, the Macedonians deserted and went over to Pyrrhus. The authority of Demetrius in Macedonia collapsed. He fled to the former capital of Cassander, Cassandreia (Potidaea), and then hurried to Greece in order to save at least his Greek kingdom. In this he succeeded, for Ptolemy was not ready to fight him and Lysimachus did not interfere. But his position in Greece was far from secure, and his last chance was to use the loyal remnant of his forces to carry out his Asiatic plans, that is, to invade Asia. He hoped to take Lysimachus by surprise (287). In this he was disappointed. It soon became manifest (286) that his army was no match for that of Agathocles, the son of Lysimachus, before which he was obliged to retire. He wished to cross the Taurus and attempt to retrieve his fortunes in the farther East. His troops refused to follow him. He then tried to get into touch with Seleucus and enlist his help against Lysimachus. But Seleucus, whatever his plans were, was too suspicious of Demetrius to accept him as an ally. Demetrius thereupon decided to fight Seleucus and invade his kingdom. But he fell ill. During his illness his army became disorganized and he was finally obliged to surrender to Seleucus (285) and become his prisoner. He spent the last years of his life at Apamea as the unwilling guest of his captor.[11]

The fall of Demetrius made a considerable change in the political aspect of the Hellenistic world. The real gainer by the struggle was Lysimachus. After Demetrius' flight from Macedonia he at first remained loyal to his understanding with Pyrrhus and was satisfied with half of Macedonia. The other half went to Pyrrhus. Lysimachus wished to make use of him against Demetrius' son Antigonus, who was still master of Athens, of many cities in Greece, and of Thessaly. With his help he succeeded in depriving Antigonus of Thessaly and endangering his position at Athens. Soon, however, in the winter of 286, when Demetrius was no longer to be feared and when Pyrrhus, realizing his perilous position, made an alliance with Antigonus, Lysimachus showed his real intentions and in 285 invaded Pyrrhus' half of Macedonia. Pyrrhus retired before him and Lysimachus remained sole master both of Macedonia and of Greece, where Antigonus led a precarious existence, confined practically to his capital Demetrias.

As master of Macedonia and Greece and of a large part of Asia Minor (excluding Pontus and Bithynia), Lysimachus aroused the suspicion and jealousy of his former friends and allies, Ptolemy and Seleucus. It was evident that there would be no lasting peace in the Hellenistic world.

In Europe Antigonus never gave up the hope of recovering his power in Greece, and Lysimachus was unable to eliminate him altogether, especially when he was joined by part of the fleet of Demetrius (see below).

In the Aegean the successor of Demetrius was not Lysimachus but Ptolemy. Demetrius had made himself master of it by creating a powerful navy. His fleet was still there, anchored near Caunus. Lysimachus made no effort to get possession of it, neither did Seleucus. The two claimants to Demetrius' inheritance were his son Antigonus and Ptolemy. It was the latter who, by no legal right but by mere bribery, secured the lion's share of it. It was handed over to him by Demetrius' admiral, Philocles king of Sidon. Some of the Greek ships, however, joined Antigonus. In this way Ptolemy became master both of the Aegean and of the Phoenician coast, wielding the greatest naval power in the Hellenistic world. He naturally became in consequence suzerain not only of the Phoenician cities but also of the Island League, and a dangerous rival both to Lysimachus and Seleucus. Seleucus, of course, was not prepared to acquiesce in the situation thus created by the death of Demetrius. The ascendancy of Lysimachus in Asia Minor and Ptolemy's control over the most vital parts of the Syrian coast were thorns in his flesh. But as long as his benefactor, the old Ptolemy, lived, and as long as Lysimachus held his kingdom together with a strong hand, Seleucus kept quiet, gradually preparing a bridge for himself into Asia Minor by building up a pro-Seleucid party in many of the Anatolian cities. In 283 both Demetrius and Ptolemy died. The successor of Ptolemy was his son by a former concubine, later his legitimate wife Berenice, Ptolemy II surnamed Philadelphus. But Philadelphus' elder half-brother Ptolemy, later surnamed Thunderbolt (Ceraunus), the son of Ptolemy I's first wife Eurydice, was alive and full of energy. He found refuge first at the court of Seleucus and then at that of Lysimachus. Deprived of his hopes in Egypt, Ceraunus decided to try his fortune with Lysimachus, now a very old man. A formidable obstacle in his way was Agathocles, Lysimachus' son. It is probable that it was Ceraunus who, with the help of Lysimachus' third wife Arsinoe, his half-sister, succeeded in arousing in the mind of Lysimachus the suspicions of Agathocles that led to the execution of the brilliant young man and of all those near to him. This event made a powerful impression on the Hellenistic world. Public opinion was aroused against Lysimachus, and the prospects of Seleucus in Asia Minor became brighter than ever before. A natural consequence was that the expedition of Seleucus against Lysimachus (Agathocles' wife Lysandra with her children had fled to Seleucus) found a favourable reception in Asia Minor (282). The two armies of the only surviving generals of Alexander met at Corupedion in Lydia (281). Lysimachus was defeated and killed. His kingdom now fell to Seleucus, who once again united under his rule the East and the West.

But it was not Seleucus' destiny to rule his empire from Macedonia. Seven months after Corupedion, when Seleucus was about to cross the Dardanelles, Ceraunus, who was now his guest and a weapon in his hands against Philadelphus, angry and disappointed in his hopes of recovering Egypt, killed Seleucus and was proclaimed king of Macedonia by Lysimachus' Macedonian army (280).

The year 280 marks the end of the period of the Successors and of the wars of succession. The forty-three years after Alexander's death were years of almost uninterrupted warfare, in which all parts of Alexander's empire were involved. None of the ruling monarchs felt himself secure and stable on his throne, for all of them had rivals and enemies disposed to increase their own kingdoms at the expense of their neighbours. From 323 to 280 there was always one of Alexander's principal generals who regarded himself as his successor, and this pretender to Alexander's succession was always opposed by the other rulers. Perdiccas and Antipater, Antigonus and Demetrius, even Lysimachus and Seleucus, all endeavoured to restore in one way or another the unity of Alexander's empire, and they all were opposed by those whom they regarded as their rebellious satraps. It was not until the second generation of the great ruling Hellenistic families came into power that the idea of separate and independent Hellenistic kingdoms and of a certain balance of power between them took firm root. It was Ptolemy Soter of the older generation who prepared the ground for this change in political mentality. His policy was followed by his son Philadelphus, and the idea was accepted by the rulers of Syria and Greece, Antiochus son of Seleucus and Antigonus son of Demetrius.

B. CONSOLIDATION OF THE HELLENISTIC MONARCHIES. THE HELLENISTIC BALANCE OF POWER

The period between the battle of Corupedion and the battle of Sellasia or between the death of Seleucus and the accession of Philip V to the Macedonian throne and of Antiochus III to that of Syria, the period when the principal Hellenistic monarchies were consolidated and a certain balance of power was established, is the most obscure in the history of the Hellenistic world. The leading historical work on this period, that of Phylarchus of Athens, is lost except for a few fragments and for the extensive use that Plutarch and Polybius made of it. None of the secondary sources which gave a continuous narrative of the events of the period, such as Diodorus or Pompeius Trogus, is preserved. Justin is not a substitute for Trogus, for his manner of presenting the historical material of his source is desultory. The only bright spots in the darkness are the biography of Pyrrhus by Plutarch, the history of the Achaean League in Polybius, Plutarch's life of Aratus based on Aratus' memoirs and on the work of Phylarchus, and the history of Sparta under Agis and Cleomenes in Plutarch's biographies of these kings, based mainly on Phylarchus. Some scattered fragments of other literary works illuminate here and there episodes in the history of the period; two of them—a fragment of a Babylonian chronicle and a fragment of a semi-literary work by an unknown author dealing with the beginning of the Third Syrian war—give passages of continuous narrative. Many inscriptions bear on certain events of the period, but few of them can be precisely dated and their interpretation is therefore controversial. The numerous papyri illustrate almost exclusively the internal life of Egypt and seldom reflect the general political situation of the time under discussion. The numismatic evidence is helpful, but does not fill the gaps in our information.

For this reason the modern attempts to reconstruct a continuous narrative of the events of the period are all of them highly conjectural, based as they are to a great extent on probabilities and not on ascertained facts. Nevertheless the general lines of the political evolution may be dimly seen and it is not impossible to indicate them. In doing this I shall not adopt the method of most modern historians of the period, who narrate the destinies of each Hellenistic monarchy separately. As in the preceding period, the political history of this time is an integral whole, the events in one monarchy being conditioned by contemporary events in the others, and the actions of the protagonists being closely interconnected. In order therefore to avoid useless and tedious repetitions, I shall try to give a general account of what happened during the forty years that followed the deaths of Seleucus I and Ptolemy I.[12]

An important event in this period, which helped very greatly to consolidate the several Hellenistic monarchies and to define their policy, was the Galatian invasion of Greece and Asia Minor. Not that the Galatians as such were a strong military and political body, capable of exerting any considerable influence on the evolution of the Hellenistic world. The Celtic tribes that invaded the Danubian region and part of South Russia at the beginning of the third century, and thence moved southwards into the Balkans and tried to cross the Straits, were not very numerous and were but loosely organized and poorly armed: they were no match for the highly developed armies of the Hellenistic powers, equipped with everything that the military technique of the day had devised. Their importance lay in the fact that they were at once utilized by the major and minor powers of that period to serve their own selfish political ends and that, settled as they were with the consent and by the efforts of the Hellenistic powers as foreign and disturbing bodies both in the Balkan peninsula and in Asia Minor, they provided an inexhaustible supply of 'allies' and mercenaries for the depleted armies of the Hellenistic rulers.

After the death of Seleucus, Ptolemy Ceraunus, recognized by Antiochus I and successful against his chief rival, Antigonus Gonatas, whom he crushed in a famous naval battle, had a good prospect of establishing his rule in Macedonia on a firm basis, for his second rival Pyrrhus was absent in Italy and Sicily. One of the most important political results of the appearance of the Gauls in Macedonia was the ill-fated battle between them and Ceraunus, which ended in the defeat and death of the latter and brought to an end the rule of the Ptolemies in Macedonia (279).

The disappearance of Ceraunus gave a chance to Antigonus Gonatas, whose fortunes at this moment, after the successful revolt of Greece against him, under the leadership of Areus, the Spartan king, were at a low ebb. The defeat of the Gauls, who had advanced to Delphi, due mainly to the Aetolians (279), greatly raised the reputation of the latter in Greece and afforded them an opportunity of enlarging their power. On the other hand, the disorderly retreat of the Gauls across Macedonia and the destruction of part of them by Antigonus (277), near Lysimacheia, opened Macedonia to him, led to his being proclaimed king of Macedonia by the Macedonian army, and gave him a certain prestige in the eyes of the Macedonian population. It was, however, to his own political and military skill that Antigonus owed his final establishment in Macedonia and the reconquest of the most important strongholds in Greece. For Pyrrhus, who at that time appeared in Greece and drove Antigonus temporarily out of Macedonia (274), proved unable to retain his hold of that country, and ended his life in an abortive attempt to add Greece to his other dominions (272). After the death of Pyrrhus Antigonus remained without a rival, and succeeded by hard work and skilful policy in establishing himself firmly in Macedonia and Greece.

The invasion of the Gauls exerted an even more important influence on the destinies of the eastern part of the Hellenistic world. In Asia Minor Antiochus I aspired for a time to be a true successor of his father and to rule over both his oriental satrapies and the whole of Asia Minor, including its northern part. It should be remembered that across northern Anatolia, along the southern shore of the Black Sea, ran the important military road that connected the eastern part of the empire of Seleucus with Macedonia, to which Antiochus had a legitimate claim. The aspirations of Antiochus I were, however, strongly opposed by the minor potentates of northern Asia Minor, the Northern League, as it was called, comprising the free and powerful cities of northern Anatolia—Heraclea, Byzantium, Tius, and Cius—and also including Mithridates II, founder of the Pontic kingdom, and the kingdom of Bithynia, a Greco-Thracian State which had never recognized the supremacy of the successors of Alexander and was at that time governed by able native rulers, Zipoites and his successor Nicomedes. Antigonus Gonatas had joined the League when, as a result of his defeat by Ceraunus and of events in Greece, he was for a short time a king without a kingdom. He certainly then hoped to create for himself a kingdom in Asia Minor. Though Antiochus succeeded in detaching him from the League (by a treaty in which Antigonus probably gave up his Asiatic and Antiochus his Macedonian ambitions), the League remained strong and powerful, not strong enough, however, to be a match for Antiochus. Nicomedes of Bithynia, therefore, and Mithridates of Pontus decided to introduce a new factor into the political situation—the Gauls, whom they helped to cross the Straits and to whom they delivered the Seleucid possessions in Asia Minor to be ravaged and plundered. Antiochus, who was occupied with a domestic sedition in Syria, and with a war against Ptolemy Philadelphus (280–279), was unable to meet the danger at once and expel the Gauls from Asia Minor. They were settled by the two kings in Phrygia, where, by their mere presence, they would protect the Northern League. They wrought great havoc in the peninsula and Antiochus never succeeded in driving them from the political horizon, in spite of the crushing defeat which he inflicted on them at the famous battle of elephants fought (probably) in 275 B.C.

After and partly in consequence of the Celtic episode the aspect of the Hellenistic world was as follows. The strongest monarchy of the time was Egypt, where the dynasty of the Ptolemies was firmly established. Next came the Seleucid monarchy, which comprised Alexander's Mesopotamian and Syrian satrapies (with the exception of Palestine, Phoenicia, and part of Syria), most of his satrapies in the farther East, and large parts of Asia Minor. The third was the kingdom of Macedonia, which claimed to be the suzerain of the Greek cities of the mainland and held some of them, e.g. Chalcis and Corinth, under a strict protectorate. Mention has already been made of Bithynia, Pontus, the free cities of northern Asia Minor (including Cyzicus), and the Gauls. Certain other Greek cities of Asia Minor and of the islands, expecially Rhodes, were also practically free. Some minor temple-states and city-tyrannies all over Asia Minor were likewise more or less independent.

PLATE IV

1. One of the bronze busts of Hellenistic rulers found in the famous collection of a Roman noble in his villa near Herculaneum, now in the Museum of Naples. Intact, with the exception of the right eye which is restored. Comparison with coins proves that it is certainly a portrait of SELEUCUS I NICATOR. It is the best Hellenistic royal portrait in existence. It shows with force and mastery the leading traits of the character of the great king: his indomitable will, his high intellectual power, his diplomatic astuteness, his unlimited ambition. (Photograph supplied by Alinari.)

The bust has been often published and discussed. It will suffice to mention the best and most recent reproductions and discussions: R. Delbrück, *Antike Porträts*, 1912, p. xli, pl. 22; A. Hekler, *Die Bildniskunst d. Griechen und Römer*, 1912, pl. 68; Arndt–Bruckmann, *Griechische und römische Porträts*, 1891– , pl. 101 f.; E. Pfuhl, loc. cit., p. 5, fig. 1; E. G. Suhr, *Sculptured Portraits of Greek Statesmen*, 1931, p. 157 f. (Suhr gives a list of statues of the king attested by our literary and epigraphical evidence.)

2. Head of a marble statue found at Cyrene. It certainly represents one of the Ptolemies. Comparison with coins makes it probable that the portrait was that either of PHILADELPHUS or of EUERGETES I. The sculptor belonged to the generation after Soter. His work is that of a period of rest and stabilization. The king is represented as a noble ruler, calm and considerate, with a certain touch of haughtiness and lordliness. The art is an imperial art somewhat similar to that of the time of Augustus. It lacks the vigour and energy so typical of the portrait art of the preceding generation. (Photograph supplied by the Sopraintendenza di Antichità di Cirenaica.)

The head was first published and discussed by G. Guidi, *Africa Italiana*, iii (1930), pp. 95 ff., cf. F. Poulsen, 'Gab es eine alexandrinische Kunst?' *Coll. Ny Carlsberg Glyptothek*, ii (1938), p. 21.

On the plastic portraits of Philadelphus and Euergetes I in general see, besides Lawrence and Noshy (quoted above, descr. of pl. II), E. Pfuhl, loc. cit., pp. 28 ff.; E. G. Suhr, loc. cit., pp. 143 ff., and F. Poulsen, loc. cit., pp. 20 ff.

1. Bronze bust of Seleucus I.
Naples Museum.

2. Head of a marble statue of Euergetes I (or Philadelphus ?). Cyrene Museum.

Each of these monarchies had its own needs and aspirations and its own plans and methods of carrying them out. The Egyptian monarchy of the Ptolemies emerged from the turmoil of the wars of succession as the strongest, the richest, and the best organized body politic of that time. Neither Soter nor Philadelphus, however, dreamt of restoring the empire of Alexander. Their main purpose was to safeguard the complete independence of their own monarchy and to secure for it a leading role in the political and economic life of the Hellenistic world. The best and easiest way of accomplishing this was to acquire the heritage of Demetrius—to obtain the hegemony over the Aegean Sea and thus dominate the principal trade-routes of the ancient world. This implied the creation of an empire of the sea comparable to that of Athens in the past. The protectorate over the Island League of Antigonus and Demetrius, first won by Soter and later consolidated by Philadelphus, gave them a partial control over Aegean waters both from a political and a commercial standpoint. In order to make his control over the Aegean more effective, Philadelphus endeavoured to establish another protectorate over the south and west coasts of Asia Minor, and an influence over the great commercial cities of the straits, the sea of Marmora, and the southern coast of the Black Sea. On the other hand, an empire over the Aegean Sea was not secure if the great Phoenician and Palestinian seaports, with their naval resources, were in the hands of another power. Hence the Ptolemies, like the Pharaohs, though not exactly for the same purpose, established their rule over Palestine, Phoenicia, and a part of Syria as soon as they could, and clung to it. Lastly—and this was a matter of no little moment—their claim to be masters of the Aegean obliged Soter, Philadelphus, and their successors to seek to establish their own authority firmly in the most important Greek ports, in order to prevent the Macedonian rulers from becoming powerful at sea.

The policy of the Ptolemies was not dictated by strictly economic considerations. Command of the Aegean they regarded as the *sine qua non* of their political existence, of their strength and independence. Isolated in Egypt, they would be helpless against Syria and Macedonia, the former holding

Anatolian Greece, the latter the mainland of Hellas. With the Aegean and Syrian trade-routes under their control the Ptolemies would have ample resources in men and money and a freedom of movement and action that would give them what they sought. Trade control was for them not an object in itself but the means of achieving a political aim.

It is evident that this policy not only ran counter to the legitimate interests of both Macedonia and Syria, but also meant vassalage and subjection for the proud and independent cities of the Greek islands and of Asia Minor. The aims of the Ptolemies could not be achieved without a strong and continuous military effort, that is to say, without war.

The Seleucids could never acquiesce in the possession of Phoenicia, part of Syria, and Palestine by the Ptolemies and, in addition to that, the establishment of their rule over the south coast of Asia Minor. If this came about, the Seleucids would be unable to build and maintain at their pleasure a strong fleet in their own Syrian harbours, and might even, at the will of the Ptolemies, be cut off from access to the Mediterranean in general. A struggle with the Ptolemies in Syria was, therefore, a stern necessity for the Seleucids. The same situation existed in Asia Minor. The Seleucids had given up (reluctantly and under compulsion) their claim to the northern part of Asia Minor. They could never willingly surrender control of its western and southern coasts and of the important military and commercial roads that led from their own Asiatic empire to the great seaports of western Asia Minor. The consequence of doing so would be that they would become a purely oriental monarchy, isolated from the Greek world altogether. If the Ptolemies wished to control the western and southern cities of Asia Minor, they must fight and fight hard for it. The importance to the Seleucids of the great roads just mentioned entailed the further obligation of making these roads safe: they had to keep close watch on the Galatians in their Phrygian stronghold, and to resist any attempt on the part of the cities of Asia Minor to take their own course and look after their own protection.

The empire of the Seleucids had not one but two or even three fronts. They ruled not only Syria and Asia Minor but also the eastern satrapies of Alexander's monarchy and the Arabian tribes of the desert. While the latter gave them but little trouble, the former were a source both of strength and of weakness. The Indian and Iranian world never became reconciled to foreign rule, and the need of having a free hand to protect themselves against their neighbours made the larger isolated centres of Hellenism in the farther East, especially Bactria, impatient of any protectorate. The consequence for the Seleucids was a permanent state of war in the East and the necessity of dividing their military forces between the East and the West.

Nor were the rulers of Macedonia, Antigonus Gonatas and his successors Demetrius II and Antigonus Doson, prepared, any more than the Seleucids, to recognize the supremacy of the Ptolemies in the Aegean. It was not from personal antipathy that Antigonus Gonatas and Philadelphus fought one another. The struggle was of a purely political character. For the Ptolemies a strong Macedonia was a revival of the maritime empire of Demetrius and meant the end of their Aegean hegemony. This hegemony a strong Macedonia would never tolerate, because it would mean that the control of the food-supplies of the Greek cities would pass from the hands of Macedonia into those of another potentially hostile power, since mastery of the Aegean would lead to mastery of the Straits. Thus the Ptolemies naturally endeavoured to support, by subsidies and in other ways, the Greek rivals and enemies of the Macedonian kings, especially Athens, the Achaean League, and Sparta. On the other hand, as soon as Antigonus had his hands free in Greece, he would mobilize his naval resources and try to drive the Ptolemies from the Aegean in order to imperil their connexions with the mainland of Greece. In this he would of course be supported by the Seleucids and he would consequently choose for his attempt a moment when success in the struggle between the Ptolemies and the Seleucids leant to the side of the latter. If the Ptolemies, in spite of being constantly menaced in the Aegean on two fronts, were fairly successful in establishing and retaining their hegemony there, this was due to the weakness of their rivals. We have seen the weak points in the position of the Seleucids. The weakness of Antigonus and the Antigonids lay in their relations with Greece on the one side and with their northern neighbours on the other. Greece was never reconciled to the Macedonian protectorate, whatever form it took, and naturally availed herself of every opportunity of asserting her full liberty. In these efforts the lead was taken first by Sparta (Areus), then by Athens (Chremonidean war), later by the Achaean League, and again by Sparta. Aetolia, like the other powers named above, varied in her attitude between friendliness and hostility according to the political situation, but in the main continued steadily to build up her own domination over as large a part of Greece as she could. At times, therefore, the Macedonian control over Greece seemed to be firmly established, at others—especially after the death of Gonatas and before the accession of Doson—it ceased to exist altogether. In any case there were few years in which some part of Greece was not engaged in war with Macedonia or in an internal struggle in which Macedonia played an important part.

Much less is known about the relations of Macedonia with the North and with the West—with Illyria, the Thracians, the Celts (especially the kingdom of Tylis and the Bastarnae), and the still existing Scythians. The Celtic invasion was but an episode in the eternal struggle between the tribes of central Europe and the two urbanized peninsulas of Greece and Italy. Possessing all the resources that a brisk commerce with the Greco-Italian world placed in their hands, the central European tribes were a great and incessant danger both to Greece and Italy. The Macedonian kings had therefore to keep themselves constantly informed of the political vicissitudes of their northern neighbours, and from time to time they were forced to repel their inroads into Macedonia or to forestall these inroads by expeditions into the territory of the northern tribes.

The situation of the minor kingdoms of northern Asia Minor—Pontus, Bithynia, and since 260 or 250 B.C. Cappadocia—was simpler if not easier after the creation of the Galatian State than that of the larger monarchies. Their chief preoccupation was to maintain their independence against possible encroachments on the part of the Seleucids. Their most efficient weapon was furnished by the Galatians. To keep these busy pillaging the western and southern cities of Asia Minor and to prevent them from treating in the same way their own territories was the principal object of their military and diplomatic activity. Apart from this main preoccupation, the northern kings were faced with the same difficult problem as all the other Hellenistic monarchies, large and small—the problem of their relations with the free and independent Greek cities situated within their territories or in their neighbourhood. This problem, however, affected Bithynia and Pontus only, and not Cappadocia.

The danger from Galatia that constantly threatened the cities of central and southern Asia Minor, the policy of the northern kingdoms towards Galatia, and the failure of the Seleucids to put an end to this constant source of dangers, provided certain ambitious half-Greek condottieri with the opportunity of creating and consolidating the State of Pergamon. A flourishing city on the Caicus and an important military stronghold, Pergamon was regarded as a valuable possession both by Lysimachus and Seleucus, especially as a large sum of money was kept in the fortress of the city. Philetaerus was governor of Pergamon both for Lysimachus and Seleucus, and succeeded in creating for himself a position which suggested that of a vassal dynast rather than of a faithful commandant. He and his successor Eumenes were obliged to defend the territory of Pergamon and of the other cities of the valley of the Caicus against Galatian incursions. The consequence was that they gradually increased their military and financial resources, and acquired ever greater independence, until in 262 B.C. Eumenes considered himself strong enough to challenge Antiochus and to support this challenge by military operations. From that time Pergamon became and remained an independent State like Bithynia, Pontus, and Cappadocia, principally concerned to isolate the Galatians in their Phrygian pastures and to protect her own territory, and implicitly the rest of Asia Minor, against their inroads. The reputation of defenders of civilization acquired by Eumenes and his successors (called the Attalids) as a result of their successful warfare with the Galatians, gave them a certain prestige among the Anatolian Greeks and inspired them

PLATE V

1. Marble bust of a young man, a talented military leader. On the head a royal diadem and a Macedonian helmet with cheek-pieces fastened by a leather strap under the chin. The helmet is adorned with an oak wreath. Various considerations, which cannot be discussed here, make it certain that the bust represents the ambitious and erratic PYRRHUS, king of Epirus. (Photograph supplied by Alinari).

The herm has been published several times in almost all the books which deal with ancient portraits (see above, description of pl. IV, 1). The latest discussion will be found in F. Poulsen, 'Bildnisse der Gegner Roms', *Die Antike*, xiv (1938), pp. 137 ff. In this article the author published another head, presumably of Pyrrhus, in the Ny Carlsberg Glyptothek.

2. Head of a marble statue found at Pergamon. The history of the head is peculiar. It represented in its original form an elderly ruler with a royal diadem, in a plain realistic style. Later was added the rich hair, which entirely changed its aspect. The portrait became idealized, heroic, and somewhat pathetic. It is very probable that the head is that of Attalus I of Pergamon, originally portraying him as he was in his lifetime, later modified to represent him as a deified hero. (Photograph supplied by the authorities of the Staatliche Museen, Berlin.)

The head has been often reproduced and discussed. A small selection of references will suffice here: F. Winter, *Alt. v. Perg.* vii, 1908, pp. 144 ff., pls. XXXI, XXXII; R. Delbrück, loc. cit., fig. 14, pl. 27; A. Hekler, loc. cit., pl. 75; G. Dickins, *J.H.S.* xxxiv (1914), pp. 302 ff.; E. Pfuhl, loc. cit., p. 46 f.; E. G. Suhr, loc. cit., pp. 171 ff. Portraits of the later kings of Pergamon (Attalus II and III): F. Poulsen, *Mél. Glotz*, pp. 751 ff.

1. Herm-bust of King Pyrrhus of Epirus.
Naples Museum.

2. Head of a statue of Attalus I of Pergamon.
Staatliche Museen, Berlin.

with the ambition of ultimately replacing the Seleucids as protectors and patrons, in other words of becoming rulers, of Asia Minor. This programme they patiently pursued by clever diplomacy and by always siding with the stronger, having of course as their principal enemies, besides the Galatians, their former suzerains, the Seleucids.

We come finally to the Greek cities of Asia Minor, whether of the islands or of the mainland, some of them permanently, others intermittently independent. Those which were not independent never gave up their efforts to become so, and proved very unreliable allies or subjects of the various Hellenistic monarchs, being always ready to resume the struggle. It is thrilling to follow the destinies of some of these cities, especially of those which were of great importance to the Hellenistic monarchs, such as Miletus, Ephesus, and Smyrna. The much-coveted control of these cities passed from the Ptolemies to the Seleucids and back again, and the cities lived through times of difficulty and hardship; they were repeatedly besieged and captured, and yet never gave up the hope of getting, sometime and somehow, from one of their temporary masters the full measure of autonomy and liberty that each had promised them while they were in the hands of his rival. Meanwhile they endeavoured to derive as much profit as possible from the changing political conditions of the time, by accepting gifts and buildings from the ruler of the day.

Similar relations existed between the Greek cities of the north-western coast of Asia Minor and the Attalids. The great cities of the Straits, the Sea of Marmora, and the southern coast of the Black Sea stood in a position of much greater freedom towards the comparatively weak kings whose territories adjoined them. Such cities were Cyzicus, Byzantium, Chalcedon, Heraclea, and Sinope. During the whole of the period under review they retained their full independence. The situation of the islands of the Aegean, except Rhodes, resembled that of the Lydian, Ionian, and Carian cities rather than that of Cyzicus, Byzantium, and the rest. Like Miletus, Ephesus, &c., they repeatedly passed from the hands of the Ptolemies into those of the Antigonids and back again, some of them keeping their federal organization (the Island League) and striving to protect themselves from robbery and pillage by the belligerents and their allies, the more or less professional pirates on land and sea.

Even more complicated was the situation on the mainland of Greece. Here armed conflict never ceased. It was in part the hereditary struggle against the Macedonians for independence. This struggle, however, was complicated by internal strife between those who stood for the new idea of Greek unity and those who insisted on the time-honoured principle of the complete freedom and independence of each of the Greek cities —between union and particularism. This second struggle was as important in the life of Greece as was that against Macedonia. Strictly speaking, during the period under consideration, except for a short time in the first years of Antigonus Gonatas, Greece was never under the direct domination of the Macedonians, was never a province of Macedonia. Antigonus and his successors were fully satisfied with less forcible measures, by which they might make Greece more or less dependent upon them. The great sources of disturbance were, therefore, the conflict of union and particularism and the struggle of the various 'uniters' of Greece among themselves. There were four champions of the union of Greece, desirous of saving her from the evils of particularism: the two recently created continental leagues (the Aetolian and the Achaean), Sparta, and the kings of Macedonia. Each offered its own form of union: the leagues wished to incorporate the whole of Greece into one federal State, while Sparta strove to restore her old hegemony, and Macedonia devised a new form of Panhellenic symmachy, an alliance between the various local city-leagues and Macedonia under the presidency of the Macedonian king.

The complicated political situation which constituted the balance of power among the Hellenistic States gave rise to almost uninterrupted warfare, which raged throughout the Hellenistic world and with special intensity on the mainland of Greece, in the Greek islands of the Aegean and in the hellenized parts of Asia Minor. A detailed description of these wars and of the political circumstances that led to them cannot be given here. A somewhat dry survey of the most important political and military events, uncertain as some points are, must suffice.

The acute conflict between Antiochus I and Ptolemy Philadelphus over the coastal cities of Asia Minor and Syria took the form of a war which, begun in 280 and renewed in 276 or 274, lasted until 271 (the First Syrian war). At the same time Antiochus I was endeavouring to check the ravages of the Galatians in Asia Minor. Meanwhile Antigonus Gonatas was consolidating his position in Macedonia and Greece in order soon to face a dangerous coalition against him of Athens, Sparta, and Ptolemy Philadelphus, which took shape in 270/269 B.C., or more probably 267/6 B.C., and resulted in a long and devastating war called the Chremonidean war (it lasted until 263 or 261). It ended in the complete victory of Antigonus and the profound humiliation of Athens, which lost for ever its leading role in the political life of Greece. Antigonus emerged from it the undisputed master of Greece, with many strongholds in his hands, especially Corinth and Athens, and the Euboean cities Eretria and Chalcis.

We may regard as part of this war the great naval victory of Antigonus over Ptolemy II off Cos. This victory (which our evidence does not date) certainly gave Antigonus a share in the control of the Aegean, which had hitherto belonged almost exclusively to Ptolemy. It is, however, equally probable that the battle of Cos was not a part but an aftermath of the Chremonidean war, and was one of the episodes of an Aegean war (otherwise unattested in our tradition) launched by Antigonus against Ptolemy in connexion with the events of the Second Syrian war.

At about this time the political horizon in the East again became stormy. Antiochus II, who succeeded his father in 261, attacked Philadelphus, in retaliation for his having supported the revolt of Eumenes in Pergamon (262). It is probable that in his struggle against Ptolemy Antiochus had the support of Antigonus. The attack was launched in Syria and especially in Asia Minor (Second Syrian war, 260 to 255 or 253). The course of the Syrian war was in the main unfavourable to Philadelphus.

Very soon, however, the fortunes of Antigonus and of the Seleucids suffered a sharp reverse. Antigonus was confronted with a new phase in the war of liberation in Greece. The

Aetolian federation since the invasion of the Gauls had been gaining in strength, and Antigonus was unable to check its growth. Even more serious was the situation in the Peloponnese. On the one hand, Antigonus' governor in Corinth, his faithful assistant, Alexander, son of Craterus, established a kingdom of his own based on the two strongholds of his chief—Corinth and the Euboean cities, especially Chalcis—and Antigonus was unable to force him into submission; on the other, an important movement in favour of liberation began in the Peloponnese, where a young Sicyonian, Aratus, inspired with new life the hitherto unimportant league of small Achaean cities (which had existed since 280) by attaching to it his own rich city of Sicyon. This city he had liberated from the rule of a tyrant, who, like many other tyrants in the Peloponnese and elsewhere, was supported by Antigonus (251). Antigonus was unable to arrest the development of the Achaean League; under the clever leadership of Aratus it increased its membership and its political importance in the Peloponnese. After the death of Alexander Antigonus had been able to recover Corinth and to keep the city in his hands for a certain time. The culminating point in the development of the Achaean League was the 'liberation' of Corinth by Aratus in 243.

By this time Antigonus had almost completely lost his control over Greece. Nor was he more successful in his efforts to retain the partial control of the Aegean which he had won at the battle of Cos. It is more than probable that Philadelphus in the last years of his reign renewed his efforts to recover his mastery of that sea. These efforts were apparently not vain. At the end of his life he was once more in a position of influence at Delos and in possession of a strong navy. But his last days may have been saddened by another defeat of his fleet off Andros, if the date generally assigned to this undated and only vaguely mentioned battle (247 B.C.) is correct.

Antiochus II died in 247 and Philadelphus in 246. The first years of Ptolemy III Euergetes, successor of Philadelphus, were stormy. Unexpected events in Syria forced him to undertake another war against that country (the Third Syrian war, 246–241). In support of his sister Berenice, the last wife of Antiochus II, against Laodice, the first wife of Antiochus, and her adult son Seleucus II, he invaded Syria and during the first year of the war overran the whole of Syria and Mesopotamia. His advance, however, was checked by Seleucus' counter-offensive in Syria, which finally obliged Euergetes to evacuate both countries, though the important city of Seleuceia in Pieria remained in his hands.

The partial success of Euergetes in Syria was probably due in some measure to events which took place in the Aegean. A war in the Aegean, which may have been started by Gonatas before the accession of Euergetes, or may have been begun in connexion with the events in the East, was in progress during Euergetes' Syrian expedition. Its course is unknown. It seems, however, that it was not Antigonus Gonatas in his last years, nor Demetrius II during his short reign, who was the most powerful ruler in the Aegean, but Euergetes. He may have lost, it is true, his hegemony at sea. It was the Macedonians, for example, who probably controlled Delos. But we find him still in possession of many islands and of the Thracian coast. We know that during this time his prestige was very high all over Greece, especially in the Peloponnese and in Aetolia and the sphere of Aetolian influence. We see the hand of his diplomats and the influence of his wealth in almost all the important events of this period. The role that he played in the career of Aratus and of Cleomenes will be noted presently. It may be added that Aetolia and her dependency Delphi had profound respect for him, as is attested by the statues erected to him both at Delphi and at Thermos.[13]

In 239 B.C. Antigonus Gonatas died. He was succeeded by his son Demetrius II. Macedonia now no longer played the leading part in Greece. Its place was taken by the two leagues, the Aetolian and the Achaean. For a while these showed a united front against Macedonia. Demetrius with rare skill and energy launched a war (the Demetrian war) successfully against both leagues. Events on his northern frontiers, however, where Macedonia was invaded by the Dardanians, stopped his advance in Greece and he was forced to leave that country for the rest of his short life to its own destinies. The result was that Macedonia almost completely lost its hold of both central Greece and the Peloponnese.

PLATE VI

1. The small head (0·24 m.) in the Museum of Alexandria presented by Sir John Antoniadis, and in consequence known as the Antoniadis head, is a beautiful product of the Hellenistic Alexandrian art which followed the lines of Praxiteles. The identification of the head as that of ARSINOE, queen of Philadelphus, recently suggested by several scholars, is very probable. There are indications that a metal diadem was once fastened to it, and over the front there is a hole which suggests a divine symbol, likewise of metal, crowning the head. (Photograph supplied by the authorities of the Alexandria Museum.)

See E. Breccia, *Alexandrea ad Aegyptum*, 1922, p. 179, fig. 84; E. Poulsen, 'Gab es eine alexandrinische Kunst?', p. 21 f., and fig. 24, and the substantial study of A. Adriani, 'Sculture del Museo Greco-Romano', *Bull. Soc. Arch. Alex.* xxxii (N.S. x. 1) (1938), pp. 90 ff., pls. VII–IX, and figs. 7–9 (with full bibliography). On the other plastic portraits of Arsinoe II see A. Adriani, loc. cit., pp. 94 ff., and below, description of pl. XXXVI. There is nothing in the fine bronze portrait head of a Ptolemaic queen in the Boston Museum (A. W. Lawrence, *J.E.A.* xi (1925), p. 186, pl. XXIII, and I. Noshy, loc. cit., p. 94, with bibliography) to suggest that it is a portrait of Arsinoe II (it is not mentioned by Adriani and Poulsen).

2. Charming head of a marble statue, partly coloured and gilt, found in 1915 in Cyrene and now in the Museum of Bengasi. The head is apparently a product of Hellenistic Alexandrian sculpture of the third century B.C., a slightly idealized portrait in the post-Praxitelean style. There is nothing about the head to prove that it is a royal portrait (no diadem), but general considerations and comparison with coins make it very probable that it represents BERENICE II, daughter of Magas and Apame, and queen of Euergetes I (for whose dramatic story see G. H. Macurdy, *Hellenistic Queens*, 1932, pp. 130 ff.). (Photograph supplied by the Soprintendenza di Antichità di Cirenaica.)

The head has been several times published and discussed. E. Ghislanzoni, *Notiz. Arch. d. Min. delle Colonie*, iv (1927), pp. 165 ff.; C. Anti, *Die Antike*, v (1929), pp. 6 ff., and *Africa Italiana*, i (1927), pp. 164 ff., and ii (1928–9), p. 218, fig. 2; cf. R. Hincks, *J.H.S.* xlviii, p. 240, fig. 1, and A. Adriani, loc. cit., p. 92. I see no reason to share the opinion of E. Pfuhl, loc. cit., p. 43, that the statue to which the head once belonged was a Roman copy (second century A.D.) of an original of the third century B.C. Why should a Roman sculptor choose the statue of a Hellenistic queen to copy? Cf. my pls. XXXVI and XLI.

1. Head of a marble statue in the Museum of Alexandria. Presumably ARSINOE II, wife of Philadelphus.

2. Head of a marble statue in the Museum of Bengasi (Cyrenaica). Presumably BERENICE II, wife of Euergetes.

It was at the time of the Demetrian war that the power of Aetolia in central Greece reached its climax. Since about 300 B.C. Aetolia had been steadily and successfully building up her federal State by incorporating in it, either by persuasion or force, cities and tribes of central Greece. At a very early stage she secured for herself a leading role at Delphi, which she endeavoured to make her intellectual capital—a rival of Macedonian Athens. Her prestige rose enormously after the invasion of the Gauls. Her influence at Delphi was consolidated, and was recognized by the leading powers. Evidence of this is to be found in the history of the victory festival of the Soteria. Celebrated annually by the Amphictions soon after 279 B.C. in memory of the defeat of the Gauls, the festival was reorganized by the Aetolians in 243 (or 246?) in order to emphasize the part that the Aetolians had played in that defeat. Invitations to the new Aetolian Soteria, sent out by the Aetolians, were accepted without reserve by the leading powers of Greece. Not satisfied with continental expansion, Aetolia, availing herself of the terror inspired by Aetolian pirates in the Aegean and Ionian Seas, extended the sphere of her influence beyond the sea by granting protection to her clients against her own pirates; and finally, by dint of clever diplomacy, came to be treated as a strong power by the leading States of the time, Pergamon, Egypt, and Rome.

While Aetolia was uniting central Greece, her temporary ally, the Achaean League, was engaged, for its part, in transforming the whole of the Peloponnese into a single federation. The Achaeans and their leader Aratus were prevented, however, from carrying their work to a successful conclusion by the development of Sparta. The conflict of Achaea and Sparta once more changed the aspect of the Greek world in favour of Macedonia.

Under Agis (245–241 B.C.) Sparta took the first steps towards the reorganization of her social and economic life. Six years later, in 235, his successor Cleomenes resumed the task where Agis had left it and carried out an important reform, which purported to be a restoration of the ancient Lycurgan conditions. The result was a considerable increase in the military strength of Sparta, which enabled Cleomenes and his

State to take a more active and more effective part in the political life of the Peloponnese. As the main effort of Cleomenes was directed against Macedonia, and the anti-Macedonian activity of Aratus was not effective enough to satisfy Ptolemy Euergetes, the latter transferred to Cleomenes the subsidies which he had been paying to Aratus. Equipped both with soldiers and money, Cleomenes started on his project of absorbing the Achaean League into a wider alliance under the leadership of the Spartan king. His success was rapid and extensive. Social revolution was then in the air and Cleomenes had the reputation of bringing with him redistribution of land (γῆς ἀναδασμός) and abolition of debts (χρεῶν ἀποκοπή), measures fervently desired by the proletariat of almost all the Greek cities. Aratus was left almost alone—his allies the Aetolians were jealous of his success and never supported him—and the Achaeans seemed to be willing to recognize Cleomenes as their permanent president. By clever diplomatic machinations Aratus thwarted the plans of Cleomenes, but he paid a heavy price for his success. Instead of an alliance under Spartan presidency he brought about an alliance under the presidency of the Macedonian king, which practically meant the restoration of the Macedonian protectorate over Greece. What Antigonus Doson, the successor of Demetrius II, required as a condition of his helping the Achaean League to fight Sparta was the restoration of Corinth to Macedonia. Aratus accepted all the conditions. Meanwhile Cleomenes lost the support of most of the Peloponnesian cities, for it became clear to the proletariat of these that he was not the apostle of a redistribution of land and an abolition of debts. The result was that in a bloody battle fought at Sellasia (222 or 221) Cleomenes' dream of uniting Greece round Sparta was shattered. Greece (with the exception of Aetolia) was once again, as in the days of Philip, Alexander, and Demetrius, in theory an independent political unit but in fact under the protectorate of the Macedonian king.

While Greece was fighting her great battles for union against particularism, the Seleucid monarchy in the East was rapidly disintegrating. About 249/248 B.C. the political career of Parthia begins. Within a very short time the Seleucids had lost a large part of their Oriental satrapies to the Parthians. About the same time, the Bactrian satrapy under Diodotus gradually asserted its independence, Cappadocia refused subjection to the Seleucid Empire and Armenia practically did the same. The Seleucids were unable to arrest this process of disintegration, at first owing to the pressure of the Third Syrian war (246–241), then because of a dynastic war which broke out soon after the Third Syrian war (235) and lasted for many years. The conflict between Seleucus II and his brother Antiochus Hierax was carried on mostly in Asia Minor, the province of the latter. Its main result was the growth of Pergamon, which under Attalus I not only succeeded in crushing the Galatians in a series of battles (the most famous being that of the Caicus in 230), but also in creating round Pergamon a real kingdom whose ruler took the title of king after his great Galatian victories and kept it after a series of victories over Seleucus III, the successor of Seleucus II (226). Although after the death of Seleucus (223) he lost the greater part of his conquests to Achaeus, who had been appointed governor of Asia Minor, Attalus and his successors retained their full independence and their royal title. The Seleucids never made any serious attempt to recover the territory they had lost in this part of Asia Minor.

After the death of Seleucus III in 223 and of Antigonus Doson and Euergetes in 221, we come to a new period in the evolution of the Hellenistic world, in which the protagonists were Philip V of Macedonia, Antiochus III of Syria, and the Romans, who from 230 onwards took an increasingly active interest in the affairs, first of the Adriatic Sea, and later of the Hellenistic monarchies in general.

Even such a brief survey of the political events of 280–221 B.C. as has been given is sufficient to show that this period, like that which preceded it, was one of nearly continuous warfare for almost all the States that composed the Hellenistic balance of power.

C. POLITICAL DECAY OF THE HELLENISTIC MONARCHIES

As regards the period next to be reviewed (that between the accession of Philip V and Antiochus III and the gradual transformation of the leading States of the Hellenistic world into Roman provinces) our information may be called good for the years between 221 and 145 and rather scanty for the remainder.[14] The events in the East from the time of the first appearance of the Romans there to 145 B.C. have been described by the great Achaean, Polybius. His work became classical soon after its publication and was extensively used by all the historians who endeavoured to describe the Roman conquest of the East. I need not here discuss Polybius. Every one agrees that he is a trustworthy guide in the tangle of Greco-Roman relations and that so long as we have his narrative we may follow it with almost complete safety. Unfortunately his history is a torso. The missing books and parts of books are known to us only from scattered fragments, of which the sequence is mostly uncertain. The gaps left in our information by the lacunae in Polybius are to a large extent filled by the narrative of Livy, who followed him more or less closely, sometimes almost translating him. But, unfortunately, Livy's work also is a torso and in some cases the gaps in the manuscripts are not covered by the extant parts of Polybius. Moreover, Livy's narrative is often marred by the use he made of Roman annalists. The Polybian history was also the source of the brief account of events written by Diodorus; but this we have only in fragments. The summary of Justin (abbreviation of Pompeius Trogus) likewise follows Polybius closely, as do also the more substantial narratives of Appian and Cassius Dio (excerpted by Zonaras). The last, however, used Polybius at second hand and combined him with the Roman annalists. Plutarch's biographies of Aratus and of Philopoemen (the latter based on Polybius' biography of Philopoemen) are for the most part reliable and from a literary standpoint excellent. His sources are different in his biographies of Flamininus ('inspired' by Polybius), of Aemilius Paulus (the question of the sources is controversial), and of the older Cato (based perhaps on Cato's own writings). Scattered facts are recorded by many contemporary and later writers, such as Cato, Cicero, Frontinus, Plutarch in his minor works, Pausanias, Athenaeus, and others. To the information derived from literary sources, inscriptions, papyri, and coins add many valuable illustrations and sometimes fill in minor gaps in our tradition. Thanks to all this, the history of the period is well known in its general outline, and most of the divergences regarding it to be found in the works of modern historians are due not to inadequate information but to differences in the interpretation of well-established facts.

Our situation as regards the history of the period that followed the great catastrophe of 145 is far less satisfactory. The attention of historians was now more than ever attracted to Rome rather than to the Greek world, and, moreover, among the hundreds of authors of that time there was no great historian like Polybius. Though a learned scholar and a brilliant writer, Posidonius, the continuator of Polybius, was probably not his equal as an historian. Unfortunately his work, though extensively used by his contemporaries and by later writers, is very little known to us. Very few fragments have been transmitted under his name.

It is probable that in his great historical work, known to us mainly from his *Geography*, Strabo, the successor of Posidonius, made large use of his predecessor's history in that part of his work which covered the same period, and so probably did Livy (the corresponding books of his history are not extant and their contents are known to us only from the *Periochae* and from later abbreviators) and Diodorus (also extant only in fragments). Their scanty evidence is supplemented by Justin's abstracts of Pompeius Trogus. The relation of some fragments of the great history of Sallust to Posidonius is unknown. Of the later authors the most important are Plutarch and Appian. Plutarch's biographies of Lucullus, Sertorius, Sulla, Pompey, Cicero, Caesar, and Antony throw abundant light on the vicissitudes of the Hellenistic States with which his heroes came into contact, but it is to the work of Appian that we owe the possibility of restoring the skeleton of the history of some of these States (especially Syria and Egypt) in the period after 145 B.C. Most valuable in this respect are his treatment of the history of Syria and of Mithridates and his books on the civil war. His sources and those of Plutarch are unknown. Under these conditions no detailed continuous narrative of the political events of the period is possible. Certain episodes, however, are well known, for instance, the history of Mithridates; for this we are in part indebted to historians who devoted special works to describing the Mithridatic war and the reign of Mithridates in general.

PLATE VII

1. Realistic portrait of ANTIOCHUS III (pl. XXIX, 7) wearing a diadem. The tetradrachm of which the obverse is reproduced here belongs to the copious series of staters, tetradrachms, and drachms minted by the king after his eastern 'anabasis', that is to say, in his most glorious days. E. T. Newell, loc. cit., p. 54.

2. Slightly idealized portrait of ANTIOCHUS IV (pl. LXXIX, 7) with the royal diadem. The coin of which the obverse is here reproduced was minted at Antioch probably soon after the king's accession. E. T. Newell, loc. cit., p. 56.

3. Portrait of DEMETRIUS I, son of Euthydemus of Bactria (pl. LXIX, 8, cf. E. T. Newell, loc. cit., pl. IX, 5) wearing a diadem and the elephant head-dress. The coins which show this highly spirited portrait of Demetrius were probably minted by him from the beginning of his reign. In this case they cannot allude to his conquest of India (as generally supposed) but manifest his desire to appear as a second Alexander. W. W. Tarn, *The Greeks in Bactria and India*, 1938, p. 131.

4. Portrait of PHILETAERUS heroized (see the *taenia* in his hair), founder of the dynasty of the Attalids. Coins bearing his portrait were minted at Pergamon from the time of Eumenes I. The portrait reproduced here forms the obverse of a tetradrachm of Attalus I. As it appears on our coin, it is slightly idealized as compared with the portraits of the coins of Eumenes I. Nevertheless it is realistic, 'displaying almost the brutal frankness of Roman portraiture' (E. T. Newell). E. T. Newell, loc. cit., p. 36.

5. Elegant portrait of PHILIP V (pl. LXIX, 9) bearded, wearing a diadem. The portrait shows him at the beginning of his reign. E. T. Newell, loc. cit., p. 30.

On the portraits of Antiochus III, Antiochus IV, and Philetaerus see also E. Pfuhl, loc. cit., pp. 24 f. and 9 f.

Enlarged coin portraits of 1. Antiochus III, 2. Antiochus IV, 3. Demetrius I of Bactria, 4. Philetaerus of Pergamon, 5. Philip V

Such works were extensively used by Strabo, Appian, and Plutarch, and by Memnon in his history of Heraclea Pontica. The same may be said of the last years of the independence of Egypt. However, for most of this period our information is scanty and often unreliable.

The history of the Jewish people offers another exception to the general rule. The works of Flavius Josephus and the Books of Maccabees give a continuous history of the Jews in their relation to the Hellenistic world and to Rome. This tradition is supplemented by certain religious and semi-religious books (for example, the Book of Daniel) which often mention historical events.

The epigraphical, papyrological, and numismatic evidence is comparatively rich and allows us to establish many facts not mentioned in our fragmentary literary evidence.

The balance of power established in the middle of the third century B.C. was shaken to its foundations by the events of the last years of that century. Certain new factors completely changed the political aspect of the Hellenistic world. Two young monarchs, men of talent and ambition, became almost simultaneously rulers of the two most important monarchies, Philip V of Macedonia and Antiochus III of Syria. Each had his own ambitious projects, and each was determined to carry them out. The main preoccupation of Philip, the successor of Antigonus Doson, was not so much with his perennial enemies the Aetolians as with a new western rival, who was beginning to exercise a powerful influence on the affairs of the Hellenistic world. That rival was Rome. For a long time she had almost completely ignored the East and the Greek world. Busy extending her sway over central Italy and forming the great Italian federation, then fighting the Carthaginians and the Celts, Rome had very little contact with the East in political affairs, although her cultural relations with it were very close, especially through the Greek cities of South Italy and Sicily.

It was owing to considerations of domestic Italian policy that Macedonia and Greece began to play a certain role in the politics of Rome. The establishment of a strong Illyrian State on the eastern shore of the Adriatic and the piracy organized by it, systematically and on a large scale, made it imperative for Rome to interfere, in order to protect the coasts of Italy and Italy's already important trade relations with the Greek world. The moment was propitious, for at that time Rome had her hands free in Italy. The result of this armed intervention (229 B.C.) was the establishment of a Roman protectorate over certain Greek cities of the Illyrian coast, of which Dyrrhachium, Apollonia, Aulon, and Oricus were the most important, and of Roman control over a coastal region behind these cities. The purpose was to secure complete command of the main line of communications between Italy and Greece, the straits of Otranto.

These measures were an encroachment on the rights of Macedonia and a grave danger to that State. Not only had the Greek cities of Illyria formerly depended on Macedonia; more important was the fact that Rome now became its neighbour and had easy access to its territory along the valleys of the rivers Genusus, Apsus, and Aôus. Moreover, Rome, both before and after her military operations, ignored the very existence of Macedonia, while entering into diplomatic relations with its enemies and its allies alike—with Aetolia, Achaea, Corinth, and Athens (228 B.C.). Neither Doson nor Philip failed to read the situation aright, and from this time onwards Rome became their principal preoccupation. Macedonia was not safe so long as part of the Illyrian coast was in the hands of the Romans.

Philip's first years after his accession (220 B.C.) were a time of war and unrest. His chief enemies, the Aetolians, decided to take advantage of the youth and inexperience of the new Macedonian king in order to carry out their plans of Panhellenic hegemony. In this they miscalculated. The young king showed both experience and boldness. In a great war—the war of the Allies—he succeeded in protecting the Hellenic League against the Aetolians and in forcing upon the latter the peace of Naupactus (217 B.C.). The conditions of this agreement were very favourable to Philip.

With the peace of Naupactus begins the determined struggle between Philip and Rome for the control of Illyria. This is not the place to describe it in detail. It led Philip to an alliance with Hannibal (215), and this alliance in turn led the Romans to an understanding with the enemies of Philip in Greece, the Aetolians, and with Attalus of Pergamon (212). The result was a long war for the control of Greece between Philip and Aetolia in alliance with Rome, a war in which Rome at first was active, but subsequently took no part whatever. The war lasted six years, until the Aetolians, weary and discouraged, made a separate peace with Philip (206 B.C.), which was soon followed by a peace between Philip and Rome (205).

Meanwhile important events happened in the East. The dominating ambition of Antiochus III was to restore the early Seleucid Empire to its former greatness. He became king of Syria in 223 B.C. as a youth of 18, a little before Philip became king of Macedonia. His first years were difficult. Asia Minor was in the hands of his cousin Achaeus, and in the East his governor Molon started (in 221) a successful revolt. Relations with Egypt were far from satisfactory. In this difficult situation Antiochus showed himself a man of energy and ability. He re-established his authority in the East, came to an acceptable understanding with Achaeus in Asia Minor, and finally tried to avert the Egyptian danger by invading Egypt. This last attempt failed. The new king of Egypt, Ptolemy Philopator, inflicted a crushing defeat on him at Raphia (217 B.C.). But Antiochus was not discouraged by this defeat. Even after it he retained Seleuceia in Pieria which he had captured in 219 B.C. (the city had previously been in the hands of the Ptolemies since the Syrian campaign of Euergetes I), and he saw clearly that the sharp blow dealt by Egypt at Raphia was but an accident which in all probability would never occur again. So he went boldly ahead in his endeavours to restore the early Seleucid Empire. But before this work of restoration could be seriously begun conditions in Asia Minor had to be radically changed. It was evident that Achaeus was acting as an independent king hostile to Antiochus, and that he was prevented from open rebellion only by the fact that his troops would not fight against the legitimate king of the Seleucid Empire. Antiochus, in alliance with Pergamon, by a war which lasted three years, settled the Anatolian question and pacified Asia Minor. He was now ready for his great and ambitious expedition to the East, his Anabasis. The authority of the Seleucids was at this moment very low in the farther East. Parthia under the Arsacids was growing rapidly; in Bactria the native Greek kings were successfully extending the limits of their kingdom; and the success of these two rebels undermined the loyalty of most of the Seleucid governors in the East. In his great expedition Antiochus did not reconquer Parthia and Bactria and did not aim at doing so. By his military operations he demonstrated the strength of Syria and re-established on a firm basis the authority of the Seleucid rule among the Asiatic satraps. It was a success, but it was not a repetition of the Anabasis of Alexander, although the subjects of Antiochus and the Greeks all over the Hellenistic world compared the exploits of the Great King Antiochus with those of his famous predecessor. In any case, his prestige after this expedition was very high, both in his kingdom and outside it, and he was regarded as a kind of second Alexander.

The conflict of Philip with Rome and the great successes of Antiochus in the East created a new situation in the Hellenistic world. Antiochus was now ready to extend his work of restoration not only to Phoenicia and Palestine, which were in the hands of the Ptolemies, but also to Asia Minor, where many cities which formerly recognized the authority of the first Seleucids were now in the power of the Ptolemies, while others were either independent or under the rule of the Pergamene kings. In carrying out his design, however, Antiochus had to reckon with Philip. Philip emerged from his struggle with the Aetolians and Rome stronger and more ambitious than ever. He had learned a bitter lesson as regards his relations with the members of the Greek leagues and was ready to revert to the policy of Cassander in dealing with his Greek allies. He had been a favourite of the Greeks, but now, after his 'change of heart' (μεταβολή), he was hated by them and regarded as a bloody tyrant. He understood, moreover, how difficult it was to fight Rome without a navy and without abundant material resources. Greece was too poor to furnish him with either, even under compulsion. The only chance Philip had of increasing his resources was to get access to the East and to re-establish in the Aegean the authority which Antigonus Gonatas had formerly won there in his struggle with the Ptolemies. The islands and the cities of Asia Minor were still rich, at least richer than Greece, and once in his hands they could provide him with the means by which he might acquire a navy and thus be able to fight the Romans. But the place once occupied by Macedonia and Egypt in the Aegean was no longer vacant. Both Rhodes and Pergamon aspired to control that sea and would hardly acquiesce in Philip's hegemony over it. Moreover, Philip's plans conflicted at many points with those of Antiochus.

Even to make a start on his Aegean venture Philip needed ships and money. And he had none. On the other hand, he realized the necessity of undermining in every possible way the prestige and the power of the Rhodians in the Aegean. Some time before (in 218) he had succeeded in improving his finances and giving trouble to the Rhodians by a device which he had learned from the Aetolians—robbery on sea and land through the medium of private corsairs, who in fact acted with his support and on his behalf. His agent had then been Demetrius of Pharos. He now employed two minor adventurers of the same type, Dicaearchus the Aetolian and Heracleides the Tarentine. They successfully raided for him a number of islands and mainland cities and tried to destroy by treachery the naval resources of Rhodes. At the same time Philip instigated in 205/4 B.C. a fierce war between Crete and Rhodes, including the allies of the latter, especially the prosperous island of Cos—a war known as the 'Cretan war' (Κρητικὸς πόλεμος). The result was that Philip was finally able to appear in the Aegean with a comparatively strong fleet, a match for the fleets of Rhodes and Pergamon.

His policy for the time being was to secure an understanding with Antiochus and to carry on a ruthless war with the Rhodians and Pergamon. Hence the scandalous treaty with Antiochus (202 B.C.), by which the two kings divided between themselves the foreign provinces of the Ptolemies without even informing Egypt or declaring war on it. They hoped that Egypt, disturbed as it was by a stubborn revolt of the natives and ruled by unscrupulous politicians who, since the death of Philopator (204), surrounded the new boy-king (Ptolemy V Epiphanes), would not offer any resistance to their plans.

The series of military operations that followed the treaty of

Antiochus and Philip resulted in a great success for the former (after some fighting he added Palestine, Phoenicia, and part of southern Syria definitely to his kingdom and probably acquired some cities in southern Anatolia) and in a catastrophe for the latter. The enemies of Philip were stronger than the adversary of Antiochus. After he had obtained some temporary successes, Rhodes and Pergamon checked his progress and forced him to mobilize all his resources, which had never been large. Finally, just when Philip was in a difficult position, blockaded in Caria by the naval forces of his rivals (201/200), his enemies, Attalus of Pergamon and the Rhodians, decided to appeal to Rome for help against him, and Rome, under strong pressure from the Rhodians and on some trifling pretexts, declared war upon him. Philip therefore, after escaping by a ruse from Caria, was obliged to retire from the East and to concentrate what remained of his forces in his own kingdom.

From this time begins the series of wars by which the Romans annihilated the forces of the two leading monarchies of the East, followed by the diplomatic and military measures which brought both Macedonia and Syria first into the Roman sphere of influence and finally into their empire. Rome's policy herein was dictated at the outset, not by any desire to increase her empire by adding to it territories in the East, but by a feeling of uneasiness aroused by the policy of Philip and Antiochus, just at the time when she had emerged victorious but exhausted from the Punic wars. Hannibal had invaded Italy; why should not Philip (a former ally of Hannibal) and Antiochus attack Rome and invade Italy in their turn? There was nothing impossible in the surmise. Alexander—such was the firm belief of the leading historians of the time—had been determined to add the West to his world empire, and since his day Pyrrhus had shown that there were men in Greece willing and able to make the attempt and to unite against Rome all who disliked her supremacy in Italian affairs. Rome was suspicious of the Hellenistic East, with its glorious military traditions and its reputation of being the home of all the great inventions in the field of strategy, tactics, and war machinery. Rome felt herself in this respect a pupil of Greece and was afraid of her teacher. This fear was never quelled in the Roman mind. Even after the great and easy victories over Philip, Antiochus, and Perseus, Rome was still afraid of Macedonia and Syria, and acted accordingly. As late as the time of Mithridates the Great, she did not feel quite safe in her Italian home, and one has only to read Horace to realize the immense relief brought by the great victory over Cleopatra at Actium, and the fear inspired by the Parthians, the successors of the Seleucids. Moreover, Carthage was still in being, and an alliance between Philip and Carthage was not out of the question. It was natural, therefore, that the Romans, after the victorious end of the Second Punic war, should without hesitation seize the first opportunity that offered of engaging one of the two allies. They had the support, material and moral, of a large part of the Greek world (especially of Rhodes and Athens, the champions of democracy) and they were encouraged by Rhodes and Pergamon to expect that Antiochus would not come to the assistance of his ally. They knew, moreover, that Philip had experienced great losses in his war with Rhodes and Pergamon and that at some later time he might emerge from a renewed venture in the East much stronger and better prepared than he was in 200 and 199 B.C.

The result was the Second Macedonian war, which was easily won by the Romans (battle of Cynoscephalae, 197 B.C.) and which brought them enormous prestige throughout the Hellenistic world. After this war Philip ceased to be, *de facto*, an independent monarch. The Romans watched him closely and would not allow him to carry out a policy of his own except in his relations with the Celtic, Thracian, and Illyrian North. Greece was proclaimed free and independent (196 B.C.). Her liberty was at least morally, if not *de jure*, guaranteed by Rome. Various explanations may be offered of Rome's policy in this matter. There is no doubt, however, that the measure was a great diplomatic success and for a time rendered the position of Rome in her dealings with Antiochus much easier than it would otherwise have been. For she thereby at least deprived Antiochus of the active support of Greece in his resistance to herself. The policy of Flamininus by which Rome secured a free Greece as her ally was as much directed against Antiochus as was that of the ten commissioners sent to settle affairs in

PLATE VIII

Stele found at Cleitor in Arcadia, now in the schoolhouse of Mazeika; in its present state very badly damaged. Here reproduced from a plaster-cast made, soon after its discovery, for the Berlin Museum. The stele is adorned with the heroized figure of a man standing, seen frontwise, the head turned to the left. He wears an exomis and a chlamys, his legs and feet are bare. In his left hand he holds a spear, behind him are his round shield and helmet. To his belt is attached a short sword. With his right hand he makes a gesture which may be that of adoration or prayer. On the lintel above the figure was engraved a distich of which the second line only was preserved when the stele was first discovered. The inscription has been restored as follows: [*τοῦτο Λυκόρτα παιδὶ πόλις περικαλλὲς ἄγαλμα*] | *ἀντὶ καλῶν ἔργων εἵσατο Πọ[υ]λụ[βίωι]* (*I.G.* v. 2, 370; F. Hiller von Gaertringen, *Historische Griechische Epigramme*, 1926, n. 112, cf. *S.I.G.*[3] 686). Statues (at Olympia and Pallantium) and bas-reliefs were erected to Polybius as a statesman after his death probably in all the cities of Arcadia (we have evidence of this for Mantinea, Megalopolis, Lykosura (?), Tegea, *I. G.* v. 2, p. xxxi, 27, 39, 70, nos. 304, 537 (?). (Photograph supplied by the authorities of the Mostra Augustea, Rome.)

Much has been written about the bas-relief, see the bibliography in *Mostra Augustea della Romanità*, Catalogo, 1938 (Appendice bibliografica e Indici), p. 30, no. 1, especially (for a stylistic analysis) H. Möbius, *J.D.A.I.* xlix (1934), p. 57 and figs. 5 (cast) and 6 (original as it is now). H. 2·15, W. 1·10 m.

Polybius, the Historian and Statesman

Greece after Cynoscephalae, who were inclined to establish an Aetolian hegemony there and to give Pergamon the supervision of the country.

We are therefore not surprised to find that the Romans after the Second Macedonian war gradually but systematically made war with Antiochus inevitable, though Antiochus tried by every means to avoid it (193 B.C.). They wanted to weaken the great Oriental conqueror while they were on more or less good terms with Greece and before Philip was willing and prepared to co-operate with him. The issue of the war was decided by the failure of Antiochus to rally Greece round him and by his retreat to Asia Minor after the battle of Thermopylae (191 B.C.). The battle of Magnesia (189 B.C.), one of the easiest victories ever won by the Romans, was merely a sequel to this failure. The result of Magnesia (the treaty of Apamea, 188 B.C.) resembled that of Cynoscephalae. Rome threw Syria out of the Greek world, won the sympathy of some of the Greek cities in Anatolia (it is noteworthy that no proclamation of liberty for all Greeks was made in Asia Minor), and established her permanent control over the whole of Anatolia, including Galatia and in fact, if not legally, Bithynia. Pontus, Cappadocia, and to a certain extent Armenia, were doomed sooner or later to submit in their turn to Roman authority.

With the appearance of Rome as an active and decisive force on its horizon the political aspect of the Hellenistic world changed completely. To begin with, that world now ceased to be a political unit. In the third century, in spite of wars, quarrels, jealousies, and so forth, it had formed a single unit both as regards politics and civilization. I have already insisted upon this unity and expressed my conviction that unless the Hellenistic world is treated as a single whole, its political development in the third century B.C. can hardly be fully understood. The Roman intervention put an end to this unity. No doubt there were still diplomatic relations between the various kingdoms and cities, dynastic marriages were still used as political weapons and were very popular among the Greeks (a prominent case was the marriage of Perseus and Laodice, daughter of Seleucus IV, 178 B.C.), but all this was now of very little importance. Rome through her agents, especially the

Pergamene kings, kept a watchful eye on these relations and would not tolerate even the possibility of a real *rapprochement* between the important Hellenistic powers.

In fact, the Hellenistic world was now split into three groups, which were in no direct contact with each other: Macedonia and Greece formed one group, Asia Minor another, Syria and Egypt the third. A few words may be said about each of these groups.

Macedonia was forced to abandon entirely her long-cherished ambition to rule over Greece and control the Aegean. These aspirations were now mere dreams. The only realities in Macedonia's political life were her relations with Rome. The proud Antigonids were not disposed to act as obedient vassals of that power, and their only preoccupation was to find a way of shaking off her heavy hand. In the last resort this meant, of course, war.

Greece for a while enjoyed her recently acquired liberty enormously. The Greeks at first took the declaration of Flamininus quite seriously, and there is no doubt that Flamininus and the Roman Senate intended it so. Achaea and Aetolia went on trying to incorporate the whole of Greece in their respective Leagues. Sparta, remodelled by Nabis on more or less socialistic and communistic lines, endeavoured to recover her Peloponnesian hegemony. But most of the other Greek cities deeply resented any encroachment by one of the Leagues or by Sparta on their new-found freedom. These diverging interests, after the withdrawal of the Roman armed forces, inevitably led to political quarrels and petty wars. It was natural that the weaker party when faced with defeat should appeal to the great protector of Greece's freedom and should send embassy after embassy to Rome, followed of course by immediate counter-embassies from their opponents. In order to secure peace and to prevent Greece from supporting Macedonia, Rome never refused to act as arbiter in these petty disputes. Her decisions always took the form of friendly advice. But such advice was almost an order. Neither of the adversaries could reject it, for behind it lay the power and authority of Rome. Thus the freedom of Greece was very like a disguised vassalage. The Greeks perfectly understood the situation and resented it deeply. There was, however, no way out of it, except by armed resistance.

Asia Minor after Magnesia in some respects resembled Greece after Cynoscephalae. It was now a country comprising larger and smaller monarchies of various types and many more or less independent cities. The largest and the strongest monarchy was Pergamon. But Pergamon was strong only so long as its kings blindly obeyed the dictates of Rome and were her faithful allies. Every independent act, every attempt to follow a policy of their own was keenly resented and harshly rebuked by the Roman Senate. Similar was the position of all the stronger States of Asia Minor: the monarchies of Bithynia, Pontus, Cappadocia, and the tribal States of the Galatians. Sooner or later, when one of the Anatolian monarchies endeavoured to pursue its own ends, whatever those ends might be, it felt the heavy hand of Rome. Here again the only way to change the situation was by war.

Syria and Egypt remained independent after Magnesia. Egypt's independence was not a menace to Rome. The Ptolemies of the second century B.C. never showed any signs of nourishing anti-Roman aspirations. The situation of Syria was different. She was deprived of Asia Minor, the most hellenized part of her empire, by the treaty of Apamea, and her relations with Greece were thereby rendered more difficult and irregular. Moreover, she no longer had a strong navy wherewith to protect her interests in the Mediterranean and the Aegean. She was therefore doomed by force of circumstances to become gradually an Oriental State.

It is unnecessary to relate once more the sad story of the gradual conquest of the Hellenistic East by the Romans. The Second Macedonian and the Syrian wars were soon followed by a Third Macedonian war, when it became evident to Rome that Perseus, the successor of Philip, was not prepared blindly to obey her orders. The result, after the battle of Pydna (168 B.C.), was that Macedonia as a political unit ceased to exist and, after a short period of semi-autonomy, was transformed into a Roman province (147 B.C.). The sympathy—passive as it was—that the Greek world showed to Perseus and the attempt—abortive as it was—of Perseus to create a Panhellenic League against Rome, so exasperated the Romans that they did not shrink from harsh measures against the Achaean League and from humiliating the glorious republic of Rhodes, thereby leaving the Aegean at the mercy of pirates. The result of this oppressive treatment was the desperate attempt of the Achaean League to assert its liberty, an attempt which ended in the temporary disappearance of this and all other Leagues and in the utter humiliation of Greece. Corinth, the chief stronghold of Greece and of the Achaean League, was ruthlessly destroyed, and Greece became a kind of pitiful appendix to the Roman province of Macedonia (145 B.C.). Thus ended the political life of Macedonia and Greece.

The group of States comprised in Asia Minor had a somewhat longer existence. Here also the leading feature in political affairs was isolation. It was purely local questions that occupied the minds of the leading statesmen in the country, such as the ever-recurring project of extending the territory of one State at the expense of its neighbours or of incorporating some free Greek city in one or other Anatolian monarchy. Territorial problems were always matters of deep concern to the several States of Asia Minor; they gave rise to permanent hostility between them, and led from time to time to wars. These wars were mostly futile, since the questions at issue were always in one way or another settled by the Romans; but the Romans allowed them to take place because they prevented particular monarchies from becoming too strong and potentially dangerous. The Romans saw to it that they should not bring to any of the combatants an undue accession of power.

The protagonists in the political activities of Asia Minor after Magnesia were Pergamon, Bithynia, which her talented king Prusias I formed into a strong and well-organized kingdom, Pontus, which after modest beginnings became under Pharnaces I one of the strongest monarchies in Anatolia, and Cappadocia. These last three States, to which we may add Galatia, were the chief fomenters of trouble. In the early years after Magnesia it was the task of Pergamon, to a large extent in its capacity of Roman agent, to hold their ambitions in check. It was Eumenes II who finally brought under restraint the brigand community of the Galatians, it was he who prevented

Prusias of Bithynia from profiting by the defeat of Antiochus III, and it was he again who in coalition with others crushed the ambitious plans of Pharnaces I. The war to which these plans gave rise lasted for four years (183–179 B.C.), and might have developed into a general conflagration of the East if Seleucus IV, the successor of Antiochus III, had not been too much afraid of Rome and if Philip had been in a position to strike. This is the reason why Rome repeatedly tried to settle the dispute and probably contributed by her authority to the peace of 179 B.C.

The role, however, of Pergamon as arbiter of Anatolian affairs soon came to an end. The turning-point in the relations between Rome and her faithful allies in Asia Minor and the Aegean (Pergamon and Rhodes) came with the Third Macedonian war, when the sympathies not only of continental Greece but also of Pergamon and Rhodes were with Perseus, although officially they all took active part on the side of Rome in the war against him. Rome was sensible of this and shaped her policy accordingly as soon as the war was over and her supremacy was re-established (as we shall see later) by mere diplomatic intervention in Syria. The last years of the reign of Eumenes II were for him years of great disappointment. Rome never allowed him again to play the leading part, to which he had become accustomed, in the political life of Asia Minor. In his heroic struggle with the Galatians, the scourge of Asia Minor, he was not supported by Rome. The Romans, in fact, encouraged the Galatians. The halo that surrounded Eumenes II after his great victories over the Galatians and the popularity he thereafter enjoyed among the Anatolian Greeks increased the suspicions of Rome, and made their treatment of him still harsher.

Even more cruel was the punishment of Rhodes for her attempt to save Perseus. By a series of measures Rome deposed her from her commercial hegemony in the Aegean, undermined her position as the protector of Hellenic trade against pirates in that sea, and deprived her of the territory on the mainland of Asia Minor that had been assigned to her after Magnesia. The result was that a state of political anarchy was created both in Anatolia and in the Aegean.

PLATE IX

1. Realistic portrait of NICOMEDES II of Bithynia (pl. XCII, 8) wearing the royal diadem.

2. Brutally realistic portrait of PHARNACES I (pl. XCII, 1) wearing the royal diadem.

3. Idealized romantic and pathetic portrait of MITHRIDATES THE GREAT of Pontus (pl. CIII, 2) wearing the royal diadem, in the style of some portraits of Alexander the Great. Note the change over to idealism from the painstaking and rather commonplace realism of his predecessors, and the Greek type of the head of Mithridates compared with the barbaric features of his ancestors.

4. Portrait of DEMETRIUS II of Syria after his return from Parthian captivity, wearing a beard in the Parthian fashion (cf. pl. XCII, 3) and the royal diadem. Cf. E. T. Newell, loc. cit., p. 61 and pl. VII, 27.

5. Superimposed portraits of CLEOPATRA THEA and her son ANTIOCHUS VIII GRYPUS of Syria. The queen wears a crown-like diadem and a veil, her hair is arranged in long ringlets; Grypus behind her in subordinate position wears a plain royal diadem. On the portraits of Cleopatra see E. Pfuhl, loc. cit., p. 43 f. On the 'Libyan' locks see below, pl. XCVI.

On the style of the coin portraits here reproduced see E. Pfuhl, loc. cit., pp. 16, 15, and 43 f.

Enlarged coin portraits of 1. Nicomedes II of Bithynia, 2. Pharnaces I of Pontus, 3. Mithridates VI of Pontus, 4. Demetrius II of Syria, 5. Antiochus VIII and Cleopatra Thea of Syria.

So long as Pergamon and Rhodes were the decisive forces in these areas, and, even after Pydna, so long as Eumenes II was alive, Hellenism continued to develop peacefully in Anatolia, despite the outbreaks of the Galatians and several local wars. Rhodes promoted it in the South, Eumenes II supported it in central Anatolia, the kings of Bithynia and of Pontus did likewise in the North. Nor were there any signs of the further political disintegration of Asia Minor, except in its southern region after the punishment of Rhodes.

A great change in the political life of Asia Minor was effected by the act of Attalus III, the successor of Eumenes II and Attalus II, who in 133 B.C. bequeathed his kingdom to the Romans. We do not know whether this act was dictated by political or personal or dynastic considerations. If political considerations were involved, they are not difficult to understand. Pergamon had become irretrievably a vassal kingdom of Rome. The glorious period of hegemony and of at least semi-independence had come to an end. Attalus III was conscious of this and felt that the position of his successors would be even worse. The kings of Pergamon bore a heavy responsibility while they enjoyed no privileges such as would attract ambitious statesmen. Why should not Rome take direct responsibility for Asia Minor?

Whatever were the reasons that impelled Attalus, the Romans accepted the bequest, and the result was that the most hellenized and the richest part of Asia Minor became, after some political and social disturbances following the king's death, a Roman province. First Pergamon, and afterwards Ephesus, was adopted as the residence of a representative of the Roman Senate and People. The rulers who had been regarded as the chief supporters of the Anatolian balance of power and the great promoters of Hellenism thus disappeared, and Asia Minor was left in the hands of Roman governors, who were but little interested in it, and regarded it merely as a source of income both to the public purse and to themselves.

A strong reaction against this state of things set in not only among the Anatolian Greeks, who were disposed to welcome any one willing and able to put an end to Roman rule, but also among the inhabitants of the kingdom of Pontus. This part of

Asia Minor had never come under the strict control of Rome, and its Iranian aristocracy, which had been only slightly hellenized, retained its martial spirit and national pride. More hellenized than Cappadocia and Armenia, less feudal in its structure than these two neighbours, richer and better organized than they, Pontus was the natural leader in a struggle against Rome which would unite in a single effort the Greeks and the Iranians both of Asia Minor and of Armenia and even Parthia. Greek hatred and the Iranian national revival were the main forces that sustained the long and obstinate struggle with Rome to which Mithridates VI of Pontus devoted the whole of his life. His failure was due not only to the strength of Rome and to his own limited ability but also to the fact that the Greeks supported him for only a short time and that the assistance of his Iranian neighbours was likewise not enduring. Cappadocia was from the outset hostile to him, and though he was supported by Armenia, which at that time was the strongest semi-Iranian power in the Near East, Mithridates was unable to supplement his coalition with Tigranes by an alliance with Parthia, the rival and enemy of Armenia.

After the disappearance of the Pergamene kingdom Mithridates' war with Rome was the first and last political act of Hellenistic Anatolia that influenced in some degree the development of the ancient world. The failure of Mithridates had as its natural consequence the transformation of Asia Minor into a group of Roman provinces and dependencies. The latter were to a large extent vassal kingdoms, more or less hellenized, which existed by the grace of Rome so long as she thought it convenient to allow these vassal kings to urbanize and hellenize the backward countries of the peninsula.

While determined to control the Greek world—Greece, Macedonia, the Aegean, and Asia Minor—in order to obtain complete security at home as well as an abundant revenue, Rome, immediately after the treaty of Apamea, seemed to be less interested in the destinies of the two eastern Hellenistic monarchies, Syria and Egypt. These Oriental States, once they were isolated from the Greek world and forced to keep aloof from Mediterranean politics, seemed harmless enough to be left to their own concerns and quarrels. But this policy of *laisser-faire* very soon gave place to one of assiduous intervention in their affairs and of diplomatic action designed to foment disorders within them and to promote their gradual disruption. The reason for this change of policy seems to have been a sudden access of fear, at the time of the war with Perseus, of a possible revival of the Hellenistic East. The eyes of the Greeks were then turned to the East, and Antiochus IV did not entirely abstain from acts which might be interpreted as directed against Rome. At a later time, constant intervention in the domestic affairs of all the Hellenistic States became for the Romans a kind of established routine.

After the battle of Magnesia Syria was too weak to start a policy of revenge. Antiochus III during his last years (he died in 187 B.C.), his successor Seleucus IV, and Antiochus IV Epiphanes, who seized the throne after the assassination of Seleucus (175 B.C.) and the suppression of the regency of Heliodorus for Seleucus' infant son, were determined to devote themselves entirely to the East and to adhere strictly to the conditions of the peace of Apamea. Indeed, this had been the policy of Antiochus III before the war: the only desire of Antiochus IV was for freedom of action within his own empire. In the affairs of the West he showed very little interest.

What Antiochus IV and his successors desired to achieve in the East was to establish their own empire on such a basis that it should be strong enough to resist any infringement by the Romans of the treaty of Apamea, that is to say, any attempt by Rome to intervene in the domestic affairs of Syria and Egypt. To achieve this a great effort was necessary. After Magnesia and Apamea the situation of the Seleucid kingdom was far from brilliant. Its solidity and unity were sapped both from within and from without.

Within it some alarming symptoms of disintegration and decay began to show themselves. The most important was the steady orientalization of the Empire. It found its expression in many and various phenomena. One was the gradual transformation of the Greek mentality of the Greek settlers in the Seleucid Empire. They became in spirit, religion, and life more and more Oriental. Another was the rise of the national spirit among the Oriental subjects of the Seleucids—the Arabs, the Jews, and the Iranians.

From outside the Seleucid Empire was threatened by many dangers. The Roman peril had not diminished. Moreover, the situation in the East and in the South was far from reassuring. Parthia and Armenia, and in the South the Nabataean kingdom, all former satrapies and dependencies of the Seleucids, were becoming increasingly powerful and enterprising.

The precarious situation of their kingdom was fully realized by the successors of Antiochus III, and their policy was dictated by their desire to consolidate and strengthen it. Of Seleucus IV we know little in this respect. Our evidence is better as regards his successor Antiochus IV. I cannot deal here at length with his domestic and foreign policy. I shall return to it in its social aspect in my fifth chapter. A few words here will suffice.

The main endeavour of Epiphanes in his domestic policy was directed against the forces of disintegration. To counteract these he made a great effort to weld together the various and disparate parts of his empire. How he set about this is uncertain. In the opinion of the present writer his policy was to knit together the various parts of his empire by extending and consolidating the net of urban communities which to some extent existed before Alexander and was further developed by him and his successors and by the early Seleucids.

These urban centres were intended to be his *points d'appui*. In them the process of amalgamation—social and cultural—of the upper classes of the population was far advanced. The idea of Epiphanes was to reap the results of this natural process and to form out of the orientalized Greeks and the hellenized Orientals, mostly residents in the cities, one political and social group, closely knit together round a city life organized more or less on Greek models, and round a common Greco-Oriental religion in which the royal cult should play an important part. With the help of this class Epiphanes hoped to solidify the old and new urban centres of his kingdom, to achieve a more reliable unity of his empire, and to secure success in his active foreign policy.

Of this foreign policy the chief aim was to re-establish the shaken prestige of the Seleucids in the East: to check the advance of the Parthians by concerted action with the new ruler, appointed by himself, of the former Seleucid satrapy Bactria; to reduce Armenia to the position of a province; and last but not least, if not to unite under his personal rule the two chief Hellenistic strongholds, Syria and Egypt, at least to establish a kind of protectorate of the former over the latter.

In all these endeavours Antiochus failed. His domestic policy of amalgamation, successful as it was among the upper classes of the population of his kingdom, met with a staunch resistance from the masses of the native population, who were disposed to defend their nationality and their religion. We know how violent was the opposition of the Jews to Epiphanes' policy of supporting the hellenized Jews and how serious were the consequences of this opposition. War became endemic in Judaea for almost a century and resulted finally in the complete political independence of that country.

Nor had Antiochus complete and lasting success in his foreign policy. Just at the time when Rome was faced with the imminent danger of conflict with Macedonia and afterwards when she was conducting a war of annihilation against her, Antiochus IV was threatened with a war on his own account. The guardians of the king Ptolemy VI Philometor, Eulaeus and Lenaeus, the rulers of Egypt at that time, were about to attempt, with the help of Palestine, the reconquest of the lost dominions of Egypt in Palestine and Phoenicia, which were of such vital importance to her economic prosperity. Whether or not the rulers of Egypt were encouraged by Rome to embark on this war, we have no means of knowing. In any case Rome left the two potential allies of Perseus to fight each other, undisturbed by any Roman intervention.

Antiochus' course seemed clear. He had probably never seriously thought of taking any active part in the struggle between Rome and Perseus. A war with Egypt, on the other hand, was welcome to him. He could not foresee how short the struggle between Perseus and Rome would be, and he hoped that before it was ended he would present Rome with a *fait accompli*, the complete incorporation of Egypt in Syria, as a

PLATE X

1. Bronze cast mask of a portrait head with royal diadem. Found at the little village of Shami near Malamir in Khuzistan (see Ch. IV, n. 237), the ancient Susiane, in the ruins of a small square temple carefully excavated by Sir Aurel Stein. In these ruins were found six large bases and several fragments of bronze statues. I cannot enter here into a detailed discussion of the identity of the portrait head. The names of Alexander the Great and Antiochus IV have been suggested. The other earlier Seleucids are out of the question: their portraits are well known and show not the slightest similarity with the head from Shami. The Seleucids subsequent to Antiochus IV are also excluded for obvious reasons. In my opinion the head shows no similarity with any known portrait of Alexander. The claim of ANTIOCHUS IV is much stronger (cf. my pl. VII, 2). But I must reserve judgement until the appearance of Sir Aurel Stein's Report. See meanwhile his article, 'An Archaeological Journey in Western Iraq', *Geogr. Journ.* xcii (1938), p. 325 and pl. IX. (Photograph of a lead cast of the mask supplied by Sir Aurel Stein.)

2. Head of Pentelic marble found in Egypt, now in the Museum of Alexandria. The head (with a diadem) certainly was made for a statue of King PTOLEMY VI PHILOMETOR, though it appears never to have been used for this purpose. A comparison with the very rare coins that bear his portrait, I mean those minted in Syria (E. T. Newell, loc. cit., p. 90), makes the identification certain. The portrait is a masterpiece of sculpture. It shows with great force certain leading traits in the king's character, some of them emphasized by Polybius (xl. 12): haughtiness and grandeur mingled with the famous Alexandrian 'morbidezza'. The sculptor must be held responsible for the somewhat pathetic and theatrical treatment of the portrait, typical of some sculptures of the time. Published and carefully discussed by A. Adriani, *Bull. Soc. Arch. Alex.* xxxii (N.S. x. 1), 1938, pp. 97 ff., pls. X–XII. (Photograph supplied by the authorities of Alexandria Museum).

1. Bronze portrait mask of a Seleucid king (Antiochus IV ?).
Pro tempore in the British Museum.

2. Marble head of Ptolemy VI Philometor.
Alexandria Museum.

result of which Rome would be faced by a united front of all the Greco-Macedonian forces of the East. He thought that in such a situation Rome would hesitate to interfere. His plan was not a bad one. With a minor as king of Egypt, a minor moreover who had a rival in his own family, with two adventurers as his opponents—guardians of the king but not regents, without authority in Alexandria and Egypt—he had a fair chance of uniting Syria and Egypt under his personal rule. His plan failed partly owing to his own mistakes, partly because of the unexpectedly rapid termination of the Third Macedonian war. During his second campaign in Egypt in 168 B.C., as he stood before the walls of Alexandria, his progress was arrested by the famous 'magic circle' of the Roman envoy Popilius Laenas. He had no choice. A war with Rome after Pydna and before he had been able to incorporate Egypt would have been folly.

The poor success of Epiphanes in Egypt was in no way such a decisive event in his personal life and such a turning-point in his policy as several scholars are inclined to believe. The magic circle of Popilius Laenas did not and could not undermine the wealth and military strength which the king displayed in his great *pompē* at Daphne—a grand political demonstration; nor did it change the main lines of his foreign and internal policy. The struggle with the Jews took its natural course, and on his eastern front Epiphanes was more active than before. His intervention in Bactria against Demetrius carried out by Eucratides (as was first pointed out by W. W. Tarn) was a prelude to his own expedition against Parthia. It was a great disaster for the Seleucid Empire that Epiphanes' Parthian expedition, which began with a series of successes, came to an abrupt end by his own untimely death. This event was the turning-point in the history of the Greek, Semitic, and Iranian East.

With his death the last serious endeavour to follow a far-sighted policy in Syria came to an end. The successors of Antiochus IV were not inactive. They did their best to maintain the unity of their empire and to check the advance of the Parthians. They were, however, faced by insurmountable difficulties. The main obstacle which prevented them from achieving their aims and plunged Syria into permanent anarchy was the policy of Rome.

The fact that Antiochus IV would have been successful but for two accidents, the rapid end of the Third Macedonian war and his own premature death, caused the Romans uneasiness, and they decided to play for safety in future and to keep the East in a state of anarchy. Accordingly they did what they could to foster dynastic troubles in Syria and in Egypt, supported with their sympathy the Jewish movement in Palestine, offered no serious opposition to wars between Syria and Egypt for the possession of southern Syria, and put obstacles in the path of the few talented and patriotic Seleucids, such as Demetrius II (captured by the Parthians in 140/39 B.C.) and Antiochus VII Sidetes (139–130 B.C.), who took seriously their position as champions of Greek civilization against the Iranian tide. It was certainly owing to the Roman efforts that none of the successors of Antiochus IV was able to achieve a single one of their chief political aims. They wasted all their strength in futile dynastic wars and for lack of the necessary resources were unable to reincorporate such States as Palestine in their empire or to stop the advance of the Parthians and Armenians.

I need not once more relate the melancholy history of Syria after the death of Antiochus IV or that of Egypt after the abortive attempt of Antiochus to unite it with Syria. The history of Syria is a medley of civil wars among members of the Seleucid house (with the addition of some intruders), of repeated attempts to re-establish the Seleucid authority in certain rebellious parts of their empire (we are familiar with the case of Palestine, which finally emerged as an independent kingdom under its own dynasty, the Hasmonaeans), of wars against Egypt connected with the above-mentioned dynastic wars, and of desperate efforts to reconquer Mesopotamia from the Parthians and check the growth of the Armenian kingdom. As vassals of Tigranes, the great ruler of the ephemeral Armeno-Syrian empire, both the Seleucids and the Hasmonaeans became involved in the last phases of the Mithridatic war and succumbed without fighting to Pompey, who in 64 B.C. brought the existence of the Seleucid Empire to an end without making any very essential change in the conditions of life in Syrian territory. The Romans in Syria simply inherited the great problems of the Seleucid Empire and had to solve them as best they could.

The last century of the life of Ptolemaic Egypt was uneventful. The history of Egypt during this period as told in our sources is practically the history of the family of the Ptolemies, of their domestic quarrels, of their terrible crimes, of their relations with their army and with the mob of Alexandria, and last but not least of their constant appeals against each other to Rome, whose obedient servants they all were. Unfortunately we know very little of their struggle with the natives, who were in almost perpetual revolt, and of the process by which they themselves became orientalized. We are somewhat better informed regarding a less important feature of their political activities, their endeavours to win back southern Syria from the Seleucids. Whereas, however, even the more prominent successors of Antiochus IV are to us mere names and shadows almost devoid of personality, the figures of the last Ptolemies stand out before us with all their individual peculiarities: the two brother-enemies, nervous and servile—Ptolemy Philometor and Ptolemy Euergetes II, with their circle of mothers, sisters, and wives; the picturesque and pitiful figure of Ptolemy Auletes; and above all Cleopatra, the last queen of Egypt, the mistress of Caesar, the wife of Antony, and the rival of Octavianus. It is curious to see how the most passive of the Hellenistic States, the State most obedient to Roman dictation, produced at last a strong, able, and ambitious woman, whose aim it was to revive the Hellenistic world in a new shape, with Egypt as its centre and with its armed forces supplied by Italy and the West—a dream, of course, which could not have been realized even if Antony had not been defeated at Actium, but a dream worthy of the glorious traditions of the great Hellenistic world.

The political decay and final collapse of the system of Hellenistic States present an important problem for the historians of the ancient world. Who was responsible for this catastrophe? Should we regard the Hellenistic States as victims of Roman imperialism and blame the Romans for the political, cultural, and moral decay of the Hellenistic world?

Or did they, while pursuing a sane and reasonable national policy and availing themselves for their own ends of the weakness of the Hellenistic system—a weakness which developed of itself and was inevitable—after all save Hellenistic civilization by incorporating the Hellenistic States in their world empire?

The problem cannot be discussed here in detail. It will serve the purposes of this book to insist on certain points. The Romans had evidently no good reason for intervention in the affairs of the Hellenistic world. The safety and the integrity of their Western empire were in no way dependent on the political development, whatever form it might take, of that world. Neither Philip nor Antiochus thought seriously of invading Italy or of interfering in the affairs of the West. Their political horizon was limited to Greece and the Near East. They knew little of the West and had little interest in it. Philip's plans were limited to keeping the Romans out of the Balkan peninsula. The political dreams of Antiochus III never extended beyond Greece. On the other hand, a lasting co-operation between Philip and Antiochus was out of the question. It was beyond the power of even a genius to reunite the Hellenistic world in a single State. Political disintegration, not unification, was the dominating tendency in the political evolution of that world.

Rome may have honestly thought that her first two wars with a Hellenistic power were necessary for her political safety. The Roman Senate certainly knew little of Eastern affairs and may have been alarmed by the successes of Philip and Antiochus. However this may be, after Cynoscephalae and Magnesia Rome was very well informed regarding the conditions that prevailed in the Hellenistic States. The Senate could not seriously think that an independent Macedonia or a well-organized Syria was a danger to Rome's Western empire. Their policy of demoralizing the Hellenistic world, of dictating to it, and of chastising any State that disobeyed their orders, was not a policy of self-defence, but of prepotency and imperialism. Imperialism does not always involve the intention of acquiring an increase of territory. The desire for political hegemony, the wish to play the leading role in the political life of the civilized world, cannot but be regarded as a form of imperialism.

To sum up. It was not to obtain security that Rome insisted on being the leading power in the East as well as in the West. Whatever her original motive may have been, once she had made up her mind to pursue this end, her ruthless and unmoral policy is easily understood. The results for the Hellenistic world were disastrous. The policy of Rome, Machiavellian, often dishonest and always strictly egoistic, her fostering of servility and dishonesty in her own political agents (such as Eumenes II), undermined the morale of the Hellenistic powers and the prestige of the Hellenistic rulers in the eyes of their own subjects. The Romans helped forward all the processes that were ruining the political stability of the Hellenistic world; separatist tendencies within the monarchies, dynastic troubles, civil wars, wars between the several States, they always encouraged, or at least hardly ever put a stop to. Rome welcomed the gradual disintegration, nay the pulverization, of the Hellenistic States. She contributed to their economic ruin. By doing this, she undermined Greek civilization throughout the Hellenistic area, and made the advance of orientalization easier and more rapid. Weak, poor, disintegrated, and demoralized, isolated in the East, Syria was unable to avert the incorporation in Parthia, Armenia, and Arabia of large territories that had become more or less hellenized. The Seleucids could not prevent the conversion of Palestine into an independent oriental State, and of many Greek cities of Syria into petty oriental monarchies. Even in the large and thoroughly Hellenic cities of Syria, the Greeks, isolated as they were from their original homeland, succumbed inevitably to the natural tendency to become oriental in social ideas and habits and in culture. The same thing happened in different forms and on a smaller scale in Anatolia, in Egypt, and in Cyrenaica.

Is it fair, however, to make Rome alone responsible for the political, moral, and cultural decay of the Hellenistic world? It is evident from what has been related in the preceding pages that even without Roman intervention the trend of development that characterized the period of the wars of succession and that of the balance of power would have continued. The various Hellenistic States would have continued fighting each other and exhausting their forces in these endless and in the main ineffectual wars. From time to time some power might have gained a temporary preponderance, but none would have been able permanently to unite the Hellenistic world into one State. It was not Rome alone that made dynastic troubles endemic in most of the Hellenistic monarchies, and it was not Rome that was responsible for the degeneration of the ruling royal families. Greece would have continued the endless struggle for liberty, revolutions would not have ceased in the individual city-states, and it is difficult to suppose that the Leagues would have arrested the disintegration of Greece and put an end to political anarchy, besides protecting her liberty against the aspirations of the neighbouring Hellenistic monarchies.

And yet it was Rome that made all these processes catastrophic. Left alone, the Hellenistic States certainly would have existed longer than they did, and would have offered a stronger and more effective resistance to the growth of Parthia and Armenia and to the rapid rise of the oriental tide. Without the 'splendid isolation' from the western world that was forced by Rome upon Syria and Egypt, they might have remained almost indefinitely a source of wealth and prosperity for Greece and so have saved that country from the cruel poverty and the depopulation by race-suicide to which she was reduced under the heavy hand of Rome. Nor can I see why the two Greek Leagues should not have existed for a long time, fighting each other and succumbing from time to time to political pressure from without, but guaranteeing on the whole an independent political existence for Greece, and developing their federal constitutions.

Rome strengthened all the forces that tended to bring about a slow and gradual decay of the Hellenistic world and accelerated their operation. She prevented the East from becoming more widely and more deeply hellenized than it actually was when she finally took over the heritage of the Hellenistic States. Thereafter she did her best during two centuries to secure peace for the East and to re-hellenize it. This is her enduring merit. But why begin by crushing Hellenism alike in the East and in the West and then try to save what little was left of it? Such questions are futile. We may say, however, that in all probability the Hellenistic world without Roman intervention would have done for the development of civilization more than it was in fact able to do. And it is very probable that Romanism in the West would have run a smoother course if it had been spared the forced union with the East imposed on it by imperialism.

II

THE ANCIENT WORLD IN THE FOURTH CENTURY B.C.

One of the most interesting products of Greek speculative thought combined with practical sagacity is the second book of the 'Economics' ascribed to Aristotle, a treatise by an unknown author written and published at the end of the fourth century B.C. and widely read and studied in later times.[1]

In the main it is a collection of financial measures and devices by which certain Greek cities and statesmen and certain hellenized Persian satraps and barbarian kings succeeded in solving temporary financial crises, a collection similar, *mutatis mutandis*, to the 'Politics' of Aristotle and to the 'Stratagems' of Polyaenus and written in the same spirit as the Pseudo-Xenophontic Πόροι.[2] It thus presents a good cross-section of the economic and financial situation, chiefly in the fourth century, of various parts of the Mediterranean world, and especially of the Greek city-states. It is unique of its kind, and therefore merits the attention and study that modern students of Greek economics have devoted and are still devoting to it.

Still more valuable, however, is the short preface in which the author gives an acute and exhaustive classification of the principal forms of economic and financial organization then existing—the first attempt at a theory of finance.

In this summary four types of financial organization (οἰκονομίαι) are distinguished and characterized: that of the (Persian) king (οἰκονομία βασιλική), that of (his) satraps (οἰκονομία σατραπική), that of the πόλις (οἰκονομία πολιτική), and that of private individuals (οἰκονομία ἰδιωτική). This classification, selecting as it does the leading types of economic and financial organization, is as characteristic of the period and of its prevailing ideas as is the choice of the stories that follow it. Persia and Greece were, to the author's mind, the only organized States of the civilized world. They alone had a well-balanced financial life worthy of study. The remaining types of organization—the tribal economy of the Thracian, Illyrian, and Celtic

States of the North, the peculiar economic life of the Etruscans, Italians, and Carthaginians, the nomadic economy of the Scythians, etc.—are completely left out of account: they are ignored as irrelevant or as unknown or of no interest to the author.

It is a pity that this theoretical summary is so short and so schematic. Yet, short as it is, it correctly defines the dominant features of the economic life of the civilized world of the fourth century B.C.

The author is right in pointing out that at this time two types of economic and political organization balanced each other in the ancient world: that of the Oriental monarchies, represented by Persia, and that of the Greek city-states. Each had behind it a long and glorious evolution, longer in the East, shorter in the West. Each was based on the strenuous creative activity of the human intellect. Each endeavoured to extend its form of economic life to the rest of the ancient world. For us, no doubt, the other parts of that world, whether they had come under the influence of the two principal civilizations or remained completely 'barbarian', present economic features of considerable interest and possess a certain importance in connexion with the economic development of Greece and Persia. But compared with these they are not only much less known but also of less consequence from an historical and economic point of view.

The author of the treatise, who was probably a contemporary of Alexander the Great or of his earlier successors,[3] stood on the threshold of a new world, a world in which the two leading economies of the past—the *βασιλική* and *σατραπική* on the one hand, and the *πολιτική* and *ἰδιωτική* on the other—were in process of merging into one, into that of the Hellenistic world. Standing before this new creation, of which he was able to perceive the first dim outlines, he looks backward and tries to summarize and to preserve for posterity what he regarded as the most useful achievements of the great men of the past. We may follow him in his endeavour and do the same from our own essentially different point of view.

I will therefore, by way of introduction to the study of the Hellenistic period, present some brief remarks on the economic

PLATE XI

1. AV Persian daric. 'Darius III.' *Obv.* Bearded king, half-kneeling, holding bow and spear. *Rev.* Incuse.

2. AR Tetradrachm of Tissaphernes, satrap of Sardis. *Obv.* Bearded head in satrapal tiara. *Rev.* ΒΑΣΙΛΕΩΣ. Persian king, half-kneeling; symbol, galley with rowers.

3. Electrum. Stater, Cyzicus, *c.* 450–400 B.C. *Obv.* Delphic omphalos with two eagles. *Rev.* Incuse.

4. AV Stater, Lampsacus, *c.* 394–350 B.C. *Obv.* Head of Zeus with fulmen. *Rev.* Forepart of winged horse.

5. AR Tetrobol, Clazomenae (?), Orontas, satrap of Mysia and Ionia, *c.* 362–348 B.C. *Obv.* Naked warrior defending himself with shield and spear. *Rev.* ΟΡΟΝΤΑ. Forepart of a winged boar.

6. AR Tetradrachm of Athens, *c.* 393–339 B.C. *Obv.* Helmeted head of Athena. *Rev.* ΑΘΕ. Owl.

7. AR Tetradrachm, Sabaces, satrap of Egypt, *c.* 333 B.C. An imitation of the preceding with the name of Sabaces written in Aramaic script (see Six, *Num. Chron.*, 1888, p. 132 f., and Newell, *N. N. and M.* lxxxii (1938), p. 62 f.).

8. AR Stater of Tarsus. Mazaeus, satrap of Cilicia, *c.* 361–333 B.C. *Obv.* Ba'altars enthroned, his name in Aramaic letters. *Rev.* Lion killing bull (emblem of Tarsus); above 'Mazdai' in Aramaic.

9. AR Tetradrachm, Philip II (Amphipolis). *Obv.* Laureate head of Zeus. Possibly copy of the Olympian Zeus of Phidias. *Rev.* ΦΙΛΙΠΠΟΥ. Boy on horse-back holding palm.

10. AV Stater, Philip II (Pella). *Obv.* Laureate head of Apollo. *Rev.* ΦΙΛΙΠΠΟΥ. Charioteer in biga.

11. AR Double-shekel, Sidon, Mazaeus, *c.* 343–335 B.C. *Obv.* Galley with rowers at sea; above, the date. *Rev.* Mazaeus (in Phoenician). The king in quadriga with charioteer, and followed by attendant.

12. AR Stater, Corinth, *c.* 350–338 B.C. *Obv.* Ϙ Pegasus. *Rev.* Helmeted head of Athena.

A few general remarks on my coin plates. The plates have been arranged and described by Miss D. H. Cox in collaboration with Dr. E. T. Newell and Prof. A. R. Bellinger. The large majority of the coins belong to the collection of E. T. Newell (New York). A few were supplied by the British Museum. No bibliographical references are added. They would be endless. With only one exception (pl. XI, 7), all the coins reproduced in these plates are included in the *B.M.C.* and Head, *H.N.*[2]

The purpose of this plate is to illustrate by a few examples the variety of coins which circulated in Greece and in the East in the last years of the fifth century B.C. and in the fourth. I have endeavoured to give specimens of the most popular and the most interesting coins.

Coins of the Late Fifth and Fourth Centuries B.C.

structure of Persia and Greece in the fourth century. For the sake of completeness I shall add a few words on the economic conditions of the rest of the civilized or half-civilized world at that time.

A. PERSIA

The great Persian Empire, heir and successor of the Sumerian, Babylonian, Egyptian, Hittite, and Assyrian Empires, was during the whole of its existence a vast complex of various types of economic, social, and political life. In this complex the most refined forms, worked out by Babylonia and Egypt, existed side by side with the most primitive, as represented by the Bedouins of the desert and by the shepherd tribes of the mountains. Persia, despite its long existence as a single body politic, never formed a natural economic and social unit. This fact was well known to the great organizers of the Persian Empire, Cyrus and Darius, and is reflected in the division of the empire into its Persian kernel and its various satrapies, each of which had its own economic and social aspect.[4]

The political leadership and military backbone of the Empire were supplied by its kernel PERSIA PROPER, supplemented by Media and the other Iranian satrapies. The background of the social and economic organization of these Iranian parts of the empire was 'feudal' and 'tribal'. The greater part of the settled Iranian population consisted of sturdy peasants devoted to their houses, fields, oxen, families, and villages. Above them stood the gentry and the aristocracy—landowners and fighters—and the influential class of priests. Though socially uniform, the Iranian kernel was far from homogeneous from the strictly economic point of view. Persis, for example, was in the fifth and fourth centuries B.C. a flourishing agricultural region, well irrigated, with developed grazing and gardening, a country that had inherited and made its own the advanced civilization of Elam and its capital Susa, first a rival, then a follower of the great Babylonian culture. The nearest relative of Persia, Media, combined agriculture with the raising of cattle on an extensive scale and of good breeds of horses. Its civilization showed a close connexion with those of its nearest neighbours, the Haldi (Nairi) of the Caucasus and the Assyrians of the Tigris triangle, while Elamitic and

Babylonian influences were less felt. Different, again, from the cultural and economic points of view were the flourishing East Iranian satrapies of the Empire: Bactria and Sogdiana, fosterlings of the river Oxus, and Margiane, nursling of the Margus. With their rich soil stretching along the rivers, their artificial irrigation, and their agricultural wealth, they may be called the Babylonia of the East. And finally, large groups of Iranians and of pre-Iranian tribes—in the Caspian and Aralian steppes, and in the Cossaean mountains—still lived the primitive life of cattle-breeding nomads and semi-nomads, of robbers and shepherds, who were sharply opposed to the settled agriculturists of civilized Iran and in whom the Iranian mind saw the incarnation of the evil, destructive forces of the world.[5]

Beyond the Iranian kernel of the Persian Empire stretched the great civilized territories of INDIA, parts of which—Gandhara and Hindu (Sind)—were for a certain time Persian satrapies, and of China. Though possessing their own civilization and art, they were not sharply separated from the Iranian world, with which they were connected by trade and probably by diplomacy. How close and important these relations were we are unable to say. There were, however, no sharp dividing lines between the three great Asiatic civilizations: the Iranian, the Indian, and the Chinese.

Quite different, and again far from homogeneous, were the economic and social background, the structure and evolution, of the Semitic parts of the Persian Empire. BABYLONIA, with its long-established civilization, its highly developed agriculture, industry, commerce, and banking, had a most complex and highly differentiated structure. This is not the place to describe its peculiar economic and social organization. Centralization, planning, and control were during thousands of years the salient features of its economic evolution. An elaborate bureaucracy, a strong body of priests attached to the various temples, groups of bankers and merchants in the flourishing cities, were the leaders and organizers of its economic life. The mass of peasants and artisans obediently followed their lead.

This ancient organization underwent some changes in Persian times. They are reflected in the thousands of business documents of the Babylonian satrapy of Persia. These changes, however, related mostly to the civil and criminal law and did not affect the main features of the social and economic structure of Babylonia. From the economic point of view some changes were brought about by the role that the Babylonian satrapy played in the economy of the Persian Empire. A larger demand for Babylonian goods caused for example a sharp rise in prices, especially in the case of agricultural products.[6]

We find a structure mainly Babylonian in the various States of MIDDLE and UPPER MESOPOTAMIA and NORTHERN SYRIA, the offspring of Babylonia, at first her rivals, vassals, and subjects and later her successors. We know very little of their economic and social life after the destruction of the last of them, the glorious Empire of Assyria. The great cities of Assyria disappeared or led a precarious life as small villages. But certain fragments of the Assyrian and of earlier empires in Upper Mesopotamia and northern Syria remained prosperous and strong, and formed important parts of the Syrian satrapies of Persia. Such were probably the great city- and temple-states of Haleb (Aleppo), Damascus, Hamath, Emesa, Tadmor (Palmyra), and the like.[7] They were saved from poverty and decay by the great caravan trade, which was another creation of Babylonia and which connected Lower Mesopotamia with Iran, India (and perhaps China), and Arabia on the one hand and with the Pontic and Mediterranean regions on the other. This caravan trade was as old as Babylonian civilization. It had its own history and vicissitudes, which cannot be dealt with here. Suffice it to say that the great caravan roads of the Tigris and Euphrates with their branches in the East, in the South (south Arabia), in the North (the Black Sea coast with its wealth of metals), and in the West (the Phoenician and Anatolian coasts) remained in Persian times as important as they had previously been, while the safety of the extensive commerce that they carried was much increased. The great caravan cities to which I have referred above were the entrepôts of this trade in Mesopotamia and northern Syria. It is unfortunate that we know so little of them. But we may legitimately reconstruct their life in its main lines from what we know of their successors of Hellenistic and Roman times—Palmyra in Syria and Petra in Arabia, with their aristocracy of merchants and caravan leaders, their *funduqs* (commercial settlements) spread all over the civilized world, their elaborate organization of huge caravans, and their widely spread diplomatic and commercial relations.[8]

To the caravan cities of the interior corresponded the great commercial cities of the Mediterranean coast in PALESTINE, PHOENICIA, and ANATOLIA. We are now gradually discovering the history and civilization of some of the Phoenician cities. Byblos, Ugarit (Ras Shamra), and Al-Mina have revealed to us their early commercial, political, and cultural relations with Arabia, Egypt, Cyprus, and the Minoan world on the one hand and with the caravan cities of the interior on the other. The history of Tyre and Sidon in later times, as it appears in our Greek tradition and as it is reflected in the history of Carthage, is known to us at least in bare outline.[9] Moreover, the range of their trade relations can be reconstructed from finds made in their far distant markets in the west and north—in Spain, Britain, and on the coasts of the Baltic Sea—and from coins discovered in Phoenicia itself.[10] But unfortunately no important written documents bearing on the social and economic structure of these cities in the fifth and fourth centuries B.C. have yet come to light, and this structure remains a matter of conjecture, if we are precluded from using for its restoration the abundant evidence relating to Carthage.

Babylonia, with its special type of highly developed economic life, and the survivals of the minor semi-Babylonian States and of the Assyrian Empire, in particular the caravan cities of Mesopotamia and north Syria and the cities on the coast of Phoenicia and Palestine were, however, but oases of an advanced civilization and of an elaborate social and economic structure. They were surrounded on all sides by a compact mass of very primitive social and economic communities, such as the numerous and ever-shifting tribes of Bedouin nomads in the Syrian and Arabian deserts, or mountain tribes of various degrees of civilization. Nor can we affirm that in Babylonia itself and in the other civilized oases of Mesopotamia and Syria the village peasantry participated to any considerable extent in the civilized life of their masters, the inhabitants of the cities and of the temples.

Mention must next be made of Palestine. Situated between Egypt and Babylonia-Assyria, Palestine had a peculiar political system and a peculiar civilization. The social and economic structure of the country is better known than that of the other parts of the Syrian and Mesopotamian world. It was a combination of a tribal and a temple State. Its economic life was based on grazing and agriculture, together with industry and commerce in rather primitive forms. The cities of the coast had, of course, their own life and their own economic development.[11]

We are better informed with regard to the Anatolian than to the Phoenician outlets of the great trade of Persia, especially with regard to those situated on the west coast of ASIA MINOR, the old Greek agricultural settlements which gradually developed into important centres of commerce and industry. These cities, though subjects of Persia in the fourth century B.C., in fact belonged not to the Oriental but to the Greek world. They were, so to speak, fragments of the Western world on the fringe of the Eastern, serving as connecting links between the two. Behind them, however, the interior of Anatolia and the adjoining parts of north Syria remained essentially Oriental. There were great industrial and trading cities, at one time strongholds of the early pre-Hittite and Hittite masters of Anatolia and northern Syria, capitals in later days of independent States broken off from the great Hittite Empire (the richest and most beautiful was Sardis, the capital originally of Lydia, later of a Persian satrapy) ; there were large temples, centres of local and caravan trade and of a flourishing industry; there were extensive domains of Persian nobles and of former Anatolian feudal lords, centring round fortified villas, similar to those of their kin in Iranian lands; and there were half-wild tribes in the Taurus mountains. Such were the constituent parts of Anatolia, the hinterland of the Greek cities of the coast.[12]

Finally we come to the great Egyptian satrapy. The role of EGYPT in the history of mankind was in some respects very similar to, and in others very different from, that of Babylonia. It was the classical land of the first attempts at centralization, at a planned economy, and at the same time a flourishing centre of developed agriculture, industry, and trade.

The life of Egypt during the first Persian domination and the following sixty years of independence and national revival (404 to 343 B.C.) and also in the time of the second Persian domination, which lasted until the conquest of Egypt by Alexander, is but imperfectly known to us.

The great Persian kings—Darius and Xerxes—showed considerable respect for Egyptian religion and Egyptian traditions. They made efforts to link Egypt to the rest of their empire and to the Mediterranean world. A splendid testimony to this is the restoration of Necho's great canal which connected the Nile with the Red Sea. They kept Naucratis open to Greek traders, most of whom now came from Athens. And, lastly, they endeavoured to improve the administration of Egypt by combating the feudal tendencies that prevailed there before the Persian conquest, especially the over-powerful clergy. In the very instructive set of Aramaic papyri found at Elephantine we have some reflections of the daily economic and social life of one part of Egypt and of the relations between the Persian overlords, their mercenary soldiers of Jewish origin stationed at Elephantine, and the native population.[13]

The following sixty years of independence, little known as they are, appear as a time of great splendour and of brilliant revival. Egypt was then, apart from Greece, the only powerful rival of Persia. It opened its doors wide to the outer world. Large numbers of Greeks entered, and some of them settled in Egypt as mercenary soldiers and as merchants and perhaps artisans. In this respect the native rulers continued the policy of the great Persian kings. Enriched by their lively trade with the Mediterranean and by a rational exploitation of the natural resources of the country, they developed a conspicuous building activity. The national revival and the wealth of Egypt led to a splendid renascence of Egyptian art, which is revealed to us by various buildings richly adorned with sculpture and painting. A late product of this renascence, which shows how much the Egyptian artists had learned from the Persians and the Greeks, is the famous grave of Petosiris, the exquisite painted carvings of which reproduce the religious and economic environment of a man of great importance in pre-Alexandrian Egypt.[14]

Of the last period, the brief term of the second Persian

domination after the reconquest of Egypt by Artaxerxes III Ochus, a few words will be said presently.

Such was the great Persian monarchy—a medley of economic contrasts and yet an economic unit in the hands of the Persian kings, who never gave up the difficult task of holding together the disparate components of their empire. Their success resulted mainly from their sound *policy of decentralization.* They seldom interfered with the social and economic life of their satrapies. At the same time they gave them the military protection that they needed and new and welcome opportunities of developing their economic relations and their interchange of goods. Excellent 'royal' roads connected the various parts of the Persian Empire; new sea routes (for example from the mouth of the Indus to the Red Sea and the Nile) were explored; and a 'royal' gold and silver currency of perfect soundness and integrity facilitated the exchange of goods. The heavy taxation to which the satrapies were subjected was not excessive if compared with the advantages that they derived from being, not independent States, but constituent parts of a world empire.

It is not surprising that Persia had the reputation of being a very rich country. We have no means of measuring its wealth. That of the Persian kings is, of course, well known. We know the amount of their yearly revenue and the quantity of gold and silver stored in the Persian capitals.[15] Royal riches do not necessarily imply the well-being of subjects. But the ever-increasing prosperity, in Persian times, of the Phoenician cities, of the caravan cities of Syria and Mesopotamia, and of Babylon is evidence that the wealth of the rulers was based on the wealth of their subjects. It should be noticed that most of the satrapies of Persia, other than Egypt and Asia Minor, enjoyed a lasting peace for at least three centuries, a rare phenomenon in the history of the ancient world.

Persia, a vast centralized empire with a flexible provincial policy, was self-sufficient and independent from an economic standpoint. She owned wide tracts of valuable forest, and mines yielding in abundance all sorts of metals (including tin and gold); she produced all sorts of foodstuffs, including wine, olive-oil, and the most delicate fruits; she was supplied with the most refined products of industry and the industrial arts by the workshops of Babylonia, Egypt, Phoenicia, and of many cities and temple-cities of Asia Minor; she was the great receptacle for all the channels of the caravan trade of Asia and Africa. She therefore needed little in the way of imports, and did not depend in any material respect on international trade relations.

And yet Persia never isolated herself from the rest of the civilized world. An active *commerce* connected her with India, perhaps China, and South Arabia. For the products of these lands she certainly paid, not in gold and silver, but largely in her own wares, especially in products of her industry. We are gradually learning how great was the influence of Babylonian and Persian art on the artistic development of India and China. Such an influence cannot be explained unless we assume well-organized trade relations between the three countries.

The commercial relations between Persia and the Western world were likewise highly developed. Through the Palestinian, Phoenician, and Anatolian harbours Persia exported to the West and to the North (including the Pontic regions) various products, some of them luxury goods and trinkets, but mostly such important commodities as incense, spices, and perfumes, which gradually became articles of prime necessity to all the civilized and uncivilized inhabitants of the northern and western world.

This commerce was certainly a brisk one, as is shown by many well-known facts. It may be useful for the purpose of this book to adduce some evidence on the trade relations between Persia and Greece in the fifth and more especially in the fourth century B.C. Highly important in this respect are the large quantities of Greek, above all Athenian, coins of the fifth and in part of the fourth century found in hoards and sporadically all over the western part of the Persian Empire: in Mesopotamia and Babylonia, in Syria, in Palestine, and in southern Arabia. Alongside of these there were in circulation, particularly in the fourth century, numerous imitations of them in Lycia, Cilicia, Syria, and Palestine, minted in various cities, and highly interesting local silver emitted in large quantities by various cities of Asia Minor, Cyprus, Phoenicia, and Palestine.

The most interesting series is the Philisto-Arabian, little known and little studied. Some of the Philisto-Arabian coins were put into circulation by the Persian satraps or by the vassal dynasts of Persia.[16]

Not less important are the many finds of Greek, especially Athenian black-glazed, black-figured, and red-figured pottery, and of Greek and Egyptian products of other applied arts made in Palestine, Phoenicia, and Syria and as far away as Uruk and Susa. Particularly striking are the objects found in the graves of the seventh to the fourth century B.C. near Atlit in Palestine, with their mixture of Greek and Iranian objects, and those discovered in the graves of Tell Far'a and the Philistinian graves of Gezer. Trade relations of Palestine with Egypt in the fourth century are attested by the splendid hoard of Egyptian bronzes found in Palestine.[17]

The spectacular development of the great seaports of the Phoenician and Palestinian coast in the time of the Persian domination under the vivifying influence of western commerce is illustrated by many striking facts: the rapid growth of these cities; the permission granted to some of them in the late fifth and the fourth century by the Persian government to mint their own silver currency; and the steady hellenization of the life and art of the leading Phoenician cities in the fourth century, accompanied by a similar process in certain regions of Asia Minor, for example Lycia. Of great interest also is the aspect presented by Cyprus at the time of Persian domination. As in Syria and Phoenicia, the intensity of Greek influence was not affected by the political vicissitudes of the various Cyprian cities which in the great struggle between the Persians and the Greeks in the fifth century sided with one or other party.[18]

The trade relations between the Greek world and the Persian Empire are excellently illustrated by the history of the trading settlement of Al-Mina, a port at the mouth of the Orontes, not far from the later Seleuceia in Pieria, which has been recently excavated by an expedition from the British Museum headed by Sir Leonard Woolley. The city had a long life which can be traced from the eighth century B.C. down to the time of the foundation of Seleuceia in 301 B.C., when it practically ceased to exist. Several cities were superimposed one on the other,

PLATE XII

1. The grave-temple of Petosiris, an Egyptian noble priest of Hermupolis Magna, of the middle of the fourth century, perhaps deified after his death, presents in its carved and painted decoration an interesting blend of Egyptian traditions somewhat modified by Greek and perhaps by some Persian influences. The choice of subjects is purely Egyptian, but the treatment of single figures and groups, the choice of certain manufactured objects shown in the scenes of industrial activity, and some traits in the composition, especially in the decoration of the pronaos, indicate that Greek art exerted a strong influence on the native sculptors and painters of Egypt. This example—part of the decoration of the base of the west wall of the chapel, showing a purely Egyptian subject: men and women bringing various offerings—keeps to Egyptian traditions but contains several Greek elements: the cock on the hand of the first personage, the baby in the arms of its mother, perhaps also the antelope with its head shown frontwise. From G. Lefebvre, *Le Tombeau de Pétosiris*.

G. Lefebvre, *Le Tombeau de Pétosiris*, 1923–4, part iii, pl. XLIX, cf. XLVIII (in colour), and part i, p. 182. Cf. P. Montet, 'Note sur le tombeau de Pétosiris' *Rev. Arch.* xxiii (5me sér.) (1926), pp. 161 ff.; E. Luys, *Vie de Pétosiris, grand prêtre de Thot à Hermoupolis-la-Grande*, 1927; Ch. Picard, *Bull. Inst. Fr. Arch. Or.* xxx (1930), pp. 201 ff.; I. Noshy, *The Arts in Ptolemaic Egypt*, 1937, pp. 43 ff., 121 ff., 140 ff.; A. Scharff, W. Otto, *Handb. d. Arch.* i, 1939, pp. 632 ff. and pl. 106, 1–3; E. Breccia, *Egitto Greco e Romano*, 1938, pp. 71 ff. Cf. note 14 to this chapter and Ch. VIII.

2. Pottery of Al-Mina. I owe the following brief description of it to the kindness of Prof. J. D. Beazley. (*a*) 'Clay vase of the shape known as "pelike" representing a young man and a woman at an altar. Attic ware of about 410 B.C.' (*b*) 'Clay krater decorated with ivy and lines. Local or at least non-Attic work of about 400 B.C.' J. D. Beazley, *J.H.S.* lix (1939), p. 23, no. 57, fig. 57. On Al-Mina see above, pp. 85 ff. Photographs supplied by Sir Leonard Woolley.

3. Sherd found at Susa (Seleuceia on the Eulaeus). Description by Prof. J. D. Beazley. 'Fragment of a clay drinking vessel. The lower part was probably in plastic form. On the upper part remains of an Amazonomachy—an Amazon (ΑVΛΑΜΙΣ) striking with the sword, and another, armed with spear and pelta, dismounting. The vase was made at Athens about 460 B.C. in the workshop of the potter Sotades.' Unpublished. See n. 22 to this chapter. Photograph supplied by R. E. de Mecquenem.

1. Section of the carved and painted mural decoration of the grave of Petosiris.

2. Vases from Al Mina.

3. Attic sherd found at Susa.

the best preserved, the richest, and the most instructive being that of the third level dated 430–375 B.C.

Al-Mina was a trading settlement which consisted mainly of warehouses and of some dwelling-houses for people of the

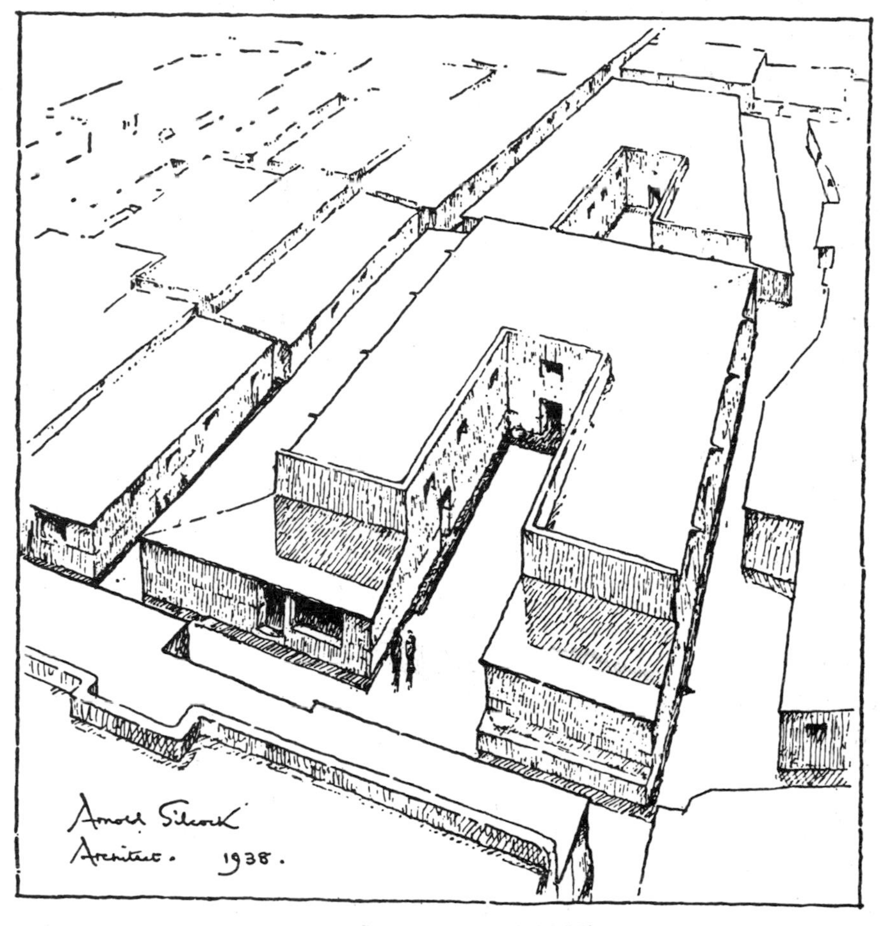

FIG. 1. Store-house of Al-Mina.

lower classes. The rich merchants who owned the warehouses lived probably, not in the noisy and unhealthy harbour settlement, but in a city built on a hill in the vicinity of the harbour, about three miles up-stream (modern Sabouni). We know that the trading city of Ugarit, which was still flourishing in the fifth and fourth centuries B.C., was organized in the same way.

From the earliest time of its existence the harbour of Al-Mina was engaged exclusively in export and import trade, serving as a connecting link between the Mediterranean world and Syria. In its early days it was chiefly dependent on Cyprus. Cyprus yielded its place in the seventh and sixth centuries to Rhodes and Corinth. Then came the predominance of Athens, which lasted until the time of Alexander.

The Athenian period in the life of the city is the best known. Athens exported large quantities of its black-figured, black-glazed and red-figured pottery, even Panathenaic vases,* choice pieces and common ware. Other goods, presumably wine and olive-oil, were exported in large jars. Finds of lead ingots and aluminium attest the variety of imported merchandise. We may form an excellent idea of this import trade from the large masses of pottery stored in the warehouses of the third level and assorted according to their character. One room, for instance, contained exclusively Attic and local lamps, another *gutti* and lamp-fillers, others were full of *aryballi*, *cotylae*, and *crateres* respectively. Large quantities of weights will show, when duly studied, how one aspect of the trade relations was organized.

Trade with Athens was not carried on by barter. While early Greek coins are absent in the ruins of Al-Mina, large quantities of Athenian silver of the late fifth and early fourth centuries were found in the ruins, mostly in hoards. The use of money as a medium of exchange was apparently introduced here, as at Aradus, by the Athenians. Attic tetradrachms appear to have been the currency used for trade transactions. Athenian coins minted at Athens prevailed in the fifth century. They were gradually replaced in the fourth by local imitations. For the local exchange large quantities of bronze were used. Most of the bronze coins found in the ruins were minted at Aradus and Sidon, but some were brought by traders from Ionia and the Greek islands.

The finds in Palestine mentioned above show the same aspect and supplement to a certain extent the picture given by Al-Mina. It is evident that the merchants of Al-Mina and Pales-

* The same is true of the other markets of Athens, especially south Russia, see below, pp. 105 ff..

tine, probably Greeks in the main, imported into the Syrian and Palestinian satrapies of Persia large amounts of mostly luxury wares. There is no doubt that they exported the products of the Persian Empire dealt with above. These products were certainly not exclusively luxuries: we know that in the fourth century Syria and Cyprus supplied Athens with grain.[19]

Similar, as regards international trade, were the conditions in Egypt in the times of the first Persian domination, of independence, and of the second Persian domination. Several coin hoards with large numbers of Athenian issues of the fifth and early fourth century B.C. and many stray coins attest almost uninterrupted commercial relations with the Greek world and especially with Athens. In the fourth century and particularly during the second Persian domination the genuine Athenian coins became rare and were replaced by local imitations of them emitted in part by the local satraps. Illuminating evidence is furnished, for example, by two coin hoards. One was found at Beni-Hassan and consisted of twenty-one Phoenician coins, more than fifty-three tetradrachms of Athens, and one drachm. It was buried in the second quarter of the fourth century. Some of the Athenian tetradrachms are genuine Athenian issues, others are local imitations. The second hoard came from Samanoud. It consisted of more than sixty imitations of Athenian tetradrachms and some coins with Persian types struck probably in Egypt by the last satrap of Egypt, Sabaces, about 333 B.C.[20]

The development of the trade with the West in Egypt is best illustrated by the history of Naucratis. In this short introductory chapter it would be useless to repeat the well-known facts about the history of this famous centre of early Greek commerce in Egypt. Nor can I mention all the controversial points regarding the history of the early settlement and its relations to the Egyptian rulers of the day. One fact, however, deserves special mention—the prevalence of Athenian influence in Naucratis in the late fifth and early fourth centuries, as attested by the finds of Athenian pottery and of Athenian coins, genuine and imitated.[21]

It is difficult to discover to what extent the balance of Greek and especially Athenian trade was in favour of Greece and of the West in general. Our information on this subject is limited. The luxury products of Greek and, above all, Athenian agriculture and industry certainly played an important role in the life of the Syrian, Phoenician, and Palestinian cities, where the consumption of wine and olive-oil was not limited to the Greeks settled in these cities. The same holds good for the products of Greek industry. They have been found in graves which apparently were not graves of Greek immigrants. A no less important customer was Egypt, where indeed Greek wine and olive-oil were probably consumed in larger quantities than in Syria, Phoenicia, and Palestine.

Greek products, however, never penetrated very far inland. The careful exploration of many cities of Babylonia and of Elam has not yielded large numbers of Athenian vases. Such finds are quite exceptional. I know, for example, only of some sherds of Attic red-figured pottery found at Susa and of a fragment of a red-figured dish discovered at Uruk. But negative evidence is not conclusive.[22]

B. GREECE

In dealing with the economic structure of Greece in the fourth century B.C. we must keep in mind two outstanding facts.[23] The first is that our written evidence—both literary and documentary—relates almost exclusively to Athens, with sidelights thrown here and there on other Greek cities by stray notices in our texts or by occasional inscriptions; and the second is that even in this period Greece was far from homogeneous in economic and social development. We are in the habit of associating the idea of Greece with that of the Greek city-state, and the idea of the city-state with that of a city more or less like our modern cities, that is to say, a centre of industrial and commercial activity. But every student of ancient history knows that large areas of continental Greece even in the fourth century B.C., for instance parts of Aetolia and Acarnania, had not developed city life at all, and that other regions, though possessing a few urban centres, had practically their whole population distributed in villages, such as parts of Arcadia and of the territory of the Ozolian Locrians. Moreover many, probably the majority, of the city-states in continental

Greece were purely agricultural communities with only embryonic trade and industry, the last mostly carried on in the home. Further, we must always bear in mind that even the more progressive city-states of continental Greece differed widely from one another both in respect of their economic resources and of the use they made of them. Finally, continental Greece was only part of the Greek commonwealth. The conditions of the island States were quite peculiar, and even more peculiar and highly individualized were those of the city-states of the diaspora, which, though they were Greek communities, lived in surroundings that differed widely from those of the Greek mainland. This is specially true of economic conditions. The Greek cities of Spain, of Gaul, of Sicily, of South Italy, of Asia Minor, of Macedonia, of Thrace, of the Pontic regions, were all of them obliged to adapt their economic life to that of their neighbours, who were sometimes their suzerains. We know of course very little of these variations and fluctuations, but we must remember their existence and be very careful, in making general statements regarding economic conditions in Greece, not to treat it as a homogeneous unit.

The chief characteristic of the economic life of the Greek city-states, especially those of continental Greece and the islands, was their dependence on other regions. Few of them were economically self-sufficient, in the sense of producing sufficient food for their population and the raw materials required for vital industries, including the manufacture of tools and weapons. Since most of the cities were in one way or another connected with the sea—and for the islands the sea was the only highway—most of them had a pressing need of shipbuilding materials: metals, timber, pitch and tar, flax (for sails), and hemp (for ropes). It is notorious that Greece is very poor in metals, that deforestation at an early date denuded most of her territory of its supply of timber, that she never produced a sufficient quantity of flax and hemp, and that in most parts the fertility of the soil is poor or mediocre, especially in respect of grain production.

Thus the first duty incumbent on every Greek city was to guarantee its citizens an adequate supply of food for consumption and of metals and other materials for the manufacture of tools and weapons and for shipbuilding. As regards military equipment it must be remembered that war was endemic in Greece, and that one of the most urgent needs of an adult citizen was to provide himself with a good panoply. His safety and efficiency in war, as well as his social standing, depended largely on this. We must also remember that the so-called luxuries (such as spices, paints, perfumes, jewels, silver and gold plate, and the like), which played a certain part in the life of even the less-developed regions of Greece, were to a large extent imported into Greece, as was also incense, which early became an indispensable requisite of Greek worship. Accordingly the exchange of goods among Greek cities, their economic interdependence, and the importation of various commodities from foreign countries were features of Greek life from very early times. And these features became more prominent in any city-state with the growth of its activity, population, and importance.

Greece never suffered from an excess of imports from abroad. On the contrary, a shortage of imported commodities was the rule. On the other hand, over-population was a salient feature of her life. It is well known that in order to find a remedy for these two enduring evils—shortage of supplies, whether produced in Greece or imported, and excess of population—Greece at a very early date, nay from the very beginning of the settlement of Greeks in the southern part of the Balkan peninsula, began an extensive and successful colonization. So long as there were good opportunities for it on the shores of the Mediterranean and the Black Sea, colonization was an effective remedy for over-population. On the other hand, the colonies, being agricultural settlements in regions rich in natural resources or important fishing stations, would in due course supply the mother country (not necessarily their respective mother cities) with foodstuffs and certain raw materials (especially metals and timber). Trade between Greek colonies and the mother country was accordingly a natural consequence of Greek colonization.

For the imported goods which Greece absorbed in ever-increasing quantities she had to pay. In early days the Phoenician traders were content to accept slaves, hides, and cattle in exchange for their goods. Soon, however, Greece was able to add to these products of a primitive economy excellent wine and olive-oil. There is no doubt that in the early stages of commercial relations between Greece and her colonies she covered her imports from them of grain, fish, and certain raw materials to a large extent by the export of olive-oil and wine. This is shown by the frequent finds of Greek wine- and oil-jars in the ruins and tombs of the Greek colonies, a type of evidence that has never been collected and published in full. Though the practice of stamping the handles of such jars began late (the earliest stamps, those of the Thasian jars, belong probably to the early fourth century B.C.) and was confined to a few Greek cities (Thasos, Cnidos, Paros, Colophon, Rhodes, Sinope, Heraclea, Chersonesus in the Crimea, and some others), a comparative study of the forms of the stamped and the unstamped jars and of the casual inscriptions on them makes it possible to establish the place of origin of some of the latter class (for instance, the unstamped jars of Chios).[24]

To wine and olive-oil Greece very soon added certain products of her industry. Evidence of this is furnished by various types of pottery found all over Greece and in the colonies, dating from their earliest times. The facts are well known, and the distribution of these various brands of early Greek pottery has been carefully studied. The same is true of Greek metal ware—vases, armour and weapons, tripods, and so forth—though the study of this material is still in its early stage.

The volume of Greek trade gradually increased. From the Greek colonies products of agriculture and industry penetrated into the lands behind them. Greek commerce began successfully to compete there with Phoenician commerce, thus renewing in some measure the trade relations that had existed between the Aegean and Mycenaean trading-centres and their customers. The natives of Sicily, the tribes of South and Central Italy, the Etruscans, the Celts of North Italy and of Gaul, the Iberians of Spain, the Illyrians and the Thracians of the Adriatic coast, of the Danubian regions and of the northern part of the Balkan peninsula, the Scythians of the steppes of south Russia, the Lycians, Lydians, Phrygians, Thracians, and other peoples of Asia Minor, Egypt, Cyprus, Syria, Phoenicia, Palestine, Arabia, Mesopotamia, and even Iran, all became customers of Greece and absorbed steadily increasing quantities of Greek wine and olive-oil and of Greek industrial products.

The climax in this evolution was reached in the fifth century B.C., after the Persian wars and after the creation of the Athenian Empire. The material available for reconstructing the economic life of the fifth century is, of course, scanty. Our literary texts relate almost exclusively to Athens, and here chiefly to the late fourth century, while the archaeological and numismatic evidence is scattered and has never been collected in its entirety and utilized by students of economic history. No wonder that leading scholars differ widely in their estimates of the character and scope of Greek economic progress during this period, some being inclined to minimize this progress, others to exaggerate it, others again taking up an intermediate position.[25] Without entering into a discussion of this problem, I may state what is accepted by every one: that in the fifth century agriculture, industry, and foreign as well as inter-state trade flourished as they had never flourished before.[26]

This period of progress, however, did not last very long. After the Peloponnesian War, the ceaseless wars of the early fourth century, and the repeated political and social revolutions within the cities, the economic aspect of Greece completely changed. Though still prosperous and still increasing and improving her agricultural and industrial production, Greece was now passing through an economic and social crisis, which gradually became more acute. The facts are well known and the evidence has been repeatedly collected and discussed by eminent scholars.[27]

The economic and social life of the time was marked by two dominant features: the lapse of the mass of the population into proletarianism and, closely connected therewith, the growth of unemployment; and secondly a shortage of foodstuffs, which sometimes assumed an acute and catastrophic form. The first is known to us from various scattered passages describing the difficult conditions of life of the many paupers in the larger cities of Greece, and the acute class-war in these cities; we also have striking evidence of it in the growing number of adult male citizens of Greek cities who were ready and willing to sell their services and become mercenary soldiers in Greek and foreign armies.[28] The second is even better attested. Food shortage and measures taken to remedy it were familiar incidents in the life of Greece in the fourth century, and references thereto are of exceptional frequency in our literary and epigraphical sources. A prominent instance of an acute and prolonged shortage of food was the famous famine that occurred all over Greece in 331 B.C. and lasted for several years, until at least 324.[29]

These two phenomena merit fuller consideration. The evidence relating to them has been more than once collected, and the data of our literary and documentary sources have been sifted and interpreted.*

The increase in the numbers of hungry and restless proletarians throughout Greece and the difficulty of feeding those of them who were citizens of Greek cities were not due to a rapid growth of population in Greece generally, in other words to over-population. We have no reliable statistical material bearing on the changes in the population as a whole. But certain data are available. It is well known that between 480 and 431 B.C. the population of Attica was increasing, and reached a very high figure at the end of the period: in 431 the number of citizens has been calculated with some probability at 172,000 and the whole population, including the metics and slaves, at 315,500. After a period of acute crisis caused by the Peloponnesian War, during which the population of Attica rapidly decreased, a new increase set in, but it was slow and never brought the total number back to the level of 480–431 B.C. Tentative figures based on more or less trustworthy data show that the maximum reached in the later period cannot have exceeded 112,000 citizens, or a total population of 258,000.[30]

Our statistical material relates only to Athens. We know that a similar development (as regards the full citizens only) took place at Sparta. But nothing is known of the other parts of the Greek world. We cannot, however, say that the conditions which prevailed at Athens were in any way exceptional. All the larger cities of Greece had the same difficulties and lived in the same general atmosphere. It is therefore probable that

* References to the sources will be found in the works quoted in notes 23 and 25, especially in the short summary in Glotz, *Hist. gr.* iii, 1936, pp. 3 ff.

the slow rate of increase of the population observable at Athens and Sparta after 400 B.C. was a general, not a local, phenomenon.

It was to a large extent war and the concomitant civil strife within the cities—the struggle between the few rich and the many poor, a true class-war—that were responsible for the slow rate of growth of the population; not so much the actual losses in the many battles fought as the general uncertainty, which may have prevented Greek citizens from indulging in the luxury of large families. There developed at the same time a growing individualism and selfishness, a strong tendency to concentrate effort on securing the largest possible amount of prosperity for oneself and one's limited family. How far the Greeks of this period had recourse to the exposure of children as a means of restricting their families, is a subject of controversy.[31]

However this may be, it was not a rapid increase in population that led to phenomena which otherwise might have been explained as its natural results. If over-population is excluded, what were the causes of the proletarianism of the masses, of the increasing unemployment, and of the food shortage in Greece in the fourth century, and especially in the second half of it?

On the subject of proletarianism and unemployment much has been written. The ruin of small landowners by wars and devastation; the concentration of the population in the cities; the rapid accumulation of wealth in the hands of a few rich people; the growth of large estates; the competition of slave labour with free labour and the growing number of slaves employed in agriculture and industry—these have been advanced as the causes. Evidence for the existence of such conditions is scanty, and generalizations are dangerous. If we admit that, as is probable, the impoverishment of small landowners and the concentration of land in the hands of a few owners were prominent features in the economic life of Greece at this time, they would certainly contribute to the creation of a rural proletariat and to the concentration of proletarians in the cities. But we should still have to account for the acute unemployment prevailing, both in the country and in the cities, among proletarians who were undoubtedly ready and willing to work. We are told that it was the growth in the number of slaves that deprived free people of work and brought them to hunger and destitution.

Certainly it cannot be denied that there were in the fifth and fourth centuries large numbers of slaves in Greece, especially in the larger and more progressive cities, such as Athens and Corinth. Their numbers naturally fluctuated, increasing in times of prosperity and decreasing in times of economic distress. Development of commerce and industry raised the demand for labour; wars and trade with 'barbarians' supplied Greece with many slaves, both Greek and foreign; servile labour was more to be relied on than free labour, for slaves were exempt from military service; and finally the comparatively large supply of slaves made their labour on the whole cheaper than that of free men and helped to lower the price of labour in general.

The existence of slave labour, however, and its gradual increase did not lead to an economic crisis in the fifth century, and it cannot be said that it was only at the end of the fourth century that servile labour became an important factor in the economy of Greece. While we have no trustworthy statistics, we know that slaves were numerous at Athens in the fifth century, probably more numerous than in the early and even in the late fourth. It is highly probable that the number of slaves at Athens did not increase greatly during the fourth century and was not exceedingly large (it is grossly exaggerated in our texts). Moreover, as is shown by many inscriptions, slave labour during that century never succeeded in ousting free labour to any great extent, especially in agriculture and in the building trade.[32]

Why, then, was it that, whereas in the fifth and early fourth centuries Greece was able to provide for her increasing free and servile population, in the second half of the fourth the Greek city-states stood helpless before the problem of growing unemployment among a population that was increasing very slowly?

The existence of a food shortage is no less difficult to account for. Dearth is never mentioned as a serious problem in Greek cities in times of peace during the fifth century. Why should it have become a matter of such grave concern to almost all of them in the fourth? We have seen that it was not due to over-population. Was it then perhaps caused by a rapidly diminishing supply of foodstuffs, home-grown and imported?

There was certainly no sharp decline in the agricultural production of Greece in the fourth century. The soil of Greece remained what it had previously been, poor but productive, if well cultivated. None of our authorities speak of anything like a general and irreparable exhaustion of the soil, though there may have been partial exhaustion locally. Nor can we say that the cultivated area was diminishing. Wars may have had a detrimental influence on agriculture. Crops were destroyed, olive-groves and vineyards cut down; but the damage, to the crops at least, was soon repaired. No doubt the wars greatly promoted the concentration of land in the hands of rich men and the concomitant ruin of the small farmers, who sank into the proletarian class. This, however, does not mean that less land was cultivated or that the yield per acre was reduced. On the contrary, agricultural production in the hands of large landowners was more systematic, better organized, and better planned. The experience of centuries had been collected in handbooks and placed at the farmer's disposal. New technical devices—better implements, more rational irrigation and drainage, more judicious rotation of crops—were coming into general use. There is no reason, therefore, to think that the downfall of small landowners—which certainly was a very slow process—had had any detrimental effect on the agricultural productivity of Greece.[33]

Nor was there any shortage of foodstuffs on the international market at that time. It is true that Italy had ceased to export large supplies of corn. But both in Thrace and in South Russia grain was produced in large quantities and in case of a failure of crops in those regions, buyers had at their disposal the grain produced in Asia Minor, Cyprus, Phoenicia, and Egypt. All these provinces of the Persian Empire were in close commercial relations with Greece, and the grain trade was well organized. Athens was still strong enough to police the Aegean Sea and to afford some measure of protection to her grain ships. Piracy of course existed and throve, especially in time of war, but it was a spasmodic rather than a permanent evil, which would not completely disorganize a well-established maritime traffic.[34]

If therefore there was a food shortage in Greece in the fourth century, it was not due to a diminution in the available supply of foodstuffs. We must seek for another explanation.

Unemployment and scarcity were not relieved by the abundance of money in circulation at that time, money which to some extent had come from external sources in the form of bribes and gifts from the Persian king and from Philip. This abundance contributed to the enrichment of political leaders and facilitated banking operations. But it also led to a rapid rise in prices, which greatly aggravated the situation of those who had little or no money. A rise in prices, though not always a sign of an economic crisis, was so in this case. The increase in coined money does not appear to have been accompanied by a corresponding increase of production. The result was a rapid rise in the price of all commodities, both foodstuffs and industrial products.

What were the true reasons of these disturbing economic and social phenomena? Wars and revolutions must certainly be taken into account, but they do not offer a sufficient explanation. In my opinion, the incipient economic crisis of the late fourth century B.C. is to be attributed in the main to the general trend of economic evolution in the ancient world. It seems to me that in the fifth century there existed a certain stable balance between production and demand, the conditions of the market were sound, and Greece was able to provide for her growing population. It was no longer so in the fourth century, for the equilibrium was disturbed, and production and demand ceased to grow at the same pace.

Since this phenomenon has not been studied by modern scholars and we are in the habit of regarding the fourth century as a period of brilliant economic progress, it is incumbent on me to set forth the grounds for thinking that the period shows, on the contrary, unmistakable signs of economic tension and unrest.

In order to understand the gradual growth of disequilibrium in the Greek economy of the fourth century, we must first review the conditions of industry and trade at that time, since it was principally these branches of economic activity that were then expanding and absorbing the bulk of the Greek labour-supply. For agriculture had reached its climax, its full capacity of employment, early in the history of Greece, and the improved methods of agriculture to which I have referred did not require more hands than the more primitive methods that preceded them. A cursory glance at the facts assembled in works dealing with the economic history of Greece suffices to show that industry in the fifth and fourth centuries was rapidly developing on 'capitalistic' lines. Production by individual artisans in their homes or in small shops for a restricted local market was, of course, still the predominant form of industry. But in the main centres much larger and much more specialized shops, approaching in character to small factories, were not uncommon. They were run mostly with slave labour as 'capitalist' enterprises and produced goods that certainly were only in part absorbed by the local and by the Greek inter-state market; in part the goods were exported to foreign countries, Greek merchants in Greek colonies serving as intermediaries. Such shops are repeatedly described by contemporaries as a common feature of the industrial life of Athens, and this evidence cannot be invalidated by even the most ingenious interpretation of the texts.

It is equally certain that there were many cities in the Greek world that specialized in certain goods. Many of them were so successful that they obtained a kind of monopoly in the production and sale of these wares and secured a market for them both in Greece and abroad. I may quote a few examples: Megara with its extensive manufacture of the commonest kind of clothing (especially *exomides*); Laconia, Boeotia, and Euboea (especially Chalcis), with their manufacture of iron armour and weapons; Delos, Aegina, and Corinth, centres of production of bronze and bronze-ware (the raw material being imported): Aegina, famous for the small wares which her pedlars sold all over Greece; the many well-known centres of pottery production, especially Athens; and several places known for their excellent woodwork, wool, and linen.[35]

It may also be noted that agricultural production became increasingly industrialized during the fourth century. I have already mentioned that larger agricultural units were now prevalent. These estates were run mostly on capitalistic lines;

their products, that is to say, were chiefly sold in the market, not consumed by the producers. This practice was not new (especially as regards wine and oil), but it now became quite general.

The increasing complexity resulting from the development of industrial and agricultural activities on 'modern' lines was accompanied by corresponding developments in the organization of trade, especially sea-borne trade. Larger amounts of capital were invested in it; larger and better ships were used; certain legal principles concerning commercial transactions, especially the very popular bottomry loans, were recognized by the courts of the more progressive city-states; effective measures were repeatedly taken against piracy, although Greece never succeeded in eliminating it completely; business intercourse became more and more systematized, as merchants came to regard their business as a profession, which was often hereditary;* and regular supplies of goods were secured by professional merchants for their regular customers, especially in the grain, wine, oil, and timber trades.

The process of regulating and systematizing trade was greatly aided by the development of banking, which assumed a professional character. Banks engaged habitually in money transactions, which included all sorts of credit operations, such as giving loans on security or mortgage, and even working a system of credit-transfer.

We must, of course, be careful not to exaggerate, not to speak of tendencies as if they were established realities. Complicated business relations were a new phenomenon in Greek life and the more recent developments were still in their infancy in the fourth century.

But why, under these conditions, did not the 'modernized' industry completely oust the antiquated forms of production by increasing its output and absorbing the idle labour that was wandering about Greece? Why, instead of this, did an acute economic crisis overtake Greece, a crisis caused in part by the country's political evolution, but which in turn

* An illustration of this may be seen in the common use of 'ship's papers', which both served as a means of identifying the ship and gave the names of the owner, his partners, and the captain.

PLATE XIII

Prof. J. D. Beazley has been kind enough to supply me with the following description of the vase (somewhat expanded by myself): 'Clay hydria. Above, "theoxenia" of the Dioscuroi: a couch with cushions and two lyres; in front of it a low table with two "cantharoi" and food; to the right and left of the couch and behind it three thuribles; above, the two stars of the Dioscuroi; to the left of the couch a priest, to the right, a priestess; behind them the two gods on horseback, and behind these a man with an ivy crown and a servant maid. Below, arrival of youths. Attic ware of about 420 B.C., by the artist known as the "Cadmus painter".' H. 0·455 m. (Photograph supplied by the authorities of the Plovdiv Museum.)

B. Filow and I. Welkow, *J.D.A.I.* xlv (1930), pp. 302 ff., figs. 18–22; I. Welkow, *Bull. Inst. arch. Bulg.* vi (1930–1) (publ. 1932), pp. 21 ff., fig. 21 and pls. V–VII; B. D. Filow, *Die Grabhügelnekropole bei Duvanlij in Südbulgarien*, 1934, pp. 73 ff., figs. 95–8, cf. this chapter, p. 113.

Attic Hydria found in Bulgaria in the Tumulus Bashova Mogila
Plovdiv Museum.

SILVER 'PHIALE' FOUND IN BULGARIA IN THE TUMULUS BASHOVA MOGILA
Plovdiv Museum.

PLATE XIV

Silver omphalos-phiale, parcel-gilt with incised figures and relief ornaments round the omphalos. Chariot-race with ἀποβάται. Outside, in Greek incised letters, the name ΔΑΔΑΛΕΜΕ, doubtless the name of the owner. Greek (Attic?) work of about 420 B.C. (according to Prof. J. D. Beazley). Diam. 0·205 m. A similar silver kylix with two handles showing on the interior, engraved and gilt, the beautiful figure of Selene (?) on horseback, and on the outside the same name of the owner, was found in the same grave. It is well known that silver vases of the same style and technique have been found in South Russia in the tumuli of the Seven Brothers (my *Iranians and Greeks*, pl. XV, 3). (Photograph supplied by the authorities of the Plovdiv Museum.)

B. Filow and I. Welkow, *J.D.A.I.* xlv (1930), pp. 288 ff., fig. 7 and pl. VIII; I. Welkow, *Bull. Inst. arch. Bulg.* vi (1930–1) (publ. 1932), pp. 13 ff., fig. 17 and pls. I, II; B. Filow, *Duvanlij*, 1934, pp. 63 ff., fig. 80 and pl. IV.

contributed largely to intensify the political crisis and make it more disastrous?

The explanation lies, in my opinion, in the conditions of the market for Greek agricultural and industrial products. This market, which had been rapidly expanding in the sixth and fifth centuries B.C., shrank considerably in the fourth, and was no longer able to absorb the goods that Greece had to offer it. The position deserves more detailed examination, for it has a direct bearing on the economic development of the Greek world in the Hellenistic period.

I begin with the home market. It is notorious that Greece never was a rich country. Its purchasing power was therefore naturally low. Besides, most of the city-states had their own flourishing industries and in most of them these industries satisfied the needs of the local market for industrial goods. In the fourth century, under the pressure of wars and of violent political strife within the cities, it was hardly possible that the purchasing capacity of the Greek city-states should show any increase. On the contrary, in most of the cities of Greece and of Asia Minor difficulties in finding the means of purchasing foodstuffs and in paying their mercenary armies led to repeated economic crises.

In addition to the home market there were the colonial and foreign markets. It was certainly to the latter that Greece owed, at least in part, her comparative prosperity in the archaic and classical periods of her existence. What was the state of this market in the fourth century?

When speaking of the Oriental countries, that is to say, the various parts of the Persian Empire, I pointed out that Greek and especially Athenian trade with the East was fully developed in the fifth and fourth centuries B.C. The products of Greek, above all Athenian, industry are found in large quantities in Egypt and in the western section of the Persian Empire, particularly Syria, Phoenicia, and Palestine, and the same is true of Greek coins, which are almost exclusively Athenian.

So it was in the fifth and early fourth centuries. In the middle of the fourth century we observe, however, a great change. Athenian pottery appears more rarely in the tombs and ruins of the cities and, what is still more important, the genuine Athenian coins minted at Athens are replaced almost entirely by local coins some of which either reproduce the Athenian coins or imitate them. We observe this phenomenon alike in Egypt and in Syria, Phoenicia, and Palestine. It is obvious that Athenian trade with the Persian Empire was declining. The demand for Athenian and Greek goods was apparently falling, and with it the commercial influence of Athens. Local products replaced Greek wares and local money was now the vehicle of trade.

We may connect this decline with the general political conditions of the time, particularly with the unsettled political situation of the early fourth century in Greece and in the East, and more specifically with the great nationalist revival of the Persian Empire in the strong hands of Artaxerxes III Ochus. In any case it is very probable that the balance of Greek trade with the East shifted considerably and not in favour of Greece. Demand for Oriental goods in Greece was not decreasing (for instance, the demand for corn was apparently rising rather than falling), while the export of Greek goods steadily declined. For her imports of Oriental merchandise Greece to all appearance had to pay in silver, which was re-minted in the East. It is an interesting fact that the Oriental silver coins of this period, except the Persian royal currency, never reached Greece: they are not found in Greek hoards of the time. Al-Mina, destroyed by fire about 375 B.C., appears to have become independent of Athens in the subsequent period of its existence. It issued its own currency. A more careful study of the imported pottery found in the second level, especially the black-glazed pottery, may show how much of it still came from Athens. It was not till the time of Alexander that the city became again an important centre of international trade.[36]

The trade of Greece with her own colonies and the lands behind them in the North-East, North, and West was much more favourable to her. We take first the northern coast of the Black Sea, a region that has been thoroughly explored, has yielded abundance of archaeological material, and has a very important bearing on economic history. It is common knowledge that the steppes of South Russia—both the agricultural territories of the Greek cities and the areas cultivated by the subjects and serfs of the Scythian kings—were the main sources of supply of grain, and the South Russian rivers were one of the sources of supply of fish, for the Greek world, particularly for Athens, in the second half of the fifth and in the fourth century. This is a subject with which I have dealt more than once elsewhere, and I will not repeat here what I have already said about it.[37] The volume of export to Greece from these north-Pontic regions has been variously estimated.[38] In any case it was very large and it follows that Greece must have exported in return a large quantity of its own goods. The customers of the Greeks in South Russia were first and foremost the Greek cities of the sea-coast: Panticapaeum, Phanagoria, Theodosia, Tanais, Chersonesus, Olbia, Tyras, and many minor Greek settlements, especially in the Crimea; also some semi-Greek fortified villages and towns along the lower courses of the Dnieper, the Bug, and the Don. Besides them there were the Scythian kings and feudal lords who lived in their camps, and to some extent in fortified towns, all over the steppes of South Russia from the Ural and the Volga rivers to the regions beyond the Dniester.

There is no doubt that the Greek cities of South Russia led a purely Greek life, at least in the sixth, fifth, and fourth centuries B.C. The cities themselves were built in the Greek fashion. A large amount of Greek building material, especially imported marble, was employed for the construction of temples and public buildings in these cities, and imported marble and bronze statues were extensively used in the adornment of temples and public squares. Some of these statues were the work of the greatest artists of Greece. Even the grave-*stelae* for the necropoleis—the cities of the dead—were some of them imported from the mother country, others made on the spot from imported material. It is more difficult to say which of the minor objects of luxury or of daily use, of a purely Greek character, that have been found in the ruins and graves of the Pontic cities, were imported and which were made in Pontic Greece. Most of the better pottery was certainly imported, as were also many lamps and some of the terracotta statuettes. It is very probable, too, that most of the armour and weapons, the gold, silver, and bronze plate, the gold and silver jewels, the gems and intaglios, were importations. Some fine textiles found in the graves of the early fourth century were certainly not made locally, and the same is true of the finest wooden furniture, especially that which was adorned with ivory and coloured glass. The famous engraved ivory plaques that were found in the tumulus of Kul Oba, and probably belonged to a richly adorned couch or a kind of baldachin, were in all probability made at Athens.

It cannot be denied, however, that some of the common objects of daily use may have been made in the Pontic cities. Common jewellery, silver and bronze mirrors, common bronze plate, armour and weapons, strigils, safety-pins, knives and spoons, may have been products of Pontic industry. But the importation of even these objects is not out of the question. It is only by a careful comparative study of their forms and of the material of which they are made (a study that has never been attempted) that we may hope to reach more or less certain conclusions.

Besides products of Greek industry many Eastern commodities, such as incense, spices, precious and semi-precious stones, were imported into the Pontic cities. Most of them reached their destination, not overland by the caravan route across Turkestan and the south Russian steppes, but through the great outlets of Eastern trade on the Aegean—the harbour cities of Asia Minor and Rhodes. The same is true of Egyptian glass and faience. Perfumes were mostly prepared in Greece, and thence likewise came articles manufactured from ebony and ivory.

Lastly—and this is a point of no small importance—there is not the slightest doubt that these Pontic cities consumed large quantities of Greek olive-oil and wine. Many earthenware jars and fragments of jars found in the ruins and graves of these cities, if studied from the point of view of form and material, would certainly be found to have come from Greece and Asia Minor. Most of the jars of a later period, when the handles were stamped, have proved to have been imported from Rhodes, Cnidos, Thasos, and probably Sinope. There is no reason to suppose that the Pontic cities consumed less foreign wine and olive-oil in the sixth and fifth centuries than in the Hellenistic period.[39]

Many objects of Greek origin have been found in the Scythian royal and princely graves of the Kuban region, between the Don and the Dnieper, and between the Dnieper and the Bug: articles of military equipment, parts of horse-trappings, gold, silver, and bronze plate, gold ornaments for dresses and rugs, choice pieces of metal and wooden furniture, and some pottery. In the earliest graves, belonging to the late sixth and early fifth centuries, the imported pieces are some of Oriental, some of Greek workmanship. In the late fifth and the fourth centuries the Oriental objects are rare (a few gems) and the Greek predominate. We must note also that in almost all the richer graves scores of Greek wine-jars were found, evidence of a large import of Greek wine into Scythia.[40]

The picture changes somewhat in the fourth century. Large quantities of local pottery are now found along with the imported Greek ware in all the Greek cities of South Russia. This pottery has received very little attention; but quite recently Mlle T. N. Knipovitch has made a careful study of the ceramic material found in the ruins of a commercial settlement at the mouth of the Don (Elizavetovskaja Staniza). This settlement was Greco-'Scythian', the local population being a mixture of Scythians and pre-Scythian inhabitants of the region; it flourished in the fifth and fourth centuries, and was probably abandoned in the third. Mlle Knipovitch identifies it with the early Tanais (transferred in the third century to another place, the modern Nedvigovka). Her analysis shows that in the fifth century black-glazed Athenian pottery appears there very frequently, and with it the Anatolian brand of the same pottery. Later, in the fourth century, these wares were replaced by a Panticapaean imitation, which coexisted with large quantities of unglazed pottery of Greek forms, undoubtedly likewise of Panticapaean make. The Attic and Ionian imports disappeared at that time almost completely.[41]

In Panticapaeum itself, which with other South Russian Greek cities was the best buyer of Attic pottery in the fourth century, the imported Attic ware found dangerous rivals in some local products. Most of the late red-figured vases of the so-called Kertch style were certainly imported, but it is not at all certain that some of them were not produced locally. The local brands of black-glazed ware have been mentioned above. And finally, contemporaneous with the late red-figured vases of the Kertch style (since they have been found in the same graves), were the so-called water-colour painted vases made exclusively for funeral use, an imitation and continuation as it were of the latest red-figured Attic vases of the Kertch style. No exact date can be assigned either to the latest red-figured or to the water-colour vases, but it is very probable that the former were contemporaneous with Alexander the Great and so undoubtedly were the earliest water-colour vases also.[42]

In the ruins of many Bosporan cities, alongside of stamped and unstamped jars of Ionian, Thasian, Rhodian, Cnidian, and Sinopic origin and belonging to about the same period, we find many jars and fragments of jars, both stamped and unstamped, which cannot be classed in any of these groups. The use of a clay similar to that of Chersonesus, and the occurrence on the stamps of names that are frequently found in inscriptions of the city, may point to the Chersonesian origin of those stamped jars, which may be assigned to the fourth and third centuries B.C., and show unmistakable Megarian affinities. The frequency with which jars that are probably of Chersonesian origin have been found in the Bosporan kingdom points to the export of wine from that city. We know from inscriptions and from the ruins of farm-houses in its territory that in the fourth century it developed a wine-growing industry and so became a rival of the wine-producing centres of Greece proper, of the islands, and of Asia Minor.[43]

Finally, recent studies of the tiles used for the buildings of Panticapaeum and other cities of the Bosporan kingdom have shown that, while in the early fourth century they were imported into the Greek cities of South Russia probably from Sinope, in the second half of that century Panticapaeum and Phanagoria began themselves to produce tiles (which were often stamped). In this industry the archons (or kings) of the Bosporus played an important part, as is shown by stamps frequently found on these tiles, mentioning the names of Bosporan kings and their relatives or (within a certain period) characterizing the tiles as 'royal' (*βασιλικὴ πλινθίς, βασιλικὸς καλυπτήρ*). Here again we see a far-reaching emancipation of the Bosporan kingdom, and probably of other cities of South Russia, from dependence on the products of the mainland of Greece. I have no doubt that a careful study of other objects of daily use (if it can be carried out with convincing results) will show the same general evolution.[44]

As regards the Scythian graves, many of the objects found in them, especially metal ware, were not imported even in the sixth and fifth centuries, but were made at Olbia by local Greek artisans. In the fourth century, most of the gold and silver objects that were buried with the Scythian kings and chieftains can be shown by analysis of their styles to be in all probability products of local (mostly Panticapaean) art, especially those which are adorned with hellenized compositions in the so-called animal style and with anthropomorphic images of Scythian gods, those which reproduce scenes of Scythian religious life, and those which reflect the Scythian heroic epos.

Iranian and especially Persian influence on the Panticapaean art of the fifth and fourth centuries was as strong as Greek. It is revealed in the form of various objects (for example, the spherical ritual bowls, so common in South Russia and Bulgaria, find their best parallels in similar bowls found in the semi-Iranian necropolis of Deve Hujuk in Asia Minor and in the famous palace of Vouni in Cyprus),* in the choice of subjects represented, and in the composition and style of treatment of these subjects. I have dealt with these products of Panticapaean Greco-Iranian art elsewhere.[45]

Thus in the fourth century the Greek colonies of South Russia, though still providing an excellent market for products of Greek agriculture and industry, became less dependent on the mother country for the supply of the latter. They gradually developed their own industry and began to compete with Greece proper in the manufacture of objects not only for their own use but also for their Scythian customers. Moreover, in the fourth century Chersonesus developed its own viticulture, and its example may have been followed by some of the cities of the Bosporan kingdom. The import of wine from Greece was considerably reduced thereby.

And yet the export of foodstuffs to Greece did not decrease.

* See note 18.

On the contrary its volume gradually increased. I have stated above that the population of Greece began once more to expand in the fourth century. Moreover, as is well known, in the same century the Italian export of foodstuffs, especially grain, was not as large as it had previously been. Egypt, Cyprus, and Phoenicia to a certain extent replaced Italy, but Cyprus and Phoenicia could not produce great quantities of grain, and Egypt had not yet assumed the prominent part in the grain trade of the world that it played in the Hellenistic period. The balance of trade with the Pontic cities became therefore in the fourth century in all probability less favourable to Greece than before. No wonder that in such circumstances Athens made the greatest efforts, by renewing her treaty with the Bosporan rulers and by bestowing on them high honours and privileges, to secure for herself at least a part of the corn exported to Greece by the crowned merchants of Panticapaeum.[46]

The history of the commercial relations between Greece (especially Ionia and Athens) and Thrace is similar. Thrace exported to Greece through the Greek colonies on the Euxine (Apollonia and Mesembria) and those on the Aegean coast (especially Abdera, Maronea, Aenus, and Amphipolis) large quantities of the same products as were exported from South Russia (chiefly grain and fish), and of metals and timber as well. The imports from Thrace in the early period were probably balanced by exports of wine and olive-oil from Greece. But the Greek cities of the Thracian coast very soon became notable centres of wine production, and the Thracians themselves were from an early date expert viticulturists. It is therefore highly probable that from very early times the exports of Greece to the Greek cities of Thrace and to Thrace itself consisted chiefly of olive-oil and manufactured goods.

There is another respect in which Thrace was similar to South Russia. The part played by the Bosporan kingdom in South Russia was played in Thrace by the Odrysian kingdom, which, if not a creation of Athens, was supported by it, in the same way and for the same reasons as was the Bosporan kingdom. We find accordingly the same general development of trade relations between Greece and Thrace as between her and the Bosporan kingdom and its Scythian hinterland. The early trade was mostly in the hands of the Ionian Greeks, while in the fifth and in the early fourth centuries the dominant influence both in politics and in trade was Athenian. I cannot dwell on this topic at length, and must confine myself to this passing remark.[47]

These conclusions, which are based on the literary and epigraphical sources, are strongly supported by archaeological evidence. The archaeological study of Thrace has, no doubt, not been so thorough as that of South Russia. None of the Greek cities of Thrace (except to a certain extent Apollonia) have been systematically excavated. The exploration of the tumuli-graves of the Odrysian kings and of their Thracian vassals is only in its early stage. Although the evidence certainly can and will be substantially increased, much material is already available, and the finds of recent years provide sufficient evidence to enable us to trace, in its general outlines, the development of trade relations between Thrace and Greece in the sixth, fifth, and fourth centuries B.C.[48]

Since there exists no general comprehensive survey of these finds from the historical and economic points of view, I may, at the risk of overburdening the reader with odd geographical names and archaeological details, present one here. Any reader who is not interested may skip the following four pages and proceed to the general remarks on the trade relations between Greece and Thrace on pp. 117 ff.

The richest and most remarkable tumuli-graves were all discovered in a single region of south Bulgaria, near Philippopolis (Plovdiv). The most important group, which has been thoroughly explored, is that around Duvanlij. All the rich graves belong to the classical period.

We may divide these graves into three sets. The earliest belongs to the end of the sixth century and the first decennia of the fifth. It consists of some graves of the Duvanlij group: Mushovitza, Kukuva, Lozarskata, and of a rich grave near Dalboki (Stara Zagora). Imported objects predominate in all these graves, especially armour and weapons, silver and bronze plate, jewellery, pottery, glass, and alabaster. While the metal ware is in all probability of Ionian origin, and the glass and alabaster came either from Egypt or are Greek imitations of Egyptian products, the pottery is Attic. The armour and weapons need a careful study. Alongside of these imported Greek objects there is a certain quantity of local products. One or two objects from the Kukuva Mogila (a breastplate and some plaques in the shape of fishes) may be Scythian, probably imported from South Russia. Relations with Scythia, I may add, are attested by a recent isolated find (near Garčinovo): a bronze press-mould for the manufacture of gold and silver plaques adorned with Scythian figures of animals.

To the next set (dating from the last decades of the fifth century and the early years of the fourth) belongs a series of very rich graves. In the Duvanlij group (in chronological order): Arabadzijskata Mogila, Golemata Mogila, and Bashova Mogila. To these we may add the tumuli of Rachmanlij and Alexandrovo and the rich grave of Urukler near Stara Zagora.

The best metal objects in these graves, the engraved and gilded silver plate, exactly similar to the plate found in the Semibratnij Kurgans in South Russia (Kuban), were imported from Athenian workshops. The choice pieces of pottery are also Athenian, and the gold rings found in many tumuli are characteristically Greek. But some of the rings are certainly local imitations of Greek originals. The jewellery has mostly an Ionian aspect. There is a very interesting iron sword from Golemata Mogila with an ivory hilt. It recalls the ivory-hilted swords which were one of the specialities of the little factory belonging to the father of Demosthenes.[49] Armour and weapons were also imported, but careful comparative study is needed to determine their place of origin. The same is true of the bronze plate. The *situla* of Urukler and similar *situlae* from other graves show Italian forms and probably come ultimately from South Italy (Tarentum?). The omphalos-cups with tongue patterns were probably of Italian origin.[50] In addition a certain number of objects of local make were found in all the graves.[51]

A third set, probably of the fourth century, consists of some peculiar graves found in the neighbourhood of Brezovo, Bedniakovo, and Panagurishte to the north of Plovdiv, and of Raduvene near Lovčen. While objects imported from Greece are common in them, these graves derive a special character from

PLATE XV

To the left three silver PHALARA in repoussé work. On the first a rosette consisting of lotus buds (diam. 0·086 m.). On the second (diam. 0·08 m.) two animals running (perhaps pigs), behind them a bird, and before them a palmette between two rosettes. On the third Heracles strangling the Nemean lion (diam. 0·088 m.). The last phalaron is of pure Greek workmanship; it is an imitation of contemporary coins of Cyzicus, like similar plaques from Kul-Oba in South Russia. Probably imported from Amphipolis. The first and second are local imitations of Greek originals. End of the fourth century B.C. B. Filow, *Röm. Mitt.* xxxii (1917), pl. 1 and figs. 26 and 30, cf. *C.A.H.*, Vol. of Pls. iii, 1930, pp. 66*b* and 68*a*.

To the right a thin silver plate in the shape of a double axe, probably a horse frontlet. In the centre a large rosette of ten dots. Above, Heracles to the l. in Thracian dress holding a club, and behind him an animal (the Erymanthian boar or Cerberus?). Above and below the rosette two winged eagle-griffins. At the bottom a Siren with a lyre. L. 0·32 m. Childish barbaric reproduction of Greek subjects with admixture of some prehistoric ornaments. B. Filow, loc. cit., p. 20, fig. 25; *C.A.H.*, loc. cit., p. 68*b*. (Photographs supplied by the authorities of the Sofia Museum.)

On the group of tumuli of Bulgaria of the same character see my *Skythien und der Bosporus*, pp. 539 ff. (with bibliography), cf. p. 116, n. 53 to this Chapter.

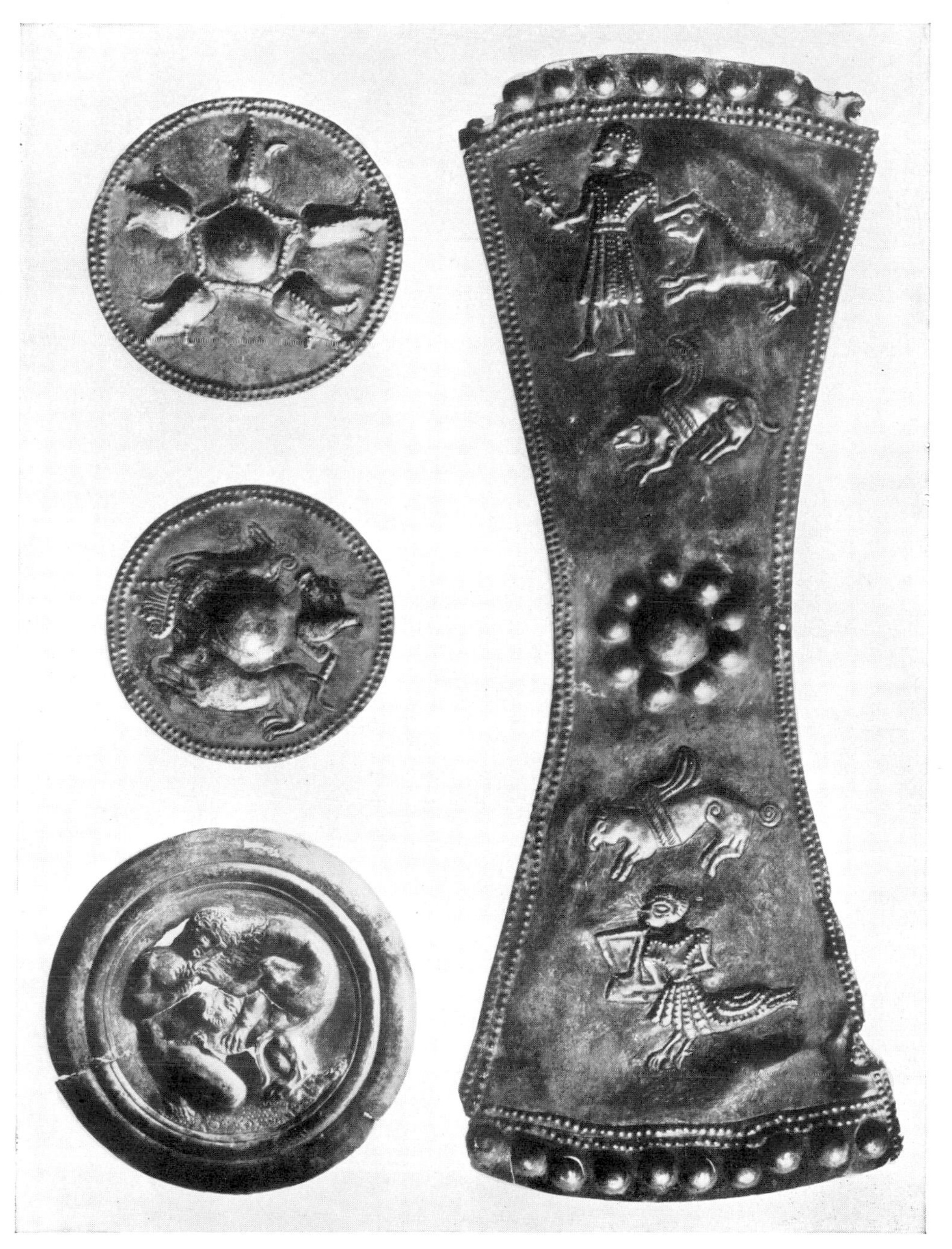

Greek and Greco-Thracian Objects found in the Tumulus of Panagurishte in Southern Bulgaria

Sofia Museum.

a, b, c, e from Craiova in Rumania, now in the Museum of Bucarest; d, found in the tumulus of Panagurishte, now in the Museum of Sofia.

SPECIMENS OF THE THRACO-SCYTHIAN ANIMAL STYLE

PLATE XVI

Silver plaques forming part of horse-trappings. (*a*) Triquetra of stylized horse-protomes. (*b*) Triquetra derived from the first, the horses' heads being transformed into imitations of Greek plant-ornaments. (*c*) Head of a stag with stylized horns. (*d*) Two lions' hind legs, the paws ending in birds' heads, crowned with a highly stylized griffin's head. (*e*) Lion's head with wide open mouth. (Photographs supplied by the authorities of the Bucarest and the Sofia Museums.)

On the find of Craiova (divided between Berlin and Bucarest) and its connexions with Scythia, see my *Skythien und der Bosporus*, pp. 491 ff. The plaque of Panagurishte, B. Filow, *Röm. Mitt.* xxxii (1917), p. 25, fig. 32; *C.A.H.*, Vol. of Pls. iii, 1930, p. 66*c*, cf. p. 70.

the presence of a large quantity of objects which are Scythian in all their distinctive features and originally formed part of horse-trappings. Certain spherical bronze and silver vases from Panagurishte and Brezovo are almost duplicates of similar ritual vases found in South Russia.[52] The grave of Verbitza, which shows no Scythian connexions, is of later date (end of the fourth or beginning of the third century).

One of the most remarkable peculiarities of these graves lies in the fact that they contained not only Scythian articles, either imported from South Russia or made in the Greek Pontic cities of Thrace, but also certain products of local workmanship, Greek or semi-Greek in character, made for the use of Thracians probably at Amphipolis and in other Greek cities of the Pontic and Aegean coast. Some silver plaques (horse-trappings?) from the tumulus of Panagurishte are of exceptional interest. Some of them are Greek, but others show a peculiar simplification of motifs of Greek art that recalls the evolution of Celtic art, especially the gradual simplification or geometric treatment of Greek coin-types in the Celtic coins of the classical and Hellenistic periods. The silver plaque of Panagurishte is typical in this respect; it probably formed part of horse-trappings and shows an almost completely geometrized figure of Heracles leading a wild boar (one of the exploits of Heracles), and simplified figures of griffins and a Siren, the whole in a geometric frame. Very similar to it is a gilded silver belt from Loveč in South Bulgaria, which has parallels in point of form both in Italy (Villanovan, Etruscan, and Samnite belts) and in the East (Luristan), while its decoration shows a curious mixture of ornamental and figure motifs partly derived from the East (the archers and the central palmette), partly Greek (the horsemen). The belt reminds me of the famous kettle of Gundestrup, which I regard as a product of eastern Celtic art under Oriental influence. The two objects mentioned above, which are probably of Thracian, not of Celtic, workmanship, show that Thrace tried in the fourth century to emancipate herself from Greek art and create her own, in this resembling the Celts and the Sarmatians, with the difference that they succeeded, especially in developing their own ornamental art, while she failed.[53]

A few words may be added here on a very interesting set of graves recently explored at Mezek in South Bulgaria, which contained a multitude of objects, many of them of great beauty. A few of the early graves of this region belong to the late fifth century B.C., but most of them to the early and late fourth. One of the peculiarities of this group, in comparison with the other similar groups, is the frequency of monumental cupola graves of the same type and the same construction as those of the corresponding period in South Russia, particularly in the vicinity of Panticapaeum. In construction and disposition these tombs are late survivals of the type of the Mycenean royal graves, while the group of royal or princely tombs in Macedonia, near the main capitals of the Macedonian kingdom, show a more advanced architectural design, inasmuch as they embody in their construction, not the traditional and primitive 'Mycenean' stepped vault and cupola, but the much more 'modern' barrel-vault, in this respect again resembling some tomb-chambers in South Russia. The general aspect of the finds made in these cupola tombs and in other less elaborate graves in the region of Mezek is the same as that of the other contemporary graves of south Bulgaria. The bulk of the objects, especially the red-figured vases and the beautiful bronze utensils (specially notable is a fine candelabrum), were imported from Greece and Asia Minor. But some parts of metal (gold and silver) horse-trappings and ornaments were certainly made locally, and are interesting products of the local Scytho-Thracian style.[54]

To sum up. Thrace in the sixth, fifth, and fourth centuries B.C. was one of the best customers of Greece. It was probably Cyzicus (whose coins circulated in large quantities both in South Russia and in Thrace) that in the earliest times supplied the Thracian market, through Apollonia, with products of Ionian metal-work. Simultaneously commercial relations sprang up with Athens, probably through Aenus, and constantly developed. In the fifth century it was Athens that dominated the Thracian market. Ionian export still existed, but no longer had the same importance as before. It was probably from Amphipolis, up the Struma (Strymon) river, that Athenian exports reached central Thrace. At the end of the fifth century we notice a new phenomenon. Alongside of imported articles we find in the graves semi-Greek local imitations of them. These gradually increase in numbers, and are accompanied in some graves (probably those of Scythian princelets or Thracian lords, vassals of the Scythians) by numerous objects either imported from South Russia or made on the spot in imitation of such imports, and by some articles of native Thracian workmanship and style. This change cannot be ascribed exclusively to the changed political conditions. Scythian influence must, of course, be attributed to the advance of the Scythians into the Balkan peninsula, which led to the well-known expeditions of Philip and Alexander. But on the other hand we must assume a change similar to that which we have noticed in South Russia. The Greek colonies of Thrace, like those of South Russia, started manufactures of their own in order to satisfy their Thracian and Scythian customers, who now preferred these local products to the expensive imported Greek goods. This must be the reason of the gradual decrease in the intensity of commercial relations between Greece and Thrace, which we see reflected in the changed aspect of the contents of the richer graves of the fourth century. In that century Thrace, like South Russia, was no longer so good a market for Greece as it had been.[55]

Nor was the situation different at the mouth of the Danube and up the Danube, in regions where the Getae formed the native population, and the Scythians were, as in Bulgaria, their overlords, having their political centres both in Transylvania and northern Hungary (on the Theiss) and in the south Russian steppes north of Olbia. Istrus on the lower Danube was the connecting link between the Getae and their Scythian suzerains on the one hand and Greece on the other. Founded, like Olbia, as a fishing colony, it developed in the sixth and fifth centuries into a flourishing commercial city, which imported large quantities of Greek goods mostly for its own consumption but partly for re-export to the lower Danubian region. Stray finds of Ionian (or south Italian ?) bronze vessels along the Danube, some of them in Greek trading settlements, afford evidence of these trade relations.

In the seventh, sixth, and fifth centuries, however, it was not through Istrus that the Scythian stronghold in the Danube region—Transylvania—had been connected with Greece. For the Agathyrsi of Transylvania the paramount Greek centre was Olbia, and it was through Olbia and through the Pontic Scythians that they received the gorgeous metal ware—Ionian, Scythian of Olbian workmanship, and Scythian of Scythian workmanship—which is such a typical feature of the contents of their graves.

We have little information regarding the economic development either of Transylvania or of the hinterland of Istrus in the fourth century. It seems probable, however, that during that century the Scythian State of Transylvania became isolated from its Scythian mother country and lost its close connexion with Olbia. It suffered heavily from the advance of the Celts and was soon absorbed by them. Consequently the eastern connexions were replaced by western. In the region of Istrus a development similar to that which occurred in the other parts of Thrace seems to have taken place. The Scythian remains found at Craiova, including silver horse-trappings, resemble those of Panagurishte and Brezovo.[56]

Another important market for the products of Greek industry in the sixth and fifth centuries was Illyria. That during those centuries the Corinthian trade in bronze ware extended to Illyria has recently been revealed by the notable discoveries in the native necropolis near Trebenishte (close to Lake Lychnitis, modern Okhrida), excavated first by Bulgarian, later by Serbian archaeologists. The richer graves of this necropolis all belong to the late sixth century. They were full of objects imported from Greece: gold funerary equipment (masks, gauntlets, etc.), beautiful bronze plate and weapons, and Greek pottery. The imported metal ware is all of Corinthian workmanship, while the imported pottery is exclusively Attic. Besides the imported things, articles of local make were found in the graves, and predominated in the poorer graves. It is noteworthy that in none of these graves—nor, it should be noticed, in any of the Scythian graves—were Greek coins found. Trade in these regions was, and continued to be, in the main conducted by barter.[57]

The character and activity of the Greco-Illyrian trade are

illustrated, not only by archaeological discoveries, but also by a casual literary reference. Strabo has preserved a statement by Theopompus that sherds of Thasian and Chian jars were frequently found in the river Naro.* The Thasian and Chian wine came to the river Naro and thence penetrated to the interior, as did the finds at Trebenishte, probably through the Greek colonies of Apollonia and Epidamnus (Dyrrhachium). It was doubtless to Illyrian trade that these two cities mainly owed their prosperity, a prosperity attested by the interesting discoveries of French and Italian archaeologists in their excavations of the ruins of Apollonia. A systematic study of these will certainly throw fresh light on the vicissitudes in the history of Apollonia and probably of Epidamnus, and will provide an instructive picture of their trade relations with Greece, South Italy, and the Illyrian region. The scanty evidence at present in our possession points to a striking development of trade in the sixth and fifth centuries. Later, in the early fourth century, when Dionysius the elder founded his group of colonies on the islands opposite the mouth of the Naro (Issa, Pharos, Corcyra Nigra, Melite), he struck a heavy blow at the Apollonian and Epidamnian trade, probably replacing the products of Greek agriculture and industry on the Illyrian markets by those of Sicily and South Italy. Still later the increase of Illyrian piracy made trade relations with Illyria very hazardous. Here again, therefore, the fourth century was a period of steady decline for Greek trade.[58]

Scattered finds in the Pannonian lands (e.g. at Savaria and Sirmium) and in Istria afford evidence of a comparatively brisk trade between these regions and Greece. While Illyria was supplied with Greek goods through Apollonia and Epidamnus, the Greco-Pannonian and Greco-Istrian trade took partly the ancient commercial route of the Axius and the Margus, but chiefly that up the Danube, the Save, and the Drave from Istrus and the Pontic regions. We have evidence of this in a passage of a Pseudo-Aristotelian treatise† which informs us that Pontic merchants brought wine from Lesbos, Chios, and Thasos to the interior marts of Istria and there bought Corcyraean jars. Trade on these long-established Balkan marts was probably

* VII, 5, 9; *F. Gr. H.* 115, Fr. 129.

† *De mir. auscult.* 104, p. 839b, 8.

conducted chiefly by barter. Here again, however, in the fifth and fourth centuries Italian competition, in this case that of Etruria, undermined the prosperity of Greek trade.[59]

In this connexion it is to be noted that it was these same Etruscans and not the Greeks of Massilia who served as a connecting link between Greece and the great Celtic world. The beautiful Celtic bronze-ware of the fifth and fourth centuries was imitated from Greek originals brought to the Celts by Etruscan, not by Greek, merchants.[60]

In the archaic and classical periods Greek goods found an important market in Italy, not only in Magna Graecia and Sicily, but also in Etruscan central and northern Italy. Our literary information regarding economic conditions in Italy during these periods is scanty. Still scantier is the evidence relating to the commercial relations between Italy and Greece. This literary evidence is, however, supplemented by an abundance of archaeological discoveries made in Italy, as a result both of the desultory and piratical excavations of the early period of Italian archaeological exploration, and of the systematic and scientific excavations of our own time. An unusually large amount of archaeological material has been accumulated in the rich museums of Italy and in almost all the museums of Europe and the United States of America. Painstakingly accurate reports on most of the scientific excavations of the nineteenth and twentieth centuries are available and have been collected[61] and extensively used in hundreds of books, monographs, and articles[62] for the reconstruction, in its general lines, of the cultural and artistic development of Italy. This archaeological material has greatly assisted the study of the development of Greek art and artistic industry, especially as regards pottery, toreutic work, and jewellery. And yet there has been no serious attempt to make use of this material, which has been thoroughly studied, classified, and dated, for the reconstruction of the economic history of Italy and of Greece from the seventh to the fourth century. Students of the economic history of Italy, with their attention centred on Rome, apparently leave this task to those engaged in investigating the economic evolution of Greece,[63] while the latter disregard archaeological evidence altogether.[64] The economic history of South Italy,

Sicily, and the Etruscan federation is therefore almost a blank. It is not the intention of the present writer to supply this deficiency. A few words will suffice for the purpose of this introductory chapter.

Some scattered passages in our texts speak of Sicily and Italy exporting grain to Greece in the fifth and fourth centuries.[65] Etruscan metal ware is referred to as highly appreciated by the Greeks.[66] Italian and especially Tarentine dyed woolstuffs were famous even in Greece, and there is mention of the import by Athens of Sicilian beds and bed-coverings.[67] On the other hand, abundant finds of all sorts of pottery, not only in Sicily and South Italy, but also in Etruria, dating back to the first settlements of Greeks in South Italy, testify to a large import of Greek pottery into Italy. There is not the slightest doubt that this pottery was imported, and was not made in Italy by Greek artisans or by hellenized natives. Signatures of Attic potters appear in large numbers on pottery found in Italy and cannot be explained away as forgeries. Moreover, our knowledge of Greek ceramics is so exact and this pottery has been so thoroughly studied that experts would at once recognize imitations and counterfeit pieces.[68] Not only highly artistic vases but also large quantities of common pottery have been found in Italy in graves and in ruins of ancient cities. This makes it impossible to assume that pottery from Greece was imported mainly to serve as offerings to the dead. There is no room for doubt that Greek pottery was extensively used from the seventh to the middle of the fifth century all over Italy, and especially in the Greek cities of South Italy and in Etruria.[69]

Besides the pottery, specimens of Greek statues and statuettes (marble and bronze), many Greek terracottas, and a large quantity of Greek silver and bronze ware and gold and silver jewels have been discovered in Italy. Most of the scholars of the nineteenth century regarded them as products of Greek art imported into Italy. In recent decades, however, a reaction against this view has set in. It is not open to doubt that most of the metal-work found in Etruria was made in Etruria itself and not imported from Greece. As regards those few pieces which show a purely Greek style, a large proportion may have been imported from the Greek cities of South Italy and Sicily.

Evidence is accumulating which shows conclusively that it was not long before the artists and artisans who came to South Italy and Sicily from Greece emancipated themselves from their mother country and started on their own account the production of statues, statuettes, terracottas, silver and bronze plate, arms and armour, jewels and articles of daily use. Their architects were able to erect most beautiful temples, public buildings, fortifications, some of them gorgeously adorned with sculptures made on the spot by native artists. Why should not Greek sculptors, toreutic artists, makers of terracotta figures (coroplasts), and jewellers, resident in Italy and Sicily, supply local customers, Greek and Italian, with the products of their own crafts, employing for the purpose imported marble, silver and gold, and native copper and iron? In fact we know, for instance, that Syracuse, Capua, and Tarentum were noted as centres of metal industry, and we are gradually learning to recognize, among the products of ancient sculpture and toreutic, statues, bas-reliefs, silver and bronze plate, that were undoubtedly made at Tarentum in the fifth and above all in the fourth century.[70]

If these inferences are correct, we shall be obliged to change our ideas regarding the volume of Greco-Italian trade. It becomes increasingly probable that, instead of importing metal ware from Greece, South Italy and Etruria began at an early date to export their own metal ware to Greece.

Nor is the situation different in other fields of production. Wine and olive-oil were probably exported to Italy from Greece in more or less large quantities for a short time only, Italy soon starting her own viticulture and her own production of olive-oil.[71] Some of the Italian regions, it is true, were rather slow in supplying their own needs in these commodities.[72] Latium probably was among these and perhaps Etruria. But there are strong grounds for thinking that it was not Greece alone that supplied central and northern Italy with wine and olive-oil in classical times. Sicily and South Italy were nearer and their brands of wine and oil were soon equal in quality to those of Greece. What is here suggested cannot, of course, be absolutely demonstrated, but probability is all in favour of an Italian as against a Greek source of supply.

The same is true of textiles. At a very early date Tarentum became known as a producer of one of the finest qualities of wool in the world and its woollen clothes had a lasting and solid reputation.

And, finally, the same development is seen in the sphere of currency. The coins of the leading Greek commercial cities—Athens and Corinth—gradually gave place to local currency in the fifth century, chiefly to that of Syracuse and certain other Sicilian cities. Next to these came cities of South Italy.

Thus Greek and Etruscan Italy, which probably in early times were important customers of Greece, soon began to free themselves from dependence on her, and before long amply supplied both their own requirements and those of their neighbours. This evolution reached its peak in the fourth century. It is well known that in that century the import of Greek pottery into Italy was for a long time discontinued. There was still a large demand for vases of Attic type both in Etruria and in South Italy. But this demand was met, not as previously by imported pottery, but by local products. Red-figured vases of local style and with local subjects, often reflecting local religious and secular life, appear all over South Italy in the late fifth and early fourth century. Apulia and Tarentum, Lucania and Campania compete with each other in this production. Etruria started her own production of red-figured vases still earlier. This peculiar type of pottery did not endure for very long, but it was never again replaced by imported articles. Its place was taken by Italian products—Apulian pottery, Campano-Etruscan ware followed by Calenian, and various types of local Etruscan make.[73]

Similar phenomena may be observed in other fields of industrial production. Capua and Tarentum took the lead in metallurgy, and their products were exported far and wide, to the Greek East among other regions. Local production of metal ware served primarily to supply the needs of Italy herself. To say nothing of the metal-work of the Etruscans, a glance at the metal objects, particularly armour and weapons, found in Samnite tombs of the late fifth and especially of the fourth century, is sufficient to show how skilfully the artists and artisans of South Italy adapted themselves to the peculiarities of the military life of the Samnites. The same may be said of what are known as 'the small bronzes' of that period, which accurately reflect the life and religion of the various Italian peoples of the fourth century.[74]

Lastly, we notice in the coin-hoards the same tendency towards emancipation. Hoards of Athenian coins become exceptional, while Corinth still holds her ground to a certain extent. But, as has been said, it was local currency that Italy used at this period. Syracusan money was replaced by that of Tarentum, and to a lesser extent by the issues of many cities of southern Italy (Thurii, Metapontum, Velia, Croton, &c.).[75]

It is probably in the development of national self-consciousness among her various peoples that we must find the explanation of the economic emancipation of Italy described above. The process was parallel to that which we have observed in Scythia and in Thrace. For Greece it was a heavy blow. Its foreign commerce, which defrayed the cost of its imported foodstuffs and raw materials, gradually declined and there was no hope of restoring the balance. In my opinion it was this crisis in the foreign commerce of Greece, together with the political conditions, that brought about the difficult economic situation in which Greece found herself at the end of the fourth century. The decline was gradual, not catastrophic. Greece was faced with the necessity of readjusting in some way her economic life.

III

ALEXANDER AND THE SUCCESSORS

It is not easy to trace the general economic development of Greece and of the Hellenistic monarchies during the three centuries that followed Alexander's death.[1] Our evidence is meagre and unevenly distributed. Each period has its own peculiarities as regards the sources on which we rely for its economic history, and must therefore be dealt with separately; and this I shall do in the following chapters.

For the time of Alexander and his Successors, which forms the subject of the present chapter, our evidence varies in quality for different regions. For Athens it is good and reliable. Menander and the fragments of other contemporary comic authors, the 'Characters' of Theophrastus, the lives of Athenian philosophers of the early Hellenistic period included in the collection of Diogenes Laertius, and the later Attic orators, combine to furnish a good picture of social and economic conditions at Athens in the late fourth and early third centuries B.C. A large number of inscriptions and the copious series of Athenian coins supplement their evidence. Finds of Athenian pottery in Greece and in other countries, though never collected in their entirety, greatly assist us in forming an idea of the extent of Athenian commerce during this period. The literary and the epigraphical sources contain much information regarding the current prices of certain commodities at Athens. We cannot establish continuous series of prices over long periods, but the evidence we possess gives us an adequate idea of the average prices prevailing at Athens and elsewhere on the eve of the Hellenistic period and during its early years.

For the rest of Alexander's empire we possess no evidence comparable to that relating to Athens. The literary sources, so excellent and so full for the time of Alexander, and still trustworthy and abundant for that of the Successors, are very little concerned with the economic conditions of this period. Here and there we come upon an instructive allusion, but nothing more. The inscriptions are almost silent as regards the reign of Alexander; they afford more, though still very scanty, information on the following period, especially for Delos. The most important epigraphical texts relating to economic conditions in the time of the Successors will be quoted and discussed later in this chapter. The numismatic evidence is invaluable: it is both abundant and trustworthy. I shall, to the best of my ability, make full use of it, as also of what little archaeological evidence has been collected and studied, in discussing certain economic problems of the period under consideration.

The economic crisis that we have seen developing in Greece in the fourth century was mitigated by the political events of the end of that century, that is to say, by the expedition of Alexander and his conquest of the Persian Empire. The state of the foreign markets of Greece in the West and in the North-East remained in most respects unaltered; but even in these regions certain new economic factors came into play during and after this expedition.[2]

The situation created by Alexander's conquest of the East has frequently been compared with that which in more recent history resulted from the discovery of America. A new world, it is said, was opened to the economic enterprise of the old. This sweeping statement is in some degree misleading. We must not forget that the East was well known to Greece at least as early as the fifth and fourth centuries, and that it was a world of long-established civilization and of highly developed economic activity. There had been trade relations between Greece and Persia long before Alexander's day, and the connexion between the East and Greece, especially during the fourth century, had become constantly closer. Witness the rapid hellenization of Cyprus and of the chief Phoenician and Palestinian cities and the increasing number of Greek immigrants in Egypt (see above, Ch. II). Alexander did not discover a new, hitherto unknown world; nor did he throw open to the Greeks a no-man's-land, or conquer a country whose barbarian inhabitants were then gradually exterminated in spite of a hopeless resistance. Alexander's achievements were great, but they were quite different from those of Columbus and his successors. Alexander created a Greco-Oriental empire, and thus succeeded

PLATE XVII

I reproduce here the well-known mosaic so familiar to many of my readers, because it shows, treated by an artist of great talent, one of the decisive moments (whether it is the battle of Issus or that of Gaugamela is irrelevant) in the great struggle between Persia and Macedonia for hegemony in the civilized world. The outcome of this conflict was what I call in the present book the Hellenistic world. My second purpose in inserting this illustration is to show the great army of Alexander in action, the spirit of this army and of its leader, their fierce determination to conquer and to dominate, expressed with such masterly skill in the head of Alexander, as contrasted with the distress, fright, and bewilderment of the former rulers of the East, the Persians and their leader Darius III. And finally, the figures of Alexander and of his companions, incompletely preserved as they are, furnish reliable information about the equipment of the Macedonian cavalry. (Photograph supplied by Alinari.)

As regards the equipment of the Macedonian cavalry of the army of Alexander and the early Hellenistic armies, the mosaic of Alexander and the famous sarcophagus of Alexander found at Sidon have recently been illustrated by P. Couissin, *Les Institutions militaires et navales*, 1931 (*La Vie publique et privée des anciens Grecs*, viii), pp. 65 ff., esp. 75 ff., pls. XXII–XXV, cf. E. Breccia, *La Necropoli di Sciatbi*, 1912, pl. XXIV. The information that we derive from the mosaic is confirmed by our literary texts and by several representations of officers and men of the heavy Macedonian cavalry in the Hellenistic armies. I refer as regards the latter, for the early Hellenistic period, to the Alexandrian painted stelae of the late fourth and early third centuries (see my pls. XIX, XXXV (XXXVII), 2, and XLVII (XLIX),1), the funeral stele of Termessus, perhaps of Alcetas, brother of Perdiccas (E. Breccia, *La Necropoli di Sciatbi*, 1912, p. 11, fig. 9), and the incompletely preserved stele of Menas who perhaps fell at the battle of Corupedion (E. Pfuhl, *J.D.A.I.* xlviii (1933), Anz., pp. 751 ff.). The early Hellenistic equipment remained almost unchanged in the later Hellenistic times. I may cite several late Hellenistic funeral stelae of Asia Minor (for example the stele of Dascylium in the Museum of Brussa, my 'Dura and the Problem of Parthian Art' (*Yale Class. Stud.* v (1935), fig. 48; cf. the stele of Leptis Magna, G. Mendel, *Cat. Sculpt. Mus. Ott.* iii (1914), p. 175, no. 962) and the peculiar stelae of Asia Minor and the islands, which show the deceased stretched on a couch and on the wall his arms and behind it his horse, E. Pfuhl, *J.D.A.I.* l (1935), pp. 15 ff. Macedonian mounted officers without cuirass, fighting or hunting, are represented several times, see my pl. LVI (LVIII). Cf., in addition to Couissin, A. Spendel, *Untersuchungen zum Heerwesen der Diadochen*, 1915, p. 10; H. Berve, *Das Alexanderreich*, i, pp. 104 ff.

The date of the mosaic and the place where it was made (whether the late fourth century B.C., or the second century, or even the time of Sulla, and whether Alexandria or Pompeii itself) are subjects of controversy. It is, however, certain that the mosaic reproduced an early Hellenistic original made by a great artist. The controversy is summarized in the light of all available evidence, literary and archaeological, by H. Fuhrmann, *Philoxenos von Eretria*, 1931, cf. A. Ippel, *Gnomon*, x (1934), pp. 75 ff. Important considerations regarding the date of the mosaics of the house of the Faun will be found in E. Pernice, *Pavimente und figürliche Mosaiken. Die hellenistische Kunst in Pompeji*, vi, 1938, pp. 90 ff. (on the exedra with the mosaic of Alexander, p. 93); cf. p. 180 (on the fragments of the Alexander mosaic in Palermo). In general, O. Elia, *Pitture murali e mosaici nel Museo Nazionale di Napoli*, 1932.

PLATE XVII

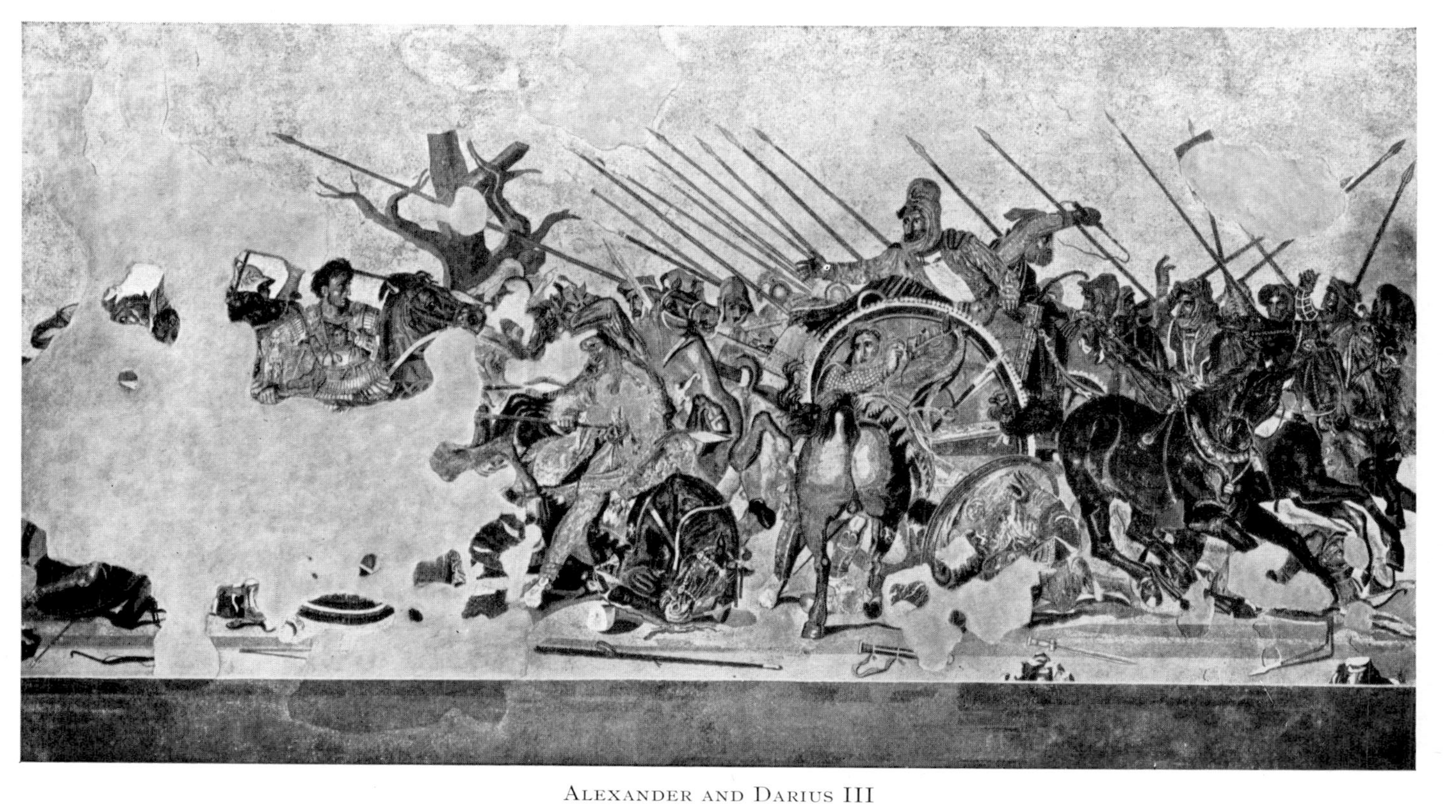

ALEXANDER AND DARIUS III

Mosaic found at Pompeii in the house of the Faun. Naples Museum.

in carrying out a plan which for centuries had been the dream of the Persian kings—that of unifying under a single rule the whole of the eastern part of the civilized Mediterranean world. Political unification was Alexander's principal achievement, if not his principal aim. Of this unified world it was not his intention that Macedonians and Greeks should be sole masters; they were to share the dominion with the former rulers of the East, the Iranians, while the other native peoples were to have an appropriate position in the new empire. The conquest of the East was thus quite different in its political, social, and economic results, from the discovery of America.[3]

The conquest of Alexander naturally had important economic consequences for Greece and the hellenized parts of Asia Minor on the one hand, and for the Near East on the other. But the western Greeks in Italy and Sicily, who had their own economic and political life, closely connected with that of Italy and Carthage, had for a long time hardly participated at all in the new possibilities opened to eastern Greece, and were little affected in their economic evolution by the changed conditions of the East.

The chief economic effects of the conquest of Alexander upon Greece and upon the East may be summarized as follows. To begin with a matter of minor importance, Alexander certainly enriched Greece in various ways; by direct gifts and grants, by providing Greeks and Macedonians with opportunities of increasing and diversifying their economic activity, and by opening new markets for Greek goods. A few words may be said on these points. Alexander's method of dealing with the booty, his lavish expenditure of the Persian hoards of gold and silver, which to a large extent were transformed into coined money, had the effect of enriching a number of men, some of whom had hitherto been paupers and proletarians. Service in Alexander's army meant for his Macedonians and Greeks not only temporary employment, but wealth and prosperity for those who survived. The extant histories of Alexander's conquest are unanimous in praising his liberality to his troops and contain occasional references to the accumulated property belonging to his generals, officers, and common soldiers that was carried in the baggage-train of the army. A substantial part of these possessions was derived from the booty, which was not appropriated by Alexander, but shared by him with his companions.

There is no doubt that the wealth that passed freely in various forms from the Persian treasuries into the hands of Alexander's soldiers was not all hoarded by them. Much of it was lavishly spent in the East and, after their return home, in Greece. The train of the army offered abundant opportunities for spending money. Many merchants, probably Greek as well as Phoenician, followed Alexander's army, bought up booty from the soldiers, and offered them in return various goods, naturally Greek goods in the main. The army was therefore for years an excellent market for Greek commodities.[4]

Besides the army in the field there were the detachments left behind as garrisons at the most important strategical points, and also the administrative officials of Alexander's satrapies. Naturally, many of Alexander's satraps were Orientals. But by the side of these stood Greek military commanders and in some satrapies Greek financial agents. All these administrators had large staffs, and since the official language of Alexander's empire was Greek, most of the members of these staffs were undoubtedly Greeks.

The Greek world found another source of wealth, and Greek goods another important market, as a result of Alexander's colonization. The extent of this colonization was somewhat exaggerated by authors of a later date. The number given by Plutarch of Alexander's colonies as being over seventy-five is not supported by the sources (Appian and Diodorus) which go back to Alexander's own time. But Alexander did create in the Near East a few large and wealthy settlements of the Greek urban type (e.g. Alexandria in Egypt), as well as some that were not Greek (e.g. Gaza in Palestine and perhaps Tyre in Phoenicia, both of them refounded after Alexander had destroyed them). His activity, moreover, infused new life into many centres of Greek export trade which existed before him and which did not need to be refounded like Gaza and Tyre, since they were never molested by him. Among these were probably several Greco-Phoenician cities, for example Sidon, of which I have spoken above and which became still more hellenized in the time of Alexander and under his successors. Witness the famous 'sarcophagus of Alexander' found there (below, note 23). The most notable example, however, of a revived semi-Greek emporium of the past is the harbour of Al-Mina, to which reference has been made in the previous chapter (pp. 85, 105). The history of this centre of Athenian export trade in the fifth and fourth centuries B.C., as revealed by the excavation of Sir Leonard Woolley, shows that, after a period of comparative decay in the early and middle fourth century, the harbour city had a new and strong, though brief, revival of activity and prosperity in the time of Alexander and his Successors, until it was superseded about 300 B.C. by the new seaport of Seleucus Nicator, Seleuceia in Pieria. This fresh spell of prosperity is attested by the ruins of the city which belong to this period, as well as by the abundance of Athenian pottery and the numerous coins of Alexander, both silver and copper, that excavation has yielded.

Alexander's military and non-military colonies, large and small, in Iranian territories, in Bactria, and in India were far more numerous. All of these had previously been native communities, some of them large and important towns. All now became urban communities of the Greek type, some at least of whose members were Greeks and Macedonians, as a rule soldiers of Alexander's army who had been wounded or disabled, or were not quite reliable politically. In default of statistics we are unable even to guess at the numerical strength of the new Greek population of these colonies, but it should not be underestimated. We must bear in mind, for example, the many mercenary soldiers that Alexander left in Bactria and Sogdiana and the many 'cities' (eight or twelve) that he founded there. We may not trust the figure of 23,000 which Diodorus gives as the number of Greek mercenaries who were massacred in Bactria after the death of Alexander when they revolted and tried to force their way back home. We may think that the true number was 3,000. In any case, the fact of the revolt shows that there were many thousands of Greek mercenaries settled in Bactria in Alexander's time, and this is supported by the later history of the country, which according to our historical tradition had a numerous Greek population and many cities.[5]

Besides Alexander's colonists we must take into account the Greeks who went to the East in the trail of the army looking for profitable business. It is permissible to suggest that many of them settled in Alexander's colonies and still more in the urban centres of Oriental life where Alexander had not made an official settlement. How many such Greeks, for instance, took up their abode in Alexander's capital, Babylon?

Thus the first result, so far as Greece was concerned, and that most apparent to the Greek mind, was an increase of wealth for the Greek world and at least a partial relief of that relative over-population which had weighed so heavily on the social and economic development of Greece in the fourth century.

But this relief of the poverty and over-population of Greece, although at that time the most conspicuous economic result of Alexander's conquests, was far from being the most important. Of much greater consequence was his attempt to bring about the economic unification of Greece (including her economic dependencies and ramifications) with what had been the Persian Empire (again including its widespread sphere of influence).

This unification did not result automatically from the conquest of the Persian Empire. In itself such a conquest would not necessarily produce either lasting political or lasting economic unity. Alexander's political system was in fact short-lived, while economic unity endured for many generations. This permanence was due mainly to certain far-reaching measures adopted by Alexander, unquestionably with the object of welding his empire into a single economic whole.

Most important from this point of view was his colonization of the East. Scores of Greek *poleis* were disseminated all over the Oriental parts of his empire. They were located at the nodal points of the great strategic and commercial roads which from time immemorial had connected with each other the most civilized and progressive parts of the Oriental world. In addition to these, communities of Greeks were established in the principal Oriental seaports (e.g. Gaza and Tyre), while newly created Greek harbour cities gave fresh outlets to the sea to such important parts of the Oriental world as Babylonia and Egypt. These new ports were first and foremost Alexandria, that excellent harbour and marvellous Greek city 'near'

Egypt, discerned by the sharp eye of Alexander or perhaps of his advisers, and in the second place Alexandria on the Tigris in Babylonia.

In itself the colonization of Alexander, as we know it, does not stand out as an important new departure in the economic evolution of antiquity. For Alexander colonization was primarily a military measure, designed to safeguard the military communications of his empire. The social and economic aims that he no doubt also had in mind were secondary. Moreover, most of the Greek *poleis* created by Alexander were not brand-new cities (as was Alexandria), nor transformations of small villages into regular commercial and industrial centres. In most cases his *poleis* were already commercial centres. Nor were the roads which connected them with each other a creation of Alexander. He inherited the roads of his empire from the Persians and we know nothing of him as a road-builder. And finally, it was not Alexander who connected the great centres of caravan trade with the sea. The chief caravan roads had led from time immemorial to important harbours in India and on the coasts of the Persian Gulf, the Black Sea, the Red Sea, and the Mediterranean.

Nevertheless, his colonization opened a new era in the economic life of the ancient world. The new and momentous feature of it was the transformation of the Oriental marts into business centres of a type hitherto unknown to the East. Most of his colonies were undoubtedly Greek city-states with all that this meant, not only from the political and social but also from the economic point of view. These Greek cities, with the roads connecting them, formed a network of channels by which Greek business life diffused itself throughout his empire, penetrating deep into the solid mass of Orientalism and bringing its transforming influence to bear on the economic structure of the East. At the same time, though set down in an Oriental environment, Alexander's colonies were not isolated from the rest of the Greek world. As Greek *poleis* they were connected by numerous ties with the city-states of their mother land, and made business relations between Greece and the East easy and convenient.

Of course what Alexander did was merely a beginning, and

his few colonies, if not supported and reinforced, would be engulfed in the surrounding Orientalism and would disappear. It depended on his settlers on the one hand and on his successors on the other whether his great design should have durable results. The event showed that the design was well conceived. Alexander's colonization did bring about a certain kind of economic union in the ancient world.

Colonization, however, was only one of the measures adopted by Alexander for this end. He intended to encourage union by improving and cheapening the means of communication by sea between the richest and most important parts of his empire. India, Babylonia, and Egypt were its three economic pillars. He sent Nearchus to explore the Persian Gulf and the sea route from India to Babylon with a view to establishing a new and secure channel for trade between India and Mesopotamia. In the same way, but with more adequate means, he intended to effect the exploration of the south Arabian coast, with the object of connecting the Indo-Babylonian area with Egypt, where, by founding Alexandria, he had opened the prospect of important economic development. The projects of Alexander with regard to these two sea routes were not new, but were inherited by him from the Persians. What was new was the combination of them with a scheme of colonization. As we learn from Alexander's methods in central Asia, the exploration of the sea routes was a preliminary step to colonization, whereby these new trade channels would have been bound up with the economic network that he was spreading over his empire.

An element in Alexander's design of unification not less important than exploration and colonization was his monetary policy. No doubt, as in the matter of colonization so in the adoption of his monetary system, Alexander was guided more by political than by economic considerations. But the measures he took in this sphere were of great importance as providing a sound foundation for the economic union he had in view. It is evident that his excellent, abundant, and uniform coinage in itself greatly assisted the development of business in his empire. But his monetary policy had a much wider scope. His currency was not a continuation of the Persian coinage, but had a special significance. In the first place, it was designed to give a Greek aspect and a Greek character to the economic life and business of the world. The types of his coins were Greek, the standard Attic. It was thus a currency adapted to his network of Greek colonies and it was intended primarily for them. Moreover, the new currency, by virtue of its excellence and abundance, was intended not only to supersede for ever the Persian imperial currency and the local currencies of the Persian Empire, but also to put an end to the monetary anarchy that reigned in the Greek world. Finally, it is probable that by providing the new Greek business centres in the East with abundant currency Alexander wished to promote the use of money as a medium of exchange in place of the trade by barter that still prevailed in many parts of the Oriental world.[6]

Without peace and security Alexander's new united economic world could not thrive and take firm root. These, during the short span of his life, he procured for the greater part of his empire. In Greece and Asia Minor peace remained unbroken during his great expedition. Professional pirates—a scourge of Greece in the fourth century—disappeared for a while. The organized piracy of Greek city-states was suppressed. The roads in Asia Minor and the Near East were improved and made safe for traffic. The Persian postal system was extended to Greece, and, though employed mainly for State purposes, certainly contributed also to the development of business and commerce.

The political and economic union of the Greco-Oriental world effected by Alexander survived him. The long struggle between his generals after his death was in the main a struggle between supporters and opponents of this union. For a long time political unity existed not only *de jure* but also *de facto*, and did not come to an end in practice until the battle of Corupedion (281 B.C.). During the whole of this period the organization of Alexander's empire endured and developed, though it was slowly modified first by Alexander's satraps and later (306 B.C.) by the kings of the constituent parts of the empire.

The peace and security that had promoted unity and prosperity under Alexander ceased, it is true, in the time of the Successors. This indeed was a period of almost uninterrupted warfare, affecting almost all parts of Alexander's empire, and

PLATE XVIII

1. AV Stater, Alexander the Great (Macedonia). *Obv.* Helmeted head of Athena. *Rev.* ΑΛΕΞΑΝΔΡΟΥ. Winged Nike holding wreath and trophy-stand; in field, thunderbolt.

2. Æ Alexander the Great, attributed to Miletus. *Obv.* Head of youthful Heracles wearing lion-skin. *Rev.* ΑΛΕΞΑΝΔΡΟΥ between bow in case and club; symbol, ear of grain.

3. AR Decadrachm, Alexander the Great (Rhodes). *Obv.* Same as preceding. *Rev.* ΑΛΕΞΑΝΔΡΟΥ. Zeus seated holding eagle and sceptre; symbol, rose.

4. AR Tetradrachm, Alexander the Great (Lycia). *Obv.* and *rev.* same as no. 3, ΛΥ beneath the throne.

5. AR Decadrachm, Alexander the Great (Babylon ?). *Obv.* Alexander on horseback with spear attacking an enemy (Porus ?) on an elephant; driver seated on elephant's neck turns to throw spear. *Rev.* Alexander, helmeted and wearing sword, holds spear and thunderbolt, in field, monogram for *βασιλεύς*.

6. AR Tetradrachm of Antigonus, 'king of Asia', of Alexander's type and with name unchanged. Mint of Sidon; ΣΙ beneath throne.

7. AR Decadrachm of Lysimachus struck at Byzantium. *Obv.* Head of Alexander the Great wearing diadem and horn of Ammon. *Rev.* ΒΑΣΙΛΕΩΣ ΛΥΣΙΜΑΧΟΥ. Athena seated holding Nike who crowns king's name; on throne ΒΥ.

8. AR Tetradrachm of same type attributed to Cyzicus.

9, 10. Bronze coins of Eupolemus, tyrant of Iasus (?), struck in Caria. *Obv.* Three Macedonian shields. *Rev.* ΕΥΠΟΛΕΜΟΥ. Sword in sheath; symbol, double axe.

On this plate are reproduced some typical coins of Alexander, Antigonus the One-eyed, Lysimachus, and Eupolemus, one of the Anatolian petty tyrants of the end of the fourth century. An excellent sketch of the evolution of Alexander's coinage will be found in E. T. Newell, *Royal Greek Portrait Coins*, 1937, pp. 9 ff., cf. my n. 6 to this chapter. On the coins of Lysimachus, E. T. Newell, loc. cit., pp. 17 ff. On Eupolemus, Ch. IV, n. 230.

Coins of the late fourth century B.C.

certainly not in the main contributing to the normal economic development of the Hellenistic world. Some facts may be adduced.

The large armies of the Successors, constantly on the move and fighting, were not an unmixed blessing to the countries in which war was proceeding. Even if a territory was not devastated—which it often was, sometimes by the army of the enemy, sometimes by professional pirates—the army in occupation evidently lived at the expense of the population, through requisitions and pillage. I may quote one instance. At the end of the Lamian war, when Antipater was preparing to invade Attica, Phocion asked him to make peace with Athens while he was still in Boeotia, that is to say, to refrain from entering Attica. Craterus objected, saying: 'Phocion is making an unreasonable request; he wants us to harm an allied and friendly country by remaining in it, while we might be living at the expense of our enemies.'*

Moreover, the Successors needed a good deal of money to pay their armies, to provide food, arms, and equipment, and to keep officers and men in good humour by means of gifts and gratuities of various kinds.[7] Their precarious political situation, their lack of any legitimate claim to power, forced them to be prodigal and ostentatious in their relations with their own court and administration and with the allied and subject Greek cities. Their prodigality in this respect was fabulous: they gave large gifts and subsidies to cities, various δωρεαί (including estates) to their friends and to their staff, and lavish bribes to the officers and soldiers of their enemies in order to induce them to betray their masters.[8] They built new cities and rebuilt existing ones. I shall refer later in greater detail to their new capitals: Antigoneia, Cassandreia, Lysimacheia, Thessalonice, Demetrias; and to their enlargement and remodelling of cities, e.g. Smyrna, Ephesus (synoecism with Colophon and Lebedos), Teos and Lebedos, Colophon, Antigoneia in Troas, and others, not to speak of the many colonies in Asia Minor and Syria.[9] And, last but not least, many of them (not, however, Ptolemy and Lysimachus) lived in unparalleled personal luxury, and spent enormous sums on household, banquets, and women.[10]

* Plut. *Phoc.* 26.

This vast expenditure could not be defrayed by the revenue from stabilized and orderly taxation, and other sources had to be drawn upon, such as war contributions imposed on the allied and subject Greek cities, the only centres where money was to be found. These contributions sometimes took the form of auxiliary troops paid by the cities or, more frequently, of ships supplied by the cities for the navy. In most cases they were paid in money in the form of regular tribute (φόροι), or of crowns (στέφανοι), or of irregular contributions (ἀποφοραί). All the Successors had recourse to these sources of supply in order to finance their military operations. Antipater did so after Triparadisos;* also Eumenes† and especially Antigonus and Demetrius. Plutarch quotes a saying of Antigonus: 'Antigonus exacted contributions with severity. When some one objected "But Alexander was not so harsh", "No doubt", he replied, "for he was reaping Asia, whereas I am gleaning."'‡ And in his letter to Scepsis Antigonus himself recognized how heavily this burden lay on the cities: 'Seeing the annoyance that you and the other allies suffer from the military service and the expenditure.'§

Some particular instances may be quoted. In a letter to Miletus Ptolemy II mentions his father's and his own various benefactions to the city, especially a benefaction of Soter: 'Having relieved you of the harsh and oppressive taxes and of the tolls that certain of the kings had imposed on you.'‖ The date of this benefaction of Soter is unknown. It has been suggested that Soter ruled over Miletus in 314–313 B.C. and that therefore the kings who subjected the Milesians to oppressive

* Ditt. *O.G.I.* 4. 10: Ἀ[ν|τιπ]άτρω γὰρ ἐπιτάξαντος χρήματα εἰς | τὸμ πόλεμον εἰσφέρην.

† Just. xiv. 1. 6: 'tunc exercitu in Aeoliam promoto pecunias civitatibus imperat, recusantes dare hostiliter diripit.'

‡ *Apophthegmata* 182: Ἀντίγονος εἰσέπραττε χρήματα συντόνως· εἰπόντος δέ τινος "ἀλλ' οὐκ Ἀλέξανδρος ἦν τοιοῦτος", "εἰκότως" εἶπεν "ἐκεῖνος μὲν γὰρ ἐθέριζε τὴν Ἀσίαν, ἐγὼ δὲ καλαμῶμαι".

§ *O.G.I.* 5. 44, Welles, *R.C.* 3. 42: ἅμα δε καὶ ὑμᾶς ὁ|ρῶντες κα[ὶ] τοὺς ἄλλους συμμάχους ἐνοχλου|μένους ὑπό τε τῆς στρατείας καὶ τῶν δαπανη|μάτων.

‖ Rehm, *Milet. Erg. d. Ausgr.* i. 3, no. 139; Welles, *R.C.* 14: καὶ φόρων τε | σκληρῶν καὶ χαλεπῶν ἀπολύσαντα καὶ παραγωγίων παρ' ὑμῖν ἅ τινες | τῶν βασιλέων κατέστησαν.

taxation were the Persian and Carian kings and Alexander or Antigonus. I do not think that Ptolemy Soter (if Philadelphus is quoting him) or Philadelphus himself would include Alexander among 'certain of the kings'; the expression implies a good deal of blame and disapproval, and he would not refer to Antigonus alone in the plural. If, however, we take the 'kings' of the inscription to be the rivals and enemies of Soter, Antigonus and Demetrius, the tone of Soter's or Philadelphus' remark is easily understood. The difficulty is that it is not easy to find time between Demetrius (295/4 B.C.) and Lysimachus (289/8 B.C.) for even a short rule of Soter over Miletus, nor is it mentioned in our sources. In itself, however, a temporary seizure of Miletus by Soter immediately after the rule of Demetrius is not at all impossible.[11]

After the short period of considerate treatment by Soter, Miletus under the rule of Lysimachus once more lived through hard times. An inscription from Miletus mentions a loan contracted by the city in order to provide the money 'of which we must pay King Lysimachus the second instalment'.* The payment to Lysimachus was probably either a contribution or a regular φόρος. The same seems to be true in the case of Eretria in Euboea, which paid Demetrius yearly 200 talents.† In addition, there were at this time Eretrian ships in the fleet of Demetrius (302 B.C.)‡. Severe pressure may also have been exerted by Demetrius on the members of the Island League. Certain inscriptions of the early third century B.C. refer to loans contracted by the cities, probably at Delos, the great money centre of the Aegean. Such a loan was obtained by the cities of Amorgos,§ and another by some other cities of the islands. Philocles, Philadelphus' admiral, assisted the Delians (about 280 B.C.) to collect these loans.|| They were probably contracted in order to pay to Demetrius the εἰσφοραί which Ptolemy Soter remitted to the Islanders.¶ We again meet another agent of Philadelphus engaged on the same business,

* Rehm, *Milet. Erg. d. Ausgr.* i. 3. 138, 7: ὧν δεῖ ἀποδοῦναι ἡμᾶς βασιλεῖ Λυσιμάχωι εἰς τὴν δευτέραν καταβολήν.

† Diog. Laert. ii. 140.

‡ *S.I.G.*[3] 348.

§ *I.G.* xii. 7. 68, 69, 70.

|| F. Durrbach, *Choix d'inscr. de Délos*, 18.

¶ *S.I.G.*[3] 390, 15.

collecting debts at Carthaea in Ceos.* It is very probable that Demetrius, in order to get his contributions paid, ordered some of the cities to introduce new taxes.† To contract a loan is not always a sign of financial ruin, but, in the ancient world at least, it betokened great financial stress. One realizes how severe this stress was when one reads the famous law of Ephesus about mortgaged property,‡ dating from about 297 B.C. The conditions were so unstable, and money was so scarce, that landowners found no buyers when they wanted to sell their land in order to pay off mortgages. In speaking of the union (synoecism) of Teos and Lebedos Antigonus mentions the foreign loans contracted by Lebedos (below, p. 155 f.).[12]

The heavy financial burden imposed by the Successors on the cities of the islands and of Asia Minor contributed to make the conditions of life in them precarious and unstable. We hear occasionally of disturbances, probably of a political and social character (ταραχαί), which took place at Carthaea in Ceos and were settled by the intervention of Philocles and Bacchon, the well-known agents of Soter and Philadelphus in the Aegean.§ Similar disturbances occurred at Ios, where some slaves escaped from their masters, and enrolled, probably as rowers, in undecked vessels (πλοῖα ἄφρακτα). They were restored to their masters by Zenon, Soter's admiral.|| The trouble did not cease with the passing of the Successors. I shall return to the subject in the next chapter.

The struggle of the Successors for continental Greece was a source of far greater evils. Greece at this time was still the prize most coveted by them. They all endeavoured, by various means, to have her on their side. The method of Antipater before and after the Lamian war was to keep garrisons in the most important cities and to establish in most of them an oligarchy or a tyranny. This system was inherited by Cassander. Their enemies protested against it, insisting on the observance of the principles of the Corinthian League: that the cities should be completely free and autonomous under the general hegemony of the king. Consequently the cities were re-

* *I.G.* xii. 5. 2, 1066.

† Poiēessa in Ceos, *I.G.* xii. 5. 570.

‡ *S.I.G.*³ 364.

§ *I.G.* xii. 5. 1065.

|| *I.G.* xii. 5. 1004; *O.G.I.* 773, cf. *S.I.G.*³ 367.

peatedly proclaimed free and independent, first by Polyperchon, then by Antigonus and Demetrius and Ptolemy, and finally by Ptolemy again. This policy kept most of the cities in a constantly recurring state of war, and each outbreak of war brought in its train civil strife within them. The conditions recall in some measure the period of anarchy that prevailed shortly before Philip's day. We may accordingly apply to them, *mutatis mutandis*, the poignant description of this last period given by Isocrates in his *Panath.* 258: 'Of all the Hellenic cities [other than Sparta], many as they are, not a single one can be mentioned or found which has not been involved in the calamities that are wont to befall cities . . . civil strife, slaughter, unlawful exile, seizure of wealth, outrage to women and children, change of constitution, abolition of debts and redistribution of land . . .'

I may quote in support of this statement a few examples drawn from the years 318–314, years that are so vividly described by Diodorus. The proclamation of liberty by Polyperchon was followed by his letter to Argos and other cities in which he recommended the execution of some of the supporters of Antipater and the exile of the rest, and of course the confiscation of their property, to deprive them of the means of supporting Cassander. These recommendations were repeated a second time, with the result that many of the Peloponnesian cities followed the advice, and that murder and exile were rife in some of them (318 B.C.).* In 315 Apollonides, Cassander's general, suppressed a revolt at Argos in a ruthless way. He shut up 500 of his opponents in the *prytaneion*, and burned them alive. Of the rest some were killed, the others exiled.† In the same year Cassander seized Orchomenos in Boeotia and captured all the friends of Alexander, son of Polyperchon, who had taken refuge in the sanctuary of Artemis. He permitted the Orchomenians to deal with them as they liked. They dragged the refugees out of the sanctuary and massacred them all, 'in violation of Greek international usage' (*παρὰ τὰ κοινὰ τῶν Ἑλλήνων νόμιμα*), remarks Diodorus—or Hieronymus.‡

* Diod. xviii. 57. 1. and 69, 3–4.

† Diod. xix. 63. 2.

‡ Diod. xix. 63. 5.

Such recourse to murder and executions was not due to any special cruelty in the character of Cassander. Aristodemus, Antigonus' general in Greece, who went there in 314 in order to liberate the cities, acted in exactly the same way. For instance, he was prevented from liberating Aegium because his soldiers began to pillage the city: many of the citizens were killed and almost all the houses were destroyed. At Dyme in Achaea, while the citizens were trying to take the acropolis and to capture Cassander's garrison, Alexander arrived and seized the city. Of the Dymaeans he killed some and exiled many. Then Aristodemus' soldiers arrived, and with their help the Dymaeans took the acropolis: almost all who were in it were killed, and many Dymaeans, friends of Alexander, suffered the same fate.* Again, Cratesipolis, the wife of Alexander, in the same year 314, after having crushed a revolt of the Sicyonians, crucified thirty of the leaders. The conduct of Demetrius himself, the great liberator, was precisely the same. In 303, when the union of hearts was proclaimed in Greece, he took Orchomenos in Arcadia and captured Polyperchon's garrison. He crucified outside the city Stromblichus, the commander of the garrison, and about eighty of those who were hostile to him.† Examples might be multiplied. One has only to read the pitiable story of Sicyon before Aratus' *coup de main*, as told by Diodorus and Plutarch, or to recall the history of Thebes in this period or the well-known vicissitudes of Athens, in order to realize what the wars of succession meant for Greece. Menander occasionally gives eloquent expression to the feelings of Greece at this time.‡ Devastation of territories, war contributions, and requisitions must be included in the sum of the sufferings of the country. In comparison with these, the fate of the islands and of the cities of Asia Minor was a fortunate one.

Yet we must be careful not to exaggerate the dark side of the picture. Greece certainly suffered heavily, for the old Greek customs of war still prevailed and these were exceedingly cruel and ruthless. The Successors in the course of their

* Diod. xix. 66. † Diod. xx. 103, 6.

‡ Men. *Περικειρ.*, 409 ff. (Allinson; 280 ff. Sudhaus): *πολλῶν γεγονότων ἀθλίων κατὰ τὸν χρόνον τὸν νῦν—φορὰ γὰρ γέγονε τούτου νῦν καλὴ ἐν ἅπασι τοῖς Ἕλλησι δι' ὅτι δήποτε. . .*

wars in Greece were sometimes obliged to adapt themselves to the inveterate brutality of their allies or enemies. But there was no tendency on their part to make war more cruel and more ruinous than usual. In the annals of their wars we find no evidence of wholesale destruction of cities, of the massacre of entire populations, or of the enslavement of women and children. In their struggles among themselves outside Greece they tried to be as humane and as chivalrous as possible. They did not extend the Greek customs of war to their new countries. And in dealing with the Greek cities, while they sowed discord and destruction with one hand, with the other they helped the cities by gifts and grants. They struck hard from time to time, but they had great regard for the public opinion of Greece and tried to avoid unnecessary cruelty and harshness. Greece was in a state of unrest, wars and revolutions were in the air, social and economic contrasts were becoming more and more pronounced. But the workless and homeless population of Greece found relief in the new territories in the East and in the armies of the Successors.

However, even war itself was not in all respects a source of evil in the economic life of the Greek and Oriental world of the period. Though seemingly a paradox, this is a fact, and a fact of some importance. This beneficent aspect of the wars of the Successors was almost entirely the outcome of the character of their armies, which was unique in its kind and in world history. The armies of the Epigoni were quite different and will be described, in their economic and social aspects, later in this book. The armies of the Successors have been compared with those of the *condottieri* of medieval history. But, in my opinion, there is not the slightest resemblance between them. I propose therefore to deal with the subject in greater detail than might be expected in an economic history because, as I have indicated, the army was, in itself, probably one of the most important factors, not only in the political, but also in the social and economic life of the period under review.[13]

Alexander's army was never demobilized after his death. It was distributed among the various satraps of the monarchy, the kernel remaining in the hands of the central government. It was kept mobilized and ready for war at least until the battle of Ipsus, and even later, alike by the central government and by those who opposed it. In a certain sense it was a permanent army under the command of one or other of the successors of Alexander. Perdiccas, Antipater, Antigonus, Eumenes, Polyperchon, and again Antigonus and Demetrius, were successively in command of the main body of the *Grande Armée*. After Ipsus, first Demetrius, then his son Antigonus, retained a part of this main body, while Seleucus, Lysimachus, and Ptolemy increased their shares of it by the addition of various contingents. The Macedonian army of Cassander was to some extent an exception. It was a revival of the Macedonian army of Philip, and of Alexander before his great expedition.

Never demobilized, the great army of Alexander was almost constantly moving from place to place, fighting or ready to fight. It would spend short periods in winter quarters, and detachments would be stationed from time to time as garrisons in various cities. This is true, above all, of the Macedonian infantry and cavalry. The auxiliary contingents—mercenaries, allies, and foreign detachments—were added to this kernel or withdrawn from it according to circumstances.

The army of the Successors was not only an instrument of war in their hands; it was in some sort a body politic, a mobile State and court, for on the support of the army depended the political existence of its commanders. This aspect of the army is especially prominent in the history of Perdiccas, and in the struggle between Eumenes and Antigonus. As long as the army—generals, officers, and men—supported the commander, he was a factor in the political life of the time. As soon as it betrayed him he was lost, until he was able to find another army to support him. Such betrayals were frequent in the annals of the Successors, the army passing with the greatest readiness to the other side after and even before a decisive battle. One of the most powerful weapons of the time in the ranks of a hostile army was a clever and well-organized propaganda, supplemented by bribes. Nor were cases of mutiny infrequent, even among the Macedonians.[14] In fact the armies of the Successors were not so much instruments in their hands as their σύμμαχοι, their *commilitones*, their associates—in this resembling the Greek cities. They obeyed their commanders

—again like the Greek cities—so long as they were well-disposed (εὖνοι) towards them.[15] This εὔνοια depended on various things. First and foremost, on good and regular pay and on frequent opportunities of spoil and plunder;[16] and, closely connected therewith, on the skill and the luck of the commander and on his way of dealing with his men.

Considerations of a higher and more ideal character played an almost negligible part in the relations between the commanders and their armies. The armies, except that in Macedonia, were large bodies, constantly on the move, of practically homeless men, fighting not for their country but to support the personal ambition of their commander and to conquer for his benefit foreign territories in which they had no interest. Their real home was their ever-shifting camp, where they bestowed their families, their money, and their belongings. This camp with its baggage (ἀποσκευαί) formed their moving *polis*, and for these they were ready to fight and to die and, on occasion, to betray their leaders. There was, no doubt, among them a certain national and professional pride, which made the Macedonians excellent fighters when they were facing in a pitched battle an equal or inferior enemy.

Loyalty to the house of Philip and Alexander (so long as this house existed) was a factor of very little importance. At the outset it influenced in some degree the behaviour of the Macedonian armies. But this attachment to the dynasty was very short-lived; nor was it as yet replaced by allegiance to any other ruling house possessing claims to power based on heredity. Again, we hear almost nothing of religion influencing in any appreciable degree the political behaviour of the army. The cult of Alexander—in some form or other—may have existed in the camps. We know nothing about it, except for the famous tent of Alexander in the camp of Eumenes. Whether the Successors encouraged displays of religious feeling (if there were any) in their favour, such as we hear of in Greek cities, we do not know. The dynastic cults of which we have knowledge were developed not in the camps but in Greek cities, subject or allied to the Successors.

The great wandering armies of these rulers were a new phenomenon in the social, and also to a certain extent in the economic, life of the Hellenistic world. Large forces of professional soldiers, well trained in military craft, were continuously maintained. The kernel of each was composed of Macedonians, but this was surrounded by contingents of different nationalities: Greeks, Thracians, Illyrians, Iranians, Anatolians, Semites, and Indians, which taken together formed a host as strong numerically as the main body of Macedonians. The camp, therefore, was a medley of nations and languages, a true reflection of Alexander's empire and of the Hellenistic world of that time. Distinctions were not lacking between classes and between rich and poor. The aristocracy was formed by the officers of various ranks (their hierarchy is little known) of the various military units. The Macedonians were, of course, richer and prouder than the rest of the army. Among them the horsemen ranked before the foot. Between the combatants and the civilians of the camp stood the large mass of technicians of various kinds: engineers and mechanics for the siege-machines and the artillery, interpreters and guides, doctors and veterinaries, and so forth.

And lastly, thousands of civilians accompanied the army: wives and concubines of the officers and soldiers, their children, their servants and slaves. Any one who reads the description of the baggage-train (ἀποσκευαί) of the army of Eumenes in Plutarch and Diodorus, or the story of the death in his camp of the Indian general Ceteus, and of the contest between his two wives for the honour of dying with him, will realize what a vast multitude of men, women, children, and animals lived in or near the camp of the army. Add to these the merchants, money-lenders, traffickers in booty, professional hetaerae, and so forth, and it will be apparent that a Hellenistic army of this period was an enormous moving city, comparable to the moving cities of the Oriental nomads in eastern Europe and in Asia.[17]

The fleets of this period were somewhat different. The ships were too small to carry the ἀποσκευαί, and the train of the fleet remained on land. The description of the fleet of Demetrius during the siege of Rhodes will show that a fleet in its own way resembled the mobile camps of the land armies. The war-ships (200) and the transports carrying troops (170) were accompanied by a much larger number of other ships: these included the pirates, faithful allies of Antigonus and Demetrius, and adepts in the arts of devastating a country and of capturing enemy merchantmen; and the ships that carried the regular supplies for the naval and military forces. In addition there were various private vessels around the fleet of Demetrius intent on earning money by one means or another, ready to sell foodstuffs to besiegers or besieged alike according to circumstances, and nearly a thousand private merchantmen prepared in case of the capture of the opulent city of Rhodes to buy booty and slaves from the conquerors.[18]

The camp of an army was thus a large moving city, or rather a moving capital, containing a population larger than that of many Greek capitals; and moreover a wealthy city. The generals and officers of the armies of the Successors were, most of them, very rich men, in this respect comparable to the generals and officers of Alexander's army. There are occasional references to large sums in coin being carried about by them.[19] Some of the common soldiers also had substantial savings which they had accumulated during their long service. This money did not lie idle. We hear of loans made to the generals by the officers, and we may safely assume that the officers lent money not only to their superiors but also to their subordinates, or borrowed from them. The whole of the army, therefore, with the civilians who accompanied it, formed an enormous business concern. Money flowed freely from the belts of the soldiers into the chests of the civilians and vice versa. Part of the money remained, no doubt, in the countries through which the army passed or where it had its winter quarters; but this part was small, for the army as a rule did not purchase but requisitioned what it needed.[20]

Though the armies of the Successors were practically on a permanent footing, the officers and men composing the various units were gradually changing. The sexagenarians who formed the body known as the 'silver shields' of Eumenes soon disappeared. Very few soldiers who had fought in the army of Alexander were still alive at the time of the battle of Ipsus, and hardly any at the time of the battle of Corupedion. Many fell in the wars. It is misleading to say that the losses in the battles of the Successors were small: in the few cases where we possess reliable information we see that they were considerable. In Cappadocia, for instance, Eumenes in 320 B.C. lost 8,000 men in the engagement with Antigonus. His army consisted of about 20,000 foot and 5,000 horse, while Antigonus had a much smaller force—10,000 infantry, 2,000 cavalry, and 30 elephants. In the battle of Paraetacene (317) Antigonus had about 36,800 men all told, Eumenes 41,000. Antigonus lost 3,700 foot and 54 horse killed, and 4,000 wounded, that is to say about one-fifth of his force. The losses of Eumenes were much smaller—about 500 to 600 killed and 900 wounded. The battle in Gabiene cost Antigonus, whose army was a little smaller than at Paraetacene, 5,000 men of his heavy infantry alone. Finally, at Gaza Demetrius' army of 17,000 lost 500 killed and 8,000 prisoners.*

It is unnecessary to refer to the frequent cases of surrender by entire armies. Those who thus became captives (αἰχμάλωτοι) were treated kindly. Wholesale massacres or the sale of the captives into slavery were exceptional during the great wars of the kings, more frequent in the small internecine wars in Greece. The prisoners either took the oath of allegiance to the victors and were incorporated in their armies, or were bought back (λυτροῦν) by their own commanders or by others who might be interested in them. Thus at the siege of Rhodes a tariff was set up by Demetrius and the Rhodians for the αἰχμάλωτοι (1,000 *drachmae* for a free man, 500 for a slave).† Surrenders were therefore always advantageous to the victors: if the prisoners did not go to swell their armies, they were at least a good source of profit, probably both for the commander and for individual officers and men.

Most of the Macedonians who were discharged on account of age or infirmity were probably settled in one of the numerous military colonies founded by the Successors, especially in Asia Minor and in Syria; some of the discharged men returned home.

* Cappadocia (320 B.C.): Diod. xviii. 40. 7; cf. Arr. τὰ μετὰ Ἀλέξανδρον 43 (Roos). Paraetacene (317 B.C.): Diod. xix. 27–31, esp. 31. 5. Gabiene: Diod. xix. 43. 1. Gaza (312 B.C.): Diod. xix. 85, 3.

† Diod. xx. 84. 6. Cf. the episode of Mallos in Cilicia, where Ptolemy sold into slavery those who survived the assault, Diod. xix. 79. 6 (312 B.C.).

Vacancies due to death or discharge were filled by new recruits, some of whom came from Macedonia. But the rulers of Macedonia soon reserved it as a recruiting ground for themselves. How the others filled the gaps in their Macedonian phalanx and cavalry is unknown. They probably recruited children of Macedonian soldiers, either born and educated in the camps or born in the earlier military colonies, especially those of Alexander. The later method of recruiting established by the Epigoni was not yet developed.

The position in Egypt is a separate question. The system of settled soldiers, military cleruchs who did not form separate communities like the military colonies of Alexander and of his Asiatic successors, was probably not a creation of Philadelphus but must be traced back to Soter. A large proportion of the first settlers of Ptolemais, the Greek capital of southern Egypt, were soldiers. We learn incidentally that the 8,000 soldiers captured at Gaza were settled in Egypt.[21]

How the Successors dealt with mercenaries when they finished their term of service or were invalided we do not know. Sometimes land was assigned to them. We have an instance of this at Cassandreia in 279 B.C., when the demagogue Apollodorus procured allotments of land in Pallene for the mercenaries of Eurydice. At Theangela (in Caria) the soldiers who surrendered to Eupolemus about 315–314 B.C. and took service with him received land or were confirmed in their rights as landholders. I am inclined to think that the same happened at Aspendus in 310–306 or 301–298, when mercenaries—Pamphylians, Lycians, Cretans, Greeks, Pisidians—received the city franchise by a special decree after a successful war, probably on the recommendation of Ptolemy Soter. I think it very probable that at least some of them received at the same time allotments of land somewhere near Aspendus, in part perhaps in the territory of the city, for it is difficult to see what value the franchise would have had for merely temporary guests of Aspendus. We have a similar case later (244 B.C.), when the soldiers settled at Magnesia on the Sipylus and at Palaemagnesia received the franchise from Smyrna.[22]

The retired officers and discharged soldiers formed a new and important class of men, many of whom did not remain in

PLATE XIX

1. A funeral stele with pediment found at Alexandria in the necropolis of Shiatby. Late fourth century B.C. On the stele, on a pinkish background is painted the figure of a young officer cantering on a spirited bay horse to the left. The horse is richly caparisoned. Note the fine saddle-cloth of purple colour. The rider wears no helmet. He is dressed in a white chiton. Over it is a fine bronze cuirass with shoulder-straps and a double row of πτέρυγες. His legs are bare. Behind his shoulders floats a cloak. In his right hand he holds a long Macedonian lance. A short sword is attached to his belt on the left side. Behind him runs his servant holding the tail of his horse in the well-known Oriental manner. Under the pediment remains of an inscription painted in black, which is variously read: . . . ξενος Μακεδών by E. Breccia, and . . . ξενος [Γ]αλάτης by A. Reinach. I accept (after inspection of the original) the reading of Breccia. The officer represented on the stele is certainly a Macedonian. H. 0·40, W. 0·37 m. (Photograph supplied by the authorities of the Alexandria Museum.)

The stele has been published and discussed several times. The best publication is that of E. Breccia, *La Necropoli di Sciatbi*, 1912 (Catal. gén. Mus. d'Alexandrie), pp. 10 ff., no. 9 and pls. XXII and XXIII. Cf. for an artistic appreciation R. Pagenstecher, *Nekropolis*, 1919, p. 54, no. 53 and p. 69; M. H. Swindler, *Ancient Painting*, 1929, pp. 345 ff. Very similar in style and composition is the stele found in the necropolis of Hadra: horseman, bareheaded, wearing chiton, armour, and chlamys. In his right hand a Macedonian lance, on his left side a short sword. Facing him his servant, who hands him his helmet, E. Breccia, *Bull. Soc. Arch. Alex.* XXV (N.S. vii. 2) (1930), p. 116, no. 22116 and pl. XII. Cf. also my pls. XXXVII, 2, XLIV, 1, XLIX, 1, and LVIII. On the equipment of the Macedonian cavalry see description of pl. XVII. I may add in this connexion that the painted funeral stelae of Alexandria have never been collected in full. See the references in the works of Breccia, Pagenstecher, and Swindler quoted above, cf. M. Rostovtzeff, 'Painted stele from Alexandria', *Mon. Mus. of Fine Arts at Moscow*, i–ii (1912), pp. 69 ff., pl. XII; W. Grüneisen, ibid. iii (1913), pp. 87 ff. (in Russian), and A. Adriani, *Bull. Soc. Arch. Alex.* XXX ii (N.S. x. 1) (1938), pp. 112 ff.

2. One of the funeral painted stelae of the necropolis of mercenary soldiers stationed at Sidon in Phoenicia. The stele has the form of a naiskos with two pillars supporting a pediment adorned with acroteria and painted ornaments. The base is painted in imitation of coloured variegated marble. Between the two pillars, in a niche, the figure of a soldier turned to the left in the attitude of combat. The body is shown from the back, the head in profile view. He is dressed in a short belted chiton of reddish-brown colour and high-laced shoes. On his head a helmet with crest of (red) feathers (cf. Men. *Perik.* 174 πτεροφόρας χιλίαρχος), visor, cheek- and neck-pieces. In his right hand an iron sword (blue), in the left a wooden oval shield with a metal boss. The sword-sheath hangs on a baldric on his left side. Under the figure a painted inscription: Διοσκορίδη Ἐξαβόου Πισίδη | Βαρβουλεῦ συμμάχων | σημεοφόρε χρηστὲ | χαῖρε | Κεραίας ὁ ἀδελφὸς ἔστησε, The man buried under this stele was a mercenary soldier from Balbura in Lycia (or Pisidia). He belonged to the detachment of σύμμαχοι and held the office of standard-bearer in his detachment. It is interesting to note that his figure is quite conventional. The Romans would represent him with the standard in his hand. Late third or early second century B.C. On the date see below, Ch. IV, n. 137, and on the Sidonian stelae in general, below, pl. LVII. More detailed description, G. Mendel, *Catal. Sculpt. Mus. Ott.* i, 1912, pp. 258 ff. H. 1·10, W. 0·57 m. (Photograph supplied by the authorities of the Ottoman Museum, Istanbul.)

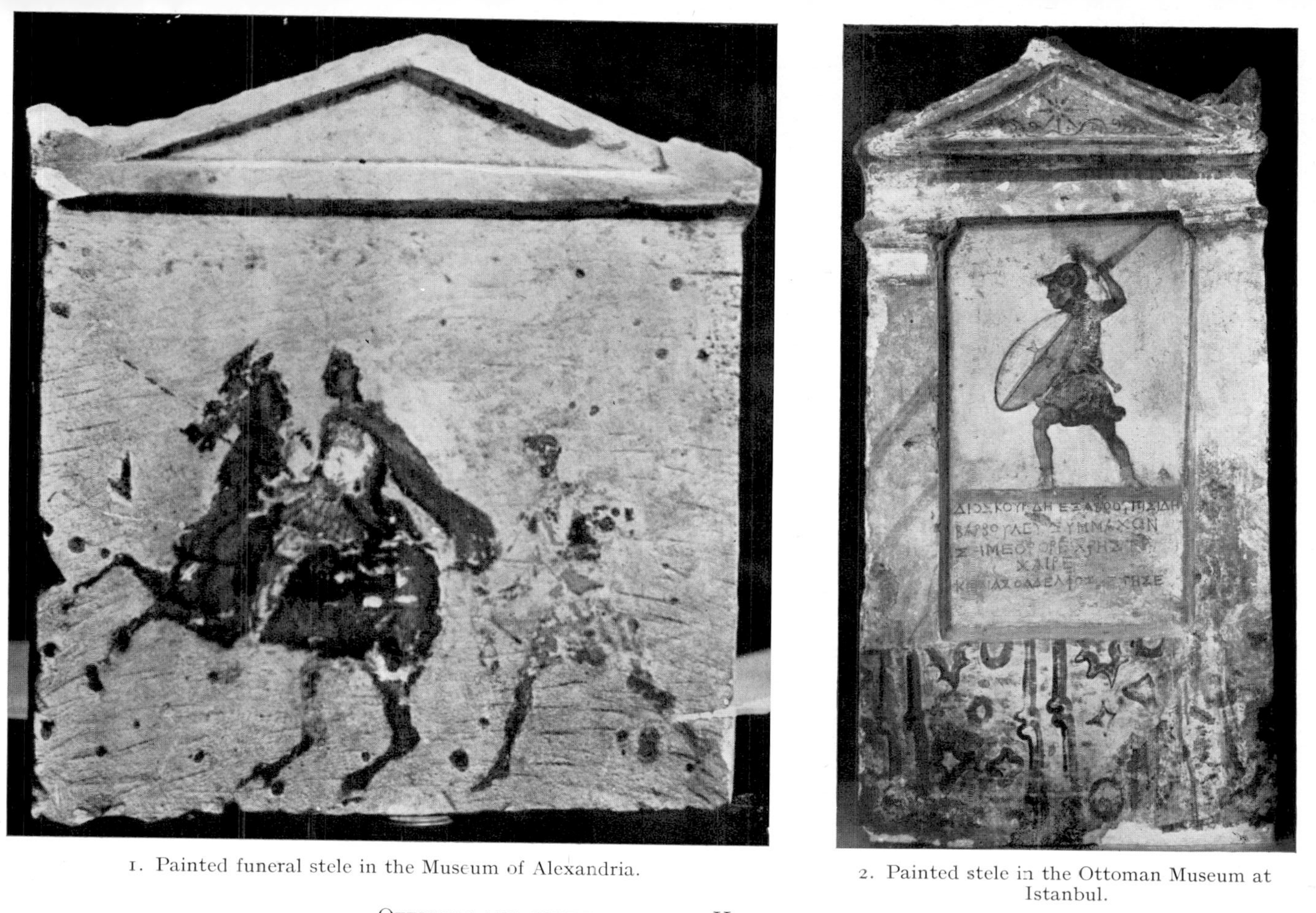

1. Painted funeral stele in the Museum of Alexandria.

2. Painted stele in the Ottoman Museum at Istanbul.

OFFICERS AND SOLDIERS OF THE HELLENISTIC ARMIES

the Eastern monarchies but returned probably to Greece and Asia Minor. They were for the most part in easy circumstances, and we occasionally hear of some of them. Such were Gorgos of Iasus, the former ὁπλοφύλαξ of Alexander,* Thersippus of Nesos,† Malusius of Gargara,‡ Laomedon from Mitylene, controller of barbarian prisoners of war (ἐπὶ τοῖς αἰχμαλώτοις βαρβάροις) under Alexander, and one of his trierarchs, later (323 B.C.) governor of Syria; his son Larichus became a highly honoured inhabitant of Priene.§ To the same group belonged the well-known Caranus, a Macedonian of noble origin, whose lavish wedding-feast was described by Hippolochus in a letter to Lynceus, the famous contemporary and pupil of Theophrastus. The wealth of Caranus was certainly fabulous, and we are justified in supposing that either he himself or his father had acquired it in the service of Alexander.|| And finally, there is much probability in the suggestion of L. Robert that the foreigners (two of them Macedonians) who in the time of Antigonus (between 311 and 306) subscribed large sums of money for the inclusion of the site of the 'old city' (παλαιὰ πόλις) in Colophon were officers of Alexander's army, who may have been impelled by public spirit or by some consideration of self-interest. While many of these officers were satisfied with being prominent citizens of their native city or of their new place of residence, others were more ambitious. In Asia Minor before Alexander's day many cities had been ruled by tyrants, who were protected and sometimes appointed by the Persian kings. The best-known instances are the dynasty of Hecatomnus and Mausolus, the tyrants of Halicarnassus, the Gongylids and Demaratids of Pergamon, the well-known tyrant-philosopher Hermeias of Atarneus, Mania the tyrant-queen of Aeolis, and Nicagoras of Zeleia. The tradition was still alive in the time of Alexander, and even in the days of the Successors there were still some tyrants of this type. It is not surprising that some of Alexander's officers, who possessed

* *S.I.G.*[3] 312; Ephippus *apud* Athen. xii. 538b (F. Jacoby, *F. Gr. Hist.* 126, fr. 5); cf. *S.I.G.*[3] 307.

† *O.G.I.* 4.

‡ *S.I.G.*[3] 330.

§ *Inschr. v. Pr.* 18; *O.G.I.* 215.

|| Athen. iv. 128c, ff.; cf. H. Berve, *Das Alexanderreich*, II, no. 412: *Κάρανος*.

wealth and military experience, should, in the turmoil of the succeeding period, become tyrants of cities where the tyrannical tradition was still alive. Such was probably Eupolemus, tyrant of Iasus in the late fourth century.[23]

These wealthy and ambitious men brought large sums of money with them, and certainly invested this money in one way or another in their cities. Money was also spent freely in the Greek cities by mercenaries or Macedonians still in military service—*milites gloriosi*—when on leave of absence or, in the case of mercenaries, looking for employment (and large groups of these are referred to as waiting in various places, especially at Taenarum, for opportunities of service).

War therefore was to a certain extent a beneficial factor in the economic life of this period. It put into circulation large sums of money which had formed Alexander's reserve fund. This money stimulated commerce, as did also the brisk traffic that developed in and around the camps. Many war-profiteers, besides officers and soldiers, became rich, and the large demand for arms, ships, and engines of war, stimulated the corresponding branches of industry. Sometimes even the supplies required for the subsistence of the army and the material for munitions may have been bought and not requisitioned from the population.

But war, important as it was, did not exert a dominating influence on the economic evolution of Alexander's empire during the comparatively short period of the rule of the Successors. Always in danger of losing their hold on the army and on the territories which they governed, always either preparing for war or actually engaged in it,[24] these rulers had little time and leisure for the organization of their satrapies or kingdoms on a stable basis. Nevertheless it is surprising how much they achieved in this respect. We know very little of the measures they adopted, but those of which we do know are important, and some of them had a decisive influence on the economic development of the regions concerned.

I can only deal briefly with this topic in the present book. The main difficulty with which the Successors were faced did not lie in their Oriental territories. There they had inherited a solid and reliable system of administration, taxation, and economic organization from Alexander, who in his turn had taken it over, at least in part, from the Persian kings. Their real difficulty lay with their Greek subjects in the East. There is no doubt that in respect of the Greek cities of Asia Minor both Alexander and the Successors regarded themselves as heirs of the Persian kings, who certainly always, and especially after the treaty of Antalcidas (386 B.C.), had dealt with these cities as with their own subjects, to whom they might or might not grant a certain degree of autonomy. Though Alexander liberated the Greek cities of Asia, he probably did not treat them as he treated the free cities of Greece proper, that is to say, he never admitted them into the Corinthian Federation and never made separate treaties of alliance with them. He granted them, as an act of grace, a certain and sometimes a large amount of liberty and autonomy, but probably nothing further. His policy in this respect was adopted by the Successors, who always regarded the old cities of Asia Minor as their subjects, and acted accordingly.[25]

The trouble, however, was that the Greek cities never accepted this state of things. They always hoped in some way to recover their full liberty, and in consequence they lent their moral and political support to one or other of the rival pretenders to the succession of Alexander according to the degree of belief that they placed in his promises, promises in which full liberty played a prominent part. It is melancholy to see how the leading Greek cities shifted their support from one pretender to another, so that stability in this respect was never attained.[26]

When one or other of the rivals enjoyed more or less undisturbed control over the Greek cities of Asia Minor, he would endeavour in various ways to give some degree of stability to his relations with them, with the object of securing their permanent support while maintaining the basic principle that the cities were to be regarded as subjects, not as allies. Some of them, for example Antigonus and Demetrius, were prepared to go very far in granting liberty and autonomy to the cities, in treating them in fact as allies, not as subjects, and in conferring on them tax exemptions and lavish gifts. On the other hand, Lysimachus and Ptolemy tried by various methods to bring home to the cities that they were not independent States but subject communities, liable to tribute and to military occupation by detachments of the ruler's army.

But the constant state of warfare defeated all attempts to find a *modus vivendi* acceptable to both parties, and reduced the situation to confusion and almost to anarchy. This instability of conditions explains the adoption of several measures which had direct or indirect economic consequences. Though they never attempted to change the type of economic system established in the Greek city-states, the Successors tried in various ways to get rid of those elements in it which were particularly unsound and mischievous. In this respect there was no difference between the more rigorous and the more liberal rulers of the Greek cities, between Lysimachus and Ptolemy on the one hand and Antigonus and Demetrius on the other.

One of the most striking features of Greek economy was its minute subdivision, hundreds of independent units endeavouring to live in economic self-sufficiency, very often to the detriment of their neighbours, and always without regard for their interests, while they in turn pursued exactly the same policy. The rulers, impatient of this state of things, tried by sundry devices to overcome it, both in its political and its economic aspects.

Much interest attaches to the various types of federations or leagues of cities in the time of Alexander and under the Successors. This is not the place to deal with them in detail: a few words will suffice. Some of the leagues had existed before, such as the Ionian, Aeolian, Ilian (?), Lycian, and Carian leagues in Asia Minor. They were certainly restored to life either by Alexander or by the Successors. Others were new creations of the latter. The best known and the most important of them was the federation of the Islanders, first created by Antigonus and inherited from him by the Ptolemies. It was undoubtedly a political organization that had economic consequences, since it helped the rulers of the time to curb the pirates of the Aegean. Much less is known of the leagues of Asia Minor. Modern scholars are not agreed about their character. Some regard them as merely religious associations, others are inclined to think that they were at the same time administrative units. However this may be, the establishment of closer contact between several cities of the same region was a device directed against the isolation, political, social, and economic, of the single cities.[27]

Of little less importance were the attempts of many of the Successors to merge several small cities into a larger, richer, and more reliable State. This was done by synoecism (συνοικισμός), of which there are several examples in the period under review. The conditions under which Antigonus intended to carry out the synoecism of Teos and Lebedos are well known. Our information is less good as regards the enlargement of Colophon at about the same time, and we know even less of the method whereby the city of Scepsis and some other minor cities were incorporated into Antigoneia, the new city founded by Antigonus in the Troad. Synoecism was carried out on a very large scale by Lysimachus in the case of Ephesus, Colophon, and Lebedos.

It is highly probable that most of such synoecisms were carried out with the object of strengthening the cities economically and financially. Small cities with small territories and a restricted population were prone—as repeatedly happened—to borrow sums which they would be unable to repay either from their own richer citizens or from foreign cities, temples, or individuals, to overload their own people with liturgies and compulsory gifts or loans, to claim rights of property over land that belonged to neighbouring cities (as for instance in the cases of Priene and Samos), and so forth. All this they did in order to secure for their own population a certain standard of material and cultural ease, if not to avert extreme poverty and starvation. This aspect of the life of the Greek cities will be more fully treated later in this book. Their economic and financial difficulties constantly led to interminable lawsuits, to civil wars, and to armed conflicts with their neighbours, which caused them to look for help from outside, naturally from their overlords, the temporary rulers of some portion of the Greek world. To them the Greek cities frequently appealed for material or political assistance.

Now the new overlords, as has been said, were keenly interested in the material prosperity of the Greek cities in their respective satrapies or kingdoms. Most of the cities were expected to pay to the overlord regular tribute and, in case of war, irregular contributions (see above, pp. 137 ff.), and they furnished the most natural market for the disposal of the surplus grain, wine, olive-oil, cattle, and the like, produced on his extensive domains, domains mostly inherited by him from the former rulers of the country. The prosperity of the cities had moreover this advantage, that they were less likely if prosperous than if indigent to betray their temporary master and go over to his rivals.

The rulers believed that one of the main reasons why the cities were poor and in distress was that there were too many of them, and for this they thought synoecism an excellent cure. They therefore tried to convince the cities of the merits of their remedy and to induce them of their own will and decision to carry out a union with their neighbours. In this they mostly failed, and thereupon had recourse to compulsion, under the cloak of benevolent guidance. This is what happened in the case of Teos and Lebedos, in that of Scepsis, and in that of Ephesus, not to speak of the creation of the large capitals of the Successors, to which I shall come presently.[28]

Such was the policy of the new overlords of the Greek world in respect of the Greek cities in their dominions, especially in Asia Minor. The situation in Greece proper and in the islands was of course more difficult and complicated.

The Successors were far less trammelled in those parts of their possessions which had had no experience of Greek political conditions and were consequently much more manageable and obedient than the liberty-loving Greeks. We have unfortunately little information with regard to their administration of these regions, but it is certain that they all took up the work where Alexander had left it and gave it a wide extension. This is true especially of the work of colonizing and hellenizing the Near East and the northern part of the Balkan peninsula.

Ptolemy Soter, who ruled Egypt during a long life, developed Alexandria on a broad and generous scale, making it both his capital and one of the largest and most beautiful cities of the Greek world. To Alexandria he added a second Greek city and a second capital, Ptolemais in southern Egypt. Alexandria was intended as a counterpart to Memphis, Ptolemais as a counterpart to Thebes, perhaps also as an Alexandria in the south, the centre of the commercial relations between Egypt and central Africa and Arabia. But Soter was not so discerning as Alexander, for Ptolemais never became a second Alexandria.

In order to rival Alexandria, the other rulers, one after another, built new capitals for their new kingdoms: Lysimacheia, Cassandreia, Thessalonice, Demetrias in Europe; Antigoneia, subsequently replaced by Antioch on the Orontes, in Syria. They also replaced some former centres of Greek trade with the East by new Greek trading cities. Such were, for example, the harbours of Antioch, Seleuceia in Pieria, and Laodicea. The first replaced the half-Athenian prosperous port of Al-Mina, of which I have spoken above; the second inherited, in one way or another, the commercial activity of the ancient Phoenician city of Ugarit (Ras Shamra), opposite Cyprus.

Other foundations of the Successors were of a somewhat different character. They were intended to be both military strongholds of the new empires and centres of Macedonian and Greek economic, especially agricultural, life. Such was for instance Apamea in Syria, the military capital of Seleucus' kingdom. Such were also the many scores of military colonies of different types, some of them rural settlements, but most of them regular cities, established all over the East and in the northern part of the Balkan peninsula. The most conspicuous work of this kind was that done by Seleucus (and continued by his two successors) in Asia Minor, Syria, Mesopotamia, and Iran. We know much less of that done by his predecessors; there is very little evidence for the colonies said to have been founded by Perdiccas in Palestine and Transjordania.

Alongside of the military colonies many purely civil settlements were established in all the kingdoms, and protection was certainly given to those settlers who, in ever-increasing numbers and at their own risk, came to the East and took up their abode in the new Greek cities, in Oriental towns, or in villages. Thus it came about that the Greek population of the East steadily and rapidly increased under the Successors, and that this growth was never arrested during almost a hundred years from the death of Alexander. It is regrettable that we have no statistics: all the attempts of modern scholars to estimate the Greek population of the East in the Hellenistic period are founded on very inadequate data.[29]

This great colonizing activity in the East and to a certain extent in the north of Alexander's empire had an enormous influence on the trend of its economic development. The rapid growth of Alexandria and later of Antioch, and the splendid expansion of the other cities near Antioch and of Seleuceia in Babylonia show that the efforts of Alexander and of the Successors bore good fruit. While war raged in Asia Minor, Greece, and parts of Syria, Egypt after the invasion of Perdiccas enjoyed peace, as did also so much of Syria as came later under Seleucid rule after the clash between Eumenes and Antigonus and the expedition of Demetrius. Thus Egypt, part of Syria, and Mesopotamia probably attained a high degree of prosperity. Though no direct evidence is available, we may take it as certain that trade rapidly developed in the Near East, that agriculture was stimulated by the new methods of cultivation imported by the Greeks, and that industry enjoyed a wider and richer market.

The wealth of what had been Alexander's Eastern empire is incidentally illustrated by two passages referring to the period soon after his death. Both of them relate to Antigonus the One-eyed. In 319 B.C.* Antigonus, who had been appointed by Antipater commander with full powers (στρατηγὸς αὐτοκράτωρ) in Asia, decided after Antipater's death not to obey the kings and their guardians. He already had a strong army, but he was confident that he could if necessary increase this army indefinitely 'since Asia was able to supply inexhaustible funds for the payment of mercenaries'. A little later, in 315 B.C., Diodorus (Hieronymus)† gives a survey of the resources at the disposal of Antigonus: besides the money deposited at Kyinda (10,000 talents), he had a regular yearly revenue from his satrapy of 11,000 talents (sixty-six million drachmas). The text is corrupt, but the figure appears to be exact.

The tide of prosperity in the East was felt throughout the empire and especially in Greece and in Greek Asia Minor. The new settlers and the soldiers of the Successors, who constituted

* Diod. xviii. 50. † Id. xix. 56. 5.

the principal market in the new world, were partly hellenized Macedonians, partly Greeks who were used to Greek life and naturally continued to live this life in their new homes. Greek life meant Greek food, Greek dress, Greek houses and furniture, Greek temples, Greek public buildings, Greek plate, Greek jewels, and so forth. For a while all these Greek products were certainly imported from Greece. Some time had to elapse before the new centres of Greek life could begin their own production of Greek goods. Thus it was that during a certain period, in some cases very prolonged, Greek imported goods were able to compete in the East itself with the products of the highly developed Oriental industry and found an easy market in the new Greek cities and other Greek settlements. This market was well supplied with money. The little we know of the Greek settlers shows that most of them were well-to-do. The military settlers received parcels of fertile land (*cleroi*) and certainly some material help towards starting life under new conditions. Some of them received their allotments after a long military service and may have saved money during this service. Civil officials were paid good salaries and had many other opportunities of earning money. Tax-farmers probably fared well in the new world. All sorts of artists and craftsmen found remunerative employment in the new and rapidly growing cities, for the inhabitants were eager to possess every kind of edifice to which they had been accustomed in their homeland, while the kings never relaxed their zeal for adorning their new capitals.

Almost all the above statements, it is true, are based on general considerations. The very few cities in the East that have been excavated have yielded mostly ruins and objects of later date. Alexander's rule was short and the period of the Successors was not much longer; taken together they did not exceed fifty years.

There are, however, certain eloquent facts. Never before had Athenian pottery been in such request as in the late fourth and in the early third centuries B.C. Athens, with her wonderful genius for adapting herself to new conditions, changed the style of her ceramic products. The demand for the red-figured pottery of the past was no longer what it had been.

Athens understood the situation, grasped the spirit of the time, and in the fourth century increased the production of some of the pottery she was already making and launched some new brands. These were mostly imitations of metal plate: wonderful black-glazed ware of both cheap and expensive qualities. I may mention some varieties of this pottery: black-glazed ware with impressed ornaments; various types of vases adorned with gilded barbotine ornaments in imitation of metal-ware, with similar decoration in inlay; a type showing applied relief-figures and medallions; and finally fine glazed pottery with painted ornaments in white and pink (which is known as 'West-slope ware').[30] These new brands of pottery are found in large quantities in various places throughout the Hellenistic world and in Italy. Many specimens have been discovered for example in South Russia, an Athenian market from time immemorial, which was as valuable in the period under review as in the fourth century. In studying the Athenian ceramic products of the types described that have been found in the rich royal graves of Panticapaeum, we must of course bear in mind that some of them may be contemporaneous with the red-figured Athenian vases of the fourth century.[31] Still more abundant was the Athenian ware in the markets of the East. The archaeological finds in Alexandria are significant. It is Athenian imports—and not only in the field of pottery—that dominate there in the late fourth and early third centuries.[32] The same is true of Palestine, Syria, and Mesopotamia. I am convinced that Antioch on the Orontes and Seleuceia on the Tigris will show in this respect, when excavated more fully, the same characteristics as Alexandria. Meanwhile we have evidence of similar conditions, for example in Al-Mina in north Phoenicia (above, pp. 85 ff.), in Samaria and many other places in Palestine,[33] and in Dura,[34] where Athenian black-glazed pottery is a typical feature in the early Hellenistic strata. At Ephesus Athenian black-glazed pottery was still regarded in the late fourth or third century as the best pottery on the market, though most of it was made locally, partly by potters who came from Athens.[35]

Charged with important economic consequences as it was, Alexander's conquest of the East did not stand alone. Philip's wars in the northern part of the Balkan peninsula, Alexander's successful expeditions in the same regions, the activity of Alexander's satraps in Thrace, and especially the expedition (ill-fated though it was) of Zopyrion against the Scythians (331 B.C.), which brought him as far as Olbia, made Thrace a part of the empire of Alexander* and enabled Lysimachus, first satrap and later king of the northern Balkan territory, to extend and consolidate the conquests of Philip and Alexander. We see evidence of this in Lysimacheia, the brilliant capital founded by Lysimachus in the Thracian Chersonese, and in his issue of large quantities of gold and silver coins which competed successfully with Alexander's coinage in the north and were for a long time the leading currency of the Balkan and north Pontic regions. It may be observed that many trading cities—Byzantium, Callatis, Rhodes, and many others—as well as the Bosporan kings, imitated the currency of Lysimachus after his death in order to secure a fair circulation for their own issues.

In the time of Philip, Alexander, and Lysimachus, Thrace and the adjacent Celtic regions were as good a market for Greek commodities as they had previously been. Consider the wide distribution of the coins of Philip, Alexander, Philip Arrhidaeus, and Lysimachus among the Danubian Celts and far beyond the regions that they gradually occupied, and the promptitude with which the Danubian Celts began to develop their own coinage on the model chiefly of Macedonian royal coins. The Celtic expansion after the death of Lysimachus, detrimental as it was to a sound economic development of the Balkan region, rather suspended than put an end to the development of trade relations between Greece (and especially Macedonia) and the Thracian and Danubian countries. I shall return to this later. It is a pity that the archaeological material found in the graves of the later fourth and early third centuries in Bulgaria and Rumania has never been completely collected and illustrated. A good example of the rich graves of this period may be seen in that of Verbitza mentioned above (p. 116), which is of early Hellenistic date.[36]

It is not surprising that in these circumstances Greece, in

* Note the beginnings of urbanization carried out in Thrace by Philip and Alexander.

PLATE XX

A highly instructive find in the Delta. It consists of one large terracotta figurine of Greek local workmanship representing a standing woman, and ten small vases. According to Prof. G. A. S. Snijder, Director of the Museum (*Allard Pierson Museum. Algemeene Gids*, 1937, p. 43, and pl. XIX), some of these vases are Attic, others of Greek forms and technique but of local workmanship, and two are imported from South Italy (Gnathian ware). Prof. J. D. Beazley, whom I have consulted on this point, regards the majority of the vases as Attic ware 'with the possible exception of the second from the right above and the left one below'. Be this as it may, the find is a striking testimony to the active commercial relations between Athens and Alexandria, and probably between Alexandria and South Italy also, in the late fourth century B.C. Cf. n. 32 to this chapter, and on the Gnathia ware imported into Ptolemaic Egypt in the fourth and third centuries B.C., below, Ch. IV, n. 198, and Ch. VIII, third section of part II. Add to the bibliography given there R. Bianchi-Bandinelli, *Scritti in onore di B. Nogara*, 1937, pp. 11 ff., and Ch. Picard, *Rev. Arch.* xii (6me série) (1938), p. 105 f. and fig. 5. The date of the find is certain: end of the fourth century B.C. (Photograph supplied by the authorities of the Allard Pierson Museum, Amsterdam.)

Allard Pierson Museum, Amsterdam.

TERRACOTTA STATUETTE AND CLAY VASES FOUND IN A GRAVE IN THE DELTA OF EGYPT

spite of wars and revolutions, rapidly recovered from the economic crisis of the late fourth century. It is sufficient to read Menander and other authors of the New Comedy to see how prosperous Athens was at that time. What we have of Menander and the reflections of his plays and of those of his contemporaries in the comedies of Plautus and Terence, the *Characters* of Theophrastus, and some of the biographies of philosophers by Diogenes Laertius which go back to contemporary sources, give us a vivid picture of the life of an Athenian citizen of the time. This typical citizen for whom Menander wrote his comedies and whom he and Theophrastus chiefly portrayed in their works is not an aristocrat by birth and wealth, nor is he a pauper, a proletarian. He is a middle-class landowner, a business man, or a *rentier*, well-to-do but not extremely rich. He draws his income from his farm, which he manages personally in a rational way with the help of slaves or hired labour, from his commercial operations, mostly marine ventures, or from money-lending. To these sources of income we may, basing ourselves chiefly on Demosthenes, confidently add industrial workshops, silver mining at Laurium, and hiring out slaves. The poor are not absent from Menander's picture, but they play a secondary part. Menander's audience consisted not of them, or at least not mainly of them, but of middle-class folk. Nor do the *nouveaux riches*, enterprising mercenary soldiers or other adventurers, figure largely in the picture of Athenian 'society'. They are there just to show the enormous difference between these upstarts and fortune-hunters and the respectable Athenians (see above, n. 16). Such members of the higher Athenian aristocracy as still existed and the millionaires of the day (if there were any) are not accepted as typical Athenians and therefore do not appear in Menander's comedies.

The Athenian *bourgeois* is well-to-do. He lives in a small but comfortable residential house, and owns one or two domestic slaves. He is not stingy, and on great occasions spends money freely; but he is careful about his affairs. His family is not very large: he generally has one or two children. To the girls he gives a decent but not excessive dowry, usually of one, two, three, or four talents of silver, sixteen being the maximum. He likes his daughter to be well dressed and buys imported frocks for her. His sons while young and before they acquire the mentality of their father have a good time: banquets and parties, wine and courtesans, some of these very highly paid (e.g. three *minae* a day). Without going into details, we can see that the standard of life of an Athenian was comparatively high, simple but comfortable. It is interesting to learn from Teles that young Metrocles, when he came to Athens to take up philosophy with Theophrastus and Xenocrates, felt ashamed of his poverty: he could not afford to dress as expensively as his schoolmates, to have slaves, to live in a large house, to eat costly food and drink choice wine.[37]

The picture drawn by Menander does not convey the impression that Athens was spending in the late fourth century what remained of the wealth she had accumulated in the past. In the tone of Menander's comedies we see reflected the outlook of men who are prosperous, confident of the present, and not afraid of the future. Menander sometimes complains of hard times, of continuous wars, but he never speaks of general ruin, poverty, and misery. And the same impression may be derived from the charming, humorous picture of Athenian society contained in the *Characters* of Theophrastus.

There is no doubt then that Athens was prosperous in the times of Alexander and the Successors. And Athens, in all probability, was no exception. That money was plentiful in Greece in the late fourth and early third centuries is shown in the first place by the frequency with which comparatively rich coin-hoards of this period have been found all over Greece. Some of these hoards were buried during the lifetime of Alexander (Kyparissia, 327 B.C.), some shortly after his death (Andritsaena, *c.* 315 B.C., and Lamia, *c.* 308 B.C.), some still later (the two hoards of Kililer in Thessaly, 285–275 B.C., the hoards of Salonica, 287–280 B.C., and of Olympia, after 250 B.C.). The contents of all have the same character—large quantities of coins of Alexander and Philip III of various mints, and in addition smaller quantities of Greek coins, mostly of Athenian and Corinthian autonomous currency. Coins of the Successors (other than those of Lysimachus) appear in the later hoards only in small numbers. These hoards show that money was steadily flowing into Greece in the times of Alexander and the Successors from all parts of the East and the North.[38]

Another sign of growing prosperity was the considerable rise of prices of all commodities and of labour throughout Greece, with occasional spasmodic fluctuations caused by the frequent wars of the period of the Successors (see above, pp. 1 ff.). In general gold and silver were comparatively cheap.*[39] Their cheapness and the concentration of large amounts of them (as well as of precious stones) in the hands of many kings and other persons is illustrated by the common use of silver and gold plate throughout the Hellenistic world, a fact well known to all archaeologists and epigraphists, and sufficiently attested by the inventories of the great Greek temples: Delphi, Didyma, Delos. A special fashion of the day was gold and silver objects, especially plate, adorned with precious stones (λιθοκόλλητοι, διάλιθοι), the earliest certainly of Oriental make. Stratonice, the wife of Seleucus I, dedicated a group of inlaid vessels and jewels at Delos; her husband did the same at Didyma. How widespread was the taste for metal plate is shown by the fact that Athenian and Italian potters changed over at this time from the manufacture of painted vases to that of vases with reliefs, imitations of metal ware. I shall speak of this later in more detail.[40]

The rise and fluctuation of prices mentioned above cannot be interpreted as the result of a kind of inflation and as a sign of bad times. It is true that large amounts of excellent and perfectly sound currency were put into circulation by Alexander and the Successors and considerably increased the quantity of money circulating in the Greek world. A certain depreciation of gold and silver, in other words a rise of prices, would be a natural result of this measure. But the main and enduring reason for the rise of prices cannot be sought in the abundance and comparative cheapness of money alone. The chief cause was the rapid increase in the demand for Greek commodities

* Especially gold; the value of gold in relation to silver fell in this period from the rate of 1 to 14 or 13 in the fifth century to 1 to 12 in Philip's time, and 1 to 10 in the days of Alexander and the Successors, while the price of all other goods in terms of silver went up considerably.

PLATE XXI

1. A votive bas-relief found at Piraeus. It shows a heroized (note the snake) actor or dramatic poet, no longer young, stretched on a couch and prepared to take part in a banquet. The table with the viands is ready, and his attendant-slave has brought in the wine for libation. A charming young woman is half stretched on the end of the couch. She draws the attention of her companion to a visitor who is entering. We may safely identify her with one of the Muses (Polyhymnia) or Skene, the personification of the Stage. The visitor is young Dionysus himself, slowly advancing from the left, half overpowered by *methe* and leaning on his attendant—a little Faun. The man on the couch is greeting his guest with his right hand. He is ready to receive from him the Dionysiac inspiration. Early third century B.C. The bas-relief has recently been interpreted in the sense sketched above, as the prototype of the well-known 'Ikarios' bas-reliefs, by Ch. Picard, 'Les Reliefs dits de la visite à Ikarios', *A.J.A.* xxxviii (1934), pp. 157 ff. (Photograph supplied by the authorities of the Louvre, Paris.)

2. The famous bas-relief of Menander, the great creator of the New Comedy. Menander—his figure is inspired by his well-known portrait, extant in many replicas—in heroic dress, is seated on a chair. His figure is turned to the right. Before him a table. Behind the table, the majestic figure of a woman, no doubt Polyhymnia or Skene rather than the famous Glycera. Menander holds in his left hand and contemplates a comic mask, that of one of the chief personages of his comedies—the youth. On the table two more masks: that of the young lady, heroine of the play, and of the father of the young man. (Photograph supplied by Alinari.)

The bas-relief has been published and discussed several times. A good description and a select bibliography will be found in M. Bieber, *Die Denkmäler zum Theaterwesen im Altertum*, 1920, p. 156, pl. LXXXVIII, and *The History of the Greek and Roman Theater*, 1939, pp. 165 ff., figs. 223 and 224 (bibliography, n. 4).

There is no need to justify the presence of these illustrations in my book. The great dramatic poets of the early Hellenistic period were the best exponents of the spirit, mentality, and creative genius of their times. It is to them that we owe, among many other things, a vivid picture of the leading class in the Hellenistic world—the *bourgeoisie* of the Greek cities.

1. Heroic votive bas-relief of a dramatic poet or actor. Paris, Louvre.

2. Bas-relief of Menander. Rome, Lateran.

ARTISTIC ATHENS OF THE END OF THE FOURTH AND THE BEGINNING OF THE THIRD CENTURY B.C.

1. One of the 'New' comedies on the stage. Bas-relief.
Naples Museum.

2. Terracotta group of two personages of a comedy.
Berlin, Staatliche Museen.

Terracotta statuette of a comic actor playing the part of a 'curly haired youth'.
Vienna Museum.

PLATE XXII

1. Background: stage scenery of the 'New Comedy' with the typical door and hangings. The moment represented is one which frequently occurs in the New Comedy. A young man of respectable family (*νεανίας ἁπαλός* or *ἐπίσειστος*) comes home after a banquet. He is in high spirits, hardly able to walk, shouting and brandishing the fillet worn at the banquets. Before him a girl-flutist. His slave is supporting him (*ἡγεμὼν θεράπων*). Present at this triumphal home-coming are the father (*ἡγεμὼν πρεσβύτης*) and his friend. The father is infuriated. He rushes towards his son, prepared to give him a thrashing with his staff or walking-stick. His friend tries to stop him. Roman period, but the types, costumes, and acting have not changed since the end of the fourth century B.C. (Photograph supplied by Alinari.)

The bas-relief has been very frequently reproduced and discussed. A good description and a select bibliography will be found in M. Bieber, *Die Denkm. z. Theaterwesen im Altertum*, 1920, p. 157, pl. LXXXIX, and *History of the Greek and Roman Theater*, 1939, p. 167 f., fig. 225 and n. 6. On the *tabellae comicae* (Plin. *N.H.* XXXV. 114) extant in painting and mosaics see A. K. H. Simon, *Comicae Tabellae*, 1938 (Die Schaubühne, XXV), pp. 66 ff. and n. 120 and p. 158.

2. Two personages of the Old or the New Comedy. Both are in good humour after a drinking bout. One is supporting the other. Both are laughing heartily. The less drunk of the two wears a red chiton and a blue cloak. The beards are red. Presumably from Tanagra. M. Bieber, *Denkmäler*, p. 132, no. 79, pl. LXIX, 1. On tipsy slaves in the New Comedy, Simon, loc. cit., pp. 145 ff. (Photograph supplied by the authorities of the Staatliche Museen, Berlin.)

3. Youth with long curly hair, wearing a dress typical of the comic actors. He is without doubt the *οὖλος νεανίσκος* of the New Comedy, not the *νεανίας πάγχρηστος* of the Tragedy. Another slightly different specimen of the same terracotta is in the National Museum of Athens and another version of the type in the Louvre, both from Myrina. (Photograph supplied by the authorities of the Vienna Museum.)

See E. Pottier and S. Reinach, *La Nécropole de Myrina*, 1887, p. 565, no. 321, pl. XLV, 1; F. Winter, *Die griechischen Terrakotten*, iii, 2. *Die Typen der figürlichen Terrakotten*, p. 430, no. 3. A. K. H. Simon, *Comicae tabellae*, pp. 49 ff., has proved against M. Bieber, *Denkmäler*, pp. 121, no. 56, pl. LXI, 1, cf. 2, and *History*, p. 152, fig. 204, that the statuettes represent the youth of the New Comedy and not of the Tragedy.

both for home consumption and export. The market was not in a position to meet it, for production had not kept pace with demand. The inevitable consequence was a rise of prices. Naturally this rise of prices affected chiefly the working classes, but these classes, on the other hand, found new outlets for their energies in the vast regions opened to them by Alexander. Ferguson has quoted texts referring to groups of Athenians who emigrated to Cyrene and to Antigoneia, the new capital of Antigonus. And Athens, in this respect also, was no exception.*

A similar disequilibrium of demand and supply, as well as the frequent wars and their consequent dislocations, account for the unsettled conditions of trade, especially of the grain trade, in the new Hellenistic world. I have already referred† to the great famine of the time of Alexander which so profoundly disturbed the economic life of Greece. It led on the one hand to wild speculation (of which Cleomenes of Naucratis offers the best known example), and on the other to striking demonstrations of Greek solidarity and general prosperity, as seen in the help given to Greece by Cyrene (*c.* 331–328 B.C.), by the kings, and by many rich private persons. But even after this crisis had passed, the grain trade remained in an unsettled state during the whole period of the Successors. A mass of epigraphical and literary evidence shows certain cities in an evil plight owing to the shortage of corn, and receiving frequent help from the kings and from private sources. Another grain crisis at Athens, which may be dated about the years 289/8 B.C., is mentioned in many inscriptions. It lasted intermittently until 282/1 B.C. The explanation may be that the ancient world, amid the political and economic disturbances of the period, found it difficult to adapt its commercial relations to the new conditions with sufficient promptitude. It appears to me probable that food shortage in Greece at this time was not due to the same causes as in the period before Alexander (above, p. 95), but that the crisis was of a purely commercial character and not a symptom of impoverishment or permanent economic distress. There was plenty of grain on the market and in most places plenty of money to buy it. The problem

* Ferguson, *Hell. Athens*, pp. 67, 69.

† Above, Ch. II, note 29.

was how to distribute and regularize the supply, and how to stabilize the price. Athens, the great corn-exchange of antiquity, was unequal to the task, and her successors, Alexandria, Rhodes, Miletus, and Ephesus, required time to discover the appropriate methods.[41]

Greece, well supplied with money in the manner described above, became in her turn an excellent market for the East. Egypt was secure of selling her grain there, as well as other commodities (papyrus, linen, glass, faience, &c.) in increased quantities. The goods that came by caravan to Asia Minor, Syria, and Egypt from the Far East, India, Arabia, and eastern Africa, found wealthy and open-handed purchasers in Greece.

Though trade with Egypt and the East enriched the large commercial cities of Greece, the centres of trade were tending to shift increasingly eastwards. Athens, which in the fourth century had been gradually forced to share her commercial hegemony with other cities, especially Rhodes and the chief seaports of Asia Minor, in the time of Alexander and of the Successors was more and more overshadowed by Rhodes, Miletus, and Ephesus, the first an excellent clearing-house for Egypt, Cyprus, and Syria, while Miletus and Ephesus were natural outlets for the caravan trade of Asia Minor.

RHODES in the time of the Successors was one of the most important commercial cities of the Greek world. Throughout the Hellenistic period she enjoyed the reputation not only of being rich and strong but also of being exceptionally well governed and of having solved, by judicious economic and social measures, the acute social problems of the time.* It was especially her situation between Egypt, Cyprus, the Syrian and Phoenician coasts, and the circle of the Greek cities, that made Rhodes an important intermediary of trade. This was true in the pre-classical and classical periods, but still more so in Hellenistic times. I may remind the reader of the well-known statement of Polybius (v. 90, 3).

It has already been stated that in the fourth century Rhodes became one of the most important corn-exchanges, especially

* Diod. xx. 81; Strabo xiv. 2, 5, p. 652, and the celebrated descriptions of Rhodes at a later date by Dio Chrysostom and Aristides, which in part depend on Hellenistic sources. For further detail see Ch. V.

PLATE XXIII

The Tanagra terracottas are too well known to require detailed treatment here. The two specimens reproduced in this plate are excellent examples of the post-Praxitelean refined Greek sculpture of the early Hellenistic period. At the same time they show us typical representatives of the well-to-do ladies of the fourth and third centuries B.C., or rather figures of young, elegant, well-dressed, and pretty women slightly idealized as the Greeks of this time would like them to be, and as probably some of them really were at certain moments of their actual life. The terracottas in this plate represent two ladies, one in meditation and in melancholy mood, the other full of life, a little aggressive, proud of her beauty and of her simple but beautifully arranged dress; she reminds us of Gorgo and Praxinoe, the two elegant Syracusan ladies of Alexandria presented by Theocritus (*Id.* xv), and of the young heroines of Menander's comedies. (Photographs supplied by the authorities of the Louvre, Paris.)

A fine stylistic analysis of Greek terracottas of this type will be found in J. Charbonneaux, *Les Terres cuites grecques*, 1936, pp. 16 ff. and figs. 44 ff., and a short bibliography, p. 24.

GREECE OF THE TIME OF MENANDER
Tanagra terracottas. Paris, Louvre.

PLATE XXIV

GREECE OF THE TIME OF MENANDER

Tanagra terracottas. Paris, Louvre.

PLATE XXIV

Two ephebes both seated, one resting after violent exercise in the palaestra and protected against the sun by a broad flat hat, the other meditating, probably not about philosophical problems. Cf. the preceding plate. J. Charbonneaux, *Les Terres cuites grecques*, 1936, figs. 47 and 48.

Photographs supplied by the authorities of the Louvre, Paris.

for the corn that came from Egypt and from the rich grain-fields of Cyprus, Syria, and Phoenicia. In the period of the Successors Rhodes became practically Egypt's chief agency for the Aegean trade in general and the grain trade in particular. This is shown by the fact that it was chosen by Cleomenes of Naucratis at the time of his great grain speculation (332–331 B.C.) as the seat of his agents and as the centre of his operations. In this connexion a very characteristic anecdote about Bion, the Cynic, and Rhodes may be quoted. When Bion was asked at Rhodes why he was teaching philosophy while the Athenians specialized in rhetoric, he replied in his pointed way, using a simile familiar to Rhodes: 'Shall I sell barley when I imported wheat?'

It is no wonder that Athens became jealous and alarmed. The close relations of Rhodes with Egypt, vital for the development of the prosperity and commercial importance of the former, were probably the chief reason why Antigonus in 305 B.C. undertook his siege of the city. He wished Rhodes to be one of his cities, and his commercial agent for the products of his own kingdom, and not an independent and neutral State, friendly both with himself and with Ptolemy. We know how greatly the siege contributed to the popularity of Rhodes in the eyes of all the freedom-loving Greek cities. There can be no doubt that, in respect of her trade also, the siege was ultimately profitable to her. The promise of safety given by Antigonus to Rhodian merchants in Syria, Phoenicia, Cilicia, and Pamphylia, provided they would not communicate with the besieged city, is proof of the activity of the trade relations between his Oriental empire and Greece, and of the great store he set by the services of Rhodian merchants.

The years of the *entente cordiale* with the Ptolemies were years of great prosperity for the island. Even our scanty evidence reveals Rhodes in the early third century as the home of powerful merchants and influential bankers. She used her money and her diplomacy, not only to promote her own interests, but also to help the Greek cities in their pursuit of independence and constitutional government, always showing herself a staunch supporter of these two pillars of Greek city life. Thus in 300 B.C. she lent money to the citizens of Priene to assist them in asserting their liberty against a tyrant. Similarly she lent 100 talents, without interest, to Argos for the strengthening of its fortifications and the improvement of its cavalry. It should be observed that the two loans, being of a purely political character, were granted not by private bankers but by the city. The city, it appears, had important reserves of money (a rare occurrence in the history of Greek cities!) stored in the treasury or kept on deposit in private or public banks in the town or elsewhere.

It was indeed more usual for such loans, even when made for political purposes, to be granted not by the city but by private citizens, rich merchants, and bankers. Thus Ephesus, which maintained most cordial relations with Rhodes, and probably depended on that city for her grain supply and no doubt for her commerce—as appears from the reform of the Ephesian coinage about this time on Rhodian models—was helped in critical times by a rich Rhodian who sold her a considerable quantity of grain at less than the very high current price.[42]

Athens had other dangerous rivals, second only to Rhodes in this respect, in the chief seaports of Ionia—MILETUS and EPHESUS. Many facts testify to the growing importance of these two cities. I may mention in the first place the great efforts of the rival Successors to obtain control of the two cities and to gain their loyal adherence. The political history of the period before and still more after Ipsus shows how strenuously Demetrius, Ptolemy Soter, Seleucus, and Lysimachus endeavoured to secure Miletus and Ephesus, and how willing they were to grant these cities the largest possible measure of autonomy. The chief efforts of Miletus were directed to two objects. One was to become, or rather to remain, the principal outlet for so much of the caravan trade from the East—from Mesopotamia and the Iranian regions, and through them from India and perhaps from China—as passed through Asia Minor on its way to Greece. From the time of the Persian Empire many merchants had preferred the safe and well-organized 'royal' overland roads leading to the harbours of Ionia to the inferior roads that ran from the Euphrates to the Phoenician and Syrian harbours. Later, the roads to the new Seleucid Mediterranean harbours, Seleuceia in Pieria and Laodicea (created by Seleucus I and Antiochus I to divert the Oriental trade from the Phoenician cities), vied with the roads across Asia Minor in safety and convenience. But it took some time for the early Seleucids to organize these new communications, and meanwhile the ancient royal road through Asia Minor was still the safest, if not the shortest. This was a source of great prosperity to Miletus and Ephesus. We have no direct information regarding the volume of this trade, but certain facts testify to its great importance.

I may quote for example the gift bestowed on Miletus by Antiochus, the eldest son of Seleucus I, about 300 B.C. He built there a portico one stadium long, the income from which was to be devoted by the city to the construction of the great temple of Didyma. The inscription recording the construction and the ruins of the portico were found by the German excavators. The portico, 190 metres long, was situated in the South Market of Miletus, and contained seventy-eight shops. It is interesting to note that the decree by which the city accepted the gift and conferred high honours on Antiochus* was introduced by Demodamas, son of Aristeides, the same man who as a general of Seleucus I made an expedition into Turkestan, crossed the Jaxartes, and dedicated there altars to Apollo of Didyma,† an expedition which certainly had commercial as well as political objects. It was probably an important increase in the volume of the Oriental trade of Miletus, promoted as it had been by Seleucus, Antiochus, and Demodamas, that suggested the construction of the new market-hall as a remunerative investment. Not less significant is the lavish gift made by Seleucus I to the sanctuary of Apollo of Didyma in 288/7 B.C. Besides gold, silver, and bronze plate, some of it of Oriental manufacture, the king gave the temple large amounts of Oriental spices—ten talents of frankincense, one talent of myrrh, two minae of cassia, two minae of cinnamon, two minae of costus.‡

While busy developing her connexions with the Seleucid kingdom (at the same time not neglecting her relations with

* *O.G.I.* 213.

† Plin. *N.H.* vi. 49.

‡ *O.G.I.* 214; Welles, *R.C.* 5, ll. 49–51: *λιβανωτοῦ τάλαντα δέκα, σμύρνης τάλαντον ἕν, κασίας μναῖ δύο, κινναμώμου μναῖ δύο, κόστου μναῖ δύο.*

Egypt*), Miletus did her best to secure another active and profitable market for her wares (goods either in transit or of her own manufacture). From time immemorial she had been connected with the Pontic regions, but for a time had been supplanted in the Pontic market by Athens. During the reign of Alexander and after it Miletus endeavoured to recover this market by making treaties of sympolity with her most prosperous and most important north-eastern colonies. We still possess the decrees adopted by Olbia, Cyzicus, Istrus, and later by Cios, and it is probable that her activity in this respect was much wider and more systematic than appears from our scanty evidence. All this makes it natural that, despite the wars and the troubles attending them, Miletus should have attained a high degree of prosperity, of which we have evidence, for example, in the work done on the beautiful temple of the Didymaean Apollo.[43]

It is regrettable that, owing to the meagreness of our material, a more detailed picture cannot be drawn of the social and economic aspect of Rhodes, Miletus, and Ephesus in the early Hellenistic period, such as has been drawn above in respect of Athens. Our literary texts are almost silent, inscriptions are few, and Rhodes has never been systematically excavated. Miletus and Ephesus have been excavated, Miletus by German, Ephesus by Austrian archaeologists. But the results of these excavations have not been published in full and Ephesus has yielded very little evidence relating to Hellenistic times. So far as they have been published I have made use of them in the foregoing sketch.

While it is impossible to form an adequate idea of the social and economic conditions that prevailed during this early period in these large and opulent cities, centres of a highly developed agricultural, industrial, and commercial life, the thorough German excavation of the ruins of a much smaller and more modest city of Asia Minor—Priene near Miletus—has yielded enough material to justify an attempt to give a general sketch of social and economic life in a city of this class.

PRIENE, like Miletus and Ephesus, was at one time a city by the sea, with a good harbour and probably some commerce and

* Welles, *R.C.* 14.

PLATE XXV

1. The Louvre bowl (another copy in the National Museum of Athens) belongs to the class of the so-called 'Homeric' bowls, that is to say, bowls illustrating in their relief decoration certain literary works, epic or dramatic. The bowl reproduced here illustrates in all probability an early Hellenistic mime. It shows a scene in a flour-mill. Work is in full swing: two millers at the two ends of the frieze are grinding corn in the peculiar hand-mills still in use in Greece. In the centre a more elaborate donkey-mill is operated by a man and a donkey. Between this mill and the hand-mill on the right a miller is sifting flour or corn. The millers are designated by the inscription: *μυλωθροί*. The peaceful atmosphere of the mill is disturbed by the entrance of five strangers, *κίναιδοι*, designated as such by an inscription. All of them wear their typical pointed caps and loin-cloths. In their usual way they are doing all sorts of mischief: two are carrying off bags, probably filled with flour, which they have apparently stolen in the mill; one is occupied with the donkey. The central scene shows a man, designated by the inscription as *τιμωρός* (avenger or executioner), who has bound one of the *cinaedi* to a pole and is about to flog him. A *cinaedus* is dragging him away from his victim. At the left hand end of the frieze is seen the figure of the owner of the mill. He is described by an inscription as *μυλωνάρχης*. Diam. 0·12, H. 0·08 m.

Drawing by H. Gute from photographs supplied by the authorities of the Louvre, Paris.

The bowl in the Museum of Athens has been published and discussed by F. Versakis, *'Εφ. 'Αρχ.*, 1914, pp. 50 ff. and pl. 1; K. Kourouniotis, ibid., 1917, pp. 151 ff.; F. Courby, *Les Vases grecs à reliefs*, 1922, p. 300, no. 207, cf. W. Ruge. *P.W.K.* xvi. 107. The Louvre bowl has been illustrated in my paper *A.J.A.* xli (1937), pp. 87 ff., where I endeavoured to show its relation to the mimes. No mention of the bowl will be found in the short discussion of the mime and related dramatic performances in M. Bieber, *The History of the Greek and Roman Theater*, 1939, p. 304 f. (Hellenistic), cf. p. 402 f. (Roman).

2. The photograph shown in this plate reproduces a similar bowl, probably illustrating a mime with the title *κίναιδος μοῖχος* (inscription on the bowl). I cannot here give a description of this unpublished bowl, which deserves to be more fully treated and discussed. I may draw the reader's attention to the punishment of the *cinaedus*: he is bound to a pole and flogged. It was Prof. R. Zahn who drew my attention to this interesting specimen of the 'Megarian' bowls. A search among the 'Megarian' bowls will probably reveal others which illustrate in their relief decoration the mimes and related works of popular dramatic art. It is highly probable that it was under the influence of the 'Megarian' bowls and similar pieces of Hellenistic relief pottery that certain Arretine factories of relief pottery such as those of M. Perennius Bargates and Ateius adorned their products with figures and scenes illustrating some mime, or perhaps Atellana, in the form either of a continuous narrative or of scattered figures. A set of fragmentary moulds of such cups from Bargates' shop was found at Arezzo (U. Pasqui, *Not. d. Sc.*, 1896, pp. 453 ff., cf. K. Hähnle, *Arretinische Reliefkeramik*, 1915 (diss. Tübingen, pp. 72 ff.). From one of these moulds modern craftsmen of that city manufactured a complete cup illustrating a mime, copies of which are on sale in the Museum. On these reproductions, A. Del Vita, *Boll. d'Arte*, xxxi (1937), 489 ff., cf. *Mostra Augustea della Romanità*, ii, 1939, lxxii, no. 256. On similar productions of the shop of Ateius see A. Oxé, *Arretinische Reliefgefässe vom Rhein*, 1933, pp. 69 ff. and pls. XI and LXIII, and R. Zahn, *Ber. Kgl. Kunsts.* xxxv (1914), pp. 301 ff., esp. 307. On Bargates' shop, A. Oxé, loc. cit., p. 87 f. and pl. XLIII.

Photograph supplied by Prof. R. Zahn of Berlin.

INDUSTRIAL LIFE IN GREECE IN THE EARLY THIRD CENTURY B.C.

Megarian bowls: one in Paris, Louvre, the other formerly in the Coll. P. Arndt in Munich.

PLATE XXVI

INDUSTRIAL LIFE IN GREECE IN THE EARLY THIRD CENTURY B.C.

Megarian 'Homeric' bowl. Paris, Louvre.

PLATE XXVI

The scene represented on the bowl (illustration of one of the epic Heracleias) shows a bearded copper-smith (χαλκεύς) seated in his forge with his instruments in his hands. To the left are the oven, with a fire burning in it, and two assistants, one bringing fuel for the oven or perhaps operating the bag-bellows (cf. the Roman lamp from Tarsus, *A.J.A.* xxxix (1935), p. 538, fig. 29, and below, Ch. VIII), the other forging a piece of metal. To the right Heracles is twice represented: receiving the club made by Hephaistos from the hands of Athena, and lifting the Erymanthian boar. A long inscription in three lines runs above the main figures of the scene. After several attempts the inscription has now been read in full and the text established with certainty: *τὸ σκύταλον τοῦ Ἡρακλέους ἐποίησε Ἥφαι-στο-ς. ἦν δὲ χαλκοῦν. δίδωσι δὲ αὐτῶι Ἀθηνᾶ εἰς | Ἀρκαδίαν πορευομένωι ἐπὶ τὸν Ἐρυμάνθιον κάπρον· ἔστιν δὲ ἆθλος πέμπτος.* Over the group of Heracles and the boar: *Ἐρυμάνθιος.* Representations of Hephaistos in the forge are comparatively common on Attic painted vases. This frieze may have been derived from them. Diam. 0·13, H. 0·08.

Drawing by M. Schmalz from photographs supplied by the authorities of the Louvre, Paris.

The bowl has been several times reproduced and discussed, W. Fröhner, *Philol.* lxxi (1912), p. 172 (who saw it and copied the inscription at Athens in 1893); F. Courby, *Les Vases grecs à reliefs*, 1922, pp. 303 ff., fig. 55 and pl. xa; S. B. Luce, *A.J.A.* xxviii (1924), p. 297, fig. 1; M. Rostovtzeff, ibid. xli (1937), pp. 90 ff., figs. 3–5.

industry. The vagaries of the Maeander deprived her of her harbour, the rivalry of her stronger neighbours of her trade and industry. The city was rebuilt about 350 B.C., with the help of Athens, far from the sea on the airy and sunny southern slope of the Teloneia, a rock forming part of the mountain range of Mycale. Thereafter Priene was a small but prosperous agricultural city of a few thousand inhabitants living on the produce of her fertile territory. This the city persistently tried to increase at the expense of her neighbour and enemy, the wealthy and powerful island-city of Samos, by the addition of some productive land in the Anaïtis or Batinetis opposite Samos.

The inscriptions and ruins of Priene give us a clear insight into the social and economic conditions of the city, conditions that in all probability were typical of those prevailing in many agricultural Greek cities of Asia Minor. There is much that is attractive and illuminating in the aspect of the city as re-founded about 350 B.C. and developed and extended in the period of Alexander and the Successors, in spite of various complications, internal and external, in its history (the short-lived tyranny of Hieron, litigations and wars with neighbours and with its own non-Greek subjects).

Priene was not a city of rich men. There were a few such, some of them foreigners who had settled there and had become (as also their descendants) full citizens. They were welcome and were highly honoured if they showed public spirit and were prepared to place their wealth at the service of the city in an emergency. But such men were exceptions. The bulk of the population consisted of well-to-do landowners and some artisans and shopkeepers. Their economic outlook was as narrow as their political horizon. They had no important export trade since they had little to export. Their industry worked for local customers and their trade was mostly local. They possessed some slaves. Men like Larichus,* son of Laomedon, a general of Alexander, one of the rich foreigners in the city, who cultivated a large area with the help of slaves, were quite exceptional.

Alongside of the actual citizens and perhaps a few resident

* *Inschr. v. Pr.* 18; *O.G.I.* 215.

aliens (*μέτοικοι*) of modest means, the territory of the city was occupied by the ancient inhabitants of the place, the native Pedieis, who were *πάροικοι* or *κάτοικοι*, not citizens of Priene. Some of them resided in that part of the territory of the city which was royal property—inherited by Alexander from the Persians and passing to his successor, whoever he might be, in this part of the world—and was probably styled *γῆ βασιλική*. They were bound to the soil and were probably called *λαοὶ βασιλικοί*. Others may have been *λαοί* of former large landowners who cultivated the land of their successors. Others again may have been tenants of the citizens of Priene. But the greater part were small landholders who paid rent or land-taxes to the city. The native rural Pedieis living in the villages had little affection for the Greeks of the city and were ready to rise against them when opportunity offered.

Thus the city of Priene was in the main an agricultural community of well-to-do landowners. We hear nothing of a large and increasing city proletariat, though it may have existed. Labour was furnished by slaves and to a certain extent by the native rural population, part of which may have settled in the city.

Narrow in their outlook, living remote from the centres of culture, and possessed of only moderate wealth, the Prieneans nevertheless maintained the traditions of Greek civilization. Their intellectual and artistic requirements were high. One of the first buildings that they erected in their new city was a charming little theatre. Their 'cathedral', the perfect temple of Athene, was a classical example of the Ionian style. It was described by its builder in a special monograph and was cited in all the ancient treatises on architecture. Its creator was Pytheus, a man eminent both in the theory and practice of architecture, who built the celebrated Mausoleum of Halicarnassus. The fortifications of the city were to be unsurpassed in technical efficiency and sober beauty. They still arouse the admiration of the rare visitors to the ruins of Priene.

The city was laid out with taste and intelligence, on the best town-planning principles of the time: straight streets crossing each other at right angles, a large and airy market-place opening on the main street and surrounded on three sides by

PLATE XXVII

The city of Priene has been described, pp. 179 ff. and n. 44. The restoration reproduced here (by A. Zippelius) is well known and has been frequently used to illustrate modern books. It shows the city as it was laid out on the 'Hippodamian' plan in the late fourth century B.C. One can easily recognize the walls surrounding it, the network of regular streets crossing each other at right angles, the spacious agora in the centre of the city, the famous temple of Athena built by Pytheus, the theatre, and in the lower part of the city the monumental Gymnasium.

The City of Priene (Restored)

porticoes, an excellent water-supply well protected against attack, a fine meeting-place for the popular assembly and the State council, and a large and well-designed gymnasium for mental and physical education—soon supplemented by a new one for the older students (*neoi*). All the public buildings and squares were adorned with bronze and marble statues by the best artists, and some of the former were painted in a simple and elegant style.

The private houses are even more characteristic of a small but prosperous *bourgeois* community, democratic in its constitution and in its social and economic structure. Each city block was divided into four parts, each part containing one house. Larger and more pretentious houses are rare and mostly of later date. The houses, though small and modest, were comfortable, hygienic, and attractive. Light and air reached the dining- and sitting-rooms and the bedrooms from the inner court. The rooms were not very large, but they were not over-crowded with furniture. The few specimens of furniture found in the houses show that the Prieneans had a high artistic standard in this field also. Fine well-proportioned couches, elegant tables, finely modelled portable ovens, exquisite statuettes in bronze and clay are characteristic features of Priene.[44]

It is impossible to enter into greater detail, but what has been said will suffice to show the typical aspect of a Greek city of this period. We have, it is true, no right to generalize. No two cities in Asia Minor—or in Greece proper or the islands—were exactly similar; each had its own peculiarities. And yet all had many traits in common, especially in their political, social, and economic system. With the political aspect of the cities I am not here concerned. But a parallel to the economic structure of Priene may be presented which is instructive alike in its similarities and in its differences.

We happen to know a little more of TEOS than of the other cities of Asia Minor, though less of it than of Priene. I have previously referred to it in connexion with the synoecism of Teos and Lebedos, which was planned and perhaps carried out by Antigonus. In a decree which deals with her sympolity with Lebedos (end of the fourth century, perhaps contemporary with the inscription relating to the *synoikismos*) are enumerated some of the taxes of the city. This list, incomplete as it may be, gives us a good idea of the economic structure of the city. Like Priene, Teos lived mostly on her agriculture and cattle-breeding: sheep and pigs were one of her main sources of income. In addition, revenue was derived from the exploitation of woods. Trees were cut and transported with the help of slaves and donkeys and probably made into charcoal. There were numerous gardens. Bee-keeping flourished, as in so many other places in the ancient world (Athens, Rhodes, Theangela and elsewhere in Caria, &c.). And finally, unlike Priene, Teos had her flourishing industry, the manufacture of certain kinds of garments, χλάνδια and ἀμπέχονα, from Milesian wool.

It is interesting to find that a substantial income was derived by the citizens from the hiring out of slaves, and that a health service was organized more or less in the same way as it was in Cos, whose laws were imposed on Teos and Lebedos by Antigonus (see next chapter). It may be added that the city, not satisfied with an extensive and diversified taxation, held private slaves and draught animals liable to compulsory public service.

The impression produced by the inscription analysed above and by that relating to the synoecism is again that of a small community of well-to-do *bourgeois*, who derive their main income from the intensive cultivation of their land and, in a subsidiary degree, from some industries. The citizens live a narrow life within their territory, consuming mainly their own products. Occasionally they export some of these; but, more often, especially when crops fail, they are in urgent need of imported food.[45]

It may be noted in conclusion that the picture of Teos is very similar to that of PIDASA in later time.*

Such were the smaller cities of Asia Minor in the period under review. The larger cities, centres of trade and industry such as Miletus and Ephesus, were, of course, different. But what we know of them, particularly of Miletus, shows that in their general aspect, that is, in their plan and architecture, especially as regards the residential and political areas, they did not differ

* *Milet*, i, 3, p. 350, n. 149; below, Ch. V.

greatly from Priene. We must, of course, picture in addition a noisy and probably dirty harbour, large crowded warehouses, picturesque quays with shops, cabarets, little restaurants, brothels, and what not. The public squares and buildings must be imagined more numerous and much larger in size. However, in the main, even a larger Greek city of that time would not be very unlike the modest and elegant city of Priene. I shall return to this topic later when I am dealing with Alexandria, Rhodes, Cos, Miletus, and Delos.

The prosperity of some, probably most, of the cities of the mainland of Greece, of the islands, and of Asia Minor was probably shared by those Greek cities which played the role of Athens, Corinth, Rhodes, Miletus, and Ephesus in the Propontis and on the Pontic coast. I shall revert to most of these cities in the next chapter—Cyzicus, Byzantium, Chalcedon, Heraclea Pontica, Sinope, Amisus and the flourishing cities of the western Pontic coast. Here I will only refer to the far distant cities of South Russia. What is true of them is true, *mutatis mutandis*, of the other cities mentioned above. They all profited by the recovery of Greece, and the late fourth century in South Russia was a very prosperous, nay, a brilliant period. Many marvellously rich graves at Panticapaeum and many splendid finds at Olbia belong to this time, as do many Scythian graves containing exquisite Greek jewellery, pottery, and toreutic work, partly imported from Greece and Asia Minor, partly made at Panticapaeum and Olbia.

It may be added that the influence of Greek prosperity was felt not only in the East, but also in the West, as we may infer from the brilliant development of certain branches of Greco-Italian industry, especially at Tarentum.[46]

The brisk exchange of goods between the constituent parts of Alexander's empire and between them and the countries of the West and the North-East was facilitated by the fact, on which I have already laid stress, that the empire of Alexander, in spite of the wars of the Successors, remained a political unit for about fifty years. This period was a repetition—on a large scale—of the glorious days of the Athenian Empire, but without the Athenian methods of compulsion. The sea was comparatively free of pirates. Alexander's measures of police were

PLATE XXVIII

1. Æ Tetradrachm, Seleucus I (Seleuceia on the Tigris). *Obv.* Head of Zeus. *Rev.* ΒΑΣΙΛΕΩΣ ΣΕΛΕΥΚΟΥ. Athena fighting in quadriga of horned elephants; in field, Seleucid anchor.

2. Æ 'Lion-stater', Seleucus I (Babylon, before 300 B.C.). *Obv.* Baal seated. *Rev.* Lion; Seleucid anchor above.

3. Æ Tetradrachm, Ptolemy I, Egypt (1st issue). *Obv.* Head of Alexander in elephant skin. *Rev.* ΠΤΟΛΕΜΑΙΟΥ ΑΛΕΞΑΝΔΡΕΙΟΝ. Athena Promachos hurling spear, at her feet an eagle.

4. *A/* Pentadrachm, Ptolemy I. *Obv.* Head of Ptolemy I wearing diadem and aegis. *Rev.* ΒΑΣΙΛΕΩΣ ΠΤΟΛΕΜΑΙΟΥ. Eagle on fulmen.

5. *A/* Octodrachm of Arsinoe (struck posthumously by Ptolemy II). *Obv.* Head of Arsinoe II, veiled and wearing stephane. *Rev.* ΑΡΣΙΝΟΗΣ ΦΙΛΑΔΕΛΦΟΥ. Double cornucopiae, filleted.

6. Æ Tetradrachm, Demetrius Poliorcetes (Chalcis, Euboea). *Obv.* Head of Demetrius wearing diadem. *Rev.* ΒΑΣΙΛΕΩΣ ΔΗΜΗΤΡΙΟΥ. Poseidon leaning on trident, resting foot on rock.

7. Æ Tetradrachm, Demetrius Poliorcetes (Salamis, Cyprus). *Obv.* Nike blowing trumpet and holding trophy-stand, standing on prow. *Rev.* ΒΑΣΙΛΕΩΣ ΔΗΜΗΤΡΙΟΥ. Poseidon wielding trident.

8. Æ Tetradrachm, Antiochus I (Antioch). *Obv.* Head of Antiochus wearing diadem. *Rev.* ΒΑΣΙΛΕΩΣ ΑΝΤΙΟΧΟΥ. Apollo seated on omphalos.

9. Æ Tetradrachm, Antiochus II (Cyme). *Obv.* Head of Antiochus II, diademed. *Rev.* ΒΑΣΙΛΕΩΣ ΑΝΤΙΟΧΟΥ. Seated Heracles, symbol, one-handled cup.

10. Æ Tetradrachm, Rhodes (*c.* 304–166 B.C.). *Obv.* Facing head of Helios. *Rev.* ΡΟΔΙΩΝ. Above, rose; below, magistrate's name.

11. *A/* Stater, Diodotus of Bactria. *Obv.* Head of Diodotus diademed. *Rev.* ΒΑΣΙΛΕΩΣ ΔΙΟΔΟΤΟΥ. Zeus hurling fulmen.

On the early Seleucid coinage see Ch. IV, pp. 446 ff., and on the early Ptolemaic, pp. 398 ff., cf. Ch. VIII; cf. the masterly sketches by E. T. Newell, *Royal Greek Portrait Coins*, 1937. On Demetrius Poliorcetes, id., ibid., pp. 27 ff., and *The Coinages of Demetrius Poliorcetes*, 1927. Diodotus I, E. T. Newell, *Royal Greek Portrait Coins*, p. 66, and W. W. Tarn, *The Greeks in Bactria and India*, 1938, pp. 72 ff. It is highly probable that the famous Nike of Samothrace now in the Louvre is an imitation of the Nike of Demetrius as shown in no. 7 of this plate. On the original site of the Louvre Nike, see A. Salač, *Socha Bohyně Vítězství v Louvru*, 1938.

The Early Hellenistic Kings

continued by Antigonus and Demetrius, who had a strong navy and the Island League at their disposal. Lysimachus, Ptolemy Soter, Rhodes, Cyzicus, Lampsacus, Byzantium, Heraclea Pontica, Sinope, and the Bosporan kings, all contributed to this security.[47]

That Alexander's empire, because it was a political unit in the days of the Successors, was also an economic unit, can only be stated with reservations. Greece even now remained what it had previously been, a loose complex of independent cities, each pursuing, by every lawful and unlawful method, a narrow policy directed to self-sufficiency and self-defence. None of the Greek cities abolished its restrictive measures against its neighbours or its oppressive customs-duties.[48] Nevertheless, Alexander's empire in the period of the Successors approximated to the character of an economic unit even more than the Athenian Empire. Our evidence is scanty but is sufficient to show this.

To begin with, I may remind the reader of the general rise of prices in the time of Alexander and the Successors all over the empire. Next comes the evidence supplied by coins. Coin-hoards buried in all parts of the empire and outside it in Alexander's own lifetime and during the rule of the Successors show that monetary unity had been almost achieved. Let me recall some well-known facts in this connexion.[49]

Alexander's currency was not only abundant but uniform in respect of types, purity of metal, and standard (Attic). After his death and for about nineteen years money of exactly the same types and standard was issued from the same mints by the Successors in the name of Philip Arrhidaeus and later of Alexander IV, for use throughout the empire, with the exception of Egypt. A certain differentiation began in Egypt and spread later to other parts of the Hellenistic world, when their rulers assumed the royal title. All of these had their own abundant coinage, the most prominent in this respect being Demetrius, Lysimachus, Ptolemy Soter, and Seleucus I. Their coins, however, as regards weight, purity, and standard (with the exception of those of Ptolemy, who finally went over to the so-called Phoenician standard), were almost exactly similar to those of Alexander. The only difference was in the types, the head of the deified Alexander and later the portraits of the Successors replacing on the obverse the well-known Alexandrian types, and new reverses being substituted for the standardized designs of Alexander.

In comparison with the royal issues the leading issues of the past were of little importance. The Persian 'archers' and other coins of the Persian Empire soon vanished. Of the city issues, the Athenian 'owls' were still abundant. Athens seems to have retained her right of coinage from the time of Alexander down to about 220 B.C., when a new style of coinage was substituted for the old. Most modern scholars are inclined to think, in opposition to the earlier view, that there was no suspension of the Athenian coinage between 322 (or 261 B.C.) and some time after 229 B.C., except for a short interruption in the days of Antigonus Gonatas.[50] Corinthian *poloi* ceased to be struck early in the third century B.C. and were never very popular in the Aegean. Mints in a few other cities were still operating, and the Greek leagues began to issue their own federal money. But many of the Greek cities preferred to issue coins of Alexandrian types. It is curious that King Areus of Sparta, when he decided (about 280 B.C.) to coin his own money, began to issue Alexander tetradrachms of Attic weight but inscribed with his own name.[51]

All these issues, however, were superseded by the royal coinage. This was the result not of compulsion or legislation, as in the time of the Athenian Empire, but of the evident convenience of monetary unity and of the abundance and excellence of the royal coinage. We have indisputable proof of this in the statistics of hoards as recorded by Noe. In all the hoards of the late fourth and early third centuries Alexandrian coins (with a certain number of 'Philippi' added) exceed the total of all the other issues. Even the coins of the Successors (except those of Lysimachus) figure only rarely and sporadically.[52] Alexander's coinage was so famous and so popular in the Hellenistic world that when, after Magnesia, many of the Greek cities recovered their right of coinage (which they had lost in the time of the Successors and of the balance of power), they mutually agreed to begin their autonomous coinage by the issue of uniform Alexandrian and Lysimachian silver money, which they struck in large quantities.* I am speaking, of course, of the great currencies of the time, those which played the leading part in commercial life and were kept by rich people in their homes and in the banks. For the expenses of daily life in the cities of Greece proper, Asia Minor, and the Near East, local currency was used almost exclusively, being only to a slight extent supplemented by the currencies of neighbouring cities. This currency was mostly copper and small silver. Its prevalence in daily life is shown by the finds made in the Greek cities of both Greece and Asia Minor, especially Priene (as was well shown by the late Dr. Regling) and Pergamon.

Everything considered, Alexander's reign and the period of the Successors were a time of great hope and great possibilities for the empire created by Alexander, including Greece. Greece lost her political independence, though she struggled desperately to retain it, but she was compensated by a material prosperity that appeared likely to endure.[53]

But this appearance was illusory. The period of prosperity, so far at least as Greece proper was concerned, was destined to be of short duration.

* This coinage is dealt with in a later chapter.

PLATE XXIX

1. Æ Ptolemy II. Egypt. *Obv.* Head of Zeus Ammon. *Rev.* ΒΑΣΙΛΕΩΣ ΠΤΟΛΕΜΑΙΟΥ. Eagle holding fulmen.

2. AV Octodrachm of Ptolemy III. Egypt. *Obv.* ΑΔΕΛΦΩΝ. Heads of Ptolemy II and Arsinoe II. *Rev.* ΘΕΩΝ. Heads of Ptolemy I and Berenice I.

3. AV Octodrachm of Ptolemy III. Egypt. *Obv.* Head of Ptolemy III, radiate, wearing aegis and holding trident-topped sceptre. *Rev.* ΒΑΣΙΛΕΩΣ ΠΤΟΛΕΜΑΙΟΥ. Filleted cornucopiae.

4. AR Tetradrachm of Philetaerus of Pergamon. *Obv.* Diademed head of Seleucus I. *Rev.* ΦΙΛΕΤΑΙΡΟΥ. Athena seated with hand on shield. In the field helmet.

5. AR Tetradrachm of Attalus I of Pergamon. *Obv.* Head of Philetaerus. *Rev.* ΦΙΛΕΤΑΙΡΟΥ. Athena seated crowning king's name. Beneath arm—A, in the field: to the left ivy-leaf, to the right bow.

6. AR Tetradrachm of Antigonus Gonatas. *Obv.* Head of Poseidon. *Rev.* ΒΑΣΙΛΕΩΣ ΑΝΤΙΓΟΝΟΥ. Apollo seated on prow of galley. This coin possibly commemorates the battle of Cos.

7. AR Tetradrachm of Antiochus III. Syria. *Obv.* Head of Antiochus III wearing diadem. *Rev.* ΒΑΣΙΛΕΩΣ ΑΝΤΙΟΧΟΥ. Elephant. Beneath monogram.

8. AR Tetradrachm. Aetolian League (*c.* 279–168 B.C.). *Obv.* Head of Alexander. *Rev.* ΑΙΤΩΛΩΝ. Aetolia seated on shields, among them the Macedonian and Gaulish shields. This is a copy of a statue set up by the Aetolians at Delphi. In the field to the right monogram.

On the royal coins of this plate, E. T. Newell, *Greek Portrait Coins*, 1937.

THE EARLY HELLENISTIC KINGS

IV

THE BALANCE OF POWER

PART I

THE CITIES: GREECE AND THE ISLANDS

THE short survey in Chapter I of political events during the period of balance of power (281–221 B.C.) has shown that, like that which preceded it, it was a time of almost continuous warfare throughout the former empire of Alexander. The region that suffered most was continental Greece, after it the islands and Asia Minor, and finally Syria. Egypt was engaged in war outside her own territory and therefore suffered least. But it was something more than a period of warfare. Except in Greece —and even in Greece to a certain extent—it was a time of great creative political activity. In this short space of time each of the monarchies formerly comprised in the empire laid the foundations of its political, social, and economic structure, a structure that was to survive almost unchanged until they were incorporated in the Roman Empire and even later.

We must therefore review separately the conditions in each of these regions, bearing in mind that they all, despite the differences that had developed between them, were still constituents of a single large unit, the former dominion of Alexander, the Hellenistic world.

To begin with Greece. Of the various sources from which our information with regard to it is drawn, the literary texts bearing on its history, both political and economic, during this period are very meagre. In the political field they are insufficient to furnish a continuous narrative of events.[1] As regards economic and social conditions they are even less informative. Even for Athens we have nothing comparable to the copious evidence relating to the preceding period.

The lack of literary sources is compensated by the data which may be gathered from epigraphic material. The inscriptions of this period are numerous and of varied character, and cannot be described as a whole. I shall discuss them group by group as I deal with the various aspects of the economic life of the Greek cities.

One group, however, the official yearly accounts of the administration of the temples of Delos rendered by the *hieropoioi*, calls for some preliminary remarks. We have substantial fragments of them for about a century, from which it is possible to compile fairly complete and trustworthy lists of the prices of commodities and domestic animals as well as of land and houses, of rents of both houses and land, and of wages and salaries. Scholars have naturally availed themselves largely of this material to reconstruct the economic history of the Aegean during the period with which we are dealing.[2] Its value certainly cannot be over-estimated, for with its help we can follow the fluctuations of prices at one place in the Aegean world, and by correlating them with contemporary political events we may be able to detect the special causes that gave rise to them. Moreover, we learn from them the real value of money in an important part of the Hellenistic world in the late third and early second centuries B.C.

Valuable as it is, the evidence from Delos has its limitations. We must not forget that it was a peculiar place, unique of its kind, different from any other city in Greece except, to a certain extent, Delphi and Olympia. A barren island containing very little fertile land, possessing no mineral or other resources, Delos lived for centuries as an appendage of its famous temple of Apollo. Later in its history it became a centre of Aegean, and still later of Mediterranean, commerce and banking, one of the clearing-houses of the ancient world.

Delos, therefore, throughout its existence depended almost entirely on imports, and the balance of its trade was distinctly unfavourable. This peculiar feature of its economy necessarily had a certain influence on the prices that ruled in the island. On the other hand in its later days—the period best known to us—it became a centre of transit trade and the residence of many aliens, merchants, business men, and bankers. This fact, together with the physical character of the island, its lack of natural resources, certainly influenced the prices of commodities, labour, land, houses, slaves, and so forth. The prices, as they appear in the temple accounts, were not arbitrarily fixed by the temple but reflect the ebb and flow of business life in Delos, of which very little is known. All this makes it difficult to regard the prices that we find at Delos as necessarily representing those current all over the Aegean, unless they are confirmed by evidence from other localities.

Moreover, the data contained in the Delian inscriptions must not be taken at their face value. There is, for instance, a tendency among modern scholars to calculate the yearly income of a family of wage-earners from the daily wages and salaries paid by the temple to its workmen and employees. But W. W. Tarn has shown that none of the wage-earners who appear in the temple accounts were employed by the temple continuously for a year. They were all employed intermittently, and in the intervals they certainly worked in the harbour or the city, or perhaps on parcels of land rented or owned by them. What remuneration they earned there is unknown. Besides, we must consider that other members of their families may have derived a certain income from their own business or work.

Thus the Delian evidence is especially valuable for the light it throws on the economic history of Delos. It may be used, with great care, to illustrate the economic conditions of the Aegean islands and perhaps of Greece. Whether we are justified in making far-reaching generalizations, and in regarding the curves of prices observed at Delos as valid for the rest even of the Aegean world, is a matter of controversy and cannot be discussed here at length. I question even more whether we are entitled to compare the curves of prices as ascertained for Delos and for Egypt during a given period* and to infer from certain coincidences in them a general uniform fluctuation of prices throughout the Hellenistic world as far as Mesopotamia and Babylonia.† Egypt was no less exceptional than Delos, and prices there were governed by many local conditions quite different from those prevailing at Delos.

I turn now to a survey of the various aspects of the social and economic life of continental Greece as reflected in our various sources, and will deal first with the influence of war and its concomitants, an important feature in the history of the

* On prices in Egypt, see below, pp. 258 ff.

† On prices in Babylonia, see below, part II, sect. C of this chapter.

Hellenistic world during the period under review. The subject needs careful consideration.[3]

It has been mentioned in the preceding chapter that the Greek customs of war were primitive and ruthless. The unwritten laws of war regarded such acts as pillage and devastation of the enemies' country as normal and lawful (see, for example, the remark of Polybius xxiii. 15, 1-3). They similarly permitted the complete destruction of captured cities; the enslavement and sale of prisoners of war, generally (but not necessarily) on the understanding that they might be freed if somebody ransomed them; requisitions of goods, foodstuffs, men, and draught animals for the needs of the fighting forces even in allied countries, not to speak of what we should call neutrals (a notion foreign to the ancient world); compulsory levies of men; and so forth.

These ideas were firmly established in the Greek world and very difficult to eradicate. I have already indicated how the Successors, when carrying on war in Greece, allowed themselves to adopt them, at least to some extent. The same is true of the rulers who followed them.

The more thoughtful opinion of Greece protested against the abuses repeatedly and vehemently. Plato gave eloquent expression to the protest,* condemning the wholesale murders and enslavement of Greeks during their internecine wars, the burning of houses, and the destruction of crops.[4] The attitude of Plato (and of Aristotle) towards war became a commonplace in early Hellenistic times. The leading schools of philosophy of this period all shared the ideas of Plato. There is no need to emphasize the Epicurean love of peace; nor were the Cynics and the Stoics less explicit. For Chrysippus peace was one of the *prima bona*. When describing the state of strife that reigns even in peace time in each house and in every man, Philo, following probably an early Stoic writer, gives a vivid description of the horrors of war:† 'They rob, plunder, sell into slavery,

**Rep*. 470 f.; cf. *Polit*. 307–8; see also *Menex*. 239 and 242, distinguishing between wars between Greeks and those with barbarians.

† *De conf*. 12, pp. 411, 412: *συλῶσιν, ἁρπάζουσιν, ἀνδραποδίζονται, λεηλατοῦσι, πορθοῦσιν, ὑβρίζουσιν, αἰκίζονται, φθείρουσιν, αἰσχύνουσι, δολοφονοῦσιν, ἄντικρυς ἣν ὦσι δυνατώτεροι κτείνουσι,* etc.

despoil, ravage, outrage, maltreat, destroy, dishonour, murder by stealth or, if they are strong enough, openly.'[5]

The attitude of public opinion towards war and peace in the third century is further illustrated by some very interesting facts. For a Greek the ideal of life was always *εἰρήνη* and *πλοῦτος*, peace and wealth; they always prayed to attain it, but never more frequently and more fervently than in the late fourth, third, and second centuries. One has only to read the prayer of Isyllus for the city of Epidaurus,* or the impressive cry of a personage of the New Comedy: 'Give us peace, o Lord Zeus, an end of strife and wretchedness.'† It finds a parallel in the prayer addressed to Demetrius by Athens in the famous ithyphallus of 291 B.C.,‡ and in the prayer of Magnesia on the Maeander to Zeus Sosipolis in 196 B.C.§ No wonder that in the lists of magistrates published in the third century and later by some of the Greek cities we often find an eloquent remark: 'In their time there was peace, order, prosperity, concord.'‖ To this general feeling of Greece Polybius gives forcible utterance when he says:¶ 'For if there is a boon for which we all pray the gods and undergo anything to secure, and which is the only one of the so-called blessings that no one questions, I mean peace.'[6]

When, after having been for a time in abeyance, the most cruel practice of war—the total destruction of cities and the enslavement of citizens—reappeared with the capture of Mantinea (223 B.C.) by the Achaeans and Macedonians, the indignation in Greece was intense. This indignation was vigorously expressed in the lost work of Phylarchus, who dedicated some striking pages to the description of the horrors which accompanied the capture of Mantinea. It is more than probable that

* Isyll. B. 22 ff.; *Anth. Lyr.* ii, p. 282 D, cf. I. U. Powell, *Collect. Alex.* 1925, p. 132 f., and I. U. Powell and E. A. Barber, *New Chapters*, etc., i. 1921, p. 46 f.

† *Nov. com. fr. in pap. rep.*, ed. Schröder, no. 1, 23: *γένοιτο δ' εἰρήνη ποτ' ὦ Ζεῦ δέσποτα [δι]άλυσις [ἔχθ]ρας [ἀθλίων τ]ε πραγμάτων.*

‡ Athen. vi. 62, p. 253 d, e.

§ *S.I.G.*³ 589, 27 ff.

‖ *ἐπὶ τούτων ἦν εἰρήνη, εὐνομία, εὐετηρία, ὁμόνοια* (or words to that effect).

¶ IV. 74. 3: *εἰ γὰρ ἧς πάντες εὐχόμεθα τοῖς θεοῖς τυχεῖν, καὶ πᾶν ὑπομένομεν ἱμείροντες αὐτῆς μετασχεῖν καὶ μόνον τοῦτο τῶν νομιζομένων ἀγαθῶν ἀναμφισβήτητόν ἐστι παρ' ἀνθρώποις, λέγω δὲ τὴν εἰρήνην . . .*

he condemned with equal vehemence other acts of unnecessary cruelty during the wars which he described. And yet the conduct of Aratus found an eloquent defender in Polybius, who appealed to the accepted laws of war (*κατὰ τοὺς τοῦ πολέμου νόμους*) to justify the wholesale enslavement of free men, women and children. He adds that the treatment of Mantinea was in retaliation for certain acts of the Mantineans which, though less cruel, did not conform with 'the laws of nations' (*τοὺς κοινοὺς τῶν ἀνθρώπων νόμους*). There is no doubt, however, that Greece in this case sided with Phylarchus and not with Aratus and the Achaeans, whose excuses Polybius was probably repeating.[7]

There is no question, therefore, that the educated opinion of Greece was unanimous in condemning the customs of war that prevailed in Greece in the third century. But Greece was helpless. 'Military necessity' was stronger than public opinion. During this period war remained as ruinous an episode in the life of Greece, as cruel and as ruthless, as it had previously been. In self-defence Greece adopted certain measures designed to make war less destructive. These are enumerated by Tarn: the creation of leagues which guaranteed peace to their members, at least within the league; inter-State treaties of a new kind, by which certain cities and temples were recognized as sacred and exempt from liability to pillage (*συλᾶν, ῥυσιάζειν*); the extensive use of arbitration for the settlement of disputes between individual cities and of conflicts within them; and treaties by which certain cities accepted the obligation not to enslave each other's citizens.[8] These compacts brought some measure of relief to some of the cities of Greece. But their very existence and their character bear witness to the persistence of old customs and to the impotence of Greece to change them. War remained, be it repeated, as cruel and ruthless as it had been, and hindered, probably even more than in the past, the normal development of the country. Some facts may be adduced in illustration.

We have no reliable information about the losses in most of the great battles. We do not know, for instance, the number of casualties in the decisive naval engagements of the period, such as those at Cos and Andros. We know, however, that at Sellasia (222 or more probably 221 B.C.), the only battle about which we are well informed, of the 6,000 Lacaedemonians who took part in it 5,800 were killed and that among Cleomenes' mercenaries the casualties were severe.* I do not think that the battle of Sellasia was exceptional in this respect.

One of the most important facts in connexion with war in ancient times is that it was universally regarded as a method not only of settling political questions but also of enriching the victors at the expense of the vanquished. To pillage a country was a common practice in ancient warfare. In this respect the period we are considering was no exception. Polybius is inclined to make the Aetolians responsible for the excessive prevalence of pillage and robbery at this time. But the other leading States adopted exactly the same methods. All belligerents were in the habit of raiding enemy territory to devastate it and to secure as much booty as possible. It is unnecessary to accumulate evidence of this. Two examples may be given which illustrate the methods of warfare practised by Phylarchus' hero, Cleomenes III. Shortly after his reform in Sparta, Cleomenes invaded the territory of Megalopolis: 'he collected much booty and wrought great devastation of the country' says Plutarch.† He did the same in his invasion of the territory of Argos after the city had been occupied by Antigonus: 'he laid waste the country and carried everything off'‡ according to Plutarch, who a little later describes a new and ingenious method adopted by Cleomenes: 'Ravaging the plain, he did not, as invaders usually do, cut the corn with sickles and daggers, but beat it down with large wooden implements fashioned like broadswords, so that his men had an amusement on the march and crushed and destroyed the whole crop without trouble.'§[9]

The great masters and exemplars in this kind of war of devastation were the pirates.[10] Piracy in this period, as in the

* Plut. *Cleom.* 28, 5.

† *ὠφελείας τε μεγάλας ἤθροισε καὶ φθορὰν πολλὴν ἀπειργάσατο τῆς χώρας* (ibid. 12, 2).

‡ *διαφθειρομένης γὰρ τῆς χώρας ὑπ' αὐτοῦ καὶ πάντων ἀγομένων καὶ φερομένων.* (ibid. 25, 4).

§ *πορθῶν τὸ πεδίον καὶ τὸν σῖτον οὐ κείρων, ὥσπερ οἱ λοιποί, δρεπάναις καὶ μαχαίραις ἀλλὰ κόπτων ξύλοις μεγάλοις εἰς σχῆμα ῥομφαίας ἀπειργασμένοις, ὡς ἐπὶ παιδιᾷ χρωμένους ἐν τῷ πορεύεσθαι σὺν μηδενὶ πόνῳ πάντα συγκατατρῖψαι καὶ διαφθεῖραι τὸν καρπόν* (ibid. 26, 1).

preceding, was an accepted feature in the life of the Greek world. The foreign pirates were of little importance. The Tyrrhenians disappeared from the Aegean after the time of Demetrius, the Illyrians carried on their business in their own waters, the Black Sea pirates never passed the Straits. The Aegean was at the mercy of domestic pirates. The leading Hellenistic States never seriously endeavoured in this period to make the sea safe from their organized depredations. The Ptolemies, in the days of their thalassocracy, made no active attempt to suppress them altogether. They may have boasted of having done so, but such claims were no more than vain boasts.[11] From time to time their admirals would retaliate on the pirates for the pillage of territories which were under the protection of the Ptolemies.[12] But Philadelphus, during the First Syrian war (274) made use of organized bodies of pirates to carry out his famous raid on the coastal cities of the kingdom of Antiochus I, in this following the practice of Demetrius as described above.[13] Exactly the same was done by Antigonus Gonatas,* and repeatedly by the Aetolians from the time of Demetrius onwards.[14] Organized bands of pirates had their own well-protected harbours (not only in Crete) and were welcomed in all commercial ports when they appeared laden with their booty.

This was the situation in the times of the Successors. The story of the capture of Ephesus by Lysimachus from Demetrius, as told by Polyaenus and Frontinus, may serve as a typical example. When Demetrius was holding Ephesus and was devastating the neighbouring territories with the help of pirates, Lycus, Lysimachus' *strategos*, bribed Andron, the chief pirate in the service of Demetrius. One day Andron appeared in Ephesus bringing with him a large number of prisoners, ostensibly to sell them. The pretended prisoners were in fact soldiers of Lysimachus, who took the city and handed it over to their master.†

Nor did the situation change in the following period. A few interesting examples will show that Greece, especially in time of war—for instance during the Chremonidean war—was at

* Polyaen. 4, 6, 18 (about 276 B.C.).

† Front. *Strat.* 3. 3. 7; Polyaen. 5, 19.

the mercy of pirates and robbers. Delphi at that time had the greatest difficulty in securing, by means of embassies to the two kings Antigonus and Ptolemy, the safety of the *theoroi* who were travelling to Delphi for the celebration of the Pythia, and, by means of embassies to all the Greeks, the safety of those who intended to go to the Pylaia.* One is much tempted to assign to the same period the decree of the Amphictions of Delphi in honour of the *hieromnemones*,† who are lauded because they made 'the assembly at Pylae inviolate and secure'‡ and rendered it possible for all the Greeks to come to the festal assembly (*πανήγυρις*, perhaps the Soteria). There is mention of ambassadors being sent out to insist that the Delphian *asylia* should be respected. The same decree quotes the decision of the Aetolians 'that ransoms be nowhere exacted and that no one be carried off contrary to the Amphictionic laws'.§ This shows that the unlawful and unauthorized action of the Aetolian free-lances contributed greatly to the insecurity of the times. The Aetolian decree mentioned by the *hieromnemones* is probably still extant.||[15]

In this connexion mention may also be made of the well-known convention (*σύμβολον*) between Pellana in Achaea and Delphi, which may be dated either between 262 and 251 B.C. or earlier, between 285 and 280 B.C. In this treaty the two cities promise each other that 'the Delphian shall not carry off the Pellanean against his will, nor the Pellanean the Delphian'.¶ If somebody buys *mala fide* a free man, he loses the price and pays a fine. Similar protection is extended to cattle and slaves. The paragraph preceding that which has been quoted deals with goods 'taken out' from ships; if a man buys them, he is fined and the goods are held not to have been sold.** This and the following paragraphs show that piratical raids were a common feature in the Corinthian gulf in the third century B.C.[16]

* *S.E.G.* ii. 261; *F.D.* iii. 1, 479.

† *S.I.G.*³ 483.

‡ *τὴν] Πυλαίαν ἄσυλον καὶ ἀσφαλῆ* (l. 6).

§ *ἵνα μηδαμοῦ λύ]τρον γένηται καὶ μηθεὶς ἄγηται [παρὰ τοὺς νόμους τοὺς ἀμφικτιονικο]ύς* (l. 15 f.).

|| *I.G.* ix. 1, 2nd ed., 171—*S.I.G.*³ 484.

¶ *ὁ Δελφὺς τὺμ Πελλανέα [μὴ] ἀ[γέ|τω] μηδὲ ὁ Πελλανεὺς τὸ[ν] Δελφὸν εἰ μὴ κελ[εύοντος]* (or *κελ[εύοντα]*).

** I would suggest reading in l. 4 *αὐτά*, not *αὐτῶι*.

It was perhaps at about the same time (*c.* 252 B.C.) that Salamis was raided by pirates, probably in the service of Alexander of Corinth, and that Heraclitus of Athmonon, commander of the garrison of Piraeus for Antigonus, had great difficulty in protecting the island.*

The Aetolians, as we have seen, were masters in the art of carrying on war with the help of pirates. Their victims were, above all, the islands of the Aegean. These and the cities of the coast were devastated by successive raids. It is not surprising that some of them tried to protect themselves by special treaties with Aetolia. The scanty epigraphical evidence includes several decrees guaranteeing safety from Aetolian raids to particular islands and cities. It has been suggested that one group of them belongs to the years 254–239, another to the end of the third century, after 224/3, both these periods being times of anarchy in the Aegean. The first group consists of a decree relating to Delos, of another to Tenos and Ceos, of a third to Chios, of some fragments which may belong to a similar decree relating to Athens, and perhaps of the treaty between Miletus and Aetolia, which, however, is attributed by its editor to the second half of the third century and may therefore belong to the second group. In the second group appear Mytilene and Teos, also Magnesia on the Maeander.[17] The wording of the decrees is the same, with minor variations, in all the above instances. The terms of that relating to the Magnesians are as follows: 'It shall not be lawful for any Aetolian or resident in Aetolia to capture anyone travelling from any part of the territory of the Magnesians by land or sea. If any one shall do so, the chief magistrate in office shall exact such property as has been visibly carried off, and for property that has been made away with the councillors shall pass sentence of such fine as they may think fit, as on public malefactors, exacting the damages awarded and indemnifying the sufferers.'†

* *S.I.G.*[3] 454.

† *I.G.* ix. I, 2nd ed., no. 4, 17 ff: *καὶ μηθενὶ ἐξουσίαν εἶμεν | Αἰτωλῶν μηδὲ τῶν ἐν Αἰτωλίαι κατοικεόντων ἄγε[ι]ν | μηθένα ἐκ τᾶς χώρας τᾶς Μαγνήτων μηδαμόθεμ ὁρμω|μένους μήτε κατὰ γᾶν μήτε κατὰ θάλασσαν. εἰ δέ τίς | κα ἄγηι, τὰ μὲν ἐμφανέα ἀναπράσσειν ἀεὶ τὸν στρατα|γὸν τὸν ἔναρχον, τῶν δὲ ἀφανέων το(ὺ)ς συνέδρους κατα|δικάζοντας ζαμίαν, ἅν κα δοκιμάζωντι, ὡς τὰ κοινὰ βλαπτόντων*

A similar set of inscriptions show the Cretans adopting the same practice. Here again our information mostly relates to times of more or less acute troubles in the Hellenistic world. In one document* the city of Anaphe and her territory are declared inviolable (ἄσυλοι) by the Cretan league (κοινόν). A decree in Cretan dialect found at Athens may, as has been suggested, be regarded as a grant of *asylia* to Athens by a Cretan city.†

It should be noted that the pirates of Aetolia were in friendly relations with the Cretans and used the Cretan harbours as rallying-points and as places where they might dispose of their captives. There is a vivid illustration of these relations in the well-known Athenian decree in honour of Eumaridas of Cydonia.‡ After the raid of Bucris (during the Demetrian war) many of the captured Athenian citizens and other prisoners were transported by him to Crete. Eumaridas supplied money to redeem them and restore them to their country. This led to the dispatch of an embassy by Athens to the two rival city-leagues of Crete in order to arrive at an understanding with them and probably to obtain the grant of *asylia* (compare the document quoted above). Eumaridas was helpful to Athens in dealing with Cnossos and its allies and with Polyrrhenia. Later during the rule of Euryclides and Micion at Athens, he and his son were still helping the Athenians to keep on good terms with Crete.§

It was perhaps a little later (but before 220) that Miletus concluded treaties with Cnossos, Gortyn, and Phaestos. One of the clauses of these treaties regulates the conditions under which slaves who were formerly free citizens of Miletus or of the above-named Cretan cities are to regain their liberty. Those who bought them *mala fide*, that is, knowing that they were free men, lose their money and pay a fine.|| To the same group,

καὶ ἐκπράσσοντας τὰς καταδίκας καὶ ἀποδι|δόντας τοῖς ἀδικουμένοις κυρίο(υ)ς εἶμεν.

* *I.G.* xii. 3. 254; *G.D.I.* 5146 (third century B.C. ?), cf. A. Wilhelm, *Wien. Anz.*, 1924, p. 154; G. Daux, *B.C.H.* lix (1935), pp. 94 ff.; lxi (1937), pp. 439 ff. See also *I.G.* xii. 2. 17 (Mytilene).

† Ibid. ii, 2nd ed., 1130; *G.D.I.* 5148.

‡ *S.I.G.*^{3} 535.

§ Ibid. 536 and 537.

|| Rehm, *Milet, Erg. d. Ausgr.* iii. 1, no. 140; *Inscr. Cret.*, Cnossos 6, Phaestos 1*.

though of a later date, belong the various documents that settle the relations between Crete on the one side and Magnesia* and Mylasa† on the other (see further below). Later, in the second century, Paros makes a special treaty with the Cretan city of Allaria.‡[18]

The inscriptions mentioned above reveal another group of facts which testify to the uncertainty of life and property in Greece in the third century. It was an immemorial custom in Greece to regard the sanctuaries of gods as inviolable (ἄσυλα). Any one who infringed this sanctity of the god's house was guilty of sacrilege (ἱερόσυλος). The same sanctity attached to the great festivals of Olympia, Delphi, Corinth, &c., and to those who were invited to them and took part in them (ἐκεχειρία, 'truce'). There was no need of special grants of inviolability for the temples and festivals. The ἀσυλία was something sacred and was universally respected.

But times changed. Politics became a more powerful force than religion and some cases of violation of the ἐκεχειρία occurred in the Peloponnesian war and in the wars of the fourth century.[19] In the third century the whole of Greece heard with horror the terrible story of the attack of the Gauls on the temple of the Delphian Apollo and rejoiced at the miracle whereby the temple was saved. Yet the priests of Delphi were not entirely safe in their own sanctuary despite the fact that Delphi now stood under the protection of the Aetolians, the chief disturbers of the peace. Reference has already been made to the inscription that shows the difficulty experienced by delegates and pilgrims in reaching Delphi at the time of the Chremonidean war, and another striking fact may be added. The Dionysiac artists of Athens as early as 278/7 B.C. felt that they could not travel with safety in Greece unless they were protected by a special decree of the Amphictions granting them in the name of all the Greeks (ὑπὸ πάντων τῶν Ἑλλήνων), as non-combatants and exempt in Athens from military service, complete immunity from molestation.[20]

We are accordingly not surprised to find that temples and organizers of games, if they lacked the protection conferred by ancient origin and venerable reputation, did their best, by

* *G.D.I.* 5153–6. † Ibid. 5157–63. ‡ Ibid. 4940.

diplomatic negotiations (especially with the most dangerous of the sacrilegious powers) to secure a recognition of inviolability. We possess a set of inscriptions in which certain cities inform kings, leagues, and individual cities (ἐπάγγελμα) of a miraculous appearance (*epiphaneia*) of their god or goddess, in consequence of which new religious celebrations have been instituted, and request that the sanctity and inviolability of the temples concerned, and sometimes of the cities containing them, may be respected. In reply the parties addressed politely acknowledge the receipt of the ἐπάγγελμα, and some of them agree to respect the sanctity of the temples and cities in question. We have many fragments of such exchanges of letters, the most complete being those which concern Magnesia on the Maeander and Teos.[21] The earliest documents of this type belong to the middle of the third century. The initiative in such cases appears to have been taken by the Amphictions.[22] The new practice spread rapidly all over Greece at the end of the third and in the second century, when cases of sacrilege (ἱεροσυλία) were becoming common. We have such incidents as the sack by the Aetolians of important and revered temples, for example of Artemis at Lusoi, of Poseidon at Taenarum, of Hera at Argos, of Poseidon at Mantinea, as early as 244; and the famous pillage by the same Aetolians of the great sanctuaries of Dion and Dodona in 219 B.C., which Philip requited by the sack of the chief Aetolian sanctuary at Thermos. These outrages brought home to the Greek communities how precarious was the immunity of most of their sacred places.

The comments of Polybius on the Aetolian ἱεροσυλίαι and the bitter words of Lyciscus of Acarnania at Sparta in 211 B.C., reported by the same historian, show how deeply Greece resented these acts of sacrilege. This indignation and the comments of Polybius show that they were a new and unheard of occurrence.[23]

The facts to which I have drawn attention indicate that methods of warfare, so far from improving, were becoming more barbarous. The measures that the cities took were measures of self-defence and cannot be adduced as evidence of a gradual humanization of war during the Hellenistic period. Moreover, they had no enduring effect. Sacrilege, on the contrary, became for more than a century a matter of common occurrence.

To return to the pirates, we find the plague of piracy raging all over the Aegean during the period 280–221. It was more acute in troubled times, especially during great wars, but even in comparative peace the pirates were active. The kidnapped citizen of a Greek city is a familiar figure to every student of Hellenistic literature, for example in the comedies of Menander as regards the time of the Successors, and in the Hellenistic epigrams as illustrating these and later times. Scores of inscriptions refer to piratical raids and to the tragic experiences of men, women, and children kidnapped by the pirates and sold into slavery. A mere list of the places mentioned in inscriptions of the third century as having suffered from their inroads gives a vivid idea of the insecurity of the coastal cities of Greece and Asia Minor: Thera, Naxos, Amorgos, Anaphe, Delos, Chios, Teos, Tenos, Ceos, Salamis, Cyprus, Magnesia on the Maeander, Miletus, Theangela in Caria, and the coasts of Attica.[24]

Here again the picture has two sides. The phenomenon was not new. Piracy had indeed been practised in Greece from time immemorial. But the frequency of the Hellenistic inscriptions that refer to it, though inscriptions of this period are comparatively rare, indicates that this ancient practice had now become very common and was carried on with cynical ruthlessness. There is further evidence of this in the fact that it was not till the fourth century that the Greek islands began to build watch-towers and refuge-towers to protect their peaceful population against pirate raids, and such activity is specially notable in the third century.[25] Public opinion reacted sharply to this new social phenomenon. The Greeks were keenly sensible of their solidarity with the unfortunate victims. Measures to put an end to the lawless raids were out of their power and they showed their feelings in a different way. It was quite a common occurrence at this time for charitable souls, who saw respectable citizens of some friendly community exposed for sale on their slave market, to come up and pay their ransom, or help them in some other way.[26]

Nor was the situation of the cities on the mainland in any respect better. There are several references in our scanty literary texts to raids of armies and of robber-bands in which thousands of men were taken and sold into slavery. Mention has been made of the case of Mantinea (223 B.C.), where the whole population, men, women, and children, were sold. Another example may be given. When the Aetolians raided Laconia, shortly before the reforms of Cleomenes, 50,000 slaves were carried off.* The figures may be exaggerated, but it is none the less certain that not only the raids of the Aetolians but all similar raids, for instance those led by the Illyrian Skerdilaidas (as described by Polybius) resulted in similar abductions of hundreds and sometimes of thousands of free men and slaves.[27] In a manner very characteristic of the conditions of his day, Plutarch quotes the remark of an old Spartan with regard to this abduction from Laconia of 50,000 men, probably *perioeci*, helots, and slaves, that the enemy had done Laconia a good turn by relieving it of a burden.†

It may be added that the practice of carrying off and selling into slavery large numbers of combatants and non-combatants was not confined to Greece. Ptolemy Philadelphus and his successor Euergetes brought home many captives taken in the course of their wars, especially in Syria. Some of these became slaves, some—who had been soldiers—may have become cleruchs (*κληροῦχοι*), others again may have been employed as 'royal peasants' (*βασιλικοὶ γεωργοί*) to cultivate the newly reclaimed lands in the Fayûm, or as shepherds to tend the royal herds of sheep and goats, which had probably also formed part of the booty.[28]

To return to Greece. The large number of prisoners of war taken in Greece during the wars of the third century may in a great measure be attributed to the poverty of the country, to the very low standard of life prevailing in most of the cities, and to the almost purely agricultural character of the greater part of the territory. The only booty with which the belligerents could defray the expense of a war—and most of them relied on doing this—consisted of men, whether free or slaves, and cattle. Note, for example, the account given by Polybius of the capture of Megalopolis and of Mantinea, which will be dealt with

* Plut. *Cleom.* 18, 3.

† *ὡς ὤνησαν οἱ πολέμιοι τὴν Λακωνικὴν ἀποκουφίσαντες.*

presently. We may take it therefore as established that life was very precarious in Greece in the third century B.C., and that personal liberty was as precarious as life. Many who were free men one day had become slaves the next.

Those prisoners of war whose families were well-to-do or who had wealthy and influential friends did not remain slaves for ever. I have already indicated that there existed among the upper classes of the population of Greece a kind of common understanding, of mutual insurance, which operated for the release of captives of these classes. But nobody cared about the metics, the proletarians of the towns, or the poor peasants: any of these once sold on the slave market remained slaves. The ransoming (λύτρωσις), it must be emphasized, was as a rule a private affair. The cities as such were helpless: their means were limited and their diplomatic measures generally futile.

The uncertainty of life, the precarious character of personal freedom, and the general instability in Greece were unfavourable to sound economic and social development. Add to this the permanent factors which, even in normal times, retarded the country's economic progress: the poverty of the soil, the scarcity of minerals, timber, and other raw materials of industry, and above all the inveterate particularism of the Greek city-states, the minute political subdivision of Greece and the ambition of each city to dominate over the rest (*Herrschaftstrieb*, as B. Keil terms it), peculiarities which found their expression not only in the political but also in the economic life of the country. Some eminent scholars have suggested that this economic particularism was moderated in the period we are considering by the formation of Greek leagues or *sympoliteiai*, especially the larger ones, such as the Achaean, Aetolian, and Boeotian Leagues. But it is not certain that a Greek league as such formed an economic as well as a political unit, that a citizen of a State-member of a given league automatically received in all the cities of that league full economic rights, in particular the right of acquiring real property, the right of holding land and house (ἔγκτησις γῆς καὶ οἰκίας), and the concomitant right of intermarriage (ἐπιγαμία). A student of Greek political life so distinguished as H. Swoboda has thought it was not so, since many Greek inscriptions of the time indicate that these rights were given in proxeny decrees by one city to the citizens of another city of the same *koinon*. It has been pointed out that the proxeny decrees are often purely honorary documents drafted in accordance with a long-established formula, and that they do not necessarily mean what they say. It is surprising, however, to find the formula used so frequently and repeating the same items, including the grant of ἔγκτησις γῆς καὶ οἰκίας and ἐπιγαμία. This repetition of the old formula suggests that the grant of these rights, even within the same league, had a certain and probably a crucial importance. In any case, the existence of the leagues, though it may have mitigated to some extent the detrimental effects of economic particularism, certainly made no radical change in the inveterate habits and the economic selfishness of the Greek cities.[29]

The most striking consequence of these political and economic factors was the impoverishment of the country, especially of certain regions, where in the second half of the third century it proceeded very rapidly. It was duly noticed and registered by contemporary observers, especially because of the contrast it presented to the flourishing conditions of the new Eastern monarchies. Here are a few examples.

Plutarch, when speaking of the wealth of the Spartan kings in the time of Agis and Cleomenes, remarks that the slaves of the Oriental satraps and of the stewards of Ptolemy and Seleucus were richer than all the Spartan kings taken together.[30]

A still more explicit and exact statement is made by Polybius in connexion with the booty taken by Cleomenes at Megalopolis. He emphatically challenges the assertion of Phylarchus that 6,000 talents' worth of spoil (λάφυρα) were taken by Cleomenes. This sum, he declares, was grossly exaggerated. 'I say,' he remarks, 'speaking not of the time when the Peloponnese had been utterly ruined by the Macedonian kings and still more through the continuous wars of its inhabitants with one another, but of our own times, in which . . . the Peloponnese is believed to enjoy the greatest prosperity, that it would be impossible to collect such a sum from the whole Peloponnese, from the movable property (ἔπιπλα) without reckoning human beings (σώματα).'* And he adds in the same passage that in fact Megalopolis and

* Polyb. ii. 62. 1.

Mantinea—large cities reputed to be rich—only yielded to their conquerors (the Lacedaemonians and Antigonus) booty to the value of 300 talents each.

In his masterly comments on this passage A. Wilhelm shows that the greater part of this sum of 300 talents consisted of the proceeds of the sale of captives, and that the value of the movable property, excluding cattle, on the farms probably did not exceed from 75 to 100 talents.

The statement of Polybius, who was much better informed on the subject than some modern scholars who are inclined to doubt him, shows how low the standard of life had fallen in some of the leading cities of Greece (both Megalopolis and Mantinea were, of course, agricultural cities possessing little industry or trade) and how small was their accumulated capital. It was certainly a new phenomenon in the life of the Peloponnese, and Polybius was certainly right in attributing it to the continuous warfare.[31]

The general causes which contributed to the gradual decline of wealth in Greece naturally affected all classes of the population. The few very rich people suffered probably less than the rest. But all the evidence relating to Greece in the fourth and third centuries shows that the solid background of Greek political, social, and economic life lay not in the few men of great wealth, but in the middle class, the *bourgeoisie*, who were mostly landowners. I have shown that this was so at Athens in the time of Menander. The same is true of the Achaean League and probably of many, if not all, the other cities. The taxes and the liturgies were chiefly borne by the middle class, a subject with which I shall deal in greater detail in the next chapter. This class certainly suffered grievously from the wars and their concomitant evils. In some cities—for example at Sparta, of which I shall speak presently—the middle class disappeared almost entirely, wealth and especially landed property becoming concentrated in a few hands. Some hitherto well-to-do families were degraded to the status of proletarians. These changed conditions, which were not confined to Sparta, were noticed by contemporaries. We possess by chance an utterance of Cercidas of Megalopolis, who was not a revolutionary, but rather a member of the well-to-do class and a prominent politician: a sentence in it sounds like a warning, addressed to the wealthy, of the coming revolution, when they will be forced to 'disgorge' (γείοθεν ἐξεμέσαι) the wealth which they have appropriated. The middle class did not, of course, sink suddenly into proletarianism: the process was slow and gradual. Nevertheless, even at this stage of development, it certainly added to the general bewilderment and unrest.

The increasing number of people who had no property or very little and who lived on what they earned from day to day by hard work, was in itself a source of danger. Add to this that in all probability, though there are no data to support the statement, opportunities of employment were constantly diminishing and the rate of remuneration for work of every kind was constantly falling.

We have no means of ascertaining the extent to which slave labour competed with free labour. I have indicated the reasons (capture of prisoners of war, piracy at sea, raids on land, &c.) which lead me to believe that slaves were abundant on the Greek market in the third century. It is unfortunate that acts of manumission, which in the second century are so numerous at Delphi, in and around Naupactus, in Thessaly, and in other parts of Greece, are exceedingly rare in the third, and that they yield no information as to the numbers and countries of origin of slaves in that century. The impression I have derived from a study of the scanty extant material is that the number of slaves was not diminishing in the third century in Greece as a whole, though it may have been falling in Athens alone.[32]

Apart from the competition of slave labour, the difficulty of finding employment for the increasing number of proletarians was intensified by a development that affected production and exchange throughout Greece. This was the decreasing demand for Greek products, especially for manufactured goods, alike in Greece itself and in foreign markets. In Greece it was a result of the impoverishment of the middle class and of the reduced purchasing power of the public, due to the causes that I have set forth; elsewhere it was due to the slow but steady emancipation of the East, especially Egypt, Syria, and Asia Minor, from dependence on Greece for industrial goods made for mass consumption. I shall return to this development later in this chapter. It certainly had an adverse effect on the demand for labour in Greece, which did not increase *pari passu* with the increasing supply of labour.

Finally, it is highly probable that owing to the competition of slave labour and the decreasing demand for hired workmen, wages were decreasing, while the prices of foodstuffs and manufactured goods were not falling in proportion. We have no data relating to continental Greece, but the curves of food prices and of wages in Delos are very illuminating, and Heichelheim may be right in affirming that these hold good for the rest of the Hellenistic world, or at any rate for Greece.[33]

Thus the contrast between the rising number of the poor and the diminishing number of those in whose hands wealth was increasingly concentrated, became more and more pronounced and fraught with greater danger, as the discontent of the proletarians grew more acute. Naturally this state of things led to civil wars and revolutions. The classical example is Sparta in the times of Agis and Cleomenes.

The story of Agis IV and of his successor Cleomenes is so well known to all students of ancient history that a short summary will here suffice. According to the trustworthy narrative of Phylarchus, the citizen body of Sparta, when Agis succeeded to the throne, had become very small. All the land was in the hands of a small group of wealthy people, among them many women. The majority of the population were paupers, men who had lost their land and consequently their citizenship. In order to restore Sparta to her former strength and perhaps to relieve the distress of the poorer classes, Agis endeavoured to carry out an economic and social reform. For a long time the idea of a reform or revolution of this kind had taken root in the minds of the Greeks. The project comprised two main and two ancillary measures. The principal measures of a positive character were abolition of debts and, as was natural in a mainly agricultural country, redistribution of landed property (χρεῶν ἀποκοπή and γῆς ἀναδασμός). As a preliminary to the redistribution of land confiscation of property was imperative, and as an effective means of achieving this, liberation of slaves was often resorted to.

Agis attempted to carry out this programme by peaceful

means. Debts were cancelled, since this suited the interests both of the landless poor and of the majority of landowners, whose land was mostly mortgaged. But it never came to redistribution of land. This, of course, could not be effected without a revolution, and Agis was unwilling or unable to go so far. He perished at the hands of his political enemies. His heritage, however, was taken up and his programme carried through by Cleomenes, who did not shrink from a *coup d'état.* I need not repeat the story of Cleomenes, or do more than recall the profound impression produced by his reforms on the rest of Greece and the revolutionary fever that rapidly spread all over the Peloponnese, almost shattering the Achaean League, which was based on the rule of the *bourgeois* class in the cities. Had it not been for the concessions made by Aratus to Antigonus and for the unwillingness of Cleomenes to carry out the full programme of his supporters, a social revolution on a large scale, perhaps throughout Greece, might have been the result of the reforms of Agis and Cleomenes, which they themselves regarded as rather political than economic and social.

The conditions at Sparta were typical of those prevailing throughout Greece in the third century. Class war was rife and the sharp social contrast between rich and poor led to acute conflicts in many cities, both in Greece proper and in the islands. I may remind the reader of the expressions used in the inscriptions quoted above, in which magistrates are praised for having maintained during their term of office peace, prosperity, legality, and concord (εὐνομία and ὁμόνοια). This formula shows that in the mind of contemporaries the principal factors that disrupted the normal life of a city and brought misery in their train were war and revolution.

The revolutions (ταραχαί in the official terminology) took various forms, the most usual being the establishment of a tyranny supported by the proletariat. The tyrants of that time—most of them protégés of Macedonia—were not all of them of the bad kind like Apollodorus, tyrant of Cassandreia, whose atrocities were proverbial, and Aristotimus, tyrant of Elea. Some were excellent rulers, such as Aristomachus of Argos and Aristodemus of Megalopolis. Yet none of them was ever able to establish his rule on a firm basis. It was generally ended by assassination, and strife began again within the city, a strife mainly of a political character, but often governed in part by social and economic considerations. The lure held out by most of these tyrants was the old one of redistribution of property and abolition of debts. But this programme was never carried out in full in any Greek city even with the help of tyrants. The proletariat by itself, without assistance from outside, was helpless, and those who had military resources at their disposal were not friends of social revolution.[34]

Most of the evidence that I have adduced relates to the Peloponnese and to the latter part of the period under review. It was certainly the Peloponnese that was the chief sufferer during this period, for wars and revolutions were less prevalent in the rest of Greece and especially in certain parts of central Greece.

We cannot therefore generalize, and we must be careful not to exaggerate. We must bear in mind that Greece, in spite of her poor natural resources, had developed these remarkably by the long and steady efforts of her people. There is not the slightest doubt that even in the third century Greece was one of the best cultivated countries in the world. Her vineyards and olive-groves, her fruit-gardens and kitchen gardens were famous. The standard of her agriculture and the quality of her pasturage were very high. Thousands of men turned to account the wealth of the sea: there was abundance of fish, salt, sponges, and shell-fish for dyeing, and their exploitation was well organized. Mines and quarries were worked as long as there were minerals and the better kinds of stone, especially marble, to extract. Greek industry had a long past behind it, and the Greek artisans were still the most efficient and the most artistic. Trade relations were firmly established between the various parts of the Greek world.

Constant wars, the competition of the East, decline of exports, diminution of purchasing power in the home market, gradually undermined the prosperity of Greece. But it was a slow process, hardly understood by contemporary observers, and, as I have shown, it did not affect all parts of Greece simultaneously. We find accordingly nothing about economic decay in the few surviving fragments of an anonymous work (sometimes attributed to Heraclides Criticus), written probably in the second half of the third century, containing witty and amusing sketches of some of the cities of central Greece—of Attica, Boeotia, and Euboea (but of none situated in the Peloponnese), though the author is keenly interested in the economic life of the cities that he describes. Attica appears in these sketches as a well-cultivated country producing the choicest foodstuffs: 'the products of the soil are all invaluable and unrivalled in point of flavour, but becoming somewhat scarce'.* Boeotia is a flourishing agricultural region. On its coast the population is busy about the sea: at Anthedon they are fishing, extracting purple, collecting sponges, building ships, and ferrying to Euboea. Oropus is full of customs-officers (of doubtful honesty), of travellers and merchants.[35] The harbour and emporium of Chalcis are no less crowded with merchants. Some of the roads are good and well provided with comfortable inns, though very few are safe from robbers. There is not a word about poverty and economic distress in these parts of Greece. Athens, it is true, is no longer the Athens of the past. She is still a glorious city, a centre of amusements, of art, and of intellectual life. But home-grown foodstuffs, though fine, are rather scarce (*σπανιώτερα*), and food shortage (*λιμός*) is a constant trouble. Nothing is said about the Piraeus, the harbour, the trade of Athens. They certainly did not impress the author. Athens is full of foreigners. But they come as tourists and students, not as business men and traders. At Oropus and Chalcis trade is the leading characteristic; not so at Athens. It is a pity that we have no description of Corinth, the Peloponnese, and Thessaly (the fragment about Thessaly does not belong to the same work and is purely geographical). But what remains is of inestimable value and highly instructive both as regards the mentality of educated men and as regards the economic aspect of part of Greece at that time.[36]

I wish that I could supplement this picture by an analysis of the social and economic conditions in particular cities of continental Greece. It must be remembered that life in these cities was highly diversified and individualistic. If we consider

* *τὰ γινόμενα ἐκ τῆς γῆς πάντα ἀτίμητα καὶ πρῶτα τῇ γεύσει, μικρῷ δὲ σπανιώτερα.*

PLATE XXX

1. An old nurse seated in a chair holding in her lap a naked baby. Tanagra.

F. Winter, *Die antiken Terrakotten*, iii. *Die Typen der figürlichen Terrakotten*, ii, 1903, p. 465, no. 12; *C.A.H.*, Vol. of Pls., iii, p. 193*c*; cf. E. Pottier and S. Reinach, *La Nécropole de Myrina*, 1887, Cat., no. 258. Known in many variations.

2. A young slave holding a child on his left shoulder. In his right hand a lantern, from his left is suspended a round basket, perhaps containing food. The child wears a crown, probably returning from a party. Myrina. (Photograph supplied by the authorities of the Staatliche Museen, Berlin.)

F. Winter, loc. cit., p. 404, no. 5; cf. E. Pottier and S. Reinach, loc. cit., Cat., no. 336 and p. 454. Type often repeated in several variations.

3. A bearded pedagogue (house slave ?) seated in a chair giving a boy instruction in reading and perhaps writing. On the knees of the boy a diptych. The lower part of the group is missing. Myrina.

E. Pottier and S. Reinach, loc. cit., Cat., no. 287 and p. 396 f., pl. XXIX; F. Winter loc. cit., p. 405, no. 5. Many variations. See for example the Br. Mus. *Guide to the Exhibition illustrating Greek and Roman Life*, 1929, p. 205, fig. 224; O. Crusius and R. Herzog, *Die Mimiamben des Herondas*, 1926—illustrations to Herondas, *Mim.* iii: *Διδάσκαλος*, &c.

4. A studious schoolgirl seated in a chair holding in her lap by her left hand a diptych; in her right hand a stilus (?). Tanagra. (Photograph supplied by the authorities of the National Museum, Athens.)

F. Winter, loc. cit., p. 123, no. 6; *C.A.H.*, loc. cit., p. 193 d. Cf. E. Pottier and S. Reinach, loc. cit., p. 415, pl. XXXIII, Cat., no. 256, cf. 257, and E. Breccia, *Terrecotte figurate . . . del Museo di Alessandria*, i, 1930, nos. 138–140. Many variations. In some cases the student is a boy.

The group of Hellenistic terracotta figurines, some specimens of which are reproduced in this, the following four, and several other plates of the present book, is a mine of information about the various aspects of the life of the people of the Hellenistic world, chiefly the Greeks of the cities and rural districts. The group is a very large one (although it is only a small subdivision of ancient figurines in general). Almost every figurine exists in replicas found all over the Hellenistic world, in Greece, in Asia Minor, in Syria, in Egypt, in Cyrenaica, and each type is known in several variations. Alongside of these Panhellenistic types we find others which are local, for instance those peculiar to Hellenistic Egypt (pl. L), or Syria (pl. LIX). Most of the figurines have been found in graves (the necropolis of Myrina in Asia Minor and that of Tanagra in Boeotia were especially rich in figurines of the type illustrated here), but many have also been found in ruins of ancient cities (for instance Priene, Pergamon, Alexandria and Seleuceia on the Tigris).

The purpose of the terracotta figurines of the type here represented and of other types is matter of dispute and cannot be discussed here. Some of them are reflections of actual life, others, such as the figurines of tragic and comic actors, derive from the stage. Since most of those represented in this and the following plates stress the comic side of a figure or group, and represent these without masks, they probably reproduce famous characters of the mimes. They may therefore be used to illustrate the *Mimes* of Herondas, and have been so used (O. Crusius and R. Herzog, *Die Mimiamben des Herondas*, 1926). A corpus of this type of figurines with comments would prove highly useful to all students of ancient life and art.

PLATE XXX

1. Paris, Louvre.

2. Berlin, Staatliche Museen.

3. Paris, Louvre.

4. Athens, National Museum.

LIFE IN GREEK CITIES. BABYHOOD AND CHILDHOOD

Terracotta figurines.

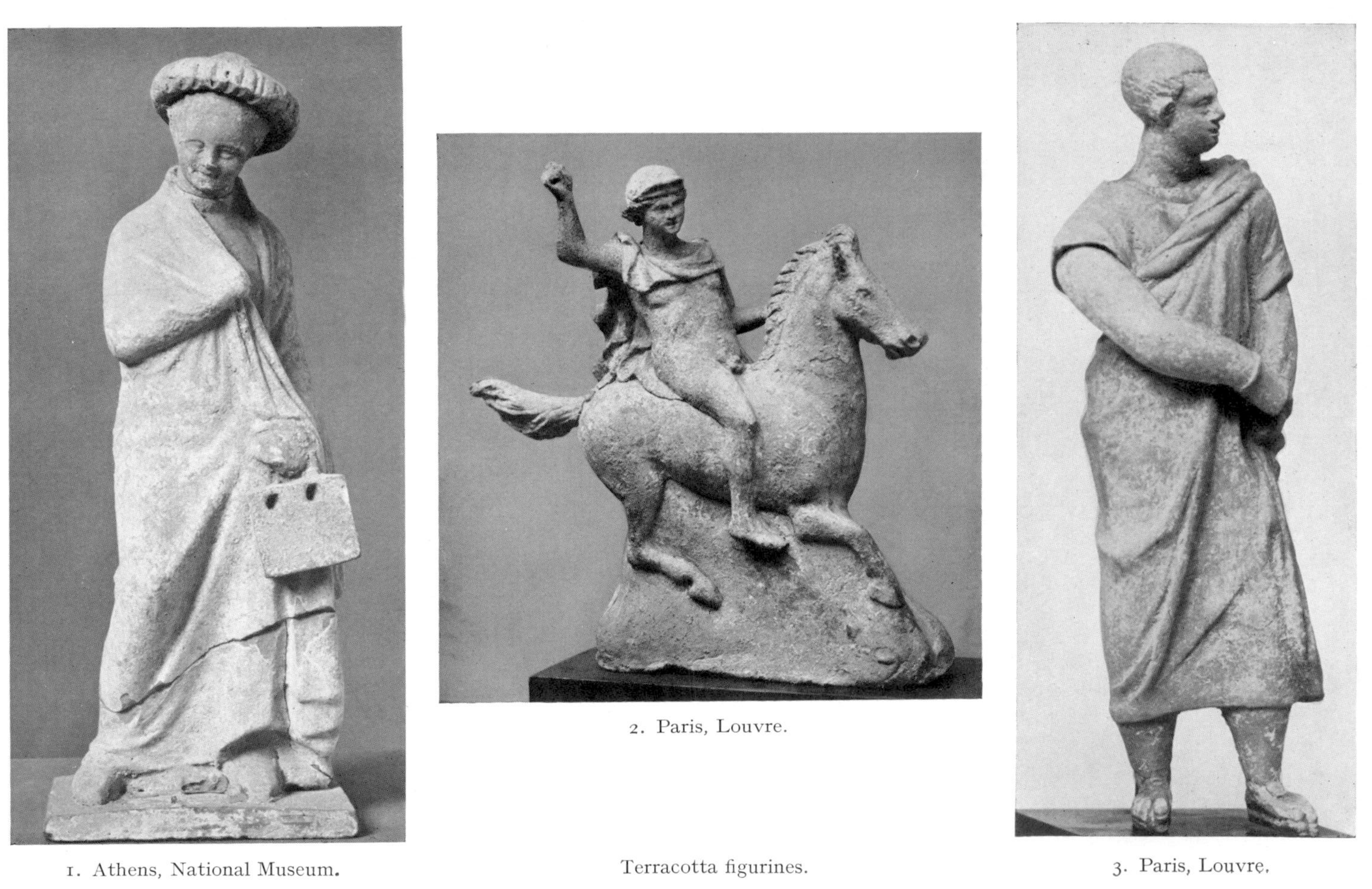

1. Athens, National Museum.

2. Paris, Louvre.

3. Paris, Louvre.

Terracotta figurines.

LIFE IN GREEK CITIES. BOYS AND YOUNG MEN

PLATE XXXI

1. A schoolboy with a crown of flowers on his head (victor in a school contest?), probably returning in winter time from the school after his victory. Dressed in a heavy cloak. Holding in his left hand his school-bag. He looks very happy. Tanagra. (Photograph supplied by the authorities of the National Museum, Athens.)

F. Winter, loc. cit., p. 240, no. 2. Schoolboys and ephebes were very popular with the Hellenistic coroplasts. A glance at the publications of Winter and E. Pottier and S. Reinach will suffice to demonstrate this.

2. An ephebe on horseback. Charming statuette from Asia Minor. The boy is naked but for a chlamys fastened on his right shoulder. On his head a cap or a helmet. His uplifted right hand probably held a lance or a dart. Military training of a noble youth?

F. Winter, loc. cit., p. 299, no. 7. An ephebe on horseback is not a very common type of ancient terracottas; see for example E. Pottier and S. Reinach, loc. cit., Cat., no. 315; E. Breccia, *Terrecotte figurate . . . del Museo di Alessandria*, i, 1930, no. 141, pl. XXXIX, 1. This statuette may be earlier than the third century B.C.; cf. for the motive J. Charbonneaux, *Les terres cuites grecques*, 1936 (the Amazon on horseback of the Boston Museum).

3. A young man apparently delivering a public speech. He is dressed in a chiton and a long chlamys; on his feet thick sandals. He is looking at his audience with pride and confidence. We may assign this figurine to the group that illustrates school life and interpret the figure as that of a member of the class of the *νέοι* in the Gymnasium, a scion of an aristocratic family delivering a speech in an oratorical contest. Or we may think that the young man is an actor in a mime, playing the part of a magistrate or a lawyer. I may remind the reader of Herondas *Mim.* ii: Battarus before the court. The statuette is a beautiful specimen of Greek art of the Hellenistic period showing in plastic form the same features that characterize the comedies of Menander, the *Characters* of Theophrastus, and the *Mimes* of Herondas; in other words, displaying the same masterly treatment of typical traits of a 'character'. Myrina.

E. Pottier and S. Reinach, loc. cit., p. 476, pl. XLVI, Cat., no. 277; *C.A.H.*, loc. cit., p. 191*c*; J. Charbonneaux, loc. cit., fig. 87, p. 20.

various categories—the sanctuaries of Delphi and Olympia, of Epidaurus and Eleusis, of Oropus, of Dodona, the Ptôion, and many others, existing in close connexion with their respective cities but not entirely absorbed by them; next, Athens and Corinth, the two great centres of commerce, industry, and banking in the past, now gradually losing their industrial and commercial importance, and the several minor industrial and commercial cities such as Sicyon, Gythium, Patrae, Naupactus, &c.; then Sparta, Argos, Megalopolis, Mantinea, Messene, and the Achaean cities in the Peloponnese, most of them almost purely agricultural communities with very little industry and commerce; Thebes and the other agricultural cities of Boeotia; the primitive communities of shepherds and peasants in Arcadia, Acarnania, and especially Aetolia—we find that all possessed their own peculiar economic and social structure, their own interests and preoccupations. The Hellenistic period brought very little change in their mode of life and did little to unify and standardize it.

Such a task, however, cannot be undertaken here, for it would involve much special study for which hardly any preparatory work has been done. We do not possess in respect of other Greek cities the abundant material that illustrates all stages of the history of Athens and Delphi. These cities, in the Hellenistic period, have found eloquent and competent interpreters in S. Jebelev and W. S. Ferguson (for Athens), E. Bourguet, P. Roussel, R. Flacelière, and G. Daux (for Delphi). The situation is quite different in respect of the other cities of Greece. Our literary texts are scanty, for the Hellenistic period was not the most brilliant in their lives. Nor is our epigraphical information abundant: the Classical and Roman periods have in this respect the advantage. Some of the cities, no doubt, have been recently excavated and have yielded important ruins, works of the great and minor arts, and inscriptions. Such are Corinth, Sparta, Olympia, Epidaurus, Oropus, the Ptôion, Dodona, Eleusis, and some others. Much excellent work has been done by the excavators of these cities. The results at Olympia have been published in full. Rapid progress is being made with Corinth and Sparta. For the other excavated cities we have excellent preliminary reports and studies based on part of the excavated material. But it cannot be said that what has been published affords a sufficient basis for an historian of the Hellenistic period. Hellenistic material is meagre and not much in favour with excavators and students of antiquity. Thus some of the discoveries, and especially those of chief importance for the student of economic history, are neglected or their publication is indefinitely postponed. I refer to pottery, terracottas, what are known as minor bronzes, bronze and iron implements, &c. Jars in general, and especially the stamped ones, which are found in all the excavations but are very rarely published, are of great significance. Until this material is published, the study of the economic life of individual cities and of Greece as a whole presents grave difficulties. And without study of this kind historians are forced to confine themselves to general sketches such as the above.[37]

I will, however, give some account of the two best-known cities of Greece, Athens and Delphi, during our period, or rather summarize what has been said on the subject by the scholars named above.

ATHENS, after her liberation from the rule of Poliorcetes and especially after Corupedion, lived a peaceful and creative life for about a score of years under the beneficent rule of Gonatas, who made the city his intellectual capital. Her cleruchies in the Thracian sea were restored to her by Antiochus I (279/8 B.C.); Antigonus, though he kept a garrison in the Piraeus, did not encroach on her political rights and autonomy; her prestige was high in the Hellenistic world and the Hellenistic rulers were glad to be of service to her. Her own mood was peaceful and she was not disposed to embark on risky and ambitious projects. Though threatened by the Celtic invasion, she had not been affected by it.

Athens was still the great intellectual and artistic capital of the Greek world, a centre of great creative activity in the fields of philosophy, drama, history, science, and art; and in all probability she kept her leading place in the economic field, though her pre-eminence here was, of course, less marked. The Macedonian garrison in the Piraeus had not only a political meaning. Gonatas wished to control this important harbour because in all probability he made it his commercial centre, his main clearing-house—a rival, as it were, to Rhodes and Delos, the great emporia of the Ptolemies, and to Miletus and Ephesus, the control of which passed to and fro between the Ptolemies and the Seleucids. The scope of Athenian trade was no doubt now more restricted than it had been, but Athens was still the principal commercial centre of the northern Aegean and the Pontus. It is, for example, significant that, soon after her liberation from Demetrius, Spartocus III, king of Bosporus, hastened to renew his relations with Athens and to contract with her a regular *symmachia* (289/8 B.C.),* and that Audoleon, king of the Paeonians, sent her his congratulations and a substantial gift (289/8 B.C.).† There is no reason to suppose that these friendly relations changed in the subsequent years. The action of Spartocus and Audoleon was certainly not dictated by sentimental reasons, but reflected the active business relations between them and Athens. Greece was still an important, nay the most important, market for Paeonia, Thrace, and the Pontus. The privileges conferred by the Delphians about 252–1 (?) on a group of seventeen persons from various places in Chalcidice, Thessaly, Macedonia, Thrace, the Propontis and the Pontus (Callatis, Chersonesus, Olbia, Panticapaeum) may have been the result of a voyage of Delphian *theoroi*. The route of the *theoroi* was probably not very different from the standard itinerary of the Athenian merchants of the time.‡ The conditions prevailing at Athens at this time were much the same as in the preceding period, for the numerous extant fragments of the New Comedy by authors later than Menander present the same type of society and display the same picture of social and economic life.

The Chremonidean war (267/6–261 B.C.) marks a break in the quiet life of the city and the beginning of a time of troubles and difficulties. This is not the place to relate the history of the agitated period during and after that war. Suffice it to say that, after the humiliation of 263 or 261 B.C., Athens remained until 229 a part of the Macedonian kingdom, faithful to her masters Antigonus Gonatas and Demetrius II. Their rule was not oppressive. The policy of Antigonus towards Athens was

* *S.I.G.*[3] 370. † Ibid. 371.

‡ R. Flacelière, *Les Aitoliens à Delphes*, p. 220 and p. 459, no. 46, a. 4.

always a liberal one, and became more liberal amid the embarrassments of his last years, when he was at war with the Ptolemies and struggling for the control of Greece. After his death in 239 his policy was carried on by his successor.

Our evidence regarding the social and economic life of Athens at this time cannot be compared with that available for the two preceding periods. We know the difficulty of her position in the last years of Antigonus and how hard pressed she was at the time of the Demetrian war. The Achaean invasions of Attica by land and the Aetolian raids on the coast (Bucris) were a severe ordeal. Both the land and sea frontiers of Attica were guarded by detachments of Athenians and Macedonians, which required a great military effort on the part of the city; yet these military measures failed to repel the invaders. No wonder that life in the city during the war was far from normal, that regular religious performances were suspended, that the grain supply of the city was disorganized, and that owing to financial stress it had frequently to resort to extraordinary measures. The acuteness of the crisis is illustrated by the numerous decrees in honour of commanders of the troops on garrison or guard duty, and by the Athenian decree of 232/1 organizing an ἐπίδοσις or subscription, 'in order that out of the sums contributed the treasurer may be able to meet the expenditure and that during the remainder of the year the harvest of the fields may be gathered in safety'—in other words, to defray the cost of the detachments of troops that guarded Attica. It should also be mentioned that Athens was forced probably about this time to have recourse to loans: a loan by Thespiae* and one by Thebes† are recorded in inscriptions of these cities.

But the evils of the situation must not be overstated nor its dark side alone presented. As a Macedonian city under the protection of the Macedonians, Athens did not lose all her business connexions, especially in the period before the Demetrian war. Macedonian Delos, for reasons not quite clear to us, was competing with Athens in the grain trade at this

* *I.G.* vii. 1737, 1738.

† Ibid. 2405, 2406. I may mention that the dates of the Thespian and Theban inscriptions are conjectural.

time, with the support, it may be, of Antigonus and Demetrius, but this competition did not seriously undermine the Athenian trade. Delos may have been patronized by Antigonus and Demetrius because the place was safer than Athens and its relations with Rhodes and the East were friendly, or they may have been influenced by political considerations. In any case Athens and her citizens were not ruined. The subscription mentioned above brought in a considerable sum, and there were still some very rich men among the Athenians. I may mention the famous Euryclides, who spent his fortune liberally for the benefit of Athens and yet was able to leave sufficient to his heirs to make them one of the richest families in the city. Wealth could hardly be acquired at Athens without active participation in commerce either directly or indirectly. Everything considered, we may say that the period of Macedonian domination, differing in this respect from that of Macedonian protectorate, was not a time of peace and prosperity for Athens; her economic life was in its decline and prosperous citizens were an exception. But it was not a time of ruin, misery, and prostration.[38]

It is very instructive to compare the vicissitudes of Athens in the third century with those of DELPHI. Our evidence regarding the latter, though abundant, relates mostly to matters of little interest for the purposes of the present history. But certain facts are known which clearly reveal its general social and economic evolution during the period in question.[39]

The most important occurrence in the political history of Delphi was her gradual absorption by the Aetolian League, her progressive dependence upon it. This absorption began very early and steadily developed until, by the middle of the third century, it was an undisputed fact, accepted, though reluctantly, by the whole of Greece. The process was accelerated, and the life of Delphi was profoundly affected, by the Celtic invasion of Greece. By their gallant defence of Delphi and Greece the Aetolians had acquired for themselves the right of assuming an important part in Delphian affairs. On the other hand, the Celts profoundly disturbed the even tenor of life at Delphi, as was manifested in various ways during the years that followed their invasion. Certain Delphian documents of this period point to very unsettled and insecure conditions. We possess, for instance, six decrees of the Amphictions granting honours to those who had helped them to detect the thieves who had robbed the temple of some of its treasures. All these inscriptions are dated about 270 B.C. These robberies in my opinion not only reflect the disturbed conditions at Delphi after the Celtic invasion and testify to the existence there of many destitute persons who took to crime in despair, but are also evidence of the troubled state of central Greece in general at this time.[40]

Then came the Chremonidean war, and again unrest prevailed not only in the territory round Delphi but also in a large part of the Greek world. I have quoted above (p. 197) documents showing the anxiety of the Amphictions to enable their own members to reach Thermopylae and the *theoroi* and pilgrims to come to Delphi for the celebration of the Pythia and Soteria. By the middle of the century, however, while many parts of Greece were suffering severely from wars and devastation, Delphi, under the protection of the Aetolians, who were now at the zenith of their political power, enjoyed quiet and prosperity. Flacelière has recently collected all the evidence relating to this period of the history of Delphi, and has shown that the Aetolians regarded the place as their intellectual capital, and, I would add, as the centre of their Panhellenic propaganda. They made Delphi an Aetolian counterpart of Macedonian Athens.

Some significant facts may be quoted. The famous Pythian festival at Delphi was celebrated at that time with much pomp. To it, as has been already stated (Ch. I, n. 12), the Aetolians added the Soteria, to which—after its transformation into an Aetolian celebration, probably in 243 B.C.—they invited by special embassies the whole of the Greek world. The invitations met with a rather cool reception and the Aetolian Soteria did not prove a striking success. Nevertheless it was celebrated regularly as a great *agon stephanites*.

During this period the sanctuary of Apollo was filled with gifts and dedications, the most notable among them being the gifts of the Aetolian *koinon* and of various influential Aetolians. I need only mention the great Aetolian monument dedicated to Apollo Pythius in commemoration of the Celtic invasion—a statue of Aetolia seated on a trophy of Celtic arms—and another in commemoration of the Aetolian victory over the Acarnanians, consisting of statues of Apollo and Artemis and of the victorious Aetolian generals. I may also remind the reader of the famous monuments at Delphi which played so important a part in the history of the Roman triumphal arch—I mean the monuments composed of two columns, of which the most famous is that of Aristaineta, probably an Aetolian lady. The two Ionic columns built by her supported statues of herself, her parents, and her son Timolaus. Some of the monuments erected at Delphi by Aetolian leaders emphasized the political connexions of Aetolia with the leading powers of the time. Such was the group of statues of Euergetes (or Philopator) and of the members of the royal family.*

The potentates of the day vied with the Aetolians in embellishing the sanctuary. The most conspicuous gift was that of Attalus: the famous portico (*pastas*) of Delphi, which was built some years before 223/2 B.C., at which date the Amphictions endeavoured by a special decree to protect it from becoming overcrowded with dedications and disfigured by pilgrims.† Friendship with Delphi was hereditary in the ruling family of Pergamon.‡

The proxeny decrees of the period bear witness to the great prestige enjoyed by Delphi throughout the Greek world and to the activity of her diplomacy, though at this time it is always uncertain where Delphi ends and Aetolia begins. Attention may be drawn, for example, to a decree in favour of Lysias, the noted potentate of Asia Minor (242 B.C.), and to decrees in favour of a Cyrenian, a Sidonian ἐγ Βηρυτέου, Syracusans, and others. I have already mentioned the relations of Delphi with the North as far as Olbia, Chersonesus, and Panticapaeum.

Finally, Delphi was still a centre which attracted leading poets and other literary celebrities. Among the *proxeni* of Delphi at this time there are several authors of poems, hymns, &c., in honour of the Delphian gods. We still possess the two hymns of Aristonous of Corinth in honour of Apollo and Hestia.§

* R. Flacelière, *Les Aitoliens à Delphes*, p. 268, note 3. † *S.I.G.*[3] 523.
‡ *F.D.* III. i. 432. § J. Audiat, *B.C.H.* lvi (1932), pp. 299 ff.

It is to be noted also that famous lecturers were welcome at Delphi. Such was Lycon the peripatetic, who is honoured in an Amphictionic decree.*

The evolution of the GREEK ISLANDS in the third century is very similar to that of continental Greece. Our literary evidence is meagre, much more so than that relating to the cities of Greece proper, and the epigraphical and archaeological material is very unevenly distributed. Very few cities in the islands of the Aegean have been carefully and systematically excavated. Good work has been done in Delos, Cos, and Thera; partial excavations of a scientific character have been and are still being carried out in Samos, Thasos, Samothrace, Aegina, Tenos, Rhodes, Carpathos, Crete, Cyprus, and some other islands. But most of the Greek islands have never been touched by the spade and have only been the subject of careful surface investigations. Moreover, even where cities have been excavated not all the material found has been published. The only exception is Thera. Next to it comes Delos. For such places as Cos and Lindos, even the epigraphic material has not yet been published in full, not to speak of what are known as minor finds.

Thus here again, especially without a background of special study, no satisfactory general picture can be drawn of social and economic conditions. It is hardly necessary to say that life on the Greek islands was as highly individualized as on the mainland. Each island had its peculiar aspect and shows a peculiar development: Delos with her temple and her thriving commercial city; Rhodes, the great trading city of the Aegean and a flourishing centre of agriculture and gardening; Cos with her health resort, her temple of Asclepius, her medical school, and her silk stuffs; Euboea with her copper mines and rich fields and pastures; Thasos with her wine and her gold, and her neighbours Imbros and Samothrace; Ceos with her *rubrica*; Paros and Naxos with their marble; the large agricultural and viticultural islands of Chios, Samos, and Lesbos—all of these present important problems for individual study, while very few offer enough material to work upon.

Moreover each of the islands had its own political, social, and

* *F.D.* iii. 3. 167.

economic connexions. Some of them were dependencies of Northern Greece; others were closely bound to Central Greece or to the Peloponnese; a large and important group were fragments of Asia Minor; while others formed, so to speak, piers of the various bridges that connected Greece and Anatolia. Cyprus, a part as it were of the oriental world, occupied a peculiar position, and so did Crete. The Ionian islands were connected mainly with the western world.[41]

In these circumstances it can hardly be matter of complaint if the following account is sketchy, incomplete, at once too general and too particular. Even so, I am aware that in my treatment of the subject I may have overlooked important evidence by which doubtful points might have been elucidated.

The islands of the Aegean were not of sufficient political importance to become the principal object of the endless wars of the rival Hellenistic kings. Their attention was centred on continental Greece and on the large and prosperous cities of Asia Minor. But, although not the main object of their strife, the islands did not remain unaffected by the vicissitudes of the wars. For a time some of them, members of the Island League, enjoyed the protection of their suzerains, the Ptolemies—Soter and Philadelphus. They had to pay for it by contributions of ships and money, and by the virtual loss of their political freedom. Nevertheless they did not obtain complete security. I have quoted evidence showing how heavily they suffered from the pirates, especially from the Aetolians and the Cretans. The time of severest trial was that during and after the Chremonidean war, which gave the pirates opportunities of carrying out raids in the name of one or other of the Cretan cities or of the Aetolians, or at any rate for the profit and at the instigation of one of the belligerents. The ordeal was renewed when in the second half of the third century the policing of the Aegean was no one's concern: the Ptolemies withdrew, the Island League ceased to exist, and consequently the sea was left at the mercy of the pirates until the Rhodians gradually took the reins into their own hands. I refer especially to the time of the Demetrian war and that of Antigonus Doson.

It is not surprising that there should be frequent mention in the inscriptions, scarce as these are, of financial and economic troubles in many of the islands. We have, in this respect, a typical situation at Arcesine in Amorgos. A set of fragmentary inscriptions* show how often the city resorted to foreign loans. In most cases the reasons for borrowing are not specified. It has been conjectured, however, with some probability, that one of the later loans (second century)† was contracted for the redemption of some citizens captured by Cretan pirates. And similar reasons may have given occasion for the earlier loans. The chief causes of financial stress in the Greek cities were always the same: bad crops and food shortage, oppressive contributions exacted by the belligerents who happened to be in possession of the city, or raids by pirates.[42]

Now, several loans were contracted by Arcesine on specially onerous conditions:‡ loans were granted by private persons on the security not only of all the property of the city but also of that of all the citizens and other residents (that is, the metics), whether it lay in the city or oversea (ὑπερπόντια). These severe conditions were not imposed in consequence of the poverty of the borrower. The rate of interest stipulated was low, and the credit of the city was good at the time of the loan. It was the general uncertainty—the dangers threatening the city from outside and apprehension of internal troubles—that made the creditors so exacting. And the city could not refuse the terms demanded because loans were one of the few sources from which it could meet emergency expenditure in unforeseen difficulties. The frequency with which such difficulties arose at Arcesine is characteristic of the conditions of the time.[43]

The case of CEOS is highly instructive. Leaving aside the earlier political status of the four Cean cities—Carthaea, Poiessa, Iulis, and Coresia—I may mention the interesting fact, known from the decrees of the Aetolians, Naupactians, and Ceans,§ that at about the time they were passed these four cities formed a sympolity. The date is disputed. I am inclined to accept the earlier date suggested by R. Flacelière and to assign them to about the same time as the similar Aetolian decrees concerning Delos and Tenos, that is, the middle of the third century. In

* *I.G.* xii. 7. 63–70.
† Ibid. 7. 63, cf. 64.
‡ Ibid. 7. 67 and 69; *S.I.G.*³ 955.
§ *S.I.G.*³ 522.

the turmoil that then prevailed the cities of Ceos may have formed a sympolity (or renewed one of an earlier date) in order to secure a recognition of *asylia* and isopolity from the most dangerous supporters of piracy, the Aetolians and the Naupactians. This sympolity, however, was dissolved, probably as soon as the danger became less acute; at any rate it did not exist in 206 B.C.* But some time in the second half of the century, perhaps in the troubled period that followed the death of Antigonus Gonatas and in the reign of Philip V, the cities of Carthaea and Poiessa on the one hand, and of Iulis and Coresia on the other, entered into close mutual relations, each pair having contracted a kind of sympolity or synoecism.† Carthaea and Poiessa may have done so before 206 B.C., the other two after this date. In any case the reasons for such measures as these are to be sought in the general insecurity of the times and in the prevalence of poverty, debt, and internal discord.[44]

Even larger and richer islands like SAMOS had their difficulties and troubles. In an inscription in honour of Bulagoras‡ the Samians bitterly complain of maltreatment at the hands of the φίλοι of Antiochus II, of lack of money, and of a severe famine which had been to some extent relieved by the intervention of Bulagoras.

Insecurity of life and economic instability led naturally to troubles within the city. I have already drawn attention to the low rate of wages current at that time and the scarcity of demand for free labour; I shall return to the subject in connexion with Delos. We are therefore not surprised to find disturbances (ταραχαί), which were of common occurrence in continental Greece, the subject of comparatively frequent mention in the islands also. Some instances of an earlier date have already been referred to. A few others may be added, all of the third century. In the time of Philadelphus a ταραχή is mentioned at Ios;§ it was settled by envoys of Philadelphus. Another broke out at about the same time at Thera.‖ During the reign of Antigonus Doson the situation in Amorgos was difficult (cf.

* *S.I.G.*[3] 562, 79–80.
† Strabo x. 5, 6, p. 486.
‡ *S.E.G.* i. 366.
§ *I.G.* xii. 5, 7.
‖ F. Hiller von Gaertringen, *Hermes*, xxxvi (1901), pp. 444 ff.

what has been said above on the loans contracted by the cities in the island)* and Ios may have had troubles again.†

However, unrest appears to have been more intermittent in the islands than in continental Greece and Asia Minor. In the former there was plenty of money in circulation, and there are many indications that the upper classes at least were fairly prosperous, while the special products of the islands were still in wide demand, especially in Egypt and Syria. I shall show presently, when speaking of Rhodes, that Chian, Lesbian, Samian, and Thasian goods were in much request in Egypt in the reign of Philadelphus (see below, p. 228), that the rate of interest on loans was low, and that there were still abundant opportunities for emigration and for profitable business abroad.[45] All this, as we now know, was temporary, and business activity was already slightly declining. In the island of Delos, for example, the general irregularity of prices, their fall in the period 270–250 B.C. and their subsequent rise may be regarded as the cause of a reduction in the number of foreigners engaged in the business of the temple.[46] It was, however, some time before this tendency towards decline became pronounced. Meanwhile the situation was bright and the prospects for the future not discouraging.

This does not mean that all classes of the population were prosperous. Over-population, which had been relieved for a time by the opening up of the East, was again a source of danger, especially as regards labour. The rates of wages current at Delos show how poorly workmen were remunerated.[47] The competition of slave labour was keen, for wars and piracy made slaves cheap and abundant, even in such minor islands as Ios, not to speak of the larger ones.[48] Egypt about this time had absorbed all the free labour that it could employ. We have here the explanation of the social and economic unrest in the islands of which I have given instances.

Of the islands of the Aegean RHODES certainly remained politically and economically the most prominent. She was still the principal emporium of the Aegean and the chief commercial partner of Egypt, especially in the grain trade. In the struggle with Demetrius Rhodes asserted her independence, both

* *I.G.* xii. 7. 221; cf. 222 and 223. † Ibid. 5. 1008.

political and economic. She asserted it a second time against Philadelphus, when in alliance probably with Antiochus II she defeated an Egyptian fleet off Ephesus (date uncertain). I can find no explanation for this course of action except on the assumption that Rhodes was fighting for her liberty; it must be supposed that Philadelphus had shown a tendency to treat Rhodes not as an ally but as a subject, in the same way that he treated the islands of the Island League and to a certain extent Delos, to which he may have shown a certain preference offensive to Rhodes.[49]

The battle of Ephesus, however, was no more than an unpleasant episode in the history of the relations between Rhodes and Alexandria. There is no record of any political or military conflict between Rhodes and the Ptolemies thereafter. On the contrary, Rhodes showed great regard for them, and although sparing as a rule in the grant of honours and statues to monarchs, she made an exception in their favour, as is shown by many inscriptions and some sculptures.[50] It seems probable that some kind of understanding was reached between Rhodes and Egypt.

The character of Rhodian business in the middle of the third century and of the trade relations that existed between Rhodes and the Egyptian Empire is illustrated by a little document which forms part of Zenon's correspondence. I shall deal with this correspondence in greater detail later in this chapter. The document in question is a note of *c.* 258 B.C. (now in the Rylands Library) sent by Zenon to Nicanor, both of them members of the staff or house of Apollonius, the 'manager' (*dioecetes*) of Egyptian economic affairs under Philadelphus. Nicanor is notified that some gifts have arrived for him together with other gifts sent to Apollonius by a certain Abdemoun, the Sidonian. The gifts had been shipped from Rhodes by Zenon, the brother of Abdemoun. Customs duties had been paid on them by Aristeus, the accountant of Apollonius.[51]

Apollonius, who was manager of the king's affairs not only in Egypt proper, but also in the king's foreign dominions, was certainly in active relations with the Syrian provinces of the Ptolemies in his official capacity. Besides he had important private interests in them: he was the owner of an estate in

Palestine and may have dealt in Syrian goods in Alexandria, and, in any case, his extensive household (οἶκος) was a large consumer of such goods, especially foodstuffs, wine, and olive-oil.[52] He naturally received regular shipments of Syrian goods: caravan-trade goods such as incense, myrrh, and the like, and foodstuffs, wine, and olive-oil. We possess lists of such shipments in the form of accounts of payments connected with the unloading of ships in the harbour of Alexandria: heavy customs duties, harbour dues, porterage, minor taxes, &c.[53]

The shipment mentioned in Zenon's note to Nicanor was, however, different: it was a gift. We know that such gifts (ξένια) were sent from time to time to the king and to influential members of his court by prominent persons in the foreign dominions of the Ptolemies. The two well-known letters of Tubias, the vassal sheikh of Transjordan, to Apollonius, refer to a gift of animals to Philadelphus and of slaves to Apollonius.[54] Another gift sent to Apollonius by an unknown person from an unknown place, certainly in Phoenicia or Syria, is described by Nicanor, apparently one of the chief agents of Apollonius for his Syrian affairs.* And finally a gift of the same character and sent apparently to Apollonius from the same city of Sidon by a magistrate of the city is mentioned in an undated memorandum, now in Michigan, of the same type as the memorandum in the Rylands Library: 'from Theodotus the archon at Sidon, of Attic honey one jar, of rose myrrh . . .'† It is regrettable that we do not know of what kinds of things Abdemoun's gift consisted. They may have been similar to those sent by the Sidonian magistrate.

Since Abdemoun was sending gifts to a person of such high standing as Apollonius, it is natural to suppose that he himself was a rich and influential man. As he had a brother at Rhodes who looked after his shipments and probably his affairs in general, we may assume that Abdemoun had important business interests there. Finally, as he was a Sidonian, it is highly probable that he was one of those Phoenician merchants who from time immemorial forwarded goods from Arabia and from

* *P.S.I.* 594.

† *P. Mich. Zen.* 3: παρὰ Θεοδότου | τοῦ ἐκ Σιδῶνος ἄρχοντος | μέλιτ[ο]ς Ἀττικοῦ | στάμνος α´ | μύ[ρο]υ ῥοδίνου . . .

Phoenicia itself to Egypt, Greece, Italy, North Africa, and Spain, making use of Rhodes in their transactions with the North and West both as a port of call and a clearing-house. It was therefore natural for a Sidonian to be in close commercial relations with Alexandria and Rhodes.

Nevertheless it is interesting to see that a shipment for Alexandria goes first to Rhodes, though it was much shorter and much more convenient to send it along the Phoenician and Palestinian coast to Gaza, Pelusium, and Alexandria. The fact shows that for Abdemoun and the Syrian merchants in general Rhodes, not Alexandria, was the great centre, the clearing-house. Here resided the agents of the great commercial houses of Sidon, Tyre, Aradus, &c. Here they received orders for Phoenician goods and gave orders for Greek goods. Here they met the Phoenician ships with their varied cargoes, discharged them if necessary, distributed the merchandise among various freighters ready to sail for Alexandria, Athens, Miletus, Cyzicus, or Italy, and dispatched to the Phoenician ports other cargoes which came to Rhodes from all parts of the world. It is possible that the gifts of Apollonius were actually sent from Sidon to Rhodes, but I should not be surprised if some of them were drawn by Zenon, brother of Abdemoun, from the latter's storehouses in Rhodes. We know that at Delos, which to some extent succeeded Rhodes in her role of clearing-house, the merchants and ship-owners (*ἔμποροι* and *ναύκληροι*) were at the same time owners of storehouses or depots (*ἐγδοχεῖς*).

The little document we have analysed gives us, therefore, a vivid picture of Rhodes as the clearing-house for the Phoenician and Egyptian trade. This picture can be enlarged if we examine some of the lists (referred to above) of shipments sent to Apollonius from Syria. The longest of them describes a shipment stated to have come from there. Yet it contains not only 'Syrian' merchandise but also goods from Cilicia, Lycia, Caria, and Rhodes on the one hand, and from Chios, Thasos, Samos, Lesbos, Athens, and the Pontus on the other. It looks as if the ships which brought all these goods to Alexandria, provided that they were the same which had sailed from Phoenicia, did not sail southwards direct to Alexandria, but moved along the oast northwards, calling at Cilician and Lycian ports and taking in more cargo, and arriving at Rhodes where they shipped further consignments. These they received from the agents of Apollonius in Rhodes, who bought there Thasian and Chian wine, Samian 'earth', honey of Theangela, Pontic nuts, Milesian and Samian olive-oil, and added thereto Rhodian products: honey, dried figs, perhaps cabbages, and so forth.[55]

Rhodes derived great advantage from the change in the political situation which resulted from the decline of the Ptolemaic power in the Aegean and the consequent establishment of the preponderance of Antigonus in at least part of that sea, a preponderance which is reflected in the Delian inscriptions. Antigonus Gonatas, so far as we know, never made any effort to attract Rhodes into his political orbit. On the contrary, it seems as if Antigonus, after the partial withdrawal of Philadelphus from the Aegean, made no serious attempt to take up the heritage of the Ptolemies and to exercise a commercial control over the seas. Our scanty evidence shows that he neglected his own navy and tacitly allowed the Rhodians to hold the dominion of the sea or to share it with the Ptolemies, with all the consequences that this implied—in particular the duty of curbing piracy. In the Aegean Rhodes stood for the 'freedom of the sea', which meant no privileges for any one, the greatest possible security afloat, a minimum of taxes and duties, and the recognition of certain general legal principles as governing maritime commerce. Those principles Rhodes endeavoured to maintain through a common understanding between all the cities that took an active part in overseas commerce, and soon acquired the reputation of being 'the protector of those who follow the sea' (προεστάναι τῶν κατὰ θάλατταν).*

The trade of Rhodes, important as it had been in the past, was rapidly developing, as we know from the distribution of the stamped handles of Rhodian jars in various centres of Greek life. I shall deal with this subject and the date of these handles in more detail in a later passage. Further evidence is supplied by the rapid spread of the coinage standard introduced by Rhodes soon after the synoecism and adopted not only by most of the islands of the Aegean and many towns of Asia Minor but also by cities on the Hellespont and the Propontis

* Polyb. iv. 47. 1.

and in Thrace; and by the extension of her alliances, especially with the islands of the Aegean, for example, with Ios.*

In the interests of her trade, Rhodes made use of her strong permanent navy to combat piracy in the Aegean, and did so successfully. As early as the middle of the third century she acted as the protector of the islands (below, n. 59), and later we hear from time to time of her energetic action against Demetrius of Pharos (220 B.C.), the well-known pirate king, and the Cretans.† The importance of Rhodes as a centre of trade and her popularity among the leading commercial powers of the time is strikingly illustrated by Polybius' account (v. 88 ff.), drawn from official sources, of the help given to Rhodes after the famous earthquake of 227 or 226 B.C. Assistance came from Sicily, from Ptolemy Euergetes, from Antigonus Doson and Chryseis his wife, from Seleucus Callinicus, from Prusias of Bithynia, from Mithridates of Pontus, and from some minor tyrants of Asia Minor. There can be no doubt that it was not from pure charity that these potentates were so lavish in their gifts nor solely from admiration of the greatness of Rhodes, but to a large extent from the desire to relieve a State which provided a convenient agency for the profitable marketing of their products.

While the general course of the development of Rhodes can, despite the inadequacy of our information, be traced with more or less certainty, the rise of DELOS to be an important factor in Aegean trade is not so easy to follow. Literary texts are almost entirely silent, and the epigraphical evidence, though abundant, is not easy to interpret.[56]

The situation of Delos was peculiar. A small insignificant island, almost devoid of fertile land and possessing no natural well-protected harbour, it became at an early date the seat of one of the most important temples of the Greek world—that of the Delian Apollo—and the centre of an important religious federation. The *panegyris* of Delos attacted large crowds of pilgrims, the treasury of the God was speedily filled with the costly dedications of the rich and the modest offerings of the poor, and the temple gradually accumulated a comparatively large capital in gold and silver and in coined money, not to speak

* *I.G.* xii. 5. 8 = 1009. † Polyb. iv. 19. 8; Diod. xxvii. 3.

of the land and houses that it owned in and around the steadily growing city. The treasury of the temple soon developed into a bank. Like other rich temples, that of Apollo lent money at interest, and the sanctity of the place guaranteed the safety of deposits.

So long, however, as the island was a subject or subject-ally of Athens, it could not look for any considerable commercial development. The situation changed when in 315/4 B.C. it recovered complete independence. This independence was of course nominal, for the prestige of Apollo was too high for Delos to be disregarded by the rulers of the time. Thus it was that Antigonus and Demetrius made it probably the centre of their Island League, and that the Ptolemies, successors of Antigonus and Demetrius in the Aegean, were careful to maintain the best relations with the sacred island. Philadelphus, in particular, showed the highest regard for it and repeatedly sent valuable gifts to the sanctuary. Under the protection of Antigonus, Demetrius, Soter, and Philadelphus, and perhaps not without their encouragement, Delos developed its customary banking activity. The accounts of the *hieropoioi* mention several loans to various cities, made through the city of Delos as intermediary. Philadelphus was keenly interested in this activity. We hear incidentally how in 280 B.C., with the help of Philocles, king of the Sidonians and admiral of Ptolemy Soter and Philadelphus, Delos collected from the Island League moneys that had been lent to it.* It has been suggested that the moneys were lent by Delos under the pressure of Demetrius for the purpose of paying the contribution imposed by him on the Greek islands. The loan was not repaid in time, and Philadelphus helped Delos to collect it in order to enable her to assist *him* in the collection of his tribute from the islands.[57] The great interest taken by Philadelphus as revealed by this piece of evidence may suggest—though this is no more than a conjecture—that it was he who, in agreement with Rhodes, made the island a kind of branch clearing-house for the trade of Egypt, especially with the northern part of the Aegean. This would explain the close business relations between Delos and Rhodes in the late fourth and early third centuries and again in the

* *S.I.G.*[3] 391; Durrbach, *Choix*, 18.

second half of the third, and also the later relations of Delos with the Macedonian kings.[58]

After the collapse of the Island League Delos developed ever closer relations with Macedonia. The role of Philadelphus and for a short time of Euergetes was now played at Delos by Antigonus Gonatas and his successors. Not content with showing his high respect for Delos and the Delian God, it appears that Antigonus further developed the commercial activities of the island by favouring its grain trade and making it an *entrepôt* for the Macedonian trade in timber, pitch, tar, and perhaps silver. Otherwise it would be difficult to account for the numerous inscriptions that speak of honours bestowed by Delos on Macedonians, and for two interesting documents, one referring to a purchase of grain in Delos by Demetrius II of Macedonia through his agent, the other to a similar purchase made at about the same time by a *sitones* of Histiaea, a subject city of Macedonia. It should be noticed that the second purchase is made out of money advanced by a Rhodian banker, probably resident at Delos. We must remember that the relations between Rhodes and Macedonia remained cordial until the early years of Philip V.[59]

If Delos was in fact constituted by Rhodes and by the Macedonian kings an important clearing-house for Aegean trade, it is easy to understand why the Bosporan king Paerisades II, the great dealer in grain, who was in close diplomatic and probably commercial relations with Philadelphus in 254 or 253 B.C., appears at Delos as the donor in 250 B.C. of a *phiale*, alongside of Antigonus Gonatas and Stratonice. About the same time we note among the *proxeni* of Delos one Chersonesite and two Panticapaeans.[60]

Finally, it is of no little interest to observe how enduring were the close relations established between Delos on the one hand and Cyzicus, Lampsacus, Abydos, Byzantium, and Chalcedon, not to speak of Olbia and Panticapaeum, on the other.[61] Noteworthy also is the gift of grain made at a later date to Delos by the Numidian king Masinissa.*

In view of all this, it is highly probable that, by the joint efforts of Rhodes, Philadelphus, Antigonus Gonatas, and his

* *Inscr. de Délos*, 442, A, 100–6.

successors, Delos in the early third century, besides being the seat of a famous sanctuary, became also an important centre of Aegean trade, a role that she retained and subsequently developed.

We know very little of the commercial activity of Delos. It is very probable that much of the trade and banking was in the hands of foreigners, while the Delians themselves took little part in these.[62] The volume of Delian trade in the early third century, when it was just beginning to develop, may be calculated from the income which the city derived from the customs duties or export and import tax of 2 per cent. (πεντηκοστή). In 279 it amounted to 14,910 drachmas (including tax on sales paid by the tax-farmers) and in 278 to 18,800. If we deduct from the latter sum the tax on sales (*eponion*), 17,900 drachmas remain as the yield of the customs. This sum implies a volume of trade amounting to a little under one million drachmas, a modest beginning indeed, if compared with the later development (below, Chs. V and VI).[63]

But if our knowledge of Delian commerce is slight, we know more of the affairs of the temple. It is appropriate to say a few words about them, for the economy of the temple of Delos is probably typical of that prevailing at this period in the other temples which stood in close connexion with a city. Our information regarding Delos is derived from the yearly accounts of special magistrates, the *hieropoioi*, who were in charge of the State treasury during the period of independence. These accounts were accurately kept and published from the end of the fourth century to 166 B.C., when Delos became a cleruchy of Athens and the character of the published accounts changed. Some of the *stelae* on which these accounts were engraved are almost complete, of others only fragments survive.

The capital and income of the temple were comparatively modest. The whole of its property, including the sacred buildings, has been estimated by Homolle (conjecturally) for 279 B.C. at about five and a half million drachmas, five millions being the value of the buildings and 300,000 that of the cult objects and offerings. The part which yielded income, therefore, may have amounted to about 200,000 drachmas. Only about one-fourth of this (50,000 drachmas) was available as floating capital for expenditure and loans, the rest representing the value of land and houses which were rented and yielded a yearly income. Later, in the first half of the second century, calculations are made more difficult by the change of the accounting system. Scholars who have studied these accounts carefully have come to the conclusion that the resources were no smaller than they were about 275 B.C. and even possibly somewhat larger, but that the funds were less liquid. Besides the sacred buildings, the temple's property consisted of farms and gardens in Delos, Rheneia, and Myconos, of houses in the city, of objects dedicated to the gods and goddesses, mostly gold and silver plate but also other things (of these an accurate inventory was kept and published every year with the accounts), and of foundations and gifts bestowed on the temple by many crowned and uncrowned donors for the purpose of sacrifices, games, and the like.

Regular income was derived from the land and houses, which were let for money rents, from sums lent to private persons and to cities (among them the city of Delos) at a comparatively low rate, from small gifts in the temple's collection-boxes (θησαυροί),[64] and from certain other minor sources. The farms and houses were rented, the first for ten, the second for five, years, to private persons. In later times a model contract (ἱερὰ συγγραφή) was drawn up to regulate the renting of real property. The money that was lent was derived mostly from gifts and foundations. The loans were made on security. The city of Delos, for example, pledged the revenue from certain city taxes.

The income of the temple defrayed its yearly expenditure. This included the construction of new buildings and the maintenance of old ones, the purchase of various materials (e.g. papyrus for the accounts), wages and salaries to employees, and sacrifices and other ritual performances, especially the various *agones* (these last involved the hiring of a number of artists—actors, musicians, singers, and so forth).[65]

While the budget of the temple is comparatively well known, we have almost no information regarding that of the city. We may obtain, however, some idea of the city's revenue from the character of the taxes collected by it with the help of tax-farmers. We find among them the above-mentioned customs duties on imports and exports (2 per cent.), a tax on metics (10 per cent. of their house-rent), fishing rights, 10 per cent. of wheat crops or of the price of imported wheat, and a tax on sales (ἐπώνιον). Like other Greek cities, Delos had no well-organized budget and had constant recourse to loans from the temple.[66]

The expenditure of the city was the same as that of other Greek cities. In a city like Delos, which produced almost no grain or other foodstuffs, great importance attached to the management of the food-supply by the magistrates. We have no information about this branch of municipal economy in the third century, but we are able to form some idea of its importance from the accounts of the grain-buyers (σιτῶναι) of the early second century, who managed a special municipal fund set apart for this purpose (σιτωνικόν). The evidence at our disposal shows that the fund was managed with great skill and contributed to make the price of grain at Delos in the early second century, though comparatively high, yet stable with few fluctuations. It is probable that measures of this kind were taken in the third century to safeguard a regular supply of grain for the population.[67]

The accounts of the *hieropoioi* are a mine of information not only on the general manner of life in a prosperous temple and in a city which was gradually becoming an important centre of commerce, but also on the prices of various commodities, on wages and on salaries. I have already more than once referred to these data. One of their most interesting features is the great instability of prices that they reveal. Wide fluctuations are noticeable from about 310 B.C. to about 270 B.C. The prices become a little more stable between 270 and 250, but fluctuations are still frequent. The general tendency of prices in the first period is upwards. From 270 to 250 they gradually fall. From about 250 or 246 B.C. the rise is renewed and continues until the end of the third century.

Since Delos was a centre of commerce closely connected with Rhodes and Alexandria, we may safely assume that the fluctuation of prices in Delos reflects the movement of prices in the rest of Greece. But I hesitate to draw far-reaching conclusions from curves of prices at Delos based on statistical data that are far from complete. We know too little of the general history of the Aegean world in the third century and more especially of the history of Delos to be able to determine the causes of the fluctuations. It seems, however, reasonable to ascribe the gradual stabilization and fall of prices between 270 and 250 B.C. to the Ptolemaic hegemony in the Aegean. With the downfall of this hegemony there was a recurrence of trouble and prices began to rise. It is likewise reasonable to assume during the period 270–250 B.C. a certain correspondence between prices in Egypt and in the Aegean, particularly as regards grain and papyrus. We may perhaps see a certain relation between the prices of pitch, tar, and timber and the vicissitudes of the Macedonian kings. Farther than this I hesitate to go.

One point, however, may be safely inferred from the Delian data. It is the exceedingly low rate of wages, alike for skilled and for unskilled labour; it remained low and constantly fell lower, irrespective of the fluctuations of prices.[68]

From the evidence assembled in the preceding pages we may infer that in the early and late third century B.C. Delos was a small but prosperous city, rapidly growing and attracting steadily increasing numbers of foreigners from all parts of the Greek world. The sanctuary benefited from the gifts of rich crowned donors who vied with each other in showing respect for the god and by their gifts and foundations sought to advertise their wealth and power and their importance in the political life of the Aegean. Less is known about the appearance of the city. Its ruins, as laid bare by the excavations of French scholars, give us a good idea of the city as it was in the second century, but very little was found to help us to picture the earlier stages of its development.[69]

Rhodes and Delos were exceptional communities, not typical of the islands of the Aegean. At Rhodes life was concentrated in the capital and hinged upon commerce and banking, while agriculture played a secondary part, except in so far as it produced wine, probably the main Rhodian export. At Delos the temple and the harbour were the sole factors in economic and social life, while the *χώρα* or rural element was practically nonexistent.

The conditions at COS, which happen to be better known than

those in any other island of the Aegean, are more typical, especially for the period under review. We have literary works which describe various features of Coan life (the *Mimes* of Theocritus and especially those of Herondas), we have some knowledge of the scientific achievements of the Coan school of medicine, and we possess a large number of inscriptions, some of them collected on the surface and admirably published by Paton, others discovered in systematic excavations of the Asclepieum by R. Herzog and the Italian Service of Antiquities, others again found in various other parts of the island by Italian archaeologists. Lastly we have the interesting ruins of the Asclepieum, carefully excavated and well described. It is, however, regrettable that not all the epigraphic material found by Herzog and the Italian Service has been published, though all documents of importance have been made known by them through one channel or another.[70]

Cos is one of the larger islands of the Aegean; with a surface of 286 square kilometres, it is inferior in size to Rhodes and Carpathos alone among the islands of the Dodecanese. Its early history is little known and does not concern us here. Its great period begins with the synoecism of 366 B.C., a measure of frequent occurrence in the history of Greek cities in the fourth century, adopted later and applied on a large scale by the Successors.

It was not, however, until the time of Alexander that Cos, freed from the domination of the Carian tyrants, reached the zenith of its prosperity. Its close connexion with Rhodes, its situation (see further below), its excellent climate, and its vicinity to Alexandria made it, after a period of dependence on Antigonus and Demetrius, one of the most privileged 'friends' and 'allied' cities of Soter and Philadelphus, who, like the members of their artistic and intellectual *entourage*, often spent their summer holiday on this fortunate island, as at the present day rich citizens of Alexandria and Cairo like to retire to Rhodes in summer. It may be noticed that Philadelphus was born at Cos during the long stay of Soter and Berenice on the island.

We have no information about the history of Cos in the critical times of the middle of the third century B.C. Being

PLATE XXXII

1. Peasant in a pointed felt cap leading a donkey laden with baskets of grapes to the city market. The donkey has stumbled on a rock and fallen on its knees. The peasant, by seizing its tail with his right hand, is trying to prevent the fall of the donkey, at the same time holding up the baskets with his left. Myrina. F. Winter, loc. cit., p. 432, no. 5. Cf. E. Pottier and S. Reinach, loc. cit., p. 489. (Photograph supplied by the authorities of the National Museum, Athens.)

2. Young peasant in a flat hat and short chiton leading a cow down a road. According to Winter (loc. cit.) one of the two figurines, now in the Louvre, was found at Anthedon (?), another, it is said, at the Piraeus. (Photograph supplied by the authorities of the Louvre, Paris.)

Peasant life was less popular with the coroplasts than city life.

1. Athens, National Museum.

2. Paris, Louvre. Terracotta figurines.

LIFE IN THE COUNTRY

PLATE XXXIII

1. Terracotta figurine. Paris, Louvre.

2. Marble statue. New York, Metropolitan Museum of Art.

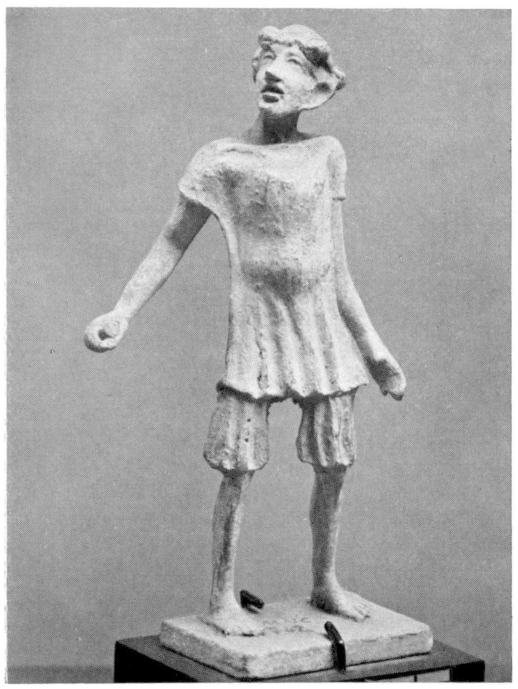

3. Terracotta figurine. Paris, Louvre.

4. Terracotta figurine. Paris, Louvre.

LIFE IN THE CITIES AND IN THE COUNTRY

PLATE XXXIII

1. A peasant, megalophallic, sturdy, old and bald, short, stout, and somewhat dwarfish, dressed in a short belted chiton and carrying on his left shoulder by a leather strap two heavy baskets of grapes, walking to the city market. In his right hand he carries a smaller basket. Probably a personage in a mime. Myrina.

E. Pottier and S. Reinach, loc. cit., p. 488 f., pl. XLVII, Cat., no. 332. Several replicas in various museums. A very popular subject with the coroplasts.

2. Statue of an old peasant woman going to market carrying in her left hand a basket containing fruit and two fowls. Perhaps part of a group (the woman with her right arm stretched forward appears to be talking to someone). The age of the woman is finely expressed in all the details of her head and body (note the bare hanging breasts) and in the movement. Parts of the feet and left breast restored. Second century (or Roman copy of an original of this time?). Found in Rome in 1907. (Photograph supplied by the authorities of the Metropolitan Museum of Art, New York.)

Several times published and discussed in connexion with other Hellenistic sculptures of old men and women. I give a short selection: D. Vaglieri, *Not. d. Sc.*, 1907, p. 325, figs. 45–6; A. Mariani, *Bull. Com.*, 1907, p. 257, pl. VII; S. Reinach, *Rép. de la statuaire*, iv (1910), p. 349, no. 7; G. M. A. Richter, *Sculpture and Sculptors of the Greeks*, 1929, p. 63, fig. 219; 1930, p. 82, fig. 219; A. W. Lawrence, *Classical Sculpture*, 1929, p. 339 f., pl. 137; Arndt–Brunn–Bruckmann, *Denkm. gr. und röm. Skulptur*, 1930, no. 730; *M.M.A.* Handbook of the Classical Collection, 1930, p. 276 f., fig. 196; M. Rostovtzeff, *A Hist. of the Anc. World*, i, 1926, pl. LXXXVIII, 2; H. T. Bossert and W. Zschietzschmann, *Hellas and Rome*, 1936, p. 142 (bibliography supplied by the *M.M.A.*).

3. A young man, barefooted, in a peculiar dress, probably that of a slave: shorts and a loose almost sleeveless chiton. In his right hand he is holding an object, perhaps a staff. His head is turned upwards and he is shouting. He may be interpreted as a public slave (δημόσιος) acting as a herald (κήρυξ) or 'town-crier', or he may be a personage in a famous mime. Pergamon (?). F. Winter, loc. cit., p. 443, no. 1.

4. A fine statuette of an old long-nosed man with large ears, thick lips, and bald forehead, draped in a heavy cloak and wearing shoes with thick soles (cf. pl. XXXI, 3; cf. also a similar statuette in the Antiquarium of Berlin, F. Winter, loc. cit., p. 440, no. 1). His posture is that of a public orator: his mouth is half open, and he looks intently at his hearers. He is probably delivering a speech. Every reader of Herondas will think of Battarus, the brothel-keeper (πορνοβοσκός), and his vulgar but efficient speech before the Coan court, a speech full of flattery, impudence, and crude jokes (Herondas, *Mim.* ii). His long nose (typical of the mimes) and his outfit make it probable that we have before us a famous character of the Hellenistic mimes; cf. the group of two slaves or beggars in the Pelizaeus Museum in Hildesheim (M. Bieber, *Denkm. z. Theaterwesen*, p. 177, no. 108, fig. 5; O. Crusius and R. Herzog, loc. cit., pl. III; G. Roeder and A. Ippel, *Denkmäler des Pelizaeus-Museums*, 1921, p. 168, no. 464, fig. 70), and an admirable statuette in the National Museum at Athens of a slave talking to someone, a beautiful piece of characterization (F. Winter, loc. cit., p. 442, no. 7). Myrina. Signature: Ἱέρωνος (one of the best coroplasts of Myrina).

E. Pottier and S. Reinach, loc. cit., p. 490, pl. XLVII, Cat., no. 324; *C.A.H.*, loc. cit., p. 193*a*; J. Charbonneaux, loc. cit., fig. 88.

to some extent a political and commercial dependency of Rhodes, Cos probably followed the latter's lead in politics and sided for a time with Antiochus II against the Ptolemies. But its connexion with and dependence on Alexandria were soon re-established. About 240 B.C. Cos sent embassies to the principal rulers of the day, especially to those with whom it was in close business relations (we know of such embassies to Euergetes I, Seleucus Callinicus, and Ziaelas of Bithynia), to ask for recognition of the *asylia* of her Asclepieum. Ziaelas in his reply lays stress on the close relations between Cos and Euergetes: 'and because King Ptolemy, our friend and ally, is well disposed towards you'.*

Later on, after the almost complete collapse of the Ptolemaic empire of the Aegean, Cos was definitely taken into the orbit of Rhodes, becoming the faithful and efficient ally of the latter, able to give assistance in various ways, especially through its well-organized fleet, which acted as an auxiliary contingent to that of Rhodes. I shall return in the next chapter to this period in the history of Cos, which was not a very happy one for the island.

By its geographical situation opposite Halicarnassus and Cnidos at the entrance of the Ceramian gulf, and by its possession of a good harbour, Cos was naturally connected with Rhodes on the one hand and the Ptolemies on the other, for both had important political and economic interests in Caria and were desirous of having a safe port of call for their ships on their northward voyages. Cos found in the connexion an excellent opportunity of becoming a commercial city and of finding markets for its agricultural and industrial products—Coan wine, which may have supplemented the wines of Rhodes and Cnidos, and Coan silks.

But Cos was mainly an agricultural community or group of communities. Its soil was fertile. Like the other larger islands of the Aegean, it endeavoured to grow enough wheat and barley for its population. Its wine had a good reputation. It produced timber in quantity probably sufficient for the needs of the island. Like many other islands of the Aegean, it derived a

* *S.I.G.*[3] 456; Welles, *R.C.* 25. ll. 22 ff.: *καὶ διὰ τὸ|τὸμ βασιλέα Πτολεμαῖον| οἰκείως διακεῖσθαι τὰ πρὸς ὑμᾶς|ὄντα ἡμέτερον φίλον καὶ σύμ|μαχον.*

considerable revenue from its fisheries. Also, like many other islands, Cos had a special industry of its own which was famous all over Greece and Italy. I refer to the silk industry which flourished here and nowhere else in the Aegean. The reader need hardly be reminded of the reputation which the *vestes Coae* had in Rome and Italy during a very long period.

The economic and social life of Cos is well illustrated by an inscription of the second century, when the island was under Rhodian influence.* The inscription is fragmentary and its character is not quite clear; but comparison with other similar texts makes it probable that the document was a kind of municipal νόμος ὠνῆς, a set of regulations respecting the sale of certain of the city priesthoods. As the main income of the priests was derived from sacrifices, and certain sacrifices were compulsory for particular groups of inhabitants taking active part in the economic life of the city, a list of these compulsory sacrifices forms part of the document. Two groups figure largely in the list. In the first are included all those who in one way or another were connected with the docks and navy of the city, that is to say, guilds of dockyard workmen or contractors—makers of oars (κωποξύσται) and dockers (νεωλκοί)—on the one hand, and on the other the personnel of the navy from the admiral (ναύαρχος) to the common sailors (ὑπηρέται τᾶν μακρᾶν ναῶν). The second list consists of the contractors who farmed the collection of certain taxes. In neither case is the list complete: the beginning of the first group and the end of the second are missing.

The text evidently reflects the conditions prevailing at Cos in the Rhodian period. Certain features are explained by the date of the document: the prominence of the navy and of the docks—ships and docks bulked large in the life of Rhodes—and perhaps the multitude of small and oppressive taxes, which may have been the result of pressure by Rhodes on her allies. However, in the main the list of taxes certainly goes back to the Ptolemaic period. Diversified and oppressive taxation was not a new feature in the fiscal system of Greek cities.

The list of Coan taxes is highly illuminating and unique in its amplitude (though it is certainly not complete; see further

* *S.I.G.*[3] 1000.

below). It is arranged—at least from our point of view—in a haphazard way, probably in accordance with official records at the disposal of the compiler of the text. The interpretation of some of the taxes is obscure and controversial, but for the most part we may class them as follows.

To begin with, it is curious to note that the list includes no taxes payable by producers—taxes, for instance, on arable land, vineyards, gardens, cattle, quarries, and industrial concerns. It does not necessarily follow that such taxes did not exist at Cos. They may have figured in the lost part of the text, or it may be that they were not farmed, or that the farmers of these taxes were not liable to compulsory sacrifices. But it must be noted that such absence of direct taxes is in conformity with the firmly established traditions of most of the Greek cities.

The only tax mentioned which may have been a tax on production is that on *τετράποδα* (cattle); but this may have been a tax on beasts of burden. On the other hand, the three taxes collected by Coan tax-farmers from the Coan dependency or deme, the island of Calymna, are all of this character ('at Calymna on vineyards, teams of draught-animals, and wool'*).[71]

The rest of the Coan taxes may be classed as follows. (1) Taxes paid by retail traders: on various foodstuffs (wheat, barley, beans, bread, salt fish, fresh fish, a special kind of Coan wine), on materials for domestic industry (wool) and for domestic consumption (wood), on requisites for religious worship (frankincense). (2) Professional and personal taxes: on prostitutes (*ἑταῖραι*), slaves in the vineyards (*ἀμπελοστατεῦντες*), female slaves of private owners (*γυναικεῖα σώματα*), and finally the medical tax (*ἰατρικόν*), which was probably a personal tax paid by the inhabitants of Cos for the maintenance of the public health service (hardly a tax paid by the doctors); we may add the *ἐνοίκια*, a tax on house-rents probably paid chiefly by metics resident in Cos (at Delos a tax bearing the same name was practically a residential personal tax paid by the metics). (3) Payments for the use of the public and private 'observation towers' (*σκοπαί*) connected with the fisheries. The

* L. 9: *ἐν Καλύμναις οἴνου ἐξ οἰ[ν]οπέδων, ζευγέων, ἐρίων.*

tax-farmers probably collected the dues paid by the fishermen for the use of these towers. (4) Payments by the contractors who farmed the revenues of certain temples.[72]

The text analysed above and some other Coan inscriptions give an excellent cross-section of the Coan community. Apart from distinguished foreign visitors, invalids who came to the Asclepieum for their health, and the exclusive group of doctors of the Hippocratean school connected with the Asclepieum, the highest class consists of the landowners, wealthy or well-to-do, the citizen-aristocracy from which the magistrates and priests were drawn. They are mentioned in several inscriptions and they are the producers of the foodstuffs referred to in the tax-list. With them we may class such inhabitants of Cos as lived in the country in villages and farms (κῶμαι and χωρία), tilling with their own hands or with the help of a few slaves land which they either owned or rented. But the number of such αὐτουργο was gradually declining all over Greece. The tax-list shows that alongside of fields of wheat, barley, and beans, vineyards played an important part in the economy of the island. These appear to have been tilled mainly with slave labour. It was the landowners again, rich, well-to-do, or poor, who produced wool and who owned the forests which yielded timber and charcoal.[73] Next in importance to the landowners outside the city were the fishermen who provided the Coan market with fresh fish.

Various industries, especially the silk industry, flourished in the city, in private households or in workshops large or small. It may be suggested that the γυναικεῖα σώματα mentioned in the tax-list were female slaves engaged in the production of silk stuffs: we know that female slaves were used for similar purposes both at Pergamon and in Egypt.

Retail traders, κάπηλοι and μετάβολοι, were numerous in the city and probably in the villages. They figure prominently in the tax-list.

Domineering over all these—producers, shopkeepers, consumers—stood the greedy crowd of tax-farmers, τελῶναι, one of the most peculiar features of Greek city life. They were deeply hated and feared by all classes of the people, for even the privacy of the house was not sacred from them: 'Every door now trembles at the tax-farmers',* says a respectable lady of Cos (Herondas, VI. 64).

We frequently meet members of these various classes in the witty sketches of Herondas and Theocritus. Phrasidemus and Antigones, owners of an estate in Cos and hosts of the literary party of Theocritus' Thalysiae (*Id.* VII), represent the higher stratum of the city population of the island. To the same class probably belonged Bitinna, the jealous lady who owned the lover-slave Gastron (Herondas, V), and certainly the highly aristocratic Gryllus, son of Matacine daughter of Pataecius, winner of prizes at the Delphic, Corinthian, and Olympic games, suitor of poor abandoned Metriche and client of old Gyllis (Herondas, I).

One step below are the petty *bourgeois* of Cos. Herondas introduces us to some of their ladies: Metrotime, the mother of the naughty boy Cottalus (Herondas, III), and Coccale and Cynno, the two visitors at the temple of Asclepius (Herondas, IV). The intellectual classes are represented by the school-teacher Lampriscus (Herondas, III) and by the doctors in charge of the health service of the city and country.

Below this respectable society of Coan citizens stand the metics. Battarus, the Phoenician brothel-keeper, is a type of this class: the arrogant, self-confident, brazen and at the same time humble metic, who knows his place in the community when he is before the citizen-judges of Cos (Herondas, II, especially l. 29: 'knowing, as I do, how to live in awe of the least of the citizens').†

With Battarus we leave the residential quarters of the city and the rural districts. We come to the harbour with all its noise and filth. Here Thales, the Phrygian, formerly Artimmes, a rich importer of grain from Ptolemais-Ake, who has saved Cos from famine, meets Battarus the Tyrian and his probably imported slave-girls. From here Mandris, Metriche's lover, has sailed for Alexandria with his cargo. Here the fleet lies at anchor and we see the κωποξύσται and the νεωλκοί of the tax-list and the ναυτικὸς ὄχλος going about their business.

At the very bottom of the scale are the hundreds of slaves

* τελώνας πᾶσα νῦν θύρη φρίσσει.

† εἰδότ' ὡς ἐγὼ ζώειν τῶν δημοτέων φρίσσοντα καὶ τὸν ἥκιστον.

working in the docks and in the harbour, in the fields and vineyards, in the shops and households. Herondas is in silent sympathy with them. The same can be hardly said of his attitude towards the members of the higher classes. The reader of Herondas and of the Coan inscriptions cannot resist the impression that the slave population of Cos was large and was not used solely for domestic service.

Cos may certainly be regarded as a typical Aegean island. Similar to it, though wealthier, were the great islands of Chios, Lesbos, and Samos. Of these CHIOS had the reputation of being the richest in the Aegean in the fifth and fourth centuries B.C. as regards both natural resources and trade.* It has never been systematically explored and none of its cities has been excavated. A large number of inscriptions, however, belonging to Hellenistic times have been found above the soil. These suggest that Chios was opulent and had extensive commercial relations. If Mlle Vanseveren (Mme L. Robert) is right in thinking that three fragmentary lists of names with *ethnica* that have been found on the island are lists of *proxenoi* and not of mercenaries, we may infer from them that close relations (probably commercial relations) existed between Chios and many cities of Asia Minor and some of Greece. One of these lists also mentions citizens of Lampsacus, Cyzicus, Byzantium, and Panticapaeum, which may point to active commercial relations with the Euxine. Moreover, the fact that Chian containers, filled perhaps with Chian and Pontic products, are mentioned more than once in Zenon's correspondence may indicate that there was commercial intercourse between Alexandria and Chios and that the latter acted as intermediary between the Euxine and Alexandria. The role of intermediary is perhaps suggested by the fact that a merchant of Chios received twice in 306/5 and again in 296 B.C. the commission of furnishing pitch to Delos.† It is clear that Chios itself produced no pitch.[74]

About LESBOS and MYTILENE in the Hellenistic period less is known. I may mention, however, an interesting list of taxes at Mytilene (*I.G.* xii. 2. 74–5) in the third century, which shows great similarities with the Coan list discussed above. In this

* Arist. *Pol.* iv. 4; Thucyd. viii. 45.

† *I.G.* xi. 2. 144 A 113 and 154 A 48.

PLATE XXXIV

1. Figurine of a slave being flogged. White slip, face pink, cheeks and body red. His ugly head with a long nose is turned upwards; he is screaming and shouting. The upper part of his body is bare. The figurine was suspended on a string and hung in the air. Crude, pathetic realism. Cf. the slaves undergoing flogging represented on the Megarian bowls, above, pl. XXV. The figurine may serve as an illustration to Herondas, *Mim.* v (*Ζηλότυπος*—the jealous woman and her slave lover). Priene. (Photograph supplied by the authorities of the Staatliche Museen, Berlin.)

Th. Wiegand and H. Schrader, *Priene*, 1904, p. 358, fig. 436 f.; F. Winter, loc. cit., p. 443, no. 5; O. Crusius and R. Herzog, loc. cit., pl. x. A similar figure of a slave being flogged is in the National Museum at Athens (F. Winter, loc. cit., p. 442, no. 9).

2. Naked prostitute displaying her beauty. She is young but not beautiful. Excellent illustration to Herondas, *Mim.* ii, *Πορνοβοσκός*. The reader will remember that Battarus produced in the Coan court his girl Myrtale (who was said to be ill-treated by Thales, the rich sea-merchant) in exactly the same posture in which the prostitute is represented in this figurine. For the correct interpretation of one passage in the Mime illustrated by our figurine see A. E. Housman, *Class. Rev.* xxxvi (1922), pp. 109 ff. Unpublished (?). My attention was drawn to this figurine and to Housman's article by Prof. J. D. Beazley. I may point out in this connexion—the subject has not been treated by me in the text of the book—that prostitution was a prominent feature in the social and economic life of the Greek cities in Hellenistic times. Sufficient information on this subject will be found in O. Navarre, art. 'Meretrix', Dar. et Saglio, *D. d. A.* iii, 1825 ff.; K. Schneider, art. 'Hetairai', *P.W.K.*, viii. 131 ff., and 'Meretrix', ibid. xv. 1018 ff. (Photograph supplied by Prof. J. D. Beazley.)

3. Fisherman standing and probably holding a fishing-rod in his outstretched right hand. He wears a soft cap and an exomis, and holds a fishing-basket in his left hand. I speak in Ch. VIII of the importance of fishing in the economic life of the Hellenistic age and of the popularity of this subject with painters, mosaicists, sculptors, and coroplasts of the Classical and still more of the Hellenistic period. Myrina.

E. Pottier and S. Reinach, loc. cit., p. 489 f., pl. XLVII, Cat., no. 330; F. Winter, loc. cit., p. 441, no. 9; *C.A.H.*, loc. cit., p. 193 *b*.

1. Berlin, Staatliche Museen

2. Gotha, Museum

3. Paris, Louvre

Terracotta figurines

LIFE IN GREEK CITIES AND COUNTRY

document Mytilene and Lesbos in general appear as mainly agricultural communities, producing wine in abundance, olive-oil, figs, all sorts of vegetables, and flowers (for ointments), and exploiting their fisheries, their woods, their quarries of marble and other kinds of stone.

The same is true of many other, even most, of the islands. A study of the few literary texts that refer to them, of the numerous inscriptions (collected in part in *I.G.* xii), and of the information relating to the several islands summarized in the relative articles of Pauly-Wissowa's encyclopaedia, makes it almost certain that there was a general similarity in their main economic features.

In conclusion, CRETE, with its singular history and its complicated social and economic development, calls for special notice. Heirs of the glorious past of Minoan Crete, the Dorian cities of the island had their own peculiar internal evolution, similar to, but in no way identical with, that of the other Dorian cities of the Greek world, in particular Sparta. The Cretan cities, organized more or less on the same lines as Sparta, with their own *perioeci* and helots (the class called ἡ μνοία), never achieved political unity. War between them was endemic. On the other hand the Cretans continued the seafaring tradition of the Minoans in their own way. Instead of being traders they became professional pirates and traders in the proceeds of piracy, above all slaves. A careful study of these two sides of Cretan life—the social and economic development of the people in their own island and their special activities at sea—is very much needed. A prerequisite is the publication of the epigraphic material derived from the long and systematic exploration of the island by Italian scholars, especially Halbherr. Until the publication of the *Inscriptiones Cretae*, now in progress, is finished, no general picture of the social and economic life of Crete can usefully be attempted. And without such a picture any general description of Hellenistic Greece will be, if not inadequate, at any rate incomplete.[75]

PART II

THE MAJOR MONARCHIES

AFTER Ipsus (301 B.C.) and still more after Corupedion (281 B.C.) there was a change in the political aspect of what had been Alexander's empire and in the principal powers that composed it. The empire was now and for a long time to come definitely split up into its constituent parts and its disintegration progressed steadily. In this disintegrated world the Greek cities played a secondary part, for they were mostly subject to, or in some way dependent on, the great monarchies of the time. Among these Macedonia, Egypt, and Syria, each ruled by a Macedonian dynasty, were the chief. Alongside of them stood, in its remote isolation, the Bosporan kingdom, a precursor as it were of the new Hellenistic monarchies. To the Bosporan kingdom were added other Pontic monarchies, former Persian satrapies and some of them satrapies of Alexander's empire—Bithynia, Pontus, Cappadocia, and Armenia. In their neighbourhood, in the heart of Asia Minor, Pergamon and the Galatian tribal State came into being and asserted their independence. A few minor *dynasteiai* similar to Pergamon sprang up from time to time in southern Asia Minor and endured for a longer or shorter period. Temple States of an oriental type here and there strove for, and in some instances attained, political independence, for example Olba in Cilicia. In the Middle East, India and some of the Iranian satrapies, the latter under the leadership of the Parthians, secured their freedom and their national character, while Bactria formed a Greek enclave between the Indian and Iranian territories. It may be added that behind the frontiers of the Hellenistic world, in the Balkan peninsula and in the steppes of South Russia, there were certain more or less Hellenized bodies politic: in the former the Thracian, Illyrian, Scythian, and Celtic States, and in the latter the Scythian and Sarmatian monarchies.

All the new 'Hellenistic' monarchies had belonged to the civilized world long before the time of Alexander, and had their own history and characteristics. Most of them had been parts of the Persian Empire and had subsequently been ruled by the satraps of Alexander and of his successors. Their social and economic systems were extremely diverse (above, pp. 77 ff.). Not less varied were their religious beliefs and their civilizations. And yet they were all justified in their claim to belong to the group of Hellenistic monarchies. In almost all of them a new phase of political evolution under new dynasties began in the period we are considering. All these new dynasties, whether Macedonian or not, organized their respective kingdoms on new models, more or less uniform, reproducing in their general lines the constitution framed by Alexander for his empire. Animated as they were by a profound admiration and respect for Greek civilization, they all had a Hellenic complexion and endeavoured to 'hellenize' more or less their respective kingdoms. This means that they all felt that they formed part of one world, the new world created by the genius of Alexander, despite the fact that they all strove for political independence and defended it against any one who threatened it on the pretext of unifying this Hellenistic world.

Their political ideas and ideals were as uniform as was the constitution that they adopted, and they were not very different from those of the Greek city-states. Political independence, political self-sufficiency (αὐτάρκεια), and as far as possible political prominence and leadership in a wider or narrower circle (hegemony) were the dominant motives of their political conduct. Their economic aims were similar. They sought the greatest possible measure of economic self-sufficiency, as a solid basis for political independence. To obtain this they strove to develop to the utmost the resources of their kingdoms, mobilizing and organizing all the creative forces of their people and adding thereto new forces, those of Greek or Hellenized immigrants. For the produce of their countries they sought to secure the largest possible market by establishing commercial connexions as widely as they could, which meant opening their countries to the rest of the world and putting an end to their economic isolation. The easiest way of achieving this was to control important commercial routes by sea or land and so secure for themselves some measure of economic hegemony as a complement of political hegemony.

Uniform as they were, the political and economic aims of the

Hellenistic monarchies were achieved by different methods according to the peculiar social and economic foundations and the political antecedents of each monarchy. There was no uniformity in this respect. A general account of the economic development of the Hellenistic monarchies taken all together would therefore be misleading and inadequate. The development of each monarchy must be studied separately: without such study a true idea of the economic evolution of the Hellenistic world as a whole cannot be obtained. The task is difficult and complicated, and our sources of information are meagre and dispersed.

A. *MACEDONIA*

Of the three principal Hellenistic monarchies Macedonia is that of which least is known. We have some information about it in the days of Philip and Alexander. Our knowledge of it during the reign of Philip V has become constantly fuller with the discovery in recent years of many new inscriptions. The intervening period, that of the reigns of Cassander and Demetrius and of Antigonus Gonatas, Demetrius II, and Antigonus Doson, remains, except for their wars, in almost complete obscurity. Something is known of their administrative system and of their relations with the Greek cities that lay within their boundaries and outside them, but there is no trustworthy evidence, either literary or epigraphical, to throw light upon the changes in the economic and social system of the country.

There appear in fact to have been few important changes. Socially and economically Macedonia remained what it had been in the past, a country of tribal, almost of feudal, structure, under a king who owned large domains in Macedonia proper as well as vast areas, if not whole provinces, in conquered territories: Chalcidice, Paeonia, Atintania, and those parts of Thrace and perhaps of Illyria which at one time or another formed part of the Macedonian kingdom.

In Macedonia proper members of the aristocracy, owners of large estates like the king himself, formed the body of the king's peers. The small landowners constituted the backbone of the country. The kings assigned from time to time 'gifts' of land to their friends, not as their absolute property, but as revocable grants. For this purpose they drew mostly on their domains in conquered territory (not in Macedonia proper). In this territory they also settled the old soldiers, some of them landless Macedonians, some of foreign origin, who had served in their armies as mercenaries.

The estates of the kings and nobles in Macedonia proper were probably cultivated by free tenants, but we have no certain knowledge on this point; nor do we know whether slaves were employed for the purpose or whether relics of earlier serfdom still survived there. In the 'provinces' the land of the kings (γῆ βασιλική) and the estates granted to their companions (ἑταῖροι) may have been cultivated by the original inhabitants of the country in one capacity or another.

A glance at the map of Macedonia will show the large number of cities included within its boundaries. Moreover, the Successors founded additional cities, mostly by synoecism, the common device of this time. Cassandreia (replacing Potidaea) in the Chalcidice and Thessalonice in Macedonia were founded by Cassander, Demetrias in Thessaly (absorbing Pagasae) by Demetrius Poliorcetes. These cities, though no longer capitals of the kingdom, continued to exist under Antigonus Gonatas and his successors. The little information we possess on the subject shows that Pella, the capital, and the other Macedonian towns became regular Greek *poleis* with the regular Greek constitution. To what extent this new status affected their economic life we do not know. Of the new creations of the Hellenistic period Cassandreia remains a mystery, but Demetrias and Thessalonice are steadily becoming better known as more archaeological material is recovered by the efforts of Greek scholars. The period of Demetrias' greatest prosperity was the third century B.C. Her ruins, her painted and carved grave *stelae*, reveal her as a flourishing industrial and commercial city, with a mixed population of Macedonians, Greeks from Greece proper, the Islands, and Sicily, and immigrants from Asia Minor, Syria, and Phoenicia. The same is probably true of Thessalonice. I shall return to the latter presently.

Macedonia was certainly a very rich country in the time of Alexander and under his immediate successors. Much wealth was brought into it by the generals, officers, and soldiers who returned home after service in the armies of Alexander or his successors. How rich these *reduces* were is shown by the well-known account given by Hippolochus (mentioned above, p. 151) of the wedding-feast of a noble Macedonian, Caranus (Athen. iv. 128 ff.). This man had certainly become rich somehow or other in connexion with Alexander's expedition; his gifts of gold and silver to his guests were so princely that after the banquet these rushed to invest them in land, houses, and other things.

True, the country was utterly devastated by the Celts, and some of the accumulated wealth was lost. But the Celts were unable to capture fortified cities, and the damage done to fields and gardens was easily repaired. More important for Macedonia were the general results of the Celtic invasion of the country and of their settlement in some parts of the Thracian regions. The patient work of Lysimachus in his Euxine empire was undermined and partially destroyed, and Antigonus and his successors were never able to restore it. The northern problem was therefore as grave and as difficult for Macedonia in the time of Antigonus and after him as it had been before Philip, Alexander, and Lysimachus. It required a good deal of attention and expenditure.

Nevertheless, the northern front and the wars of Antigonus in Greece and the Aegean of which I spoke in the first chapter did not affect the general economic situation of Macedonia. The country, as I have pointed out, was certainly prosperous in the reigns of Antigonus Gonatas and his successors. This prosperity may be explained by the general trend of their economic policy. Their personal requirements and expenses were modest, for they never indulged in Oriental luxury like their richer neighbours in the East. The bulk of their revenue was derived from their domains, and taxation does not appear to have been oppressive. It is to be borne in mind that the royal domains included, besides large and fertile fields and meadows, the silver- and gold-mines and the forests, which last yielded excellent timber for building, in particular for shipbuilding, and abundant tar and pitch.

Though no direct information is available, we may safely

assume that Antigonus did his best to develop the rich natural resources of his native land, and above all of his domains, in order to increase his revenues without oppressing his subjects. At the same time he certainly was anxious to take his share in inter-State trade in competition with the other commercial powers of the time. His efforts in this direction are attested by the abundant and reliable gold and silver coinage issued by him and his successors. Antigonus' coinage was certainly intended to play an important part in the world currency of the time. In standard (Attic) and types it was a continuation of the coinage of Alexander. And it had a great success: Macedonian coins circulated far and wide in the Hellenistic world. It is interesting to observe, however, that in his coinage Antigonus did not follow the example of the Ptolemies and the Seleucids. He never issued coins bearing his own portrait (as his father had done), and his immediate successors followed his policy in this respect. In this we may recognize a concession to Greek ideas and an endeavour to facilitate the circulation of his coins in Greek cities. As regards these cities his monetary policy resembled that of the Seleucids. His subject cities were not allowed to issue gold or silver of higher denominations; their coinage was limited to small silver and copper for local circulation. The Greek *κοινά* and cities which were legally independent of Antigonus continued, of course, to strike their own money.

Another important feature of his economic policy was his relations with Rhodes and Delos.

I have already pointed out that after his victories over the Ptolemies Antigonus entered into close political and commercial relations with Rhodes and Delos; and these relations were maintained by his successors. The port from which the grain of part of Macedonia and the produce of Macedonian forests were principally shipped was in all probability Thessalonice. It may be noticed that Aristobulus, the corn-factor (*σιτώνης*) of Demetrius II,* was a citizen of Thessalonice, apparently a man with business experience, and that Admetus the Macedonian, whose place of residence was apparently Delos, was highly honoured both at Delos and Thessalonice, where statues of him were

* *I.G.* xi. 4. 666; Durrbach, *Choix*, 48.

PLATE XXXV

I need only add a few words to those in the title of the plate and to what I have said about the mosaic on p. 196 and n. 11 and on p. 380 and n. 178. The mosaic has never been fully discussed from the technical, artistic, and historical points of view, a necessary preliminary to the dating of this important monument of art. In my opinion, though the mosaic found at Thmuis may have been laid in late Hellenistic times, it was not an original creation of that time but probably a copy of a much earlier original. It is of course impossible to say whether the immediate original was a mosaic or a rug with the bust of Alexandria inwoven, in the style of the rugs with inwoven heads of the Ptolemies described by Callixeinus. The author of this immediate original, a product of industrial art, can hardly have been the creator of the impressive head of Alexandria in the mosaic of Thmuis. This head appears to me to hark back to some great artistic work, not a mere piece of decoration, perhaps to a famous symbolical painting in which the personification of thalassocracy, as represented on the Thmuis mosaic, was the principal feature. The painting may have been the creation of some place other than Alexandria, and may have celebrated the naval exploits and the resulting thalassocracy, not of the early Ptolemies, but of their rivals. But it is more reasonable to suppose that it was the work of an Alexandrian artist and was intended to exalt the naval achievements of the early Ptolemies. Whether Sophilus was the name of this artist or of the copyist it is impossible to say. The plate is reproduced from the same original that served for the illustration in the Memoir by E. Breccia. For permission to use it I am indebted to Prof. A. Adriani, Director of the Museum of Alexandria.

PLATE XXXV

Bust of Alexandria

represented as mistress of the seas (with naval crown on her head, a military cloak on her shoulders and an *aphlaston* in her left hand). Part of a mosaic found at Thmuis in the Delta. Signed by Sophilus. Now in the Museum of Alexandria. (See ch. IV, notes 11 and 178.)

erected.* Since no mention of the king is found in the inscriptions in honour of Admetus nor any suggestion that the latter held any official position, it is more than probable that he was a rich business man who organized regular commercial relations between Macedonia and the Greek world. Autocles of Chalcis, on the contrary, described as 'a friend of King Demetrius' (φίλος ὢν τοῦ βασιλέως Δημητρίου), was probably a Macedonian officer, perhaps of the navy.†

All this Delian evidence points to the rapidly growing importance of Thessalonice as a trade centre and probably to the endeavour of the Macedonian kings to organize the commercial business of their country on the latest lines.[76]

B. *EGYPT*

1. Sources of Information

The Macedonian monarchy about which we are best informed is undoubtedly Egypt, where the dynasty of the Ptolemies firmly established itself for three centuries. Our knowledge of it, derived from literary, epigraphic, papyrological, and archaeological sources, is unusually full, especially if compared with our knowledge of Macedonia and Syria. And yet our sources of information even about Egypt are not really abundant and are most unequally distributed. Literary passages bearing on the social and economic life of the country are as haphazard as those relating to the rest of the Hellenistic world. Inscriptions are poorer both in number and in content than in Asia Minor. The papyri constitute our main source of information. But Greek and Demotic papyri are comparatively scarce for the time of the Ptolemies (they are estimated at about 10,000 published texts, while those of the Roman period are much more numerous), and the light thrown by them upon the various parts of Egypt, the several centuries, and the different aspects of its life, is most unevenly spread.

The best-known period is that now under our consideration, comprising the reigns of Philadelphus and Euergetes I. Our

* *I.G.* xi. 4. 664, 665, and 1053, cf. 1076; Durrbach, *Choix*, 49; Philemon, his son, was buried in Rheneia, *C.I.G.* 2322b.

† *I.G.* xi. 4. 679, 680; Durrbach, *Choix*, 47.

knowledge of the later reigns is much less complete and very irregular. I shall speak of the documents of this later period in the subsequent chapters; here we are concerned with the papyri belonging to the time of Philadelphus and Euergetes I.

Of these very few have reference to general conditions or emanate from the central government. Such documents as that which embodies the royal orders or laws of Ptolemy Philadelphus regulating the farming of certain royal revenues (perhaps officially styled διάγραμμα or νόμοι τελωνικοί, while the first editors of the document called it 'Revenue Laws'), or the directions (ὑπομνήματα or ἐντολαί) of the *dioecetes*, or economic manager, to his subordinates in the time of Euergetes I or Philopator, are exceptional. To these two may be added the extracts of certain laws and regulations (mostly of the city of Alexandria) collected by a party to a lawsuit and styled by the editors of the document δικαιώματα. Unfortunately we have only bad copies of these three documents; they are incomplete and lacunary, and the last two are not original documents but extracts.

Of the other numerous papyri, certain connected groups of documents which once belonged to the records of a single person or a single office are of exceptionally high value. Such are, in particular, the documents of the archives of Zenon, one of the trusted assistants of Apollonius, the great 'manager' (διοικητής) of the financial and economic affairs of Philadelphus. Specially illuminating are those belonging to the early period of Zenon's life, when he was managing the affairs of Apollonius in Palestine and subsequently assisting him in Alexandria and on his tours of inspection. Later, when he had been appointed manager of the large estate of Apollonius at Philadelphia in the Fayûm, he was no longer in touch with his employer's wider interests, but devoted all his attention and energy to this estate. Next to Zenon's archives in point of interest and importance are the documents of the same period from the office of the engineers Cleon and Theodorus, who were in charge of the reclamation work in the Fayûm. And finally we have among the documents of the reigns of Euergetes and Philopator those known as the papyri of Magdola and Ghoran in the Fayûm, which once formed part of the archives either of the *strategos* of the nome or of the chief police officer (ἐπι-στάτης) of a village.* I may also mention the set of documents which come from the archives of Tebtunis in the Fayûm, of Ankyronpolis, modern Hibeh, in Middle Egypt,† and those which were found at Elephantine in South Egypt.‡

But these groups of connected papyri are exceptional. The bulk of the Greek documents written on papyrus consist of disconnected records of miscellaneous character. Many of them are official or semi-official, illustrating the relations between the government and the various classes of the population of Egypt, such as orders and other pronouncements of the kings and their ministers, various official papers (surveys, accounts, &c.) connected with taxation and the management of royal revenues, petitions and complaints of the inhabitants of Egypt addressed to the king or his officers and officials, records of law-suits, tax receipts, and so forth. No less numerous than official documents are those recording various transactions between private persons, especially contracts of various sorts. And finally there is a fair number of private letters.

Besides Greek papyri an ever-increasing number of documents in Demotic have been discovered in Egypt, especially in the ruins of temples and of private houses connected with the temples. Some of them form continuous series, representing the contents of private archives: such are, for example, the series of documents from Gebelen beginning with the sixth century B.C. and another set illustrating the economic condition of a family from 317 to 217 B.C. Most of them belong to a later time and will be mentioned in subsequent chapters. They are of the greatest importance, in particular for the light they throw on the economic organization of the temples. The wealth of Demotic papyri accumulated in our museums and libraries is attracting the attention of scholars to an increasing extent, and there is hope that many more Demotic documents will soon be published with good translations and adequate comments.

Large and important as it is, the papyrological evidence has

* O. Guéraud, *'Εντεύξεις*, 1931–2.

† Grenfell and Hunt, *The Hibeh Papyri*, i, 1906.

‡ O. Rubensohn, *Elephantine Papyri*, 1907.

its limitations. We must not forget that our papyri come only from some parts of the so-called 'country' (χώρα)—from the Fayûm, from certain places in Middle Egypt, and from others in Southern Egypt. They have been recovered from the ruins of cities and villages, from the rubbish-heaps of various settlements, and especially from the sarcophagi and wrappings of mummies, for which waste paper was used as material. There is no hope that papyrological documents of any period or of any kind will ever be found at Alexandria. But we may expect that, as happened at Abusir el Melek, archaeologists may once more discover Alexandrian documents exported from Alexandria as waste paper to some place drier and nearer the desert. Nor is it likely that many papyri (apart from carbonized papyri) will be found in Lower Egypt, except in its borderlands on East and West, which have been very rarely touched by the spade of papyrologists.

On the other hand, it is mere chance that Middle and Southern Egypt have yielded few documents as compared with the Fayûm, and that those found there belong mostly to the late Ptolemaic period. Here, and especially in Southern Egypt, important discoveries of Ptolemaic documents may be made at any time. The finds at Elephantine and the many Greek and Demotic documents of our period which come from south Egypt, and which I have mentioned above, show that this region is full of promise.

Moreover, as has been said, very few of them bear upon Egypt as a whole. The enormous majority reflect local conditions, which certainly varied from one place to another, since the economic aspect of Egypt and historical traditions were far from uniform. And finally the documents belong only in part to official archives. Most of them relate to the life of individuals. To use such material for general statements is very hazardous.

One instance will suffice. Besides other valuable information on economic matters, the papyri—in this respect comparable with, but differing from, the Delian accounts (see above, p. 190 ff.)—supply us with a large amount of statistical data of various kinds. These data are of course discontinuous, but they belong to a class of documentary evidence which is rarely at the disposal of modern students of ancient history. They are very valuable, but they must be used with great prudence. Those of them which relate to the prices of commodities and of land, houses, labour, rents, &c., are of exceptional importance. They have been frequently collected and studied by modern scholars. But this material has its limitations, and we must not over-estimate its value. It must be remembered, in the first place, that the documents in which the prices are mentioned vary greatly in character. We possess nothing similar to the official records of Delos. Some of the prices occur in official, some in private, documents; some are prices fixed by the government, some by private agreement; none necessarily represent current prices, and most relate to particular localities only and to the interests and economic circumstances of individuals, which in the majority of cases are unknown to us.

Moreover, the comparative study of prices in Egypt and even in parts of Egypt (a nome, a toparchy, a village) is rendered very difficult by many peculiar circumstances. This is true, for example, of the prices of such a basic commodity as grain. In the statistical lists compiled by modern scholars the price of grain is shown per *artaba*, as if the *artaba* were a constant measure. In fact, as has been proved by Wilcken and Tarn, many *artabae* of various sizes were in use at the same time and in the same region of Egypt.

Despite its limitations, the papyrological material is of enormous value to the student of economic history. For no other country have we such abundant and trustworthy information for the Greco-Roman period. In the field of ancient history the Babylonian cuneiform tablets and cylinders alone furnish material comparable to this.[77]

Next in importance to the evidence of papyri is the archaeological material. Every one knows that the ruins and tombs of Egypt are a mine of wealth for archaeologists, as regards both the earlier periods of its history and the Hellenistic, Roman, and later periods. Large quantities of objects of Hellenistic times are stored in the museum at Cairo and still more in that of Alexandria, and many are distributed among European and American museums. In most of the museums the finds made in Alexandria itself form a large proportion of those relating to the Hellenistic period in general. Sculpture and decorative painting, bronze and terracotta figurines, silver and bronze plate, jewels, fragments of dresses and shoes, objects of wood, bone, and ivory, pottery of various kinds, and glass have been found in large quantities both in Alexandria and in the cities and villages of the χώρα, especially in the Fayûm. In addition we have an abundance of remains of articles in common use: weapons and armour, agricultural implements, household utensils such as baskets, ropes, brooms, and brushes, fragments of looms and of other industrial equipment, harness for horses, donkeys, and camels, fishing and hunting implements, and so forth, in great variety and of various periods.

Some of these finds have been studied and published in the catalogues of the Cairo and Alexandria museums and in various other publications, but many which perhaps have the most important bearing on the economic history of Egypt (for instance, the agricultural and industrial implements) still await publication. We hope that the excavators of Karanis, where the largest quantities of such objects have been found, will furnish a comprehensive comparative study and technical analysis of them.[78]

Lastly, we have a rich set of coins—gold, silver, and copper—which are of the greatest importance for the economic history of Ptolemaic Egypt. I shall speak of them in detail later in this section.

In spite of its fragmentary character, the wealth of material that Egypt presents to the historian of economic conditions is overwhelming, and it is increasing rapidly. Scientific investigation of the accumulated material tries to keep pace with its rapid increase, but a great deal remains to be done, as is evident if we consider the enormous quantity of unpublished papyri alone which are stored in the various museums of the Old and New Worlds. Even such a sensational find as the Zenon correspondence, divided as it has been between various museums and some of it still in the hands of professional dealers, is not yet completely published. It is difficult to estimate the number of unpublished papyri of the Ptolemaic period, but they certainly amount to thousands if not to scores of thousands. And every year brings a fresh supply from the inexhaustible soil of

Egypt. The same is true of the archaeological and numismatic material. In these circumstances an exhaustive treatment of the economic evolution of Egypt in the Hellenistic period will not be expected here. All that can be attempted is a short survey of the results already achieved. The reader, however, must bear in mind that the generalizations contained in this and the next chapters concerning this economic evolution are to a large extent conjectural. There are very few points of Egyptian economy of which we can claim exact and final knowledge. Every fresh publication of papyri, every additional inscription, throws light on old problems and raises new ones; every important aspect of Egyptian economic activity is still, and will long remain, under discussion.[79]

2. Egypt before Philadelphus

It was not an uncivilized country that became the field of the political, social, and economic activity of Ptolemy Soter and his successors. Egypt had a long and glorious history, a highly developed civilization, and strong traditions reaching back thousands of years and concerned with all aspects of its life, religious, political, administrative, juridical, intellectual, social, and economic. Nor had Egypt been in the past a country closed to external influences. In the Saïte period, during the two Persian dominations, and still more in the sixty years of independence between them, Egypt had adapted herself to the new political and economic conditions then prevailing in the ancient world. In this period Egypt was closely connected with the Greek world, and was an important element in the political and economic situation. But beyond the fact that during her independence she admitted comparatively large numbers of Greeks, soldiers and merchants, to her territory, and that Persian domination opened the country to many foreigners, both Persian and other subjects of the Persian king, our information does not go. We do not know how far the political and economic structure of Egypt was affected by Persian influence or how extensively Egyptian customs were modified, especially during the rule of the XXVIIIth, XXIXth, and XXXth dynasties.[80]

Nor do we know very much of the proceedings of Alexander's

agents in Egypt (except for certain transactions of Cleomenes) or of the conditions that prevailed there during the long rule of Soter. The literary sources are almost silent and documentary evidence fails us almost completely. It is not until the reign of Philadelphus that we begin to perceive the general outlines of the organization of Egypt, and since it is manifest from the evidence that Philadelphus displayed a feverish activity, we are inclined to give him credit for most of what we know and perhaps to under-estimate the achievements of Cleomenes and Soter. It is, however, certain that Philadelphus inherited his main problems from his predecessors. The political and economic condition of Egypt under Alexander and Soter could not have remained exactly what it had been under the Persians, for the course of events had introduced new elements into the situation. As one of the satrapies of Alexander, Egypt may conceivably have continued her traditional mode of life. The Persian army was replaced by a detachment of the Macedonian army and the tribute that Egypt had formerly paid to Artaxerxes Ochus and Darius III went into the treasury of Alexander.

Under Soter the conditions changed. Egypt became an independent Macedonian kingdom, engaged in a hard struggle for independence and for a leading role in the affairs of the world. The prerequisites of independence and international prestige were, obviously, a strong army and navy and ample resources, especially a large revenue in gold and silver. In the contest for power a native Egyptian army would be useless. The other Successors had at their disposal well-trained armies of Macedonians and Greeks, the best soldiers of the day, led by expert officers and equipped with everything that Greek military technique could devise. The superiority of such forces even to the excellent Persian army had been proved by the campaigns alike of Alexander and of the Successors. It was the same with the navy. Without a well-equipped and up-to-date navy, equal to those of the other Greek powers, Egypt's political existence was doomed. But Egypt possessed no national navy or naval tradition when Soter became ruler and subsequently king of Egypt. To attempt to create from native elements a loyal and well-equipped army and navy would have been a hazardous experiment. In the conditions of the time it was not seriously to be thought of. Soter was accordingly forced to rely upon the Greco-Macedonian army and navy inherited from Alexander, and to increase, strengthen, and discipline them in every possible way. This could not be done unless officers and men were assured of good pay, sufficient to enable them to maintain themselves and their belongings (ἀποσκευαί), and unless they were in some way bound to their new country, that is to say, assured of a privileged position in it.

Soter was himself a Hellenized Macedonian; his education had given him a Greek outlook and he can hardly have known much of the Egyptian language or of the glorious history of the country of which he was now master. If he placed natives in charge of the civil administration of the country he would scarcely be able to understand his own ministers and other officials. There is nothing to show that he discriminated in principle between Macedonians, Greeks, and natives. But his attempt to employ natives as assistants, of which there is good evidence, probably convinced him, as it had convinced Alexander, of the difficulty of making extensive use of the native aristocracy in the administration of the country, however well trained they might be, and though they might even prove to be perfectly loyal. Thus he would naturally surround himself with a civil staff composed in the main of officials possessing the same training and mentality as his own, and therefore congenial to him. To these Greek and Macedonian assistants, no less than to his military forces, he was bound to assure good pay and a privileged position.

For his army, his civilian staff, and his foreign policy Soter needed money, gold and silver, in vast quantities. Egypt, as we shall presently see, was a very rich country, economically almost self-sufficient, and yielding regularly to its rulers a large revenue. The use of money, especially foreign money (above, p. 89), as a medium of exchange was not unknown in Egypt before Alexander. There were large quantities of gold and silver in the country in the possession of temples and in private hands. But, in the main, the business of Egypt was conducted on a basis not of money but of barter. To secure for himself a regular inflow of gold and silver Soter was obliged to change this custom. Gold and silver had to be put into circulation on a greatly increased scale, and the commodities that were produced in Egypt in abundance and for which there was a demand in the world market had to be made available there in much larger quantities than before. Egypt must be thrown wide open to the Mediterranean lands through Alexandria, the wonderful new gate. All this could not be done without the co-operation of foreigners, men who were used to a money economy and who understood the commercial system of the Mediterranean world. This meant not only admitting foreigners into the country, which had been done before and on a large scale, but making them welcome there, incorporating them in it, and assuring them a leading part in its affairs.

The economic potentialities of Egypt were very great, but the pace of economic activity was slow, as in most oriental countries. Soter required a larger yield from its resources, in particular a more intensive exploitation, better organized and better planned. This involved an improvement of the economic machine that he had inherited from his predecessors. For this work of readjustment and improvement he needed faithful assistants, capable of understanding him and willing and ready to help him. No such help was to be expected from the natives, and he was forced to rely upon his Macedonian fellow countrymen, and upon Greeks and hellenized Semites.

Lastly, Soter needed prestige in the eyes of the Greek world. Such prestige a new Pharaoh of Egypt could never acquire, however large the sums of money he spent in Greek lands. Egypt must have at least a Greek façade, it must figure as a Greek, not as an Egyptian, monarchy. A Greek capital for the new Egypt was imperatively required. Memphis, however international her population may have been, would not serve the purpose, nor would Thebes. Alexandria, the foundation of Alexander, was the ideal place. It linked Soter with Alexander and was from the outset a Greek city. And it was necessary that Alexandria should be not only the political and economic façade of the country but also a great Greek city, a centre of Greek art, learning, and life. There is no need to assume a change in Soter's policy in order to understand his transfer of the capital from Memphis to Alexandria. Memphis was his capital so long as he did not feel secure from external attack. As soon as his army and navy were strong enough to make his position in Alexandria safe, he moved to this Greek city and by so doing made it the capital of Egypt.

A Greek superstructure had thus to be built up in Egypt, as any successor of Alexander in Egypt, Ptolemy or another, would have found. Without it the kingdom of the Ptolemies would not be a 'Hellenistic' kingdom, a prolongation, within its boundaries, of Alexander's monarchy.

But the Greek superstructure in Egypt, important as it was, was no more than a superstructure. As I have said, there were foreigners settled, in groups of various sizes, in all parts of the country long before the days of Alexander. There were compact settlements of them in the Greek cities of Naucratis and perhaps Paraetonium, and other groups in Memphis and perhaps Thebes. There was a large Jewish colony of civilians as well as soldiers at Elephantine in south Egypt, and there were many other foreigners who came to Egypt with the Persians. This foreign population increased in numbers and importance in the times of Alexander and Soter. I have spoken of Alexandria. To Alexandria Soter added Ptolemais as his southern capital, to balance Thebes. Macedonian and Greek garrisons were stationed all over the country, and with them came new settlers.

Native Egyptians, however, formed the main body of the population. Though we have no statistics, there can be no doubt that this population numbered millions, while the immigrants numbered thousands. We have too little information about the social conditions of Egypt in the fourth century B.C. to tell whether there was at that time a sharp dividing-line between the rich and influential temple-lords of the type of the well-known Petosiris and the lay aristocracy. What happened to the latter under and after Soter we do not know. It is rarely mentioned in extant texts in the time of Soter and almost never later. Some of its members may have merged with the temple aristocracy. The temples continued to be the centres of religious life, with their numerous priesthood and its stable organization, with their traditional economic and social system going back thousands of years. Demotic documents of the late fourth century, under Ptolemy Soter the satrap, show no change in their traditional customs. The temples and the clergy were a great force in Egypt, as Soter certainly knew. The gods of Egypt were its real lords, and all the successive rulers of the country, except perhaps Artaxerxes Ochus, recognized this. In relation to the gods and the temples, Soter stepped into the position of the last Pharaohs, and was officially recognized as their successor by the priests, whatever their real feelings may have been.

Next to the temple communities in pre-Hellenistic Egypt stood the powerful body of royal officials, the scribes of various grades. The upper stratum of these gradually disappeared, the lower scribes remaining as representatives of the population before the crown. They had to learn Greek and to adapt themselves to their new masters and their new overlord, and this they did. It is unfortunate that we know so little of this class during the rule of Soter. It was one of the chief successes of the new government that it was able to educate afresh this backbone of the country's administrative, financial, and economic system—to teach it the Greek language and the Greek system of accounting. A discovery of early documents from the archives of a village scribe may one day enable us to understand the process.

Last in the social scale were the millions of natives in the thousands of towns and villages of Egypt: peasants, artisans, traders, soldiers settled in the country, and it would be of the highest interest to know their manner of life in the time of Soter. The systematic excavation of one of the villages, not of the Fayûm but of Lower, Middle, or Upper Egypt, may some day give us the information we so much need. From the Fayûm there is little to hope for in this respect. The inhabitants of the new villages on the fringe of the desert—the only villages that yield an abundance of papyri—were, whether Greeks or natives, mostly new settlers, immigrants.

Although we have no positive information on the point, it is obvious that Soter could not regard the native population of Egypt as a negligible element, as semi-slaves obliged to toil for him and for the men who came to Egypt with him. It was to his interest to keep them in good humour and to ensure them a fair amount of prosperity and happiness. He was their king, as he was king for his countrymen and for the Greeks. The chief problem that faced Soter as ruler of Egypt was therefore to find an acceptable *modus vivendi* for the two sections of the population, to reconcile the antinomy inherent in the peculiar structure of his 'Hellenistic' monarchy. In other words his problem was to turn to the best advantage, for his own ends, a situation resulting from causes outside his own will and choice. How he solved this problem, we must admit that we have no evidence to show.[81]

3. Philadelphus' Reform of the Economic and Social Systems

Much more is known about Egypt in the time of Soter's successor Philadelphus, who was faced with the same fundamental difficulties. How much of the situation revealed by the thousands of documents of his time was of his own creating and to what extent its main lines had already been laid down by Soter are questions that we are as yet unable to answer.[82]

The power of the Ptolemies in Egypt, as reflected in the documents of the reign of Philadelphus and of later times, had three different aspects. Heirs of Alexander—and they insisted on a direct connexion with Alexander in their genealogy—they were kings of the Macedonians who were with them in Egypt, originally soldiers of Alexander's army, who had helped to conquer the country. Egypt, from the point of view of the Ptolemies, the Macedonian kings, and of their Macedonian army, was a land 'won by the spear' (δορίκτητος χώρα), that is to say, an estate of the Macedonian kings.

But, once established in Egypt, the Ptolemies (like Alexander) claimed to be the legitimate successors of the Pharaohs, and were recognized as such by the priests of the national cults. According to the ancient political and religious conception of kingship prevalent in Egypt, the king was the son of Ammon-Ra, a god residing temporarily on earth. Since the god or the gods were the real masters and owners of Egypt and were entitled to use the land and its inhabitants as they pleased, the kings of Egypt, in the period of its independence, were regarded as the supreme owners and masters both of the land and of their subjects. This supreme ownership the Ptolemies, as successors of the Pharaohs, claimed for themselves.

Finally, the Greek subjects of the Ptolemies gradually recognized them as descendants of gods and as gods residing on earth, and an official cult of the Ptolemies was established both in their capital and in the country, supplementing an equally official cult of the deified Alexander. I cannot discuss here the hotly debated problem of the history and character of the ruler-cult of the Ptolemies. There is, however, no doubt that it was from the very beginning a religious and political institution of purely Greek character, organized as such by the kings and imposed by them on all the inhabitants of Egypt, Greek and native. The official cult of the living ruler was added, certainly by Philadelphus (not later than 271/0 B.C.), to the equally official cult of the deceased rulers. I cannot interpret this institution in any other way than as an endeavour of the Ptolemies to give to their absolute rule over the Greeks a religious sanction acceptable to the Greeks. The acceptance of the institution by the Greeks was equivalent to the recognition of the kings as their divine masters and of themselves as their subjects.

Moreover, Greek philosophy in early Hellenistic times added to this political and religious conception, for the benefit of Greeks who had some philosophical education, the theory that kingship was the best form of government and that kings were identical with the State and, as it were, an incarnation of it. Various schools, which contributed powerfully to shape Greek mentality in Hellenistic times—Stoics, Neo-Pythagoreans, Peripatetics, even Epicureans—vied with each other in finding arguments to prove that monarchy, from the philosophical standpoint, was the best possible form of government. Some of them went so far as to declare that kings were the 'living law', to be blindly obeyed by their subjects.

The theory of the kingship of the 'best man', who by this very fact *is* king, was completely adopted by the Ptolemies. Whether or not Philadelphus received any special training in philosophy, and particularly in moral philosophy, we do not know. But it is certain that he read the treatises on kingship, and it is probable that his father Soter had read them likewise, for he had been advised to do so by Demetrius of Phaleron. In their own eyes, as in the eyes of the Greek population, the Ptolemies, like other Hellenistic monarchs, were 'Saviours', 'Benefactors', 'Gods manifest', applying themselves to the good of their country, promoters of justice, patrons of the sciences and arts, generous employers and paymasters of the Hellenes and especially of their soldiers, strong defenders of their country against enemies, courteous and civil in their daily intercourse with their subjects, devoted worshippers of the immortals; in a word, true kings and not tyrants. We have definite evidence of this point of view in the idylls of Theocritus, in a lately discovered political treatise of the third century B.C., and later in the ethico-political discussion at the banquet of Greeks and Jews described in the Epistle of the so-called Aristeas, in many sentences and expressions that occur in royal orders and instructions and are repeated with modifications by royal officials and by subjects of the kings in their petitions.[83]

Being recognized by all the constituent parts of the population of Egypt as the absolute rulers of the State, the Ptolemies acted accordingly. Absolute rule meant, alike from the Egyptian and from the Macedonian point of view, the ownership of the State, of its soil and subsoil, and ultimately of the products of the soil and subsoil. The State was the 'house' (οἶκος) of the king, and its territory his estate (χώρα, οὐσία). So the king managed the State as a plain Macedonian or Greek would manage his own household. It should be noted that many titles of the king's officials in the sphere of finance and economics were terms borrowed from Greek private law and Greek public and private economy. The chief assistant of the king in finance and economics was his manager (διοικητής), who was represented in the country by local managers (διοικηταί or ὑποδιοικηταί). In the subdivisions of Egypt—the nomes (departments)—the king's interests were looked after by his stewards (οἰκονόμοι). The accounting was done at Alexandria by the chief accountant of the king, the ἐκλογιστής, and in the nomes the accounts of the steward were checked by an ἀντιγραφεύς (*contrascriptor*, checking clerk, controller).

To the Greeks, indeed, the ideal of a State being in the private ownership of some one was an alien notion. But Greek

PLATE XXXVI

1. Head of a Ptolemaic queen found at Naucratis in 1885–6. Greyish-white clay; greenish-blue glaze covering the whole of the head except the eyes and the base. It is certainly the portrait head of a queen. She wears a melon coiffure, a thin diadem and ear-rings (the diadem and the ear-rings are glazed lemon-yellow to represent gold). The identity of the queen is not quite certain: Arsinoe II and Berenice II have the strongest claims. I am inclined to accept the former identification. The head may have belonged to a statuette or may have served another purpose (there are similar but smaller heads, probably of Euergetes I, in the Br. Mus.). Photograph supplied by the authorities of the British Museum.

Br. Mus. Catal. of Roman Pottery, K 7; R. Hinks, *J.H.S.* xlviii (1928), pp. 239 ff. and pl. xv, cf. E. Pfuhl, *J.D.A.I.* xlv (1930), p. 42, and A. Adriani, *Bull. Soc. Arch. Alex.* xxxii (N.S. x. 1) (1938), p. 94 f. H. 0,059.

2. Fragment of a greenish-blue glazed royal *oenochoe* (on vessels of this kind see description of pl. XLI), showing the figure of Queen Berenice II, wife of Euergetes I (cf. the description of pl. VI, 2). A fine piece of miniature sculpture. Photograph supplied by the authorities of the Allard Pierson Museum, Amsterdam.

Several fragments of royal *oenochoai* are known and have been published. Almost identical with this fragment is that in the Museum of Alexandria, C. Anti, *Die Antike*, v (1929), p. 15, fig. 5, cf. R. Pagenstecher, *Gr.-Aeg. Samml. E. von Sieglin*, ii. 3, pp. 118 ff., figs. 129 and 130. The fragment here reproduced is published in *Allard Pierson Museum. Algemeene Gids*, p. 177, no. 1633, pl. LXXXII. H. 0·133.

3, 4. Similar fragment of excellent workmanship, the best that I know. I am inclined to identify the queen with Arsinoe II, whose figure frequently appears on the royal *oenochoai*, for example on the famous *oenochoe* in the Brit. Mus. often published: see the bibliography quoted in n. 163, and cf. R. Vallois, *C. R. Ac. Inscr.*, 1929, pp. 32 ff., and a good reproduction in J. H. Macurdy, *Hellenistic Queens*, 1932, p. 134, fig. 6. Note however, that on the Brit. Mus. *oenochoe* Arsinoe II wears a different type of coiffure. The fragment reproduced here appears to be unpublished. Photographs supplied by the authorities of the Louvre, Paris.

1. London, Brit. Mus.

2. Amsterdam, Allard Pierson Museum.

3. Paris, Louvre.

4. Paris, Louvre.

FAIENCE PORTRAITS OF PTOLEMAIC QUEENS

citizens in general imbibed from their earliest days the doctrine that the interests of the State were supreme and the private interests of the citizens subordinate thereto, the fundamental doctrine of Greek political philosophy. Now the same Greek political philosophy that had taught and was still teaching this doctrine proclaimed the king to be identical with, and, as it were, the incarnation of, the State. The Greeks could therefore, provided they accepted the philosophical theory of kingship, reconcile with their conscience the idea of the king being the owner of the State.

As owner and supreme manager of the State the king, according to Egyptian ideas, had at his disposal not only its material resources but also the labour of the population, with which they actively assisted him in the exploitation of his estate. Ownership of the land by the king, and compulsory labour for his benefit as the representative of the deity and the realm (and therefore as a rule for the benefit of the community as a whole), were the twin pillars supporting the fabric of the Egyptian State and of Oriental States in general. This idea of compulsory service to the State was familiar to the Greeks also. For them the supremacy of the State implied the active assistance of all the citizens, especially in case of emergency, of war or of any need connected with war. The citizens had then to serve the community with their labour and their substance, to perform a 'liturgy' (λειτουργία) if called upon by the State.[84]

Whether this conception of the relations between the king of Egypt and his country was ever formulated by contemporaries, whether it was fully understood by them, and became the guiding principle of their activity, we do not know. In all probability not. But the two leading notions that it comprised formed the basis, perhaps the subconscious basis, of the activity of the Ptolemies in Egypt, and were taken for granted both by the kings and by their subjects. In formulating them we are not merely propounding a modern theory to explain the facts, for the ideas, whether formulated or not, did really prevail, acceptable or repugnant according to tastes.

In seeking to make Egypt politically independent, economically self-sufficient, and a leading power in the civilized world, the Ptolemies, and probably the satraps of Alexander before them, could not fail to observe that the productivity of the country might be greatly increased. A stricter, more efficient, and more logical economic system was required. A reform of some kind was imperatively called for, and it was carried out. We see the new organization partly at work, partly in making, in the hands of Ptolemy Philadelphus. This new economic organization is known to us in general outline from the papyrological material described above. In it two systems were to be blended, so as to form one well-balanced and smoothly working whole: the immemorial practice of Egypt and the methods of the Greek State and the Greek private household.

The reform presents two aspects to the student. On the one hand, it endeavoured through a stricter and more thorough organization to concentrate the efforts of the people on an increase of production. On the other, it sought to develop the resources of the country by the adoption of the technical improvements that had come into use in other parts of the civilized world. The ultimate object of this reform was evidently to increase and to stabilize the royal revenues, on which depended the safety and the strength of the king himself and of his kingdom. I will first deal with the former aspect.

The economic, social, and financial reform carried out by the first two Ptolemies which I am going to describe was based, as I have said, on the chief principles underlying the fabric of an Oriental State, viz. identity of king and country, ownership of the country by the king, unrestricted obedience of the people to the dictates of the gods and the king. These principles led in most of the Oriental monarchies to a more or less planned economic organization, verging on State control (*étatisme*) designed to increase production over a wide range of industries. But in none of these monarchies was this system carried out logically and systematically. It found itself restricted by the power of the priests, the cities, and the aristocracy, and by the strong tendency of the Oriental monarchies to become feudalized, a transformation that was in fact effected to a greater or less extent from time to time. Yet even in the feudalized Oriental monarchies the principles in question predominated in each of the constituent parts of the monarchy. The Ptolemies took over and developed to the full these main principles of Oriental economy, principles that were, of course, diametrically opposed to those on which the Greek city-state was founded.

And yet in organizing the Egyptian economy on these Oriental bases the Ptolemies were strongly influenced by their Greek training and by the Greek experience of their assistants. The new economic system of the Ptolemies was Oriental in essence, but it was strongly Hellenized. The Greek influence is seen, to begin with, in the practice of regulating the various departments by stringent written laws, orders, and instructions of an elaborate character. Written documents of this kind were not unknown to the Oriental monarchies, and some of the Ptolemaic financial and economic legislation goes back to Oriental prototypes. But the regulations are strictly Greek in their spirit, their logic, and their coherence. Greek influence is seen likewise in much of the system, terminology, and organization of taxation, in its highly diversified and inquisitorial character. From Greece was borrowed the idea of introducing between the taxpayers and the government officials a class of middlemen 'tax-farmers' (τελῶναι), guaranteed by sureties (ἔγγυοι) and acting sometimes in groups or societies. They helped the State to a certain extent to collect its revenue, but their main function was to act as underwriters, guaranteeing the full collection of one or other of the king's revenues. And, finally, the administrative control of the various royal revenues was Greek in character, especially the system of accounting, utterly different from that hitherto prevalent in Egypt and much more logical and efficient.[85]

Nevertheless the Ptolemaic reform almost entirely ignored the essence of the Greek economic system: private property recognized and protected by the State as the basis of society, and the free play of economic forces and economic initiative, with which the State very seldom interfered. These could not be suppressed altogether, for they were among the factors that helped the Ptolemies to achieve their second object, the improvement of technical devices and the development of the natural resources of the country, but they were limited and curtailed in order to bring them into harmony with the general Ptolemaic scheme of centralized State control. Restricted and curtailed as they were, these features never disappeared from the economic system of Egypt, and by the mere fact of their existence they created within it a kind of antinomy of which the Ptolemies were never able to get rid, but which, on the contrary, became more and more apparent as time went on.

The economic organization of Egypt created by the early Ptolemies can be perceived by us in its main outlines only as its features dimly emerge, one by one, from the scattered documents of the time. It was assuredly not created all at once as the result of a sweeping reform based on certain theoretical and philosophical conceptions. It is almost beyond question that the problems to be solved were taken up successively or simultaneously and that one branch of economic life after another was regulated in such a manner as suited best the interests of the king. We have no means of following this evolution. What we are more or less able to do is to draw the general outlines of the organization and to characterize its chief features. This, of course, is the fruit of patient work in collecting the relevant texts, restoring them, and interpreting them. Such a detailed presentation of evidence and inferences cannot be attempted here: it would require at least a volume to itself. What follows is a mere sketch adapted to the purpose of this book as a whole. For a fuller treatment of the subject the reader must be referred to the special studies cited in my notes and to the books devoted to Ptolemaic Egypt which are mentioned there, especially to the most recent and most detailed of them, that of Mlle C. Préaux.

AGRICULTURE

Agriculture was the foundation of the Egyptian economic system. It is well known how favoured the country is in this respect: its climate is excellent, its water supply in normal years, if judiciously managed, is sufficient to secure an abundant harvest, its soil is very fertile and adapted to a great variety of crops: cereals, vegetables, grass, oil-producing plants of all kinds, vines and olive-trees, fruit-trees and berries. Egypt in the eyes of the rest of the ancient world was an agricultural Eldorado, a gift bestowed by the bountiful Nile on its people.

Water-supply. It is natural that every ruler of Egypt should have turned his attention especially to agriculture. But agriculture in Egypt was impossible without a careful management of the water-supply and a planned system for its conservation and distribution after the flood. This involved a far-reaching control over agriculture in general and a thorough organization of the labour of the nation for the construction and maintenance of a network of canals and dikes. Organized work, of course, means compulsory work, and such it has been in Egypt for the purposes of the irrigation system from time immemorial, the whole of the population with their draught-animals being mobilized at certain seasons for the common task. So it was in Pharaonic Egypt and so it remained under the Ptolemies. There is no doubt that the Ptolemies took over the Pharaonic system, and it is very probable that they extended and improved it: to what extent and in what direction escapes our knowledge. With the irrigation system the Ptolemies inherited from their predecessors the method of maintaining it by the seasonal compulsory labour of the whole people. Like the Pharaohs, they granted, of course, some exemptions from this liability to personal service. Certain classes were privileged to the extent that they were allowed to replace work by payments. Such a privilege was probably granted in the Ptolemaic period to the immigrants, the 'Greeks' as they were called, whether to the whole of them or perhaps only to certain groups. The same privilege continued to be enjoyed by the priests.

Registration of the land. Another necessary branch of agricultural administration, also inherited by the Ptolemies from the past, was the careful registration, based on measurements (*γεωμετρία*), of all the land of Egypt. The land registers were compiled in Ptolemaic times by the village administration, the village chiefs (*κωμάρχαι*) and the village scribes (*κωμογραμματεῖς*) under the vigilant supervision (*ἐπίσκεψις*) of higher officials (the 'royal scribes', *βασιλικοὶ γραμματεῖς*). They were renewed yearly and great attention was paid to them. The purpose of the various types of surveys (best represented by the documents found at Tebtunis) was to maintain a record of the arable land showing the character of its various parcels (which often changed from year to year) and the persons responsible in a given year for their cultivation. The parcel may be sown (ἐσπαρμένη) or not, it may be over-inundated (ἔμβροχος) or dry (ἄβροχος), that is to say, the parcel may be in perfect condition from the point of view of crops and the payments due to the crown (τὸ ἀπηγμένον) or liable to a reduced rent or not subject to any rent at all (ὑπόλογος). The village surveys were tabulated from the fiscal standpoint by the toparchs (officers of the *topoi*, subdivisions of the nome) and sent to the nomarchs (νομάρχαι), special officers of the nome responsible for the cultivation of the royal land. They in turn sent their reports for the whole nome to Alexandria, where they served as material for the preparation of a general *rôle de perception*.[86]

Classes of land. Well irrigated and carefully recorded, the soil of Egypt was handed over to its actual cultivators. There had been from time immemorial different types of land-tenure and different classes of land according to the status of those responsible for its cultivation and their relation to the land. We have no exact information on the pre-Ptolemaic conditions in this respect. Nor is our information for the Ptolemaic period entirely clear and definite. We must not forget that it was reserved for Rome to create a precise terminology in the field of public and private law. In this respect Greece fell short of Rome, and Ptolemaic Egypt was even less strict. It appears that, at least in later times, two classes of land were distinguished: the γῆ βασιλική, the land managed directly by the king, and the γῆ ἐν ἀφέσει, the land 'granted' or 'released' by the government and handed over to other persons, passing thereupon from the direct care of the king and his agents. A third class may have been constituted by the γῆ πολιτική, land assigned to the new Greek cities of Alexandria and Ptolemais, and land in the possession of Naucratis. We have little information about its status under the early Ptolemies. According to Greek ideas γῆ πολιτική should be the private property of the city and of its citizens, a Greek enclave as it were in the γῆ βασιλική. But in this particular case we may think of the γῆ πολιτική as a subdivision of the γῆ ἐν ἀφέσει.

It is impossible to give even an approximate idea of how much land in Egypt belonged to the first class and how much to the second. Our information relates to conditions in the Fayûm, where newly reclaimed land, which of course was 'royal land', predominated. The situation in this respect was probably different in other nomes. To what extent we are not even able to guess.

To the 'granted' land belonged: the land which was in possession of the temples (γῆ ἱερά or ἱερὰ πρόσοδος and γῆ ἀνιερωμένη) and that used for remunerating the various servants of the State (γῆ ἐν συντάξει) including soldiers (γῆ κληρουχική) and civil servants of various grades; the highest of the civil and military assistants of the king received large plots of land as 'gift estates' (γῆ ἐν δωρεᾷ). Finally, there were areas of land held in private ownership: κτήματα and γῆ ἰδιόκτητος.

This terminology, as has been said, was not precise. The general term γῆ ἐν ἀφέσει appears in our documents sometimes as including the γῆ ἱερά and the γῆ ἐν συντάξει and ἐν δωρεᾷ and sometimes not; it had, that is to say, sometimes a broader, sometimes a narrower meaning.[87]

Our information about the various classes of land is unevenly distributed. The system of exploiting the γῆ βασιλική is comparatively well known to us, we have some information about the γῆ κληρουχική, and Zenon's correspondence throws much light on the γῆ ἐν δωρεᾷ. We know much less of the γῆ ἱερά and the private land. One thing, however, is clear: the king regarded himself as the real owner of all the land of Egypt, and property or use of land was not a right vested in private individuals, as (with some restrictions) it was in Greece, but a concession of the kings.

Royal land. The royal land (γῆ βασιλική) was cultivated by the royal peasants or farmers (γεωργοὶ βασιλικοί). This also was a heritage from the past. The bulk of the royal peasants lived scattered all over the country in thousands of towns and villages. They were registered as such in some village or town, which was their home or their place of residence (ἰδία). A royal peasant was supposed to remain in his ἰδία, but he was not strictly bound to his village and to the soil. We hear frequently that many 'foreigners' (ξένοι), men whose ἰδία was another village, resided in a village which was not their own. The practice was so common that special collectors of arrears were appointed to look after these 'foreigners' (πράκτορες ξενικῶν), while other collectors (πράκτορες ἰδιωτικῶν) were concerned with those who remained in their own village or ἰδία. Whether special permission was required for such migration is unknown.

The royal peasants were free men, not serfs or bondsmen. This is shown by many facts. I have mentioned their freedom of movement. Their status is also attested by the relations of the holders of gift-estates (*doreai*) and cleruchic land with the royal peasants. Gift-estates granted by the king to his grandees never consisted of one or more villages with their land and inhabitants, as in Asia Minor, but always of so many (mostly 10,000) *arourae* of land. In the few known instances this land was tilled not by those who had been hereditary holders of its parcels, but by cultivators of various types, especially tenants who rented the land, mostly for a short term, from its holder. The same is true of the holders of smaller parcels of granted land, for instance the cleruchs. All such tenants belonged to the class of 'royal peasants', for although this class comprised people who had cultivated the 'royal land' for generations, the name 'royal peasant' was also given to all who in one way or another cultivated royal land, as being ultimately lessees of the king. Finally, the relations between the king and the royal peasants were based not on tradition but on regular written contracts. In the early Ptolemaic time the contracts were mostly short-term contracts. Though no direct information is available on this point, so far as concerns the royal land managed by the king directly, this practice is well established for the gift-estates and for the holdings of the cleruchs, which were both ultimately parts of the royal land. It must, however, be borne in mind that in the late second century the leases were often for longer terms and sometimes for no fixed terms at all, the land being cultivated under existing conditions until a new general lease was announced and brought into force by the government (διαμίσθωσις). It is by no means certain that such forms of contract were unknown in the early Ptolemaic period and were first introduced in later times under the pressure of circumstances. They appear to me to represent an old practice which may have been in use in Egypt from time immemorial, and which may have been followed by the early Ptolemies concurrently with the new practice of short-term contracts.

For the plots of royal land that they cultivated the royal

peasants paid a yearly rent to the king (ἐκφόριον). We may think it probable that in pre-Ptolemaic times this rent paid by the peasants was a *pars quota*, 20 per cent. of the crop (πέμπτη),* though this cannot be regarded as an ascertained fact. In Ptolemaic times, however, it was a *pars quanta*, not *quota*; it was determined by several considerations, and was subject to alteration according to the condition in which each parcel was found to be after the yearly inundation.

In addition to the rent, the peasant paid a countless number of different taxes for the privilege of cultivating his land. The list of these taxes, incomplete as it is, is imposing. The number of *artabae* paid as rent for each *aroura* and the quantity of grain paid in respect of the various taxes is often mentioned in the documents at our disposal. But we are reduced to uncertain guesses when we try to figure out what part of the crop the royal peasants paid to the king. It was certainly not less, and perhaps more, than half.

Bound by his lease to cultivate the parcel of land which he had rented, the peasant was expected to stay in the village during the agricultural season until he had discharged his liability to the king. This obligation he expressly acknowledged under oath when receiving his seed-corn from the king.

During the agricultural season he was closely watched by a number of government officials: various guards, the head of the village (κωμάρχης), the village scribe (κωμογραμματεύς), and especially the representatives of the king in the nomes (the οἰκονόμοι) personally or through their agents. His seed-corn he received from the crown. One of the objects of the government in making this obligatory loan was to secure that the parcel should be sown whatever the peasant's circumstances might be and that the seed should be of good quality. It was the duty of the *oeconomus* to prevent the use of seed-corn for other purposes.

The peasant was not free to cultivate his land as he pleased. A special instruction (διαγραφὴ σπόρου) regulated the cultivation according to the planned economy of the State. The order was strict, and the *oeconomus* was required to enforce it. For this purpose, and to see that the land was well tilled, this official inspected the crops when they were sprouting.

* Test. Vet., *Genesis*, xlvii. 24–6.

At the time of the harvest the peasant was again closely watched. He gathered the crops, transported them to the threshing-floor, threshed them, all under the watchful eye of the administration, responsible guards (γενηματοφύλακες) being specially appointed for this purpose. The grain on the threshing-floor was inspected and divided between the crown and the peasant, and what remained after the claims of the former were satisfied (ἐπιγένημα) was released (ἄφεσις) and carried home by the peasant. The government grain was then transported to royal barns scattered all over the country and handed over to the keepers of grain (σιτολόγοι). From the local barns it was transported by water or land to the larger central stores and from there in part to the huge granaries at Alexandria. The procedure to be followed in the collection of the grain was laid down in a special royal διάγραμμα (περὶ τῶν σιτικῶν or σιτολογικόν).[88]

Special crops other than grain were treated in a similar way, e.g. grass and flax. As regards grass sown after the harvest (χλωρὰ ἐπίσπορα) or as a rotation crop and used for feeding cattle, special contracts, valid for one season only, were made by the government, the γῆ ἐν ἀφέσει (we know this at least for the cleruchic land) being treated in this respect exactly like the royal land.[89]

Sacred land. A large part of Egypt's cultivated and cultivable land belonged in the pre-Ptolemaic period to the temples (γῆ ἱερά or ἱερὰ πρόσοδος). The land was regarded as the estate of some deity, as his or her 'sacred revenue land'. It was tilled by 'slaves' of the deity, ἱερόδουλοι in Greek. Some of it was in the hereditary possession of priests, who were free to sell, to rent, or to mortgage it, as if it were their private property. The parcels tilled by the 'slaves' of the god were also apparently assigned to them for an indefinite time, the tenant being free to dispose of them. It should be added that the whole of the population of a temple were 'slaves' of the god, regardless of their professions. Even the minor priests, such as keepers or feeders of sacred animals, were termed ἱερόδουλοι.

The organization as sketched above is known to us—very imperfectly it must be admitted—from documents of Hellenistic and to a large extent late Hellenistic times, mostly Demotic.

It may therefore have been the result of an evolution which took place in the Hellenistic period. It appears to me, however, much more probable that it was inherited by the Ptolemies from the past and was not changed by them in its essential features.

We see how chary the Ptolemies were of modifying the immemorial customs of the temples. They certainly did not secularize the temple property. We hear nothing, for instance, of any confiscation on a large scale, that is to say, of any transformation of γῆ ἱερά into γῆ βασιλική. On the contrary, all sorts of grants to the temples, including land (γῆ ἀνιερωμένη), were of frequent occurrence during the rule of the Ptolemies, and that from the very outset.

Nevertheless certain changes appear to have taken place in the relations between the crown and the temples. Defective as our information is, some of these changes are known to us; and first as regards the terminology. Γῆ ἱερά is a term of exactly the same type as γῆ βασιλική. It appears in the later documents alongside of the latter in such a way as to suggest similarity of treatment. The same applies to the term ἱερὰ πρόσοδος. It is evident, therefore, that in Ptolemaic times the land and income of the temples formed one of the departments of the royal economy, part of the king's household property. A close connexion between the king and the temples lies behind this terminology. This connexion may have been first established by the Ptolemies and may not have existed in earlier times. We may think that it was the Ptolemies who first did away with the economic independence that the temples had probably enjoyed under the later Pharaohs. But it is possible that the Ptolemies found the temples already deprived of this independence by the Persians. Mention has already been made of the measures taken in this respect by the great Darius and Xerxes (p. 82). It is well known that Artaxerxes Ochus and Darius III showed little respect for the Egyptian gods and the Egyptian priesthood. It may even be that the Ptolemies in settling their relations with the temples showed themselves more liberal than the Persian kings. Many other features in the organization of the temples point to the same close connexion between these and the crown. Here are a few of them.

I regard it as very probable, for instance, that it was the Ptolemies who first founded a new office, that of president of a temple, ἐπιστάτης. He was in all probability a nominee of the king and was his representative in the temple, being especially responsible for the financial obligations of the temple to the crown, for example in the field of industry and manufacture. Another instance of State control over the affairs of the temple is the management of the priestly offices of various kinds from the economic point of view. These offices were assets of no small value. They had prebends attached to them and yielded a certain amount of revenue, as was probably the case in Oriental temples generally (for instance in those of Babylonia). Before the Ptolemies they and the income connected with them were in all probability assigned by the temples to priests and to temple slaves in the same way as land was assigned to them, that is to say, they were sold or rented to the highest bidders. The same system was practised under the Ptolemies; but now it was the administration, not the temples, that sold the offices, and the leases were not hereditary as they may have been previously.

It is highly probable that the temple land, of whatever class it may have been, was subject to a similar system of management. It seems certain, at least as regards the Fayûm and the later Ptolemaic period, that the local administration kept the sacred land recorded in its register just as it did the royal land, that it kept close watch over its cultivation, and treated the revenue from it—the rent which was paid in one form or another for its use—as part of the royal revenue, seeing to it that the rent was paid in full and that the land remained in cultivation. This system of management can hardly have been an innovation of the later Ptolemies, for they were not strong enough to encroach in this way on the rights of the temples (see below, chs. V and VI). In all probability the close connexion between temples and government in respect of the sacred land was established or restored by the early Ptolemies. What they insisted upon was good and efficient cultivation and prompt and full payment of the rent into the State treasury. The title of the cultivators to their holdings was a matter of less importance to them, and probably in most cases they did not interfere with the temple traditions in this respect.

The main concern of the king was to see that the temples did not cost more than they brought in, that they were not dependent on grants and gifts from the government, and further than this to secure that there should be a surplus of income, which would accrue to the king as part of his regular revenues. How large this surplus was, we are unable to say. The maintenance of the temples was an expensive affair and it is probable that the larger part of the income from them went back to them in the form of σύνταξις, paid to the temples by the government. We find a very similar situation in respect of what was known as the ἀπόμοιρα, a tax amounting to one-sixth of the yield of the vineyards, which had been collected before the reign of Philadelphus by the temples from the owners of the vineyards. By a special order of Philadelphus, as the chief manager of divine affairs on earth, this revenue was assigned to the new cult of Philadelphus' consort Arsinoe, and a special law (νόμος) carefully regulated the collection of this tax by the government. Without it the government would have been unable to collect the revenue in full and thus to provide for the requirements of the new cult. No doubt part of the revenue was spent for the purpose for which it was collected. If the cult of Arsinoe was introduced into all the temples of Egypt, as is probable, each temple would receive its share. If not, the money would be spent on the new temples of the new goddess. In any case, if there was a surplus, the government would spend it as it pleased, and in fact did so.*

Though our information is scanty, the probability is that the γῆ ἱερά was in all respects managed in accordance with the same policy and by the same methods as the γῆ βασιλική, the main object being to support the temples as a State institution, to make their existence safe and easy. If, as a result of careful administration, the sacred land yielded a surplus to the government, it was fair that the government should use it as it pleased. Everything considered, it is uncertain whether the temples lost or gained by the change of conditions. They certainly resented the new order, for it deprived them of their

* *P. Col. Zen.* 55.

ancient paternal superintendence of their revenues, it diminished the influence of the priests in temple affairs, and it threw open the doors of the temples to government agents, who were mostly foreigners. This state of things could not be agreeable to the priests even if it was not entirely new to them.[90]

Cleruchic land. The royal peasants on the one hand and the temples and priests on the other had both been closely connected from time immemorial with the agricultural life of Egypt. The army presented the Ptolemies with a problem of no less importance. It was out of the question to reform the ancient native militia (in Greek terminology μάχιμοι) and to transform them into a standing national army. On the other hand, it was dangerous and exceedingly expensive to maintain a permanent army of mercenaries, who would most of the time be kept idle in barracks. The solution of the problem adopted by the Ptolemies was suggested partly by Egyptian traditions, partly by the practice of Alexander and the Successors, and was framed to some extent on the model of Greek, especially Athenian, cleruchies.

The Ptolemies maintained a permanent army of Macedonians and mercenaries of various origin by paying the greater part of them, not in money and kind as was usual (above, p. 137), but in kind alone, and that by assigning them plots of land. The income from this land was supposed to provide the soldiers and their families with the means of subsistence. The men who received from the king such a plot of land were called cleruchs (κληροῦχοι).

Of the inauguration and application of this scheme in the time of Soter and Philadelphus we know very little. It is certain that the Ptolemies did not adopt the system of Alexander and the Successors, methodically carried out by Seleucus and his successors, of settling the soldiers in considerable groups in cities or in special settlements (κατοικίαι), which enjoyed a kind of self-government. The soldiers of the Egyptian army were scattered all over the country. The plots of land assigned to them lay in the territories of ancient villages or in those of recently created villages and towns. An example of the last type was the settlement of a large group of soldiers, both newly recruited (νεανίσκοι) and older men (πρεσβύτεροι), foot and horse, in and around the town of Philadelphia, newly founded by Philadelphus, his *dioecetes* Apollonius, and the latter's steward Zenon. The land assigned to them was probably not part of the gift-estate of Apollonius.

The military allotments (*cleroi*) were of different sizes according to the rank and perhaps the seniority of the officer or soldier. Two scales are known to us, which shows that there was no uniformity in this respect. The largest plots rarely exceeded 100 *arourae*. The land, whether it had always been cultivated or was recently reclaimed, was handed over to the soldiers in such a condition that agricultural work could be started at once, the necessary irrigation and drainage, at least of a part of it, having already been done. Further improvements were sometimes carried out by the soldiers themselves at their own expense (with the king's assistance, in the form of loans).

Since the soldiers were mobilized or summoned (ἐπάγγελμα) very frequently—for war, for garrison service in Egypt and abroad, for service in the capital, or for manœuvres—they were certainly, especially in early Ptolemaic times, unable to attend personally to their plots and generally rented them to local tenants. Zenon, Apollonius' manager at Philadelphia, regularly took charge of many such plots for the cleruchs of Philadelphia and the neighbouring villages. In exceptional cases, especially before land was definitely assigned to soldiers, the government itself undertook the cultivation of the allotments and handed over the produce to the soldiers.* Some details in connexion with the *cleroi* still await interpretation and explanation. Such are, for instance, the cases where the plot was divided into two *hemicleria*, one of which was treated like other *cleroi* (taxes, not rent, being paid on it by the *cleruch*), the other as if it were a piece of royal land subject to rent (ἐκφόριον).†

Besides allotments, quarters (σταθμοί) were assigned to the soldiers. In new villages like Philadelphia, brand-new houses were built for them by the king, in older towns and villages where the population was dense and building-space was scarce the soldiers were billeted in the houses of the inhabitants. This

* *P. Freib.* 7; Hunt-Edgar, *Sel. Pap.*, ii. 412. † *Teb.* 746.

often led to ill feeling, endless litigation, and sometimes bloody quarrels. From the earliest times the system of billeting was a serious defect in the Ptolemaic military organization and a source of irritation to the native population.

In the third century it was not the intention of the Ptolemies that the soldiers should be owners of their plots. The plots and the quarters were royal property and the grants were revocable at the pleasure of the crown. The cleruch had no right to sell, mortgage, or bequeath his allotment. In practice, however, if all was well, he would be left in undisturbed possession of it until his death, and then his son would take it over. In fact in some cases we find the son in the position of co-tenant (σύγκληρος) alongside of his father.*

The cleruchs paid several taxes in respect of their land (partly the same as those paid by the royal peasants): crown money (στέφανος), a moderate tax on the sown land (ἀρταβιεία), taxes for the upkeep of embankments (χωματικόν), for the guard service (φυλακιτικόν), for medical service (ἰατρικόν), and probably others, besides the regular taxes paid by the population of Egypt, of which more presently. They were not liable to compulsory labour, but the king was free to require from them extraordinary service (λειτουργία) in an emergency.

This system of assigning pieces of valuable land to soldiers in order to provide them with a regular income and make them self-supporting required a good deal of administrative supervision. The holder of a *cleros* was responsible to the government for its cultivation and was closely watched by his superiors and by the regular civil administration of the crown: for instance, the rule about seed-corn supplied by the government as a loan was applicable to him also. The cleruch, however, was freer than the royal peasant in his management of his allotment. The διαγραφὴ σπόρου, or official distribution of crops, was not applied to military holdings. Except for certain crops (oil-producing plants and perhaps grass), the cleruch was free to cultivate his land as he pleased. We know that some of them, instead of growing grain, transformed their plots or parts of them into vineyards, olive-groves, or gardens. They did this probably with the special permission of the government and on

* *P. Cairo Zen.* 59001, with Edgar's notes on ll. 46 and 51.

the usual conditions applicable to the planting (καταφύτευσις) of land.

The king, however, regarded himself as the owner of the *cleroi*. His claim on the produce of the land came first. As in the case of the royal peasants, the crops were put in sequestration until the various taxes were paid by the cleruch. His portion of the crops he was not permitted to carry home from the fields and threshing-floors till he was granted 'release' (ἄφεσις) by the royal officials.

In creating cleruchies the Ptolemies were guided by various considerations, partly political, partly economic. I have already referred to some of them, and I may mention a few others. Scarcity of coined money may have been a motive, though not a prime one. Of far greater, indeed of dominating importance, were considerations of a different order, first and foremost the desire to bind the personnel of the army to Egypt, to make Egypt their country, and to establish close and permanent relations between the king and the army. Next came the intention of introducing new methods of work and cultivation, a new economic spirit, into the country. It is certain that the cleruchs were not absentee landowners with little interest in their holdings. Many letters in the correspondence of Zenon show how keenly interested they were in their new houses, in their cattle and poultry, and in the cultivation of their land. Used to the life of the country in their own homelands, some of them experts in agriculture, viticulture, olive-growing, and cattle-breeding, they were happy to become landowners again and to return, even if intermittently, to their customary work. We must remember that Greece and Asia Minor were still to a large extent countries whose economic life was based on agriculture. Lastly, the Ptolemies wished that the money which their soldiers received either as pay or as their share of the booty, in other words their savings, should not be exported but should remain in the country and be invested in land which otherwise might have remained uncultivated. Agricultural labour in Egypt was always rather scarce, while the extent of agricultural territory in the country is very elastic. The more money, men, and energy available, the more the cultivated area expands.[91]

PLATE XXXVII

1. Painted funeral stele found at Alexandria in the necropolis of Gabbari. It has the form of a *naiscos* with pediment, supported by two pillars. On the architrave the inscription *Διονύσιος Βιθυνός Χαῖρε*. In the niche are painted two figures. The larger represents the deceased, head and body in front view, feet in profile. The upper part of the lower half of his body is missing and therefore the character of his dress is uncertain. He appears to wear a straight-sleeved jacket over a chiton, and high shoes. On his head, a crown. With his right hand he holds a long spear (probably the Macedonian *sarissa*) which rests on the ground. Behind him his boy-attendant seen in profile, wearing on his head a conical cap or helmet (that of his master ?) and carrying in his hands his master's arms—two darts and a tall oval, so-called Celtic, shield. Photograph supplied by the authorities of the Alexandria Museum.

Unpublished(?). Mentioned by E. Breccia, *Bull. Soc. Arch. Alex.* XV (N.S. iv. 1) (1914), p. 60, no. 5 (the brief description of the stele speaks of a horseman). Cf. the painted stele of another Bithynian (*Σωτ]ήριχος Βιθυνός*), R. Pagenstecher, *Nekropolis*, 1919, p. 48, no. 35, fig. 31 (Hadra). His figure is badly preserved, but he also is represented in front view and in civilian(?) dress. As already mentioned (pl. XIX, description), there is no full collection of the painted stelae of Ptolemaic Egypt. A corpus of stelae showing figures of soldiers would greatly assist the study of the Ptolemaic army. Cf. description of pl. LVII. H. 0·55, W. 0·32.

2. The best, from the artistic point of view, of the painted stelae found at Alexandria. It is a pediment stele found in the necropolis of Hadra. Of the inscription the letters . . . ΕΛΟΤ . . . only are preserved. The painting in the niche represents three figures on a rose ground. A chestnut-coloured horse, rearing and attempting to break away from a young man who wears a conical cap covering his red hair, a yellowish belted chiton, and perhaps a sword. Behind this group, a boy with reddish hair and dressed in the same way as the grown-up man, looking at his master or father. 'The horse', says Miss Swindler, 'is done with spirit, his head thrown upward, his ears back and his eyes full of fire.' A. Reinach has suggested that the man mastering the horse is a Galatian, and has drawn far-reaching conclusions from this suggestion. I see nothing Galatian in the human figures nor in the style of the painting; cf. n. 342 to this chapter. Photograph supplied by the authorities of the Metropolitan Museum of Art, New York.

The stele has been several times published and described: A. C. Merriam, *A.J.A.* iii (1887), pp. 261 ff., pl. XVII (in colour); A. Reinach's papers quoted in n. 342; R. Pagenstecher, *Nekropolis*, 1919, pp. 54 and 69; M. H. Swindler, *Ancient Painting*, 1929, p. 345, fig. 551.

1. Alexandria Museum.

2. New York, Metropolitan Museum of Art.

SOLDIERS OF THE PTOLEMAIC ARMY. TWO FUNERAL STELAE FROM ALEXANDRIA

Doreai. The same considerations led the Ptolemies to assign land to their civil employees (γῆ or κλῆροι ἐν συντάξει, to which category the κληρουχικὴ γῆ also belonged) and to create large δωρεαί, 'gift-estates' granted by the first Ptolemies, especially by Philadelphus, to their chief assistants in military and civil affairs. Many such *doreai* are mentioned in our sources, and one is well known to us. It is that of Apollonius, the chief *dioecetes* of Philadelphus. I have already dealt with the origin and character of the *doreai* in general and I shall speak of the *dorea* of Apollonius later in this chapter. It is sufficient to say here that, apart from the natural tendency of a wealthy proprietor to attach his chief assistants to himself by lavish gifts, the principal motive that led the Ptolemies to make these grants was the desire to try the Macedonian and Persian system of large estates, alongside of the old-fashioned Greek system of small *cleroi*, as a means of improving the exploitation of Egypt. Such estates were granted to the most active and most thrifty assistants of the king, men capable of applying to a substantial estate—an Egypt in miniature—those methods which the king had adopted for Egypt as a whole. It must be noted that, like the *cleroi*, the *doreai* were revocable and remained part of the king's land. Their holders were in fact a sort of blend of land-owners and royal stewards, who would act on the king's behalf and on his instructions.

Private land. Finally we come to the κτήματα and the γῆ ἰδιόκτητος, that is to say, land held in private ownership. There is not the slightest doubt that, in addition to such holdings in the area of the temple land, there existed, scattered all over Egypt, many pieces of land which were owned by private persons. Houses, vineyards, and gardens were termed κτήματα in the earliest period of Ptolemaic rule. Besides these, certain areas of grain land, especially in Southern Egypt, were freely sold, bought, mortgaged, bequeathed, &c.; that is to say, were treated, with the knowledge of the government, in the same way as private property. The origin of this land is not known. It probably existed in Egypt in Pharaonic times and its increase was certainly promoted by the Persian government. In any case, so far as we know, the Ptolemies did not resort to confiscation or similar measures in respect of this land, but accepted the *de facto* situation. In this sphere, as in the sphere of civil law in general, they never attempted to introduce substantial modifications or violent changes.

Indeed, from the very outset they encouraged the development of private property in land. The γῆ ἰδιόκτητος or land sold by the government was their creation, and it was they who regulated emphyteutic (or cataphyteutic) tenure. The existence of a body of thrifty and energetic landowners, who would increase the planted area and transform parts of the kingdom into vineyards and gardens, was in their interests. They needed a class of men of property from whom to draw officials, contractors, sureties for these, and such like, in considerable numbers, who could guarantee the efficiency of their service by pledges of their land. Of course, private land did not remain untaxed and the government kept strict watch over its careful cultivation (for instance, the sowing of special crops on it if required) and insisted on the regular payment of taxes. In case of default the king had recourse to confiscation and sale of the land.[92]

Such were the various forms of land-tenure in Egypt. It is evident from my short survey how closely the government supervised and how strictly it controlled the agriculture of the country. This is not surprising, for it was from the cultivated land that the government derived its principal revenue. The rent (ἐκφόριον) and the minor taxes paid by the royal peasants, the various taxes paid by the cleruchs and private owners, the $33\frac{1}{3}$ per cent. tax from the vineyards and in addition thereto the ἀπόμοιρα of one-sixth (or one-tenth) of the produce, the taxes on gardens and kitchen gardens, all these together formed an important item in the highly diversified revenue of the Ptolemies. All classes of landholders contributed their part to it.

And yet we cannot say that in organizing the agricultural life of the country the early Ptolemies carried out a preconceived plan based on theoretical premises. It is evident that in their reorganization of this branch of Egyptian economy they were guided by many various considerations, some of which I have specified above. They desired to intensify production in order to increase their own revenue. They wished to reserve for themselves the largest possible part of the agricultural produce, but they were equally desirous not to go too far in this direction, in order not to arouse too much passive (or eventually active) resistance on the part of the people. They apparently modified and improved the mode of collecting their land-revenues by making the machinery of collection better and more efficient. But they were loath to abandon the existing traditions, to break with the deeply rooted habits and customs of the country. They tried to bring under their direct control as large agricultural areas as possible, but again they were careful not to do too much damage to the interests of important sections of the population, above all, the body of priests and large groups of private landowners. Indeed, the Ptolemies themselves were led both by political and by economic considerations to create many new islands of private property at the expense of the land under their direct control—gift-estates, cleruchic holdings, privately owned land. From this 'private' land they secured for themselves a handsome revenue and always exercised a certain control over its management, but so far as possible without prejudice to the interests of the landholders. They regarded themselves as all-powerful masters of the country who had to be blindly obeyed, and they invested their civil officials with some of their powers, and yet even in the direct management of their own land (the 'royal land') they tolerated the traditional practice adopted by the agricultural population—their own 'royal peasants'—of protesting against certain unjust acts of the administration by recourse to 'secession strikes' (ἀναχώρησις, flight to a temple, or ἐκχώρησις, migration to another part of the country, to another 'nome'), which were generally settled not by compulsion but more or less amicably by mutual understanding. The result was the establishment of a system which reminds one of the State control (*étatisme*) of modern times, but this control was not rigid and strict.

The same system of management was applied by the early Ptolemies to other departments of economic activity concerned with the exploitation of the other natural resources of the country which were likewise under their control.

Pasture land. In addition to the arable land and the land planted with vines, fruit-trees, &c., they were owners of all the pasture land (νομαί) and claimed for themselves the right of disposing of the green forage grown in cultivated meadows (χορτονομαί) and in the fields as rotation crops and as catch-crops after harvest (χλωρὰ ἐπίσπορα). Possessing such ample resources in forage, the Ptolemies naturally maintained large herds and flocks of various domestic animals: cows and oxen used mostly for cultivating the fields, donkeys used for transport, sheep and goats kept especially for their wool and their milk, pigs, and geese. To these traditional domestic animals of Egypt must be added all sorts of poultry, large studs of horses, from which the cavalry were supplied with mounts, parks of elephants for war purposes, and rapidly increasing numbers of camels.[93]

Domestic animals. The most important domestic animals were those used for the cultivation of the fields and for transport: oxen, cows, donkeys, occasionally camels. The king needed large numbers of them for the cultivation of his land and for the transport of his goods. He could not rely upon the draught-animals in private hands. Most of the tenants of royal land had very few and these not in the best condition, and there were many peasants who possessed no such cattle at all. The first concern of the king was to know exactly how many oxen, cows, and donkeys there were in a given place. We know from *Teb.* 703 (ll. 69–70) that for this purpose a careful registration (ἀναγραφή) of all the royal and private draught-animals was carried out yearly in each nome by the *oeconomus*. The registers were kept up to date by means of frequent inspections. This supervision is easily explained. A shortage of such animals or their poor condition was as detrimental to efficient agricultural work as were defective dikes and canals, and the regular transportation of officials and of goods belonging to the State depended largely on the supply of them. A knowledge of what draught-animals were available and of their condition was essential for the king's planned economy.

Particular attention was paid to the rearing of calves, whether 'royal' or raised by private persons; they were kept in special 'nurseries' (μοσχοτροφεῖα) under the care of expert attendants (μοσχοτρόφοι).* Some of them, it should be remem-

* *Teb.* 703, ll. 183–91, cf. 66–70.

bered, were used for sacrifices, as is frequently mentioned in documents of the third century.

How exactly the king managed his oxen, cows, and donkeys, we do not know. It appears that they were distributed among the royal tenants, who were probably responsible for them. The distribution of draught-cattle to tenants was one of the chief concerns of Zenon, the manager of the gift-estate of Apollonius. It should be added that *pigs* were treated in more or less the same way, since they were used for agricultural work (to trample the seed into the earth) as well as for sacrifice. Special swineherds, who belonged to the class of 'men connected with the revenues' (ἐπιπεπλεγμένοι ταῖς προσόδοις), took care of the 'royal' pigs (perhaps renting them from the king). But, of course, private people also possessed pigs. We hear occasionally of special pigsties being built in Philadelphia. It must be added that this department of the royal economy was organized in much the same way as was usual in Pharaonic times.[94]

Horses and *elephants* occupied a special position. The elephants were kept solely for war purposes. Horses were probably not used at all for agricultural work and very seldom for heavy transport. The king and the notables travelled sometimes in horse-drawn carriages or on horseback, but most of the horses were bred for the use of the army. From time to time fresh supplies of them came from abroad: from the Cyrenaica, from Syria and perhaps from Palestine, and in all probability from Carthage and Sicily as well (see below, p. 396.) In what way the army was supplied with horses, whether or not the 'royal' horses were distributed among the soldiers in actual service and the cleruchs and on what conditions, there is no evidence to show. The existence of special 'inspectors of horses' (ἱπποσκόποι) and of special payments made in respect of horses—a horse tribute (φόρος ἵππων) and a tax called ἀνιππία (the meaning of which is obscure to me)—suggests that the royal horses may have been distributed among the soldiers and officers who had no horses of their own. In any case all the cleruchs apparently paid special taxes (mentioned above) designed perhaps to cover the king's expenditure in connexion with the breeding and transport of horses.[95]

Sheep and *goats* were kept chiefly for their wool and their milk. I shall speak of wool presently. Cheese was a staple food of natives and Greeks alike. Meat was eaten by the former occasionally and by the latter more frequently. Large flocks of sheep and goats were owned by the king and by private people. The care devoted by the kings to the breeding of sheep and goats will be spoken of later in this section. Side by side with sheep and goats large flocks of *geese* are often mentioned in our documents. The royal flocks were tended by expert shepherds and gooseherds (ποιμένες and χηνοβοσκοί), who sometimes, if not always, rented them, paying in money or in kind. Such was also the practice of private owners of small cattle, for example Apollonius.[96]

A special and very important part in the agricultural economy of Egypt was played by *pigeons*. They were not only the cheapest luxury in the diet of the people, but they were very highly valued for the excellent manure that they produce in large quantity. Pigeons figured prominently in Egyptian life from time immemorial, and pigeon-houses still form a marked feature in the landscape. In the villages of Ptolemaic and Roman Egypt these occupied a large space: for proof it is sufficient to mention the large specimens excavated by the Michigan expedition at Karanis. The kings certainly possessed some pigeon-houses, and at Philadelphia they were no doubt as numerous as they were at Karanis. Most of them, however, were private property. The king derived large profits from taxing them: the third of the produce (τρίτη περιστερεώνων) was probably calculated on the basis of the number of pigeons and of their yearly progeny sold on the market; the πηχισμὸς περιστερεώνων, a high tax paid in money and assessed according to the space occupied by the pigeon-houses, was probably a tax chiefly on the manure produced by the pigeons. The first tax, which was arbitrary and extremely difficult to assess, led to misunderstandings, oppression, and quarrels, of which we catch a glimpse in an interesting document. It was therefore soon dropped in some parts of Egypt. But the second, which was less arbitrary and easy to collect, lasted until Roman times at least.[97]

Private domestic animals in general were carefully registered by the administration for the purposes of taxation. This was an important duty of the *oeconomus*. Every year, at the time of the Nile flood, all animals were counted and listed (ἀναγραφή, *Teb.* 703, ll. 165–74). The lists were probably used to check the individual declarations or census returns (ἀπογραφαί) of cattle made for the purpose of taxation. The same procedure is attested for Syria in Ptolemaic times. The main tax levied on cattle—a very important item of the king's revenue accruing to him from his ownership of all the pasture-land—was the ἐννόμιον, a tax similar to that of the same name levied throughout the Hellenistic world (see below, Ch. VI), and to the Roman *scriptura*. The people were required to pay a tax in money for the management of the pasture-land by the government. The payment of this tax was perhaps a condition of acquiring the right enjoyed by owners of cattle to ask permission to use special pastures under payment of special rents, which varied according to the class of pasture-land (either χορτονομαί or χλωρὰ ἐπίσπορα,* or νομαὶ ἐκτὸς μισθώσεως) and according to the status of the applicant (the royal peasants and the priests may have occupied a privileged position). An additional tax was perhaps paid on each head of domestic animals.[98]

Bee-keeping. An important branch of semi-agricultural work was bee-keeping. Bee-keeping played an important part in the economy of the ancient world in general: honey was the sugar of antiquity. It is no wonder, therefore, that it was practised on a very large scale all over the ancient world and was carefully studied by ancient scholars. Discourses on bee-keeping formed a very important part of treatises on agriculture in general. We know from various documents in the correspondence of Zenon that many apiaries existed in the Fayûm and in the neighbouring nomes. We hear of an owner of 1,000 bee-hives scattered over the Heracleopolite and the Memphite nomes in the time of Euergetes; 5,000 are mentioned in another letter in Zenon's archives. Greeks and natives were busy in this branch of industry. A special class of trained bee-keepers (μελισσουργοί) was included among the ἐπιπεπλεγμένοι ταῖς προσόδοις. Many bee-hives belonged to the king, but no attempt was made to monopolize this branch of the economic

* See above, pp. 280, 292.

activity of Egypt. We hear of many private owners of apiaries. They paid a high tax (25 per cent. of their income) and perhaps also a licence duty; but they were free to sell their goods at the market price and they were protected from the competition of foreign producers by high customs duties on imported honey (25 per cent.).[99]

HUNTING

The Nile, the lakes, and the marshes were parts of the king's property. It is probable that sometimes the king would organize hunting expeditions in the marshes and in the desert, which were carried out by expert hunters (*κυνηγοί*), some of whom were pressed into the royal service. We know that this was the way in which the capture of elephants was organized by the Ptolemies (below, pp. 383 ff.). In Egypt itself the king, in accordance with ancestral traditions, would from time to time take an active part in such expeditions. It must not be forgotten that hunting was not only the most cherished sport of all the Oriental kings, but also the chief pleasure of king and nobles in Macedonia. It is enough to recall the so-called sarcophagus of Alexander, the painting of Hellenistic date in a grave near Marissa in Palestine, and the hunting scene (of Alexandrian workmanship) on the dish from Trasilico in Calabria. The correspondence of Zenon shows that he himself and probably his master Apollonius were very fond of the sport.

But as a rule hunting was treated by the Ptolemies from the fiscal point of view, hunting rights being rented to special concessionaires (*τελῶναι* or *οἱ ἐξειληφότες τὴν θήραν*), who either carried out expeditions themselves with the help of hired labour or allowed private people to do so on payment of certain dues. So much may be gathered from the few documents which relate to hunting in Egypt. This branch of royal economy was not unimportant, for the marshes of Egypt were full of game (especially waterfowl) and game formed from time immemorial an important part of the diet of the population.[100]

FISHING

Still more important was fishing, which was carried on in Egypt by expert fishermen on a large scale. The catches were transported from the fishing grounds to the markets. That fish was a very important element in the diet of the Greeks in their homeland is a well-known fact. Fishing conducted on capitalistic lines in Egypt itself would therefore serve the same purpose as the production of wine and olive-oil: it would provide the new settlers with an abundant supply of a food to which they were accustomed without recourse to import. A fragmentary document of 235 B.C. found at Tebtunis (*Teb.* 701) informs us of the manner in which fishing and the transport and sale of fish were organized by a large enterprise, which was either a royal concern or one managed by the holder of a gift-estate. The accounts recorded in this document show how large was the amount of profit falling to the king or the holder of the *dorea* and how small a share went to the actual fishermen. In most cases, however, fishing was managed by the Egyptian administration on another system, similar to that used by the Ptolemies in organizing the exploitation of other sources of revenue: fishing rights were leased to special *telonai* who underwrote the fishing contract (ἰχθυικὴ ὠνή), which was carried out by expert fishermen liable to pay to the crown 25 per cent. of their catch (τετάρτη ἁλιέων or ἰχθυικῶν) besides minor taxes.[101]

MINES AND QUARRIES

No less exclusive than the king's rights over the river, the lakes, and the marshes, was his right over mines and quarries, which were situated mostly in the desert. Egypt is very poor in minerals. It appears that the copper mines of Sinai were exhausted at an early date, and the Harvard expedition to these mines found no trace of their having been worked in Ptolemaic or Roman times.* Cyprus and Syria were without doubt the sources of Egypt's copper supply from the time of the New Kingdom and probably earlier. Copper mines in the Fayûm are occasionally referred to. Some iron was mined in the eastern desert. Gold mines were worked in the eastern desert and in Nubia. Silver occurred in small quantities in Egypt itself and in Cyprus. Egypt was much richer in various kinds of building stone, and the beautiful Egyptian granite was especially famous. Many semi-precious and precious stones were found in various places on the borders of the country. Finally, salt was

* See Appendix II.

extracted from lakes, from salt-pans on the coast, and from salt mines; and the shores of lakes furnished Egypt with nitre* (νῖτρον) and alum (στυπτηρία).

We are not well informed about the exploitation of these natural resources, but it is certain that the king reserved the exclusive right of working them. The exploitation of gold mines in Egypt and Nubia was carried out by the forced labour of prisoners of war and criminals, who were treated like slaves. They were supervised by a technical staff and by officers and soldiers of the army (below, pp. 381 ff.). The system of exploiting quarries was similar, but as the quarries were situated nearer to the cultivated part of Egypt, the use of prisoners and criminals was not so common as in the gold mines. Generally the work was done by specialists in the craft, members of the guild of stone-cutters (λατόμοι), who undertook to extract from a given quarry a certain quantity of stone. The contracts were worked out in the office of the chief engineer of the nome, who depended on the *dioecetes*. The work was done by the stone-cutters themselves and by their hired workmen under the supervision of an overseer (ἐργοδιώκτης) and under the protection and with the collaboration of soldiers, for whom service in the quarries was a burdensome liturgy. The tools were supplied by the king (iron being scanty in Egypt, below, p. 362). In case of need the king would supply the contractors with labour also (mostly that of prisoners and criminals). Work in the quarries was hard and dangerous, and the conditions of life were abominable. The products of the mines, quarries, salt-pans, &c., were used or disposed of by the government, although metal ware was certainly produced by artisans and artists and sold by them to the people of Egypt and probably to foreign merchants as well. The artisans were not all in the service of the government and probably worked under licence on material that they bought or received on commission from the government. We possess no exact information on this point.[102]

ARBORICULTURE

Lastly, I may mention in this connexion the management of what we should call forestry. Egypt was not a treeless country.

* Cf. *S.E.G.* viii. 366 (Jews working ἐν Νιτρίαις).

Many sorts of trees grew there and some of them could be used as good material for the construction of buildings and ships, for carts and wagons, for agricultural implements, for baskets and other domestic utensils. Such were the sycamore, the persea-tree, the acacia, and the different kinds of palm-tree. Even forests or groves were not unknown in Egypt. Theophrastus (*Hist. Pl.* iv. 2; 8) mentions a grove of acanthus and oaks in the Thebaid. But the needs of Egypt for timber were large and the area available for growing trees was very limited. In consequence the rulers of Egypt always paid great attention to tree-planting and to the systematic cutting of trees. Our information on this subject is very inadequate, but the correspondence of Zenon shows how anxious he was to obtain a sufficient supply of wood, and the importance he attached to tree-planting in his programme of the work to be done on the estate of Apollonius. Moreover, a paragraph in the instructions of the *dioecetes* to the *oeconomi* recorded in *Teb.* 703, 191–211, and one of the ordinances (προστάγματα) of Euergetes II (*Teb.* 5, 200 ff.), together with some inscriptions and papyri of the Roman period, yield very valuable, if meagre, information on the planting and cutting of trees.

The only large area available for planting trees was, and still is, to be found on the banks of the Nile and the canals, which served at the same time as roads. Extensive tree-planting was carried out on the embankments by the administration. It was done probably by the compulsory labour of the population under the supervision of the administration and under the guarantee of special contractors. Trees (willow, mulberry, acacia) and shrubs (especially tamarisk) were first planted in nurseries and afterwards transplanted to the embankments. Measures were taken to protect the young trees against sheep and, of course, goats and other domestic animals. The cutting of the older trees and of the branches and the handling of fallen trees were also strictly regulated. The government also issued orders regarding the use of trees that grew on private land. There is very little evidence on this point.[103]

Agriculture, grazing, fishing and hunting, arboriculture, mining, and quarrying yielded large quantities of foodstuffs and raw material to the government. The bulk of it consisted of grain of various kinds. Next in importance came wine and the seeds of oil-producing plants. Grain was used by the government as currency. Various obligations to it were discharged by payments in grain (wheat and barley). The method of payment in kind was firmly rooted in Egypt, and the Ptolemies never thought of replacing it entirely by payment in money. The grain surplus was placed on the market, but not on the internal market; for it was much more profitable for the king to export the grain and offer it on the international market, a subject to which I shall return. Other foodstuffs were sold to the population. We shall see presently how this branch of State economy was organized.

INDUSTRIES

A large part, however, of the produce in the possession of the government could not be consumed directly. This consisted of raw materials for industrial production: seeds for making vegetable oils, barley for brewing, milk for cheese-making, hides for leather, flax and wool for textiles, hemp for ropes, &c., papyrus for making mats, baskets, and especially paper. The same may be said of mineral ores, salt, nitre, various kinds of stone, and lumber. The manipulation of raw materials, in the Greek world, was a matter left, with few exceptions, to private enterprise. Private artisans working for their own profit and selling their products to consumers or to other artisans and merchants, private industry and manufacture, were characteristic features of Greek commercial life. The government of a *polis* would never think of occupying itself with such trivial concerns.

The situation in Egypt and probably in other Oriental monarchies of pre-Hellenistic times was different. Here the needs of the royal household were supplied by royal shops, in which thousands of artisans were employed in making beer, vegetable oils, cheese, and the like, or working in metal, wood, or stone, weaving, or embroidering. Household production on a large scale was a typical feature of royal economy in Egypt. The houses of the great gods of Egypt vied with the royal house. Each temple had its own shops which supplied the needs of the gods and of the temple population. The houses of the minor gods and of some of the wealthy nobility reproduced these great houses on a smaller scale. The sculptures and paintings in royal and other Egyptian graves of various times plainly indicate the importance of industry in the life of Egypt and the pride taken by the rulers in their workshops. All these shops may have been disposed to sell their products to the public, especially articles of finer workmanship.

Alongside of this household production on a large scale there existed in the villages and towns of Egypt home industries carried on by members of a family for their own needs. Besides these there were probably in the larger towns many artisans, grouped by professions and supervised by the government, working partly for the king and partly for the people and producing mostly simple articles of daily use.

It was most probably the example of the temples that influenced the Ptolemies in dealing with the question of industrial production. They found in Egypt an abundance of trained craftsmen and craftsmen of first-rate ability. Some of these used to work in the past for the temples, others for the courts of the king and his noblemen, others again for the inhabitants of towns and villages. With Alexander and Soter the courts disappeared, but the temples remained, and the artisans who had worked for the courts probably joined those of the temples, towns, and villages. We have little information about the industrial activities of the temples in pre-Ptolemaic times. Their linen manufactures were especially famous, and some other crafts may also have flourished in them. It is probable that in the time immediately before Alexander the temples had secured for themselves so predominant a position in respect of certain commodities that we may speak of the existence of something like a monopoly. The manufacture of oil—expensive to establish and maintain—may have been organized in the temples on a large scale and their produce may have dominated the market. Some special textiles may have been manufactured in temples only, for example fine linen—the famous *byssos*.

The part played by the temples in the economic system of Egypt may have suggested to the first Ptolemies the organization of Egyptian industry adopted by them and known to us through several documents. The two prerequisites for its establishment on a profitable basis were in their hands: they had enormous quantities of raw material concentrated in their storehouses and they had at their disposal a large supply of skilled labour. A skilful combination of these two elements produced what we call, using a modern term, the Ptolemaic 'monopolies', or more precisely their planned economy in the field of industry.[104]

Vegetable oils. The best known of these MONOPOLIES is that of vegetable oils, in Ptolemaic terminology the ἐλαικὴ ὠνή. A copy of a law (νόμος) of the time of Philadelphus (259/8 B.C.) regulating this branch of royal economy is extant. It formed originally a part of a general νόμος τελωνικός, which contained a section dealing with the farming of the contracts (ὠναί) in general, and special νόμοι regulating the management of particular contracts. How many such special 'laws' the document originally contained is not known. The fragments that we possess contain, besides the general section, the almost complete text of the νόμος ἐλαικῆς, substantial parts of the regulations concerning the temple wine-tax (*apomoira*, above, p. 283), and badly preserved fragments of those dealing with the textile industry (ἐριηρά, ὀθονιηρά, στύππιον), banking (τραπεζιτική), the beer industry (ζυτηρά), and the pasture tax (ἐννόμιον). The law as we have it is a revision of the original law, which may go back to the early years of Philadelphus, or even to the time of Soter.

The section of the Revenue Laws of Ptolemy Philadelphus, as the document is generally called, relating to the vegetable oils (ἐλαική) is unique in its completeness and affords us a deep insight into the policy and practice of Philadelphus, and possibly of Soter.

The νόμος ἐλαικῆς regulated the manufacture of the vegetable oils most widely used in Egypt: sesame, castor-oil (*croton*), safflower (*cnecos*), round gourd (*colocynthos*), and linseed (λίνου σπέρμα). The raw material was furnished by the farmers. Every year the surface to be planted with oil-bearing crops was distributed by the central government among various nomes, by the local administration of each nome among its several villages, and by the village administration among the individual farmers (διαγραφὴ σπόρου). So many *arourae* had to be planted with one or other of the oil-producing plants, and outside the allotted areas no one had the right to grow these specified plants. The responsibility for the exact execution of the 'sowing-plan' lay with the administration. Each farmer received from the government the necessary seed, which was paid back by him to the government. The crops were gathered under the watchful eyes of the administration and the contractors, the underwriters or guarantors responsible for the yield of the ὠνή. The produce of the fields was measured, one-fourth of it was paid as a tax and the rest was taken over by the contractor, who paid to the farmers the price of the amount delivered by them. The rate of payment was fixed by a tariff (διάγραμμα) published by the king. The contractor had then to deliver the amount collected to the government. It was transported to the government's barns and thence to the government's oil factories, located in towns and villages. No private mills were tolerated, with the sole exception of those belonging to the temples. They retained their oil-presses, but they had to register them and they were permitted to manufacture, under the control of the contractors and the officials, a certain quantity of sesame oil in their own mills and for their own use during two months only. The rest of the year their mills remained sealed. If in need of castor-oil, they had to buy it from the contractors. No sale of oil by the temples was permitted.

The oil mills in the service of the king were under the strict supervision of the administration and of the contractor. All the mills were registered, and a seal was affixed to those which were not in use, as well as to all idle machinery in the mills. The work done in them was organized by the contractor and the administrative officers. They were supposed to furnish each mill with a sufficient quantity of raw material, no less and no more than its actual working capacity required. They were also responsible for the efficiency of the work done in each mill.

The workmen (ἐλαιουργοί) were free men, not slaves nor serfs, but nevertheless closely controlled. They worked in the mills during the manufacturing season, and while at work they were bound to their work and to the place where the mills were situated, that is to say to a certain nome. The contractor and the administrative officials were (for the working season) their 'masters' (κύριοι) and the masters of the mills. Whatever this term exactly means from the juridical point of view, the use of it shows that the workmen during the working season and the mills were at the complete disposal of the agents of the government. For their work they received remuneration, so much for an *artaba* of seed. If at the end of the working season there was a surplus (ἐπιγένημα), they were given a bonus.

The exact status of the oil-makers is not quite clear. They belonged to the large class of those 'who were connected with the revenues' (ἐπιπεπλεγμένοι ταῖς προσόδοις), a class which shared certain privileges and certain restrictions with the royal peasants. This, however, does not define their legal status. Though we have no exact information on the point, it is probable that they were men trained in the craft, perhaps organized by the government as a kind of guild, who had been doing the same work for generations.

The fact that in the time of the early Ptolemies there probably existed mills and machinery owned but not used by private people (whatever their legal status may have been) shows that in a not far distant past the oil-makers may have worked, at least partly, in their own mills. At some time—perhaps under the early Ptolemies, perhaps earlier—the private production of oil was entirely forbidden to the professional oil-makers and oil-making became the exclusive privilege of the crown. There was no choice for the craftsmen but to enter the service of the government. Their peculiar legal status—their half-bondage—I hesitate to regard as an innovation of the Ptolemies. I should rather suppose that it was a heritage from the past, from the time when the guilds in the temples and in the towns and villages worked, at any rate in part, for the gods and the king in mills that mostly belonged to them.[105]

Vegetable oils were sold all over the country in the villages and towns, including Alexandria, exclusively by licensed merchants (κάπηλοι and μετάβολοι in the 'country', παλινπρατοῦντες in Alexandria), who bought them from the government and sold them to the customers. The relations between the vendors and the contractors were minutely regulated. The retail price of oils was fixed, and no one was allowed to sell them at a higher or lower price. Each retailer received a certain quantity for sale. The distribution of oil and the control of the retailers were in the hands of a special contractor (εἰληφὼς τὴν διάθεσιν καὶ τὸ τέλος τοῦ ἐλαίου), who was responsible for the tradesmen and was required to keep careful watch against attempts to sell at higher prices than those fixed by the crown and against smuggling, for which a heavy penalty was provided. The price of oil was outrageously high, much higher than that of the best olive-oil in Greece, and the king made an enormous profit from his monopoly, to protect which a high customs duty (50 per cent.) was imposed on imported olive-oil, even on that which came from the Ptolemaic dominions. Moreover, the concessionaires of the meat trade (μάγειροι), who had plenty of fats at their disposal, were carefully watched and their trade was subjected to special regulations. Not satisfied with his profit, the king levied from the public a special tax (ἐλαική), perhaps a tax per head, for the right of using the monopolized oil. The tax was probably intended to cover the cost of production.[106]

It was natural that these minute regulations, which were in constant conflict with the interests of the people, should lead to repeated infringements of the law by retail traders and consumers. Spying, denunciations, house-searches, and violence were the order of the day. Many documents give a vivid picture of the way in which the oil monopoly worked in the Fayûm.

Textiles. The manufacture of textiles presented a more complicated and more difficult problem. Linen fabrics were an ancient speciality of Egypt. Next in importance came woollen cloth, and finally the various products for which hemp was used, required especially for ships' tackle. In dealing with textile manufacture one must bear in mind the extent to which spinning and weaving were carried on in private households and the great development of the textile industry of the temples. Naturally in the laws of Philadelphus the three departments of textile manufacture—wool, linen, and hemp (ἐριηρά, ὀθονιηρά, στύππιον)—are treated under one and the same heading. But in the instructions of the *dioecetes*, given in *Teb.* 703, linen manufacture alone is dealt with. I am therefore inclined to think that the three departments were organized on the same general lines but had each its peculiar features.

The best-known department is that of the linen industry, and yet even in this many points remain obscure. The general scheme of organization presented by *Teb.* 703 (our best source of information) appears coherent. The organization was very similar to that for the manufacture of vegetable oils. It is probable that the production of flax was not unlimited but was controlled by the government (*Teb.* 769), a certain quantity being delivered to the State while the rest of the production was free. To supply the requirements of the State and perhaps also for purposes of sale and export, the king had his own linen factories. Specially trained weavers, scattered all over the country, worked for him, some in government factories, but the great majority in their own houses, where they had their own looms. Every year the manufacture of a certain quantity of cloth and garments was assigned by the central administration to each of the nomes; the work was then distributed among the towns and villages of the nome, and their shares were portioned out among individual weavers. With these weavers contracts were made by the government. Each of them received a separate order for a certain quantity of carefully specified cloth and garments, sometimes to be adorned with embroidery. The yarn and nitre and *kiki* for washing the cloth were apparently furnished to the weavers by the government. Who spun the yarn is unknown. After delivery of the cloth and garments as ordered, and their careful examination by the *oeconomus*, the weavers were paid according to a tariff (διάγραμμα). In case of defective quantity or quality the weavers were charged with the difference according to a διάγραμμα (probably the same as that just mentioned). The looms while not in operation were taken away from the weavers and kept under seal in the storehouses of the capital of the nome.

Evidence concerning the sale or use of the fabrics delivered by the weavers is very meagre. *Teb.* 703 is silent on the subject and the information derived from other documents is contradictory. I cannot discuss the problem here. In my opinion the stuffs and garments made in the royal shops or made for the king in private shops were intended to supply first and foremost the king's own needs and the needs of his enormous household. Some finer fabrics may have been sold to foreign merchants. How much was disposed of on the Egyptian market and on what conditions, we do not know. Nor is there any evidence about the restrictions imposed on home-production and on private factories. The temples still produced, probably on a large scale, the fine linen called *byssos*. Part of it was for delivery to the king, who was very strict in requiring the exact execution of his orders as regards both quantity and quality. Like the royal weavers, the temples were charged for the cloth they failed to deliver, and had to pay certain fines for cloth that was not up to the prescribed sizes and quality. It is not improbable that some of the private weavers had a permit or licence (for which they certainly paid) to produce fabrics for the general market. Whether or not such fabrics were sold at a price fixed by the government and by merchants specially licensed by the government, we do not exactly know. The temples had certainly the right of selling their *byssos* to foreign merchants. An inscription informs us that an Arab merchant who was at the same time priest of an Egyptian temple imported some *aromata* from Arabia and delivered in exchange *byssos* from his own temple (below, p. 388).[107]

Even more meagre is our information regarding the manufacture of woollen cloth. In this field the Ptolemies had to be very careful. Woollen garments, rugs, carpets, and mattresses were used, especially by the Greeks. The Egyptians wore linen garments and used mats of reed, palm leaves, and other material. Now the Greeks brought with them the habit of having their clothes made for them and their families by their own wives and maids. Every one remembers Theocritus' description of a housewife in Alexandria who was furious with her husband for buying dirty and inferior wool for her in the market. In these circumstances I very much doubt whether the Ptolemies imposed far-reaching restrictions on the wool trade or on the home-production of woollen cloth and garments. They may have had their own wool factories in Alexandria and elsewhere. There is evidence of this as regards Alexandria in the first century B.C.* But it is improbable that they created

* Oros. *Hist. adv. pag.* vi. 19, 20.

anything like a royal monopoly of wool-weaving and the wool trade. There is no doubt that certain special requirements of the government (for instance a supply of the special kind of woollen stuffs called Syrian (συρίαι), much used in the army) were met by compulsory manufacture carried out by specialist craftsmen, and organized in the same way as that of linen cloth and garments. But this was an exception. We possess many documents which speak of the wool trade in terms that suggest its freedom. For instance, we know from the Zenon correspondence that Apollonius had workshops at Memphis and perhaps at Philadelphia in which woollen stuffs were produced in large quantities; and we know that these shops worked both for the needs of those whom Apollonius employed on his estate and for the general market. I do not think that his case was exceptional. Many documents speak of clothes, perhaps mostly woollen clothes, sold by various people. On the whole it appears probable that the manufacture of woollen stuffs was organized on the same general lines as that of linen, but with fewer restrictions.[108]

Beer. Second in importance only to the vegetable oils as an article of consumption was beer brewed from barley. Beer was the national drink of Egypt. It was certainly consumed, especially during the hot season, in large quantities. From time immemorial a special craft of professional brewers had existed in Egypt, who certainly made a much better beverage than home-brewed beer. In the Ptolemaic period these professional brewers formed local guilds which were in the service of the State. Whether the State permitted home brewing is unknown. It was no easy matter to stop it, even for the Ptolemaic government. In any case the commercial production of beer and the sale of it in beer-shops were concentrated in the hands of the king. Brewers of beer (ζυτοποιοί) were concessionaires of the government. They received from the king a certain quantity of barley (σύνταξις), and the beer brewed from it they either sold direct to customers or handed over to retail dealers. Special agents of the government (πιστολογευτής and ταμίας) had charge of the accounting. Besides paying a high price for beer, the public paid for the right of buying it; a special charge was perhaps also made for permission to brew beer at home. As in other ὠναί, special 'contractors' underwrote the collection of this revenue by the government.[109]

Salt. The important part played by salt in the history of taxation is well known, for instance in France before the Revolution, in Italy (the famous 'sale e tabacchi'), and in Russia. In ancient times we hear of salt being subject to special regulation in many States, among them the Roman Republic and Empire and several of the Hellenistic monarchies (see below, n. 258, on the Seleucids). It was so easy and so profitable for the government to monopolize the production and sale of salt, and certainly no single commodity was more extensively used by consumers. It is not surprising, therefore, that the salt monopoly was strict and complete in Egypt. How the production of salt was organized is quite unknown to us. Salt was obtained from salt mines, salt lakes, and sea-water. No doubt the salt-pans belonged to the government and were operated in the same way as mines and quarries. Thereafter salt was dealt with in much the same way as oil and beer. It was sold to the public by the government through special licensed traders all over the country and also in large quantities and at a reduced price directly by the government to such privileged bodies as the army, the priests, and the officials. Every inhabitant of Egypt (with the exception of special classes of people who were exempted by royal orders), besides paying for the salt he consumed, paid the salt tax (ἁλική); many receipts for the payment of this tax are extant. The rate was high and the tax weighed heavily on the population, especially as it was very strictly administered. In the second century B.C. the hated tax was probably reorganized. In Roman times it still lingered on in the Arsinoite nome. The abundance of our evidence about this tax is probably not due to chance. It is almost certain that it was much more oppressive than the other similar taxes connected with the monopolies (if we may assume that the existence of such taxes can be taken as proved), playing almost the part of a poll-tax.[110]

Nitre and alum. Nitre and alum were treated in similar fashion. As soda mixed with castor oil was used as soap mainly by fullers (γναφεῖς, στιβεῖς) and washers (πλυνεῖς), these artisans all paid a special tax (νιτρικὴ πλύνου) for the right of buying soda from the crown.

Leather. Of less importance was the leather trade (δερματηρά), which was organized by the government in a manner similar to the linen trade.

Paper. The production of paper from the famous Egyptian papyrus reed was a matter of not only local but international importance. The demand for papyrus, both in Egypt and abroad, was very large. That it was so in Egypt we know with certainty. Thousands of official documents and alongside of them many fragments of books and private letters, all written on papyrus, have been found in the country. It is interesting to find that the use of papyrus rapidly increased in Egypt in the Ptolemaic period: while documents of the time of Soter are rare, under Philadelphus they become very common. This is certainly not accidental. Undoubtedly during the reigns of Soter and Philadelphus the production of papyrus was improved and increased, and the price of papyrus rolls went down correspondingly.

This supposition is confirmed by a recently published document from the archives of Zenon: an account of 258/7 dealing with the purchase of papyrus rolls (χάρται) and the distribution of them among the various offices of Ptolemy II's general economic manager, Apollonius (*P. Col. Zen.* 4). The rolls were very cheap, 3½ obols each. They were used not only for writing but as wrapping paper also (i. 10: εἰς ἐνειλήματα καρπάσ[ων]). Unfortunately we do not know the size of the standard rolls used in the offices of Apollonius. In any case two facts are indicated by this document: there was mass production of papyrus rolls in Egypt in the reign of Philadelphus and their price was very low.

Nor was the consumption of papyrus in the Greek and Latin world decreasing. No doubt in Syria and in Pergamene Asia Minor, after Attalus I, parchment was chiefly used, and it is not improbable that some restrictions were imposed by the Seleucids and Attalids on the importation of papyrus into Syria and into the Pergamene kingdom. The rest of the world, however, used papyrus. We know, for instance, that the Delian temple administration bought a yearly supply of papyrus for the purpose of its accounts. The same was being done by thousands of cities and temples in Greece, and by scores, if not hundreds, of thousands of private persons in all parts of Greece, throughout the area of Greek colonization, and in Italy.

Thus the demand for papyrus was rapidly increasing, and the supply followed the demand. How this supply was organized in the time of Philadelphus is a matter about which we know very little. We do not know by whom the papyrus groves were cultivated. In all probability they were rented from the government by special farmers who looked after them. They delivered the papyrus to local factories, where paper rolls of different qualities and sizes were made; the stems of papyrus could not be transported long distances as paper was made exclusively from fresh-cut stems. In these factories were employed many trained craftsmen whom the Ptolemies had inherited from former times. How these factories were organized, and how the finished product was sold is imperfectly known. A document of 159 B.C. (*Teb.* 709) shows that at this time there existed a special 'department of paper', a special ὠνὴ χαρτηρά. In this department an official styled 'supervisor of the sale of royal paper' (ὁ πρὸς τῆι διαθέσει τῶν βασιλικῶν χαρτῶν) looked after the sale of the 'royal paper', which was carried out by special retailers who rented from the crown the exclusive right of sale. These merchants had compulsory clients, for instance the notaries public, who were not allowed to buy paper from private dealers (ἰδιωτικὰ φορτία). In the second century B.C., therefore, there was a sort of partial monopoly of papyrus. The king produced his own papyrus in his factories or had it made by order in private establishments. This paper was sold in his own shops to compulsory clients. Side by side with it there existed paper privately manufactured and sold by private (probably licensed) dealers under the supervision of the management of the ὠνή.

Such was approximately the state of things in the second century. For the third century we have no information. The correspondence of Zenon shows that Apollonius and Zenon bought their supply of papyrus on the free market. Some paper was made for them on special order. On the other hand, the existence of the 'department of paper' or 'paper contract' (χαρτηρά, sc. ὠνή) is an established fact. We also know of the existence of a special tax called χαρτηρά, a tax perhaps similar to the ἁλική. We may think that in the early Ptolemaic times the government was satisfied with a strict control over private production and with a share in its produce, and did not possess its own factories. Whether or not at that time and later the temples retained the right of manufacturing paper for their own needs and perhaps paper of special quality, as they manufactured *byssos*, there is no evidence to show.

Nor have we any exact information regarding the organization of the foreign trade in paper and on the part taken in it by the king. The Delian material is difficult to interpret. There is no doubt that in 296 B.C. the price of one roll (χάρτης) at Delos was about 3 obols, while in 279 it rose to 2 drachms or a little less. The price dropped again after 267 B.C. This sharp rise of price has been explained by Glotz as due to the establishment of a papyrus monopoly in Egypt by Philadelphus. But there are many objections to this theory. We do not know whether there was a monopoly on papyrus in Egypt in the early Ptolemaic times, nor do we know what kind of rolls were bought at Delos in 296 and in 279 respectively, that is to say, whether the rolls were of the same size and of the same quality; and finally we cannot compare the prices that prevailed in Egypt with those that ruled at Delos, since a 'roll' varied in size and in quality.[111]

Baths. A large income was derived by the king from the baths (βαλανεῖα). Our evidence on their management, though abundant, is contradictory and obscure. We know that the baths paid to the king the third part of their income (τρίτη). At the same time there are frequent mentions of the payment of a φόρος. We do not know whether these two payments are identical. The high tax paid on the baths, apparently by the private owners of them, may suggest that the king regarded the permission given to private persons to build and manage baths as the cession to them of one of his rights. There are some indications in our sources that the king himself owned several baths, which he rented to private business men. The large supply of fuel at his disposal and the free use of the water-supply in towns and villages may have induced the kings, especially in the early years of their domination, to build several baths. I may remind the reader that public baths were a Greek innovation and that the building of such establishments was, in the early years of Ptolemaic rule, a risky undertaking, a kind of pioneer work. The king, however, did not prevent private people from taking a share in this business, provided they were ready to pay a very high tax.[112]

Aromata. Finally, I may mention the king's control of the trade in frankincense, myrrh, cinnamon, cassia, &c., known as *ἀρώματα*, most of them imported into Egypt from Arabia, East Africa, and India. Both the home consumption of these commodities as raw material or in the form of scents, ointments, and so forth, and their export were to a large extent, if not completely, under royal management. The prices charged for them by the retail dealers were apparently fixed prices.[113]

It appears certain, therefore, that besides the strict control of agriculture, which yielded him a large income in foodstuffs and raw materials, and of mining and quarrying, fishing and hunting, &c., the king exercised a control, in some cases complete, in others partial, over many other important branches of economic activity. The production and sale of basic commodities were thus in his hands and were managed on a well-devised system. A very large revenue accrued to him from this source.

It is impossible to state exactly how many branches of production were organized in the manner described above. But it is important to note that the scanty evidence at our disposal has not so far indicated any branch of production, either agricultural or industrial, which was not regulated and to a large extent managed in one way or another by the government. The same is true of trade. We have seen how some of the 'monopolized' goods were made accessible to the population. It was done through retail traders who were, in effect, agents of the government. The same is true of practically all the other branches of production regarding which chance has preserved us some information. The traders we meet with in the documents are all of them concessionaires of the government, men who on payment of a fee received a licence and alone had the right of dealing in certain commodities. We hear occasionally of such concessionaires selling wine, cheese, bread, meat, salted meat and fish, even boiled lentils and roast pumpkin seed, bricks, and jewels. For some commodities there were fixed prices, for others not, but all branches of trade were controlled by the government. There is a very instructive passage in *Teb.* 703, l. 174 ff., in which the *dioecetes* gives these directions to the *oeconomus*: 'See to it, too, that the goods for sale (ὤνια) be not sold at prices higher than those prescribed. Make also a careful investigation of those goods which have no fixed prices and on which the dealers may put what prices they like; and after having put a fair surplus on the wares being sold,* make the . . . dispose of them.'[114]

Transport. Such was the management of production and sale within the country. The business of transportation was organized on the same general principles. Of course private transport was not strictly regulated, though taxes were paid on draught-animals, especially donkeys, and special payments were exacted from those who were professionally engaged in the transport business (ὀνηλάται). The same was probably true of transport by water on boats of various sizes. There is mention in many texts of privately owned ships, and also of privately owned draught-animals. Apollonius, for example, owned many means of transport by land and water, which he used for himself, for his staff, and for the conveyance of goods produced on his estates. A special commander was in charge of his fleet. But the case of Apollonius may have been exceptional. As in many other departments, so in the matter of ships, we cannot tell whether he had so many at his disposal as the king's *dioecetes* or in his private capacity, the ships being part of his *dorea*.

The question of transport was an important one in the economy of the Ptolemies. Military requirements in time of peace and war, the frequent journeys of the king, his staff, and his various employees, the government postal service, and especially the movement of enormous quantities of grain and other commodities from the places where they were produced to the royal storehouses in Alexandria and in the country outside it (χώρα)—all these called for thousands of beasts of burden and

* The 'surplus' added to the cost makes the selling price; the contractor's gain is what remains after deduction of the sums paid to the government.

drivers, and hundreds, if not thousands, of ships large and small, with their crews.

Like other owners of 'houses', the kings had at their disposal for their own service their own means of transport—horses, camels, donkeys, mules, and carriages, carts, &c., on the one hand, and boats of various kinds, from gorgeous dahabiyehs to modest grain ships, with their crews, on the other. On the organization of this department of the royal household, except as regards the postal service (which cannot be discussed here), we are very imperfectly informed. The drivers and rowers were probably free natives who served under contract, but in case of necessity were pressed into service.

In time of war, however, of important movements of troops within the country, or of long tours of inspection by the king, and every year at harvest-time, when millions of bushels of grain and other produce were moved by road, river, and canal, the means of transport owned by the king were insufficient. In these circumstances the Ptolemies made full use of the government's immemorial right of requisitioning for these purposes men, draught-animals, and ships. In normal times the mobilization of private means of transport was effected by means of contracts with their owners; contracts were made in particular with professional donkey-drivers (ὀνηλάται) and professional shippers (ναύκληροι). But in cases of emergency the Ptolemies would have recourse to the ancient system of ἀγγαρεῖαι and would press into government service draught-animals, men, and ships—a very much dreaded and hated form of liturgy.[115]

Requisitions. Closely connected with the organization of transport were requisitions of foodstuffs and other supplies for the king, the army, and the higher officials when moving. Such requisitioned supplies were known as ξένια ('gifts') or παρουσία and κοίτη. How far requisition was used for feeding detachments of soldiers on the march or stationed in the country we do not exactly know, especially in the time of the early Ptolemies.* It is, however, very probable that, if payment was made for whatever was requisitioned, it was on the basis of prices fixed by the government. This was, for instance, the practice

* Some information on this subject will be found in *P. Ryl. Zen.*, 9 (251 B.C.) and *Teb.* 729 (2nd cent. B.C.).

in cases of purchase of grain by the government, which was often a form of requisition (ἀγοραστός, συναγοραστικός, βασιλικὸς πυρός or σῖτος).[116]

Taxation. To the numerous burdens of the population that have been described was added regular taxation. Many taxes have already been mentioned, such as those paid by farmers and landholders of various types, by artisans, and by the public at large (taxes per head connected with the 'monopolies'). In addition to these there was a great variety of other taxes, but the enumeration and classification of them would have no direct bearing on the subject of this book. It may, however, be said that no personal poll-tax appears to have been imposed on the people under the early Ptolemies. On the other hand, there were elaborate taxes on property, for example, on houses and on slaves; on legal acts connected with property, such as the registration of private documents and the καταγραφή,* sales (ἐγκύκλιον), auctions, and inheritances; on foreign trade, both export and import; on internal commerce, so far as concerned the exchange of goods between Upper and Lower Egypt; on the use of harbours, landing places, roads, and so forth. I have already pointed out that taxation was highly diversified and therefore all the more oppressive.[117]

ECONOMIC AND SOCIAL CONDITIONS IN EGYPT

The economic system of the Ptolemies as sketched above was inspired by one motive, the organization of production, with the main purpose of making the State, in other words the king, rich and powerful. All the efforts of the people were concentrated on this principal object. Every one was required to work first and foremost for the State, according to a plan devised by the government, carefully worked out by the administration, and strictly enforced by all kinds of sanctions, material responsibility and personal responsibility being judiciously combined.

The native Egyptians. Very little initiative or opportunity

* The meaning of καταγραφή is hotly disputed by modern scholars. On the present state of the controversy, see A. B. Schwarz, *Actes du Vme Congrès Pap.*, 1938, p. 381 ff.; E. Schönbauer, *Arch. f. Pap.* xiii (1938), p. 39 ff.; C. Préaux, *L'Écon. Lag.*, 1938, p. 286 ff. (who translates 'droits de mutation'); cf. F. E. Brown, *A.J.A.* xlii (1938), p. 613.

of furthering their private interests was left to the various classes of the population. The margin of individual profit was very narrow. For the native Egyptians it was almost nil, since on them lay the heaviest burden. I must remind the reader that the majority of them were in one way or another bound to work for the government, whether they were royal peasants or constituted the various groups of 'tax-payers' (ὑποτελεῖς) and 'men connected with the revenues' (ἐπιπεπλεγμένοι ταῖς προσόδοις)—workmen in the factories, retail traders, keepers of flocks and herds, professional hunters and fishermen, professional drivers, rowers, and sailors, labourers in the mines and quarries, and so on. Besides their usual work they were liable to much obligatory service. Compulsory work on canals and dikes, and from time to time in mines and quarries, probably also in fishing and hunting, on tree-planting and transport, very often interrupted their daily routine. We do not know exactly what legal forms these relations assumed. It is probable that in most cases they were of a contractual character. But the contracts between the government and those who worked for it were of a peculiar kind. They regularly contained a significant *clausula* that in case of non-payment of debts 'execution shall be made as usual in the case of royal claims' (ἡ πρᾶξις ἔστω πρὸς βασιλικά in the case of debts to the government, and ὡς πρὸς βασιλικά in the case of private debts). A recently discovered document shows that this formula implied the right of the government to exact what was due to the crown by means of execution against the person, which meant imprisonment and enslavement. The document in question relates to conditions in Syria. It deals with the λαοί, the working classes only. Does this mean that the liability to enslavement was limited to them? The same rule probably applied to Egypt proper.

Still more dependent on the government or the king, and overworked and overburdened with responsibility, were those of the natives who were pressed into the royal service as guards of various kinds. These, in their various spheres, were supposed to keep a watchful eye on all who were working in any capacity for the State, especially in the field of agriculture. Their responsibility, both personal and material, was heavy, their work

PLATE XXXVIII

1. This mosaic reproduces the most characteristic features of Ptolemaic Egypt. The upper part of it is a sort of zoological atlas of the Egyptian Sudan with all the fabulous and real animals of that region and their names in Greek (cp. Philostr., *Vit. Apoll.* vi. 24 and Ael., *De Nat. Anim.*). The lower part gives the general aspect of Egypt, especially the Delta, in time of flood. In the right-hand corner a peasant's house is shown, with a dove-cote near it. In the other (left) corner are hippopotami and crocodiles. The centre of the lower part is occupied by two buildings. One of them is a pavilion with a large curtain, behind which is seen a tower-villa with a large garden in an enclosure. In the pavilion a group of soldiers is preparing to celebrate a festival. At the head of the group a laurel-crowned officer sounds the horn; he is greeted by a woman with a palm-branch, who offers him a garland or a diadem; and he appears to give a signal to a company of soldiers approaching in a military rowing-boat. Near the military pavilion a party of civilians, including women, gathered under a pergola, are drinking to the strains of music. Behind these buildings are two more bands of decoration. In the lower of the two is seen a small shrine with a religious procession moving through it. Behind the pergola we see a sacred enclosure and an osier-barn, perhaps a *μοσχοτρόφιον* or a barn for cattle; round the barn ibises are flying. The upper of the two bands is occupied by large temples. The largest has two pylons and colossal Egyptian statues near the main entrance; in front of it is a man riding a donkey, followed by his servant with his baggage. Behind the pergola and the barn are three other temples: the first is a shrine of ibises (*ἰβιών*, cf. *P. Fouad* i, 16), the next a typical Egyptian shrine with two towers, and the third a Greco-Egyptian temple. In the water are seen various animals, flowers, natives in canoes (one loaded with lotuses), and two large pleasure and hunting boats with cabins. The whole mosaic is the best and most realistic of the extant pictures of Egypt in the Ptolemaic and Roman periods and gives a vivid idea of its aspect. The date of the mosaic is controversial. I agree with Miss M. E. Blake, who says: 'my contention is that . . . the Nile and the fish mosaic of Palestrina are Hellenistic, and not Roman, and may have been laid at any time between Sulla and Hadrian. The subject . . . is thoroughly Hellenistic in spirit.' I may add that the points of similarity between the mosaic and Aelian, *De Nat. Anim.*, pointed out by O. Marucchi (cf. description of pl. XLII), and between them and the animal frieze of the Hellenistic tomb of Marissa (pl. LVIII) makes it more than probable that all go back to a Hellenistic source, perhaps an illustrated treatise of zoology. From A. Engelmann, *Antike Bilder aus römischen Handschriften*, 1909, pl. 29.4.

I cannot quote here all that has been written on the mosaic. It will suffice to mention the most modern works, which contain up-to-date bibliographies: O. Marucchi, *Bull. Com.*, 1895, p. 32 ff.; 1904, p. 258 f.; *Diss. Pont. Acc.*, ser. 2, x (1912), pp. 177 ff.; S. Reinach, *Rép. d. peint.*, p. 374; M. H. Swindler, *Anc. Paint.*, p. 318, n. 336; M. Rostovtzeff, *Soc. and Ec. Hist. R.E.*, pl. XLI; Eva Schmidt, 'Studien z. Barberinischen Mosaik in Palestrina', *Zur Kunstg. d. Auslandes*, no. 127, 1929; M. E. Blake, 'The pavements of the Roman buildings' &c., *Mem. Am. Ac. Rome*, viii (1930), pp. 139 ff.

2. The paintings here reproduced (they belong to a wall decoration of the third style) represent, the first a monumental entrance to a sacred grove, the second perhaps an entrance to a royal park. Some peculiarities of the architecture suggest that what is represented are not buildings appertaining to Roman villas but constructions of the Hellenistic period either in Asia Minor and Syria, or in Ptolemaic Egypt. I have discussed these and similar Pompeian paintings in my article 'Die hellenistisch-römische Architekturlandschaft', *Röm. Mitt.* xxvi (1911), pp. 47 ff., figs. 26–8. Photographs supplied by Prof. A. von Gerkan.

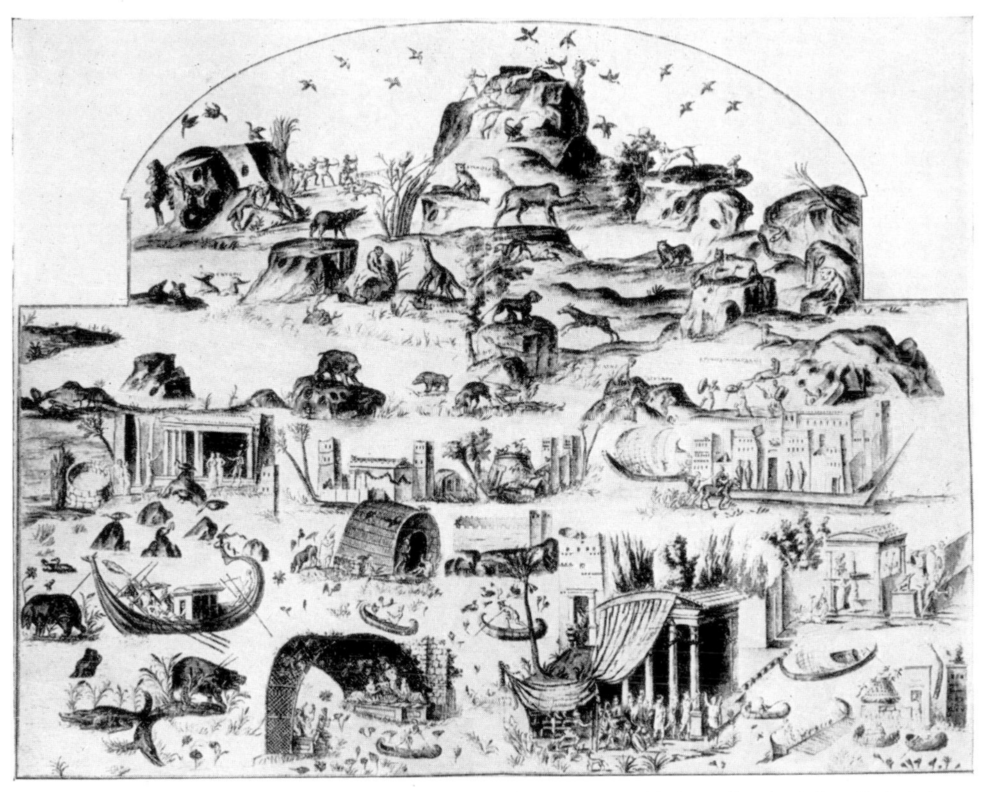

1. Mosaic found in Palestrina (ancient Praeneste), now in the Palazzo Barberini at Palestrina

2. Paintings from Pompeii (house IX, 7 (13), 3).
Drawings in the German Archaeological Institute in Rome

1. Cairo Museum. 2. Alexandria Museum.

3. Alexandria Museum.

LIFE IN THE χώρα OF EGYPT

PLATE XXXIX

1. Elegant votive stele of Attic type with pediment, found at Philadelphia in the Fayûm. On the upper front of the stele is carved in low relief the figure of Anubis facing to the right, holding in his left hand the *crux ansata*, in his right the sceptre. Before him a *thymiaterion*. The body of Anubis was painted. Above to the right, inscription in hieroglyphs: 'Anubis the master of the two earths', an unusual variation of the usual formula 'master of the Necropolis'. Below, an inscription in Greek in elegant letters of the third century B.C.: *ὑπὲρ Ἀπολλωνίου | καὶ Ζήνωνος | Πασῶς κυνοβοσκὸς | Ἀνούβι εὐχήν*. Since the stele was found at Philadelphia and must be assigned to the third century B.C., it is very probable that this Apollonius is the great *dioecetes*, owner of the Philadelphia *dorea* and builder of the 'city' of Philadelphia, and Zenon his Philadelphian steward. The dedicant is an Egyptian, keeper of the sacred jackals, cf. Strabo xvii. I. 40, p. 812: *ἑξῆς δ' ἐστὶν ὁ Κυνοπολίτης νομὸς καὶ Κυνῶν πόλις, ἐν ᾗ ὁ Ἄνουβις τιμᾶται καὶ τοῖς κυσὶ τιμὴ καὶ σίτισις τέτακταί τις ἱερά*. The stele is an eloquent testimony to the reverence paid by the Greek masters of Egypt to Egyptian religion. It is probable that the *Ἀνουβιεῖον* was built in Philadelphia with the support of Apollonius and Zenon. H. 0·52, W. 0·15. Photograph supplied by the authorities of the Cairo Museum.

G. Lefebure, *Ann. Serv. Ant. Ég.* xiii (1914), pp. 93 ff.; *S.B.* 5796 (wrongly assigned to Theadelphia); U. Wilcken, *Arch. Pap.* vi (1920), p. 222; M. Rostovtzeff, *Out of the Past of Greece and Rome*, 1932, p. 126.

2. Terracotta figurine found in Alexandria (?). A peasant (not a slave) in a conical felt hat gathering dates from the top of a palm-tree, which he has climbed by means of a rope; the basket for the dates hangs from his shoulder. Photograph supplied by the authorities of the Alexandria Museum.

E. Breccia, *Terrecotte figurate greche . . . del Museo di Alessandria*, i, 1930, p. 72, no. 465, pl. XXXIII, 8, cf. P. Perdrizet, *Les Terres cuites grecques de la Collection Fouquet*, 1921, ii, pl. XCIX, 2, and i, pp. 129 ff., no. 354, and pl. XCIX, 4, no. 355 (with an excursus on date-palms in Egypt); M. Rostovtzeff, *Soc. and Ec. Hist. R.E.*, pl. XLII, 4.

3. Terracotta figurine showing a cart drawn by two oxen or cows and driven by a peasant-boy in a thick cloak with a hood. The wheels of the cart are heavy and primitive. The cart is protected by a canopy. M. Rostovtzeff, loc. cit., pl. XLII, 3. The figurine belongs to Roman times, but the carts and drivers were the same in the Ptolemaic period. Photograph supplied by the authorities of the Alexandria Museum.

repugnant. No wonder that they tried hard to escape this obligation. More responsibility than profit was also implied in the tenure of the minor offices in the royal administration that were open to the natives, such as those of the heads of villages (κωμάρχαι) and the village scribes (κωμογραμματεῖς). These enjoyed, of course, a prominent position in the villages, but their work was hard and complicated; there was a certain possibility of profit connected with it, but in the main the village offices were *munera*, not *honores*, and the tenure of them involved more danger and responsibility than enjoyment of prestige and profit.

There is, of course, no ground whatever, as I have already stated (pp. 277 ff.), for speaking of the working classes as serfs comparable to the serfs of the Oriental monarchies and temples, or to those of whose existence in the Greek world and among some of the Central European tribes we have occasional evidence. The Egyptian λαοί were not strictly bound to their professions or to their place of residence, they possessed a good deal of social and economic freedom in general and of freedom of movement in particular, and their normal relations to the government so far as their economic activity was concerned were contractual; the compulsory service that was exacted from them was remunerated (though at a low rate). And yet they were not entirely free. They were bound to the government and could not escape from this bondage, because on it depended their means of subsistence.

This bondage was real, not nominal. Royal officials and tax-collectors pried into the domestic affairs of those who worked for the government, since every action of the workers might affect the 'revenues' of the king, a sacred thing in official eyes, the ultimate goal towards which the efforts of all should be directed. These workers understood very well that the government was interested in their existence mainly because the safety of its revenues depended on their work. Thus in their frequent petitions they appealed not only to the justice of the king and to his equity, but very often to the fact that the unfair treatment of the petitioner might prevent him from doing his work and so be detrimental to the king's revenues. It is not surprising that under such conditions the λαοί showed little enthusiasm or energy and creative activity in their work.

What proportion of natives were not in some way bound to the government cannot be said. Priests, officials of the crown (including a very few of higher rank), and owners of private land stood more or less outside the circle of direct bondage, and free artisans, if such existed in Egypt, would be in the same position. I very much doubt whether there were many natives who earned their living as hired labourers, having no other profession at the same time. Women and children were, of course, not directly bound to the government.[118]

Slaves. The part played by slavery in the economic and social life of Egypt is inadequately known. Two forms of slavery must be distinguished, the native and the Greek. The first was the result of some form or other of bondage, and we have very little information about it. The second was imported into Egypt by the Greeks. The native form of slavery best known to us is that which is found in the temples—the *hierodulia*, which I have spoken of above and shall mention below. It was the economic foundation of their activities and certainly prevented imported slaves and the Greek form of slavery from penetrating into them. In the life of the masses of the Egyptian population slavery—in whatever form it might appear—could not play any important part. A royal peasant or a workman in one of the monopolies was not rich enough to maintain slaves, whether native or imported, and they were poor enough to provide with cheap labour everybody who was in need of it. This made the development of slavery of either kind on any large scale almost impossible in Egypt.

The only important group of the inhabitants of Egypt willing and able to have slaves, natives or imported, were its new masters and rulers: the king and his court and household, the higher officials, the officers and soldiers of the army (who often appear on their tombstones accompanied by slaves), and the members of the gradually growing Greek and hellenized native *bourgeoisie*. They all were accustomed to the use of slave labour and many could not exist without it. They found in Egypt, especially during and after the great foreign wars of Soter, Philadelphus, and Euergetes, a slave market well provided with human material and they knew how to reduce to slavery some of the natives with whom they were in business relations. Their slaves they employed chiefly for domestic work, but they certainly tried also to use servile labour in industry and trade, particularly in Alexandria. I see no reason to think that in such concerns as the gift-estate of Apollonius slave labour would not be used alongside of hired labour. We must not, however, overestimate the number of slaves in the houses of the masters and rulers of Egypt. Their increase was not encouraged by the kings, who imposed considerable restrictions on the spread of the Greek form of slavery by opposing the enslavement of natives, by limiting the numbers of exported and imported slaves, and by levying high taxes on the internal trade in them.

In sum, slavery, as an economic factor, was of far less importance in Ptolemaic Egypt than in other parts of the Hellenistic world.[119]

Priests. Like the minor royal officials, the priests formed a privileged class of the natives. They enjoyed certain important privileges, such as freedom from compulsory labour, which in fact were not always respected by the administration; they were allowed a certain degree of self-government; and they attended to their own professional business without interference by the government. Moreover, they derived some income from their professional affairs, from agriculture as landowners within the boundaries of the sacred land, and as supervisors of the temple industries and of such trade as was left in their hands. But, as we have seen, a large, perhaps the larger part of their income went into the royal treasury (*βασιλικόν*).

Hieroduli. We should like to know more of the '*slaves' of the gods*, *ἱερόδουλοι*, who did not belong to any grade of the priesthood but worked for the temples as tillers of the sacred land (*γῆ ἱερά*), workmen in the temple factories, keepers of the temple herds, and manual workers (of either sex) who performed divers functions connected with the management of the temple buildings and the various religious performances. To call these slaves in the Greek sense of the word is certainly misleading. Further light on their peculiar position is much needed and will no doubt be furnished by Demotic documents still awaiting publication or careful study. Were the temple farmers a group of royal peasants (*βασιλικοὶ γεωργοί*)? Were the temple artisans classed with the *ἐπιπεπλεγμένοι ταῖς προσόδοις*, the workmen 'connected with the revenues'? To such questions there is at present no answer.[120]

Foreigners. Thus the natives of Egypt, with the exception of the government officials, a few owners of land, and perhaps the priests and some artisans, had small chance of enriching themselves by thrift, energy, and business ability. In this respect the situation of another 'privileged' class, the foreign immigrants who by settling in Egypt became subjects of the Ptolemies, was far more favourable.

I cannot discuss here the political and legal status of the foreigners in early Ptolemaic Egypt. The subject is controversial, and many solutions of the problems connected with it have been suggested. There is, however, no doubt that we may speak of the foreigners, of whom thousands of varying standing and various professions poured into Egypt in the third century B.C., as a separate part of the population, sharply divided from the mass of the natives and subdivided into various groups, chiefly ethnical. The transference of an individual from the group of natives to that of foreigners and *vice versa*, or from one subdivision of the foreigners to another, without the special permission of the king was strictly forbidden.

While they formed a separate group, nevertheless from the point of view of the kings and of the government the foreigners were legally as much subjects of the king as the natives, although they enjoyed certain privileges granted to them by the will and decision of the king. Those of them who were not temporary residents or visitors—such was for a time the status of most of the foreigners in Egypt in the early days of the Ptolemaic régime—but who settled down permanently in the country were liable, like the natives, to the payment of the taxes imposed on them, they were not exempt from the monopolies, they had to take their share of the extraordinary financial burdens imposed on the people, and they were expected to perform any work which was demanded of them by the government.

However, in the organization of their life and their *de facto* situation there were certain peculiarities which sharply distinguished them from the natives and which we may safely call privileges. The largest and the best organized group of them, the Ptolemaic army, lived its own peculiar and privileged life, governed by firmly rooted traditions and by regulations laid down for officers and men by the king. Second in importance were large groups of ancient pre-Ptolemaic settlers and of immigrants who formed the citizen bodies of the few Greek cities of Egypt, old and new—Naucratis and perhaps Paraetonium, Alexandria and Ptolemais. They were without doubt allowed some measure of self-government, and their organization was not very different from that of the Greek *poleis* in general.

Most of the Greeks who lived in rural Egypt (the χώρα) had apparently no self-government recognized by the State. But they had their own educational institutions (*gymnasia*), which enjoyed certain privileges, such as that of owning land and receiving its income, and they formed associations of a religious, national, or social character. The most interesting and important of these associations, though very little known, were the national πολιτεύματα, most of them connected with the army. Each of these πολιτεύματα may have been granted special rights and privileges. For example, the πολίτευμα of Jews in Alexandria had its own houses of prayer and perhaps its own jurisdiction. Next in importance to the πολιτεύματα, and perhaps connected with them, were the associations of the 'alumni' of the gymnasia (οἱ ἐκ τοῦ γυμνασίου), which supported by their contributions and administered these basic institutions of Greek life in Egypt. These groups were also closely connected with the territorial army of the Ptolemies. Special courts were organized for the foreigners, and the validity of Greek civil law as embodied in the legal code of Alexandria and probably of other Greek cities in Egypt and perhaps of certain national associations (πολιτικοὶ νόμοι) was recognized by the king; though it must be emphasized that recourse was had to this law by the Greek judges—*chrematistae*—and by the royal officials who sometimes acted as judges, only in such cases as were not provided for by the laws or by various orders (προστάγματα, διατάγματα, διαγράμματα, &c.) of the king. But in this respect the situation of the natives was similar. These retained their native courts (λαοκρίται, judges for the λαοί), which based their verdicts on national Egyptian civil law in default of royal orders or regulations. Finally, by special favour the foreigners, or more precisely some of the non-native subjects of the king, immigrants or descendants of immigrants, were probably exempt from compulsory labour, and certain classes of them as well as individuals had special privileges as regards taxation.

All these 'privileges', however, these peculiarities in the treatment of the foreigners, were just what the word privilege means—grants by the king to individuals or groups, and of course revocable. They were not rights recognized as such by the king.[121]

We must also bear in mind that a large part of the foreign population of Egypt was in one way or another in the service of the king. I have already spoken of the army. Here the relations were peculiar, but I must again emphasize the fact that the army was the army of the king and had no obligations whatever to the country. It was not the army of Egypt, but the army of one or other of the Ptolemies. As regards the foreign civilians, the greater part of them, or at least of those about whom we have some information, belonged to the private household (οἶκος) of the king. They were his private servants. And each of them had his own οἶκος, again with a set of dependents. Apollonius, the *dioecetes*, had at his disposal his own men (οἱ παρὰ Ἀπολλωνίου or οἱ περὶ Ἀπολλώνιον or even οἱ ὑπὸ Ἀπολλωνίου); the manager of his gift-estate at Philadelphia, Zenon, had in turn his own οἶκος; and so had his subordinates. Except for the Greek cities, it is hard to detect in the χώρα foreigners who did not belong to one οἶκος or another, and were not under the protection (σκέπη) of their employers. Those who were not were drawn into the same circle of οἶκοι by the part which was reserved for them in the economic system of the Ptolemies. I shall speak of them presently.[122]

Moreover, the *de facto* situation of the foreigners socially, politically, and economically, was quite different from that of the natives and much more advantageous. The higher civil officials were all of them foreigners, as were also the officers and soldiers of the army. The citizens of Alexandria and its foreign population were given an exceptional 'political' status and abundant opportunities of increasing their prosperity. In agriculture the foreigners had a better chance than the natives of becoming landowners and of getting a substantial income from the land.[123] In industry they were the contractors, not the workmen. In the management of the taxes, again, they were the supervisors, guarantors, underwriters, not the minor agents. Most of the 'royal' and private banks were managed by them. In short, the foreigners, though legally subjects of the king like the natives, were practically his associates and assistants, who shared with him his rule over the natives. The régime of the early Ptolemies in Egypt in this respect reminds us to a certain extent of that established in modern times by European countries in their colonies, especially in the early period of European colonial development. The relations of the Europeans to the natives at that time were those of domination rather than association, and the aim of the colonizers was in the main the exploitation of the colonized territory for their own material benefit. And so it was in a certain measure with the early Ptolemies and their entourage, however benevolent and liberal their rule over the natives claimed to be and really was.

The power of the foreigners must not, however, be overestimated. The higher officials had, of course, great influence in the affairs of the country, but they were entirely dependent on the king or on their superiors. Their responsibility both material and personal was great. The demi-god of to-day might be disgraced, imprisoned, executed to-morrow, and his accumulated wealth confiscated by the king. Even the scanty records that we have contain many examples of such downfalls. The same might be the fate of officials of the second rank, as we see from instances in the Zenon correspondence. They were stewards of the king and, if they proved dishonest or inefficient, the king never hesitated to indemnify himself by confiscating their property. How often this happened we cannot say. But it might happen to any official at any moment.

Officers and soldiers. A few words may be added about some of the various classes of foreign residents. The officers and soldiers of the army had some chance of enriching themselves. Service in the bodyguard of the king and in the garrisons was probably well remunerated. A successful war might bring substantial profit to the victorious army. We do not know how the

Ptolemies dealt with the question of booty, though we are informed that Philopator after Raphia gave a liberal bonus to his soldiers, and officers of Euergetes and Philopator boasted that they had received gifts of gold from the kings.[124] Finally, when settled in the country and in possession of a good *cleros*, they had a fair opportunity of developing their land, of improving it by hard work, of adding to it plots of *γῆ ἰδιόκτητος*, of planting vines, olive-trees, and fruit-trees. The taxes which the cleruchs paid were not so high as those of the royal peasants (under the head of *ἀπόμοιρα* they paid one-tenth instead of one-sixth of the wine they produced) and they had much more economic freedom. Some of the cleruchs were successful as landowners; how many it is difficult to say, though I should not suppose the proportion was a small one. The cleruchs were Macedonians, Greeks, Thracians, Syrians, and Anatolians; they belonged, that is to say, to stocks that produced hard workers and men of energy and initiative. And yet there were many impediments to their economic success. Service in the army in the reign of Philadelphus was no sinecure, and the soldiers were very often on duty. During their absence their plots were sometimes taken back by the government or they were managed by strangers. They were not completely free in their agricultural work. They were carefully watched and they suffered almost as much as the natives from the dishonesty and inefficiency of officials and from the difficulties to which the planned economy of the Ptolemies gave rise. They were sometimes forced to sell even their grain, not in the open market, but to the government at a fixed price (above, p. 316).

Owners of land and houses. That there existed a class of well-to-do owners of land and houses apart from the officers and officials of the crown and from the soldiers settled in the country is attested, not only by the evidence adduced above, but also by a peculiar feature in the economic system of Egypt. We derive our knowledge of this from certain interesting documents, the introductory part of the so-called Revenue Laws of Philadelphus, which contained the general rules concerning the farming of the taxes (*ὠναί*)—the *νόμος τελωνικός par excellence*—and a similar later document of the time of Epiphanes (203/2 B.C.) which contains a set of regulations affecting all taxes that were farmed by contractors in the Oxyrynchite nome (*U.P.Z.* 112). The information gleaned from these two documents is supplemented by that derived from several other documents which bear in one way or another on the ὠναί.

We have seen above how the economic life of Egypt was organized. Millions of producers, consumers, and tax-payers, some of the first bound to the government by contracts, contributed to the wealth of the king. Their contributions to the king's treasury (βασιλικόν), to his banks (τράπεζαι), and to his store-houses (θησαυροί), were collected by thousands of officials of various grades down to the modest agents of collection, the λογευταί. These officials were responsible to the king for the fulfilment of the obligations contained in the contracts that bound the cultivators of land and the various classes of the ἐπιπεπλεγμένοι ταῖς προσόδοις to the king.

Tax-farmers. Into this well-balanced system, with the payers on one side and the collectors on the other, the Ptolemies introduced a third body of men connected with the collection of revenues: a group of middlemen, τελῶναι, tax-farmers, individuals or associations, who were assigned a special role in the collection of the royal revenues.

In Greece such middlemen were the actual collectors of the revenues. They paid a lump sum to the State and thus acquired the right of collecting some particular revenue from the tax-payers. In Egypt it was different. The actual collection of the revenues was the duty of State officials, who delivered the sums or goods collected by them into the royal banks and store-houses. The τελῶναι of Egypt had very little to do with the actual collection; but they had a lively interest in it and took an active part in watching both the producers of revenue and the tax-collectors, since by their contracts with the king they guaranteed and underwrote to him the full collection of a particular revenue, that is to say, a specified quantity of goods or a certain sum of money. In case of deficiency they, their partners (μέτοχοι), and their sureties (ἔγγυοι) were required to make it good. In case of insolvency the property pledged by the contractors and by their sureties was taken by the government and sold. On the other hand, if all went well and the actual collection of the payments yielded a surplus (ἐπιγένημα), this surplus was their profit and in addition they received from the government a bonus or salary (ὀψώνιον).

This Ptolemaic system of revenue-farming, based in the main on the Greek system, was ingenious. By introducing middlemen between the tax-payers and the collectors the Ptolemies protected their interests very efficiently. Two groups—the collectors and the tax-farmers—both responsible to the crown, were employed in extracting revenue from the tax-payers. Their interests in this respect were identical and their collaboration made it practically impossible for the tax-payers to evade their obligations. On the other hand, dishonesty or laxity on the part of officials affected the interests of the tax-farmers' group. The tax-farmers therefore served as effective checks upon the officials. The losers by this arrangement were the tax-payers. The officials and tax-farmers were bound under heavy penalties to collect the revenue in full, and whether or not at the end of the operation the tax-payer was ruined was of very little concern to them. To the king, of course, this was a matter of great concern, and he insisted upon the tax-payers not being maltreated, despoiled, or cheated. But as a rule officials and tax-farmers combined were stronger than the king.

The profession of tax-farmer, though risky, was probably remunerative on the whole. There were, in the early Ptolemaic period, plenty of applicants for the contracts and they found no lack of sureties. The number of contractors appears to have been comparatively large, for the farmed revenues were numerous, though we cannot say how many there were. Although a rich man here and there might undertake several contracts at once and concentrate a large part of the business in his hands —as perhaps Zenon did, especially after his retirement into private life—the rule probably was dispersion of the contracts rather than concentration. We must bear in mind that the ὠναί were farmed out locally, in respect of small districts never larger than a nome, and that a thorough knowledge of local conditions was required if the farmer was to estimate the yield of a tax successfully. His work was no sinecure and required his personal presence at innumerable operations connected with the assessment and collection of the individual charges. Most of the tax-farmers were therefore local men, men who were well acquainted with both the payers and the collectors. They were all certainly well-to-do men with wide business connexions. They and their sureties had to offer good security, and this security usually took the form of real property: houses, vineyards, gardens, land.

The Greek bourgeoisie. The existence of the system of farming out taxes and monopolies shows, therefore, that there was in Egypt in the reign of Philadelphus a considerable class of well-to-do men, most of them owning real property, men who had savings and were desirous of investing their money in profitable business. The great majority of them were Greeks. We may infer accordingly that by this time a Greek *bourgeoisie* had grown up which was not identical either with the officials in the actual service of the crown (these were forbidden to bid for the tax-contracts or to act as partners or sureties of the tax-farmers) or with the cleruchs.

Of a lower grade, but engaged in similar business, were the thousands of retailers who leased from the government the right of dealing in special kinds of goods and were responsible to it. A certain amount of capital was needed for such business. This class did not consist of Greeks alone. The retail traders were chiefly natives; but their existence attests the growth, side by side with the higher *bourgeoisie,* of a class of petty *bourgeois* closely connected with the new organization of Egypt.

Who were the members of the Greek *bourgeoisie*? Some of them may have been retired officials, officers, or soldiers, and their descendants, others the descendants of Greeks who had settled in Egypt before Alexander's conquest. But many did not belong to either of these categories. They were in all probability immigrants from Greece who came to Egypt, not as soldiers or officials, but as men possessing some property and seeking a good investment for it. I have shown in a previous chapter how large, in all probability, was the number of those who acquired some measure of wealth in the times of Alexander and the Successors. I have endeavoured to show at the same time the insecurity of life in Greece and in the islands. No wonder that many Greeks were attracted by the peaceful conditions of Egypt and by its reputation as an Eldorado for emigrants.

In any case a Greek *bourgeoisie* was in course of formation in Egypt. The Ptolemies were aware of the fact and opened the doors of their new economic system to this new class. The prospect of sharing profits with the government may have been very alluring to these Greeks. Some of them were expert tax-farmers in their own country and they hoped to carry on the profession as successfully in Egypt as in Greece. Besides, there were not many other openings for business activity in Egypt. The opportunities for trade were limited: Alexandria and foreign trade were open to them, but a large part of the internal trade of the country was chiefly in the hands of the government. Industry was in the hands partly of the government and to a large extent of the natives, again with the possible exception of industry at Alexandria. What remained was investment in land and an active share in the management of the *πρόσοδοι*, the royal rèvenues.

Foreigners of lower standing. Besides the upper strata of the foreign population of Egypt there were certainly many immigrants who earned their living by hard work in agriculture, industry, and trade as workmen, artisans, clerks, and so forth. We may safely assume the existence of such a class in Alexandria. But groups of men of the same standing were also scattered all over the *chora*. A glance at the list of men engaged in different types of agricultural, industrial, and domestic work compiled by W. Peremans, mostly from the Zenon papyri, shows how many Greeks were engaged in economic activities of various kinds on the Philadelphian estate of Apollonius, activities in which they competed with the natives. Of course some of them may have been men of some means—contractors who undertook to carry out a certain work or persons who invested their money for example in viticulture and corn-growing. They must be classed with the *bourgeoisie*. But some of them probably were common artisans and workmen.[125]

It would be interesting to know the number of foreigners domiciled in Egypt in various capacities. Unfortunately we possess no reliable data on this subject. An attempt has recently been made by A. Segré to calculate the numbers of the Greek population of Egypt on the basis mainly of the reported strength of the armies mobilized in Egypt by the Ptolemies, especially that of Philopator's army at Raphia, which is trustworthy. Segré's conclusions are that Egypt had absorbed almost 150,000 adult males of the population of Greece and Macedonia, and that Syria and Asia Minor had absorbed twice as many (on this see below, note 275), that is, one-fifteenth of the population of Greece. These figures, however, are based on very slight and debatable evidence. He miscalculates the strength of Greek horse and foot at Raphia, and he does not take into account the Greeks of Alexandria and those outside it, who were not military settlers. We have not the least idea whether any of these Greeks were mobilized alongside of the military settlers and, if so, what proportion of them. Moreover, it is very probable that the number of Greeks in Egypt in 217 B.C. does not represent the number of the original migrants from Greece and Macedonia. Even the foreigners were very prolific in Egypt.[126]

4. The Egyptian Dominions

A large revenue was derived by the Ptolemies, not only from Egypt, but also from their dominions outside it. Egypt in the third century B.C. had many external possessions. The more important and the more permanently connected with Egypt were Cyprus, Cyrene, and the Cyrenaica, and the so-called Coele-Syria with Phoenicia and Palestine. Lycia with her valuable forests, Caria with her trade, manufactures, flourishing viticulture (Cnidus), and bee-keeping (e.g. Theangela), parts of Ionia (especially Miletus, Samos, and Ephesus), a group of Aegean islands formed into a league, the large and rich island of Lesbos, parts of Crete, Thera, and certain places in the Peloponnese, for many years formed (some of them intermittently) part of the Ptolemaic Empire. Finally Egypt held for a time a part of Thrace, with the Chersonese, and Samothrace. The acquisition and loss of these provinces have been occasionally referred to above and cannot be dealt with here.

Our main problem is to discover what were the economic relations of the Ptolemies with their foreign dominions in the third century, and especially to what extent (if at all) the Ptolemies applied to their provinces the principle of a planned economy which was the foundation of their policy in Egypt itself. I am afraid that no satisfactory answer can be given to this question as regards most of the provinces. Evidence is exceedingly meagre and scattered.[127]

Of these provinces Cyrenaica occupied a peculiar position. It was a kind of appendage of Egypt, ruled by a member of the Ptolemaic dynasty. Economically it was of great importance. It was a very rich agricultural country, one of the granaries of the ancient world, and the home of one of the best breeds of horses (and of horses the Ptolemies had urgent need). From the time of her foundation Cyrene had been an important centre of commerce. We know very little of its economic organization or of that of the Cyrenaica. There was, however, a striking similarity between the social structure of Cyrene and the Cyrenaica as described by Strabo* and that of Alexandria and Egypt. The city had a large non-Greek population, mainly Jewish; side by side with full citizens and citizens possessing limited rights, there was a mass of foreigners (metics) who were not citizens at all, in part probably native Libyans; the rural population consisted of 'husbandmen' (*γεωργοί*) who tilled the land belonging either to the city or to the king. The last class may well have included soldiers settled as cleruchs.[128]

The position of the Aegean islands was also exceptional. The islands included in the Island League were never treated by the Ptolemies as a regular province. Of this League the Ptolemies were the powerful allies, not the masters. The contributions of the Allies went into the treasury of the League, not into that of the Ptolemies, and the funds of the League, though under the control of the kings (represented by their nauarchs, nesiarchs, and *oeconomi*), were spent chiefly on the maintenance of its fleet, an important element in the Ptolemaic naval forces. Apart from these obligations, the members of the League were free to manage their own affairs as they chose and they were apparently not supposed to pay any royal taxes.†

Much less liberty was left to the Greek cities in the regular dominions or provinces of the Ptolemaic Empire: in the main-

* *ap.* Joseph. *A.J.* xiv. 115 ff.

† On the League see above, p. 154; cf. W. Peek, *Ath. Mitt.* lix (1934), p. 57, n. 13.

land of Greece (Methana), in Ionia, Caria, Lycia, the Thracian Chersonese, in Samothrace, Samos, Lesbos, Thera, and Crete. Our information, of course, is very defective and scattered, but we are able to form a general idea of the relations of these cities to the Ptolemies. This question cannot be fully dealt with here; I shall limit myself to its economic and financial aspect.

All the Greek cities under Ptolemaic rule were supposed to have the primary duty of taking their share in the defence of the Egyptian Empire. All had strong royal garrisons stationed in them. About these garrisons we have some evidence from Thera and from Cyprus. Of Cyprus I shall speak presently. In the case of Thera a group of inscriptions sheds a vivid light on the military occupation of the island and on various aspects of the life of the detachments stationed there.[129] From the economic point of view the presence of garrisons in the cities involved an obligation on the part of the cities to provide the soldiers with lodging (*σταθμοί, ἐπισταθμία*) and to supply food for them and fodder for their horses. A glimpse of the situation is afforded by one of the letters of Zenon's correspondence.* At Calynda in Caria the soldiers of the garrison were billeted on the citizens, and certain landowners were required to supply fodder for the horses of some of the cavalry.

Still heavier were the obligations of the cities in respect of the royal navy. A large part of the fleet was supplied by the cities of the empire, Greek and Phoenician, on the method of the Greek trierarchy. The burden was not limited to provincial cities: Alexandria and Naucratis had an important share in it.[130]

But the main burden imposed on the cities was the royal supervision of their finances and the royal taxation. All the Greek cities in the Ptolemaic dominions retained, of course, their self-government and their right to tax their citizens and other residents (*πάροικοι*) and to spend the money which they collected for their own needs. But even in this respect they were apparently not entirely free. Their expenditure was watched and controlled by the financial agents of the central government, and their economic freedom was restricted. A few instances may be quoted. Halicarnassus sent an embassy

* *P. Cairo Zen.* 59341b.

to the king to obtain permission to build a new gymnasium for the *neoi* called the Philippeion.* The reason for sending the embassy apparently was that the city had to organize a subscription and to contract a loan for the construction of the gymnasium and was in financial difficulties.† In Samothrace it was for the king and his governor to allow or forbid the importation of wheat from the other provinces of the empire.‡[131]

More burdensome for the cities than the financial supervision were the new royal taxes imposed on their inhabitants in addition to the traditional taxes levied by the cities themselves. Although we have little evidence concerning these royal taxes, their existence and their importance in the economic life of the cities are beyond doubt. Here are a few instances. A fragmentary papyrus of the fourth year of Epiphanes§ contains extracts from letters addressed by the *dioecetes* of Alexandria to the *oeconomi* of several Ptolemaic provinces (Thrace and Lesbos, Lycia, perhaps Caria). While these letters reflect to some extent the troubled conditions of the time (that of Philip V's expedition), in general they give a good picture of the routine of provincial fiscal administration as established by the first Ptolemies. One of them addressed to the *oeconomus* or agent of the *dioecetes* in Thrace and Lesbos and likewise in Caria, is an emergency demand for the dispatch of money, corn, and other goods|| stored in these provinces in order probably to save them from Philip. Though this is an emergency document, it shows that large sums of money and large supplies of corn and other goods (probably wine and olive-oil) were stored in the provinces, having been collected from the population in the form of taxes. Even more interesting are the summaries of letters written to Nicostratus in Lycia. The first letter informs him that the *dioecetes* has succeeded in farming out the money-taxes of Lycia for more than before, the increase being 6 talents, 1312 drachmas and 4 obols. On the other hand the gate-toll (διαπύλιον) showed a diminution of 2 talents 1366 drachmas. The main commodity on which the

* A. Wilhelm, *Jahreshefte*, xi (1908), pp. 56 ff., no. 2.

† Ibid. pp. 53 ff., no. 1, and 56 ff., no. 2. Cf. *O.G.I.* 46 and below, n. 132[a].

‡ *S.I.G.*,[3] 502.

§ *Teb.* 8 (Wilcken, *Chr.* 2).

|| I suggest that we should read τῶν ἄλλων φορ(τίων) not φόρ(ων).

gate-tax was paid was wine. The next letter deals with the ξυλική, probably revenue derived from the exploitation of forests: we must remember that Lycia was rich in timber and that a regular supply of timber was a matter of great concern to the Ptolemies. The last letter relates to the revenue derived from purple (πορφυρική, sc. ὠνή), which was leased for five years, the yearly payment of the contractors being 1 talent 1800 drachmas.

Similar conditions prevailed in the large and fertile region of Lycia that had as its capital the flourishing city of Telmessus. The history of this region in early Ptolemaic times is very peculiar. It is revealed by many inscriptions mostly found at Telmessus and by occasional notices in literary texts and has been reconstructed in the following way. The region consisted of the city of Telmessus with its territory and the adjoining royal land (γῆ βασιλική). During the rule of Philadelphus it formed part of the province of Lycia, which he had inherited from his father. Some time in the reign of Philadelphus a part of the royal land was granted as a *dorea* to Ptolemy, son of Lysimachus and Arsinoe, a talented and energetic young man who played a certain part in the events of the time. After the death of Philadelphus and the end of the Syrian war of Euergetes I the latter transformed the region of Telmessus into a kind of *dynasteia* or vassal kingdom, like Cyrenaica and at a later date Cyprus, and many *dynasteiai* within the Seleucid kingdom (see note 230); and he handed over this *dynasteia* in 240 B.C. to the above-named Ptolemy, son of Lysimachus. This may have been done for political and military or for dynastic reasons, or perhaps both.[131a]

Ptolemy, son of Lysimachus, found his *dynasteia* in an unprosperous condition. A decree of the city in honour of Ptolemy* furnishes detailed information about it. The city and its territory had suffered severely during the wars, and the citizens were hard pressed.† The new ruler took certain measures to relieve their distress, which give an interesting picture of the fiscal administration of the city as organized by Philadelphus. The region of Telmessus was mainly a land of orchards and pastures. The owners of the orchards paid a tax to the

* *O.G.I.* 55 (*T.A.M.* II, 1).

† L. 11–12, ἐν πᾶσιν [θλιβο]μένους.

crown (ξυλίνων καρπῶν) and the owners of flocks and herds paid dues for the right of pasturage (ἐννόμιον). These two main taxes were remitted by Ptolemy (probably for a definite period only). They may have been paid in money, as in Egypt. In addition the landowners of the city (citizens and πάροικοι) paid an ἀπόμοιρα, apparently a sort of ἐκφόριον, a *pars quanta* of the produce of their fields: corn, beans, millet of two kinds, sesame, and lupin. These payments had been strictly (σκληρῶς) collected by tax-farmers in accordance with a special law (νόμος, sc. τελωνικός), undoubtedly similar to the νόμοι τελωνικοί of Philadelphus (above, p. 302) and to the *lex Hieronica* of Sicily. No remission of these payments was made by Ptolemy, but he changed the character of the tax and the system of its collection to that which prevailed in Asia Minor and was familiar to the landowners of Telmessus, by substituting the payment of a tithe (δεκάτη) to the tithe-farmers (δεκατῶναι), probably on the basis of agreements (συγγραφαί) between the landowners and the tax-farmers, as in Sicily and later in Asia Minor (below, Ch. VI). Certain minor taxes connected, as in Egypt, with the σιτηρὰ ἀπόμοιρα* were remitted.[131b]

It is evident from the fragmentary evidence adduced above that Caria and Lycia, the Thracian possessions, some of the larger and smaller islands of the Aegean, and Ionia were organized by the early Ptolemies from the fiscal point of view on more or less the same lines. The cities were heavily taxed. They, of course, continued as before to collect the usual taxes from citizens and other residents to cover their own expenditure. But they were also supposed to contribute their share to the royal revenues. This contribution may in some cases have taken the form of a tribute, a lump sum (φόρος, σύνταξις), but in most cases it was made by payment of royal taxes imposed directly on the inhabitants of the cities and the country. These taxes were probably as heavy and as diversified as in Egypt, comprising imposts on the produce of vineyards, orchards, olive groves, fields, forests, and fisheries, on cattle, on industry, on commerce (customs duties, gate-tax), and so forth. A text of a later date (below, Ch. V) suggests that even a poll-tax was paid in the second century B.C. by the inhabitants

* τῶν συνκυρόντων τῆι σιτηρᾶι ἀπομ[οίραι] ἀφῆκεν πάντων ἀτελεῖς.

of the region of Telmessus, perhaps only by the country people, the *laoi* of the royal land. Possibly this was a heritage from Ptolemaic times.

Besides cities and their territories which were under royal control, there were in all the provinces large tracts of royal land. I have spoken of this in the region of Telmessus. It was a characteristic feature in the Thracian Chersonesus and the Thracian possessions of the Ptolemies. These Thracian domains passed from the Ptolemies to the Attalids (*agri Attalici*) and from them to the Romans (below, Chs. V and VI). Nothing is known of the Ptolemaic management of the royal land in the provinces we are dealing with. It was probably based on the same traditional principles as in the Seleucid kingdom, where we have some information on the subject (below Sect. C). Like the Seleucids, the Ptolemies occasionally granted parts of this land to members of their family* and probably to some of the grandees of their kingdom. Parts of it may also have been given away to cities. I may quote for instance the case of Miletus, though the exact status of the land granted by the king to the city is unknown.†

The taxes paid by the residents in the Greek cities were farmed out. The tax-farmers, mentioned in the documents cited above, were local people, but the contracts for the collection of the taxes were granted to the contractors, not in the provinces, but at Alexandria, as we may infer from several documents of the Zenon correspondence (especially *P. Cairo Zen.* 59037), which make it probable that the picture drawn by Josephus (*Ant.*, XII, 169 ff.) of an auction of the provincial taxes of Syria Coele is on the whole accurate. Josephus describes how the candidates for contracts—the richest men of Syria—gathered in Alexandria and how the auction was held.[132]

In the provinces the interests of the kings were looked after by special agents of the *dioecetes* of Alexandria, styled *oeconomi*, as is attested in the case of Thera (n. 129) and of Cyprus (below, p. 339). The dependence of the provincial cities on the *dioecetes* is illustrated by many letters in Zenon's correspon-

* See above on Ptolemy, son of Lysimachus.

† A. Rehm, *Milet, Erg. d. Ausgr.*, I, 3, no. 139; Welles, *R.C.* 14; *Milet*, loc. cit., no. 123 and p. 305, n. 1, on the estates of Eurydice.

dence, which were written to him as the trusted assistant of Apollonius by his friends in the Carian cities of Halicarnassus, Caunus (Zenon's native city), and Calynda. The writers ask for Zenon's support when their cases are considered by Apollonius. The evidence furnished by these letters is supplemented by that derived from some inscriptions.[132a]

It is highly probable that the provinces in which city life was undeveloped, or developed on Oriental lines, were treated in a different way from those where Greek city life was predominant. Of the former group CYPRUS was a prominent example, with its rich copper-mines and timber and flourishing agriculture, and its cities semi-Phoenician and semi-Greek in character, centres of agriculture, industry, and commerce. The mines were probably regarded as the property of the king. We learn from an inscription that a special governor with military power, an *antistrategos*, had charge of them.* Nothing is known regarding the forests. In the later part of the Ptolemaic period, according to Polybius (xviii. 55), the royal revenues of Cyprus were collected by the *strategos* of Cyprus and passed on to the *dioecetes* at Alexandria. But we know from certain Zenon papyri† that in the third century the *dioecetes* of Egypt had his own agents in Cyprus—*oeconomi* and *grammateis*—who probably had charge of the revenues of the king. The correspondence of Zenon points to a close connexion between Cyprus and Phoenicia.

What we know of Cyprus is mostly derived from documents of later date. Not all of them have been published. The impression produced by them is that Cyprus was not only in close economic relations with Phoenicia, as it had been since the times of the flourishing kingdom of Ugarit (Ras Shamra), but also was probably organized on the same lines as the Ptolemaic province of Syria and Phoenicia, in other words in much the same way as Egypt itself (see below). A recently discovered inscription of the time of Euergetes II shows, for example, that an amnesty decree by that king was published not only in Egypt but also in Cyprus and in similar terms: for instance, the paragraph dealing with strikes (ἀναχώρησις) appears in the same form.[133]

* *O.G.I.* 165. † *P. Cairo Zen.* 59016; *P.S.I.* 505, cf. 428, 56.

We are better informed about the Ptolemaic administration of SYRIA and PHOENICIA, and of PALESTINE than of the other provinces. It is again from Zenon's correspondence that we derive the bulk of our knowledge. Zenon was for a time (in 259 B.C.) the chief agent of Apollonius in these provinces, and it is difficult to distinguish in his letters between his doings as agent of the *dioecetes* of Alexandria and as representative of the private interests of his employer.[134]

We have, in addition, a recently published document of the Rainer collection in Vienna: it consists of fragments of two orders (προστάγματα) of Philadelphus relating to the return (ἀπογραφή) to be made by the population of Syria and Phoenicia of their movable property for the purpose, at least in part, of taxation. The fragments refer to cattle (λεία) and a special group of *laoi* (σώματα λαϊκὰ ἐλεύθερα). The two orders quote various other documents by which various branches of the economic activity of Syria and Phoenicia were organized: a royal letter ordering the registration of cattle (left col., 25), a διάγραμμα (left col., 6–7, 26, 30–31) regulating the fines imposed on those who did not conform with the royal orders regarding the *apographe* of cattle, and lastly a 'law regarding lease' (νόμος ὁ ἐπὶ τῆς μισθώσεως) (right col., 21–22) relating to the λαϊκὰ σώματα ἐλεύθερα. This shows how active Philadelphus was in Syria and Phoenicia in reorganizing the economic and social life of these provinces. The Syrian legislation was contemporary with, and similar in character to, the legislation applying to Egypt of which the 'Revenue Laws' (dealt with above) are such a fine specimen. I should not be surprised if Syrian νόμοι τελωνικοί similar to the 'Revenue Laws' were one day found among the Ptolemaic papyri of Egypt.[135]

To these early documents is to be added the famous account of Josephus (quoted above) of the proceedings of a Palestinian notable named Josephus in connexion with the assessment and collection of taxes in Syria and Palestine; and further valuable information relating to Palestine is furnished by the well-known letter of Ps.-Aristeas, the Books of the Maccabees, and later by the New Testament. It is highly probable that the Seleucids inherited the fiscal organization of

Palestine from the Ptolemies, and the Romans from the Seleucids (below, Chs. V and VI).

It appears from this evidence and especially from the Vienna papyrus that the fiscal organization of the Ptolemaic province of Syria and Phoenicia (as it is officially styled in the document) was on much the same lines as that of Egypt, or at any rate the rural part of it. Syria and Phoenicia were divided into *hyparchies* instead of nomes, a system probably inherited from the Persians, Alexander, and the Successors; and the hyparchies in turn were divided into villages.[136] As in Egypt, the population consisted of 'Greeks' and of natives, λαοί. The Greeks included the royal officials, the army of occupation,* and perhaps the soldiers settled in the country (cleruchs), the many immigrants from Greek or hellenized parts (οἱ κατοικοῦντες in the Rainer document†), and probably the hellenized population of the Syrian and Phoenician cities. I have referred to the last in dealing with Rhodes and its relations with some notables of Sidon. The best-known examples of hellenized Phoenicians of high standing are the well-known Philocles, king of the Sidonians, and Diotimus, son of Dionysius, who appears as victor in horse races at the Nemean games in an inscription of Sidon of the late third century B.C. Sidon, in the Ptolemaic period, was in many respects a centre of Hellenism: a city with a hellenized aristocracy, a Greek or hellenized constitution, extensive trade, and a population of international merchants and business men, a strong garrison and πολιτεύματα of foreign soldiers or foreigners in general. It may be mentioned here that the territory of Sidon was very large and that we have evidence of colonies of 'Sidonians', in part Greek Sidonians, in Palestine.[137]

We have no direct information regarding the situation of the privileged classes, but it was probably the same as in Egypt. As for the λαοί (natives in general or only one section of them, the tillers of the soil?), the second *prostagma* of the Vienna document contains some important information about them; but this unfortunately relates to only one particular feature in their life. The *prostagma* concerns only those *laoi* (σώματα λαϊκά) who were held in possession (as slaves) by other persons,

* Rainer pap., right col., 12–13.

† Right col., 13–17.

having been bought by them or otherwise acquired (the reconstruction of the mutilated text is uncertain). It directs that such *laoi* shall be declared to the *oeconomus* of each hyparchy within 20 days. Those who fail so to declare shall forfeit their slaves and pay a fine of 6,000 drachmas for each slave. Those, however, who can prove that they have bought the slaves ὄντα οἰκετικά (the meaning of this term is controversial, see below) shall have their slaves returned. It is not stated what would happen to those slaves for whom no such proof could be brought forward. In all probability they were restored to liberty. The *prostagma* proceeds to forbid in future the purchase, pledging, or acceptance as pledges, of free σώματα λαϊκά.

The interpretation of this *prostagma* is very difficult. Was it merely an endeavour of Philadelphus to liberate those natives or peasants who during the disorder of war time had been unlawfully enslaved, a measure similar to that which, according to the Pseudo-Aristeas, he took with regard to the Jewish prisoners of war (αἰχμάλωτοι) in Egypt? Or had the measure a wider scope and a more general character? Was it an endeavour to put an end to attempts to enslave free people in general and especially to transform into regular slavery certain local forms of servitude closely connected with oriental bondage and resulting from various kinds of contractual obligation, including self-enslavement and the sale by parents of their own children? Moreover, and this is of especial importance, was the ordinance of Philadelphus confined to Syria and Phoenicia, and here to the *laoi* only, or was it the extension to one of the Ptolemaic provinces of a regulation of wider scope, not limited to *laoi*, which was already valid in Egypt?

I cannot enter into a detailed study of this problem, but I may briefly state my opinion. I am inclined to think that the measure was not confined to Syria but applied to Egypt also (above, n. 119). It was primarily an attempt to protect the working classes of both countries against the endeavours of certain people to enslave free workmen, chiefly by transforming Oriental bondage resembling slavery into regular slavery of the Greek type. This may be the basis of the distinction made in the Vienna papyrus between the σώματα λαϊκὰ ἐλεύθερα

(Oriental bondage) and the σώματα ὄντα οἰκετικά. It may be suspected that the institution of Oriental bondage lay behind some of the purchases of slaves by Zenon on his Palestinian tour. The act of Philadelphus is easy to interpret. He was opposed to the enslavement of free men and especially of the working population of Syria and Egypt, because this enslavement would deprive him, the king, of valuable free labour, especially that of the *laoi* in agriculture and industry. I have pointed out how scanty was the supply of labour in Egypt and probably also in Syria, and how anxious Philadelphus was to increase its amount and efficiency. But the question is difficult and complicated and for the time being insoluble, for the subject of Oriental bondage and slavery, including that of the sacred slaves (ἱερόδουλοι), and of its evolution in Hellenistic times, is in great need of special and thorough investigation. In any case it is evident that Greek ideas and Greek practice in the matter of slavery did not agree in many respects with those prevailing in the East, and that the Greek rulers of Eastern kingdoms were faced in consequence with problems which were new to them and which they had to solve in some way.[138]

Liberal as were the provisions of the *prostagma* of Philadelphus in respect of the natives, it contained one exception. It did not apply to those *laoi* who were sold into slavery by the agents of the crown; in their case the financial agent of the king in Syro-Phoenicia (ὁ διοικῶν τὰς κατὰ Συρίαν καὶ Φοινίκην προσόδους) retained his general right of 'execution against the person' and of selling into slavery any who were liable to such execution under the νόμος μισθώσεως.

In connexion with the question of the personal liberty of the *laoi* (σώματα λαϊκά) the same *prostagma* makes what appears to be special provision for the case of the cohabitation of Greek soldiers and foreign residents in Syro-Phoenicia with native women. It directs that these λαϊκὰ σώματα shall not be treated in the same way as *laoi* who have been unlawfully enslaved, that is to say, they shall not be declared. It is significant to find the concubines of the Greeks and other foreigners thus identified with the λαϊκὰ σώματα who have been bought as slaves. Was it because most of the concubines were acquired in a manner similar to that by which other λαϊκὰ σώματα became slaves? And did the order of the king confer a privilege on the women by changing their legal status, or on the men in whose possession they were? And finally, have we any ground for supposing that the measure was an encouragement of mixed marriages? All these questions will remain open until new evidence is discovered.

The king was represented in Syria and Phoenicia by a *strategos*, at least so far as concerned military government and administration. In the field of economics and finance his representatives were probably a local *dioecetes* (in charge of the royal revenues, πρόσοδοι) and certainly one *oeconomus* for each hyparchy. The organization is almost that of Egypt. I should not be surprised if a document similar to *Teb.* 703 should one day be found, regulating the functions of the Syrian and Phoenician *oeconomi*.*

Some passages of the Vienna document raise important questions and throw light on the status of the rural population of Syria and Phoenicia.

In his second πρόσταγμα Philadelphus quotes 'the law concerning the farming' (right col. 21–22: καθότι ἐν τῶι νόμωι τῶι | ἐπὶ τῆς μισθώσεως γέγραπται) in connexion with the regulation regarding the right of the Syrian *dioecetes* to use execution against the person (πρᾶξις καὶ ἐκ τοῦ σώματος) in the case of the *laoi*. Another passage of the same document (first *prostagma*, left col. 17–20) dealing with the *apographe* or return of cattle says: 'Those who have leased the villages and the comarchs shall register at the same time the cattle in the villages liable to tax and exempt from it.'† 'Those who have leased the villages' are certainly equivalent to the κωμομισθωταί known in Palestine at Bethanath and in Egypt at Tebtunis.[139]

A detailed discussion of these passages cannot be given here, but I may briefly state my view. It is evident that in Syria and Phoenicia and in Palestine the fiscal and economic unit was the village inhabited by the *laoi*. Each village as a whole

* Vienna papyrus, left col. 1; left col. 37, and right col. 1; right col. 19.

† Ἀπογράφεσθαι δὲ καὶ τ[οὺς] με|μισθωμένους τὰς κ[ώμ]ας κα[ὶ] τοὺς κωμάρχας ἐν τ[ῶι] αὐτῶι | χρόνωι τ[ὴν] ὑπάρχ[ουσαν ἐν] ταῖς κώμαις λείαν ὑποτελῆ | καὶ ἀτελῆ, κτλ.

was in all probability leased, in accordance with the prescriptions of a special law, to general farmers of revenue, styled κωμομισθωταί, who ranked higher in the life of the village than the village chiefs. In the Vienna document they occupy the place which in Egypt was reserved for the village scribes. Their functions are not specified, but it appears that they were in general charge of all the revenues of the king from a given village and were responsible for them. They are concerned with the status of the villagers and their liabilities, and with the cattle which are in their possession. It is tempting to regard the κωμομισθωταί as a blend of farmers and royal officials. In addition to their financial duties they may have acted as stewards of the king, charged with the duty of making contracts for the cultivation of the king's land with the individual *laoi* in the same way as in Egypt. In this case we must assume that the *laoi* of Phoenicia were treated like the λαοὶ βασιλικοί of Egypt, as free tenants of the parcel of land which they rented from the crown through the κωμομισθωτής. If this be correct, the *chora* of Phoenicia tilled by the *laoi* had the same status as the crown-land (χώρα βασιλική) in Egypt and not that of *ager stipendiarius* in Roman terminology. It must, however, be emphasized that we have no direct evidence bearing on this question.

In any case the existence of κωμομισθωταί may help us to a better understanding of the statement of Josephus (above, p. 338). He speaks of tax-farmers in Syria responsible for one or other city, and of the possibility of one general farmer of all the payments due from a whole province. Whether these contractors for the villages, the cities, and the province were responsible for the collection of all the taxes without exception (including the royal 'monopolies', if such existed in Syria and Phoenicia), or of the land tax only, we do not know. It is highly probable that they played the same role of 'underwriters' as in Egypt, and that the aim of the Ptolemies was, as in that country, to make the richer classes of the population take a share of responsibility for the collection of the king's revenues.

The character of the taxes which are known to us and the method of their collection were exactly the same as in Egypt.

The portion of the Vienna papyrus that deals with the registration of cattle as a preliminary to the collection of the cattle-tax and the pasture dues (ἐννόμιον) contains the same regulations as those we find in *Teb.* 703. Nor were the regulations about the registration of slaves very different from those in force in Egypt. The registration (ἀπογραφή) was intended not only to prevent the illegal enslavement of free citizens, but also to keep a record of the slaves with a view to the collection of the slave-tax.[140] Finally, there is evidence that the taxes levied by the Seleucids in Palestine and mentioned as being especially burdensome to the people (below, p. 348) all existed in Egypt with the exception of the poll-tax. It should be noted that the salt-tax in Palestine was organized on the same lines as in Egypt, and was no less unpopular. I shall return to this in the next section of this chapter.

In addition to the evidence adduced above, certain documents, especially those that form the correspondence of Zenon, throw a vivid light on various aspects of business activity in Syria and Phoenicia in the time of Philadelphus. The information they give relates chiefly to the activity of the foreigners, those agents of the central government and private business men who came to Syria from Egypt, generally in order to buy local and imported goods and to export them to Egypt. I will revert to this subject later in this section.

Much as we know, there remain many important gaps in our knowledge. We must await the discovery of new documents to obtain a better idea of the conditions of land-tenure, of the division of land into various classes, of the management of the crown land (χώρα βασιλική), the economic situation of the *laoi*, the relations of the priests and temples to the crown, the social structure of the larger cities, and similar matters. In the present state of our knowledge it appears highly probable that Syria and Phoenicia were in many respects reorganized on much the same lines as Egypt.

The little we know of PALESTINE suggests a similar conclusion, with the difference that in Palestine the Ptolemies were builders of cities. Palestine proper, a country organized from very ancient times and now in a recalcitrant mood, they surrounded with a screen of fortified cities of the Greek type:

the line of coastal cities from Gaza to Phoenicia, another line east of the Jordan, and a third in the south in the country of the Idumaeans. Some of these strongholds kept their native names, in this resembling the cities of Phoenicia, others received new dynastic names (Ptolemais-Ake); others again were recent foundations, some of them pre-Ptolemaic (dating from Alexander and the Successors), probably all of them military colonies, which were given Macedonian or dynastic names. This is illustrated especially in Transjordan, where we find Philadelphia (Rabbat-Amman), Philotera on the Sea of Galilee, and perhaps Arsinoe on the one hand, and Pella, Dion, &c., on the other. The Ptolemies had purely military and political objects in view in the measures they took on the borderlands of Judaea and were in no way influenced by economic considerations. They aimed at the effective occupation of a country which otherwise might serve as an important military base for the enemies of Egypt. We have an excellent picture of a Ptolemaic stronghold on the frontier between Judaea and Idumaea in the small but flourishing fortified city of Beth Zur which has recently been excavated.[141]

For the purpose of administration and perhaps taxation Palestine was probably subdivided into regions. We know the names of several of them. Idumaea with its capital Marissa, a flourishing city with a large Greek and Phoenician population and with an important trade to which Zenon's correspondence testifies; Ammanitis with its capital Philadelphia, another important military and civil centre of the Ptolemies, and several other regions mostly with names ending in *-itis* (e.g. Galaaditis). On the other hand, we hear that in later times Palestine was divided into *nomes* and *topoi* or *toparchies*. There are also instances of the use of the term *meris*. The evidence is neither abundant nor clear, and most of it applies to later times. But the choice of terms points to the Ptolemaic period and suggests an administrative system similar to those of Syria and Egypt. It may also be mentioned that Palestine appears in the correspondence of Zenon as being full of various agents of the Ptolemies both military and civil.[142]

If, however, the country was actually subdivided into uniform areas of varying size and was thereby given administrative unity, such unity could hardly conceal the strong social and economic contrasts that it presented as a Ptolemaic province. It included the sacerdotal or temple-state of Judaea, with its theocratic organization, and its numerous villages under their sheikhs (there is no evidence of the existence of cities within its boundaries); it included also many flourishing cities, of Greek or Oriental type, occupied with commerce and industry or entirely with agriculture; there were native tribes or aggregations of tribes such as those which in the day of Philadelphus lived in the Ammanitis under their own sheikh, the famous Tubias, well known to us from various sources.[143] There were Greek settlers in the various parts of Palestine (with the exception probably of Judaea). I have mentioned the military colonization of the Ptolemies. We know some details of one such colony combined with a native settlement at Birta, the stronghold of Tubias in the Ammanitis.* We should probably assign to another military settlement or to one of the garrison cities of Palestine the Greeks enumerated in one of the documents of Zenon's correspondence:† military men (ἀκροφύλαξ, φυλακάρχαι) and civilians (δικαστής, γραμματεύς, ἀρχυπηρέτης, and a man termed ὁ παρὰ τοῦ βασιλέως). It should be noticed as regards Judaea that, according to Josephus (*A.J.* xii. 159) Euergetes I threatened Onias, son of Simon, 'that he would turn their land into holdings . . . and send soldiers to occupy them'.‡

On the subject of taxation our information is scanty. It is interesting to observe that the law and regulations of Philadelphus regarding the taxation of Syria and Phoenicia did not apparently apply to Palestine. The fiscal administration of the latter was probably different. We may suppose that the taxation of the vassal borderlands, such as the Ammanitis, was not reorganized on new lines by the Ptolemies. The sheikhs of these borderlands, it may be presumed, were subject to certain military obligations and perhaps paid a kind of tribute. On the other hand, there is no reason to think that the fiscal system of the coastal cities was unlike that of the

* *P. Cairo Zen.* 59003: note the δικαστής, l. 18.

† *P. Cairo Zen,* 59006; cf. 59007.

‡ κληρουχήσειν αὐτῶν τὴν γῆν . . . καὶ πέμψειν τοὺς ἐνοικήσοντας στρατιώτας.

Phoenician cities. They probably retained their own fiscal organization and paid tribute to the king. We hear, at a later time, that tax-farmers played a very important part in its collection.[144]

The organization of Judaea was in all probability somewhat different. The story of the tax-farmer from Judaea told by Josephus shows the king-priest in the role of a general contractor responsible to the Ptolemies for the revenue of that region. The same system is described in the account which he gives of the peace between Antiochus III and Epiphanes.* His narrative also shows that the same system prevailed earlier.†[145]

I doubt, however, whether in Palestine the Ptolemies were satisfied with levying tribute, a lump sum paid to them by the king-priest on behalf of Judaea and perhaps by the representatives of the self-governing cities of the coast on behalf of these cities, that is to say, whether Palestine was treated in the matter of taxation like the Ammanitis. It is highly probable that in Palestine—and in all probability in Syria also—besides the tribute, collected from the people by the local authorities according to ancestral traditions, a series of new 'royal' taxes, which did not form part of the tribute, was imposed by the Ptolemies on the people and collected by special tax-farmers. We may guess from the famous letter of Antiochus III, which exempted the Jews from taxes for three years as a reward for their help,‡ that he had retained in the main the Ptolemaic system of taxation. Now, the taxes mentioned by Antiochus III and those which were subsequently remitted to the Jews by his successors (below, Chs. V and VI), as being specially hateful, include some which are typical royal taxes of the Hellenistic period and are common to all the Hellenistic kingdoms. They were hardly innovations of the Seleucids; in all probability they were inherited by them from the Ptolemies. Their existence suggests that the Ptolemies carried out in Judaea a reform of taxation on lines similar to those which they followed in Syria and Phoenicia.

Moreover, in the time of Jesus Christ Judaea and Galilee were full of τελῶναι (wrongly translated 'publicans'), who were

* *A.J.* xii. 155. † Ibid. 158–9. ‡ Ibid. 138 ff.

hated because of their oppressive treatment of the people and their unscrupulous denunciations. I pointed out long ago that the condition of Palestine as depicted in the New Testament strikingly recalls that of Ptolemaic Egypt and, like the division of Judaea into eleven toparchies, probably goes back to the Ptolemaic fiscal reform. I drew attention to the large part played by denunciators (μηνυταί) both in Egypt and in Syria and Phoenicia during the reign of Philadelphus. Whether the tax-gatherers of Judaea were local collectors of taxes in general (one collector or a group of them for each village),* as in Syria and Phoenicia, or local collectors of single taxes, it is impossible to say.[146]

In any case, it seems reasonable to suppose that the early Ptolemies (probably Philadelphus) organized Judaea and probably other parts of Palestine for purposes of taxation more strictly than before. As might be expected, the rural population, which was probably treated in the same way as that of Egypt and Syria, resented the new system and hated the new taxes and their collectors, while the privileged city population was satisfied with the new régime and became rapidly hellenized. We find an echo of the feelings of the people of Judaea in the utterances of the author of *Ecclesiastes*, who, about 200 B.C., though himself an aristocrat, described the land as full of the tears of the oppressed and regarded the dead as happier than the living. The spies of Ptolemy, who are so ubiquitous that 'a bird of the air shall carry the voice' of him who cursed the king in secret, were presumably both fiscal and political μηνυταί.[147]

A vivid idea of economic conditions in Palestine in the time of Philadelphus may be derived from the correspondence of Zenon. Zenon, the agent of Apollonius, was in Palestine on business from the end of 260 to the end of 259 B.C. He travelled all over the country in grand style with a large staff of Greeks. Besides visiting Gaza and other cities of the coast, Judaea and Galilee, he or his agents penetrated as far as Idumaea, the Ammanitis, the neighbourhood of Damascus, and the frontiers of the Nabataeans. On his travels Zenon transacted business of many kinds: he occasionally lent money, he bought slaves

* See above, note 139.

(these purchases occupy an important place in his correspondence), also horses, and products of the Nabataean caravan trade. Was this Greek commercial penetration of Palestine a blessing or a curse to the population, or was it both?[148]

It was not only as merchants and business men that the Greeks penetrated into Palestine and Syria. I have spoken of Greek cities founded by the Ptolemies, and of cleruchs settled by the Ptolemies in Palestine, and perhaps also in Syria and Phoenicia. Thus new elements were introduced by the Ptolemies among the landholding classes. Besides the cleruchs there were new civilian landholders. We have reason to think that Apollonius owned an estate in Palestine at Bethanath and drew a good income from it. In all probability he was not an exception. Was his estate granted to him by the king or did he acquire it otherwise?[149]

Apart from taxation and exploitation of the rich resources of the Syrian provinces (e.g. the forests of the Lebanon), the Ptolemies undoubtedly derived a substantial revenue from the flourishing industry of the Phoenician cities. Unfortunately we have practically no information on the subject. Even more important was their revenue from the customs duties and, above all, from the caravan trade with Arabia. I shall speak of this later in this chapter.

Finally, I may mention that under Soter and Philadelphus the Greek and the Phoenician and Cyprian cities of their dominions contributed a large proportion of the ships of the Egyptian navy and that the Greek system of trierarchies was adopted for this purpose (see especially *P. Cairo Zen.* 59036).

5. Development of the Natural Resources of Egypt

We now return to Egypt and devote our attention to the second important problem that faced the Ptolemies there: that of developing the rich natural resources of the country, of increasing and systematizing its production, and of improving the industrial opportunities and methods of its population. The objects in view, as I have pointed out, were twofold. The first was to make the country self-sufficient, as little dependent as possible on foreign imports. This was not easy, for Egypt,

PLATE XL

1. Central part of a floor mosaic in a bath of the fourth century A.D. at Antioch. Like many other bath-mosaics of the Roman period, this mosaic is chiefly designed to illustrate the beneficent powers of water. The central oblong panel (about one-third of it is missing) is surrounded by four square panels placed at the corners, showing busts of rivers and countries which owed their prosperity to them, and by oblong panels showing personifications of the sea—Tritons and Nereids—all with their names appended. The composition of the central panel is skilful. The central group consists of the majestic figure of the Earth (inscription: *Γῆ*) reclining and resting her left arm on a sphinx, and another female figure opposite her with the elephant cap on her head and the elephant's tusk in her left hand, certainly representing Egypt (inscription: *Αἴγυπτ*]*ος*). Associated with the figure of Earth are two *putti*. Seven other *putti* styled in the inscription *Καρποί* (fruit) connect the figure of Earth with another female figure seated in the right-hand corner of the mosaic and called in the inscription *Ἄρο*[*υρα*], cultivated fields. Of the seven *putti* one is plucking ears of corn, while five are carrying a heavy garland of ears, and the last is embracing the figure of Aroura. The missing part of the panel may perhaps be restored with the help of a mosaic of an earlier date (second century A.D.) from Leptis Magna showing the triumphal progress of the Nile; the Nile is riding a hippopotamus and is conducted by *putti* (*Καρποί*) carrying a garland. The procession is headed by two Nymphs (sources of the Nile) and is met by priests standing near the Nilometer. If the figures of the Nile and of the *Καρποί* be restored to complete the mosaic of Antioch, it would strikingly illustrate the fertility of Egypt (*Καρποί*), resulting from the common action of fertile Earth, careful cultivation (Aroura), and the fertilizing power of the Nile during the annual flood (the sixteen *Καρποί* being equivalent to the sixteen cubits of the rising Nile as shown, for example, in the famous statue of the Nile in the Vatican). I have discussed the two mosaics in more detail elsewhere (*Mél. G. Radet*, in print), and have endeavoured to show that they go back to a famous Alexandrian composition of Hellenistic times. Photograph supplied by Prof. C. R. Morey.

The mosaic of Antioch has been published by R. Stillwell, *Antioch-on-the-Orontes*, ii. 1938, p. 180, no. 33, pl. 23, cf. G. Downey, 'John of Gaza and the mosaic of Ge and Karpoi', ibid., pp. 205 ff., and C. R. Morey, *The Mosaics of Antioch*, 1938, pp. 36 ff., pl. xv. For the mosaic of Leptis Magna G. Guidi, *Africa Italiana*, v (1933), pp. 1–56.

2. One of the four square panels of the mosaic which decorated the *tepidarium* of a bath in a Roman villa near Leptis Magna. The four panels are disposed crosswise. They all glorify the blessings conferred on mankind by water. The first pair deals with fresh water: one of the pictures (described above) exalting the generative power of rivers, as illustrated by the Nile, the second the inspiring power of spring water (Pegasus, the inspirer of poets, at the spring Hippocrene). The second pair takes the sea as its subject: one picture shows the sea as generator of fish, several fishermen on the shore and in boats catching fish by various devices; the other, the sea as carrier of maritime trade. It is this last which is reproduced here. Its right extremity shows a harbour and behind it a palatial building. *Putti* are hurrying to the harbour, conveyed in all sorts of comical ways, all bringing fruit and flowers. Among them is seen a war-ship manned by two *putti* and loaded with fruit and flowers. I have shown elsewhere (*Mél. G. Radet*, in print) that, though of Roman make the four mosaics breathe the Hellenistic Alexandrian spirit, the same that we find in Hellenistic poetry, especially the epigrams. They all deal apparently with Alexandria and Egypt: the Nile, the Museum—sphere of Pegasus, the sea-shore rich in fish. The picture represented here exalts the thalassocracy of the Ptolemies (the war-ship) devoted to the service of Ptolemaic commerce, the two together safeguarding wealth, merriment, and abundance for Alexandria, Egypt, and the king himself (the palace in the harbour ?). Photograph supplied by the Sopraintendenza degli scavi in Libia.

See G. Guidi, loc. cit. Cf. in the present work pp. 407 ff., and n. 206.

1. Mosaic found at Antioch.

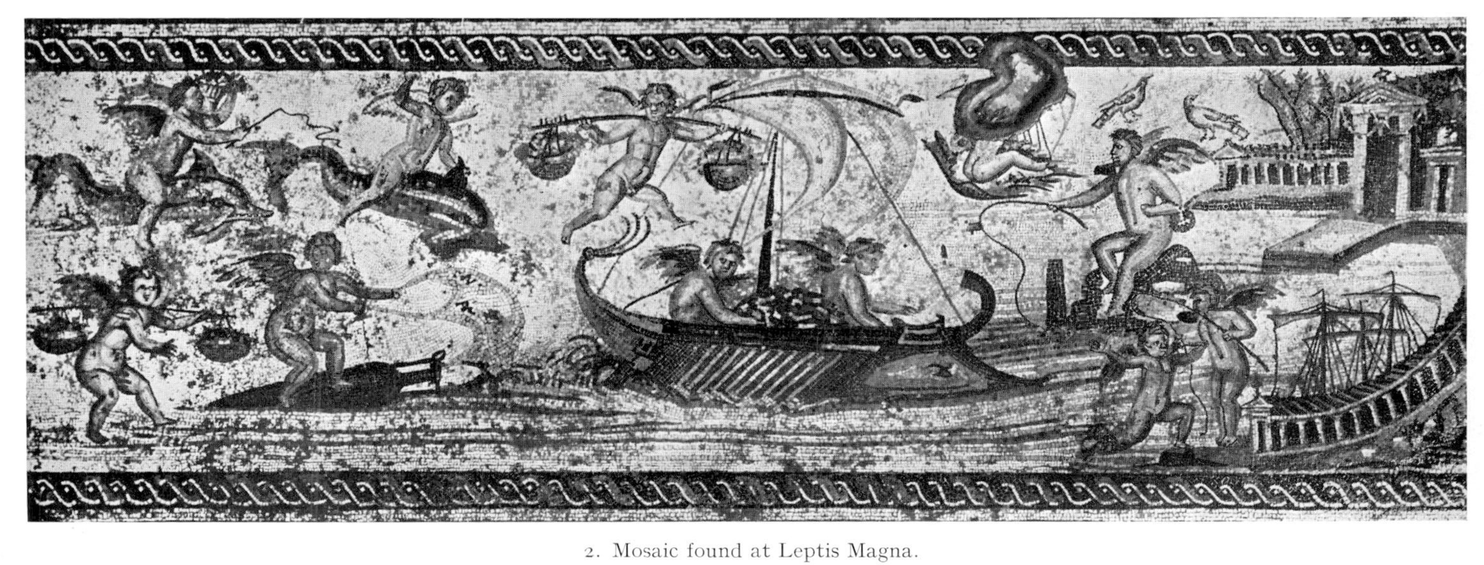

2. Mosaic found at Leptis Magna.

FERTILITY AND WEALTH OF PTOLEMAIC EGYPT

we must remember, now had a large and growing Greek population, whose peculiar needs could not be satisfied by local production unless special measures were taken to that end. The second object was to obtain for Egypt a favourable balance in international trade and thereby to secure a good influx of gold and silver from abroad. This object could only be attained by increasing the quantity and improving the quality of those Egyptian commodities for which there was demand abroad. It was, moreover, necessary that Egyptian products, especially manufactured goods, should be adapted to the rapidly changing tastes of Egypt's foreign customers.

The first object was achieved, so far as concerned the production of foodstuffs, by increasing the cultivation of certain plants which, though known in Egypt, had never been grown to an important extent, and by introducing and acclimatizing new plants practically unknown in Egypt before this time.

Vines. To the first class belonged the vine. Vineyards existed in Pharaonic Egypt and wine was used by the Egyptians, but the national drink of Egypt was beer. One of the earliest steps taken by the Ptolemies to satisfy the ever-growing demand of the Greek inhabitants for wine was an extensive planting of vines of various kinds, especially on the recently reclaimed lands. There is evidence of this in many documents. Our fullest information relates to the Arsinoite nome. This nome in the time of Philadelphus was covered with vineyards large and small, some planted by the kings, but most by immigrants, not by natives. We hear of one which yielded as much as 898 1/6 *metretae* of wine (Petrie, iii. 67). Vines were planted with feverish activity on the *doreai* (gift-estates) of Apollonius the *dioecetes*. Many sorts of vine were tried. In 257 B.C. Apollonius sends messengers to a certain Lysimachus, perhaps himself the owner of a *dorea*, to get cuttings of vines and fruit-trees from him. Nicias, Lysimachus' manager, replies to the message from Apollonius and attaches a list of cuttings. Eleven varieties of vine are named, among them Cilician, Mendean (from Mende in Chalcidice), Maronean (from Maronea in Thrace), Phoenician, and Alexandrian, and some others, all famous for their quality.* Many of Apollonius' letters

* *P. Cairo Zen.* 59033.

to his managers Panacestor and Zenon deal with the planting of vines, olive-trees, fruit-trees, flowers, and so forth. In one letter Apollonius speaks of 10,000 vinc plants (φυτὰ ἀμπέλινα) and 1,700 shoots (μοσχεύματα),* in another of 20,000 φυτά, part of them at least vine-cuttings,† and there is a long passage in a memorandum about the conveyance of vine-cuttings by donkeys and mules;‡ others were sent by ship.§ The plantation of vines was taken up on a smaller scale by other Greeks, some of them cleruchs. For example, in a letter Alcaeus informs Sosiphon that he has planted 300 vine roots and some trees among them (Petrie, i. 29).

It was natural that the Greeks of Egypt, familiar from childhood with the management of vineyards, should plant vines in their new home. The demand for wine in the new Egypt of Soter and Philadelphus was large, and the production of wine certainly remunerative. Moreover, the planting of vines was undoubtedly encouraged by Soter, Philadelphus, and Euergetes. They granted many privileges to planters. Plots of land planted with these and with other trees became, according to the Ptolemaic practice, the private property of the planters. Part of the *apomoira* was remitted to the cleruchs: they paid one-tenth instead of one-sixth of the produce. The Ptolemies, of course, did not neglect their own interests: vineyards were subject to heavy taxes: one-third or one-half of the produce was paid in cash, and in addition one-sixth or one-tenth as *apomoira*, besides some minor taxes.|| They carefully watched the vintage and the making of the wine in order to safeguard for themselves and the temples the dues demanded of the vine-planters; they regulated minutely the collection of the taxes in kind or in money, piling responsibility on responsibility: the vine-growers, the tax-farmers (underwriters), and officials of various grades were all responsible to the king for the full collection of this part of the royal revenue. It is instructive to read and analyse the portion of the νόμοι τελωνικοί of Philadelphus which relates to the *apomoira* and certain documents that illustrate the collection of the main wine-tax.

* *P. Cairo Zen.* 59159, 59162.
† *P. Cairo Zen.* 59222.
‡ *P. Cairo Zen.* 59736; cf. *P.S.I.* 499.
§ *P.S.I.* 568.
|| *P. Cairo Zen.* 59236; cf. 59357, 59361, 59367.

The spirit is the same as in the case of the monopolies, the methods are somewhat different. On the other hand, the king guarded vine-growers against competition by imposing heavy customs duties of a compensatory* or protective character on imported wine.[150]

Olives. The Ptolemies and the Greek settlers did what was practically pioneer work in Egypt by planting olive-trees. I need not emphasize the importance to the Greeks of olive-oil, for which they would accept no substitute. They had been accustomed to genuine olive-oil from childhood, and this they were determined to have. Olive-trees were not unknown in Pharaonic Egypt, but these were planted mostly to produce olives for eating. In some places the practice of planting olives had become well established. Thus Theophrastus† knows of olive plantations in the Thebaid, probably in the oasis of Khargeh in particular (where such plantations still exist), and he says that olive-oil produced in Egypt was not inferior to that of Greece.

It was reserved, however, for the Ptolemies to extend the area of olive-groves in Egypt and to foster production of native olive-oil. Our evidence on olive plantations in the third century B.C. is meagre, but the correspondence of Zenon shows that Apollonius planted many ἐλαιῶνες on his estate and desired gradually to extend these.‡ As a result he certainly became one of the producers of olive-oil for sale. It is possible that an interesting letter written by him to Zenon has reference to this subject.§ In this letter Apollonius instructs Zenon to discharge a cargo of olive-oil on its arrival at the emporium at Alexandria from his οἶκος and to keep it under careful custody in a safe storehouse until Apollonius is able personally to attend to it. Edgar thinks that the olive-oil came from the Syrian estate of Apollonius. This may be, but it may perhaps be regarded as a consignment sent from the Fayûm to the river-harbour of Alexandria and unloaded there.

* i.e. equalizing the price of imported and home products.

† *H.P.* iv. 2. 9.

‡ *P. Cairo Zen.* 59072, 59125, 59157, 59184, 59244, 59734, 59788, ll. 18 and 27; *P. Mich. Zen.* 45, l. 26.

§ *P. Col. Zen.* 14, supplemented by C. C. Edgar, *Arch. Pap.* xi (1935), p. 218.

In planting olive-trees extensively Apollonius was doing nothing exceptional. According to Strabo (xvii. I. 35), the Arsinoite nome produced in his day large quantities of olive-oil, while round Alexandria there were many olive-groves which furnished that city with olives for eating. This bears out the existence of olive culture on an important scale in Hellenistic, especially late Hellenistic, times. Strabo's statement is confirmed by numerous documents attesting the abundance of olive-groves in the Fayûm in Roman times and their presence in other parts of Egypt. It should be noted, however, that according to Strabo Egyptian olive-oil was of very poor quality.

We do not know to what extent the production and sale of Egyptian olive-oil were controlled by the government. Olive-oil was not dealt with in the law of Philadelphus regulating the production and sale of other vegetable oils. This does not mean that in his time the quantity of this oil produced was too small to require the government's attention. It is more probable that olive-oil was dealt with in special regulations. If my interpretation of the above-mentioned letter of Apollonius is correct, some restrictions were imposed on the import of olive-oil into Alexandria from the country. Apollonius appears to have wished to attend in person to the formalities and payments connected with the import of a large consignment of native oil, which at that time may have been a novelty (the date of the letter is 257 B.C.). Whether olive-oil was subjected *mutatis mutandis* to rules similar to those which governed other vegetable oils, there is no evidence to show. Its price was certainly not lower than that of vegetable oils as fixed in the νόμος ἐλαικῆς; what its price was, however, is completely unknown to us, the term ἔλαιον in the accounts being used for all the vegetable oils. The high tariff on imported olive-oil (50 per cent.) was intended to protect all the native oils, including olive-oil. How long this protection lasted we cannot say. In the second century it was not so strict as in the third (*Teb.* 728).

In any case, it is certain that an attempt was made by the first Ptolemies to provide the Greek population of Egypt with native olive-oil and thus to make Egypt, in this respect also, independent of foreign supplies.[151]

Other foreign plants. The first Ptolemies experimented on the acclimatization of other foreign plants hitherto unknown or little cultivated in Egypt. This was done with the same object of meeting the demand of the Greeks for the vegetables and fruit to which they were accustomed, and of reducing imports. Various fruit-trees were planted on the Philadelphian estate of Apollonius with the same energy as vines and olive-trees: figs of the best foreign sorts,* quinces, pomegranates, early and late apples, apricots (?), and nuts. There are reasons for thinking that pistachio trees were first grown in Egypt about this time. Similar steps were taken as regards vegetables. We know, for example, that garlic was introduced, a root still much consumed by Greeks and Italians at the present day. Two sorts of garlic were cultivated on Apollonius' estate, the famous kind from Tlos in Lycia and a kind that grew in one of the oases of Egypt.† An attempt was made about the same time to improve the quality of cabbage grown in Egypt by importing seed from Rhodes.‡[152]

I may refer, moreover, to one of the documents in Zenon's correspondence, a letter from Apollonius to Zenon (*P. Cairo Zen.* 59157) in which he recommends him to plant at least three hundred fir-trees all over the park (*παράδεισος*) at Philadelphia and round the vineyard and the olive-groves, adding, 'for the tree has a striking appearance and will be of service to the king' (as C. C. Edgar translates). By 'service to the king' Apollonius has in mind the ultimate employment of the trees as timber. In the same park there were large plantations of roses, certainly not grown merely for decorative purposes.§

Live stock. The same policy of innovations may be observed in the rearing of live stock. Great attention was paid in particular to providing Egypt with wool of the highest quality. As I have already pointed out, Greeks wore almost exclusively woollen garments, and were accustomed in their own country to excellent cloth made of the finest qualities of

* *P. Cairo Zen.* 59033.

† *P.S.I.* 428. 85 and 433; cf. 332 and *Lond. Inv.* 2097, ll. 14 ff.

‡ Diphilus of Siphnos (a contemporary of King Lysimachus) in Athen. ix. 9, p. 369 f.

§ *P. Cairo Zen.* 59269, 59735, and 59736, 23.

wool. The Ptolemies accordingly endeavoured to produce in Egypt wool equal to that of Greece, Asia Minor, and Arabia. The easiest way of doing this was to import foreign sheep and acclimatize them in Egypt.

In this matter as in others Apollonius was of assistance to the king. He owned a very valuable and much admired flock of Milesian sheep, of which there is frequent mention.* A letter from Apollonius to Zenon and Panacestor of 254 B.C. (*P. Cairo Zen.* 59195) is of especial interest. Apollonius was sending a trained shepherd, Maron by name, to Philadelphia to take charge of the Milesian flock. Panacestor and Zenon were to hand over to him the sheep and sheepfold, and all the material (*κατασκευή*), and to place the shepherds and four apprentices under his orders. There was a good prospect of acclimatizing the Milesian skin-covered breed (*ὑποδίφθερα*), for the marshy pastures of the Fayûm were not very different from those of the banks of the Maeander.

Even more successful were the attempts to acclimatize Arabian sheep. Arabian sheep and Arab shepherds (*P. Cairo Zen.* 59433, 22 ff.) are frequently referred to in Zenon's correspondence and elsewhere.† It may be noticed that in the great procession organized by Philadelphus and described by Callixeinus‡ Arabian, Ethiopian, and Euboean sheep were displayed to the public, certainly as evidence of the great efforts that the king was making to supply the needs of his Greek subjects.

It has been mentioned that pigs were used extensively for sacrifices. We know, moreover, that pork was a favourite dish of the Greeks when they treated themselves to the luxury of eating meat. It is accordingly not surprising to hear of Sicilian pigs in Egypt. They are mentioned in one of Zenon's accounts, relating to foodstuffs for various domestic animals.§ They may have been kept in the special pigsty built at Philadelphia (*P. Mich. Zen.* 84).

* *P. Cairo Zen.* 59142, 59195, 59430.

† *P. Cairo Zen.* 59430, cf. 59405, 59406, and perhaps 59404; *P.S.I.* 429. 17; 377. 14; *Hib.* 36. 6. 11; Arabian wool, *P. Cairo Zen.* 59287, cf. *P. Edg.* 107.

‡ Athen. v, p. 201 c.

§ *P. Cairo Zen.* 59710 and 59711.

The same accounts mention dogs, which were favourite animals of Zenon's; for he was an ardent hunter, resembling in this other Macedonians and Greeks.* The dogs mentioned in the accounts, however, were probably sheep-dogs, not hunting-dogs, and, like Zenon's Indian hunting-dog, of an imported breed.†

Finally, I may mention the attention paid by the Ptolemies to horses, to the improvement of the breed of donkeys by importations from Syria,‡ and to the increase of the number of camels, which were commonly employed, for instance in the *dorea* of Apollonius, as beasts of burden.§ In this connexion I am certainly of opinion that the animals, mostly domestic, given to Philadelphus by Tubias, the Transjordan sheikh, were intended, not as an addition to the king's zoological garden, but as a contribution to the improvement of the breeds in Egypt.[153]

Grain. The second object—AGRICULTURAL PRODUCTION—was taken up seriously from the outset by the Macedonian conquerors of Egypt. Egypt had begun to export grain under the Persians, if not earlier. The Persians appear to have been the first to introduce into Egypt the cultivation of a better quality of wheat, the Median, alongside of the inferior wheat of the country. The experiment of Cleomenes, the satrap of Egypt in the time of Alexander, showed how great a profit might be derived from the grain trade by the masters of that fertile corn-land. In the days of the first Ptolemies grain, especially wheat, was in large and ever-increasing demand in Greece. At that time Italian and Sicilian grain rarely appeared on the Greek market. Before Alexander's day Thrace and South Russia were the chief sources of Greek supply, and so they remained in his time and in the lifetime of Lysimachus, whose wealth was probably derived in part from large exports of grain to Greece. But the supply of Thracian and south Russian grain was not unlimited, and largely depended on good crops, which in their turn depended on a sufficient rain-

* *P. Cairo Zen.* 59532.
† *P. Cairo Zen.* 59075, cf. Athen. V, p. 201 b.
‡ *P. Cairo Zen.* 59075.
§ *P. Cairo Zen.* 59143, 59207; *P. Mich. Zen.* 103, cf. *B.G.U.* 1351, 1353.

fall. Moreover, the invasion of the Balkan peninsula and South Russia by the Celts and of Scythia by the Sarmatians disorganized the Thracian and south Russian production and export of grain. All the other principal grain-producing countries, Cyprus, Phoenicia, Cyrenaica, were in the hands of the Ptolemies. The Ptolemies consequently had an excellent opportunity of securing control of the Greek grain-market, and they did not fail to take advantage of it. In order to be in a position to place large quantities of grain on the Greek market, they had first to increase its production in Egypt and secondly to make a considerable change in the quality of the Egyptian produce.

Increase of cultivated area. For the former purpose the Ptolemies not only reorganized the Egyptian agricultural system as described above, but took in addition certain other measures. To begin with, they increased the area of cultivated land in Egypt. Additional land was reclaimed by the extension and improvement of irrigation, by the drainage of marsh lands, and by the careful irrigation of the sandy and stony borders of the desert. We know fairly well how these measures were applied in the Arsinoite nome. The correspondence of Cleon and Theodorus, the chief irrigation engineers in the Fayûm in the reigns of Philadelphus and Euergetes, vividly depicts the execution of the work there by the joint efforts and technical knowledge of Greeks and natives. The picture given by Cleon's correspondence is enlarged and filled in by numerous documents illustrating the progress and the various aspects of the improvements carried out on Apollonius' estate of 10,000 *arourae*, partly by Cleon himself, partly by specialists in the service of the owner. And, finally, a thorough investigation of the region of Caranis, one of the new cities of the Arsinoite nome, which has been carefully excavated by the Michigan expedition, by Miss G. Caton Thompson and Miss E. W. Gardner, has enabled us to see on a modern map the result of the measures taken by the first Ptolemies. In this investigation special attention has been paid to the irrigation system, which is proved to have been started in the reign of Philadelphus.

This is not the place to describe the methods by which the improvements were carried out. The technical side must be investigated by a specialist familiar both with modern practice and with the history of the science and technique of ancient times. For the economic history of the period it is important to point out that the work was done mainly with free labour by contractors paid by the government or by landholders who employed hired workmen. Compulsory labour appears to have played no important part in the execution of this great enterprise, though there was some employment of criminals in custody (δεσμῶται).

The work was begun without delay. The Italian investigation of the region around Tebtunis appears to have produced conclusive evidence of an early settlement of cleruchs there, which means that the work in this region dates from the time of Soter. It was carried on there and in the Fayûm in general with the utmost vigour by Philadelphus, and was still proceeding under Euergetes I.

We have no statistics that would enable us to form an exact idea of how much land was reclaimed in the Arsinoite nome under the early Ptolemies. But Apollonius' estate of 10,000 *arourae* near Philadelphia gives an idea of the scale of reclamation. We must remember also that much land was assigned in the same region to cleruchs. It would therefore be wrong to form a low estimate of the results achieved here by the first Ptolemies. And Philadelphia did not stand alone. A glance at the map and at a list of the names of the various towns, villages, and hamlets of the Arsinoite nome will suffice to show the many new centres of life similar to Philadelphia founded in this part of Egypt in the third century. The settlements bear names of various types. Some of them are purely Greek, dynastic or religious, some are Egyptian. Almost all these settlements, however, even those with Egyptian names, were either new creations of the Ptolemies or became large and prosperous in consequence of the measures taken by them. We have examples in Philadelphia, Caranis, Tebtunis, and especially the capital of the nome, Crocodilopolis or Arsinoe. It should be observed, moreover, that many settlements with Egyptian names are homonyms of villages in Middle Egypt and the Delta. This suggests that they were inhabited by native emigrants from those villages.

Was the Arsinoite nome an exception? We have no direct information on this point, but it is reasonable to suppose that similar work was carried out in many places. There is no doubt, for instance, that the flourishing state of the region around Alexandria, with its famous Mareotic wine, was due in the main to the activity of the early Ptolemies. And the same was probably true of many other parts of the Delta. We should like to know more of the borderlands of the Delta, especially on the West.[154]

The Ptolemies applied the most recent devices, some of them the outcome of Greek scientific investigation, to the extension of the cultivated area. The question arises how far in the same period Egyptian agriculture benefited by similar technical inventions. Our information on this point is meagre. There is hardly any literary evidence; the papyri occasionally mention agricultural implements, but the references are not easy to interpret; and the agricultural implements themselves, though found in large numbers, have never, as I previously remarked, been collected, described, and analysed from the technical and historical standpoint. For the early Ptolemaic period it is again Zenon's correspondence that furnishes the best information.

Provision of iron. One of the greatest achievements of this period in respect of agriculture was the introduction of the 'iron age'. The supply of iron was scanty and it had been used only sporadically in Pharaonic Egypt. The Ptolemies were the first to supply Egypt with iron, most of it imported, in sufficient quantity to enable the people to use it extensively in their daily life.

It is interesting to see how carefully the provision of iron was organized on Apollonius' estate at Philadelphia. A long account (*P. Cairo Zen.* 59782 a), supplemented by other documents, details the daily issues of iron by the management to various members of the staff of the estate: those dealing with agriculture (including irrigation) and transport, with the building and decoration of houses and other edifices, and with various crafts requiring iron instruments (e.g. barbers, *P. Mich. Zen.* 54). In the department of agriculture iron was used for making and repairing various implements and fitting cutting edges into the blades of certain tools. Iron implements were extensively used at Philadelphia. Most of the agricultural implements that were made of wood in Pharaonic times now appear on Apollonius' estate as made partly or entirely of iron: ploughshares now have iron sheaths (ὕνεις); mattocks and shovels (σκαφεῖα and ἆμαι) and probably hoes (δίκελλαι), reaping-hooks of various forms for different purposes (δρέπανα and ψέλια) have iron-edged blades; axes (ἀξῖναι, πελέκεις) are made of iron, and iron is extensively used for wagons, especially for the wheels. So extensive a use of iron in Egyptian agriculture was almost tantamount to a revolution. It is not surprising that Zenon should be so careful of his iron.[155]

Mechanisms for irrigation. Next in importance were the improvements in the devices used for irrigating land beyond the reach of the Nile flood. During thousands of years Egypt had been content to water such land by hand (διὰ χειρός) or by primitive *shadufs* (κηλώνια). For some parcels of land this was the most economical method of irrigation, and it is still employed in Egypt.

But many plots of otherwise valuable land could not be irrigated in this way. Some better device, a more scientific mechanism, was needed. For the Greek science of mechanics, developed as it was in the fourth and third centuries B.C., it was an easy task to construct a simple and efficient water-wheel by a combination of cog-wheel and endless rope. Thus the well-known *sakiyeh* and the similar machines of the region of the Euphrates and Orontes came into being and are still extensively used in Egypt and in Syria. In the Greek documents of Hellenistic and Roman Egypt the sakiyeh is called μηχανή or μηχανὴ ἀντλοῦσα, ὄργανον, μηχανικὸν ὄργανον. It is first mentioned in a papyrus of the second century B.C. (*P. Cor.* 5), then in one of 5 B.C. (*B.G.U.* 1120. 27), and frequently in documents of the Roman period.

Less use was made of a pump based on the principle of the Archimedean screw, because it was less efficient for agricultural purposes. Diodorus (i. 34) states positively, and there are no serious grounds for doubting his statement, that the Delta was irrigated by means of such a special machine, 'which was invented by Archimedes of Syracuse and was called because of its form "snail" (κοχλίας)'. This contrivance appears to have come into common use in the Delta in Hellenistic times and is still employed in some parts of Middle Egypt. In the correspondence of Zenon neither the sakiyeh nor the κοχλίας is mentioned, but there is evidence of the latter in early Roman times, and it is represented in certain paintings and sculptures as used for irrigating gardens.[156]

Sowing-plough. Other mechanical devices for making agricultural work easier and more efficient were used in Egypt in early Roman times: such was the sowing-plough, which had been known to the ancient world for centuries and was used extensively in Babylonia; and the *norag*, a threshing drag still in use in Egypt and elsewhere and called by the Romans *plostellum punicum*. The former implement is expressly mentioned in documents of the Hellenistic period. The latter is probably referred to in a third-century document (*B.G.U.* 1507) connected with what had formerly been the *dorea* of Apollonius.[157]

Oil- and wine-presses. It is to be regretted that we know so little of the oil- and wine-presses of the Ptolemaic period. From a fragmentary document (*P.S. I.* 624) we may infer that Zenon was well informed about the progress made in viticulture in Hellenistic times. It is very likely that he used for his own information and for the instruction of his subordinates one of the many treatises then current on agriculture in general and viticulture in particular. If screw-presses of the new type, which were introduced into Italy in the early first century A.D., were known in Greece before they appeared in Italy, he certainly was aware of their existence and may have employed them. The problem of the date of the screw-press, however, is far from being settled. Pliny (*N.H.* xviii. 317) regards it as a new invention of his own time. On the other hand, Heron knew about presses of all types and describes them minutely. Unfortunately the date of Heron is disputed. If he belonged to Hellenistic times, the screw-press (not the '*prelum* and screw press' that was well known all over the Hellenistic world) was familiar to the Greeks before it was introduced into Italy.[158]

Water-mills. A problem related to those dealt with above is presented by the history of the water-mill for grinding grain. Strabo (xii. 556) refers to a water-mill at Cabeira in Pontus in connexion with the palace built by the great Mithridates. This type of mill was well known in the early Roman Empire under its Greek name *hydraletes* and is described by Vitruvius (x. 257) and Pliny (*N.H.* xviii. 97). Remains of water-mills have been found in some places—I may mention the ruins of one discovered in the Athenian agora, and the wooden mill-wheels found in Italy and elsewhere. Are we to ascribe the invention of the water-mill to the East, or to connect it with the progress of Greek technical science in the Hellenistic period? It is interesting to find that there appears to be no mention of water-mills in the papyri either of Hellenistic or Roman times found in Egypt. Are we to explain this by the difficulty of using the Nile for the purpose of a water-mill? It is even more surprising, in view of the progress made by ancient technique in the matter of irrigation, not to find windmills used either in Egypt or in the other parts of the Hellenistic and Roman world.[159]

An increase in the agricultural production of Egypt in general and in the production of grain in particular was the natural result of the innovations above described. We must undoubtedly ascribe to the need for such an improvement, both in the quantity and the quality of the output, the technical progress of Egyptian agriculture in early Ptolemaic times.

We must explain in the same way certain other agricultural improvements of a different character introduced by the Ptolemies. One of Apollonius' letters informs us that the king bade him adopt on his estate the system of two crops a year (*P. Cairo Zen.* 59155). The system was not new. It had been extensively used in various parts of the world—in Greece, in Syria, and in Arabia—and was probably not unknown or untried in Egypt. It is, however, characteristic of the reforming zeal of Philadelphus that he wanted to have it applied on the estate he had given to Apollonius.[160]

Lastly, it was certainly due to the desire of the first Ptolemies to bring about a great increase in the exportation of grain that they changed the type of grain grown in Egypt. In pre-Ptolemaic Egypt *olyra* (rice-wheat, *triticum dicoccum*) was cultivated in preference to wheat, for *olyra* was the staple food of the population. But there was no demand for it in other countries: what was there required was wheat, and wheat of the best quality, capable of competing with that of South Russia, Thrace, and Asia Minor. By their planned system of agriculture the Ptolemies found it easy to increase the production of wheat. At the same time they experimented with a view to improving the quality of Egyptian wheat, and tried many kinds of seed. We hear of Calyndian wheat, and we know that Syrian wheat was very popular in Egypt in the third century.[161]

In these endeavours they were successful. We have no statistics, but by careful interpretation of such data as we possess we are able to infer that in normal years Egypt was not only able to feed her population and their live stock, but also to export a large surplus, probably not less than ten million *artabae* a year.[162]

The situation in regard to INDUSTRIAL PRODUCTION was almost the same as in regard to agriculture. From time immemorial Egypt had produced various manufactured goods both for her own population and for export. In many branches of industry, such as papyrus, linen, glass, and faience, she had no rivals; and to these may be added articles made from the ivory, ebony, spices, &c., brought by caravan, which also were for a long time a speciality of Egypt.

When the Ptolemies took over the country from the Persians they were faced with the same problems in respect of industry as of agriculture. New customers appeared in Egypt who had their special requirements and would not be satisfied with the alien products of Egyptian industry: these were the immigrants, mostly Greeks or persons accustomed to the Greek mode of life. They would have been glad to buy goods imported from their own country, but the Ptolemies would not allow them to do this. I have already explained that one of the main objects of their policy was self-sufficiency. On the other hand, the purchasing power of foreign countries and the demand for Egyptian goods were steadily increasing. The Hellenistic market, however, was not easy to satisfy. It had its peculiar preferences, to which producers had to adapt themselves. It was evident, therefore, that in order to obtain a good return from Egyptian industry it was not sufficient to monopolize some of its branches and to control production and sale in others. The output of many commodities had to be increased and its character adapted to the needs of customers who were Greeks or had Greek tastes and habits. A hellenization of Egyptian industry was required.

We are even less well informed about the industry of Egypt than about its agriculture. The documents reveal its organization by the Ptolemies, as indicated above, but they are silent on the character of its products and its technical processes. For some branches of industry the archaeological material is abundant and will be described below. On one point, however, the evidence, especially that of the papyri, speaks with certainty: the Ptolemies did not neglect any of the ancient industries of Egypt. I have shown above how they developed the papyrus industry and with what excellent results. Of other branches of industry I shall speak presently, but I may say at once that it was the Ptolemies who practically introduced the woollen industry on a large scale into the country.

The results achieved were remarkable. Egypt became self-sufficing in almost all branches of industry and was able to export in the third century some manufactured goods. I shall describe these results in the several industries so far as we know them from literary, documentary, and above all from archaeological evidence. The archaeological material assembled by me is no doubt incomplete and will, it is hoped, be soon supplemented by competent archaeologists.

Pottery. I shall begin with pottery, the best-known branch of Egyptian industry. I have already explained how Alexandria became in the late fourth and early third centuries one of the best markets for Athenian and South Italian potters (see above, p. 160). The import of foreign pottery, of course, never entirely ceased. Imported ceramic goods are found in Alexandria from time to time throughout the Hellenistic period. But in the later part of this period imports were relatively rare. Very early in the third century Alexandrian potters began to compete with foreign importers. They started this competition by imitating the various Athenian and South Italian models. They soon went further and manufactured for the Alexandrian market new types of pottery, some of which

PLATE XLI

1. Funerary black-glazed amphora with white ornaments (stylized ivy) found in the Necropolis of Hadra. A very common type of Alexandrian pottery made in imitation of similar black-glazed Attic vases. Photograph supplied by the authorities of the Alexandria Museum.

E. Breccia, *Bull. Soc. Arch. Alex.* XXV (N.S. vii. 2) (1930), p. 119, no. 22028, pl. XVI, 1. On Alexandrian pottery in general see n. 163 to this chapter. On the b.-g. Alexandrian vases, R. Pagenstecher, *Gr.-Aeg. Samml. E. von Sieglin*, ii. 3, pp. 54 ff.; C. W. Lunsingh Scheurleer, *Griekische Ceramiek*, 1936, pp. 155 ff.; recent finds *Le Musée Gréco-Romain*, 1925–31 (1931) pp. 34 f., 89 l., cf. 88 (Western Necropolis).

2. One of the royal faience *oenochoai* with greenish-blue glaze (cf. above, pl. XXXVI) and traces of gold and painting, found at Benghazi. The relief decoration shows Queen Berenice II wearing a royal diadem and holding in her left hand a cornucopia full of fruit and ears of corn, performing a libation over a rectangular horned altar adorned with a garland. On the front of the altar, inscription: *Θεῶν Εὐεργετῶν*. Behind Berenice, a conical betyl on a cylindrical base similar to those represented in the landscapes of the second style (for instance that of the Livia house on the Palatine) and in the so-called 'landscape bas-reliefs' of Hellenistic and early imperial times. To the left of the head of the queen, inscription: *Βερενίκης βασιλίσσης | Ἀγαθῆς Τύχης*. O. Rayet and M. Collignon, *Hist. de la Cér. Gr.*, 1888, pp. 371 ff., fig. 139. Several other intact *oenochoai* of the same type, besides many fragments, have been found in Egypt, Cyrenaica, Cyprus, and South Italy. They all show the same plastic decoration (with two exceptions—one at Corpus Christi College, Cambridge, which is without reliefs and bears the inscription of Philopator, and another in the Ottoman Museum, Istanbul, showing a scene of sacrifice) and bear inscriptions of the same character mentioning Arsinoe II, Berenice II, and Philopator. It appears very probable that *oenochoai* of this type were sold in Egypt and the Ptolemaic dominions in temples and shrines devoted to the royal cult, and served for the performance of libations to the deified rulers. After use they were taken home as a kind of souvenir. There is a representation of an *oenochoe* of this form being used for the above purpose on the bronze bas-relief from Delos reproduced below, pl. XC, 1. Since all the known *oenochoai* apparently belong to the third century B.C. and no other queens and kings except the above-named are mentioned in the inscriptions, the fashion must have been shortlived.

See bibliography in n. 163, cf. R. Pagenstecher, *Gr.-Aeg. Samml. E. von Sieglin*, ii.3, pp. 207 ff., and pls. XXXI–XXXII; R. Vallois, *C.R. Ac. Inscr.*, 1929, pp. 32 ff.; C. W. Lunsingh Scheurleer, *Griekische Ceramiek*, 1936, p. 171, pl. LIII, fig. 163.

3. B.-g. funeral amphora with painted (white) and plastic appliqué decoration and a cover crowned by a statuette of a standing woman. The appliqué decoration consists of groups of young women holding medallions bearing the head of Athena. Found in the Necropolis of Ibrahimieh. Photograph supplied by the authorities of the Alexandria Museum.

E. Breccia, *Bull. Soc. Arch. Alex.* ix (1907), p. 58, fig. 17, and *Alexandrea ad Aegyptum*, 1922, p. 251, fig. 165; R. Pagenstecher, loc. cit., p. 53, fig. 59, cf. pl. XIX. This type of vases (called 'plaquette' vases) is found exclusively in Egypt and Crete. Similar vases, however, are common in Athens, Pergamon, and especially in South Italy. See n. 163, and below Ch. VIII; cf. C. W. Lunsingh Scheurleer, loc. cit., pp. 155 ff., fig. 145 (a fine specimen in the Berlin Antiquarium, cf. K. A. Neugebauer, *Führer d. d. Antiquarium*, ii, Vasen, 1932, p. 170, n. 2885, pl. 91, found in Crete).

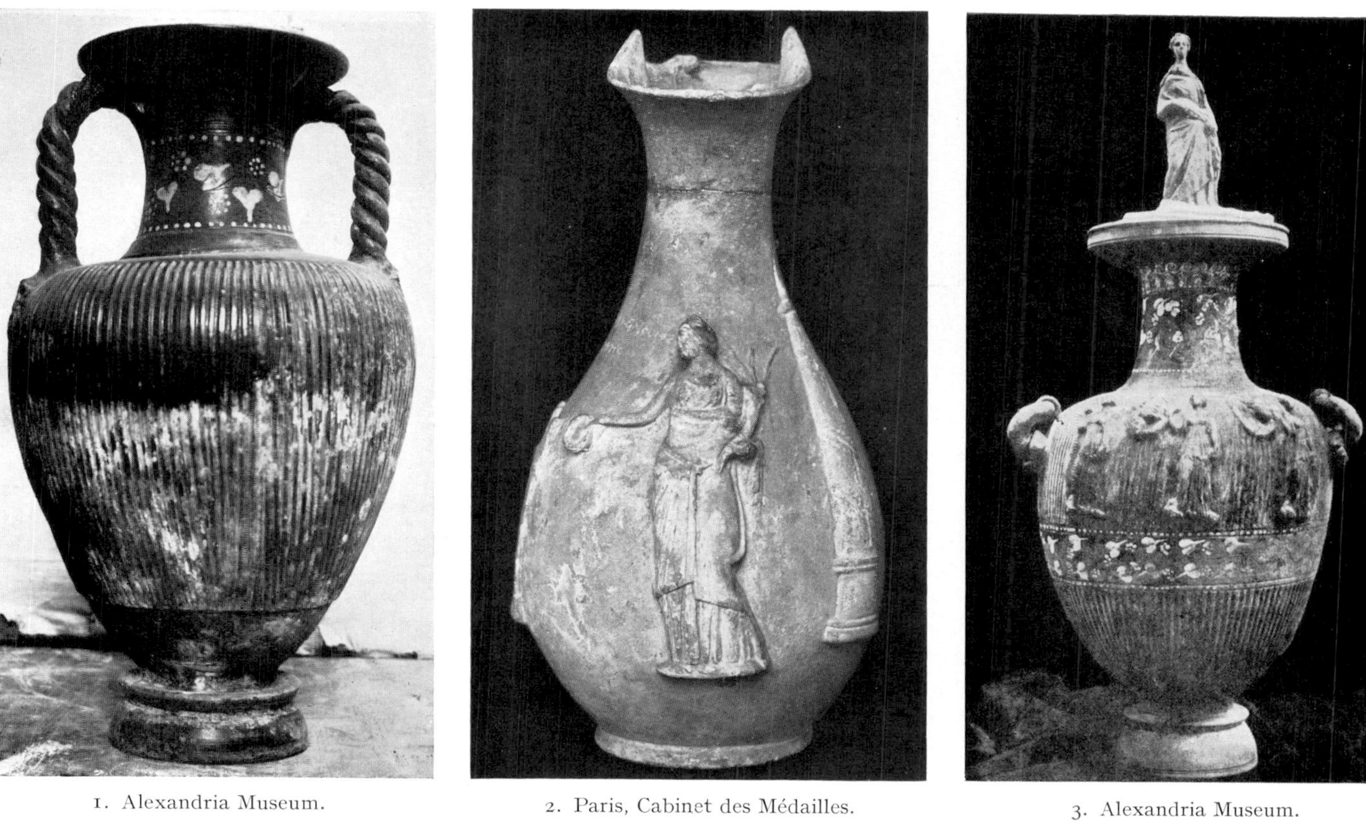

1. Alexandria Museum.

2. Paris, Cabinet des Médailles.

3. Alexandria Museum.

EARLY HELLENISTIC POTTERY MADE IN EGYPT

PLATE XLII

1. New York, Metropolitan Museum of Art.

2. Alexandria Museum.

3. Alexandria Museum.

4. Alexandria Museum.

EARLY HELLENISTIC POTTERY MADE IN EGYPT

PLATE XLII

1. Blue-glazed faience bottle almost intact (the upper part of the neck is missing) adorned with six decorated zones or friezes with figures and ornaments in bluish-green. On the neck are seen, in metopes formed by clusters of papyrus stalks, human figures with pendent abdomens and heavy breasts, probably the Nile god. The next zone containing figures shows birds (not aquatic) and fish, and between them flowers and fruit. The most interesting zone is the lower one, in which real and fantastic animals are represented: a griffin facing a hare and to the left a goat with lowered horns, a lioness(?), a hyena(?), perhaps an antelope, and finally a lion, which completes the circle. The two friezes described above should be compared with the fauna and flora of the mosaic of Palestrina (pl. XXXVIII) and with the animal frieze of the paintings in the grave of Marissa (pl. LVIII). H. 0·155. I have to thank Prof. L. Bull for a detailed description of the bottle which I have used extensively above. Photograph supplied by the authorities of the Metropolitan Museum of Art, New York.

2. Blue-glazed faience bottle of about the same shape as No. 1, intact, with mixed plastic and painted decoration. To the former belong the three appliqué heads of Bes and a complete figure of the same god standing between the shoulder and the mouth; to the latter the decoration of the zones of the body of the bottle—a mixture of Greek and Egyptian elements; note the curious griffins in metopes facing each other. E. Breccia, *Alexandrea ad Aegyptum*, 1922, p. 271, fig. 181. Reproduced from a coloured drawing.

3. Funeral amphora of the so-called Hadra type with decoration in black: running Pegasus between two columns. The figure of Pegasus is the symbol of the apotheosis. There are similar vases with the same decoration in the Metropolitan Museum. Photograph supplied by the authorities of the Alexandria Museum.

R. Pagenstecher, *A.J.A.* xiii (1909), p. 402; id., *Bull. Soc. Arch. Alex.* xiv (N.S. iii, 3) (1912), pls. XV–XVI; F. Cumont, *Bull. Soc. Arch. Alex.* xx (N.S. v. 3) (1924), pp. 193 ff., pl. XXIV, cf. Ch. Picard, ibid. xxxii (N.S. x. 1), pp. 3 ff.

4. Funeral amphora of the same Hadra type but with different decoration: polychrome on white ground. Garlands are painted above and a cuirass and Macedonian round shield below. R. Pagenstecher, *Gr.-Aeg. Samml., E. von Sieglin*, ii. 3 (1913), p. 49f., fig. 56, cf. 55 a–b. Photograph supplied by the authorities of the Alexandria Museum.

The two classes of Alexandrian vases, most typical of Ptolemaic Egypt, illustrated on this plate (cf. pl. XLI), cannot be discussed here. See pp. 367 ff. and n. 163. Cf. below, Ch. VIII and C. W. Lunsingh Scheurleer, *Griekesche Ceramiek*, 1936, pp. 168 ff., figs. 161–2 (Faience), and pp. 146 ff. (Hadra). It is interesting to see how the ancient faience ware of Egypt was adapted to the requirements of the new customers of the Egyptian potters. Most of the faience vases of the types illustrated above belong to the third century B.C. As regards the Hadra vases they may be divided into two classes: the earlier, with designs mostly of ornamental and symbolical character in black on yellowish ground (late fourth and early third century B.C.), and the later, with polychrome decoration of more diversified character on white ground. The Hadra urns were used to hold the ashes of Greek residents in Alexandria, chiefly soldiers of the Ptolemaic army, and of θεωροί (sacred envoys) who came to Alexandria from abroad, as we learn from the inscriptions on the urns, which contain the names of the deceased and the dates of the burial. Hundreds of Hadra urns have been found in the Ptolemaic necropoleis of Alexandria and a few in the Ptolemaic dominions and in places where Ptolemaic influence was strong, and are now preserved in various museums of Egypt, Europe, and America. They yield important information on the religion and life of the Greek population of early Ptolemaic Egypt. No full collection of them exists.

were exported (especially to the Egyptian dominions and to Italy). I cannot enter into details, and some points are still controversial. But there is no doubt that Alexandrians buried the ashes of their dead in special painted *hydriae*, known as Hadra vases, made in Alexandria, perhaps in partial imitation of certain kinds of Boeotian and Apulian pottery. It is likewise probable that it was Alexandria that took up a special type of relief pottery, produced in continental Greece and known as 'Megarian bowls', Egyptianized it, and contributed to its enormous success not only in Alexandria and Egypt in general, but also in almost all Greek centres outside Egypt. It must, however, be noted that very few Megarian bowls have been found in Alexandria or in other urban settlements in Egypt (for instance Canopus), especially specimens of early date, most of them being late and perhaps imported. The whole question of Megarian bowls needs careful investigation. The same is true of the portable ovens and incense-burners with relief decoration. Their history is little known. They may have originated in South Italy, but may have been remodelled in Alexandria and have spread from there over the whole Hellenistic world. In imitation of metal ware a special type of pottery widely distributed over the country, known as 'relief vases with light background', was manufactured in the rural districts of Egypt for the use of the Greek and hellenized population. Finally, it was Alexandria that modified the ancient faience of Egypt (including beads and scarabs), adapted it to the Greek taste, and started a large and very successful production of it. A curious example of this pottery is seen in the typically Alexandrian *oinochoai* bearing the names of queens and kings (Arsinoe, wife of Philadelphus, Berenice wife of Euergetes I, and Philopator).[163]

Glass. Glass had been from ancient times a speciality of Egyptian industry. The somewhat fossilized and old-fashioned craft received new life in the Hellenistic period. A new kind of glass vases, imperfectly known from some specimens found in South Russia in graves of the second and first centuries B.C., which were either cast in moulds and polished or hewn out of solid blocks of cast glass in imitation of metal ware (some of them mounted in bronze or in gold inset with precious stones), may have been first made in Egypt, perhaps some time in the third or early second century, and later imitated in the East. The specimens of this type of glass found in Russia recall certain votive offerings in the temples of Delos.[164]

Various glass vases of somewhat different make—bowls, cups, and dishes, all with gold ornaments—are certainly of Alexandrian origin. The ornaments of these vessels are of thin gold pasted on a background of coloured or uncoloured glass, and sometimes covered with a layer of colourless transparent glass. The best bowls of this type are close reproductions of Megarian bowls or of their metal prototypes. Beautiful specimens of this style and technique have been found in Palestine and in South Italy. Some fine fragments, however, have been found in Egypt and testify to the Alexandrian origin of the class. All students now agree in assigning this type of glass vessels to the early and late Hellenistic period. They disappear from the market in the early Roman Empire, to reappear in large quantities in the late Roman Empire (fourth and following centuries after Christ).[165] It was probably the invention of blown glass that ousted the glass vases with gold ornaments; they were replaced by painted glass vases.[166]

Along with the glass vases above described Egypt produced large quantities of glass ware of what is known as the *millefiori* technique, which had been a speciality of Egypt at least since the time of the New Kingdom. Beads of this kind were exported as far as China and gave rise there to a local production of similar beads. Pieces of *millefiori* glass were commonly used as substitutes for precious stones in the manufacture of jewels. Square plaques of the same technique, mostly with floral ornaments, were made to adorn the walls and ceilings of public buildings and private houses, pieces of furniture, and other wooden articles. All these hellenized products of ancient Egyptian glass-craft had a very long life, and were in great demand throughout the Roman Empire in the first three centuries of its existence. But most of those found in ruins of cities and in tombs all over the civilized world are local, especially south Italian, imitations of the original Egyptian ware.

All that we know of glass in Egypt we learn from some

PLATE XLIII

1. The beautiful glass amphora from Olbia is a unique specimen of early Hellenistic glass (about 200 B.C.). It is described in note 164. Photograph supplied by the authorities of the Staatliche Museen, Berlin.

2, 3. The gold glass bowl of the British Museum (one of two found at Canosa in Apulia) is one of the best specimens of early Alexandrian gold glass. It is mentioned in note 165. H. 0·140, diam. 0·195. In shape and decoration it is similar to the contemporary Megarian and faience bowls. There is not the slightest doubt that the bowl must be assigned to the third century B.C., and not to Roman times. Photograph and drawing supplied by the authorities of the British Museum.

Published by O. M. Dalton, *Arch. Journ.* lviii (1901), p. 247, no. 23, pl. v, cf. W. Deonna, *Rev. É.A.* xxvii (1925), pp. 15 ff.; and P. Wuilleumier, *Le Trésor de Tarente,* 1930, p. 30, pl. x, 5.

4. Sherd (0·07 × 0·08) of a bowl (diam. of the entire bowl 0·133). The bowl was decorated with a garland of vine in gold and berries in purple between two layers of glass. *Bull. Metr. Mus. of Art,* xx (1925), p. 183. On this sherd of the late (?) Hellenistic period, which attests the gradual transition from gold glass to painted glass, see below, Ch. VI, n. 198. Drawing supplied by the authorities of the Metropolitan Museum of Art, New York.

1. Berlin, Staatliche Museen.

2. London, British Museum.

3. London, British Museum.

4. New York, Metropolitan Museum of Art.

HELLENISTIC GLASS MADE IN THE PTOLEMAIC EMPIRE

1. Reggio, Calabria, Museum.

2. Moscow, Archaeological Museum (formerly coll. Goleniščev).

HELLENISTIC GLASS MADE IN THE PTOLEMAIC EMPIRE

PLATE XLIV

1. Gold glass dish found at Trasilico in Calabria. In a frame of three rows of ornaments two hunting-scenes are represented. A Macedonian horseman, dressed in chiton and high shoes and crowned, riding a spirited horse, is aiming his long lance at a leopard which is moving away but is turning its head towards the rider ready to attack him. To the right a tree, in the air a flying bird, probably an eagle (symbol of victory?). Below, a crowned young boy seated near a tree on a tree-trunk(?) is shooting an arrow at two antelopes or gazelles pursued by a dog (or perhaps a hare, in flight like the antelopes). The style and the composition of the two scenes are surprisingly similar to those of the painting in the Ptolemaic grave of Marissa (below, pl. LVIII). There is little doubt that both were made by artists of Alexandria or trained in Alexandria. For bibliography n. 165. About 200 B.C.(?). Photograph supplied by Alinari.

2. The sherd from the Moscow Museum certainly belonged to a dish similar in shape to that described above. The ornaments are the same, cf. the preceding plate nos. 2, 3, and B. Pharmakovsky, *Bull. Comm. Imp. Arch.* xiii (1906), p. 181, fig. 133 (sherd of a bowl or dish from Olbia in South Russia). On the bottom of the dish is represented a Greco-Egyptian vaulted temple or *aedicula*, the flat vault supported by papyrus-columns. In the back wall the usual niche; before the niche an altar or *thymiaterion*. Near the temple a column with the figure of a hawk on the top, a base supporting the statue of a sphinx, a horned altar, and a tree. Cf. the little temple of the mosaic of Palestrina, above, pl. XXXVIII. I have no doubt that the sherd must be assigned to the Ptolemaic period. I published this specimen of gold glass in my paper 'Die hellenistisch-römische Architekturlandschaft', *Röm. Mitt.* xxvi (1911), p. 63, fig. 38, cf. W. Weber, 'Ein Hermes-Tempel des Kaisers Marcus', *Sitzb. Heidelb. Akad.*, Phil.-hist. Kl., 1910, 7, p. 27, fig. 6. Cf. n. 165 to this chapter. Drawing made from a photograph supplied by the authorities of the Moscow Museum.

literary texts and from archaeological finds. The papyri are silent on the subject. Even in the correspondence of Zenon there is no mention of glass. It is therefore probable that it was a luxury, very little used in Egypt. It was produced chiefly in Alexandria for export, as a kind of expensive curiosity. In Egypt itself rich people apparently preferred metal ware.[167]

Metal industry. The metal industry, especially the production of gold, silver, and bronze plate, had flourished in Pharaonic Egypt. There is not the slightest doubt that Hellenistic Egypt inherited and carried on the splendid traditions of these earlier times. There is much evidence of this, especially in the copious finds of gold and silver plate, cult utensils and jewels of the early third century B.C. made in Egypt. I may quote some examples without aiming at completeness. The richest of these, dated with precision by coins of Soter and of the early years of Philadelphus, was made in 1905 in the ruins of a temple at Toukh el Qarmous in the northern Delta. It consisted of a beautiful set of gold and silver plate, ritual objects and jewellery, of local make and of Greek, Egyptian, and Greco-Persian style. Similar, though earlier, is the find at Mendes.[168]

A little later than the find at Toukh el Qarmous are the interesting plaster casts made from metal vases and other metal objects found recently at Mit-Rahineh. The majority of them are rightly assigned to the third century B.C. They certainly belonged originally to large and well-furnished metal shops at Memphis. Many moulds and models (of plaster, clay, and stone) for various metal objects were and still are frequently found in Egypt (I may mention for example the beautiful stone models for helmets of the third century B.C. discovered at Memphis). The largest number of those belonging to the Hellenistic period come from workshops of Memphis. Together with the plaster casts they are invaluable for students of ancient art and ancient technique. The abundant discoveries made at Memphis testify to the importance of this city as a centre of metal-ware production. Another important centre was Hermupolis. The frequent finds of beautiful silver plate here (of late Hellenistic and early Roman times) attest the existence of a flourishing metal industry which probably began earlier than the late Hellenistic period.[169]

The popularity of metal ware in Egypt in the period under review is further illustrated by various imitations of metal plate in clay. I may remind the reader of the above-mentioned Megarian bowls and their faience counterparts with Greco-Egyptian vegetal decoration in relief (a mixture of acanthus and nymphaea leaves). They are certainly reproductions in clay of metal vases of the same shape and decoration made in Egypt. Such metal bowls have occasionally been found in Egypt, and one of Egyptian make was excavated recently in Syria at Ras Shamra.[170] Casts of vases of similar shape and with similar ornamentation are among those found at Mit-Rahineh, and the same type of decoration may be observed on the silver lid of a *pyxis* from Tarentum and on several bowls from Cività Castellana, which probably belong to the third century B.C., and may be regarded as imported from Egypt. Several other types of pottery made in Egypt certainly go back to metal originals.[171]

I may further draw attention to the fact that metal vases with *niello* decoration of Hellenistic and Roman date, some of them partly adorned with Greco-Egyptian figures and designs, testify to the revival of this old Egyptian technique in the Hellenistic period. This ware, like the other types of metal plate, was at least in the later period exported from Egypt. The best specimens have been found at Egyed in Hungary.[172]

Great interest attaches to some bronze models of toilet articles, mostly hairpins with elaborate tops in the form of figures or other ornaments, found recently at Galjub near Cairo, and now in the Pelizaeus Museum. These bronze models served as samples in the shop of a gold- and silversmith, and were reproduced in gold or silver as ordered by his customers. A business of this kind was carried on, for example, in the workshop of Mystharion in Alexandria in early Roman times. The objects found at Galjub are assigned in the work describing them to the second century B.C.[173]

The importance and the influence of Alexandrian metal work in the Hellenistic period may be gathered from these few examples. Though specimens of Hellenistic silver and bronze plate, and of its later derivatives are not very numerous, a careful analysis of them will certainly lead us to assign to Alexandria several types of them.

We must not, however, exaggerate the part played by Alexandria. The time is past when all the products of Hellenistic toreutic art were attributed *en bloc* to that city. Etruria, Campania, Sicily, Tarentum, Corinth, Chalcis, Delos, and Athens were famous centres of metallurgy in the classical period, and there is no reason to suppose that all of them ceased working in Hellenistic times. Their traditions were taken over, not only by Alexandria, but also a little later by Pergamon, which was soon to enter into competition with its older rivals. In the East—in Babylonia, Assyria, Phoenicia, Armenia, and Iran—the toreutic art was as old and as flourishing as in Egypt. There is no doubt that the gold and silver vases and other objects inlaid with precious stones which I have mentioned above (ch. III) were made also by artists who resided not only in Egypt, but also and perhaps chiefly in the Seleucid Empire, and that Seleucid Syria was another rival of Ptolemaic Alexandria in this field. In his famous *pompe* Antiochus IV displayed to the people of Antioch a profusion of gold and silver plate, most of it undoubtedly made within his empire.[174]

Yet the evidence taken all together shows that the Alexandrian production of gold, silver, and bronze plate was very large. Without doubt it amply covered the needs of the population of Egypt, and some of it was exported. To realize the number and the splendour of the pieces of gold and silver work in the possession of the Ptolemies, most of them, it must be supposed, of local workmanship, one should read Callixeinus' description of the *pompe* and banquet organized by Philadelphus in the early days of his reign. Hundreds if not thousands of gold and silver vessels and other objects were displayed at these gorgeous functions. No less important than the description of Callixeinus is the account which Ps.-Aristeas gives of the gifts of expensive plate that Philadelphus presented to the temple of Jerusalem. Like so many things in this letter, the description is based on observations, though probably no such gift was ever sent to Jerusalem.[175]

Textile industry. We know very little of the products of the textile industry in Hellenistic Egypt. No woollen or linen materials of any artistic value have hitherto been found in Egyptian graves of the Hellenistic period. The famous 'Coptic' stuffs found in such quantities in Egypt are all of a much later date, although in technique and decoration they may go back to Hellenistic times. But numerous papyri which speak of the textile industry in Egypt, especially a large group of early Ptolemaic documents, bear eloquent testimony to its flourishing condition at that time. Linen fabrics, under the control

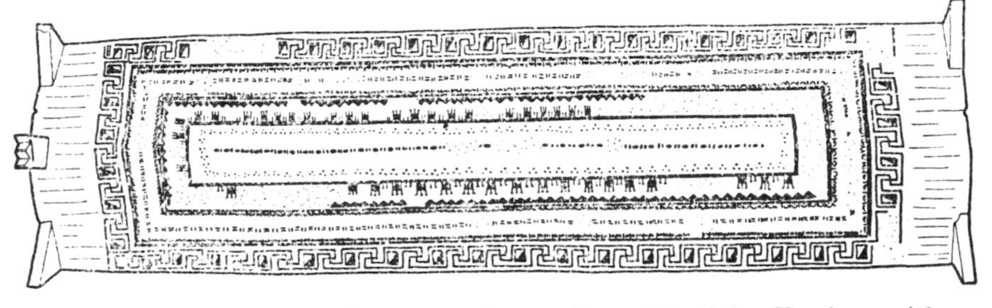

FIG. 2. Lid of a wooden sarcophagus from Magdola, Fayûm, with painting representing a rug. Cairo Museum.

and supervision of the government, were produced in large quantities and of fine quality: fine *byssos*, garments embroidered or with inwoven ornaments, and all sorts of plain materials are frequently mentioned in the papyri. Large quantities of linen tissues and garments were made to the order and for the use of the king. Since flax was scarce in the other parts of the Greek world and Egypt was famous for its linen, there is no doubt that part of the linen goods in the king's possession was sold to foreign merchants. The remainder and all that was made by the weavers on their own account supplied the home demand. The manufacture of woollens was not a speciality of Egypt in ancient times, for the Egyptians as a rule used linen materials. In the Ptolemaic period, as I have stated above, efforts were made to start a woollen industry on a large scale under the supervision and with the protection of the government. I mentioned that Milesian, Euboean, and Arabian sheep were imported and bred in Egypt. This was done without doubt to provide the industry with better raw material than the wool of Egyptian sheep. Egyptian wool was protected by compensatory tariffs against the competition of

PLATE XLV

1. One of the plaster casts found at Mit-Rahineh (Memphis), taken from an *emblema* of a patera or dish, probably in silver. In the centre, bust of Athena in front view wearing a Corinthian helmet with three crests; the bust is surrounded by two circles, the first showing palmettes and lotus buds, the other a row of ducks flapping their wings. From this cast Herr Blume, a goldsmith of Hildesheim, has made a reproduction in silver and restored the whole of the patera with the help of another ancient plaster cast from Mit-Rahineh taken from handles of a similar patera (Pelizaeus-Museum, Inv. 1139). Diam. 0·15. O. Rubensohn, *Hellenistisches Silbergerät in antiken Gipsabgüssen*, 1911, pp. 13 ff., nos. 1 and 1a; G. Roeder and A. Ippel, *Die Denkmäler des Pelizaeus-Museums zu Hildesheim*, 1921, p. 140, no. 1109, figs. 51 (the ancient plaster cast) and 52 (modern restoration), cf. n. 169 to this chapter and description of pl. XLVII. Stylistic considerations and several casts showing portraits of various members of the ruling house (Inv. nos. 1119, 1120, 1121, 1147) beginning with Soter (*Die Denkmäler*, &c., p. 143, figs. 56—ancient cast, and 57—modern reproduction in metal, cf. the description of pl. II) make it certain that the majority of the casts must be assigned to the early Ptolemaic period. Note the mixture of Greek and native motifs (the flapping ducks) in the ornamentation of the dish. Photograph supplied by the authorities of the Pelizaeus-Museum, Hildesheim.

2, 3. Silver armlets said to be from Balamun (Diospolis Inferior) in the Delta. One has the form of coiling snakes, and the other (one of a pair) consists of wire wound in a serpentine design ending in snake and uraeus heads and adorned with many rings. Unpublished. Not dated, but probably late Hellenistic. The snake bracelets are common in Greek art. The peculiar shape and ornamentation of the second bracelet finds parallels both in Mesopotamia and in Egypt (and also in early Celtic art); see for Egypt B. Segall, *Museum Benaki, Katalog der Goldschmied-Arbeiten*, 1938, no. 180, pl. 39, pp. 118 ff. Cf., for Ptolemaic toreutics in general, the interesting Ptolemaic silver bottle recently acquired by the M.M.A.: A. Lansing, *Bull. Metr. Mus.* xxxix, 1938, pp. 199 ff. Photographs supplied by the authorities of the Metropolitan Museum of Art, New York.

A few words may be added on the finds of Mit-Rahineh in general. The many plaster casts and stone models of helmets (see pl. XLVII), now for the most part in the Pelizaeus-Museum, but some distributed among other museums (for example the Allard Pierson Museum in Amsterdam and the Museum of Alexandria), were found 'in a continuous set of houses of the type of storehouses in the ruins of Memphis', in all probability houses of the goldsmiths' quarter of the city (we know that in Roman times—and probably earlier also—craftsmen of various kinds lived close to each other in special streets and wards of the Egyptian cities, see the works quoted in Ch. VIII, n. 25). The large number of these houses and of the models found in them shows the importance of metal industry in the life of Memphis and probably of the rest of Egypt in the Ptolemaic period, and gives some idea of the extent of the production of Alexandria. All sorts of metal objects were made at Memphis: plate, jewels, mirrors, weapons, horse trappings, &c. The plaster casts (some of them were hung on the walls of the shops) were probably taken from metal originals, both old and new, and served as models for the craftsmen and as specimens for the customers.

1. Hildesheim, Pelizaeus-Museum.

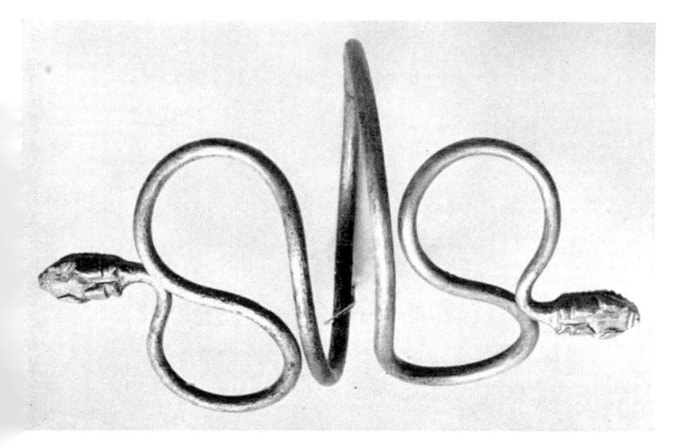

2. New York, Metropolitan Museum of Art.

3. New York, Metropolitan Museum of Art.

TOREUTIC ARTISTS AND JEWELLERS IN PTOLEMAIC EGYPT

1. Alexandria, restoration of the funeral couch in tomb no. 3 of the Necropolis of Mustafa Pasha

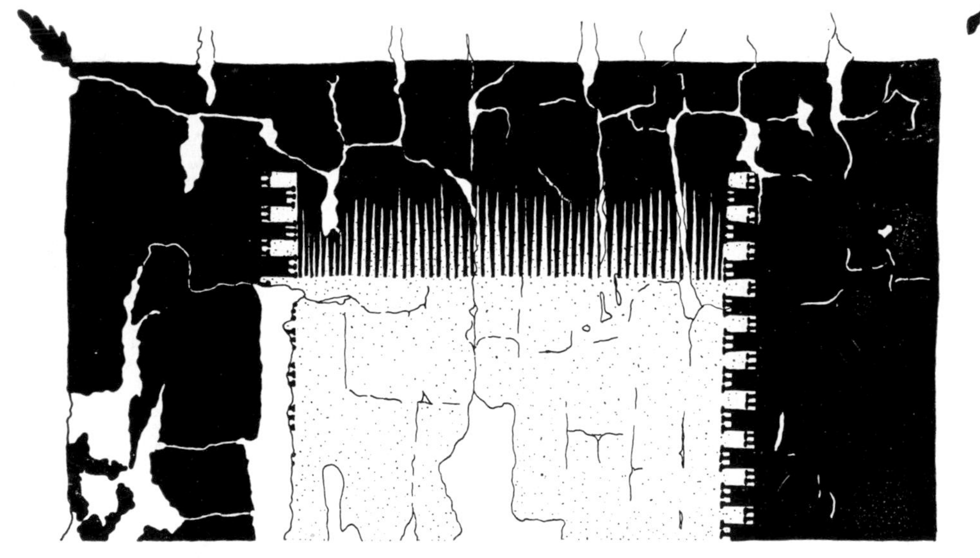

2. Taman peninsula, South Russia, rug painted on the ceiling of the grave-chamber of the tumulus Vassjurinskaja Gora

TEXTILE INDUSTRY IN PTOLEMAIC EGYPT

PLATE XLVI

1. An excellent idea of the achievements of the textile industry of Ptolemaic times in Egypt may be derived from the carved and painted funeral couches commonly found in many hypogaea of the various necropoleis of this period at Alexandria. They have been recently studied in the light of parallel material from other parts of the Hellenistic world by A. Adriani, *Annuaire du Musée Gréco-Romain* (1933–4 and 1934–5), 'La nécropole de Moustafa Pacha', 1936, pp. 101 ff. I give here a brief description of two of them, both in the recently discovered graves of Mustafa Pasha, one more elaborate, the other plainer but elegant. For all details the reader is referred to the description and study by A. Adriani. I am not concerned with the form and ornamentation of the wooden couches reproduced in the graves, marvels of the carpenter's craft, inlaid with metals, ivory, and precious wood (for which see the references in A. Adriani, loc. cit., p. 101, n. 1): I confine myself to the pillows, mattresses, and hangings. In grave no. 2 (Adriani, loc. cit., pl. D, in colour) there are three pillows at each end of the couch, a thick stiff mattress, and a rich hanging. The stuffs used for the pillows and the mattress are of purple colour with broad yellow and narrow blue stripes. On some sections of the mattress figures of women are inwoven, presumably in gold. Even more refined is the hanging, with its blue centre and red borders adorned with tassels and inwoven golden ornaments and figures. Similar is the couch in grave no. 3 (here reproduced; Adriani, loc. cit., pl. XXXIII) with its two pillows at each end, a fine mattress, and a hanging without tassels but with a set of human figures inwoven in its lower border, probably representing a mythological subject. Cf. pp. 376 ff. and nn. 177 and 179; and on the mosaics reproducing rugs, ibid. and n. 178.

2. Section of the rug painted on the barrel-vault of the grave-chamber of the Kurgan Vassyurinskaja Gora in the Taman peninsula (South Russia). The centre of the rug is blue, the border with its tassels on the outer side and fringes on the inner side is of deep red colour. The grave must be assigned to the end of the fourth century B.C. Note the far-reaching similarities of this painted rug and its purely textile ornamentation with the Alexandrian, Delian, and Pergamene mosaics of the Hellenistic period (pls. XXXV, LXXIV, and LXXXIX) and with the hangings of the couches described above. Reproduced in colour and discussed at length by myself, *Ancient decorative Painting in the South of Russia*, 1914, pp. 30 ff. and pl. XV; cf. my brief remarks in *J.H.S.* xxxix (1919), p. 148.

foreign wool. There is evidence that there were workshops for the manufacture of woollen cloth on the estate of Apollonius, and that these were regarded as an innovation. All this was done in order to provide the Greek population of Egypt with woollen materials without recourse to importation, and it is certain that Egyptian woollen fabrics very soon found customers in foreign countries.[176]

Since both linen and woollen fabrics were intended partly for export, partly for the use of the Greek population of the country, the Egyptian weavers had to change their style of production and to adapt themselves to the new requirements. This they did with great success, witness the mattresses, pillows, and rugs that are often represented on funeral couches in Alexandrian painted tombs of the third and second centuries B.C., and on the lids of wooden sarcophagi of the same period. The ornaments and patterns in these representations are Greek, not Egyptian, and their originals were certainly not imported from abroad.[177] We find likewise Greek style and Greek ornaments in certain early floor mosaics of Alexandria, which certainly reproduced woollen rugs.[178] And finally Callixeinus' description of the banqueting tent of Philadelphus and of the floating villa of Philopator, which were both of them gorgeously decorated with coloured and ornamental rugs, testifies to the Greek character of the rugs and to their local manufacture (though some rugs—no doubt by way of contrast—are described as Persian and Phoenician).[179]

Sculpture. With the products of industry and the applied arts may be classed those of sculpture, particularly decorative and sepulchral sculpture (grave *stelae* and statues). Here again the earliest products were made of Attic marble by Athenian artists, either at Athens or more probably at Alexandria, but at a very early date local sculptors created their own (purely Greek) style and supplied the needs of the Greek population of Alexandria and the 'country' (χώρα). The Alexandrian school of sculptors excelled particularly in portrait sculpture. Alongside of them native artists continued to produce for their temples, shrines, and tombs in their old-fashioned style. In some few cases, however, a mixture of the two styles may be noticed.[180]

6. Commerce, Coinage, and Banking

The skilful commercial policy of the first Ptolemies, by which they systematically developed Egypt's trade relations, contributed to their great success in reorganizing Egyptian agriculture and industry, and added to their wealth. Their trade policy was dictated by considerations similar to those which directed their internal policy, their principal object being to strengthen and consolidate their position in Egypt and to acquire hegemony, or at least as great an influence as possible, in the civilized world. I need hardly repeat that the basis of Ptolemaic strength and influence was their economic prosperity, which enabled them to maintain a strong and well-organized army and navy, and to carry on a successful foreign policy. This last rested to a large extent on subsidies in money and grain granted to their supporters in the Mediterranean world.[181]

TRADE WITH THE DOMINIONS

Egypt was a very rich country, and the Ptolemies by their efforts made her almost self-sufficing. But her self-sufficiency was not complete. I have already pointed out that Egypt was poor in respect of certain fundamental needs of the army and navy—metals, horses and elephants, and good timber. The four basic metals—iron, copper, silver, and gold—had to be imported, at least in part. By their foreign policy, though this was not directed exclusively by economic considerations, the Ptolemies succeeded in satisfying some of their requirements. These were supplied by their most important foreign dominions and dependencies: Cyprus furnished copper; Syria, Cilicia, Lycia, and again Cyprus, furnished timber and some silver; Cyrenaica, horses; Nubia, a certain quantity of gold; Meroe, some iron (inferior in quality) and gold, the latter imported probably from Abyssinia; while eastern Africa, especially Somaliland, supplied elephants. A few words may be said first of all with regard to Nubia, Meroe, and Central Africa.

Gold. Gold was mined for Egypt in two regions: in the Nubian desert south of Egypt, and in the Eastern desert between the roads which led from Coptos and Apollinopolis to Berenice on the Red Sea. The Nubian mines are known to us from a wonderful description of them by Agatharchides in the second century B.C.* They were situated east of Dakke in Wadi Alaki. The discovery of some inscriptions in this place, and references to it in Egyptian texts, show that the Nubian mines had been worked for a very long time before they came into the hands of the Ptolemies. The description of Agatharchides, on the other hand, shows the difficulties under which the exploitation of these mines was carried on in the waterless and torrid desert. The conditions were appalling and indeed fatal to the miners—criminals and prisoners of war. The problem of labour for these mines was evidently one of great difficulty. Moreover, they lay practically outside Egypt and their retention called for a considerable military effort on the part of the Ptolemies. It was not only labour that was required: a strong detachment of soldiers was needed to maintain discipline among the miners and guard the mines from attack by robbers and enemies. How rich the mines were is hard to say. As they had been worked for hundreds of years, their yield, even with a somewhat more advanced technique, cannot have been very great. The interest, however, shown in them by Agatharchides and the great efforts made by the Ptolemies to keep them working show that they were the most important gold mines under Ptolemaic control. It is highly probable therefore that the mines of the Egyptian eastern desert, known from modern archaeological exploration, those of Barramîja, Dunkash, and Fawakhir, were not of very great importance. Hence I very much doubt whether the yield of the gold mines controlled by the Ptolemies covered their requirements in gold. The balance had to be supplied from other sources.

It was not merely the necessity of protecting the gold mines that led the early Ptolemies to strive to retain Nubia and to extend their influence to Meroe. They probably had important commercial interests in Meroe: archaeological exploration has shown that some iron was mined there and that the Meroites had some gold (imported from Abyssinia?). They can hardly have used it all locally. Part of it was probably exported to Egypt, though we have no direct information on this point.

* Agath. *De mar. Er.*, Phot. 23–9, and Diod. 23–9 (*G.G.M.* I, pp. 122 ff.), cf. Diod. III, 12–17.

Other merchandise may have come to Egypt through Meroe from Central Africa: ivory, ostrich feathers, ostrich eggs, and some slaves.

In the light of these considerations we may better understand the relations of the two first Ptolemies with Nubia and Meroe. The first information about Meroe was obtained for Soter, or for Philadelphus in the early years of his reign, by Philon.* Thereafter Philadelphus first intimidated the Nubians by marching into their territory† and established his rule over their gold mines, and he subsequently kept Meroe under close observation by a succession of expeditions which went to Meroe and beyond.‡ These expeditions and similar explorations by hunting parties § were certainly not carried out for purely scientific ends. Their object was doubtless at the same time commercial and diplomatic, and they kept Meroe open to Ptolemaic influence. The main purposes, in my opinion, of these relations with Meroe, besides the protection of Egypt's southern frontier, were to safeguard the gold mines of Nubia, to reserve the Meroitic supply of iron and gold for Egypt, and to protect the hunting parties that visited the country regularly under Philadelphus.[182]

Elephants. No less valuable to the Ptolemies than the gold and iron of Nubia were the elephants of eastern Africa. It must be remembered that the use of elephants was the culmination of military technique. The rivals of the Ptolemies, Seleucus and his descendants, had them in abundance and of the highest quality, obtaining them from India. The Ptolemies could not submit to remain inferior in this respect. The reputation of war-elephants among military experts of the day was very high and had not been diminished by their failure in Pyrrhus' expedition, for their sensational success when used against the Celts had compensated for their failure in Italy. We have evidence of this in the confidence shown in these animals by so great a general as Hannibal. Now elephants were numerous in Africa, and there appeared to be no reason why expert trainers imported from India should not tame and train the fierce beasts of Africa. Such were probably the

* Plin. *N.H.* xxxvii. 108.
† Diod. i. 37. 5.
‡ Plin. *N.H.* vi. 183.
§ Agath. *De mar. Er.*; Diod. 78.

considerations that led Philadelphus to undertake the formation of a contingent of African elephants.

It would be out of place to repeat here the story of his venture. It is enough to say that he carefully explored the west coast of the Red Sea and the coast of Somaliland and established a number of stations for hunting elephants, of harbours for shipping them, and of other harbours where they could be landed in Egyptian territory. The two chief harbours on the Egyptian coast were Philotera and Berenice, which were connected with the Nile by caravan roads; these were well organized, well guarded, and well supplied with water. They have been carefully explored by modern travellers and a recently discovered document illustrates the movement of the caravans along these roads and their organization in the time of Philopator. The caravans consisted of heavy carts carrying among other things official correspondence with the chiefs of the elephant-hunting expeditions. To the two harbours mentioned above a third, Myos Hormos, farther north, was soon added. The elephants, when they reached Egypt, were kept, fed, and trained in special parks.[183]

Grain, &c. Besides some gold and silver, some iron, a large supply of copper, horses, and elephants, the Ptolemies could rely upon their dominions for an abundant supply of grain in case of a shortage in Egypt itself: import of grain from Syria and Cyprus is mentioned in the decree of Canopus. We know the fertility of the soil of Syria, Cyprus, and Cyrenaica. In addition Syria produced wine and olive-oil of a high quality, and Lycia and Caria (especially Cnidus) could supply wine and excellent honey, besides other commodities of less importance.

How the trade with the dominions was organized is very little known. Our only source of information—the correspondence of Zenon—relates to Syria and Palestine only, with some side-lights on Asia Minor and Rhodes. Of Cyrenaica and Cyprus we know practically nothing. So far as the evidence goes, we may assume that the trade was in the hands of private merchants. Export of merchandise from Palestine and Syria was in general apparently free, although there were naturally some restrictions. Export duties were in all probability levied, and for some objects of export, for instance slaves, a special export licence was required.

There are, however, some vital points on which we have no information. The first is by what means the Ptolemies secured for themselves the exclusive or preferential import from their provinces of certain essential commodities, such as metals, timber, pitch and tar, horses and the like, and grain when needed. We may assume that corn came from the royal land, and that the mines and forests in the dominions were their property and were exploited by them directly. We may think that they had large horse-studs in Cyrenaica. But this is no more than a guess.

As regards other merchandise, the merchants of the dominions had probably a free hand in their relations with foreign countries. But as regards Egypt they were certainly subject to many restrictions of various kinds. Egypt with its peculiar economic system, with its numerous monopolies of all sorts designed to enforce the consumption of home-produced goods, could not be allowed to maintain free trade relations even with the dominions of the Ptolemies. The Ptolemies fenced themselves off effectively from their own dominions by customs barriers. From the νόμος ἐλαικῆς and from some documents of Zenon's correspondence we know well how the import of olive-oil from Syria to Alexandria and Pelusium was subjected to high customs duties and other taxes, with the object apparently of safeguarding the interests of the oil monopoly of the Ptolemies. Without entering into details which have been carefully studied by myself and others and which strikingly illustrate the policy of the Ptolemies in this respect, I must point out that in the matter of customs duties distinctions were made between the products of the Ptolemaic dominions and those of foreign cities and kingdoms. Thus in the oil law of Philadelphus 'Syrian' and 'foreign' oil (Σύρον and ξενικὸν ἔλαιον) are distinguished (*R.L.* 52, 25 ff.). But our information on this point is very vague. We do not know exactly what is meant by ξενικόν as opposed to Σύρον. One thing is very probable. The Ptolemies discouraged their subjects from buying goods from the dominions in order to assure a steady and undisturbed market for the goods that they themselves produced in Egypt.[184]

FOREIGN TRADE

What I have said of the exchange of goods between Egypt and the foreign dominions of the Ptolemies shows that with the help of the dominions they were, as regards all vital commodities, almost independent of foreign imports. There remained, however, some urgent requirements which could not be supplied by imports from the provinces. The supply of gold was probably not sufficient for the needs of the Ptolemies, they had little silver within their empire, no tin, and hardly any iron. These commodities had to be imported from abroad and in large quantities. Silver and gold were required for the Ptolemaic coinage and for payments which the kings had to make in Egypt and abroad, and without large quantities of tin and iron the needs of the army and of agriculture and industry in Egypt and the empire could not be supplied. This, together with the natural desire of the Ptolemies to have at their disposal a large reserve, accounts for their efforts to develop their commercial relations with foreign countries.

Egypt had commercial relations with foreign countries in three directions: on an important scale with eastern Africa, Arabia, and India, and not less so with the Aegean Sea and the Euxine; while, thirdly, her trade with the West and North-west was gaining steadily in volume.

The South and East. Her trade relations with the South and East were of a peculiar character. She needed southern merchandise, it is true, for consumption within her own territory, in her temples, in the king's household, and among the population at large. But the Ptolemies desired to attract goods from the South mainly for the purpose of re-export to the North-east and North-west, partly as merchandise in simple transit, partly in the form of manufactured articles produced in the workshops of Alexandria and Egypt in general. The imports from the South that the Ptolemies encouraged were, as is well known, of a very special character: from Trogodytike and Somaliland ivory, myrrh, frankincense, and cinnamon; from Arabia the same (with the exception of ivory) and in addition nard and balsam, pearls, coral, and gold. Finally India supplied Egypt with ivory, tortoise-shell, pearls, pigments and dyes (especially indigo), rice, and various spices, e.g. pepper, nard, costum, malabathron, some rare woods, various medicinal substances, and cotton and silk.

How to attract these goods to Egypt was a problem of some difficulty. There were two routes by which African, Arabian, and Indian goods were conveyed thither. One—not very extensively used before the time of the Ptolemies—was the sea route along the coasts of Arabia or Africa respectively and up the Red Sea to the Heroonpolite or to the Aelanitic Gulf. The other was the ancient land route from south Arabia along the western coast of Arabia to the country of the Nabataeans and Petra, and thence to Gaza or across the Sinai peninsula to Egypt.

The second route was much more important than the first. In Persian times it was controlled by the Nabataeans, a strong, thrifty, and well-organized Arab tribe. So long as the Ptolemies were not in firm possession of Palestine and Phoenicia, they were dependent on the Nabataeans for their supply of caravan goods. The Nabataeans could direct these, according to their wish and profit, either to Egypt or to some place which was beyond the reach of the Ptolemies. It should be noted that they were also in possession of the Aelanitic Gulf and were daring pirates as well as traders. As soon, however, as the Ptolemies had firmly established themselves in Palestine and Phoenicia, the Nabataeans were at their mercy and had to submit. Philadelphus showed them his strength by sending a naval expedition against them and by founding (probably, the point is disputed) a military and naval station called Berenice in their own Aelanitic Gulf.

In order, however, to have a completely free hand in dealing with the Nabataeans, Philadelphus explored and developed the Red Sea route described above and tried by making it safe to recommend it to the merchants. It was in order to make it safe that the naval expedition was sent against the Nabataeans, and that Berenice was founded on the Aelanitic gulf; that the western shore of Arabia was explored by Ariston for Philadelphus, and perhaps that a Greek harbour city—Ampelone—was founded opposite the great trading centre—El-Ela by name—first of the Minaeans and then of the Lihyanites. In particular it was for this same purpose that the harbours and desert roads constructed for the importation of elephants were adapted to commercial purposes also. The crown was set on this patient and expensive work by the restoration about 275 B.C. of the ancient Egyptian and Persian canal connecting the Heroonpolite gulf with the Nile. The Ptolemaic Suez received the name of the great consort of Philadelphus, Arsinoe.

For a time the new route was certainly used. I have already mentioned the Minaean funeral inscription from the Fayûm, probably of the reign of Philadelphus, which tells the story of a Minaean merchant who at the same time was priest of an Egyptian temple and imported myrrh and calamus for the temple in his own ship in exchange for *byssos*. Another inscription from Redesiyeh in south Egypt was dedicated by a Greek named Zenodotus, son of Glaucus, who returned safely to Egypt from the land of the Sabaeans. By the same sea route embassies were exchanged between the great Asoka of India and Philadelphus.

And yet in early Ptolemaic times this route appears never to have become very popular with the Greek and Arabian merchants. The Red Sea is treacherous and inhospitable and was very little known, while the land route, though expensive, was well organized by powerful Arab tribes both in the South (Minaeans and Sabaeans) and in the North (Lihyanites and Nabataeans). It led to ancient commercial cities in Palestine and Phoenicia, which had established trade connexions and were accustomed to deal with the complicated business of the caravan trade.

It is therefore not surprising that Philadelphus adopted a peaceful policy towards the Nabataeans in place of his former hostility and found a way of regulating satisfactorily his relations with the Phoenician cities as regards Arabian and Indian merchandise. The results were excellent. Zenon's correspondence repeatedly refers to caravan goods bought in Palestine, and occasionally to dealings with the Nabataeans. Moreover, it seems to have been an accepted fact among the contemporaries of Philadelphus that the Ptolemies derived an enormous revenue in gold from the Arabian caravan trade with the help of Phoenician cities.*[185]

* Agath. *De Mar. Er.* 102, probably borrowing from the treatise of Ariston, who has been mentioned above.

While thus the Arabian trade very soon resumed its traditional character Philadelphus certainly succeeded in diverting all the African trade to his new commercial and hunting stations. It is a very interesting suggestion made by W. W. Tarn that the reason why the price of ivory fell on the Delian market between 264 and 250 was that Philadelphus, in competition with the king of Syria, offered for sale large quantities of African ivory.[186]

We have no precise knowledge of the treatment applied to the goods imported into Palestine and Phoenicia and thence into Egypt, or to those which were imported directly into Egypt from Arabia and Africa. Trade in Arabian and Indian goods in Palestine and Phoenicia appears to have been free. I have referred to the dealings of Zenon and other agents of Apollonius in these goods in Palestine and Phoenicia. Of course the goods paid customs duties on entering the territory of Palestine and Syria and probably also on leaving it for export to Egypt. No information is available on the relations between the Syrian and Palestinian merchants in Arabian and Indian goods and foreign states (including perhaps the other dominions of the Ptolemies). We may think that such direct trade was not tolerated and that all the Indian and Arabian goods were supposed to pass through Alexandria before reaching the foreign markets. A new set of customs and harbour duties was paid on the Arabian and Indian goods when they came from Syria and Palestine to the harbours or to the land-frontier of Egypt.

As soon as the merchandise of India, Arabia, and Africa reached the soil of Egypt it had to be delivered to the crown at prices fixed by a special tariff. How the goods thus purchased were afterwards dealt with, we do not know exactly. Our evidence is meagre and ambiguous. Part of them went apparently to the royal storehouses in Alexandria and to the royal workshops. From the storehouses the merchandise was exported, while in the workshops it was transformed into scents, ointments, perfumes, medicines, and so forth. We may suppose that another part was delivered to the temples. The rest may have been reserved for private manufacturers and dealers. In any case there was no free trade in these goods.

PLATE XLVII

1. Small necklace or pectoral of gold inlaid with precious stones, of Egyptian type and workmanship. Made probably for a statuette of a god or goddess. Photograph supplied by the authorities of the Cairo Museum.

2. Two gold bracelets, one with ends shaped as foreparts of sphinxes with wings of Oriental type but coiffure of the Ptolemaic fashion, and the other with a clasp in the form of a knot with a hovering Eros in the hollow of the knot and wavy tendrils overhead. Photograph supplied by the authorities of the Cairo Museum.

3. Beautiful silver drinking-horn of Greco-Iranian workmanship, with the protome of a winged eagle-griffin. Here reproduced, after thorough cleaning by Mr. P. André of Paris, from a photograph supplied by Prof. A. Adriani.

4. Silver bowl similar in shape to the Megarian bowls, but of pure Egyptian style and workmanship. Photograph supplied by the authorities of the Cairo Museum.

The find of Toukh el Qarmous (probably the treasure of a temple which may have been the place of worship of a detachment of the Ptolemaic army encamped on the eastern border of the desert) has never been thoroughly cleaned and published and studied in its entirety. Some pieces have been reproduced and illustrated by C. C. Edgar, *Le Musée Égyptien*, ii (1907), pp. 57 ff. The find—exactly dated by a set of coins of the time of Soter found with the other objects, but never published (see p. 374 and n. 168)—is an excellent illustration of the social and cultural aspect of early Hellenistic Egypt. Products of Egyptian toreutic art and jewellery predominate, accompanied by wonderful jewels of pure Greek style. The best is the knot bracelet so fashionable in the Hellenistic period and of which many examples have been discovered in South Russia, Thessaly, and elsewhere (see B. Segall, *Museum Benaki, Katalog der Goldschmied-Arbeiten*, 1938, pp. 31 ff., pls. 8 ff.). Prominent among the objects, finally, are products of Greco-Iranian art, such as the drinking-horn (no. 3), the torc with Persian griffins' heads (Edgar, pl. XXIII) and the sphinx bracelet (no. 2), the last perhaps a Greco-Egyptian imitation of a Greco-Iranian original. The presence of this element in the find of Toukh el Qarmous has been recently stressed by H. Luschey, *J.D.A.I.* liii (1938), Anz., p. 758. I cannot agree with A. Adriani, *Bull. Soc. Arch. Alex.* xxxiii (N.S. x, 2) (1939), pp. 350 ff., who is inclined to see in the rhyton of Toukh el Qarmous a Greco-Egyptian and not a Greco-Iranian work. Rhyta with animal protomes are known from prehistoric times both in Egypt and Mesopotamia (see my *Animal Style in South Russia and China*, 1929, pl. I, 1, and p. 7 f., and n. 12, overlooked by A. Adriani). In later times they are typical of the Iranian and Greco-Iranian world. I may remind the reader of the splendid rhyton of the Semibratnij tumulus (my *Iranians and Greeks*, pl. XII) of the fifth to fourth centuries B.C., and of the similar rhyton of the Oxus treasure of the fifth century (O. M. Dalton, *The Treasure of the Oxus*, 1926, pl. XXII, no. 178). A glance at these beautiful products of Iranian art and at the rhyton of Toukh el Qarmous shows how similar the three objects are in shape, style, and conception, though the rhyton of Egypt is more hellenized. The same is true of the torc (cf. Dalton, loc. cit., pl. I). Cf. A. U. Pope, *A Survey of Persian Art*, i, 1938, pls. 113 and 114.

1 2

3 4

TOREUTIC ARTISTS AND JEWELLERS IN PTOLEMAIC EGYPT. FIND MADE AT TOUKH EL QARMOUS IN LOWER EGYPT

Cairo Museum.

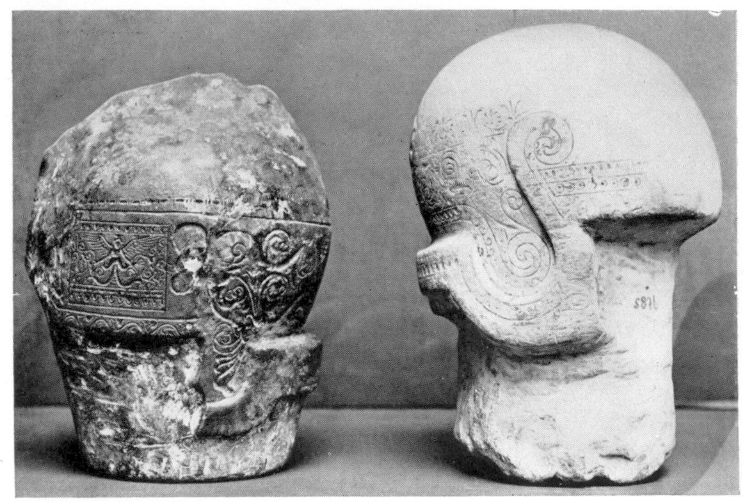

1. Amsterdam, Allard Pierson Museum.

2. Amsterdam, Allard Pierson Museum.

3. Hildesheim, Pelizaeus-Museum.

4. Hildesheim, Pelizaeus-Museum.

METAL WORK IN PTOLEMAIC EGYPT

PLATE XLVIII

1, 2. Two limestone models of Macedonian helmets found in the ruins of ancient Memphis (above, pl. XLV). Many similar models have been found in the same place, and have been bought by various public museums and private collectors (there are excellent specimens at Cairo, in the Pelizaeus-Museum, at Bonn, in the State Museums of Berlin, and in the Allard Pierson Museum). Most of the helmets are richly decorated, all in the same technique and style: incised ornaments mostly floral. The decoration is confined to the lower zone of the surface of the helmet and to the neck- and cheek-pieces. Figure 2 shows a section of the decoration of the helmet, figure 1, to the left (photograph from a modern plaster cast). Besides the helmets, one stone model of a typical round Macedonian shield was found in the same place (now in the Allard Pierson Museum). Around the boss is the inscription ΠΤΟΛΕΜΑΙΟΥ (name of the soldier or of the eponym of a detachment of the Ptolemaic army?). The purpose of these models, besides serving as specimens for customers, may have been, as B. Schröder has suggested, to enable wax forms of the ornamented parts to be made from them for casting the helmets. It has been suggested that the models served for the manufacture, not of actual helmets, but of cheap and thin substitutes for funerary use (cf. my pl. LXXVIII). All the models must be assigned to the third century B.C. They are very important for the light they throw on the equipment of the Ptolemaic soldiers (above, pl. XXXVII and F. N. Pryce, *Brit. Mus. Quart.* xii (1938), p. 6). Photographs supplied by the authorities of the Allard Pierson Museum, Amsterdam.

See O. Rubensohn, *Hell. Silbergerät*, &c., 1911; B. Schröder, *J.D.A.I.* XXXV (1920), Anz., pp. 3 ff. (valuable study of the Hellenistic helmets); G. Roeder and A. Ippel, *Die Denkm. d. Pelizaeus-Museums zu Hildesheim*, 1921, p. 163, nos. 1101, 1851–4; Van Essen, *Bull. van de Vereeniging tot bevordering der kennis van de antike beschaving*, i (1926), pp. 18 ff.; Fr. W. Freiherr von Bissing, *Eurasia Septentr. Ant.* ix (1934), pp. 221 ff. (the shield); *Allard Pierson Museum. Algemeene Gids*, 1937, pp. 65 ff.

3. Plaster cast of an oval horse frontlet (*prometopidion*), found in two fragments at Mit-Rahineh, showing Neoptolemus taking refuge at the altar of Delphi. Excellent purely Greek style and composition going back to the great creations of the fourth century B.C. Early third century B.C. H. 0·158. Photograph supplied by the authorities of the Pelizaeus-Museum, Hildesheim.

G. Roeder and A. Ippel, *Denkm. d. Pelizaeus-Museums*, p. 145, fig. 59; A. Ippel, 'Guss und Treibarbeit in Silber', 97 *Winckelmannsprogr.*, 1937, pp. 3 ff., pl. 1 and figs. 1–4.

4. Fragment of a plaster cast of a dish found at Mit-Rahineh. Decoration similar to that of the Megarian bowls and still more to that of the faience vases. On the bottom a rosette of palmettes and lotus buds. Then follow two friezes, one showing a procession of Dionysiac Erotes carrying thyrsoi and wine amphorae (note the melon-shaped coiffure), the other a horse race of Erotes riding in *bigae*. H. 0·105, W. 0·085. O. Rubensohn, loc. cit., p. 67 f., no. 51, pl. X. Photograph supplied by the authorities of the Pelizaeus-Museum, Hildesheim.

Licensed retail traders alone were permitted to sell the products of the spice monopoly (ἀρωματική).[187]

The Aegean. The trade of the Ptolemies in the Aegean can be briefly described. I have already referred to it in connexion with Rhodes, Delos, and Cos, and I shall speak later in this chapter of the evidence we have regarding the trade with Pergamon, Bithynia, the cities of the Straits, of the Sea of Marmora, and of the Euxine. The policy of the Ptolemies in the Aegean, the Straits, and the Euxine was dictated by political considerations. But, like the policy of the Athenians in earlier days, it also had, in great measure, mercantile ends in view. Political and commercial interests went hand in hand in the Aegean policy of the Ptolemies. We know that this policy resulted for a time in the establishment of a Ptolemaic hegemony over the Aegean Sea, which was of both a political and a commercial character. This hegemony did not last very long, nor was it uninterrupted even in the reigns of Philadelphus and Euergetes I. Yet while it lasted, it enabled the Ptolemies to achieve enduring results. They succeeded in making Alexandria one of the most important commercial cities of the world, equal in importance to Rhodes, and far superior to the other commercial cities of the time. Foreign merchants came thither in large numbers, and Alexandrian merchants were no doubt familiar figures all over the Aegean and probably as far as the Euxine. The relations between Paerisades of Bosporus (see below, p. 598) and the kings of Bithynia (see below, n. 335) on the one hand and the Ptolemies on the other are significant. But I much doubt whether in the times of Philadelphus and Euergetes Alexandria played the same part in the commerce of the Aegean as did Athens in the fifth and during part of the fourth centuries B.C. Our meagre information suggests that Rhodes, as a clearing-house for the Aegean commerce, was as important as Alexandria. Moreover, the rivals of Rhodes—Miletus and Ephesus—were only intermittently in the hands of the Ptolemies. Nor must we underestimate the progress that Antioch and her harbours were making at this time in respect of trade.

However this may be, Alexandria in the time of Philadelphus and Euergetes certainly controlled a very important part of the commerce of the Aegean, a commerce that was undoubtedly of great volume. It must be remembered that at this time the Aegean market was still the dominating centre of world trade.

The principal commodity that this market absorbed in large quantities was grain. Its capacity in this respect was very great. It is hardly appropriate therefore to speak of competition between the chief producers of grain in the Aegean. Yet their interests no doubt in some respects conflicted. It was probably such conflicting interests that were settled at Alexandria by the envoys of Paerisades of Bosporus, and led to active diplomatic relations between Bithynia and the Ptolemies. But the affair had rather a commercial than a political character, and in all probability some *modus vivendi* was arranged, not by diplomatic negotiations, but by the merchants and bankers of Rhodes.[188]

We have no means of estimating the volume of the Aegean trade in grain. The prices, at least at Delos, are known. They fell steadily after 270 B.C., a fact which testifies both to the abundance of supply and to the sound state of the market.[189] We have other evidence that these conditions prevailed. Whereas in the time of the Successors the grain trade was unsettled and the cities of Greece and Asia Minor suffered frequently from a shortage of corn and were forced to have recourse to the help of kings and rich merchants, in the time of the Ptolemaic hegemony we have very little indication of famines or scarcity of food. From time to time we hear of some city being in financial difficulties, which were adjusted in some way, but the general impression we gain is that the supply of grain was abundant and regular and the Greek cities rich enough to feed their populations. To secure this regularity of supply the cities frequently had recourse to the assistance (by the method of liturgy) of the well-to-do citizens, but the burden on the *bourgeoisie* does not appear to have been very oppressive.[190]

Grain was not, of course, the only commodity that was exported from Egypt to the Aegean Sea and to the Euxine. No direct information (except about papyrus) is available, but it seems certain that some specialities of Egypt and the commodities obtained through her trade with the South continued in great demand. In disposing of Arabian and Indian produce the Ptolemies certainly had strong competitors in the Seleucids, and to a certain extent—so far as Chinese and perhaps Indian goods were concerned—in the kings of Bosporus.[191]

The question arises how Egypt paid for her southern imports and what was the balance of her trade with the Aegean. On the first point we have no definite information, though as regards eastern Africa we may be certain that the imports were compensated by products of Egyptian industry. For Arabia the problem is more difficult. More systematic excavations in Petra and archaeological exploration in south Arabia may furnish some much-needed evidence. As regards Greece, the balance of trade was certainly in favour of Egypt. Greece and Asia Minor no doubt exported to Egypt certain kinds of agricultural and industrial produce in spite of protective or compensatory* tariffs. We hear of wine, olive-oil, wool, and certain special foodstuffs: honey, pickled fish, fish-sauces, special kinds of meat, nuts, fruit, vegetables, cheese, and so forth. On manufactured goods the papyri afford no information. But the volume of such exports cannot have been very large. The protective tariffs greatly raised the price of imported goods and made them inaccessible except to rich people, a small fraction of the Greek population. On the other hand, Greece was unable to supply Egypt with the raw materials that the latter needed. Marble, it is true, was certainly exported to Egypt in large quantities and probably works of art made of marble and bronze: statues, statuettes, decorative vases, capitals for columns. But it is often observed that in many statues the heads alone are made of marble and even the heads not entirely, part being of plaster; and this suggests that marble was expensive at Alexandria, in other words, that it probably paid high customs duties. Besides marble, some iron may have been exported from the Peloponnese. For the rest, Greek imports were without doubt paid for in good silver, of which the Ptolemies had such pressing need. So it came about that it was in great measure her Aegean trade that supplied Egypt with silver.[192]

The West and North-west. If we now turn to the West and North-west,[193] we find that Egypt under Philadelphus was

* Cf. p. 355, note.

the first Hellenistic power to establish diplomatic relations with Rome, a fact that has always perplexed students of Hellenistic and Roman history. It is known with certainty that as early as 273 B.C. an embassy from Philadelphus came to Rome with the result that an agreement (*homologia*) was concluded between the two powers. Egypt and Rome had no political interests in common and even the failure of Pyrrhus to humiliate Rome is not a satisfactory explanation of the dispatch by Philadelphus of a political mission to that city.[194]

This transaction, however, does not stand alone. It was only one link in the policy of Philadelphus. It is well known that about the same time friendly relations existed between Syracuse and Egypt. It has been frequently pointed out that Agathocles minted coins of the Ptolemaic standard and that Hiero II did the same. Moreover, Hiero's friendly relations with Philadelphus are attested by the remarkable coincidences between the tax law of the former (*lex Hieronica*) and the *νόμοι τελωνικοί* of Philadelphus. It is more than probable that the legislation of Philadelphus was the earlier.[195]

Even closer were the relations between Philadelphus and Carthage. If Carthage asked Philadelphus to lend her a large sum (2,000 talents) during the first Punic War (Appian, *Sic.* 1), it meant that Carthage had good hopes of getting this money. There is no doubt that there were constant relations between Carthage and Alexandria before and probably during the first Punic War. Some scattered references to Timosthenes, one of the great admirals of Philadelphus, and to the information about the harbours of the North African coast west of Carthage, which he incorporated in his geographical work on harbours, show that Timosthenes with his fleet had been at Carthage at least once, and perhaps more than once, and had received the permission of Carthage, a jealous guardian of her western trade-monopoly, to sail west of Carthage as far as the Straits of Gibraltar. There is evidence of these friendly relations also in the finds of Ptolemaic coins in Tunisia and in the fact that when Carthage first instituted a regular coinage she adopted the Ptolemaic standard.[196]

These relations cannot be explained solely by the fact that Philadelphus was the master of Tyre, the mother city of

Carthage, and that Alexandria therefore inherited the close trade connexion between Tyre and Carthage that had existed without interruption for many centuries. Philadelphus had more urgent reasons for attempting the diplomatic feat of keeping on friendly terms both with Rome and Sicily on the one hand and with Carthage on the other.

It is more than probable that his connexions with the West were not political but commercial. I am convinced that the commercial genius of Philadelphus suggested to him how greatly the western market might contribute to the prosperity of his kingdom. Carthage, as is well known, was rich in horses, and so was Sicily. No doubt Cyrenaica, a famous horse-breeding country and a province of the Ptolemies, partially supplied Egypt with the horses she required, but a subsidiary supply from both Carthage and Sicily was of supreme importance. South Italy, Sicily, and the Lipari islands produced sulphur, which was used alike in agriculture (especially in viticulture) and in the industry of Egypt.[197] More important was the silver of Spain, which in early Hellenistic times was monopolized by Carthage. Through Carthage and Massilia Philadelphus may have received much-needed tin from Britain. And after the Samnite wars it was Rome that possessed the richest iron mines, which had formerly been worked by the Etruscans, the remainder of Egypt's supply being obtained from Massilia. We must also bear in mind that Rome now controlled the Tyrrhenian, that is to say, the Etruscan pirates, the chief plague of the Aegean Sea in the early third century.

We have some indirect indications of active commercial relations between Italy and Egypt. I have already mentioned that these began before the time of Philadelphus. The presence of the 'Gnathia' pottery in Alexandria and of Alexandrian pottery in Apulia is significant. I have also adduced some facts relating to other Alexandrian products (especially glass and metal plate) found in south Italy.[198] It is regrettable that the Hellenistic objects found in Italy, Sicily, Gaul, and North Africa have never been carefully collected and studied, for they would certainly yield important evidence. So far as North Africa is concerned, such a study would present no difficulty. A glance at the treasures of art and artistic industry exhibited in the Musée Lavigerie at Carthage and in the Bardo Museum at Tunis will reveal the strength of Alexandrian influence at Carthage. The same is true of such ancient Punic towns as Hadrumetum and Hippo Regius. I am convinced that Alexandrian influence at Pompeii began long before the imperial period.[199]

ORGANIZATION OF ALEXANDRIAN COMMERCE

It is very unfortunate that we know so little of the organization of Alexandrian commerce. The king certainly held large quantities of merchandise for sale. How did he dispose of it? We know that Apollonius had a sea-going fleet. We know that his ships sailed to the Syrian and Phoenician ports and it is probable that they sailed if required to ports in the other Ptolemaic dominions, to Rhodes and even further. Had the king his own commercial fleet also, and was the fleet of Apollonius perhaps part of his fleet? We have no direct information on this point.[200]

We know, however, from a curious document in Zenon's correspondence, which will be dealt with presently, that there were many foreign merchants in Alexandria who came there for the purpose of buying goods and were well provided with silver and gold for the purpose. We are told that they did not confine their dealings to Alexandria but used to go out to the country and make purchases there also. The last statement is rather puzzling, unless we suppose that they were saving money by sailing up the Nile in their own ships and buying from the crown or from private persons in the country and not in Alexandria the supplies which they wished to export. There are, no doubt, many other possible explanations.

In any case the presence of many foreign merchants, shipowners, and warehousemen in Alexandria is just what we should expect. There was no need therefore for the king to export his merchandise in his own ships, unless he wished to make some profit out of the transport, which of course is not impossible. Moreover, in later times we hear of the existence of Alexandrian corporations of shipowners and warehousemen, who had business relations with Delos, and there is no reason to suppose that they did not exist under the early

Ptolemies. But their relations with the royal administration are unknown. Were they completely free, carrying on their own business for their own account and paying the usual customs dues? Or are we to suppose that, like the shipowners on the Nile, they worked chiefly for the crown, serving under contracts and carrying goods that belonged to the king? In

FIG. 3. Restoration of the lighthouse of Alexandria (Pharos), built by Sostratus of Cnidus. After Thiersch.

this case the corporations would be the precursors of the *navicularii* of Roman times—shipowners who, if required, would work for the king, carrying, or perhaps receiving for sale on commission, goods that were royal property.

COINAGE

The economic policy of the first Ptolemies found admirable expression in their abundant, beautiful, and peculiar coinage. The coinage and the monetary system underlying it were unique in the Hellenistic world, differing in many respects from those of the other Hellenistic monarchies. I will deal with it briefly.*

* What is here said about the successive changes of standard is hypothetical and disputable, being based on a more or less systematic and extensive weighing of the extant coins. I follow the views of E. S. G. Robinson of the British Museum (see his Excursus at the end of this book).

While he was still satrap and during the first years of his reign, Soter naturally followed the monetary policy of Alexander and minted the same gold and silver coins of the Attic standard as were used by the rest of the Hellenistic world. Soon, however, he initiated a new policy. He altered the standard by issuing silver coins of lighter weight, probably with the object of adjusting them to the current prices of the precious metals which were steadily rising in the case of silver and falling in that of gold. The new standard did not coincide exactly with any of the accepted standards of the time, but approximated most nearly to the Rhodian of the late fourth century (before the siege of the city); and it may have been intended to facilitate trade relations with Rhodes. For a time it was popular: Cyrene for instance probably adopted it.

Later in his reign Soter took a further step which almost completely isolated Egypt from the rest of the Hellenistic world. He reduced the weight of his silver still more by adopting a standard which was practically identical with that used in the Phoenician cities, and this new standard was maintained until the end of the Ptolemaic dynasty. It was in all probability adopted by Rhodes after the siege, and it came to be used throughout the maritime empire of the Ptolemies as well as by all those who fell in one way or another under its sway. This sharp separation from the rest of the Hellenistic world may be partly explained by considerations of a commercial character (cf. above, pp. 381 ff.). The Ptolemies needed large amounts of currency for their caravan trade, which, at least in their early days, was to a large extent in the hands of the Phoenician cities, now their subjects. Moreover, caravan goods and other Egyptian merchandise found an excellent market in the West, and there the main customer was Carthage, the great Phoenician trading city.

It was natural that this new coinage should be minted not in Egypt but in the leading Phoenician cities, Tyre, Sidon, Ptolemais-Ake, Joppa, and Gaza, and later in Cyprus; and coins of these mints were easily recognized by mint-marks and by the special form that was given to the name of the king (Πτολεμαίου Σωτῆρος, not Πτολεμαίου βασιλέως). We may suppose that the mint-mark of one of the Phoenician cities—old customers of the Arabs—made the new currency for the caravan trade more acceptable to them.

Besides the Phoenician standard, there was another peculiarity in Ptolemaic monetary policy which separated Egypt from the rest of the Hellenistic world and gave it a peculiar monetary system. While in early days Ptolemaic coinage was based on the same bimetallic (silver and gold) foundation as that of all the other Hellenistic countries, and copper was used practically as token money, at a later date—in the second half of the reign of Philadelphus—a momentous change was made. Heavy copper coins with heads of Egyptian gods were struck in Egypt, coins which were no longer tokens but regular, standard coins accepted at their metal value. Thus a trimetallic system, unknown in the rest of the Hellenistic world, was introduced. For this innovation there were apparently two main reasons. In the first place the former system was not popular with the natives. They took the silver coins, of course, but treated them as bullion, as is shown by the hoards of that time. They were unfamiliar with silver and unaccustomed to the use of it: from time immemorial they had used copper only (and gold) as their means of exchange. The new heavy Ptolemaic copper was, therefore, a concession to them, and it became very popular with them. From the time of its appearance on the market silver coins almost disappeared from coin-hoards in Egypt, their place being taken by the new copper. The copper coinage of Philadelphus was consequently another symbol and expression of the dualism which was established in Egypt by the Ptolemaic system of organization: old Egypt, the Egypt of the natives, with its heavy and clumsy old-fashioned copper, co-existed with the new Egypt, that of Alexandria and the Greeks, with its elegant and handy silver and magnificent gold. But to satisfy the requirements of the natives was not the only aim of Philadelphus in introducing the new bronze coinage. He foresaw that the new coins would drive silver and gold out of circulation, and that the coins made of these two metals would gradually come to be hoarded in the royal treasury and used by the king for his own purposes. And that, without doubt, was what happened, especially after his time.

As has been said, the coinage of the Ptolemies was in the first instance intended to serve the needs of their commerce and of Egypt as they had organized it. This intention found expression in the issue of the imposing heavy copper coins that were destined to become the main currency of the 'country' (χώρα), and of the abundant and modest silver tetradrachms of a standardized character and stable value that were almost exclusively reserved for the use of Alexandria, the dominions, and foreign countries. But at the same time the Ptolemaic coinage was a means of international propaganda, of which gold was the medium. Gold was not very much used in the home trade, especially the most beautiful issues: the pentadrachms (*trichrysa*) of Soter and later the octodrachms (*mnaeia*) and tetradrachms (or 'pentekontadrachms', as their equivalent in silver) of Philadelphus and Arsinoe with the fine portraits of the ruling kings. These coins were used chiefly for foreign commerce and political subsidies, and they could not fail to impress contemporaries by their slightly barbaric magnificence and the wealth and strength that they symbolized.

Proud of their currency and confident in their wealth and power, the Ptolemies did not hesitate to take another step towards separation from the rest of the Hellenistic world. They wanted their empire to be a well-knit unit, a solid structure with a uniform organization and a uniform currency. This tendency toward uniformity and self-sufficiency was manifested by several of their measures. Like Athens in the past, they endeavoured to make their own currency the exclusive currency for the whole of their vast empire, in this respect differing from their neighbours the Seleucids. The first step which they took to achieve this aim was to force their own monetary system and their own coins on their foreign dominions. As a rule the Greek cities under their control were not allowed to retain their own currency or, in the rare cases where this was permitted, they were obliged to convert it to the Phoenician standard. The same exclusive use of the Ptolemaic coinage was enforced upon the cities of Phoenicia and Palestine; their own coinage ceased and the most important of them became the chief Ptolemaic mints. As a result of this policy the Ptolemaic currency became the only one used in the Egyptian dominions. No other coins have been found in the Ptolemaic strata of those Palestinian cities which have been carefully excavated, for instance, Gezer, Marissa, Samaria, and Beth Zur. There was nothing unusual in such unification of currency.

The Ptolemies, however, were not satisfied with this. They took another more important and more unusual step in the same direction. While the Seleucids tolerated the circulation of foreign coins of the same standard as their own within their empire, Philadelphus took certain measures to exclude foreign coins from the Egyptian market. It is in this way that I am inclined to interpret a document belonging to the archives of Zenon, a letter in which a certain Demetrius, probably a royal official connected with the Alexandrian mint, reports to Apollonius on certain difficulties that had arisen in connexion with the king's order to re-mint all worn-out local gold coins and also gold coins of foreign mints imported into Egypt. This letter (as M. E. Bikerman has pointed out to me) furnishes clear evidence of the establishment in Egypt of a kind of royal monopoly of exchange, at least as regards gold, very profitable for the king and burdensome for the merchants: no private money-changers, no private or even royal banks were allowed to carry out this operation. The whole business was concentrated in Alexandria in the hands of a special royal official. Similar measures were not unknown to the Greek world of the past. The mere existence of such a monopoly practically meant the exclusion of foreign gold from the market. The royal order to re-mint it made this exclusion still more strict; it meant that the king took it for granted that all important business transactions in Egypt, in which gold was used as the medium of exchange, were supposed to be carried out in Ptolemaic currency. Such a restriction of the freedom of trade, aggravated by bureaucratic red tape, which made the process of exchange and of re-minting slow and irregular, naturally aroused the indignation of foreign merchants.[201]

The monetary policy of the early Ptolemies as we have described it presents two aspects. On the one hand it stressed the point that Egypt was the property of the king, his estate, which had a separate existence, and was connected with the rest of the Hellenistic world through the king alone. This was the meaning of the introduction of the Egyptian copper currency. On the other hand the Ptolemies claimed for themselves an exceptional position in the Hellenistic world. They did not wish to be mere members of the Hellenistic balance of power. They insisted upon living in splendid isolation, unless they should be able gradually to bring the rest of the Hellenistic world within their sphere of influence. In this direction tended their acceptance of the Phoenician standard and their enforcement of the royal monopoly of coinage on the whole of their empire. Their policy was crowned with success. Although they were never able to enforce their hegemony upon the Hellenistic world, they certainly isolated Egypt from the rest of it and this isolation gradually became the leading feature of the life of the country.

The currency of the Ptolemies, though in the main an instrument of their foreign policy and of their commercial dealings with their own provinces and with the rest of the world, considerably altered economic conditions in Egypt itself. The use of money was not unknown in pre-Ptolemaic Egypt. Large quantities of coined money, both foreign and local, circulated in the country. But its use as currency was confined to the upper classes of the population and chiefly to foreigners. Among the natives barter was firmly established. After Alexander's conquest the use of coined money began to replace barter. Among the Greeks it was adopted as a matter of course. But to what extent and how rapidly it took the place of barter among the natives, it is difficult to say. Our information on this point, though abundant, is insufficient. Besides Zenon's archives—especially the accounts—hundreds of official documents and certain features of the internal policy of the Ptolemies (for example, the part-payment of soldiers, employees, and workmen in kind and the assignment of *cleroi* to the soldiers), suggest that in the reign of Philadelphus there was some shortage of currency in Egypt. On the other hand the natives apparently still adhered to their old habits. This led to the persistence of barter in many branches of economic activity in Egypt. Thus in Zenon's archives money accounts and accounts of commodities issued figure to an almost equal extent. Similarly in the early Ptolemaic fiscal system we find many taxes paid in kind (for instance, the rents of the royal peasants, several land taxes, the *apomoira*, &c.), side by side with taxes paid in money. It was scarcity of coined money that accounts, in my opinion, for the high rate of interest on loans both from the royal banks and from private persons, the rate being probably fixed by the government. This rate of interest, 24 per cent., was much higher than the current rate in Greece where coined money was plentiful.[202]

BANKING

The peculiar situation in Egypt as regards the circulation of money, and the slow and gradual spread of its use as a medium of exchange, is illustrated by the development of banking in the country. The chief owners of money were the kings. We know little of the financial affairs of the Ptolemies, but allusions here and there in our literary texts show that in early times members of the dynasty lent money both at home and abroad: we hear of a loan by Soter of fifty talents to the priests of Memphis for the burial of the Apis,* and of the request of Carthage to Philadelphus for a loan of two thousand talents.† A recently published papyrus belonging to Zenon's correspondence (*P. Cairo Zen.* 59503), as interpreted by U. Wilcken,‡ makes it probable that the foreign money transactions of the Ptolemies were conducted by the royal bank in Alexandria (βασιλικὴ τράπεζα), which may have been at the same time the central treasury of the kings, although it is to be distinguished from the βασιλικόν, which is the general term by which the king's financial administration, including the treasury, is designated. If we accept the interpretation of the document suggested by Wilcken, it was probably Apollonius, the *dioecetes* himself, who managed this bank.

The royal bank had branches distributed over the country under the general management of the *dioecetes*: offices in the capitals of the nomes and local sub-offices in the villages. Of the management of these banks we have some slight know-

* Diod. i. 84. 8.

† Appian, *Sic.* i, cf. above, p. 395.

‡ *Arch. Pap.* ix (1930), p. 233 f.

ledge from the few fragments of a special law regulating banking business in the country which was incorporated in the so-called *Revenue Laws* of Philadelphus (fragments of col. 73–8) and from several documents which illustrate the activity of certain local bankers, especially Python, the director of the royal bank of Crocodilopolis–Arsinoe, a contemporary of Apollonius and Zenon, and Clitarchus, the banker of the *topos* Koites in the time of Euergetes I. The evidence is scanty and difficult to interpret. The banks as such were closely connected, if not identical, with local branches of the royal treasury (both styled *βασιλικὴ τράπεζα*) to which went all payments due to the king—a curious mixture of a treasury office and a regular Greek bank of the kind well known to us, for instance, at Athens, in the fourth century B.C. The money collected in the treasury offices was employed by the bankers. All sorts of banking business were carried on by the royal banks of Egypt on a comparatively large scale: exchange business, various types of deposits, current accounts, loans of various kinds strictly regulated by royal ordinances, transfer of credit, payments in cash, every kind of business that we know was conducted in Athens in the fourth century. The royal banking in Egypt is an interesting and unique phenomenon in the history of the ancient world, furnishing another instance of the dualism in the economic and social structures of the country. Ptolemaic banking in its organization goes back to, and at the same time far beyond, that of the Oriental monarchies, and in some of its private operations shows both dependence on the banking system of the Greek *poleis* and many improvements on it. I cannot go into details, but I may mention that one of the most striking novelties in comparison with the practice of the Greek banks was the complete change from oral management (partly used in the Greek cities) to written management of banking business. Refined accounting, based on a well-defined professional terminology, replaced the rather primitive accounting of fourth-century Athens.

The royal bankers were primarily managers of the royal money, agents of the king. It is probable that, like the *telonai* or 'underwriters' in the collection of taxes and in the management of the 'monopolies', they were concessionaires of the State, underwriters of the τραπεζιτικὴ ὠνή, dealt with in the section of the *Revenue Laws* already mentioned. Whether as such they managed the royal money exclusively or invested their own money and the money of their clients in the banking operations (for instance in loans and mortgages), it is impossible to say. Nor is there evidence enough to show whether, alongside of the royal banks, there were private banks in Alexandria and in the rest of Egypt, that is to say, whether the banking business was completely or only partially monopolized by the king. There is no reason to deny *a priori* the existence of such private banks. Money transactions between private persons—loans, mortgages, and so forth—were common in Ptolemaic Egypt. Why should not private capitalists organize regular banks of the Greek type to carry out such transactions, presumably with a special licence and under supervision of the State?

The existence of a network of banks and such information as we have about their transactions show once more the predominant position of the king in the economy of the country. Most of the money belongs to him and he knows how to use it for his own profit. But the very fact that banks existed makes it certain that, despite all restrictions, the use of money as the basis of private business was fairly well developed under Philadelphus. There were savings in the country which looked for safe investment and the business spirit was awake. It is true that the banking business was concentrated almost entirely in the hands of the Greeks: almost all the bankers were Greeks, and so were the customers. Was this because the natives were too poor and too little familiar with the use of money or because they preferred to keep their savings in the temples under the protection of their gods, as of old?[203]

Storehouses. It must be borne in mind, however, that in addition to the banks there were θησαυροί, royal storehouses, forming a network as developed as that of the banks, or perhaps more so. The operations of these storehouses were of the same kind as those of the banks, or even more diversified, especially as regards transfers of credit. This shows that dealings in kind played an important part both in the business of the king and in that of the people. And so it remained until the end of the Ptolemaic period.[204]

7. THE PROSPERITY OF EGYPT

The economic reforms and other measures of the first Ptolemies produced wonderful results. The Ptolemies were certainly regarded by their contemporaries as the richest kings of the time. We have exceptionally good evidence of this. The picture drawn by Theocritus of the splendour of Philadelphus (*Id.* xvii. 95, and xiv. 58 f.) may be regarded as a piece of advertising, like that clever piece of political and economic propaganda, the description by Callixeinus of the grand procession (πομπή) arranged by Philadelphus. Nevertheless no historian of Ptolemaic Egypt can disregard the evidence contained in their direct and indirect descriptions of Egypt at that time. These are in the main exact.

We may dwell for a moment on Callixeinus' description, for it admirably illustrates the motives and achievements of Philadelphus in his foreign and commercial policy. Since the *pompe* was probably organized to celebrate the political successes of the king in his Syrian war, we are justified in seeing in most of the religious and symbolical groups which were displayed in the procession, allusions to his achievements that would be easily understood by the people of Alexandria. Such were the picturesque chariots exhibiting the wealth and wonders of India, Arabia, and eastern Africa. Naturally enough they illustrated the deeds of Dionysus; but every one in the crowd realized that it was the ruling king who, by his military and diplomatic successes, made the spectacular gifts of the East and South accessible at that time to Egypt and to the Greek world. Attention was next forcibly drawn to another leading motive of Philadelphus' policy, the establishment of strong ties between Egypt and the Aegean, linking the land of the Nile with Greece, headed by Corinth, and the Greek cities of Asia Minor and the islands which had been liberated from the Persians by his 'ancestors', Alexander and Soter. Very striking is the passage referring to the countries of the South and East and their exotic products, which shows how proud the king was of his successes there, successes equal to if not

PLATE XLIX

1. Mural painting in the peristyle of the gorgeous tomb no. 1 recently discovered at Mustafa Pasha near Alexandria (A. Adriani, *Annuaire du Musée Gréco-romain* (1933–4 and 1934–5), 'La nécropole de Moustafa Pacha', 1936). The painting is placed above the central entrance door of the south side of the peristyle, a door which led to the most important grave-chambers (Adriani, loc. cit., pl. XXVIII). The picture (Adriani, loc. cit., pl. XXVII and fig. 2) represents three horsemen in three-quarter view on prancing horses turned to the right. They are all wearing military dress: sleeved chitons, cuirasses, high shoes, and perhaps swords (cf. above, pl. XIX). The figure to the right has in addition the chlamys. The same figure wears a Macedonian crested helmet, while the two others have the causia or petasus. All three hold paterae in their right hands and are performing a libation, the central one over a cylindrical altar which is represented behind him to the left. Between the three riders stand two ladies with apparently cult objects in their right hands (twigs?). The picture is not easy to interpret. I am inclined to see in the five persons heroized members of a noble Macedonian family of Alexandria buried in the loculi of the grave: the central figure may represent the father, the lateral figures his sons (one of them an officer of the royal army in actual service) with their respective wives. We have a good parallel to this picture in the well-known fragmentary funeral carved stele from Alexandria in the Bissing Collection (R. Pagenstecher, *Nekropolis*, 1919, p. 5 f., fig. 2, note 17): before a funeral altar or a grave monument in altar form is seen a horseman in Macedonian military dress: chiton, cuirass, chlamys, and high shoes. Around his head is a diadem. Early third century B.C. On altars as grave-monuments in Alexandria, Pagenstecher, ibid. But other interpretations of the Mustafa painting are equally possible and have been suggested (for example by Ch. Picard, *Rev. Arch.*, 6 sér. xi (1937), p. 269). Unfortunately of the two inscriptions painted on the walls of the hypogaeum, one (Adriani, loc. cit., p. 18 f., fig. 5) is illegible, the other (ibid., p. 43 f., figs. 18 and 19; *S.E.G.* viii. 365) gives a list of names, partly Syrian and Anatolian, perhaps of members of a σύνοδος which may have consisted of the members of the household of the family. For a more complete description and discussion of the picture from the technical and artistic points of view, Adriani, loc. cit., pp. 37 f. and 109 ff. Photograph supplied by Prof. A. Adriani.

2. Restoration of the banqueting tent of Ptolemy Philadelphus as described by Callixeinus (cf. above, pp. 415 ff. and notes 179, 205). The restoration is by F. Studniczka, see his paper 'Das Symposion Ptolemaios II', *Abh. Leipz. Akad.*, Phil.-hist. Kl., no. ii, 1914, where the reader will find a detailed analysis of Callixeinus' text in the light of the archaeological evidence. Much has been written since on Alexandrian architecture. A useful summary will be found in L. Noshy, *The Arts in Ptolemaic Egypt*, 1937, pp. 16 ff., cf. F. Poulsen, 'Gab es eine alexandrinische Kunst?', *Coll. Ny Carlsberg Glypthotek*, ii (1938), pp. 1 ff., quoted in n. 214, cf. our pl. xxxviii, 2 and 3.

1. Painting in grave no. 1 of the necropolis of Mustafa Pasha, Alexandria

2. Banqueting-tent of Philadelphus, after Studniczka

LIFE IN ALEXANDRIA

greater than those of his predecessors, the great Pharaohs and of Dionysus himself.* 'These were immediately followed by carts drawn by mules. These contained barbaric tents, under which sat Indian and other women dressed as captives. Then came camels, some of which carried three hundred pounds of frankincense, three hundred of myrrh, and two hundred of saffron, cassia, cinnamon, orris, and all other spices. Next to these were Ethiopian tribute-bearers, some of whom brought six hundred tusks, others two thousand ebony logs, others sixty mixing-bowls full of gold and silver and gold dust'† There follows a display of exotic animals, birds, and trees.[205]

While the encomium of Theocritus and Callixeinus' description of the *pompe* have advertisement as their object, and probably contain a good deal of exaggeration, the humorous, but appreciative and perhaps even slightly tendentious enumeration of the wealth, beauty, and attractions of Egypt and Alexandria in the first mime of Herondas (ll. 23ff.) represents certainly the ideas prevailing among the Greeks of the time of Philadelphus. We may note his emphatic statement: 'all that exists and can be produced anywhere on the earth *is* in Egypt', and the prominence attached to wealth (πλοῦτος) and gold (χρυσίον), in the enumeration of the blessings that await Mandris in Egypt.

There is, however, no advertising at all in the well-known remark of Teles (Περὶ πλούτου καὶ πενίας, 29, 6). He takes it for granted that the young men in the service of Ptolemy acquire wealth. The same is true of the statement of Athenaeus (V, 203 c) which follows the description of the *pompe* of Philadelphus and reproduces ideas current in Hellenistic and Roman times regarding the wealth of Egypt. These ideas first grew up in the time of Soter § and were still prevalent under Euergetes I

* Athen. v. 200 f–201 a: αἷς ἐπηκολούθουν ἀπῆναι ὑφ' ἡμιόνων ἀγόμεναι. αὗται δ' εἶχον σκηνὰς βαρβαρικάς, ὑφ' ὧν ἐκάθηντο γυναῖκες Ἰνδαὶ καὶ ἕτεραι κεκοσμημέναι ὡς αἰχμάλωτοι. κάμηλοι δ' αἱ μὲν ἔφερον λιβανωτοῦ μνᾶς τριακοσίας, σμύρνης τριακοσίας, κρόκου καὶ κασίας καὶ κινναμώμου καὶ ἴριδος καὶ τῶν λοιπῶν ἀρωμάτων διακοσίας. ἐχόμενοι τούτων ἦσαν Αἰθίοπες δωροφόροι, ὧν οἱ μὲν ἔφερον ὀδόντας ἑξακοσίας, ἕτεροι δὲ ἐβένου κορμοὺς δισχιλίους, ἄλλοι χρυσίου καὶ ἀργυρίου κρατῆρας ἑξήκοντα καὶ ψήγματα χρυσοῦ

† Loeb translation slightly altered.

§ Plut. *Reg. et. imp. apopht.*, 181 f.

and Philopator, in whose days an officer of the army is glorified as having received gifts of gold from the 'kings of Egypt, rich from early times' (παλαίπλουτοι βασιλῆες Αἰγύπτου). Some of the political enemies and rivals of the Ptolemies, however, who had received subsidies from them for a time, were or pretended to be rather sceptical, for instance Aratus in his sarcastic remark concerning the wealth of Euergetes I.*

As late as the reign of Soter II, if that is the date of Isidorus, whose hymns to Hermuthis Isis have recently been discovered at Ibion near Tebtunis, we have a local poet drawing an enthusiastic picture of the wealth of pious kings and of the prosperity of the country. We read in his third hymn:† 'All that live most blessed, men of highest worth, sceptre-bearing kings and all that are rulers, these being heedful of thee hold sway even to old age, leaving to their sons and grandsons and those who come after abundance of wealth, brilliant and glorious. But he whom our Queen (i.e. Hermuthis-Isis‡) has held dearest among rulers, he rules (not only over Egypt but) also over both Asia and Europe; and he brings peace, and the *Fruits* of the fields and the *Fields* that bear the fruitage load him with blessings of every kind.' The reference to the kings in the plural suggests that we should assign the hymns of Isidorus not to the time of the Roman Empire but to the end of the Ptolemaic period. However this may be, the lines quoted recall various works of art celebrating the fertility and prosperity of Egypt, such as the mosaics of Antioch and Leptis Magna, in which Καρποί and *Aroura* are represented by the side of the Nile and Egypt, and perhaps the well-known bas-relief found at Carthage.§ [206]

* Plut. *Arat.* 15. 3.

† Published by A. Vogliano, *Atti IV Congr. Pap.*, 1936, p. 491 ff., 1. 7 ff., and *Primo Rapporto degli scavi di Mādīnet Mādī*, 1936, p. 37: *S.E.G.* VIII. 550; *S.B.* 8140.: ὅσσοι δὲ ζώουσι μακάρτατοι, ἄνδρες ἄριστοι σκαπτοφόροι βασιλεῖς καὶ ὅσσοι κοίρανοί εἰσι, | οὗτοι σοι ἐπέχοντες ἀν⟨ά⟩σσουσ' ἄχρι τε γήρω[ς] | λαμπρὸν καὶ λιπαρὸν καταλείποντες πολὺν ὄ[λβον] | υἱάσι θ' υἱωνοῖσι καὶ ἀνδράσι τοῖσι μεταῦ[τις]. | ὃν δέ κε φίλτατον ἔσ⟨χ⟩ε ἀνάκτων ἡ βασίλε[ια](?) | οὗτος καὶ 'Ασίας τε καὶ Εὐρώπης τε ἀν⟨ά⟩σσει | εἰρήνη⟨ν⟩ τε ἄγων καρποὶ βρίθουσιν ἐπ' αὐτῶι | παντοίων ἀγαθῶν καρπόν τε φέροντες ἄρ[ου]ρ[αι(?). The second sentence is a little involved but there is no doubt about its meaning.

‡ Cf. *S.E.G.* VIII. 548, 1. § See Pl. XL and the description of this plate.

The wealth of the king was certainly shared by many of the Greek immigrants. Not only men of high position such as Apollonius and the other holders of 'gift-estates', prominent civil and military assistants of the king, but men of more modest station, such as Zenon, the faithful steward of Apollonius, and probably many other members of his staff, were either rich or well-to-do. All these Greek civil officials belonged to the οἶκος of the king or to the οἶκοι of his assistants. We have seen how they invested their property during and after their term of service. They became landowners, progressive farmers who bought or rented large tracts of land or took a share in some form of business connected with the new economy of the Ptolemies: in building-contracts of one kind or another, in contracts connected with taxation and with the king's 'monopolies', in banking business, or in money-lending. We have no direct means of knowing how far they were successful in these ventures. But since we never hear in the time of Philadelphus of any lack of 'contractors' willing to collaborate with the government, we may infer that on the whole their business was not unremunerative. Zenon, as revealed by the letters he wrote in his retirement in the reign of Euergetes I, was a typical representative of a wealthy man of this period: first a member of an influential οἶκος, then a successful farmer, breeder of sheep, 'contractor', money-lender.[207]

We know very little of the natives. We cannot tell how the economic system of Philadelphus affected their prosperity. The only thing we know positively is that they did not greet it with enthusiasm. Conflicts in the sphere of agriculture were frequent. Some of them, as we know chiefly from the correspondence of Zenon, ended in ἀναχωρήσεις, that is to say, withdrawals of the peasants into the temples under the protection of the gods. Not less frequent were the conflicts that arose in connexion with the new organization of industry and commerce. Smuggling and sale of goods without licence were of common occurrence as soon as the new system was started. Finally, the various kinds of work and service of a compulsory or semi-compulsory character inevitably led to conflicts and strikes. The government disliked this opposition. The punishments inflicted on 'rioters' (στασιασταί) were heavy, and informers (μηνυταί) flourished.[208]

But we must probably not seek the cause of these conflicts in any impoverishment brought about by the new economic system. We know that in the reign of Philadelphus wages, if the prices of foodstuffs and other commodities are taken into consideration, were higher in Egypt than in Greece, while the general trend of prices was very similar in the two countries. This does not suggest general poverty.[209] The causes of the conflicts lay deeper. In the first place, they may be explained by the natural defects of every new system, by the fact that neither those who managed it nor those to whom it was applied were yet familiar with it in all its aspects. It was the experimental stage. But these slight defects cannot account altogether for the troubles. There were in the system itself many peculiarities which irritated the natives.

I have already spoken of the priests. It was natural that they should resent the new system. Holding, as they had long done, a dominating position, they first became slaves of the Persian overlords, and then, when they expected with the advent of Alexander to have their power restored, they were bitterly disappointed by the policy of Soter and Philadelphus. Officially they showed nothing but enthusiasm for the new régime and expressed it in the decrees adopted at their meetings. But resentment certainly was there.

The situation of the native populace (λαοί) was not exactly similar. They had always blindly obeyed the king and his officials, and they were inured to working, not for themselves, but for somebody else. But centuries of evolution had accustomed them to a rather mild paternal form of pressure. Besides, within the Pharaonic system there was room for much liberty in social and juridical relations. And the rulers were, after all, their compatriots (not always, but as a rule), and in any case they were men who spoke their own language, who had the same religion, the same ideas, and the same mode of life.

With the Ptolemies came a marked change. The system remained the same in the main and the natives retained their social and to a certain extent their juridical independence. But now the old system was managed in a different way. It was carried on by a huge, complicated, and rather dull and impersonal bureaucratic machine, in which foreigners played the most important part, foreigners who regarded themselves as far superior to the natives, who did not speak their language and had no intention of learning it, but compelled at least some of the natives to learn theirs. They brought with them their own gods whom they worshipped in their own temples, and they had in general a mode of life and habits of business quite different from those with which the natives were familiar. In particular, the government endeavoured by control and heavy taxation to force the native population to work more, and more energetically, than before. European standards of efficiency to which they were unaccustomed were applied to them—a policy always fraught with danger. The characteristic Oriental rejoinder was the strike in its peculiar Oriental form—*secessio*, ἀναχώρησις.

Thus under the new régime the natives were expected to toil hard and painfully, and that not for their own gods and their native king, but for a foreign conqueror, surrounded by foreigners to whom he gave all the best posts and abundant opportunities of enrichment. Almost all these foreigners were comparatively rich, while the natives were poor. If a native wanted to borrow money or grain, he generally borrowed it from one of them; if he wanted to rent a piece of land, it was usually land that belonged to them; and so forth. The foreigners were not always harsh and overbearing; the kings were very considerate to the natives and so were many of their assistants. But the natives, in fact, understood—and this did not require much intelligence on their part—that they were no longer at home in Egypt, but were expected to be obedient tools in the hands of foreigners.

In this atmosphere even an increase of prosperity would not have relieved the tension. Slight inequalities of treatment would lead to grave conflicts, and these conflicts would in some cases be settled not by mutual concessions but by violence or compulsion. Naturally the resentment of the natives grew more and more acute. They saw better than we can all the defects and inconsistencies of the new régime and sharply criticized it, not only among themselves. The government reacted rather harshly, and every expression of opinion was regarded as a crime. Thus the rift between the rulers and the natives became ever deeper.[210]

Slight indications here and there in the papyri show that all these causes of discord, which existed under Philadelphus, were rapidly becoming more pronounced in the reigns of his successors, Euergetes I and Philopator.

The short-lived successes of Euergetes I in Syria and the final results of his efforts to maintain his supremacy in the Aegean maintained the prestige of the Ptolemies in the Greek world, and the great victory of Philopator at Raphia certainly added to their fame in foreign countries.[211] These exploits, moreover, brought gold and silver in some quantity into the royal treasuries. Part of the booty was distributed among the officers and soldiers of the victorious armies, but the bulk was appropriated by the kings. However, the successes of Euergetes and Philopator were not enduring, and the increase in the store of money and precious metals had no influence on the general economic tendencies of the time. These appear to have been rather in the direction of a decline. The economic situation in Egypt in the second half of the third century is not well known to us, but even the scanty information that we have includes some significant facts.

The great efforts called for by the wars of Euergetes I involved an increase of the government's pressure on the population. We hear occasionally of native Egyptian militia (μάχιμοι) being mobilized, of natives being pressed for the hated naval service, of increasing harshness in the methods of the bureaucracy, of the royal tenantry being subjected to extortionate rents (ἐκφόρια). As a result, there were instances of people fleeing from their homes, of the desertion of recently founded villages, and even of armed resistance. It was under Euergetes, during his Syrian war, that we hear for the first time of disturbances in Egypt. This was very probably a native revolt. There were similar occurrences later, after the battle of Raphia.[212]

At the same time certain facts lead me to think that the free initiative of the population, even of the Greeks, was gradually and systematically restricted. Some gift-estates (δωρεαί) still survived and some new ones were granted, but many others had been taken back by the crown and were now managed by officials on purely bureaucratic lines. Faithful servants of the king were now often rewarded not with large estates—fields for all sorts of new experiments—but with the right of collecting various minor dues and taxes, certainly to the detriment of the people. With the confiscated gift-estates disappeared many of the opportunities for the display of energy and enterprise. What still remained of the old-fashioned, personal, paternal management of Egypt was more and more replaced by pure bureaucracy, impersonal and exasperating by its very impersonality.[213] Of the new tendencies shown by the policy of Philopator in respect of the natives before and after Raphia I shall speak later in this book.

8. ALEXANDRIA AND PHILADELPHIA

The sinister phenomena of which I have been speaking were, however, hardly perceptible to contemporaries, even if good observers. The dominant note was splendour and rapid progress. This progress was strikingly manifested in the marvellous growth of new urban settlements.

The most spectacular of these was, of course, ALEXANDRIA.[214] With startling rapidity it became the largest Greek city in the world, larger than the greatest cities of the past—Athens, Corinth, Syracuse, and at least as large as the Seleucid capitals, Antioch on the Orontes and Seleuceia on the Tigris. This is not the place to draw a detailed picture of this splendid capital of the Ptolemies, with its peculiar organization and its rather strange relation to Egypt. It was not the capital of Egypt. It did not lie *in* Egypt, but *by* Egypt (πρὸς Αἰγύπτωι or κατ' Αἴγυπτον). It was the residence of the king, his city, and at the same time a city-state (πόλις), which acted as if it were a free and autonomous Greek city. As it appears in descriptions of the time, in the eyes of Theocritus and Herondas, Alexandria is first and foremost the world-city, the chief manifestation of the Ptolemaic power. It is resplendent in its unique beauty. No idea of its appearance can be formed from the remains of buildings, which are hidden under the flourishing modern city, but some of the striking features in its aspect are known to us from the literary

PLATE L

1. A terracotta figurine showing a bearded pedagogue with his right hand on the head of a boy. Variation of a well-known type. F. Winter, *Typen*, &c., ii, p. 403 (the nearest is no. 3). Photograph supplied by the authorities of the Cairo Museum.

2. Terracotta lamp in the form of an oldish man with a pointed beard wearing a hooded cloak and holding in his right a lantern, in his left a ladder. The lower part is missing. Apparently a lamp-lighter (λυχνάπτης, *lampadarius*). Another version of the same type is represented by a terracotta figurine found in Alexandria and now in the Museum of Alexandria. E. Breccia, *Bull. Soc. Arch. Alex.* xx (N.S. v, 3) (1924), pp. 239 ff. and *Terrecotte figurate*, &c., i, 1930, p. 72, no. 463, pl. U, 2 (in colour), cf. no. 464. The lamp and the figurines may represent the lamplighters in the streets of Alexandria. While λυχνάπται are not attested by our literary and papyrological evidence for the city of Alexandria, they are well-known figures in the Serapea of Egypt and Athens. U. Wilcken, *U.P.Z.* i, p. 49, paragraph 35, cf. W. Otto and H. Bengtson, 'Zur Geschichte des Niederganges des Ptolemaerreiches', *Abh. Münch. Akad.*, N.F. xvii (1938), p. 155, n. 6; J. Zingerle, *Commentationes Vindobonenses*, iii (1939), pp. 103 ff., and my *Soc. and Ec. Hist. R.E.*, p. 527, n. 6. On the various types of λυχναψία in use in Egypt in Ptolemaic and Roman times see M. Hombert and Ch. Préaux, 'Pap. Fond. Reine Élizabeth', *Chr. d'Ég.* xxix (1940), p. 145 f.

3. Ugly old woman with a *lagynos* in her left hand. A similar statuette in Berlin has on the base the inscription τιθηνός (nurse). The statuette here reproduced may be of Roman times, but it goes back to Hellenistic originals (F. Winter, loc. cit. ii, p. 461, 2 and 6; p. 466, 8). Especially famous was the well-known statue by Myron (third century B.C.) of a seated woman with a *lagynos*; it has been frequently reproduced, see A. Rumpf in Gercke und Norden, *Einleitung*, ii. 1, 3, 4th ed., 1932, p. 70 f.; cf. the well-known terracotta figurine derived from Myron, F. Winter, loc. cit., p. 468, no. 8. Photograph supplied by the authorities of the Cairo Museum.

4. Lamp in the form of a slave carrying a lantern. Perhaps of Roman times. It represents, however, a well-known type of a slave with a lantern seated or standing, generally a negro. Photograph supplied by the authorities of the Cairo Museum. F. Winter, loc. cit., ii, p. 450, n. 1; cf. E. Breccia, *Terrecotte figurate*, &c., i, pl. LVI, 2, and F. Poulsen, 'Gab es eine Alexandrinische Kunst?', p. 34, fig. 36. Survival in Roman times (?), E. Breccia, loc. cit., ii, 1934, nos. 378, 379, pl. LXXIV.

1. Cairo Museum.

2. Paris, Cabinet des Médailles.

3. Cairo Museum.

4. Cairo Museum.

LIFE IN ALEXANDRIA

descriptions, from some Hellenistic epigrams of the third century B.C., from some of the papyri, and from representations in contemporary and later painting, sculpture, and minor artistic work. We hear of Alexandria's harbours and of the famous lighthouse, one of the wonders of the world. The royal palace, an immense block of buildings occupying one-third of the city, was its most conspicuous quarter: every one had heard of the Mausoleum of Alexander, of the Library and the famous Museum, the royal 'Academy' of science and letters, of the parks and walks, of the magnificent 'Zoo', all included in the precincts of the palace. The royal buildings were richly adorned inside and out: their walls were built either of slabs of coloured stones, especially alabaster, or of brick covered with such slabs; the rooms were full of elegant wooden furniture decorated with ornaments and figures made of ivory and precious metals and upholstered with beautiful rugs; the floors were adorned with fine mosaics. No less rich and stately were the high tower-like houses of the aristocracy. We may derive an idea of the appearance and furniture of the royal and private palaces from some Pompeian pictures, from the painted decoration of Alexandrian tombs of the Hellenistic period, and from some terracottas. In the royal parks and gardens stood beautiful monumental fountains. One such fountain is described in an epigram, written probably by Posidippus or a poet of his school, as built of expensive material—Hymettian and Parian marble and the famous Egyptian syenite—and adorned with portraits of Philadelphus and Arsinoe, to whom the fountain was dedicated. Another epigram describes a shrine of Homer built by Philopator and probably connected with the Museum.

Nor were the other features of the great city less imposing: the two large avenues crossing each other at right angles and leading to the four gates of the city with their porticoes illuminated at night, the minor streets with their peculiar names (some of them dynastic), the parks and squares, the gymnasia and palaestrae, the spacious hippodrome, the theatres, the stadia, the temples—among them the great Serapeum—and the synagogues. Outside the walls were the gorgeous cities of the dead with their richly painted mausoleums and their gardens, the villas and gardens of the suburbs, and Canopus, noted for its gaiety, so often mentioned in ancient literature and reproduced in miniature by Hadrian in his villa near Tibur.

This city was inhabited by a peculiar society, composed of the king and his court, the army, the high officials, the magistrates and priests of the city, the members of the City Council (*Boule*), the scholars, poets, writers, and philosophers of the Museum and the Library, ephebes and schoolboys and girls, Greek and native priests, rich business men (subjects of the king or foreigners), modest shopkeepers, artisans, pedlars, lamp-lighters, longshoremen in the docks and harbours, sailors, and slaves.

Many languages were spoken here: Greek in its various dialects was, of course, predominant, but in the native quarters Egyptian was the language of the inhabitants, while in the Jewish wards Hebrew or Aramaic was still the prevailing tongue. Besides Hebrew, one might hear in the streets and the harbour various other Semitic languages and perhaps even some Indian dialect.

A detail here and another there, in a private letter, in a document written on papyrus, an inscription, or a literary text, in a terracotta, a picture in one of the tombs, or on a grave *stele*, a bas-relief or a sketchy painting on pottery, a graffito—these serve to light up a part of the picture, but it is only a corner and it is lit up only for a moment. We get a glimpse of the official aspect of the Ptolemaic Empire when we read Callixeinus' description of the great celebration of Philadelphus, his magnificent *pompe*—the soldiers of his army, the statues of the gods, the symbolical display of the king's achievements at home and abroad, the gorgeous marquee which served for a great banquet and struck the imagination of contemporaries. We get other glimpses of this aspect when Aristeas in a letter describes a banquet at the court, or when Flavius Josephus so vividly depicts an auction of the taxes and tributes payable by the provinces. And lastly Theocritus in his *Adoniazusae* shows us a great religious ceremony, the mystery of Adonis' death and resurrection celebrated in the palace and open to the public, a ceremony in which the leading part was taken by a world-famous opera star of the day.

We have a miniature of the Ptolemaic court in the vast household of Apollonius. Zenon's correspondence throws a flood of light upon it. The figure of the great *dioecetes* is in the background. Before us are his staff of employees of various grades and different kinds: stewards, treasurers, managers of his household, commanders of his ships, his commercial agents abroad and in Egypt, and the rest. It is impossible, in respect of these, to distinguish between the *dioecetes* and the head of a large private house. Alongside of the staff of Apollonius stood his personal servants, many of them slaves. Of these many kinds are mentioned, especially in Zenon's accounts: cooks and bakers, porters and butlers, coachmen and drivers, even musicians who played at his banquets. Strange to say, in this wealthy establishment the main preoccupation of staff and servants was in one way or another to obtain their wages, which were always in arrear. Thus Satyra, the harpist (κιθαρωδός), bitterly complains of receiving no money and no clothes: she will be 'naked', she says.* The two fine linen frocks (χιτῶνες βύσσινοι) which she finally receives† have made her more dressy, though not less 'naked'. In the same documents we find mentions of Apollonius' house or houses‡ and of the furniture in their rooms.§ The journeys of Apollonius (and he made frequent tours of inspection) were again probably almost exact reproductions of those of the king. Apollonius travels on his *dahabieh*, a floating villa,|| or on horseback, or in a coach, surrounded by his assistants, a large staff of scribes, and his servants. They descend like a cloud of locusts on the country, though officially Apollonius paid for his supplies.[215]

The *Aetia* of Callimachus shows us another corner of the picture: a banquet of the literary men of Alexandria and some foreign guests. In his famous idyll already mentioned Theocritus takes us into the private house of one of the Greeks of Alexandria: we meet his wife, her guest, her child, her slave-

* *P. Cairo Zen.* 59028, cf. 59059.

† Ibid. 59087.

‡ Ibid. 59326, 189 ff., cf. *Large Estate*, Index, ss. vv. 'Artemidorus,' and 'House,' and *P. Cairo Zen.* 59150 and 59398.

§ e.g. *P.S.I.* 483, cf. *P. Cairo Zen.* 59059.

|| e.g. ibid. 59053 and 59054, cf. 59242 and *P.S.I.* 533.

girl, and we go with them on an excursion through the crowded streets and squares of Alexandria.

Alexandrias in miniature were strewn over Egypt. These were the recently founded city-like settlements of Philadelphus. And they had around them their own little Egypts—the large *doreai* or gift-estates granted by the king to his assistants, probably scattered all over the country. We are well acquainted with one of these towns, PHILADELPHIA, and with one of the gift-estates, that of Apollonius, closely connected with Philadelphia. I have made extensive use of the evidence furnished by the correspondence of Zenon, the manager of Apollonius' estate, in reconstructing various features of the economic and social structure of Egypt. I will now add a few words about the *dorea* of Apollonius and the town of Philadelphia in general.

The estate of Apollonius was, in fact, a reproduction on a small scale of the new Egypt of the Ptolemies. Philadelphia was a miniature Alexandria, with its chess-board plan, its straight streets crossing each other at right angles, its brand-new Greek and native temples, its public buildings, its baths, its private gardens, and the large park (παράδεισος) of Apollonius filled with ornamental trees, vines, fruit-trees, and flowers, and the spacious, carefully built, and finely decorated houses of the new settlers. These were mostly Greeks, holders of offices in the Ptolemaic administration, or officers and soldiers of the army.

It resembled Alexandria also in its social aspect. The administration of the estate, with Zenon at the head of it, and the officials, officers, and soldiers with their large households (οἶκοι), formed the aristocracy of the place. Next to them stood the minor employees of the estate and the various artists and artisans of foreign origin attracted by the fame (δόξα) of this splendid new 'city', as one letter to Zenon calls it, and by the opportunities that it offered. At the bottom of the scale came undoubtedly a large number of natives who furnished the labour required for the construction and service of the town and for the development and management of the estate.

Like Alexandria, Philadelphia too was encircled by its own Egypt—the territory of the town partly included in the estate of Apollonius, partly distributed among the civil and military settlers of the place. On his estate Apollonius carried out, on behalf of the king as well as for his own profit, a work very similar to that which he carried out on a larger scale in Egypt as a whole at the order and on behalf of his royal master. In Philadelphia he acted through his representative Zenon. He and Zenon reclaimed the land and made it fit for cultivation. With the help of Greek and native contractors they cultivated the fields and produced large quantities of grain of various kinds, of oil-producing plants, of flax, of hemp, and of grass. They planted, again with the help of farmers, mostly of Greek origin, large areas of the reclaimed land with vines, olive-trees, fruit-trees, and vegetables, They organized bee-keeping on new lines. They kept large flocks and herds of agricultural cattle, draught-animals, sheep, goats, pigs, and various fowls. To the crops, trees, and domestic animals native to the country they added new species, making of the estate a sort of experimental station. They established and organized workshops and factories of a new type, using partly native, partly imported skilled labour, and for some branches, in accordance with Greek custom, slave labour. They created a large staff for the sale of the produce of the estate. Finally, with the help of the regular Greek and native officials, they supervised the organization of the inhabitants of town and estate in their relations with the government.[216]

The study of Zenon's archives is specially important because they show better than any other documents the interaction of the various forces and principles that were at work in Ptolemaic Egypt: the long-established customs of Egypt on the one hand, and on the other the new spirit, new mentality, new energy of the invaders from a quite different world who had come to reorganize its life. Was the aim of the Ptolemies to amalgamate the old world and the new in Philadelphia and likewise in Egypt, or to superimpose one on the other? We cannot tell. In any case, in the time of Philadelphus the Greeks in and around Philadelphia, like the Greeks of Alexandria and of the rest of Egypt, kept intact their Greek mentality and their Greek mode of life. Their mentality was not exactly the same as that of their fellow-Greeks in continental Greece, on the islands, and in Asia Minor. The *homo politicus*, still alive in Greece, yielded place to the *homo oeconomicus* and to the *homo technicus* in Egypt. The Greeks in Philadelphia and in Egypt in general were, or were gradually becoming, specialists in one field of activity or another—intellectual, military, administrative or economic. It is the *homo oeconomicus* that dominates in Philadelphia. Material interests are uppermost in his mind, and his feverish activity is devoted mainly to enrichment, regardless of ways and means. I do not mean, of course, that these tendencies were exclusive. The Greeks in Philadelphia wanted to become rich—that was why they came to Egypt—but at the same time they wished to maintain their high intellectual standard, to remain Greeks themselves in this respect and to train their children to be like them, that is to say, to be educated men. They read Greek classics in their hours of leisure, they were fond of the theatre and of music and as enthusiastic about sport as their fellow-Greeks in the homeland. And they wanted their children to have the same tastes. This was the reason why they spent much of their money on giving a good 'gymnasial' education to their boys and girls.[217]

The experiment that is brought so clearly before our eyes in the *dorea* of Apollonius was repeated by Philadelphus in many other *doreai* and on a lesser scale in the thousands of small estates granted by him to his officials, officers, and soldiers. Unfortunately none of these is known to us in the same way as the *dorea* of Apollonius. Let us hope that the future will place at our disposal the domestic archives of one of the cleruchs of Soter or Philadelphus.

C. *THE SELEUCID EMPIRE*

We have been able to present the general outlines of the economic structure and evolution of Egypt in the time of the early Ptolemies. Nothing similar can be done in respect of Syria, the empire of Seleucus I Nicator and his successors, for our information regarding it, especially in the early Seleucid period (under Seleucus I, Antiochus I Soter, and Antiochus II Theos) is miserably inadequate.[218]

I. Sources of Information

The literary sources are almost silent. The epigraphical evidence cannot be compared in volume and importance with the combined papyrological and epigraphical evidence relating to Ptolemaic Egypt. It is, moreover, very unevenly distributed. Most of the inscriptions on stone that furnish information about the Seleucids have been found in Asia Minor and are concerned chiefly with the vicissitudes of the Greek cities of that region. The inscriptions of Hellenistic times found in the rest of the Seleucid Empire are very few and most of them of little significance. In Syria proper, Antioch has yielded only one important stone (the excavations now in progress there have produced few inscriptions, and these of later date); Seleuceia in Pieria has been a little more productive, while Apamea (now in process of excavation) and Laodicea ad mare have not contributed anything worthy of note. Outside Syria proper, Seleuceia on the Eulaeus, where excavations by a French expedition have been proceeding for many years, has supplied a little group of epigraphic texts of the Hellenistic period (most of them manumissions), and Seleuceia on the Tigris and Babylon, though partly excavated, have added hardly anything to our knowledge. Nor is Dura-Europus in Parapotamia, the most important part of which has been thoroughly and systematically excavated, rich in Hellenistic inscriptions.[219]

For this scarcity of inscriptions on stone one would expect to find compensation, especially in Babylonia and in certain cities of Mesopotamia, in an abundance of documents written on clay tablets, since these are so characteristic of the pre-Hellenistic period, not only in these two countries but also in Asia Minor, Syria, Phoenicia, and Palestine on the one hand and on the Iranian plateau on the other. In this expectation we are unfortunately disappointed. Very few documents in cuneiform on tablets of the Hellenistic period have been found in Babylonia and none, so far as I know, outside it. Most of them come from Orchoi (Uruk-Warka), while Babylon has added only a small group. Some of these tablets are still unpublished.[220] The use of the cuneiform script and of clay tablets, which was already in its decline in the late Assyrian,

PLATE LI

1. The famous marble statuette in the Vatican (head and some other parts restored but extant in other replicas), one of the many reproductions of the famous statue of the Tyche of Antioch, made in bronze by Eutychidas, a pupil of Lysippus. The statue of Eutychidas showed the 'Good Fortune' of Antioch seated on a rock, wearing a mural crown, and holding in her right hand a bunch of ears of corn. Her right foot rested on the right shoulder of the god of the river Orontes, represented as a naked boy in the act of swimming. The statue of Eutychidas cannot be discussed here. Suffice it to say that the type of a city goddess created by him became immensely popular in the ancient world and remained so until the late Roman Empire. In my opinion the figure of the Tyche of Eutychidas was an attempt to merge into one Greek artistic creation the Semitic idea of the Gad (male or female), protector of a city or other corporative body, the Baal or Baalat of this body, origin of its creative forces, with the Greek idea of the mysterious goddess of Good Luck and Success, the Tyche, who played such an important role in the religious conceptions of the Hellenistic period. It is probable that in Hellenistic times the statue existed both as a single statue and grouped with the two founders (*κτίσται*) of Antioch, Seleucus I and his father Antiochus. See my paper 'Le Gad de Doura et Seleucus Nicator', *Mél. Syriens R. Dussaud*, 1939, p. 291 f. (with bibliography); for a stylistic analysis, cf. J. D. Beazley and B. Ashmole, *Greek Sculpture and Painting*, 1932, p. 73. Photograph supplied by Alinari.

2. A bas-relief of gypsum, one of the three which served as cult images in the Palmyrene temple built at Dura-Europus to the gods protectors (the Gaddé) of Palmyra and Dura. In the bas-relief are represented: in the centre a majestic figure of Zeus Olympius—Baalshamin, seated on an eagle-throne, wearing a diadem, and holding a bunch of ears of wheat in his right hand and a sceptre in his left. He is being crowned (with a laurel crown) by a standing youthful figure in Macedonian military dress, wearing a diadem and ear-rings and holding a lance upright. To the left a figure in Palmyrene priestly dress is burning incense on an altar. The names of the three figures are written in Palmyrene on the base of the bas-relief: (1) under the figure of the dedicant—'Image of Hairan, son of Maliku, son of Nasar' (over the figure the same in Greek: *Αἱρά[νη]ς [Μ]αλί[χου]*); (2) under the figure of Zeus—'The Gad of Dura; made by Hairan, son of Maliku, son of Nasor, year 470 (A.D. 158–9); (3) under the figure of the armed youth—'Seleucus Nicator'. The divine group of the bas-relief therefore represents the god protector of Dura and of the Seleucid Empire—Zeus Olympius—crowned by the founder of Dura and the Empire, Seleucus Nicator. I have endeavoured to show in a special paper (*Mél. Syr. R. Dussaud*, 1939, pp. 281 ff.) that the group goes back probably to Hellenistic times and reflects the cult statues, carved by Greek artists, which stood in the temples of the many Greek and hellenized cities of the Seleucid Empire, the 'Capitols' of these cities in which the cult of Zeus Olympius was combined with that of the ruling king, his family, and his ancestors (*πρόγονοι*). See F. E. Brown, *Yale Dura Exp.*, Rep. vii–viii, 1939, pp. 258 ff., pl. XXXIII, and my paper cited above, pls. I, II. Note that the second bas-relief of the Dura temple (pl. II of my paper) represents the Tyche of Palmyra, according to the Antiochene tradition, as a combination of Atargatis and the Greek Tyche, crowned by a Nike. The same type was later adopted by Dura also, see my *Dura-Europos and its Art*, 1938, pl. I. Photograph supplied by the Yale Dura Expedition.

1. Rome, Vatican

2. Yale Gallery of Fine Arts.

The Seleucid Empire and its protectors

neo-Babylonian, and Persian periods, was certainly dying out in the Hellenistic period and completely ceased in Parthian times. The more convenient and less complicated Aramaic alphabet ousted the cuneiform signs, and with the Aramaic alphabet came ink and parchment or papyrus. Moreover the Greeks, the new masters of the land of the two rivers, were as much accustomed to the use of ink and parchment and papyrus as the Aramaeans and those who borrowed their script from them. Now papyrus and parchment are very rarely found in the ruins of Babylonia, Mesopotamia, and the remaining countries of the Near East other than Egypt. The exceptions are few. In Dura we owe to peculiar circumstances the preservation of a number of parchments and papyri. Only one of these belongs to the Hellenistic period. In Avroman (Kurdistan) some parchments of the Parthian period were found in a jar. Fragments of papyrus have been found at Seleuceia on the Tigris. That is all. But there was undoubtedly an abundance of documents on papyrus and parchment in all the inhabited places of the Seleucid Empire. This obvious fact is illustrated by two finds made in Babylonia. At Orchoi (Uruk) there were found in some rooms of a temple of the Hellenistic period, alongside of cuneiform tablets, many stamped clay seals which had once been attached to parchment or papyrus documents, and also stamped clay *bullae*, serving as envelopes for the same type of documents, all of them of Hellenistic date. A similar find was made in Seleuceia on the Tigris in a large and sumptuous private house. It is evident that these were the remains of temple and house archives consisting of documents mostly or exclusively written on parchment or papyrus.[221]

Besides inscriptions, tablets, and parchments and papyri, we possess many sets of coins minted by the Seleucids. They are of great importance in connexion with the political, and to some extent the religious, history of the Seleucid monarchy. Their contribution to the economic history of the time will be dealt with below.[222]

Finally we have the archaeological evidence. Asia Minor, Syria, Phoenicia, Palestine, the Hauran, Transjordan, Mesopotamia, Babylonia, and the Iranian plateau are an Eldorado for archaeologists. In few countries of the world have such beautiful ruins of temples, palaces, and cities been preserved. We owe this to a cause that is evident and need not be discussed here. As in Roman Africa and in Egypt, so in these regions, the great civilization of the pre-Hellenistic and Greco-Roman periods was for many centuries in full decline and the once flourishing urban centres and villages were only partially inhabited in the later times.

An imposing group of cities which were of great importance in the Hellenistic age have been excavated and thoroughly studied by modern archaeologists in Asia Minor. I may quote some examples, Pergamon, Miletus and its temple of the Didymaean Apollo, Ephesus and its temple of Artemis, Heraclea on the Latmus, Magnesia on the Maeander, Priene, Aphrodisias, Assus, Angora, Aezani, Ilium, Sardis with their respective temples, beautiful and sometimes well-preserved structures, have all of them been carefully and more or less fully investigated, with due attention to the Hellenistic period of their history. In all of them a large number of monuments and minor objects have been discovered, most of which have been published. The same applies to certain rich cemeteries (I may mention those of Myrina and Cyme as well as those of some of the cities named above). Most of the antiquities found in Asia Minor are preserved in the Ottoman Museum at Istanbul, the Museums of Smyrna and Brussa, the British Museum, the Museum of Berlin, and the Louvre.[223]

The situation in Syria is different. There most of the extant ruins date from Roman or Byzantine times, for example the beautiful ruins of Palmyra and Baalbek. Palmyra was insignificant in Hellenistic times and no pre-Roman remains have been found at Baalbek. The same is true of the Hauran, of whose splendid ruins hardly any have been excavated.[224] Gerasa in Transjordan and Petra in Arabia did not become prominent until the Roman period. The only Hellenistic ruin of great interest in Transjordan is Amir el Araq near Amman. Careful excavations here may yield important results. But during the period with which we are dealing Transjordan and Petra were in the sphere of influence, not of the Seleucids, but of the Ptolemies, and so were Palestine and Phoenicia. It was not until the reign of Antiochus III that they became Seleucid satrapies. Antiquities found in Palestine and in Transjordan are preserved in the National Museum of Antiquities at Jerusalem, with the exception of a few in European and American museums.[225]

In Mesopotamia and Babylonia the Hellenistic age was a short episode in the many centuries of their history. Here, and especially in Babylonia, a number of cities have been excavated. Some of them were not inhabited or were small communities in the Hellenistic period and consequently very few or no remains of that period were found in them. Others, such as Babylon and Orchoi, were important in Hellenistic and Parthian times. These yielded some material of Hellenistic date, which was neglected by the excavators of the past but has been very carefully collected in our own day.[226] The great Hellenistic centre of Babylonia—Seleuceia on the Tigris—is now being explored by an expedition of Michigan archaeologists. Important discoveries have already been made there, and many others may certainly be expected. The antiquities found in Babylon and Orchoi are partly in the Museum of Bagdad, partly in Berlin, while those of Seleuceia are in the Bagdad Museum, Michigan University, and the Toledo Museum.[227]

The only Hellenistic and Roman city of Mesopotamia that has been well excavated is Dura-Europus, one of the military colonies founded by Seleucus I. It existed as a more or less flourishing centre of urban life for almost six centuries, and was captured and destroyed soon after A.D. 256 by the Sasanian king Shapur. The most brilliant period of its history was that of the Parthian domination. Most of the important monuments discovered in the city belong to this and to the last, that is, to the Roman period of its existence. Little has been found in the city dating from the Hellenistic period. The antiquities found at Dura have been divided between the Museum of Damascus and Yale University.[228]

The Hellenistic cities of the Iranian plateau, of Bactria, and of India have contributed even less to our knowledge. Bactria has proved especially disappointing, for coins are the only vestiges of this flourishing State in its Hellenistic phase. Some reflections of its civilization may be found in the contemporary monuments of India, especially of Northern India, where the most important source of information is the city of Taxila. Remains, capable of being dated with certainty, have been found in abundance at Sirkap, the second city of Taxila, that of the Hellenistic and of the Saka and Pahlav kings. Still less do we know of the cities of the Iranian plateau. The only exceptions are Persepolis in Persia and Susa in Elam, the last refounded by Seleucus I as Seleuceia on the Eulaeus. But the Hellenistic monuments of Persepolis are not yet published and Seleuceia in Hellenistic times was a small and insignificant city and its ruins of this date are badly preserved and of little importance. Persepolis and Susa were at their zenith in Persian, and Susa especially in pre-Persian Elamitic times. The importance of the Hellenistic remains of these cities lies in their suggestion that other political and commercial urban centres of the Iranian plateau, if carefully explored, may yield similar or richer monuments of the same period.[229]

Besides materials derived from systematic excavations, a wealth of what are called minor antiquities is to be found in the Hellenistic graves of this region. But no important cemetery of this period has hitherto been discovered and excavated by archaeologists. Chance excavators, natives who dig with a view to the sale of what they find, have been more enterprising and successful. Thousands of objects found by them are included in various public and private collections in Europe and in the United States. There is a large group in the Ottoman Museum, and the local museums of Syria are rapidly accumulating treasures of minor antiquities, some of them of the Hellenistic period: I mean the museums of Beirût, Damascus, Latakieh (Laodicea), Antakieh (Antioch), Alexandretta, and Suweida in the Jebel Druse.

Under present conditions, as indicated above, no trustworthy account can be given of the economic structure and evolution of the Seleucid monarchy. No more than a somewhat meagre outline is therefore attempted in the following pages. The interpretation of the few known facts is, as a rule, necessarily conjectural.

2. General Policy of the Seleucids

The area of the Seleucid Empire was enlarged in the time of Seleucus I but shrank rapidly under his first four successors. Seleucus occupied Babylonia in 312, and very soon added to it the Iranian satrapies, later Syria and Mesopotamia (in 301) and Cilicia (in 296). After Corupedion (281 B.C.) he became master of Asia Minor, with the exception of Pontus, Bithynia, and some of the Greek cities. He lost India, however, in the early days of his rule (304 B.C.)

After his death the disintegration of his kingdom began and never ceased until the last days of the dynasty. The Galatian wars started the process in the western part of the empire, and it was intensified by the Syrian wars, as they are called, of the Seleucids and the Ptolemies. During these wars many important cities of Asia Minor passed, for a longer or shorter time, into the hands of the latter. Part of Phrygia was occupied by the Galatians. Pergamon and the valley of the Caicus asserted their independence under the leadership of Philetaerus and his successors, and this was finally secured in the war begun by Eumenes and won by him in 263/2 B.C. About the same time Cappadocia ceased to recognize the sovereignty of the Seleucids, and even before this petty tyrants of the type of Philetaerus succeeded in establishing their rule temporarily over various cities of Asia Minor (Eupolemus at Iasus (?), Hieron at Priene, Timarchus at Miletus), but unlike the Pergamene kings they failed to maintain the position they had gained. After Asia Minor came the turn of the East. The Iranian satrapies were never very loyal to Seleucus and his successors, and the Greek settlements in the richer of these satrapies always tended to be separatist in order better to protect themselves against the Iranian tide. Thus insubordination of satraps and secession of some parts of the kingdom under Iranian rulers were the order of the day. Persis appears to have become independent (probably only for a time) early in the reign of Antiochus I. While Antiochus II was engaged in regaining territory in the West, Bactria gradually asserted her 'autonomy' and finally seceded from the kingdom under Seleucus II, when he was occupied first in recovering his kingdom from Ptolemy Euergetes I and afterwards in fighting his own brother. It was probably a little earlier that Parthia revolted under Andragoras and an Iranian nomad tribe, the Parni, under the leadership of its king Arsaces, invaded some parts of the Seleucid kingdom and subsequently conquered Andragoras and seized Parthia, thereby creating the nucleus of the great Parthian Empire of the future under the dynasty of the Arsacids. Finally, amid the turmoil of the dynastic war under Seleucus II, a new group of petty tyrannies sprang up in Asia Minor, and certain temple-states declared their independence or semi-independence. We have as examples several tyrannies in Cilicia, Pisidia, Phrygia, and Caria, and the famous temple-state of Olba in Cilicia ruled by the house of Teucer.[230]

It is difficult to describe the character of the great empire of the Seleucids in its economic aspect. It was the heir of the Persian Empire and, like it, consisted of many regions which had very little in common and never could be welded into anything like an economic unit. I have already given (see above, Ch. II., pp. 77 ff) a general description of the conditions in the various parts of the Persian Empire, and this holds good for the Seleucid period. It was impossible to apply to the Seleucid dominions any general organization such as that which was introduced in Egypt by the Ptolemies, and no attempt was made to do so. What economic cohesion the empire possessed depended entirely on its political unity, and the economic policy of the Seleucids was merely a part of their general policy—military, religious, and social—which aimed at keeping the various portions of it together.

The political unity of the Seleucid Empire was created by Seleucus I and its maintenance depended on him and his descendants. The rule of the Seleucids, like that of the Ptolemies, was personal and dynastic. It rested to a large extent on their ability to maintain a record of victory in their external and internal wars. The military successes on which their rule was based were due ultimately to the personal qualities of the rulers and to their close association with their 'friends' and their army and the support received from them.

This situation is reflected in many documents of the time, for instance in the speech (probably spurious) of Seleucus I to his friends and troops reported by Appian (*Syr.* 61) and in a decree passed by the city of Ilium in honour of Antiochus I for having secured peace for the cities and enlarged his kingdom 'thanks mainly to his personal valour (ἰδίᾳ ἀρετῇ) and to the devotion of his friends and troops'.*

For this personal rule over the countries that formed their kingdom the kings found an additional legitimization of a higher, though secondary, kind in religious institutions and philosophical doctrine which supported the dynastic principle. They claimed to be not only the successors but also the descendants of Alexander, thereby sharing in his victory over the East. In this respect the Seleucids did not differ from the Ptolemies nor, to a certain extent, from the Antigonids. Descendants of Alexander, they were at the same time descendants of the gods. From the days of Seleucus I, certainly from those of Antiochus I,† they publicly declared, perhaps through the medium of the oracle of Didyma, the divine descent of Seleucus I from Apollo.

This descent from Apollo made it possible for many Greek cities to set up spontaneously a cult of the ruling king. This was done for example at Ilium. We know, moreover, that divine honours were paid first to Seleucus and afterwards to his successors in cities that were founded by them. Very soon there was probably no Greek city in the Seleucid Empire without a cult of the reigning sovereign, his family, and his ancestors (πρόγονοι) in some form or other.

Alongside of the municipal cult of the living and dead kings we find from the time of Antiochus III a State royal cult organized by the king himself and served by priests and priestesses appointed by the king for each satrapy, and perhaps for the subdivisions of the satrapies, with an official residence at least in the most important cities of the various satrapies. The relations of this State cult to the municipal cult is little known. It is possible that the two were separate institutions, the municipal temples, priests, and ceremonies of the royal cult coexisting with those of the State cult. It is, however, equally probable that the new State cult was grafted in one way or another on the municipal cult, sharing in the individual cities

* *O.G.I.* 219.

† *Ibid.* 219, 26, cf. 227, 5–6 and 237, 5.

PLATE LII

1. Restoration of a monumental mausoleum, very similar to the famous grave of Maussolus at Halicarnassus, recently excavated by Prof. J. Keil and his associates near Ephesus. The mausoleum was built on the road leading from Ephesus to Sardis (12 km. from Ephesus) near a tumulus grave probably of Hellenistic times. It was never finished. It consisted of a Doric base and a cella with a *prostasis* of Corinthian columns. Over the columns ran a sculptured frieze (Amazonomachy), in the coffers were carved Centaurs fighting the Lapithae and scenes of gymnastic contests. The border of the roof was adorned with figures of winged and horned Persian lion-griffins in pairs facing each other and separated from each other by decorative marble vases; at the corners stood statues of horses and men. The sepulchral chamber contained a carved *kline*-sarcophagus richly adorned with sculptures; on the couch reclined a male figure (unfinished). All parts of the monument were gorgeously painted. No funeral inscription was found. Analysis of the architecture and sculpture of the monument and of one inscription led Prof. J. Keil to assign the monument to the middle of the third century B.C. Since the grave was so grandiose and expensive, Keil has suggested that it was the Mausoleum built by Laodice for her husband Antiochus II Theos, who died at Ephesus in 246 B.C. It must be remembered that political conditions hardly permitted Laodice to transport the body of Antiochus to Antioch. J. Keil, *Jahreshefte*, xxix (1934–5), Beibl., pp. 104 ff.; xxx (1936–7), Beibl., pp. 173 ff. (with copious illustration). Photograph supplied by Prof. J. Keil.

2. Terracotta statuette found at Myrina representing an Indian war-elephant covered with a heavy rug and carrying on its back a square wooden crenellated tower (*θωράκιον*). The tower is reinforced below the crenellation by two Macedonian metal shields. On the neck of the elephant is seated his driver. The elephant wears under its neck a large bell (cf. the coins of Seleucus I, E. T. Newell, *The Coin. of the Eastern Sel. Mints*, 1938, p. 125). It is striking with its trunk a Galatian soldier armed with sword and shield. Frequently published, see P. Bienkowski, *Les Celtes dans les arts mineurs gréco-romains*, 1928, pp. 142 ff., no. 1, fig. 212 (with bibliography; another replica at Athens, ibid., no. 2, fig. 213); for details regarding the military equipment cf. P. Couissin, *Institutions militaires et navales*, 1931, pl. XL, 1. The Myrina statuette certainly represents a scene in one of the battles against the Galatians fought by the Seleucids or the Attalids, perhaps the famous elephant battle of Antiochus I. For other monuments representing Indian war-elephants cf. my pls. LIII and LV. I may remark that figures of African war-elephants of the Ptolemaic army are familiar to the minor arts of Ptolemaic Egypt, see P. Bienkowski, loc. cit., pp. 145 ff. On p. 146, no. 13 (cf. C. W. Lunsingh Scheurleer, *Gr. Cer.*, p. 169), Bienkowski describes a sherd of a faience vase representing a war-elephant driven from behind by a horseman and charging a Galatian (third century B.C.). I may tentatively suggest that the curious scene represented an episode in the sad story of the destruction of 4,000 rebellious Celtic mercenaries by Ptolemy Philadelphus in 274 B.C., E. Bevan, *Hist. of Egypt*, 1927, p. 63; cf. the story told in III Macc. of the persecution of the Jews by Philopator, ibid., p. 229 f. I may remind the reader that one of the war-elephants of Pyrrhus is painted on the bottom of a South Italian dish of the Pocolom class, E. Q. Giglioli, *Corp. Vas. Ant.*, Italia, iii, 1928 (Villa Giulia), cf. J. D. Beazley, *J.H.S.* xlviii (1928), p. 257, and my *Hist. Anc. World*, ii, pl. XI, while the well-known *emblema* of a Calenian dish represents an African war-elephant (Bienkowski, fig. 214). On war-elephants S. Reinach, Dar. et Saglio, *D. d. A.* ii. 537 ff., and G. A. S. Snijder, *Bull. v. d. Vereen. tot bevord. d. kennis v. d. ant. beschaving*, ii, 1 (1927), pp. 8 ff. and ii, 2 (1927), p. 4.

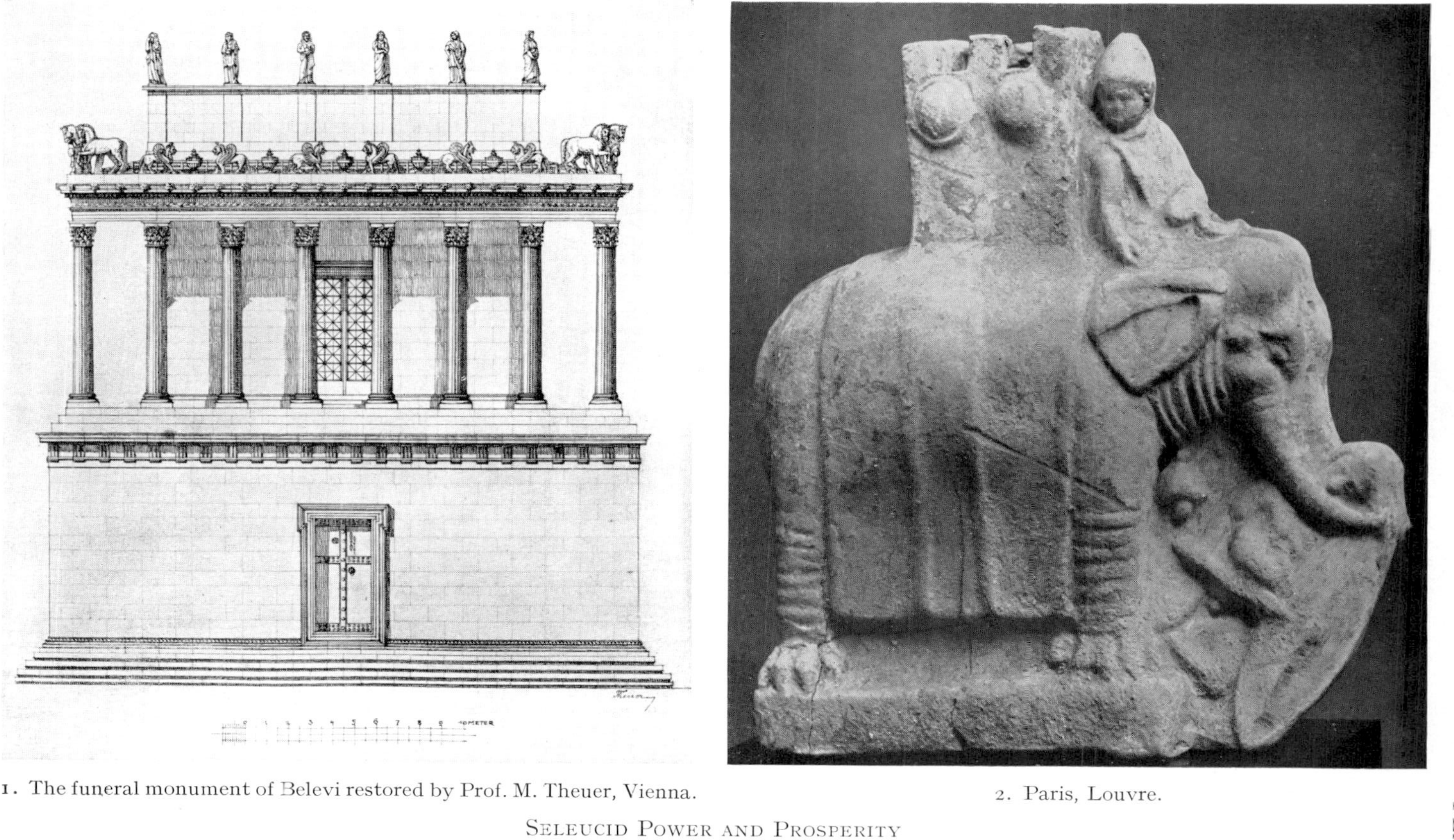

1. The funeral monument of Belevi restored by Prof. M. Theuer, Vienna.

2. Paris, Louvre.

Seleucid Power and Prosperity

1. Leningrad, Hermitage.

2. Athens, National Museum.

INDIAN ELEPHANTS IN THE SERVICE OF THE SELEUCIDS

PLATE LIII

1. One of the two silver *phalerae* (perhaps originally *emblemata* of silver dishes) of unknown origin acquired by the Hermitage in 1725. The centre of the circular *phalera* is occupied by the figure of a war-elephant very similar to that of the Myrina terracotta reproduced in the preceding plate. Note, however, that the tower is shaped like a little fortress and is occupied by two soldiers with lances, one wearing a Macedonian helmet. Note also that the driver is represented with his driving hook in his right hand, and that the rug which covers the back of the elephant is embroidered. The dragon which adorns this rug is the forerunner of the Chinese and Sasanian dragons. Smirnov has pointed out that the ears of the elephant were apparently cut to protect it against the enemy, for the ears of an elephant are its most vulnerable part. The picture of the elephant of the Hermitage *phalera* is by far the most realistic and exact representation of a war-elephant. The artist was certainly thoroughly familiar with war-elephants and their military equipment. Early Hellenistic Bactrian or Syrian work. N. Kondakoff and I. Tolstoi, *Antiquités de la Russie Méridionale*, p. 427, fig. 382; J. Smirnov, *Argenterie orientale*, 1913, pl. CXX (which is reproduced here).

2. Terracotta statuette from Myrina. Amor and Psyche, half naked and wearing crowns of flowers, are seated on the back of an Indian elephant on a pillow and fringed rug. Amor is holding in his left hand a round Macedonian shield with the boss in the form of a Medusa head (a common feature of Macedonian shields). There is another version of the same subject in a similar terracotta from Myrina in the Louvre. The elephant's saddle is fastened by a saddle-strap. On the back of the elephant are two girls, one embracing the other. It has been suggested with great probability that the statuettes of the Athenian Museum and the Louvre may be regarded as representing scenes of some great pageant of the Hellenistic kings. Since the elephants of the two terracottas are Indian, we must connect the figurines not with Ptolemaic Egypt but either with Syria or Pergamon. There is no need to remind the reader of the great pageant of Antiochus IV Epiphanes. In the *pompe* of Philadelphus described by Callixeinus elephants played a prominent part. Dionysus himself was represented riding on one of them, the role of driver being played by a Satyr. The groups here considered may have had a symbolical meaning; note especially the Macedonian shield in the hand of Amor in the Athenian replica. The Louvre statuette has been published and interpreted in the sense sketched above by S. Reinach, Dar. et Saglio, *D. d. A.* ii, p. 537, fig. 2620. For the Athenian replica see F. Winter, loc. cit., p. 229, no. 8. Photograph supplied by the authorities of the National Museum, Athens.

the same temples, sacred precincts and groves, ceremonies, and so forth as the municipal cult. Our evidence is meagre and no certain conclusions can be drawn from it.[231]

Simultaneously with the institution of this cult various philosophical schools vied with each other in giving a philosophical sanction to the royal power in general. The Seleucids, like the other Hellenistic kings, eagerly accepted the pronouncements of the philosophers and made use of them on many occasions. For instance we may detect an echo of such a pronouncement in the speech of Seleucus I to his army to which I have referred above. Spurious or not, the speech goes back to an early Hellenistic source and accurately represents the ideas of the time. In this speech, explaining the marriage of Antiochus I with his own stepmother, Seleucus I says: 'It is not the customs of the Persians and other peoples that I impose upon you but *the law which is common to all*, that what is decreed by the king is always *just*.'[232]

Such were the foundations of the royal power of the Seleucids in the eyes of their Greek subjects and allies. What kind of doctrine, if any, they found for the non-Greek inhabitants of their empire we do not exactly know. Over them they ruled by right of conquest, as descendants of Alexander. This was especially emphasized in the coinage of Seleucus I, a continuation, as it were, of the coinage of Alexander. Moreover, it is probable that the Seleucids, like the kings of the Pontic monarchy and later the kings of Commagene, in order to conciliate the Iranian population of their empire, emphasized their connexion with the extinct Persian dynasty of the Achaemenids. In this it appears that they were not successful, and that the Iranians never recognized their claim. There is also reason to think that in the figure of the supreme god of their monarchy—Zeus Olympius—a figure which they inherited from Alexander, they intended to set up a universal god of their composite empire, more or less like the Ptolemaic Sarapis—Zeus and Ahura Mazda and Bel all in one. This tendency became prominent later, in the time of Epiphanes, when Zeus Olympius was supposed to play in the destinies of the Seleucid Empire the same role that Jupiter Capitolinus played in those of the steadily growing Roman Empire.

In general the early Seleucids, like the Ptolemies, were careful not to offend the religious feelings of their subjects.[233] In Babylonia they displayed deep reverence for the native gods, of which we have sufficient proof in the ambitious project entertained by Alexander the Great and Antiochus I of rebuilding the great temple of Babylon, Esagila, and the restoration of Ezida in Borsippa by Antiochus I (268 B.C.). The same attitude finds expression in the gift of land made by Antiochus I in 279 B.C. to what remained of Babylon in his time (after the foundation of Seleuceia), a gift withdrawn from the Babylonians, Kuthaeans, and Borsippaeans five years later. I may also cite the story of the final cession to the temples of Babylon of the gift made by Antiochus II to Laodice and her sons. Finally, I may mention the tentative suggestion of E. T. Newell that a series of tetradrachms of Seleucus I with the figure of the seated Baal on the obverse and the lion on the reverse, a continuation of a pre-Alexandrian series of coins but certainly minted at Babylon between 306–281 B.C., may have been temple-money coined by the priests. Similar coins occur at Susa and Ecbatana.[234]

The same policy was adopted by the Seleucids in other cities of their Babylonian satrapy. We have good evidence of this at Uruk-Warka, the holy city of Babylonia, which became once more in the times of the Seleucids an important centre of Babylonian religion, learning, and science. The great temples of Uruk had been badly neglected by the Persian kings, and by the time of Alexander probably lay in ruins. In Seleucid days they were again the scene of much building activity. One temple after another was rebuilt from the foundation. The work was not carried out by the kings themselves but, certainly with their approval and support, by the representatives of the royal power in Uruk. Our rather meagre and incomplete evidence, which certainly will soon be enriched by further discoveries, shows that the Bît-rêš—the complex of buildings round the temple of Anu—was restored, or rather completely rebuilt, by Anu-uballit the 'second officer' of the city in 243 B.C., under Seleucus II. The second name of this officer—Nicarchus—was Greek and was granted to him by Antiochus II Theos. A little later, in 201 B.C., under Antiochus

III, a man of the same Babylonian name, perhaps a member of the same family, Anu-uballit, whose second Greek name was Kephallon and who was 'the great, the city-lord of Uruk', built in the same group his famous temple of Anu and Antum. It was the same man who infused new life into another great sacred precinct of Uruk, the so-called 'Südbau'. This restoration of Uruk from its state of decay to its former splendour by representatives of the government, who probably played at Uruk the same role as the *epistatai* and the *strategoi* played in other cities of the Seleucid Empire, is a striking episode, for these representatives acted undoubtedly with the permission and probably with the support of the ruling kings, whose faithful servants they were.

Private contracts and other documents of the Seleucid period written in Accadian on tablets and probably in Aramaic or Greek on parchment and papyrus, and some semi-literary and literary texts written on tablets in Accadian, which have been found in the temples of Uruk in comparatively large numbers, make it clear that under the Seleucids these temples regained their past prosperity and played once more their former important part in the life of the city and perhaps of Babylonia in general. It was certainly due to the liberal policy of the Seleucid administration that the temples transacted their own business in their own language and according to their own law, that they were free from the obligation to register their contracts in the royal *chreophylakion*, and that their archives served as a depository not only of documents in cuneiform relating to the life of the temples but also of documents in Greek and Aramaic which probably, at least in part, had no relation to it. The example of the kings was followed by those Greeks who lived at Orchoi. In the temple documents they appear not only as devotees of the local gods—Ishtar, Anu, and Antum, and the rest—but also as active participants in the cult and business of the local sanctuaries.[235]

Nor was the policy of the Seleucids different in Elam. The recent French excavations at Susa—the Hellenistic Seleuceia on the Eulaeus—have shown the prosperity and influence at that time of the famous temple of Nanaia in this city; it was a large and handsome building, which certainly was not neglected either by the kings or by their local representatives. Among the stones of the temple, which were used later by the Sasanians for the construction of their palace, were found scores of Greek inscriptions of the Seleucid and Parthian periods, among them several manumissions; which shows that at this time the temple was the chief centre of the city, the place where important documents were published, statues erected, and so on.[236]

The documents that refer to the reconstruction of Esagila and Ezida and many other documents of the Seleucid period at Babylon and Uruk show that in the official terminology the Seleucids were represented there as the legitimate successors of the Babylonian kings, as rulers who, like Alexander, had received their power from the hands of Bel and Marduk.

It is more than probable, moreover, though we have little information on the subject, that a cult of the kings was instituted in some form in the Babylonian and Elamitic temples. On a tablet found at Uruk of uncertain date (after the year 100 of the Seleucid era, that is to say, under Antiochus III or after him) there is a mention of offerings of meat before the statues of the kings on the days of the regular sacrifices. It is well known that such offerings and some sort of royal cult were not foreign to the Babylonian religion.[237]

In Syria, the kernel of their empire, Seleucus and his descendants adopted a similar attitude in regard to the local gods and traditions. Malalas (p. 198 Bonn), in his well-known account of the foundation of Seleuceia in Pieria and Antioch on the Orontes by Seleucus Nicator, tells us how Seleucus, looking for a site for his projected harbour city, sacrificed to Zeus Casius, a local god of storm and thunder, who showed him where to found it. Three days later Seleucus organized a religious celebration of the local god Zeus Ceraunius in the sanctuary said to have been founded for him by Perseus near Iopolis, and performed a sacrifice to him on the first day of Artemisius. The story testifies to the reverence shown by Seleucus I for the local gods and especially for the god of the sky, storm, and thunder, who was at the same time the great military god of Syria, Anatolia, and Phoenicia—Teshub–Hadad–Baal. His policy is the same here as in respect of the

Iranian Ahura Mazda and the Babylonian Bel. It may be noticed in this connexion that the cult of the local supreme gods was in all probability the origin of the cult of the military hellenized gods of Syria, the triad of Bel, Jahribol, and Aglibol, gods of light and victory, with whom the monuments of Palmyra and of Dura have made us so well acquainted. To the same group belong the Arabian, Syrian, and Anatolian military gods figured on horseback and camel-back. We know them from sculptures and dedications of Roman times, but the military dress in which they are represented is not purely Roman but shows some Hellenistic features. The gods were probably creations of the late Seleucid period, gods of the Seleucid army, which by that time had become strongly orientalized.[238]

Next to the god of lightning and victory in the Syrian pantheon came the great Atargatis, wife and consort of Hadad, the *Συρία θεά* of the Greeks and the 'dea Syria' of the Romans. Like the cult of Hadad–Teshub–Baal, her cult was adopted and hellenized by Seleucus I. Her famous temple at Bambyce (Hierapolis) was rebuilt by Stratonice, wife of Seleucus I (Luc., *de dea Syria*, 17–19). This building was certainly Hellenistic, comparable to the temples of the same goddess at Baalbek and of Bel at Palmyra, both of the early Roman Imperial period. It is unfortunate that no thorough excavation of the ruins of the temple of Bambyce is possible, its site being occupied by a mosque. The results of some trial excavations made by Perdrizet and Seyrig on the site have never, to my knowledge, been published. Greek artists of Hellenistic Syria created images of the goddess, as they did of Hadad–Teshub–Baal. In these images she appears as another version of the great Anatolian mother-goddess, whose sacred animal was the lion, while Hadad's animal was the bull. The predilection of Seleucus for the bull's horns and the frequency with which they appear on his coinage are well known.

I may note in passing that the Ptolemies followed the same policy in their Syrian and Phoenician dominions. The popularity of the cults of Astarte, Adonis, and Atargatis–Hadad in Egypt, alike in Alexandria and in the 'country' (χώρα), certainly reflects the high regard in which the Ptolemies held these gods in Syria and Phoenicia. As regards Egypt, it will be sufficient to remind the reader of the reverence that the great Arsinoe paid to the mysteries of Adonis (Theocritus), and of the papyri testifying to the popularity of Adonis, Astarte, and Atargatis in the 'country'.[239]

It is not improbable that in Syria and Mesopotamia, as in Babylonia, some form of dynastic cult was connected with the worship of the local gods patronized by the Seleucids. If so, the practice of the Seleucids in Syria in this respect was not unlike that of the Ptolemies in Egypt. But, so far as I know, we possess no direct or indirect evidence bearing on this point.

Seleucus and the Seleucids probably followed the same policy of benevolence and protection in their relations with the rich and important temples of Asia Minor, but of these relations we know very little. A stray inscription found at Nysa* shows that Seleucus I and Antiochus granted to the city of Athymbria several important privileges for their Plutonium, in all probability an old native sanctuary; and it is specifically stated that in so doing they were guided both by their piety and by their desire to be agreeable to Greek cities. Another inscription† attests the rebuilding by Seleucus I of the temple of Zeus Olbius at Olba in Cilicia. And there is not the slightest doubt that Seleucus and his successors held the great temples of Asia Minor in general in high esteem, for example that of Artemis in their capital, Sardis, and those of Ephesus and Miletus. We know that the temple of Artemis at Sardis was very rich,‡ and we hear occasionally of lavish gifts bestowed by Seleucus I and his successors on the temple of Didyma.[240]

The unity of the empire of the Seleucids found expression first and foremost in the uniformity of its military and administrative organization, which the Seleucids inherited in the main from the Persian kings and from Alexander. It would be outside the scope of the present work to discuss this topic at length. All the material relating to it has been recently collected and expounded by E. Bikerman in his *Institutions des*

* C. B. Welles, *R.C.* 9.

† A. Wilhelm, *Denkschr. d. Wien. Akad.*, phil.-hist. Kl. xliv (1896), no. vi, pp. 85 ff.

‡ Buckler, *Sardis, Gr. and Lat. inscr.*, no. 1.

Séleucides, where the reader will find reliable information about what little is known of the organization of the central and provincial administration of the empire in general, of the Seleucid army, of the royal court, of the financial agents of the king, and other matters.

Suffice it to say here that the Seleucid administration shows a general unformity, with slight variations from place to place. Its terminology is almost identical with that of the Ptolemaic administration with only slight differences, a blend as it were of Greek and Persian terminology: satraps, *strategoi*, *hyparchoi*, *toparchai*, *meridarchai*, &c., for the provincial administration; *βασιλικόν, ὁ ἐπὶ τῶν προσόδων, ῥισκοφύλαξ, γαζοφύλαξ, διοικητής, οἰκονόμος* for the central and provincial financial administration; *βασιλικοὶ δικασταί* for the courts; *χρεοφύλακες* and *βιβλιοφύλακες* for the record officers, &c.[241]

3. Economic and Financial Policy

(*a*) Ps.-Aristotle, *Oeconomica* II

Not very abundant and no less difficult to interpret is the information we have concerning the economic and financial policy of the Seleucids. To this we now turn our attention.

We may begin our study of the economic and financial organization of the early Seleucid Empire by analysing the very interesting treatise on economics which forms the second book of Aristotle's 'Economics', and which, though Peripatetic in character, certainly cannot be regarded as a work of Aristotle (above, p. 74). The treatise consists of two parts. The second is practical and historical: it contains a set of stories illustrating the various emergency devices adopted by Greek cities and tyrants and by Persian satraps to relieve acute financial crises in their cities and satrapies. On the other hand the first part is purely theoretical. Intended as a kind of preface to the second, it endeavours to give a theory of finance in brief outline. In fact it classifies the different types of economy both public and private, and briefly characterizes each, viz. royal economy, satrap economy, city economy, and private economy.

The author and the date of the treatise are not precisely known. The writer certainly used early sources not later than the late fourth century. None of his stories is subsequent to Alexander, and the theoretical part is undoubtedly based on a study of the late Persian Empire and Alexander's monarchy. The treatise would therefore seem to have no bearing on the subject dealt with in the present chapter. This, however, is not my opinion. To begin with, there is reason to think that the author of the treatise, though he used exclusively sources not later than the fourth century B.C., lived himself probably in the time after Alexander, in the last years of the fourth and the early years of the third century B.C. In addition to what I have said before on this subject (above, p. 74), I may point out that the treatise as we have it suits the literary atmosphere of the early Hellenistic period very well. It is evidently not a purely theoretical and historical literary production. It was in all probability intended to serve practical purposes, to be a kind of manual or guide for those who were confronted with problems of an economic and financial kind, whether in the cities or in the monarchies of the time. This was nothing unusual. Various philosophical schools of early Hellenistic times vied with each other in producing similar manuals in various fields. It is sufficient to mention the numerous treatises *περὶ βασιλείας*, some of which were written by the early successors of Aristotle (e.g. Theophrastus).

If I am right and the book was published as a sort of guide or vade-mecum in the early Hellenistic period, and in all probability not in Greece but perhaps in Asia Minor, for the use of contemporaries who were faced with economic and financial problems, the author in his classificatory and theoretical preface certainly had in view not the past only, the structure of the Persian kingdom and of Alexander's empire, but also the present, the economic and financial organization which he himself observed in the world in which he lived. This world could not possibly be Ptolemaic Egypt and Antigonid Macedonia. What we know of these countries shows that their economic and financial organization was very different from that described in the preface. The world that the author had in mind and tried implicitly to characterize, alongside of Persia and of Alexander's empire, may have been the kingdom of Antigonus the One-eyed.[242]

If so, it seems appropriate to set forth and analyse the evidence furnished by *Oecon.* II before discussing the meagre information which we have concerning the economic and financial structure of the Seleucid Empire. The survey will reveal the general outlines of an economic and financial organization that was in all probability very similar to, if not identical with, that of the Seleucid Empire, or at least of the same type. Moreover, in discussing the Seleucid Empire it seems to me opportune to leave aside modern classifications and follow the subdivision into types and the description of each type suggested by the author of our treatise, an acute observer who was perfectly familiar with the conditions of the time with which we are dealing.

I have mentioned above that the writer distinguishes four types of economic and financial organization: the *οἰκονομία βασιλική*, that is to say, the general management of economic and financial affairs by the king personally; the *οἰκονομία σατραπική*, the economic and financial organization of each satrapy; the nearly autonomous *οἰκονομία* of the *polis*; and the basis of all these 'economies', the management of their own affairs by private people, irrespectively of their nationality and their political status.

The royal economy dealt, according to the author of the treatise, with very few matters. His description of these summarizes very well the main departments of financial administration that were necessarily managed by the king personally, or by the chief of his *βασιλικόν*, alike in the Persian and in the Hellenistic monarchies. The first sentence* deals with monetary policy: how much money should be minted at a given time and of what kinds (gold and silver in Persia; gold, silver, and copper in the Hellenistic monarchies) and when dear or cheap (perhaps a reference to variations of standard, such as is attested in the case of the first Ptolemy; above, p. 398). We know that coinage was an almost exclusive monopoly of the Persian kings and of Alexander. We have seen the attention paid by the Ptolemies to this question, and how strict was their monetary monopoly. We shall see presently that in their coinage the Seleucids inherited the traditions of Persia and Alexander.

* *ποῖον (νόμισμα) καὶ πότε τίμιον ἢ εὔωνον ποιητέον* (II. 1. 3, p. 1345b23).

The next sentence* has been interpreted by modern scholars in various ways. In my opinion it should be translated as follows: 'as regards the exported and imported goods: which of the goods the king has received from his satraps as their stipulated amount (ταγή) it will be profitable for him to sell, and when'. The interpretation of this paragraph is evident. It deals with the commercial policy of the king, especially as regards his trade with foreign countries. It was for the king to decide how much of the merchandise that he received from his satraps he would sell and export and what imports his kingdom required. No satrap was competent to do this. I have shown above the importance of the foreign trade of Persia, and I have emphasized in the preceding section of this chapter the prominence of foreign trade in the economy of the Ptolemies and its close connexion with their monetary and their general economic policy. It was no less important for the Seleucids and the Hellenistic monarchs in general. I shall return to this subject presently.

What follows—the third and last sentence† of the section on royal economy—deals with expenditure. According to our author (at the end of the theoretical section) the chief requirement in every type of economy is to balance the budget. In the case of the king the best way of doing this is to reduce expenditure. Next comes the question how most profitably to use the revenue of the kingdom in money and kind to cover the expenditure. It is evident that these were vital problems both for Persia and for the Hellenistic monarchies.

The king therefore dealt with matters of prime importance only. Taxation—the assessment and collection of the revenues—in Persia and probably in Alexander's monarchy was the business of the satraps. In Egypt, as we have seen, it was otherwise. In all probability the Seleucid monarchy was organized in this respect more or less in the same way as Persia. In *Oecon.* II the οἰκονομία σατραπική is mainly concerned with the revenues (πρόσοδοι). Six classes of revenues are distin-

* *περὶ δὲ τὰ ἐξαγώγιμα καὶ εἰσαγώγιμα, πότε καὶ τίνα παρὰ τῶν σατραπῶν ἐν τῇ ταγῇ ἐκλαβόντι αὐτῷ λυσιτελήσει διατίθεσθαι* (ibid.).

† *περὶ δὲ τὰ ἀναλώματα, τίνα περιαιρετέον καὶ πότε, καὶ πότερον δοτέον νόμισμα εἰς τὰς δαπάνας ἢ ἃ τῷ νομίσματι ὤνια.*

guished: revenues from the land, from other property of the State, from trade and commerce, from land-tolls and taxes on various transactions, from cattle, and from personal taxes. In describing these various classes of revenue the author is very brief, and brevity makes him obscure. I cannot discuss all the controversial points, and will merely state briefly my opinion. The state-revenues from the land are described as ἐκφόριον and δεκάτη. The meaning of this statement is not clear. We know that in Egypt ἐκφόριον meant rent, a *pars quanta* paid by the tillers of the soil to the landowners; the meaning of δεκάτη is obvious. It is possible that the author found in his source the two types of payment distinguished and described in detail. He disregarded this and used the terms ἐκφόριον and δεκάτη, without discriminating between them, to cover the royal income from the land. His chief concern was to emphasize the importance of land revenue in the budgets of the satrapies and in the satrap economy. In any case the passage does not help us to a better understanding of the system of land-taxes as established in the Persian Empire or in the satrapies of Alexander.

The next sentence deals with the ἴδια, the revenue from which consisted in gold, silver, copper, or other products. The most probable interpretation of this passage is not that which I suggested some years ago. The ἴδια are probably the private possessions of the king other than agricultural land, his ἴδιος λόγος: first and foremost mines, then quarries, salt-pans, forests, lakes, and so on. In Egypt these were the private property of the king and were exploited by him. I see no reason to suppose that it was otherwise in Persia and in the empire of Alexander. Seleucus and his successors made no change in this state of things.

Next follows the income from the ἐμπόρια, revenues which the satraps collected for the king from the internal and foreign commerce of their respective satrapies in the form of customs duties, harbour dues, payments connected with fairs, duties levied at the frontiers of the satrapies.

The next sentence, which enumerates τέλη κατὰ γῆν and ἀγοραῖα τέλη, is obscure. The former have been explained as tolls levied for the use of the roads, and this may be correct; the latter may be regarded as taxes paid in the ἀγορά, that is to say, on transactions such as are carried out as a rule in the market-place of cities and villages—all kinds of taxes on sales, taxes on the registration of documents, and so forth. The following item,* the revenue derived from the βοσκήματα (cattle) calls for no comment, except that I do not know whether the ἐπικαρπία and δεκάτη mentioned as revenues from the βοσκήματα were identical. The absence of the ἐννόμια or pasturage tax may be due to the fact that the pastures were royal property and were meant to be included in the second sentence.

Last come the personal taxes: ἐπικεφάλαιον and χειρωνάξιον. The latter is the payment made by artisans for the right of exercising their craft. Whether by ἐπικεφάλαιον was meant a general poll-tax is very uncertain. We shall see later that there is evidence of a tax of this name in Palestine.

I may observe that no mention is made under the heading of οἰκονομία σατραπική of the revenue derived by the king from the tribute (φόρος) paid by the cities. Nor is this item mentioned in the description of the οἰκονομία βασιλική. Our author is likewise silent on the subject of the expenditure of the satraps. In all probability the satraps were not empowered to deal with this side of the provincial budget. In *Oecon.* II they appear as mere collectors of the king's revenues. This does not accord with the little we know about the powers of the Persian satraps, but may be true of the provincial governors of the Seleucids.

The city economy is dealt with briefly. It appeared of minor importance to the author, and so it certainly was during the Hellenistic period and in a treatise concerned mainly with the structure of the Persian Empire. The revenue of a city was derived from its property in the territory belonging to it, from taxes on commerce (ἐμπόρια καὶ διαγωγαί), and from the ἐγκύκλια, various taxes connected with the business transactions of the inhabitants of the city. I have dealt with the subject of city economy above (pp. 241 ff.). The author's enumeration of municipal sources of revenue is correct.

The author is a little more explicit on the matter of private economy. The fact that in his view the income of a

* ἡ ἀπὸ τῶν βοσκημάτων, ἐπικαρπία τε καὶ δεκάτη καλουμένη (II. 1. 4).

private person is chiefly derived from land is interesting as an indication of the mainly agricultural character of the economic system of his time. Next come the enigmatic ἐγκλήματα (ἐγκτήματα?), a unique term of unknown meaning. Ἐγκτήματα may be connected, as Prof. C. B. Welles suggests, with ἔγκτησις in its technical sense—the right to own property in land or houses. Last comes ἀργύριον, money-lending.

That we may see how far the economic policy and the revenues of the Seleucids accord with the sketch in *Oecon.* II, I shall set out such information as I have been able to derive from the available sources.

(*b*) *Coinage, Weights and Measures*

The Seleucids, like the Ptolemies and the other Hellenistic kings, paid great attention to their *coinage,* which succeeded without discredit the coinage of Alexander. Like him, the Seleucids kept strictly to the Attic standard. Like him again, they endeavoured to make their coinage abundant, stable, reliable, and of excellent quality. The issues from the various Seleucid mints were widely distributed not only over their Anatolian, Syrian, Mesopotamian, and Iranian Empire, but also over the rest of the Hellenistic world.* The coinage was much simplified by Antiochus I and became the basic currency of the East. Its popularity there is shown by the fact that after the secession of Bactria and Parthia the independent coinage of these kingdoms was in fact a continuation of that of the Seleucids. Moreover, coins of the first Seleucids were 'widely circulated far into Asia and were copied again and again, as had been the case with the coins of Athens in the fifth and fourth centuries' (Milne). Their coinage, it may be observed, was of a more personal character than that of the Persian kings and the Ptolemies. Each king issued coins bearing his own likeness.[243]

The kings of the Seleucid dynasty coined in three metals: gold, silver, and copper. Gold was regularly minted until the second half of the third century, when minting stopped and was resumed from time to time by the later Seleucids on special

* Note the imitation of this coinage by Cleomenes III and Nabis of Sparta, and the circulation of over-stamped Seleucid coins in Byzantium and Callatis.

occasions only. The explanation of this curious history of their gold coinage (the Ptolemies coined gold regularly till a much later date, almost until the end of their rule in Egypt) may be found in my opinion in the scarcity of gold in the Near East in general. The main supply of gold—I disregard the gold of the northern Balkan peninsula, which never reached the Near East—came either from Egypt (Nubia), or from the Asiatic North, from the gold mines of Siberia and the Altai. The Ptolemies, of course, kept their gold supply jealously for themselves. Thus the only abundant sources of gold for the Seleucids were Siberia and the Middle East (Asia Minor hardly produced much gold at that time). Since Siberian gold reached Bactria first, it was natural that gold currency should be issued in large amounts especially in the Seleucid satrapy of Bactria. As soon as Bactria became independent and was itself cut off from Siberia, while the Parthians inserted themselves between the Seleucids and the Asiatic North, gold became very scarce in the Seleucid kingdom and the kings subsequent to Seleucus II had to give up their coinage in that metal. We may, by the way, suppose that the question of the gold supply was one of the reasons for the Oriental expedition of Antiochus III.[244].

The main currency of the Seleucid kingdom was silver. As long as Asia Minor with its abundant silver mines was in the hands of the Seleucids, they never suffered from a shortage of silver. The loss of Asia Minor by Antiochus III changed the situation: I shall speak of this in my next chapter. I have already mentioned that the minting of the tetradrachms of the early Seleucids was distributed over their extensive Empire, many mints being established. This does not mean, however, that the cities of the Seleucid Empire had any right of coinage. They minted for the king and in the name of the king. The early Seleucids regarded the minting of gold and heavy silver as their exclusive privilege and, like Alexander and the Successors, they would not tolerate any competition from the Greek cities of their empire. Some exceptions to this rule are known, but occasional concessions to the cities in this respect, due to special political considerations, only serve to confirm the rule.

Much more liberal was their policy as regards copper. Copper (and sometimes small silver) was regularly minted by most of the Greek cities of Asia Minor for local and regional circulation. The careful study of the material found at Priene carried out by the late Dr. Regling proves this with full certainty. And Priene, of course, was not an exception. It must be emphasized that the Seleucids never recognized, like the Ptolemies, the trimetallic system. The copper of their empire was always intended for local exchange with a very limited circulation.

While the old Greek cities of Asia Minor were granted the privilege of coining their own small change, this privilege was never given to the new cities founded by Alexander and the Seleucids in Syria and in the eastern satrapies. Like gold and silver, copper was royal currency, minted in the name of the kings. It seems very probable, however, that the coins were occasionally produced not in one of the royal mints but in municipal mints, which acted as concessionaires and on behalf of the kings. Large quantities of such local copper were emitted in the various cities of Syria and of the East, as may be gathered from a study of the coins found at Dura–Europus, Seleuceia on the Eulaeus, and Seleuceia on the Tigris. Like the copper of the Anatolian cities, the Seleucid copper of Syria and the East had not merely a local circulation within cities. As small change it circulated over comparatively wide areas.[245]

One of the most interesting features of the circulation of coins in the Seleucid Empire is revealed by the study of many hoards found in Syria and Mesopotamia on the one hand and in Asia Minor on the other. These hoards, in contrast to some found in the houses of various cities, are a striking illustration of the way in which money circulated throughout the empire, representing as they do the savings of richer people. They show that the bulk of the savings of the inhabitants of the Seleucid Empire consisted, not so much of Seleucid silver and occasionally gold, which do not form a very prominent element of third century hoards, but of issues of Philip, Alexander, and Lysimachus with a certain mixture of coins of the other Successors. Coins of Alexander and Lysimachus are the most prevalent. They are partly issues made during their lifetime, but mostly posthumous issues by various mints outside as well as inside the empire. Besides these coins and the Seleucid gold and silver, coins of the other independent kings of the

Hellenistic world in the third century, especially the Pergamene rulers, are often found (in small quantities) in these hoards. The only exception is the Ptolemies. In none of the third century hoards outside Greece is Ptolemaic silver or gold found, so far as I know. The Ptolemaic currency was apparently carefully excluded from the Seleucid kingdom.

The character of the hoards, as briefly described above, reflects some important features of the economic life of the third century and in particular of the economic policy of the Seleucids. It appears that the Seleucids—in this respect so different from the Ptolemies—made great efforts to maintain the monetary unity of the Hellenistic world. By a sort of mutual accord all the leading mints of the time kept strictly to one and the same standard—the Attic—and emitted large quantities of international currency in the shape of posthumous Alexanders and Lysimachi. These coins circulated freely all over the Hellenistic world, apparently without restriction—in the Seleucid kingdom, in the Anatolian monarchies, in Greece, and in the Balkan peninsula. The only exception was the Ptolemaic Empire. When the Ptolemies changed their standard to the 'Phoenician' and introduced a strict monetary monopoly throughout their empire, they isolated themselves from the rest of the Hellenistic world. No coins of foreign mints or of Attic standard are found in hoards of the third century B.C. discovered in Egypt or in the Ptolemaic dominions, and, as I have already said, no coins of Ptolemaic mints are found in any Syrian or Anatolian hoard. The Hellenistic world of the third century was sharply divided into two spheres of economic activity: the Ptolemaic with its expansion chiefly to the West, and the Seleucid with its mainly Oriental connexions.[246]

The tendency of the Seleucids to maintain unity of currency is attested by another important trait of their monetary policy. The bulk of the coins of Seleucus I in his early years consisted of gold and silver which practically repeated Alexander's coinage, with the sole difference that the names of Alexander and Philip III were gradually, though not completely, replaced by that of Seleucus. In the last ten years of Seleucus' rule, however, his coin-types became more diversified and of a more personal character. A reaction against this set in with Antiochus I and II, who again issued large quantities of Seleucus' Alexander coins and even reminted some of the later coins of Seleucus as coins of the Alexander-Seleucus type, thereby stressing the international character of their economic policy and the demand for such a policy inside and outside the kingdom.[246a]

It is certain that the coinage of the Seleucids was intended both to promote the use of money in their empire and to serve as a powerful instrument for the development of their foreign trade. To what extent they succeeded in the first of these aims we do not know. We have no evidence comparable to the Greek papyri of the Ptolemaic period in Egypt. The few tablets from Babylon and Uruk that have been published have been very little studied from the point of view of economic history. We hope, moreover, soon to have a large number of tablets from Seleuceia; no one would venture to base general conclusions on the scanty material now available, knowing that hundreds of tablets still await publication. The impression left by such documents as have been published and translated is that the use of money was firmly established in Seleucid Babylonia, though it had not entirely displaced barter. In any case money circulated freely and was extensively used for all sorts of transactions; how much more extensively than in the Persian period we are unable to say. It is interesting to note that in the cuneiform documents of the Seleucid period payments were reckoned, according to the ancient method, in minae and shekels, though they were effected in Seleucid staters, probably at an official rate of exchange (there are frequent references to the 'Babylonian rate').[247]

If these conditions prevailed in Babylonia in spite of its immemorial traditions, they must have prevailed likewise in the hellenized parts of the Syrian Empire, not only among the Greek inhabitants of those districts but also among the native population. The Greeks, of course, conducted their business on a money basis. We should probably know much more on the subject if the same strict attention were paid to finds of coins in the excavations of Syrian, Mesopotamian, and Babylonian cities as has been paid in many of those of

Palestine. The number of coins of the Ptolemies, and later of the Seleucids, that have been found in Palestinian cities is surprising, and the same is true of the excavations of Seleuceia and Dura, where all coins found have been and are being carefully collected, cleaned, identified, and published. The proportion of Seleucid, and especially of early Seleucid, coins is indeed small, and it could not be otherwise; but they are sufficiently numerous to show the prominent part they played in the affairs of Seleuceia and Europus-Dura, and that no other currency was in use in the two cities at the time of Seleucid domination.[248]

Closely connected with the coinage and its management was the organization of a rational system of weights and measures. Many systems were in common use in the Seleucid kingdom: the Babylonian, the Phoenician, the Attic. Did the Seleucids follow any definite policy in this respect? Did they attempt a kind of unification?

Our information on this subject is very meagre. Except for the tablets of Uruk we have no written documents to throw light on the problem. The Babylonian tablets of Hellenistic date suggest that there was no change as regards the weights and measures used in Babylonia in the Hellenistic period: the traditional weights and measures were still in exclusive use.[249] But two bronze weights of the Parthian period (56/5 B.C. and A.D. 72/3), one found near Babylon bearing the name of the city *agoranomos*, the other in Seleuceia with the monogram of the chief of the city police (the *paraphylax*), seem to testify to the use of the Attic standard in Parthian Babylonia, along with the Babylonian one.[250]

For Syria we possess no documents similar to the tablets of Uruk and Babylon. By way of compensation, however, we have a unique series of bronze, lead, and stone weights of various dates and places. Many of them are precisely dated and belong to the period of Seleucid rule. The series of dated weights begins with the reign of Antiochus III, and goes down to the last days of the Seleucid régime. These weights may be divided into two classes. The first, which is very small in number, may be called the group of royal weights. Inscribed on them are the names of the ruling kings (Antiochus IV,

PLATE LIV

1. Square lead weight. Winged Nike flying to the left with crown and palm branch between two stars. Inscription: ΒΑΣΙΛΕΩΣ | ΑΝΤΙΟΧΟΥ ΘΕΟΥ | ΕΠΙΦΑΝΟΥΣ | ΜΝΑ. *Rev*. Square network in relief to prevent adulteration of the weight. 519 gr.

E. Babelon and A. Blanchet, *Cat. d. bronzes ant. de la Bibl. Nat.*, p. 679, no. 2245; E. Michon, 'Pondus', Dar. et Saglio, *D. d. A.* iv, p. 555, no. 19, fig. 5738 (assigned to Antiochus IV Epiphanes); O. Viedebandt, *Z. d. d. Palästina-Vereins*, xlv (1922), p. 13, no. 97, and p. 22 (assigned with little probability to Antiochus I Theos Dikaios of Commagene).

2. Square bronze weight. Zebu turned to the right. Above: ΑΝΤΙΟΧΕΙΟΝ, below: ΤΕΤΑΡΤΟΝ. *Rev*. Network as above. 122 gr.

Babelon-Blanchet, loc. cit., p. 682 f., no. 2267; E. Michon, loc. cit., p. 555, nos. 11 and 12, cf. *Bull. Soc. Ant. Fr.*, 1906, p. 195.

3. Square lead weight. Found at Antioch. Anchor. Above: ΒΑΣΙΛΕΩΣ | ΑΝΤΙΟΧΟΥ | ΦΙΛΟΜΗΤΟ|ΡΟΣ ΜΝΑ *Rev*. Network. 0.105–0.105. 674 gr. Antiochus VIII Grypus (125–95 B.C.). Another copy found at Kurye (Koseir), now in the Museum of Antioch. 0.103–0.10.

Unpublished. For acquaintance with these weights, descriptions and photographs of them, and permission to publish them I am indebted to M. H. Seyrig, Director of Antiquities in Syria.

Two other weights with the names of kings are known to me. One—in the Museum of Antioch (lead)—is described by M. H. Seyrig, to whom I owe the information, as follows: Square lead weight. Inscription: Β[Α]ΣΙΛΕ[ΩΣ] | ΔΗΜΗΤΡΙΟΥ | ΣΩΤΗΡΟΣ. In the field to the right: ΗΜΙΜΝΟΥΝ. Poseidon naked standing to the left, his foot on a rock, the trident in his hand. To the left in the field an anchor. Around a frame (knotted string). *Rev*. Damaged. 258 gr. Unpublished (in bad condition). The figure of Poseidon does not appear on the coins of Demetrius I Soter (162–150 B.C.). The other is in Paris, Louvre, and was published by E. Michon, *Mém. Soc. Ant. Fr.* li (1890), pp. 11–13, no. 3; *D. d. A.*, loc. cit., p. 555, no. 16. Square lead weight. *Obv*. Anchor. Above: ΒΑΣ]Ι[ΛΕ]Ω[Σ] ΑΝΤΙΟΧΟΥ; below: ΕΥΣΕΒΟΥΣ | ΦΙΛΟΠΑΤΟΡΟΣ. *Rev*. Network. ΕΤΟΥΣ ΚΕ | ΑΓΟΡΑΝΟΜΟΥΝΤΟΣ | ΔΙΟΝΥΣ[Ι]ΟΥ ΜΝΑ. 614.4 gr. Antiochus X Eusebes, 92 B.C.

On the weights of the Seleucids, see pp. 446 ff. of this chapter and notes 250, 251.

1. Paris, Cabinet des Médailles.

2. Paris, Cabinet des Médailles.

3. Beirut, Museum.

Royal Weights of the Seleucids

PLATE LV

1. Paris, Louvre.

2. In the possession of Count Chandon des Brialles, La Cordelière, Chaourche (Aube), France.

Royal Weights of the Seleucids

PLATE LV

1. Square lead weight. Indian elephant bridled turned to the left. Above: ΣΕΛΕΥΚΕΙΟΝ | ΓΚ - Ρ; below, ΔΙΜΝΟΥΝ ΕΠΙ ΔΕΛΦΙΩΝΟΣ. *Rev.* Network. 1143 gr. Found at Sidon. E. Michon, *Bull. Soc. Ant. Fr.*, 1906, p. 193 f.; id., *D. d. A.*, loc. cit., p. 556, no. 1. Cf. *Bull. Soc. Ant. Fr.*, 1903, p. 355, no. 45. Date—123 Sel. = 189 B.C., Seleucus IV.

2. Square lead weight. Standing anchor, two heraldic dolphins to the left and right, and another in the field to the right. Above: ΣΕΛΕΥΚΕΙΟΣ; across the anchor ΒΞΡ - ΕΠΙ | ΕΥ-Δ - Ω - ΡΟΥ; below: ΜΝΑ. *Rev.* Network. 0·98–0·101. Date—162 Sel. — 150 B.C. Demetrius I Soter or Alexander Balas. I am indebted to M. H. Seyrig and Rev. P. Mouterde for making me acquainted with this weight, and to its owner for the photograph here reproduced and for permission to publish it. *Σελεύκειος* in the legend means *Σελεύκειος χαρακτήρ*. See my 'Seleucid Babylonia' (*Yale Cl. Stud.* iii, 1932) p. 23. Photograph supplied by Count Chandon des Briailles.

The meaning of the designation of the weights as *Σελεύκειον* and *'Αντιόχειον* is discussed in n. 251 to this chapter. I have mentioned there the suggestion of M. H. Seyrig. I must add that I still regard the interpretation 'weights of Seleuceia and Antioch' as more probable because on several dated weights the designations *Σελεύκειον* and *'Αντιόχειον* appear at a time when the ruling king was not a Seleucus or Antiochus. The names accompanied by the preposition *ἐπὶ* are those of the *ἀγορανόμοι*. Two other dated weights of Antioch of the Hellenistic period are known to me. One (*μνᾶ*)—in two specimens (in Berlin and in the Musée de Notre Dame de France in Jerusalem)—bears the date *θιρ'*, 119 Sel. = 193 B.C., Antiochus III (E. Michon, *D. d. A.*, loc. cit., p. 555, no. 15); the other—a *τέταρτον*—now in the Museum of the Amer. Univ. at Beirut (copied by myself and by the Rev. P. Mouterde) is unpublished. I may give here a short description of it. Square lead weight. *Obv.* Tripod, between anchor and caduceus; above ΑΝΤΙΟΧΕΙΟΝ; to the right and left of the tripod: Λ - Ρ | ΕΠΙ ΙΦΙΣΟΥ; below: ΤΕΤΑΡΤΟΝ. *Rev.* Network. The date is 130 Sel. = 182 B.C., Antiochus III. A Seleuceian dated weight (hemimnaion) with the date 155 Sel. = 157 B.C., Demetrius I Soter, is in the Louvre, see E. Michon, *Mém. Soc. Ant. Fr.* li (1890), p. 14 f., no. 4; *Bull. Soc. Ant. Fr.*, 1906, p. 195, no. 7; *D. d. A.*, loc. cit., p. 556, no. 2, cf. a weight of 153 B.C. (without the name Seleuceion), F. de Ridder, *Catal. Coll. de Clercq*, iii, p. 364 f., no. 681. I cannot mention here all the weights with the above designation and those which by their dates fall within the Seleucid period. We must await a Corpus of these weights from the hands of either M. H. Seyrig or the Rev. P. Mouterde.

Demetrius Soter, Antiochus VIII Grypus, and Antiochus X (Eusebes), the denomination (*mna*), and on the latest of them the name of the *agoranomos*. On the obverse there are also some official symbols which likewise appear on the coins: Poseidon and anchor, the Seleucid Victory and the anchor.

The second class consists of what appear to be city weights, which are more numerous. Some of the dated specimens are of the Hellenistic period, others are earlier and later. They were made in various cities of the Seleucid kingdom, Antioch, Seleuceia in Pieria and Laodicea, Damascus, and many cities of Phoenicia—Aradus, Byblus (?), Tripolis, Berytus, Sidon, Tyre. A few were found at Gezer in Palestine.

The most interesting of those which certainly belong to the Hellenistic period come probably from Antioch on the Orontes and Seleuceia in Pieria. They show a striking similarity to the royal weights. We see inscribed on them the name of the city, the date, the denomination (*mna* and its subdivisions), and the names and titles of the magistrates who were in charge of this department of the municipal administration, almost exclusively the *agoranomoi*, while the larger part of the surface is occupied by one of the heraldic devices of the Seleucids: the anchor, the tripod, the prow, the elephant, the horse, the zebu, the Victory, the Tyche. They sometimes bear countermarks similar to those of the coins.

From this brief description of the royal weights and of those of Antioch and Seleuceia we may perhaps infer that they were standard official weights, controlled by the government, although the majority of them may have been issued by the cities under the supervision of municipal magistrates. They may suggest the existence in the Seleucid administration of a department of weights and measures which issued the royal standard weights and controlled those issued by the magistrates of at least the most important cities of the kingdom.

Unfortunately there is no complete collection of the numerous weights of the Seleucid kingdom nor any careful study of them. My remarks are therefore necessarily somewhat vague and tentative. A question of great importance is the standard of the royal and semi-royal weights which I have described. Not being a specialist in metrology and not having weighed the extant weights myself, I do not venture to offer even tentative suggestions on this matter. The natural inference would be that they represent the Attic standard, but this need not be the case. What is common to most of those which certainly belong to the Hellenistic period is their official and royal character.[251]

(c) *International trade*

I have referred to the importance of the Seleucid currency in the international trade of the time and particularly in Asiatic trade. The trade of Syria with the rest of Asia (especially India and the Middle East) and Arabia on the one hand, and with the West and North on the other, was certainly of great consequence to the kingdom as a whole and to its inhabitants. Though we have very little information on the subject, we are in a position to form a general idea of the commercial relations maintained by Syria with Arabia and India. The policy in this respect of Alexander the Great, to which I have already alluded, was taken over with some changes by Seleucus I and his successors. They had two objects in view. The first was to attract Indian, central Asiatic, and Arabian merchandise to Syria, so that the transit trade in this merchandise should pass through their own territory instead of Egypt. The other was to find good markets for the merchandise in transit as well as for the products of the kingdom, in other words to develop Syria's commerce with the North and West. Historians of the Hellenistic period are inclined to attribute the relations between the Seleucids and the Ptolemies, their unceasing warfare, solely to political motives, to the exclusion of economic rivalry between the two kingdoms. But political and economic considerations are so closely connected that I find it difficult to discriminate between them.

It has been shown that the Ptolemies devoted great attention to the development of their commerce with Arabia and India, and that this would be greatly promoted if they held the Palestinian and Phoenician seaports and exercised political control over Transjordan and the Nabataeans. The revenue of the Ptolemies from Syria, Phoenicia, and Palestine must have been very large, and it certainly was not from military and political motives alone that they endeavoured so obstinately to secure the harbours of those countries.

The Seleucids showed no less interest than the Ptolemies in the trade with the East and South. Their policy in those directions was dictated partly by political and military considerations, partly by the wish to secure the largest possible share of the Indian, central Asiatic, and Arabian transit trade. Central Asia and India were connected with the West and especially with Syria by many routes, of which two lay in the North. One of these—the central Asiatic trade route—ran along the northern coast of the Caspian Sea and ended in the Bosporan kingdom. It may have served to some extent for the conveyance not only of central Asiatic but also of Indian goods, but its importance was principally as one of the later Chinese silk routes, and it was never under the control of the Seleucids. The western section of the other ran along the southern coast of the Caspian Sea and then along the river Cyrus (Kura) to the eastern coast of the Black Sea. This route is imperfectly known. It was never very popular with merchants and its western portion was never fully under the control of the Seleucids. Seleucus I and Antiochus I may have been interested in the possibility of developing it. The military expedition of Demodamas of Miletus across the Jaxartes was, it is clear, primarily intended to protect the Seleucid Empire on the north, and the partial exploration by Patrocles of the Caspian Sea was certainly suggested by military and political considerations. But these two enterprises may to some extent have been prompted by the wish to establish shorter and more convenient communications, partly by river, partly by sea, between the north-western and north-eastern parts of the Seleucid Empire, thereby facilitating the defence of the north-eastern frontier against the nomads of the north and secondarily serving commercial purposes.[252]

The routes of immemorial antiquity which connected India with Babylonia were, for the most part, far more frequented, more important, and better developed. They converged on Seleuceia on the Tigris, the great political and commercial city of Seleucus I, the eastern capital of that king and his successors, the inheritor of Babylon's pre-eminence.

One of these routes was the sea route, or rather routes, along the shores of the Persian Gulf. I shall speak presently of the route along the western shore of that Gulf. The second, that along the eastern shore, certainly existed and was in use, but very little is known about it, especially during the early Seleucid period. The existence of some harbour cities on the Persian Gulf—Antioch in Persis (Bushire), Seleuceia 'on the Erythraean Sea', and Antioch-Charax—does not necessarily imply that this route was of importance in early Seleucid times, and any extensive Greek colonization of either the east or the west coast of the Gulf is very poorly attested. If the route along the Seleucid satrapies of Persis and Carmania had been extensively used and a lively direct traffic by sea had existed between the India of Chandragupta and Asoka and the Seleucid kingdom, we should expect the number of Seleucid coins found in India to be greater than it is (see above, n. 243). As the evidence stands at present, it is probable that the main connexion between the early Seleucid Empire and India was partly by the land routes, one (the northern) running through Bactria, another (the southern) through Gedrosia and Carmania, Persis and Susiana, and partly by the western sea route through Gerrha. It is possible that later, when Babylonia became part of the Parthian Empire, more use was made of the eastern sea route. This would account for the decay of Gerrha in the Parthian period (below, p. 458), and for the rise and development at that time of an important trading-centre on the Gulf of Ormuz, which successfully competed with Gerrha. The evidence on the trade between the Gulf of Ormuz and India in the second and first centuries B.C. has recently been collected by W. W. Tarn.

The sea route along the western or Arabian coast of the Persian Gulf, supplemented by the ancient land route along the same coast, was much more important and more frequently used. This combined sea and land route, like the similar route along the eastern shore of the Red Sea, was in the hands of powerful Arab tribes, who were actively engaged in a highly developed trade. On the Red Sea these tribes were the Nabataeans, the Lihyanites, and the Sabaeans, on the Persian Gulf the Gerrhaeans. The last were a well-organized Arab State, whose commercial relations extended to South Arabia and India on the one hand and to Babylonia and the Nabataeans on the other. The Seleucids found the Gerrhaeans in possession of the sea route along the western shore of the Persian Gulf and of the great caravan roads of Arabia—one of which connected Gerrha, the capital of the Gerrhaeans, with Arabia Felix, and the other with Petra, through Dumaetha and Taima.

It is important to note that the bulk of our information about Gerrha is derived from Hellenistic sources and goes back in the main to Aristobulus, Eratosthenes, Artemidorus, and Agatharchides.* We may infer that Gerrha reached its zenith in the days of the Seleucids, and that its decline began with the Parthian domination.

The Seleucids dealt with the Gerrhaeans in much the same way as the Ptolemies with the Nabataeans. In order to prevent the Gerrhaeans† from robbing the Seleucid ships that plied between Babylonia and India, they maintained a flotilla in the Persian Gulf. At the same time they endeavoured, by diplomatic action and military intervention, to keep the Gerrhaeans more or less under control and to obtain from them a large proportion of the Arabian and Indian goods held by their merchants. In this light we are better able to understand the account given by Polybius (in the fragmentary form in which we have it)‡ of the expedition of Antiochus III against the Gerrhaeans. It was a military demonstration on a large scale, which did not and could not lead to the conquest of Gerrha, but was imposing enough to frighten the Gerrhaeans and make them increase the quantity of merchandise that they sent to Seleuceia, at the expense probably of the Nabataeans and the Ptolemies.§

From the scanty information we possess we may conclude with reasonable certainty that it was mainly through the

* Str. xvi. 766 (Aristobulus and Eratosthenes), 776–8 (Artemidorus); Diod. iii. 42 (Agatharchides), cf. Plin. vi. 147; xxxi. 78.

† The Gerrhaeans possessed an important harbour on the Persian Gulf and transported their wares not only by land but also by sea.

‡ xiii. 9, cf. Plin. vi. 152.

§ Note that the Gerrhaeans in their letter to Antiochus insisted that they had enjoyed in the past ἀΐδιον εἰρήνην καὶ ἐλευθερίαν.

Gerrhaeans that the Seleucids received their chief supply of Arabian merchandise and at least a fair amount of Indian goods. The importance of this trade must not be underestimated. Syria received an abundance of Arabian commodities, of which a large proportion was consumed locally, while a substantial part was re-exported. We have evidence of this, for example, in the gifts that Seleucus I and Antiochus I bestowed on the Didymaean temple of Miletus: ten talents' weight of frankincense, one talent's weight of myrrh, two minae of cassia, two minae of cinnamon, and two minae of costus.*

A channel of Indian trade not less important than that by the Persian Gulf was provided by the ancient roads across the Iranian plateau to Seleuceia. These are so well known and have been so often described and mapped that I need not repeat the description. They were the chief military means of communication between the western and the eastern parts of the Seleucid Empire. The Seleucids did not neglect them but maintained and increased the number of fortified and strongly garrisoned towns that guarded them. Though they were military in their character and purpose, they also served commercial needs. Transport by these routes, long and difficult as it was, was nevertheless safer and perhaps cheaper than by the Persian Gulf, since their whole course lay in Seleucid territory. It was probably to secure the safety of these routes that Seleucus I gave up his claims to part of India and preferred peaceful traffic with Chandragupta and his empire of Magadha to continuous and ruinous war. Through cordial relations and repeated embassies (such as those of Megasthenes and later of Daimachus) the Seleucids ensured a steady supply of war elephants and of Indian wares. When their communications with India were endangered by the secession of Bactria and of Parthia, Antiochus III launched his famous expedition, which led to an *entente cordiale* with Bactria and a temporary withdrawal of the Parthians, and re-established for some time the supremacy of the Seleucids along the routes in question.

The importance of the above-mentioned land routes from the political and commercial points of view is emphasized by the

* Welles, *R.C.* 5. 49 ff.

PLATE LVI

1. Fragmentary bronze lamp (the lower part is missing) in the form of a crouching camel, saddled and harnessed, found in Syria. The lamp is not dated. It may be Roman, but I am rather inclined to assign it to the Hellenistic period. A. de Ridder, *Les bronzes antiques du Louvre*, i, 'Les figurines', 1913, no. 428, p. 65, pl. 34. Similar representations of camels, carriers of the desert trade, are frequent among the terracottas and small bronzes of the Hellenistic and Roman periods. Cf. the bronze lamp in the form of a standing saddled camel from Syria in the Ashmolean Museum, Oxford (my *Soc. and Ec. Hist. R.E.*, pl. XXXVIII, 1) and A. de Ridder, *Collection de Clercq*, iii, 'Bronzes', 1904, no. 372, pl. LVII, 1. H. 0·063.

2. Bas-relief of a stone sarcophagus of Roman times. The sarcophagus was found intact in one of the *hypogaea* of Sidon. It is decorated on three sides in the usual manner with carved garlands suspended from rings fastened in the mouths of lions' heads. The decoration of the second short side of the sarcophagus is different. This side, covered with an elaborate design in very low relief, shows a sailing merchant-ship floating on the waves of the sea, in which are seen leaping dolphins and fish. The ship, though carved in the second century A.D., retains the leading features of the ancient Phoenician ships. (A. Köster, *Das antike Seewesen*, 1923, pp. 45 ff.) The ship drawn by an amateur on the walls of a private house in Dura (*Yale Dura Exc.*, Rep. iv, 1933, p. 222, no. 3, pl. XXIII, 1) has the same form. The Sidonian ship was first published by G. Contenau, *Syria*, i (1920), pp. 35 ff., pl. VI, and fig. 10 f., and has since been often reproduced and discussed, see for example Fr. Moll, *Das Schiff in der bildenden Kunst*, 1929, p. 25, pl. b–iv, 95; my *Soc. and Ec. Hist. R.E.*, pl. XXXVIII, 2; *Mostra Augustea della Romanità, Catalogo*, 1939, Sala XIX, no. 45. Photograph supplied by the authorities of the National Museum, Beirut.

1. Paris, Louvre.

2. Beirut, National Museum.

CARAVANS AND SHIPS IN THE SELEUCID KINGDOM

fact that their principal key towns were notable mints of the early Seleucids. The main supply of coins came from the extremely active mint of Seleuceia on the Tigris. The southern route to India was supplied with money by the mints of Susa (Seleuceia on the Eulaeus) and Persepolis. Still more important were the mints of the northern Bactrian routes: Ecbatana, the capital of Media, the chief source of the supply of horses for the Seleucid Empire (it is to be noted that the mint mark of Ecbatana was the forepart of a horse feeding); Alexandria in Areia (modern Herat), capital of the fertile satrapy of Areia and a nodal point of the route to Bactria and to India (through Drangiana); and the great city of Bactra, of which more will be said below. All the mints enumerated above issued money which satisfied alike the administrative and military and the commercial needs of the Seleucid kingdom. It may be mentioned that, in order to facilitate Bactrian trade with India, Antiochus I at the time of his joint rule with Seleucus (285–280 B.C.) made a special issue of coins of the Indian instead of the Attic standard.

The clearing-house for all the merchandise that reached the Seleucid Empire from central Asia, India and Arabia was Seleuceia on the Tigris, which in consequence grew rapidly and soon became the largest and probably the richest city of that empire. Our information about it dates mostly from the Parthian and Roman period of its history, but the foundations of its prosperity were undoubtedly laid in Seleucid times. It was certainly the trade of Seleuceia that enriched its inhabitants, not only the natives, who had accumulated capital and experience of the caravan trade in pre-Persian and Persian times, but also the Greek residents.

From Seleuceia Arabian and Indian goods were conveyed to the North and West by the roads that from the earliest times had connected Babylonia with those regions, running along the Tigris and the Euphrates and thence to the Phoenician and Syrian coasts. These roads were well organized and thoroughly secure. They were guarded throughout their course by chains of strong and prosperous Greek colonies, which at the same time provided convenient resting-places for the caravans. We know one of these—Dura-Europus on the middle Euphrates.

As the Phoenician towns were in the hands of the Ptolemies, the early Seleucids developed their road system in such a way as to prevent the caravans from going to Tyre or Sidon or to other Ptolemaic seaports. Some of the early Seleucid roads led from Mesopotamia across Asia Minor to the Anatolian harbours, but most of them converged on the new capital of the empire, Antioch on the Orontes, and on its ports—Laodicea on the Sea and Seleuceia in Pieria. The route across the desert to Palmyra and thence to Damascus was probably very rarely used by the early Seleucid caravans.[253]

Of the commercial relations between the Seleucid Empire and the Aegean Sea and western Mediterranean we know very little. The empire had plenty of merchandise to export. We shall see later in this section how plentiful and various were the products of Syrian agriculture and industry, to which must be added the goods in transit from Arabia and India. But their export presented difficulties in the time of the first Seleucids. The sea was in the hands of the Ptolemies. Even Seleuceia in Pieria was lost to Euergetes I (in 246 B.C.) and remained in the hands of the Ptolemies until 219 B.C. The great outlets for their caravan trade in Asia Minor—Ephesus, Smyrna, and Miletus—were only intermittently in Seleucid hands. The third century was therefore not a very brilliant period in their history. And yet there are several reasons for believing that, in spite of all these unfavourable factors, Seleucid trade by the Anatolian land routes and by sea was important and made no small contribution to the prosperity of the kingdom.

I have already pointed out that the Seleucids were anxious to keep strictly to the Attic standard in their coinage and that many foreign, especially Anatolian, coins are found in the Syrian hoards of early Seleucid times. I have also emphasized the fact that Ptolemaic currency was carefully kept out of the regions where coins of the Attic standard were predominant. These facts seem to me to indicate the existence of steady, uninterrupted commercial relations between Syria on the one hand, and Anatolia, the Aegean, and the Pontic world on the other, even though the monetary *entente cordiale* between Syria and the Aegean and Pontic regions may have not led to special treaties. The same trade connexion is attested by the political relations of the Seleucids with the other powers of the Hellenistic world in early times.

On the sea it was Rhodes that was the leading commercial power of the time. For a while dependent on Egypt, Rhodes soon recovered its commercial freedom (above, pp. 225 ff.), and the ships of the Seleucids were as welcome there as those of the Ptolemies. The relations between it and Syria are very imperfectly known. In the early days of Seleucus I, he and Demetrius had employed a Rhodian as their ambassador to Ephesus and other Greek cities.* We have no further information until the reign of Seleucus II or III. Though the Seleucid grant or sale of Stratonicea in Caria to the Rhodians† probably belongs to a later date, trade relations between Syria and Rhodes are well attested for the last decades of the third century. When the city suffered heavily from the famous earthquake (227/6 B.C.?), all the leading powers of the time came to its help. Among them was Seleucus II or rather Seleucus III. The character of his gifts is interesting:‡ he grants the Rhodians ten quinqueremes, a large amount of material for building ships, a substantial quantity of corn, and *ateleia* (perhaps exemption from customs duties only, not a general exemption from taxes) to the Rhodians 'who sail to his kingdom' (εἰς τὴν αὐτοῦ βασιλείαν πλοϊζομένοις). A study of the Rhodian jar handles found at Antioch and the other cities of Syria, Seleuceia on the Tigris, Uruk, Dura-Europus, and Tarsus would be of much interest, and might show whether any of them are earlier than the reign of Antiochus III.

Whereas commercial relations between Rhodes and Syria were never completely interrupted, the early Seleucids were not very popular in the sacred island of Delos. No Seleucid before Antiochus III was honoured with statues there, and Seleucus I and Stratonice alone appear as donors in the Delian inventories. A gift by Seleucus (of the model of a ship) was probably connected with one of his naval victories.[254]

This sketch of the foreign trade of the Seleucids, notwithstanding its deficiencies, fully justifies my interpretation of the second paragraph of the summary of the royal economy in *Oecon.* II. Export trade undoubtedly played a very important

* *O.G.I.* 10. † Polyb. xxx. 31, 6. ‡ Ibid. v. 89. 8.

part in the economy of the Seleucid Empire and yielded a large revenue to the kings and much profit to many of the Greek and native inhabitants. It is very unfortunate that we know nothing of the Seleucid customs duties and of their tariff policy.

(*d*) *Revenues from land*

The section of *Oecon.* II which deals with 'satrap economy' gives the impression that all satrapies were uniformly organized in respect of the revenues derived from them. Two alternative inferences may be drawn from this: either that such a uniformity existed in the Persian Empire and was inherited from Persia by Alexander and the Seleucids; or that the author (or his source) did not in fact know the practice in all the satrapies and extended to the other satrapies information relating to Asia Minor, the part of the Persian Empire best known to the Greeks. For it is difficult to believe that the same system of taxation was applied in exactly the same way throughout an empire such as the Persian and Seleucid, whose parts varied widely in history, institutions, and economic conditions. Apart from this general consideration, we have little to guide us in our choice between the two alternatives. We know very little of the system of taxation of the Persian Empire and not much more of that of the Seleucid Empire.

I have mentioned above that the author of *Oecon.* II, in speaking of the revenues of the kings and of the satraps, never mentions the tribute (φόρος) paid by the communities which were constituent parts of the satrapies of the kingdom—the cities, the temples, and the tribes. We know that all these self-governing bodies paid in one form or another a *phoros* or a *syntaxis*, which in all known cases was a larger or smaller lump sum. The principle on which this *phoros* was assessed and the mode of its collection are little known; they will be discussed presently.

For the author of *Oecon.* II the main revenue accruing to the State from each satrapy was derived from the land taxes. He mentions this revenue briefly. It was probably so familiar to his readers that no details were needed. He states only that it was termed ἐκφόριον and δεκάτη. It is typical of the defective character of our evidence that we can hardly add anything substantial to his brief statement.

We know, mostly from epigraphical sources, that in Asia Minor and probably in other satrapies of the Persian and subsequently the Seleucid Empire the land was divided into various classes, more or less in the same way as in Egypt. On the one hand there was the land that depended directly on the kings, the χώρα βασιλική or perhaps the χώρα in general, the χώρα βασιλική being only one part of it, the private estates of the kings. On the other hand there was the land that was the property of the Greek cities, of the temples, and probably of some tribes. Between the two groups stood the land that was assigned by the kings from the *chora* or the *chora basilike* to various institutions, groups of individuals, or individuals under various conditions, that is to say, to cities founded by the kings, to gods and temples, to groups of κάτοικοι or κληροῦχοι, some of them settled soldiers, and to private persons who were members of the royal house, officials of the crown, or friends of the kings.

Concerning the payments, collective or individual, made by these various types of landholders very little is known. We are best informed about the χώρα or χώρα βασιλική of Asia Minor. Land of this class was cultivated under the supervision of royal officials by hereditary tenants termed *laoi*, men bound to the soil or to their place of residence (mostly villages). It was probably these officials, not general contractors (*telonai*), who collected the payments of the *laoi* or *laoi basilikoi*, the Anatolian peasants or royal peasants. Our information about these officials is very slight. It is not very probable that there was a special administrative class charged with the management of the χώρα or χώρα βασιλική. In all probability the charge of the χώρα and of the λαοί was entrusted to the general managers of the satrapies and of their subdivisions and to the officers whose special duties were of a financial character.

We hear occasionally that the *laoi* paid their *phoroi* to the kings either in kind or in money. The former method prevailed on the χώρα βασιλική near Teos and Lebedus, the latter on Laodice's estate in the Troad and on Mnesimachus' estate near Sardis. How the payments in kind were reckoned is not known:

they may have been a *pars quota* (δεκάτη) or tithe of the harvest, or a *pars quanta* (ἐκφόριον). The payments in money on the estates of Laodice and of Mnesimachus may have represented the equivalent in money (*adaeratio*) either of a *pars quota* or a *pars quanta*.

Some scattered texts may suggest that in some way or other the assessment of the *phoroi* of the Greek cities in Asia Minor was made in connexion with the yield of the land-tax, one part of which was collected for the treasury of the city, the other for the royal treasury through the royal financial administration (βασιλικόν). In my book on the *Kolonat* (pp. 244 ff.) I pointed out that the *chora* or the territory of the cities was liable to the payment of a *phoros*. Thus Seleucus II* 'granted to the Smyrnaeans freedom and immunity for the city and the *chora*'. In the well-known farming law (νόμος πωλητικός) of the φυλὴ Ὀτορκωνδέων of Mylasa,† belonging perhaps to the time when Mylasa was a city of the Seleucid kingdom, the payments of the citizens of the city, landowners, and hereditary tenants are clearly divided into two groups: those due to the royal treasury (βασιλικόν) and those due to the city treasury (πολιτικόν). Lastly, in a fragmentary inscription of Seleuceia–Tralles,‡ recording a letter of Antiochus III, a tithe (δεκάτη) is remitted to the city, which had hitherto been paid to the royal treasury.§

The evidence here adduced is scanty and obscure and may be differently interpreted. Later, however, in Roman times, the government collected the *phoros* from the cities of the province of Asia on the basis of a uniform δεκάτη which was imposed on the land that formed the territory (*chora*) of a given city (below, ch. VII). Was the Roman practice perhaps a return to the Seleucid tradition after the Attalids had introduced some modifications of it? May we suppose that the *phoros* was collected from the cities according to an assessment based on the *adaeratio*, or money value, of a land-tax imposed on the territory of the city? Or was the royal land-tax, like

* *O.G.I.* 228, 7 f.: ἐπικεχώρηκε δὲ τοῖς [Σμυρ]ναίοις τάν τε πόλιν καὶ τὰν χώραν αὐτῶν ἐλευθέραν εἶμεν καὶ ἀφο[ρο]λόγητον.

† Le Bas–Waddington, v. 404.

‡ Welles, *R.C.* 41.

§ Cf. Welles, loc. cit. 48, D, 3.

other royal taxes (see below, pp. 469 ff), an addition to the *phoros*, which last was assessed on the basis of calculations unknown to us, for instance according to the amount of the general income received by the cities from various sources, especially from various taxes collected by them?

Still scantier is the evidence relating to other bodies and individuals liable to a land-tax. Nothing certain is known about the relations between the temples and the king from the fiscal point of view. Some temples in Asia Minor may have been liable to the payment of a certain tax on the land in their possession, perhaps a δεκάτη. A tithe was also probably paid by the military settlers: we hear of this payment being sometimes remitted to them. And finally the individual holders of land received from the king were not tax-free.[255]

The only reliable information about the land-taxes in parts of the Seleucid kingdom other than Asia Minor relates to Palestine in the time of the Maccabees. In the two letters by which Demetrius I promises, and Demetrius II grants, various favours (φιλάνθρωπα) to Jonathan and the Jews, the first speaks among other things of remission of the usual land-taxes which were paid by Judaea and also by what were known as the three νομοί or τοπαρχίαι, as well as by parts of Samaritis and Galilee, which were apparently connected in fiscal matters with Judaea before the time of Demetrius I. These taxes* were one third of the yield of the sown crops (τρίτον τῆς σπορᾶς) and one half of the καρπὸς ξύλινος (grapes, olives, other fruit, especially dates, &c.). Demetrius II apparently refers to the same taxes when he says in his letter: 'and all things appertaining unto them, for all such as do sacrifice in Jerusalem, instead of the king's dues which the king received of them yearly aforetime from the produce of the earth and the fruits of the trees.'†[256]

The land-tax collected by the Seleucids in Judaea was certainly very high, much higher than the tax which was usual in Asia Minor in Roman times (a *decuma* or a tithe) and which,

* 1 Macc. x. 29–30.

† 1 Macc. xi. 34: *καὶ πάντα τὰ συγκυροῦντα αὐτοῖς πᾶσι τοῖς θυσιάζουσιν εἰς Ἱεροσόλυμα ἀντὶ τῶν βασιλικῶν ὧν ἐλάμβανεν ὁ βασιλεὺς παρ᾽ αὐτῶν τὸ πρότερον κατ᾽ ἐνιαυτὸν ἀπὸ τῶν γενημάτων τῆς γῆς καὶ τῶν ἀκροδρύων.*

as stated above, may have been inherited by the Romans from the Seleucids. However, the Palestinian land tax was not much higher than the payments in kind made by the *βασιλικοὶ γεωργοί* in Egypt.

Since the payments of the tillers of the soil in Judaea in Caesar's time were about the same in amount as those made by the rural population of Judaea in the time of Demetrius I and II (below, ch. VII), I am inclined to think that these payments were traditional in Judaea, and that the innovation of the Seleucids consisted perhaps in collecting these taxes directly and as an addition to, not a part of, the tribute (*phoros*) of Judaea.

This interpretation I regard as more probable than that of Bikerman,* who is inclined to explain the heavy payments exacted from Judaea as a punishment imposed by the Seleucids on the people for their revolt in the time of the Maccabees. According to him the kings treated the territory of Judaea after this revolt not as *ager stipendiarius* (to use the Roman terminology) but as *ager regius* (*χώρα βασιλική*), and the tillers of the soil not as landowners but as tenants of the kings.

About the system of land taxation that prevailed in Babylonia in Hellenistic times nothing is known. We may conjecture that it descended to the Arsacids and the Sasanids, and that the land-taxes described by the Talmud for the Sasanian period were inherited from the Seleucids. But the data of the Talmud, abundant as they are, give no connected and intelligible picture, and we cannot be sure that the Seleucid system had not been changed considerably by the Arsacids and the Sasanids. In any case it is difficult to decide whether the 'taska' of the Talmud was a rent or a tax and whether it was paid in kind or in money. The problem is complicated by a reference to the 'king's portion', which may be the same as the above or an additional payment.[257]

The few facts that I have adduced may suggest that there was no uniformity in the assessment of land-taxes and land-rents by the kings of the Seleucid dynasty. The payments for the use of the land, which was ultimately regarded as the property of the king, whether it was cultivated by his own

† *Inst. Sél.*, p. 179.

tenants (*laoi basilikoi*) or by members of communities such as half-independent tribes, cities, and temples with their population of men and women who regarded themselves as slaves of a god or goddess, were collected according to ancient traditions which varied from satrapy to satrapy, and within the satrapy from one group of landholders to another. I doubt very much whether even in any one satrapy the rents of one and the same group were uniform, that is to say, whether all the *laoi basilikoi*, all the temples, vassal tribes, and cities had the same obligations to the crown. The rent or taxes were collected as *pars quanta* or *pars quota* sometimes in kind, sometimes in money. It may be for this reason that the author of *Oecon.* II is so inexplicit on the subject.

(*e*) *Royal taxes*

Our information about the other revenues of the king as set forth in *Oecon.* II is no better than about the land-taxes and land-rents. There certainly existed in the Persian, and later in the Seleucid, kingdom a class of royal taxes which were organized in the same way throughout the empire, being probably levied by agents of the crown. The payments made in respect of these taxes may have varied from satrapy to satrapy in some cases, for instance in that of the poll-tax, but in most cases they were probably uniform, assessed and collected on the same principle and in the same way.

We may obtain some idea of the character of those taxes from certain texts relating to Palestine before, under, and after Antiochus III. According to a letter of Antiochus III (Jos., *A.J.* xii. 138 ff.) the royal taxes, in addition to the tribute, paid by the people of Judaea in his own time, that is to say, inherited by him from the Ptolemies, were the poll-tax, the crown tax (στεφανιτικὸς φόρος), and the salt tax (περὶ τῶν ἁλῶν). There were also some indirect taxes. Few people were exempt from these royal imposts.

Similar taxes were collected in Judaea in the time of Demetrius I. In his letter of 152 B.C. promising favours (φιλάνθρωπα) to Jonathan and the Jews (I Macc. x. 29–30) he speaks of the land-tax mentioned above, of the 'tributes', which may be the salt tax and the crown tax, and of the 'price of the salt' (τιμὴ τοῦ ἁλός). Difficult to interpret are (ibid. 31) the 'tenths' (δεκάται) and the 'tolls' (τέλη), and (ibid. 33) the 'tributes of their cattle' (φόροι καὶ τῶν κτηνῶν αὐτῶν). At a later date Demetrius II in his letter (1 Macc. xi. 35) speaks of the 'tenths' and 'tolls' (δεκάται καὶ τέλη), and in addition of 'salt-pans' (τὰς τοῦ ἁλὸς λίμνας) and of the 'crowns' (στέφανοι).

Salt tax. Of the three royal taxes mentioned in these texts the best known is the salt tax. The mentions of this tax in Josephus and in the books of the Maccabees suggest that the revenue from salt was one of the most important revenues of the crown. It is very probable (1) that the crown regarded the salt-pans as its property, (2) that the people paid a special salt tax, probably as their contribution to the management of the salt-pans, and (3) that they received an allowance of salt from the government on payment of a certain amount of money each year in addition to the salt tax.

This organization is similar to that which, as we know from many documents, existed in the third century B.C. in Egypt (above, p. 309). In Egypt, as in Palestine, the salt-pans were the property of the crown, the people paid a salt tax closely resembling a poll-tax, and received their salt (probably a prescribed amount) at fixed prices from the crown. It is very probable that it was the Ptolemies who organized the salt monopoly in Palestine, adopting the system that they had established in Egypt. The main features of this system may have been inherited by them from the Persian financial administration.

In Babylonia the method of collecting the revenue from salt was much the same, as we know from certain stamps impressed on clay *bullae* found in the temple of Anu-Antum at Uruk and in a private house at Seleuceia. I have dealt with these stamps in a special memoir and need not repeat here what I have said there. Suffice it to say that the ἁλική, that is, the ἁλικὴ ὠνή, the salt revenue department, existed in Babylonia from the time of Seleucus II till at least the last years of the Seleucid domination there, and that in all probability this ὠνή was organized on the same lines as in Egypt and in Palestine. This suggests that both Ptolemy Soter and the Seleucids inherited the revenue and the main features of the system of collecting it from the Persians.[258]

Poll-tax and Crown tax. Much less is known about the poll-tax and the crown tax mentioned in the texts quoted above. The poll-tax was temporarily revived at a later date by the Romans in Cilicia and elsewhere in Asia Minor as an emergency tax (below, ch. VII). This may indicate that it was one of the royal taxes levied by the Seleucids in all their satrapies. The crown tax is known in Egypt and had a long life. In Seleucid times it appears to have been a general royal tax. Like the salt and poll-taxes, it was probably a personal tax. The same is true of the χειρωνάξιον, a tax payable by artisans which is mentioned in *Oecon.* II and occurs in Egypt, but is not referred to in documents of the Seleucid period. Finally, there was the cattle tax noted in *Oecon.* II, which is found in Hellenistic Egypt and in Attalid and Roman Asia Minor (the Roman *scriptura*) but is not mentioned in Seleucid documents.[259]

Ἀνδραποδική. The nature of the tax called ἀνδραποδική, which was levied in Babylonia and is attested by some *bullae*, is disputed. It may have been a general tax on slaves or a special tax levied in connexion with the sale of slaves. Various taxes connected with slaves are known in Egypt.[260]

Customs duties. I have already said that several other taxes which were certainly royal in character existed in the Seleucid Empire. Such were the different customs duties, inherited from the Seleucids by the Romans (*portoria*, below, chs. VI and VII), and various taxes of the same kind, for example that exacted for the use of the royal roads. Similar to the last in all probability was the tax πλοίων Εὐφράτου, which is mentioned on one of the *bullae* of Uruk.

Tax on sales. To the same group may be assigned the ἐπώνιον, a general tax on sales levied in Uruk, and the taxes for the registration of documents, which are well attested in Uruk and elsewhere and were collected by the χρεοφύλακες and βιβλιοφύλακες. It may be noted that a provincial ἐπώνιον was imposed by Piso in Macedonia and Greece (below, ch. VII).

Mines, &c. Lastly, the Seleucid rulers certainly derived a large income from the various natural resources of their vast empire. I have pointed out that they were owners of the salt-pans, and there is reason to believe that they also owned many mines, quarries, forests, fisheries, &c. These sources of revenue are mentioned in *Oecon.* II, but not in documents of the Seleucid period.

Meagre as it is, the evidence at our disposal allows us to form a general idea of the fiscal policy of the Seleucids. Their fiscal system they certainly inherited from the Persian kings, Alexander, and the Successors. How far they changed it, how many innovations they introduced, we are unable to say. It appears, however, very probable that they were more conservative than the Ptolemies and that their fiscal system was less elaborate and more flexible than theirs.

Of the total amount of their revenues no idea can be formed. The Seleucids were certainly as rich as the Ptolemies and they were as lavish as their Egyptian rivals. We know very little about their expenditure, but the little we do know shows that they spent large sums of money on their army and navy, on administration, on colonization (see below), and on foreign policy, in which gifts and bribes played an important part.[261]

How heavily the burden of taxation pressed on the people of their empire, is a question that cannot be answered. The situation in Judaea as we know it was probably typical. Yet even in the case of Judaea we cannot say whether it was the burden of taxation in itself or the humiliation of paying taxes to foreign rulers that roused the greater resentment.

4. Social Policy

(*a*) *Colonization*

The economic and social development of the Seleucid Empire was greatly influenced by the so-called Seleucid colonization, the policy of superimposing a Greco-Macedonian stratum on the native population by the foundation of settlements of Greeks and Macedonians, in the form of cities and villages. This policy was initiated by Alexander and Antigonus, and greatly extended by Seleucus I and his first two successors, Antiochus I and Antiochus II. Seleucus I was most active in Syria, Cilicia, and Mesopotamia, and Antiochus I devoted his main attention to the Iranian countries; all three of them pursued the policy in Asia Minor.[262]

We know how diverse were the elements of the empire of Seleucus I and his successors. It included States and regions possessing immemorial and firmly rooted traditions, nations and peoples that looked back to days when they all had been independent, and some of them had themselves ruled over empires. Such were above all the Iranians, and next to them the Babylonians and the Aramaeans. The Phoenician cities and the Jews, likewise proud of a glorious past, were at the time under review not yet subjects of the Seleucid kings. To build up a political, social, and economic unit out of these States, nations, tribes, and cities, unconnected with each other and naturally tending in different directions, was a difficult task. But the successors of Alexander fully realized that, unless it was unified, the Seleucid Empire, the successor of the Persian Empire and of that of Alexander, could not be preserved. The predecessors of the Seleucids had behind them forces that helped them to keep together the disparate constituents of their empires. The Persian kings had a solid foundation for their rule in their Iranian, and especially their Persian, subjects, who had always been the dominant nation in the Persian Empire despite the liberal policy of the Persian kings. Alexander had behind him his own people, the Macedonians, and upon them and upon the glamour of his own personality his power was practically based until his death. With the Macedonian nation behind him Alexander could indulge in the luxury of experiments. We know how he endeavoured to merge his Macedonian and his Iranian soldiers in a single highly trained and well-disciplined body, and how desirous he was to extend this experiment and to try the same policy of amalgamation in other fields and with other nations. He appears to have contemplated an organic fusion of the best elements of his empire, irrespective of their nationality, and the creation thereby of a new ruling class essentially devoid of and superior to national prejudices. This class, in his imagination, would possess all the endowments of civilization, among which those of the Greek civilization were, from his point of view, pre-eminent. This, in my opinion, was the sum and substance of Alexander's intended 'hellenization' of the East. It is not impossible that his dream was wider, and that he

PLATE LVII

1. Painted funerary stele found at Sidon of the form described above, pl. XIX: pediment, acroteria, niche. Below the pediment three garlands. The niche is occupied entirely by one figure, that of a soldier standing frontwise. He is dressed in a chiton with short sleeves and high shoes and wears over his chiton a cuirass and on his head a large crested bronze helmet with visor, cheek- and neck-pieces. In the left hand he holds an oval so-called Celtic shield, in the right a long lance. The sword (not visible) hangs from a baldric. On the base, inscription (rightly restored by L. Robert, *B.C.H.* lix (1935), p. 428 f.): *Σάλμα Μολ*[. . .*'Α*]δαδεῦ | χρησ[*τέ, χαῖρε*]. A detailed description will be found in G. Mendel, *Cat. d. Sculpt. Mus. Nat. Ott.* i, 1912, pp. 264 ff., no. 105. H. 0·86, W. 0·485.

2. Painted funerary fragmentary stele, found at Sidon, of the form described above, pl. XIX. The niche is occupied by a group of three soldiers. The one to the left is represented in profile, turned to the right. He wears chiton, chlamys, crested helmet, high shoes. In his left hand a long lance, in his right an oval shield. He is shaking hands with another soldier represented in profile, turned to the left, dressed and armed like the first. The third soldier, a little smaller in size, is dressed and armed in the same way. He stretches his hand towards the first soldier waiting for his turn to shake hands with him. Inscription not extant. G. Mendel, loc. cit., pp. 267 ff., no. 107. H. 0·75, W. 0·48.

Photographs supplied by the authorities of the National Ottoman Museum, Istanbul.

On the Sidonian stelae in general see the works quoted by G. Mendel and L. Robert, locc. cit., cf. L. Robert, *B.C.H.* lx (1936), p. 191 f., and E. Bikerman, *Inst. Sél.*, pp. 88 ff. From the point of view of the history of painting the stelae have been discussed by M. H. Swindler, *Anc. Painting*, 1929, p. 346 (with bibliography). The military equipment of the Hellenistic foot-soldiers has been still less studied than that of the horsemen (above, pl. XIX). The abundant material relating to this subject has never been collected in full. Some remarks will be found in P. Couissin, *Les Institutions militaires et navales*, 1931, ch. x, pp. 74 ff., cf. A. Schober, *Der Fries des Hekataions von Lagina*, 1933, p. 74 and notes 31 and 32. In addition to the material used by Couissin and Schober, I may draw the attention of the reader to an interesting terracotta statuette in the Boston Museum representing a standing bearded soldier wearing helmet, cuirass, oval shield, and a sword with curved handle. D. Burr, *Terracottas from Myrina*, &c., 1934, p. 76, n. 112, pl. XLI. The soldier is not necessarily a Galatian. The sword with curved handle, first perhaps introduced into the Hellenistic world by the Celts, became (like the Celtic shield) very popular and appears on many monuments of Asia Minor which have nothing to do with the Galatians. Cf. my remarks on pl. LXI, 1. In studying the Hellenistic war equipment with the help of archaeological material one must take into consideration that the Hellenistic funerary art, in this so different from the Roman, created here a certain *κοινή*, a standardized type of warrior. The same standardized type appears in the mythological scenes of the Hellenistic period: see, for example, the warriors of the 'Homeric' Megarian bowls or the sculptures of the temple of Lagina. The conventional soldiers in mythological scenes survived the Hellenistic period and were still repeated in Roman illustrations of literary works; see the remarks of C. Hopkins on the 'Homeric' shield found at Dura, *Yale Dura Exp.*, Rep. vii–viii, 1939, pp. 331 ff.

1. 2.

MERCENARY SOLDIERS OF THE HELLENISTIC ARMIES

Istanbul, National Ottoman Museum.

was thinking of creating ultimately a world State in which national distinctions would be effaced (cf. above, pp. 126ff.).

Seleucus I and his successors were in a far more difficult situation. They could not resume and pursue Alexander's policy. Experiments were dangerous in the prevailing atmosphere of incessant warfare, and Alexander's experiment had met with too little success even in his own day to be repeated. Seleucus I always hoped to be able to return to his own country, Macedonia, as its sovereign. But it was quite impossible to found any practical policy on what was no more than a hope. Macedonia as the solid basis of his power was a possibility of the future, not an actual fact; and for his successors even this possibility vanished. Failing the Macedonians, there was no nation in the dominions of the Seleucids that could serve as the mainstay of their rule. Seleucus and Antiochus were certainly convinced by long experience that the Iranians, the only nation accustomed to exercise authority and capable of fighting efficiently, were quite unsuited for this purpose. The Iranians had supported Alexander, though with reluctance. But they would not support one of his generals as their king, even if Seleucus had decided to let his Macedonians be gradually absorbed by the Iranians. Seleucus might live on good terms with them and employ some of them as auxiliary detachments in the royal army, but to found his dominion upon them was out of the question.

The only policy left to him and his successors was that followed by their neighbours and enemies the Ptolemies. This was to rely upon those elements of the population which from the outset had been closely connected with the rulers and had helped them to acquire their empire: the Macedonians and the Greeks of the army, the Macedonian and Greek settlers, military and civil, who were scattered all over their territories, but were mostly concentrated in the few cities founded by Alexander and Antigonus, and finally their own civil and military staff—their personal friends. This foundation was numerically not very strong, but it was trustworthy and flexible, and it could be steadily and rapidly increased. The problem that lay before Seleucus and the Seleucids was therefore the same as that which confronted the Ptolemies, how to increase the number of Macedonians and Greeks permanently residing in their kingdom, and how to organize the relations of the new immigrants with the ruler on the one hand and the natives on the other, so that of the latter they should hellenize and absorb as many as possible.

We have seen how the Ptolemies dealt with this problem. Seleucus and his successors adopted a different solution. While the Ptolemies discontinued in Egypt Alexander's practice of founding cities, the Seleucids took up and carried on the tradition of Alexander and Antigonus; indeed they were the first to give to these traditions the character of a definite policy with a definite aim.

It should be observed that in a very few instances only can we trace the history of post-Alexandrian settlements back to Antigonus. Such cases as those of Europus (Dura) and Antioch Arabis,* which last may be identified either with Edessa or with Nisibis, are typical. It has been suggested on insufficient evidence that the founder of these two cities, Nicanor, who according to Pliny, was prefect of Mesopotamia, was the Nicanor, satrap of Media under Antigonus, who succumbed to Seleucus. Now we know that Europus-Dura was founded by order, not of Antigonus, but of Seleucus I (see pl. LI, 2), and the same is certainly true of Antioch Arabis. Nicanor, the prefect of Mesopotamia, founder of Europus and Antioch Arabis, was probably one of the two regents of the East—Nicanor and Nicomedes—appointed, according to Malalas, by Seleucus I, both of them his nephews, sons of his sister Didymea.† Their task, it may be supposed, was, in the first place, to prevent an attack on Mesopotamia by rivals of Seleucus, similar to those of Demetrius and Antigonus in 310–308 B.C., and secondly to protect the empire from its warlike neighbours, the mountaineers of the North and the Arabs. For the latter purpose a group of strongly fortified colonies was established along the most important strategical

* Pliny, *N.H.* vi. 117.

† This appointment was the beginning of the Seleucid policy of choosing the governor-general of the East from members of the royal house; Nicanor and Nicomedes were probably succeeded by the son of Seleucus, the future Antiochus I (in 292 B.C.).

roads. We know for example that Edessa—a very important fortress—was founded in 302 B.C.[263]

The measures taken by Seleucus I and his early successors in respect of the military and civil colonization of their empire are too well known to need detailed description here. It is enough to say that by relentless systematic work, carried on with speed, energy, and skill, the three first kings—Seleucus I, Antiochus I, and Antiochus II—succeeded in forming in Asia Minor, in Syria, in Mesopotamia, in Babylonia, in Elam, and in parts of their Iranian satrapies, large aggregations of Greek and Macedonian settlers; these were established in Greek and Macedonian cities and villages, and the settlements were connected by good roads.[264]

Though modern maps of the Seleucid Empire contain many lacunae, and the identification of ancient with modern sites is incomplete and in some cases uncertain, a glance at them will show the general distribution of these settlements and the character and intensity of the colonization of the various regions. The groups of Greco-Macedonian cities founded by Seleucus and his first two successors extended from the coasts of the Aegean right through Asia Minor, Syria, Mesopotamia, Parapotamia, and Babylonia, to Bactria and Sogdiana.

Starting from the West, the Lydian, Phrygian, and Carian group was the first. It included several cities and many military settlements (κατοικίαι) of the nature of villages, scattered all over the country partly along the great military and commercial roads, but chiefly in the most fertile regions. The capitals of this group were the ancient flourishing cities of Sardis and Celaenae (Apamea Cibotos), which by the time of Seleucus already had a large Greek population and probably a Greek organization. Next came the Cilician group. Besides many native towns, some of them temple states (Castabala–Hieropolis), which in some cases were reinforced by Macedonian settlers, it contained cities newly founded by the first two rulers. Of these, Seleuceia on the Calycadnus and Antioch on the Pyramus were the most prominent in Cilicia Tracheia, Aegeae and Alexandria on the gulf of Issus the most prominent in Cilicia Pedias.

No less important than the Anatolian groups were those of

Syria and of northern Mesopotamia. In this region, the centre of his power and the seat of his great capitals, Seleucus certainly endeavoured to give full development to the policy I have described. His main aims and leading ideas are reflected first and foremost in the administrative reorganization of the kernel of his empire. His four main bases in what was called 'Seleucid Syria' (Σελευκίς) were his four Greco-Macedonian capitals: of which Antioch on the Orontes, easily accessible from the sea but not on the sea, was his political capital; Apamea, farther inland, was his military capital and base; and Seleuceia in Pieria and Laodicea on the sea were his two harbour capitals, which would keep open his communications with the Greek world even if the western coast of Asia Minor were completely lost. These four spacious and beautiful cities, all newly constructed, became each the capital of a satrapy —the richest and the best cultivated satrapies of the empire.

It was the constant policy of Seleucus and his successors to protect Seleucid Syria on the south, the north, and the east. This is one reason why they strove to wrest southern Syria and Phoenicia from the Ptolemies, and began, during the short period of their success, a somewhat ineffective attempt to transform Coelesyria, in the same way as their other dominions, by the foundation of Greek and Macedonian cities. South Syria soon passed into the hands of the Ptolemies and it was a satrapy of the Ptolemies, not of the Seleucids, that bore for a while the proud name 'Syria' (above, pp. 340 ff.). On the north Seleucid Syria was protected by Cilicia, and on the north and east by another intensively hellenized region, the satrapy of Mesopotamia, to which we may add Parapotamia along the Euphrates and perhaps some parts of the Arabian desert, at least such as were occupied by tribes recognizing the supremacy of Seleucus and his successors.

Seleucid Syria and Mesopotamia with Parapotamia were studded with new settlements, which all bore Greek and Macedonian names. It is interesting to note that the regions in which the settlements were concentrated were known by two sets of names. Officially they were called Seleucis (with its four satrapies), Mesopotamia, and Parapotamia. But certain parts of these satrapies were known among the settlers by other, purely Macedonian, names. The coastal region together with Seleuceia was called Pieria, in imitation of the coastal region of Macedonia, the region between Mt. Amanus and the Euphrates and one part of Mesopotamia were proud to bear Macedonian names—Cyrrhestica and Mygdonia.

The names given by Seleucus and his successors to their new urban settlements were similar. They were either geographical, repetitions of Macedonian and Greek names, mostly the former—Europus, Pella, Beroea, Edessa, Cyrrhus, Perinthus, Maroneia, &c.—or dynastic, derived from the names of their founders, or the mothers or wives of these: Seleuceia, Antioch, Apamea, Laodicea, &c.

These facts make it clear that the Seleucids intended to transform the kernel of their kingdom into a new Macedonia, with capitals, principal seaports, and hundreds of cities and settlements bearing Macedonian and Greek names and occupied by a Macedonian and Greek population. The area of this new Syrian and Mesopotamian Macedonia was not much smaller than that of its original. How large its European population was we cannot so much as conjecture. We do not even know the exact number of settlements, much less the population of each.[265]

It has been stated that this region was connected with Babylonia by a chain of strongholds along the Euphrates and by another along the Tigris. Babylonia was to a certain extent the counterpart of Seleucid Syria. Here, on the site of the ancient Opis, stood Seleuceia on the Tigris, the new eastern capital of the Seleucid empire, the residence of the viceroy of its eastern satrapies.

To what extent Seleucus and his immediate successors endeavoured to surround Seleuceia, as they had surrounded their western capitals, with other cities of Greek character is not known. It was not necessary to urbanize Babylonia: Babylonia had been urbanized from time immemorial, and there was hardly room, indeed, for many new foundations of Macedonian and Greek type. There may have been, from early Seleucid times, attempts either to resettle the abandoned Babylonian cities or to transform some existing ones into Macedonian or Greek settlements. Our evidence mostly relates to the reign of Antiochus IV, who did his best, for example, to hellenize such cities as Babylon and perhaps Uruk. In any case, by founding Seleuceia, Seleucus contributed in no small degree to the hellenization of Babylonia.

Great efforts were made to protect Babylonia on the east against attack by the hordes of eastern Iran. Many Macedonian strongholds were created in Media (from which the Seleucids drew horses for their cavalry), Susiana, and Persis, the richest and most civilized parts of the Iranian world. Rhagae (Europus) and Ecbatana (later Epiphaneia), the two greatest centres of Media, will probably, if excavated, be found to resemble Susa, which, as we know from its excavation, after being first the capital of Elam and later one of the capitals of the Persian Empire, was refounded by Seleucus I as a Macedonian city under the name of Seleuceia on the Eulaeus. Antioch in Persis was another Seleucid city: it was founded by Antiochus I and is known to us as a 'colony' of Magnesia on the Maeander from two inscriptions found there, one of them a decree of the city.*

Little is known of the activities of the Seleucids in the eastern portion of their empire. It must be remembered that this part of Asia was in the hands of Seleucus and his successors during only fifty years. Seleucus and Antiochus appear to have foreseen the future role of Parthia, and attempted to prevent a Parthian invasion from the north by founding there several military colonies.†

The above sketch is based mainly on scattered literary, epigraphical, and numismatic evidence, from which we learn chiefly the names, and sometimes the approximate date of the foundation, of various Macedonian and Greek cities in the empire of the Seleucids. The names alone, however, do not enable us to form an adequate idea of what their policy in founding cities really was.

Antioch on the Orontes was the chief capital of the empire, and therefore may be supposed to have presented social and economic features similar to those of the better known Alexandria in Egypt. The king, his court, his administration, his

* *O.G.I.* 231 and 233; *Inschr. v. Magnesia*, nos. 18 and 61.

† App., *Syr.* 57.

'friends', a substantial part of his army, formed the nucleus of the population. This nucleus was supplemented, from the very foundation of the city, by many Greeks and Macedonians, rich and poor, landowners, merchants, retail traders, artisans, &c., and a large and ever increasing population of natives. The city grew quickly, and we hear of new wards being added to it in rapid succession.

Antioch and its sister cities, Apamea, Seleuceia, and Laodicea, were, as I have said, the centres of large and prosperous satrapies. What we know of these satrapies in the Roman and early Byzantine periods must have been true of them under the Seleucids. The country was rich, well cultivated, and thickly populated long before Seleucus, and it certainly remained flourishing and prosperous under him and his successors. As in the later times, it must have been thickly set with native villages and farm-houses of rich landowners, and with wealthy and important temples. In what kind of relations villages, landowners, and temples stood to the city of Antioch we do not know.

But Antioch and its sister cities were not only capitals of rich satrapies. Like all the Greek cities, they certainly had their own 'territories', that is to say, considerable areas of cultivable and cultivated land. How large these were is unknown. A late text suggests that the territory of Antioch was very large. The emperor Julian speaks of the city owning ten thousand *cleroi* in this territory.* These *cleroi* may have been an inheritance of the remote past. It may be supposed that immediately after the foundation of Antioch the territory assigned to it was measured out and divided into allotments, *cleroi*, as was done in Greek colonies in general. Some of these *cleroi* may have been given to the city in its corporate capacity, and the rest may have been divided among the first settlers of the city, Greeks and Macedonians, nobles and common people, soldiers and civilians. What happened to the native population of the city territory, to their villages and hamlets, and to their temples, we cannot say. We shall see later that in Asia Minor the new owners of the land were superimposed on the earlier native population.

* *Misop*. 362 C; cf. 370 D; 371 A.

If this was the procedure of Seleucus I, it certainly implies that, like Ptolemy I in Egypt, he regarded himself as the owner of the country which he had conquered with his spear (δορίκτητος χώρα). His companions in this conquest were his fellow Macedonians and Greeks, who naturally claimed their share in the land that had been conquered.[266]

We know very little of the relations between the central government and the larger cities of the kingdom. An inscription of the time of Seleucus IV shows Seleuceia in Pieria organized as a regular Greek city with its δῆμος, perhaps its βουλή and its ἄρχοντες. There can be no doubt that alongside of the city-archons there was a royal governor in the city, and probably a royal garrison; and that, where the interests of the king were involved, very little freedom was left to the city. The king's πρόσταγμα could not be disregarded. But the order of the king was carried out in constitutional form, as if it had been a free decision of the city. The relations of Seleuceia to the government were probably those, *mutatis mutandis*, of all the larger cities of the empire, including Antioch on the Orontes and Seleuceia on the Tigris.[267]

Of the minor cities—the many cities with Macedonian and dynastic names—we know little more. It is idle to speculate whether the settlements with Macedonian and those with dynastic names belonged to different classes, either of military and more or less civil colonies respectively, or of settlements organized as villages (κατοικίαι) and regular cities. The two settlements that we know best—Europus (Dura) in Parapotamia, as it was officially called, on the middle Euphrates, and Seleuceia on the Eulaeus (Susa), show in fact no difference as regards their constitution. Seleuceia, as we know from documents of Parthian times, was a Macedonian stronghold just like Europus, and Europus probably had the constitution of a regular Greek *polis* (below, pp. 485 f.), in the same way as Seleuceia or Antioch in Persis. Until more information is available hasty generalizations must be avoided.[268]

Europus. The best known of the minor foundations is Seleucus' colony Europus. Systematic excavations over a period of twelve years have revealed the history of the city. I have mentioned above that from a combination of literary, archaeological, epigraphic, numismatic, and papyrological evidence we know with certainty that Europus (known previously and also in later times as Dura) was founded by Nicanor, governor of Mesopotamia under Seleucus. It is interesting to note that the new city was called Europus, after the birth-

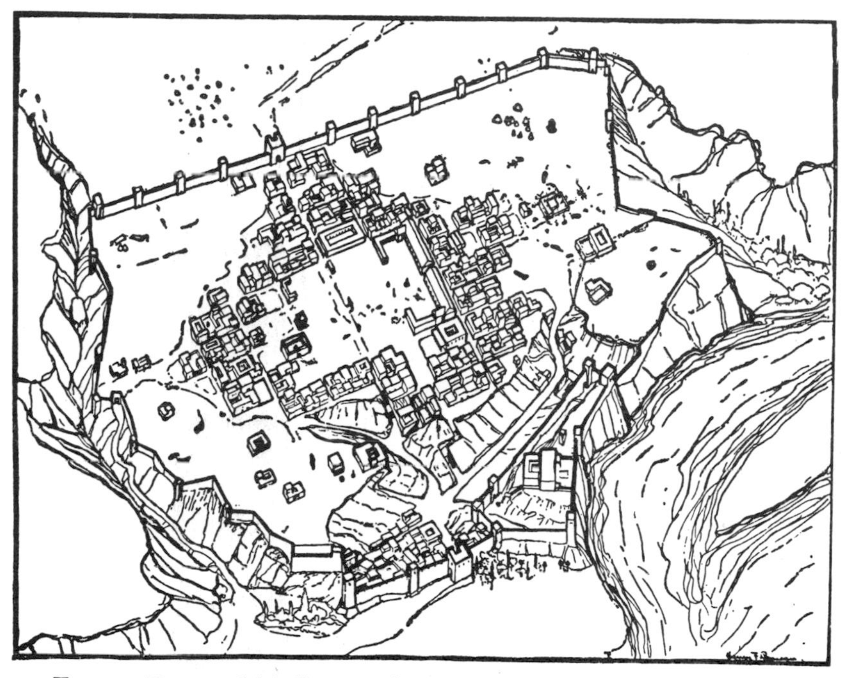

FIG. 4. Restored bird's-eye view of Hellenistic Europus. Drawn by H. Pearson.

place of Seleucus. It is probable that at least some of the first colonists were compatriots of Seleucus, like him natives of Europus in Macedonia. In any case the aristocracy of Europus in Hellenistic, Parthian, and Roman times bore almost exclusively Macedonian and Greek names.

We know little of the city in the early period of its existence. It attained its greatest prosperity under the Parthian domination, when it was thoroughly rebuilt on Oriental lines. But what we know of its earlier plan, buildings, and constitution shows that the Europus of the early Seleucids was not a mere stronghold or military village, but a combination of strong fortress and regularly planned, well-constructed city.

The city stood in a position of great natural strength, on a rocky plateau overhanging the Euphrates, and flanked by two deep ravines. It was surrounded by strong walls of stone with a superstructure of mud bricks, pierced by three monumental gates and including a citadel on the river front.

It will be apparent from the map of the city and the surrounding territory that Europus was in fact situated at a point which controlled the military and commercial road along the Euphrates, and that by closing its gates it could easily interrupt communication between lower and upper Mesopotamia. For the rocky plateau protruding into the river at this point forced the road to leave the bank of the Euphrates which it had followed above Europus, ascend to the plateau, and then descend again to the river. The wadi by which the road descended was included, where it approached the river, in the fortifications of the city. Europus was thus the strategical key of the Euphrates road in middle Mesopotamia, and for this reason was protected by its founders with imposing fortifications, the strongest parts of which were the desert wall and gate and the citadel, the former protecting the city against all attack from the desert, the latter commanding both the Euphrates road and the river. Within the citadel a large palace was built in early Hellenistic times, and extensive barracks were planned to accommodate the garrison of the city. The palace may have been that of the governor (*strategos*) of Parapotamia, and Europus may have been the capital of this province, or it may have been built for the commander of the garrison, the *phrourarch*. It must be added that the ambitious plans of Seleucus and Nicanor were never carried out in full: the fortifications of Europus were never finished and the barracks of the citadel never even begun. The original design of Seleucus I and Antiochus I was abandoned by their successors probably in consequence of the political situation.

The history of the citadel shows that the powerful fortress of Europus in Parapotamia, first intended to be one of the most important strongholds of the Euphrates road and therefore probably occupied by a garrison of soldiers in active service, was soon after the foundation of the city left entirely in the care of its citizens, who apparently were supposed to be strong enough and sufficiently trained to defend their own city from the attacks of the neighbouring Arabs and of any other enemy. Since the task of finishing the fortifications appears to have been entrusted to them alone, it is probable that the kings considered them to be rich enough to afford it.

Inside the walls the spacious city was laid out on what was known as the Hippodamian plan, a characteristic feature of most of the early Hellenistic cities: Priene, Miletus, Alexandria, and, in Syria, Damascus, Aleppo, and Latakieh.* Two main streets ran from north to south and from east to west, and the narrower side streets ran parallel or at right angles to these, forming quadrangular blocks. A large *agora* opened on the north side of the main east-to-west street, a widening, as it were, of this street. Temples occupied some of the quadrangular blocks. One was dedicated to Apollo and Artemis, the great protectors of Seleucus.

Opposite the citadel, beyond the above-mentioned wadi, a rocky spur, part of the main plateau of the city, formed the acropolis. The slopes of this spur were strengthened by fine supporting walls. On the top was built a palatial peristyle house. I think it probable that this house was the headquarters and official residence either of the Macedonian *epistates* (governor) of the city or of the chief magistrate, the *strategos*. Unfortunately no inscriptions of the Hellenistic period were found in the ruins of this palace.

Behind it on the same spur stood a Greek temple, later dedicated to Zeus Megistos. It may be suggested that it was originally a temple of the great Zeus Olympius, god of the Seleucids, and was perhaps built in the time of Antiochus Epiphanes.

We have no contemporary evidence relating to the constitution of the city in the Hellenistic period. But inscriptions and parchments enable us to form a fair idea of it in Parthian times. It is difficult to believe that it was the Parthians who endowed Europus with a Greek constitution, for this would not accord with their custom. It is much more probable that

* The topography of Damascus and Latakieh has recently been studied by Sauvaget (below, ch. viii).

they allowed the city to retain the constitution that it had possessed from the time of its foundation. Nor is it likely that the Romans changed the constitution in any essential respect.

We have evidence of a city council (βουλή) in Roman times. At the head of the city under the Parthian and the Roman domination stood the chief magistrate and the commander of the garrison, known as the *strategos* and *epistates*. There are grounds for thinking that this combination was a Parthian innovation. In the early period of its history Europus, like Seleuceia in Pieria in Hellenistic times and Seleuceia on the Eulaeus in Parthian times,* may have had its elected magistrates with a *strategos* or *archon* at their head, and alongside of these a royal governor. We know of several minor magistrates at Dura in the later times: ἀγορανόμοι, ταμίαι, σιτῶναι, and their apparitors, for example κήρυκες. Besides the city magistrates there were a group of royal officials discharging various functions. We hear of royal judges in charge of a royal court organized on the Greek model. In the χρηματιστήριον and χρεοφυλάκιον sat the keepers of archives and registrars, royal or municipal officials. Finally, documents have recently been discovered which show that late in the Roman period there were still at Europus eponymous priests, similar to those known to have existed in many other Seleucid cities of the Hellenistic period. The group of priests at Europus included priests of Zeus, probably Zeus Olympius, of Apollo, and of the long-extinct Seleucid dynasty. In the formula of Roman times the reigning king was of course omitted but his ancestors (πρόγονοι) remained. Last among them came the priest of the founder of the city, Seleucus Nicator, whose cult was always kept alive at Europus, as is shown by an interesting bas-relief of Parthian times (pl. LI, 2). This survival of the dynastic cult is very suggestive. It shows the great prestige of the Seleucids in their dominions, especially among the descendants of the Greeks and Macedonians, and the care taken by the Parthians and the Romans to avoid offence to the Greek population of the former Seleucid Empire.

The constitution of Europus, as reconstructed above mostly

* *S.E.G.* vii, no. 1.

from later evidence, is almost identical with that of other royal cities of the Seleucid Empire, so far as they are known to us. I have already referred to Seleuceia in Pieria, Antioch in Persis, Seleuceia on the Eulaeus and Seleuceia on the Tigris; and as regards Asia Minor, we find the same similarity in the little we know of the constitutions of Antioch in Pisidia,* Antioch in Caria,† and Laodicea on the Lycus.‡ We may therefore infer that the Seleucid policy was to give their new cities a uniform constitution, based in all probability on that of some of the cities of Asia Minor.

The population of Europus in the early period consisted apparently of various elements. The garrison of the citadel was in all probability a detachment of the regular royal army. The soldiers composing it may, however, have been conscripted from among the Macedonians settled at Europus, as was probably the case at Seleuceia on the Eulaeus in Parthian times (below, p. 489 f.).

The kernel of the population was formed by the early settlers, all of whom bore either Macedonian or Greek names, and their families. To this kernel were very soon added constantly growing numbers of Greek and native immigrants and of slaves. Although we have no direct evidence of this, it was a natural process.

Unfortunately there is no evidence to show who were the original settlers of Europus. But from the fact that they bear almost exclusively Macedonian names it is legitimate to infer that they were either veterans or soldiers, not in active service for the time being, of the army of Seleucus I. The earliest extant parchment from Europus,§ an extract from a contract of sale, shows that the inhabitants who bore Greek and Macedonian names were in possession of *cleroi* or allotments, and were therefore κληροῦχοι. We may perhaps draw the same inference from the well-known law, or regulation, of inheritance of which a fragment was found at Europus.|| The text that we possess is late, but in its original form the law probably dated from Seleucid times. We may regard it as one of those general laws or orders

* *Inschr. v. Magn.* 80 and 81. † Ibid. 90. ‡ Michel 543.

§ *D. Perg.* 1, of 190 B.C.; F. Cumont, *Fouilles*, pp. 286 ff.

|| *D. Perg.* 5; F. Cumont, loc. cit., pp. 309 ff.

(προστάγματα or διαγράμματα) by which the Seleucids regulated the life of the new settlers in their empire. References to similar laws frequently occur in parchments and papyri found in the same city and show that in this respect also the Seleucid traditions remained alive long after the dynasty had come to an end. The fragment of the law of inheritance contains the rules of inheritance *ab intestato*. At the end it prescribes that, failing the heirs specified in the preceding lines, the οὐσία or estate of the deceased shall lapse to the king (βασιλικὴ ἡ οὐσία ἔστω). This general prescription may have special reference to the property of the cleruchs, their *cleroi*. These, having been assigned out of royal territory (χώρα βασιλική), were treated in a special way prescribed by the law and not according to the general law regarding the *bona caduca*.

In the earlier parchment (*D. Perg.* I) there is mention of *cleroi* and of *hecades*, the former being subdivisions of the latter. Both the *cleroi* and the *hecades* are distinguished by personal names (*hecas* of Arybbas, *cleros* of Conon). This shows that a *hecas* in the Hellenistic period was a division of the cleruchic land of Europus, while the *cleroi* were subdivisions of the *hecades*. In later times, however, we find the territory of Europus divided into villages and not into *hecades*. Many of these villages are referred to in the parchments and papyri of Dura belonging to the Parthian and Roman period; they have local names and certainly were not creations of that period.

It therefore seems probable that, when the new colony of Europus was first founded, a certain 'territory', that is to say, a considerable tract of land along the Euphrates, including a group of villages, was assigned to it. Part of this territory was measured and divided into *hecades*. These were subdivided into *cleroi* and the *cleroi* were assigned to the new settlers. This means that some at least of the land assigned to the new city was taken from its former holders and given to the new-comers, unless we are to assume that the new settlers received land that had formerly been waste but had been reclaimed and irrigated by the new rulers of the country.* Whether taken from the ancient owners or recently reclaimed,

* Cf. the epiphyteutic land of *D. Perg.* 23; C. B. Welles, *Münch. Beitr.* xix, pp. 380 ff.

the land became the private property of the settlers. They had the right to sell, mortgage, and bequeath it. It could be owned by women as well as men. How they cultivated it we do not know. In *D. Perg.* I the *cleroi* appear as prosperous farms, with farm-houses, fruit gardens, vineyards, and perhaps palm-groves. Later documents speak of many vineyards in the territory of Dura, and of fields sown with barley; and similar conditions undoubtedly prevailed in early Seleucid times. These gardens, palm-groves, and vineyards may have been planted by the new settlers, or they may have already been planted when taken from the former owners. The settlers may have cultivated their *cleroi* themselves or by means of slave labour; they may, again, have rented them to the former owners.

Though a minor city in comparison with such important cities as Antioch on the Orontes, Laodicea on the sea, Apamea, Seleuceia in Pieria, and Seleuceia on the Tigris, Europus certainly played a not unimportant part in the life of the Mesopotamian lands. It was a military stronghold and administrative centre, and at the same time a prosperous city, a centre of agriculture, horticulture, viticulture, and cattle-breeding, and of local trade; and it was also a stopping-place for the caravans. All this is reflected in its monuments and is emphasized by the fact that Europus was one of the minor Seleucid mints, at least in the time of Antiochus I. Recent discoveries have shown that there were at least three issues of bronze coins at Dura during his reign. Whether the mint of Europus was a purely local one for regional small change, managed by the city, or had a wider scope, is a question which cannot be answered without further evidence.[269]

Seleuceia on the Eulaeus. Seleuceia on the Eulaeus was similar in all respects to Europus on the Euphrates. I have already mentioned that it had a regular city constitution in Parthian times, very similar to that of Seleuceia in Pieria, Antioch in Persis, and Europus.* Its laws and regulations were certainly of the same kind as those of Europus. The temple manumissions of Seleuceia follow purely Greek models.† Moreover Seleuceia, like Europus, was an important military centre.

* *S.E.G.* vii, no. 1; C. B. Welles, *R.C.* 75. † *S.E.G.* vii, nos. 15 ff.

Under the Seleucids it certainly was strongly garrisoned.* And again as at Europus, at least part of the foreign population consisted of military settlers. In two metrical dedications of the Parthian period† the Parthian administration is praised by the 'guardians of the ἄκρα'‡, inhabitants of the city, for the benefit conferred on them by the restoration of the irrigation system. As a result, they say, the *cleroi* which had become dried up, have been restored to fertility. It is probable that the ἀκροφύλακες or ἀκροφυλακῖται of Seleuceia were descendants of former Seleucid cleruchs to whom allotments had been assigned in the territory of the city and that, as such, they performed active military service in defence of the city.[270]

There are good grounds for believing that other Seleucid colonies of Mesopotamia, those planted along the Euphrates and the Tigris and in the Iranian countries, belonged to the same category as Europus and Seleuceia. Support for this view may be found in the contracts of sale on parchments found at Avroman, the earlier of which are of Greek type and recorded in Greek, while one of a later date is of Oriental type and recorded in Pehlevi. In my opinion the parties to these contracts were descendants of Seleucid colonists of Iranian nationality.[271]

Our information, however, is insufficient to enable us to draw the general inference that the early Seleucid foundations in Syria, Mesopotamia, and Iran, with the exception of the larger cities, were *all* of the same type as Europus in Parapotamia and Seleuceia on the Eulaeus. Even the scanty knowledge we have enables us to see that the colonization of these countries by the Seleucids was not uniform. It is certain, for instance, that in some of the colonies the majority of the settlers, if not all of them, were Macedonians and that in some others (for instance Larisa with its Thessalian population and Antioch in Persis founded by emigrants from Magnesia on the Maeander) they were Greeks. We hear occasionally of colonies that were neither Greek nor Macedonian but Jewish, established, for example, in Asia Minor (below, p. 492).

Some of the colonies were planted in already existing Oriental

* *S.E.G.* vii, no. 4. † Ibid. vii, nos. 12 and 13.

‡ Cf. the ἀκροφυλακῖται of Babylon, *O.G.I.* 254.

cities of considerable size and importance, such as Hamath, Halab, Edessa, Nisibis, Susa, &c., while others absorbed little known native villages or hamlets. To the latter class belonged certainly Europus and probably some of the cities in Seleucid Syria with Macedonian names. We now know that the Oriental name of Europus, Dura, was that of a native village which fifteen centuries before had belonged to the kingdom of Hana.

Most of the colonies, as has been shown above, had a city constitution and were regular Greek *poleis*. We shall see presently, however, that in Asia Minor many, if not most, of the Macedonian settlements were rural communities (κατοικίαι) with a special organization. There is nothing to prevent us from supposing that such κατοικίαι existed in Syria also, though no certain instance is known.

Nor do we know which of the colonies were military and which civil settlements, that is to say, in which of them the early residents were taken from the ranks of the Seleucid army and in which they were recruited from civilians of Greek communities in the Seleucid kingdom. The former was probably the case at Europus and Seleuceia on the Eulaeus, the latter almost certainly at Antioch in Persis. The inhabitants of this city, in a decree replying to a letter from Magnesia on the Maeander (*O.G.I.* 233), mention that the Magnesians are their relatives and friends, since it was they who at the request of Antiochus I, the founder of the city, had sent a colony to Antioch to increase its strength and prosperity.* We hear of a similar colony being sent to Antioch in Pisidia.†

The most important question, however, is that of the relations of the above-described urban and rural centres founded by the Seleucids to the king who founded them and his successors, especially as regards the part they played in the military affairs of the empire. I shall discuss this problem after reviewing some of the features of the Seleucid colonization of Asia Minor.

The Seleucids were no less active in settling Macedonians and Greeks in Asia Minor. Some of their new colonies were organized as regular Greek cities, others were rural settlements

* Antiochus had made the request φιλοτιμ(ο)[υ](μ)ένου ἐπα[υξ]ῆσαι τὴν πόλιν ἡμῶν.

† Strabo, xii. 8. 14, p. 577.

(κατοικίαι). The case of Magnesia by the Sipylus shows that even ancient Greek cities might be used for the settlement of Seleucid colonists and yet keep their old population.*

Of the constitution and mode of life of the Seleucid colonies in Asia Minor we know very little, and what we know relates mostly to later times.[272] A passage in Josephus,† which has been the subject of much discussion, gives us a vivid picture of the foundation of a colony in Asia Minor by Antiochus III. According to this passage, Antiochus decided to settle two thousand Jewish families from Mesopotamia and Babylonia in Lydia and Phrygia. Whether this is an historical fact or a mere invention, and whether the letter of Antiochus to Zeuxis quoted by Josephus is genuine or not,‡ is here immaterial.[273] The letter undoubtedly gives us exactly the normal procedure when the Seleucids founded a colony. It fits in very well with what I have said of Europus. It was decided by a resolution of the council of the king's 'friends' to settle two thousand families with their effects in certain fortified posts. The settlers were granted autonomy, sites for houses, allotments for agriculture and vineyards, immunity from taxation upon their lands for ten years, grain for the subsistence of themselves and their dependents during the first year, and security against attack—presumably in the form of fortifications.

Most of the colonists throughout the Seleucid Empire, in Asia Minor and elsewhere, were settled in groups in newly founded cities and villages; a few were superimposed in groups on the population of existing cities and villages. I have referred to the instance of Magnesia on the Sipylus, and in the preceding chapter to the incorporation of a group of mercenary soldiers in the citizen body of the ancient Greek city of Aspendus; and other methods of settlement may have been resorted to exceptionally. The inscription of Mnesimachus§ conveys the impression that individual *cleroi* may have been assigned to officers and soldiers out of royal land that did not form part of the territory of a city or of a κατοικία. Land for this purpose

* *O.G.I.* 229.

† *A.J.* xii. 148.

‡ Its style is singularly like that of the letter of the same Antiochus to the city of Amyzon, Welles, *R.C.* 38.

§ *Sardis, Gr. and Lat. Inscr.*, no. 1.

was sometimes taken from a temple, as it certainly was in the case of the colonists who received their *cleroi* out of what had formerly been the property of the Zeus of Aezani,* and as it may have been in the case of Mnesimachus.

Some of the cities and settlements created in Asia Minor by the Seleucids were certainly not military. We hear for instance of the foundation of Nysa on the Maeander by Antiochus I.† The king formed this city by settling there the population of three neighbouring communities. This was the ordinary method of synoecism and was frequently resorted to. The temple connected with the city (the Plutonium, see above, p. 439) received the privilege of *asylia*, afterwards confirmed by Antiochus III. We find a similar procedure at Lysimacheia,‡ the former capital of Lysimachus, destroyed by the Thracians and restored by Antiochus III. The king summoned together the former inhabitants of the city (among them prisoners of war, whom he redeemed), invited new settlers, gave them cattle and agricultural implements, and fortified the town at his own expense.

It was not only by the grant of portions of the royal territory (χώρα βασιλική) to cities, rural settlements (κατοικίαι), and individual cleruchs that foreigners, mostly of Macedonian or Greek origin, were superimposed on the native population. We hear of many other methods. Sometimes large areas of royal land with the villages and population included therein were sold to Greek cities, to members of the royal house, or to members of the higher aristocracy of the empire. We have, for example, purchases by the city of Pitana in the reign of Antiochus I§ and by Queen Laodice in the time of Antiochus II.|| The land in possession of Mnesimachus besides the *cleroi* referred to above (pp. 465, 492) may also have been such a purchase. In other cases tracts of royal land were given as royal gifts (*doreai*) to persons of eminence in the empire, for instance to Aristodicides of Assus in the time of Antiochus I,¶ to Meleager, and to Athenaeus, the last an admiral under Antiochus I.** Royal gifts of this type and also of another kind

* *O.G.I.* 502.
† Steph. Byz. *s. v.*; Strabo xiv, 1. 46, p. 650.
‡ App. *Syr.* i. 1.
§ *O.G.I.* 335.
|| Ibid. 225; Welles, *R.C.* 18.
¶ *O.G.I.* 221; Welles, *R.C.* 10–12.
** Ibid.

(grants of cities with their territories) remained common in later Seleucid times, for example the gift by Demetrius I of the city of Ecron to Jonathan and that by Antiochus IV to his mistress. I may also recall in this connexion the well-known grant of land by Philadelphus to Miletus.*

In some cases we find royal land in the possession of Greeks, but do not know in what way it passed into their hands. We have an example in a certain Demetrius, son of Demetrius, grandson of Mnasaeus, who was for a time the owner of the sacred village of Baetocaece in the Apamaean satrapy. The *dossier* of this land recorded in the inscription of the temple of Zeus Baetocaecenus near Tartus† does not state how he came to own the village. Nor do we know how Larichus acquired his large estate in the territory of Priene (see above, p. 178; possibly by buying parts of the χώρα πολιτική or parcels of the χώρα βασιλική), nor in what circumstances the most prominent 'friends' of Antiochus II divided among themselves the territory known as Anaitis, which was the property of the Samians.‡ Sometimes a purchase may have been a disguised gift (as in the case of Laodice) or a gift a disguised purchase.

The sales, assignments, and gifts of tracts of royal land were not confined to Asia Minor and Syria. We hear incidentally of a gift of land and cattle being bestowed by Antiochus I in 279 B.C. on the groups of inhabitants of Babylon living around the temple of Bel (all that remained of the city after the creation of Seleuceia on the Tigris) and being taken from them again for the royal house by the governor of Babylon five years later. A copy of an inscription on stone of 236 B.C., preserved on a Babylonian tablet of 173/2 B.C., records gifts of land and other property in Babylonia by Antiochus II to his wife Laodice. His sons Seleucus and Antiochus ceded the land to the Babylonians, Borsippaeans, and Kuthaeans, and later it became the property of Babylonian temples. The land in question had belonged to Seleucus I and Antiochus I before it passed into the hands of Antiochus II.§ The tablet has never been carefully published and studied, and it is uncertain whether the land formed part of the χώρα βασιλική, like that

* Welles, *R.C.* 14.

† Ibid. 70.

‡ *S.E.G.* i. 366.

§ Above, n. 234.

disposed of by the early Seleucids in Asia Minor and Syria, or part of the private estates of the early kings which the Seleucids owned as successors of the Persian kings and of Alexander, the conditions of land tenure in Babylonia being perhaps different from those in Asia Minor.

Lands bought by individuals from the king became in most cases their private property; but inasmuch as outside the Greek cities the property rights of individuals were highly precarious, a condition of the purchase was that the land must be ascribed to the territory of some city. In some cases gift land, like bought land, became private property under the same condition of ascription to the territory of a city. We have an instance of this in the case of Aristodicides. Very often, however, gift lands were held as fiefs, and might be resumed from the holders at the pleasure of the king. Demetrius of Baetocaece, and Meleager, the former owner of the land assigned to Aristodicides, held subject to this liability.

The case of Mnesimachus was peculiar. He may have received part of his estate near Sardis from the king as a fief in consideration of the payment of a lump sum. Very interesting information on the composition of his estate, which was probably typical of many other similar properties, may be derived from the inscription found at Sardis to which I have referred. The inscription contains fragments of a deed of sale 'subject to redemption', or, to apply modern terms, of a mortgage whereby Mnesimachus conveys to the goddess Artemis on behalf of himself and his descendants the lands specified in the deed in return for a loan that has been granted to him by the temple. This loan may have been contracted in order to pay the king. The estate consisted of several villages and of two allotments (*cleroi*). With the villages and allotments went the dwellings, the serfs with their households and belongings, the wine vessels (or perhaps the output of the pottery factories, as Prof. C. B. Welles suggests), and the dues (of the serfs) payable in money and in labour (φόρος ἀργυρικός and λητουργικός). Before the estate was finally assigned to Mnesimachus a division (διαίρεσις) was made (in what circumstances and by whom we are not informed). As a result of this, two men with Greek or Macedonian names—Pytheus and Adrastus—received in the territory of two of the above-mentioned villages their separate property (ἐξαίρημα), which consisted of a farmstead or manor-house, houses of the serfs and slaves, and gardens, in one village, and dwellings, gardens, and slaves in another. Whether the ἐξαίρημα of Pytheus and Adrastus consisted of their *cleroi* we are not told. In any case it is evident that the document distinguishes sharply between villages and *cleroi*. It is regrettable that we cannot discern what constituted the difference between the two. So far as dues were concerned, there was none. Both pay rent or a tax to the king in gold; both form part of the estate of Mnesimachus; and both are cultivated by native λαοί, who after the purchase of the estate by Mnesimachus became his serfs. The difference probably lay in the title of the holder to the land and in the different conditions under which the land was given to him and under which it could be taken back from him by the king. The *cleros*, moreover, was generally situated outside the native village and was generally given by the king to foreigners, not to natives.

There may have been other ways, besides those described above, of establishing islands of Greek farming in various parts of the royal land. The Seleucids may well have rented plots to immigrants and encouraged them, as did the Greek cities and the Ptolemies, to plant with vines and trees land that had hitherto produced little or nothing (καταφύτευσις, ἐμφύτευσις). The king may also have sold parcels of royal land, not only to cities and to wealthy purchasers, but also to members of the recently created Greek *bourgeoisie* of his new settlements.[274]

In any case, by their policy of settling groups of immigrants on the crown land and of creating holdings, large and small, for individual Greeks, the Seleucids, like the Ptolemies in Egypt, introduced a new element into the economic system of the empire. It would help us greatly to estimate the various consequences of this measure if we could form even an approximate idea how much land was assigned to the new settlers, and how many of them remained permanently established in the empire.

On the former point there is no evidence, and the question cannot be answered. We do not even know the exact number of the new settlements and we know very little about the extent of land assigned to each. We have even less information about the gift lands. It is certain, however, that large tracts of territory, probably the major part of it, remained in the hands of the natives.

Nor can an adequate answer be given on the second point. It is impossible to arrive at any probable estimate of the number of foreigners who settled in the empire under the early Seleucids (cf. above, p. 479). We have, it is true, certain figures. We know that the Macedonian phalanx numbered 20,000 men at Raphia, and that the phalanx was 17,000 strong at Magnesia, and 20,000 at the review held at Daphne under Antiochus IV. If we add the Macedonian cavalry, the garrisons of cities, and the military police, we may form a very approximate and general idea of the minimum numerical strength of that part of the Seleucid army which was recruited from immigrants who called themselves Macedonians and Greeks. But what proportion of the settled foreign population of the various satrapies was liable to military service is, we must remember, unknown to us (below, pp. 499 ff.). We cannot even conjecture what proportion of men of military age and liable to military service was mobilized at critical moments in the history of the Seleucid dynasty. In deciding the size and composition of the army the kings and their staff were guided by many considerations, both military and economic. The provision of food, transport, and accommodation for a large army with its baggage and belongings (ἀποσκευή) was a matter of no less importance than difficulty, and the larger the army, the greater the difficulty. Moreover, there were tactical objections to a phalanx that was disproportionately large: cavalry of various types and special troops were as important as the Macedonian infantry, and the best cavalry and special troops were drawn from sources other than the Macedonian settlers. For all these reasons, we are not justified in basing on the reported numbers of mobilized 'Macedonians' any conclusion as to the size of the Macedonian and Greek population of the Seleucid Empire.[275]

The study of Dura-Europus warns us against an exaggerated estimate of the number of Macedonian military settlers in the military colonies of the Seleucids. We may form an idea of the number of Macedonian families in Parthian Dura from the numerous inscriptions, and especially from the names of the ladies of the leading families of the city, most of them Macedonian, inscribed on their seats in the theatre-like *pronaoi* of the three leading temples of the Great Goddess. The information thus derived is not exact. It is true that many families of the early settlers may have died out, and that no new settlers of Macedonian origin were added in late Seleucid times to those who resided at Europus in the early Hellenistic period. Nevertheless it is surprising to find how few Macedonian families, not more than a score or at most two score, were living at Dura in the Parthian period. Even if this number be multiplied by ten or even twenty, the total will not be large. This is not astonishing, for the Macedonians in the armies of Alexander and his successors were never numerous. Distributed among many scores of military colonies, they could furnish at most a handful of settlers to each, who formed in later times no more than a small aristocratic minority of the population.

Failing statistics for the Seleucid period, we may perhaps look for help from certain data of later times. We possess some more or less trustworthy figures relating to the population of Antioch on the Orontes and of Seleuceia on the Tigris under the early Roman Empire. These give Antioch a population, in round numbers, of *c.* 500,000 and Seleuceia of 600,000.* But it is hardly possible to derive from these figures any approximate idea of the Greek population of the two cities in early Seleucid times. We do not know how many natives and non-Greek immigrants they contained, and we must remember the long period that had elapsed and the many changes that had occurred between the Seleucid and Roman dominations. We are somewhat better informed as regards Apamea. According to the census of Quirinius (of A.D. 6/7) there were 117,000 citizens (of both sexes and all ages) in this city and its territory. This no doubt is a surprising number, but we must take into consideration that the territory of the Roman city of Apamea was very large and included hundreds of towns and villages. Moreover, in Roman times many natives became citizens of Apamea. And finally we must take into account

* Pliny, *N.H.* vi. 122.

that the cities of Seleucid Syria never ceased growing, and that this growth was perhaps as rapid in the troubled times of the later Seleucids as it had been in the quieter times of the immediate successors of Seleucus. We must therefore reduce the above figure considerably to arrive at that applicable to the early Seleucid period; by how much it is impossible to say.[276]

However this may be, the 'Hellenes' in the early Seleucid Empire were undoubtedly very numerous, and their number was constantly increasing. Yet it is certain that in comparison with the natives the Hellenes formed a small minority. We know nothing of the size of the total population of the Seleucid Empire. Calculations based on modern statistical data suggest a figure between 25 and 30 millions. Of these the Hellenes certainly were a very small fraction.

In conclusion we return to the basic question which I have stated above. What was the general character of Seleucid colonization and what were the aims of the Seleucids in carrying it out? Was their object mainly military? Did they wish to have in the Macedonian and Greek settlements of their empire as large a reservoir as possible from which to draw a well-trained and reliable nucleus of armies? Or was their aim more political than military? Did they regard their colonies mainly as meshes of a Greek net spread all over their empire to hold together its disparate parts and thus to assure their domination over it and secure it from internal disintegration and external attacks? Or, again, in founding their colonies and creating Greek islands in their empire, were they pursuing a policy of hellenization in the hope that these islands of Hellenism would absorb the native population?

The scantiness of our material prevents us from giving a definite answer to this question. Some scholars are inclined to think that a large part of the Seleucid colonies, both urban and rural, were military settlements, their population being regarded as soldiers of the Seleucid army who were temporarily not in active service but were ready to join the ranks of the field army or act as garrisons at the call of the king. This would be practically the same system as that of the Ptolemies, with the difference that the reserve soldiers of the Seleucids were settled in groups in cities and villages, while the Ptolemaic reserves were scattered all over the country in already existing towns and villages or in recently founded settlements, mostly villages, which, however, were not purely military settlements.

This opinion has been recently challenged by E. Bikerman.* If I rightly understand him, he does not admit that the urban settlements of the Seleucids were of a military character, that is to say, that the citizens of these cities were in any way liable to military service in the royal army or ever fought in the phalanx and in the Macedonian cavalry. Like citizens of all Greek cities, they were of course citizen-soldiers. Each of them was armed and received military training for the purpose of defending his city in case of necessity. The citizens of every city not only formed a body politic, but were also organized as a potential army, a local militia. This militia, however, only occasionally took part in the wars of its overlords, and when it did so, it fought in an allied, not a subject capacity. In short, so far as military obligations were concerned, the Seleucid colonies were in exactly the same position as the ancient Greek cities of the kingdom, especially those of Asia Minor.

While therefore the city-colonies of the Seleucids were 'civic', not military, settlements, the Seleucids nevertheless made provision for a military reserve on which to draw at need. This reserve was the Macedonian settlers scattered over the empire in rural communities, in *κατοικίαι*. These men, who did not belong to any city, were liable to military service and were conscripted or mobilized whenever the Seleucids needed to increase their permanent army. They were enrolled in the phalanx or in the Macedonian cavalry. The status of the Thessalian *κατοικία* of Larisa was more or less similar, and so perhaps was that of the Cardaces in Lycia (see below, Ch. V, n. 61). The system was, in the main, the same as that which obtained in the Macedonia of Philip, Alexander, and the Antigonids. For the purpose of mobilization, it may be added, the empire was divided into several mobilization districts, which were perhaps the *chiliarchies* mentioned in the inscription of Mnesimachus.

This view cannot be discussed here in detail. It seems to

* *Inst. Sél.*, pp. 72 ff.

me too logical, too redolent of the jurist rather than the historian. It is hard to believe that the Macedonians of Europus were treated by the Seleucids like the citizens of Miletus and Ephesus. My impression is that from the military point of view Europus was treated as a κατοικία, not as a *polis*, although it was in all other respects a regular *polis*; and so, in my opinion, were the other settlements of the same kind. Their inhabitants received their *cleroi* from the crown as potential soldiers of the army and were bound to answer the king's call in case of mobilization. Whether the larger urban foundations of the Seleucids were treated in the same way, in other words, whether they had a nucleus of *cleruchoi* liable to military service, cannot be said. I am convinced that the Seleucids had no rigid scheme in this respect, but acted according to circumstances. And, as I have stated above, they did not require very many soldiers for their fighting forces, particularly soldiers spoilt by the life of large cities. Nevertheless I see no reason why they should not, in case of need, have mobilized the better trained and more vigorous citizens of their capitals and of the larger cities of their empire, which were founded by themselves. We hear for example of Antiochenes fighting in the ranks of the army.*

Military considerations were, therefore, an important factor in the colonizing policy of the Seleucids. But they were not the only considerations: political motives were probably equally important. It is certain that in spreading a net of Macedonian, Greek, and other colonies the Seleucids intended first and foremost to lay a solid foundation for their rule over their disparate empire. The settlers of the new cities and communities, organized as Greek *poleis* and as Macedonian villages, stood in a close relation to the king, who had helped them to start a new life and was the semi-divine founder (*ktistes*) of their communities. Many of them had served under his command and were accustomed to carry out his orders. From the king they received their means of subsistence, and they were very well aware that their prosperity and safety depended entirely on the security of his empire. Their fortunes were bound up with those of the king. At the same time they were sons of Greece

* E. Bikerman, *Inst. Sél.*, p. 72.

and Macedonia, and they brought to their new abodes the mentality of Greeks and Macedonians, above all, a profound devotion to their home, whether it was a real city or a quasi-urban community. For this home and all that it meant to Macedonians and Greeks they were ready to die, if necessary. Thus in their new colonies the Seleucids found a solid and unfailing support of their domination.

In colonizing their vast empire did the Seleucids also aim at hellenizing it, at unifying it by the spread of one particular manner of life and one civilization? When we speak of hellenization, we are really using a modern, not an ancient, conception. The Greeks in their long history never tried to hellenize any one: the notion was foreign to them. Greek colonization in Classical and Hellenistic times produced a certain amount of hellenization that was the result of a natural process independent of the wishes and aims of the Greek settlers in foreign countries. And so it was in the case of the Seleucids. Natives became hellenized and Greek and Macedonian settlers became orientalized. It was inevitable. But the Seleucids never realized the importance of this process. They never tried to accelerate or to arrest it. They never dreamt of a national Greek and Macedonian State resulting from the colonization of their Oriental empire.

Military and political in its very essence, the colonization of the East had nevertheless important economic and social consequences, though such considerations were entirely foreign to the Seleucids, who never thought in economic and social terms. What these consequences were, we shall see presently.

(*b*) *The royal land: temples, large estates, villages, native towns*

In the terminology of the various overlords, including the Romans, that ruled the Near East, the political units with which they had dealings and which therefore were regarded as possessing more or less sovereign powers were kings (βασιλεῖς), minor rulers (δυνάσται), cities (πόλεις or δῆμοι), and 'peoples' (ἔθνη). These terms could be and probably were applied, not only to political units outside the Seleucid Empire, but also to the more or less self-governing State-like formations within it: the vassal kings, the vassal dynasts, the cities, and the semi-independent tribes, more or less civilized and urbanized, some of them organized on the lines of the Hellenistic κοινά (on the one hand certain mountain tribes in Asia Minor and various tribal states in the Semitic and Iranian parts of the East, and on the other the Lycians, the Carians, and perhaps the Galatians in Asia Minor).[277]

The above enumeration of self-governing units in the Seleucid Empire is not intended to be an exhaustive list of its constituent parts. It naturally omits the territories devoid of self-government, which were regarded as the property of the king, as parts of his 'house' (οἶκος), the so-called χώρα or χώρα βασιλική. The *chora* certainly formed as large a part of the Seleucid Empire as the territories that retained, or received from the kings, a certain measure of self-government. Both divisions of the Empire were inhabited by subjects who were bound to render unquestioning obedience to the king. The difference between them lay in the fact that each retained peculiarities of structure inherited from the past. A short survey of the two divisions may begin with the conditions of life in the royal territory.

The social and economic structure of the χώρα may have been different in the different satrapies of the Seleucid Empire. The little we know about it relates to two regions only: Asia Minor and Babylonia. For Syria and Mesopotamia our information is very slight, and for the Iranian satrapies we have none.

I will therefore briefly summarize what is known of the above-named regions. In Asia Minor, apart from the self-governing bodies already mentioned, and the military rural settlements, we find three main types of social and economic structure. They are: (1) the temples (many of them temple-states with their peculiar organization); (2) the large pre-Hellenistic estates that are especially characteristic of Asia Minor in the Persian period; and (3) the native villages.[278]

Temples. The temples had their own religious, economic, and social organization, firmly established from remote times.[279] There were many of them scattered all over Asia Minor. Some had been absorbed by, or brought into close association with, the ancient Greek cities of that region long before Alexander and Seleucus. Outwardly they presented a Greek appearance, for instance in respect of the names of their gods and goddesses, their architecture and their statues, their votive offerings, and so forth. Their social and economic relations with the cities varied in different parts of Asia Minor. This is not the place for a close examination of the questions connected with them, since the Hellenistic period was no more than a brief phase in the centuries of evolution of sanctuaries of this type, such as that of Artemis at Ephesus or Artemis at Sardis or Apollo at Clarus.

Many temples, however, had no relations whatever with any Greek city. Some of them were probably modest sanctuaries closely connected with native villages. Very probably the natives regarded the village as the property of the god or goddess whose shrine stood within it, and the priests of the god or goddess no doubt played a very important part, not only in the religious, but also in the social, administrative, judicial, and economic life of the community. The close relations between temple and village are sometimes attested by the theophoric names of villages such as Menokome, Hermokome, Dioskome, Atyochorion, and the like. One of the best known sanctuaries of this type, that of Apollo Helios Laerbenus on the Maeander in Phrygia, has been more than once carefully explored in modern times. The sanctuary itself and the village around or near it may have been assigned, either in Hellenistic or in Roman times, to the city of Hierapolis (not to Dionysopolis), which lies at no great distance from it. The sanctuary may, perhaps, before this absorption by the city, have been connected with the village or town of Motella. In any case the change of status did not affect the business of the temple or the part taken by the priests in the life of the district.

It is unfortunate that we know practically nothing of sanctuaries of this type and their villages during the Hellenistic period. All the information we have relates to late Roman times. But the organization and life of the temples in Roman times were highly archaic and thoroughly Oriental, except for the hellenized names of the deities, the architecture of their temples, the aspect of their images, and the language of most of the dedications, consecrations, and confessions, written by the worshippers or by professional scribes for them, mostly in Greek. It is therefore safe to assume that the Seleucids did not interfere with the traditional religious system of these temples nor probably with their social and economic organization, and that they left them still playing a leading part in the life of their respective villages.[280]

It is impossible to draw a sharp dividing line between the village temples of various sizes and varying importance, and the large, rich, and influential sanctuaries, enjoying a wide reputation, attended by thousands of worshippers, provided with imposing buildings and a numerous clergy, temples that we may safely call temple-states, since their territory was large and their organization resembled that of a State. The difference between them was probably not so much in organization and structure as in size, wealth, and importance. The most celebrated temples of the second type were situated, not in the Seleucid Empire, but in Pontus, Cappadocia, Armenia, and Phrygia, and will be dealt with later in this book. How many similar temples in Asia Minor were constituent parts of the Seleucid Empire we cannot precisely say. The best known is that of Olba in Cilicia, the sanctuary of Zeus Olbius near Seleuceia on the Calycadnus, a city founded by Seleucus I. We probably have a similar temple-state in the early phase of Commagene, which later became a regular Hellenistic monarchy. Another temple of great importance was that of Zeus Chrysaoreus in Caria, which was for a time part of the Seleucid Empire (until it became first Rhodian, then Macedonian, and then again Rhodian). The Plutonium near Nysa in Caria was also a temple of considerable size and prominence. But it was closely connected with the city of Athymbria probably before Caria became temporarily part of the Seleucid Empire.

The relations between the Seleucids and these larger temples are very little known, and still poorer is our information about the smaller, mostly village, temples. I have already referred to the reverence displayed by the kings for such temples as that of Zeus Olbius and the Plutonium. They certainly made no important changes in the organization of the temple of Olba, for the ancient dynasty of the Teucrids was still ruling in the temple-state of Olba at the very end of the Seleucid period. We may therefore assume that the Seleucids did not interfere with the social and economic organization of the larger temple-states any more than with that of the village temples.* We may suppose that the elaborate hierarchy of the temple clergy was maintained. The high priests and their colleagues continued to be the lords and masters of all the inhabitants of the temple itself, the temple town, and the temple villages. All these were ἱερόδουλοι, 'slaves' of the god or goddess, and all were required to work for their divine master or mistress, as attendants of the temple (a term that included singers, musicians, and dancers), as temple prostitutes, as artisans and artists, as tillers of the soil or in charge of cattle and poultry. Excellent pictures of the conditions prevailing in a temple-state will be found in Strabo's descriptions of the temples of Pontus, Cappadocia, and Armenia, in the inscriptions of Nimrud Dagh in Commagene, and in Lucian's treatise on the *dea Syria*.[281]

Nevertheless, the Seleucids, like the Ptolemies in Egypt, regarded themselves as overlords and owners of the temples of Asia Minor. They would not have hesitated, had it seemed advisable, to impose taxes on the temples, to take away from them substantial portions of their land and bestow it on their favourites or distribute it among their soldiers, to grant or refuse recognition of their *asylia*, or to demand large sums of money from them in emergencies.[282] We hear of instances in which they tried to 'urbanize' the temples. By this I mean the compulsory subordination of a native temple to a Greek city, such as had been carried out in certain early Greek cities of Asia Minor. Our information is scanty and open to different interpretations, but the following are among the better attested cases. I have mentioned the possibility that the sanctuary of Apollo Laerbenus was joined to the city of Hierapolis as early as the time of the Seleucids, and not subsequently under the Pergamene kings or the Romans. Antioch in Pisidia may have received the land assigned to it at the expense of the temple of Men Ascaënus, which stood near the city.† Stratonicea

* The attitude of the Seleucids, it may be remarked, was in marked contrast to the arbitrary treatment of the same temple by the Romans.

† Str. xii. 3, 31, p. 557, and 8, 14, p. 577.

in Caria, founded by Seleucus I and named after his former wife, at that time the wife of Antiochus I, may have originally been a military κατοικία* and probably had assigned to it some villages belonging to the σύστημα Χρυσαορικόν, that is to say, the organized group or amphictyony of villages of which the centre was the temple of Zeus Chrysaoreus. The temple-state of Castabala in Cilicia may have been transformed into a semi-Greek city with the name Hierapolis.[283]

The question arises whether the facts adduced above point to the adoption by the Seleucids of a deliberate policy towards the temples, or should be regarded as isolated measures dictated by some emergency. The evidence is meagre, but so it is on all aspects of Seleucid history, and the facts, to my mind, are eloquent. Seleucus and his successors never offended the religious feelings of their subjects, but they would not, so long as they were strong and self-confident, tolerate any insubordination or any far-reaching autonomy. By their treatment of the temples, especially by their occasional disposal of the temple lands, they made it clear to them that they were regarded as parts of the State, administrative units like the villages and nothing more. If they enjoyed certain privileges, it was by the permission of the kings. This appears to have been the policy, at any rate, of the first Seleucids. In more difficult times, in periods of trouble under Seleucus II and Antiochus III, the situation changed. As in Egypt, the temples, and likewise the cities, were striving for greater independence. The result was the appearance of tyrannies or 'dynasties' in the cities, and of government of the same type in the temples, where the role of the dynasts was played by the high priests.

Large estates. So much of the royal land as was not in possession of the temples and was not sold or given to the cities or to private persons who incorporated it in the territory of some city, retained its primitive economic and social structure. Most of this land in Persian times consisted of large estates of local barons. When the Seleucid dominion was established, some of these estates were given to new Macedonian or Greek barons, others were managed by the financial officers of the king. In both cases the structure of the estates was probably

* Str. xiv. 2, 25, p. 660, cf. Steph. Byz. *s. v.*

retained. Most of them centred in fortified manor houses, which are called in the Laodice inscription* and in an inscription from Magnesia† *bāris* (an Anatolian word), like the castle of Tubias in the land of the Ammonites. Other names for them were *tyrsis* (perhaps a Hittite word), and in Greek *pyrgos, tetrapyrgion, aule, epaulion*, &c.[284] Around the manor were the villages (*mandrai*) of the native population. Their inhabitants and the cultivators of the land around them were no doubt *adscripti glebae* or *adscripti vicis* and were required to render to the owner of the estate a certain proportion of the harvest, or a fixed payment in money or kind, and also probably a certain amount of labour. More exact information as to the obligations of the villagers is lacking. The technical word used by the administration to designate the population of the villages was, as in Egypt and Ptolemaic Syria, *λαοί* or *λαοὶ βασιλικοί*. It is regrettable that we know so little of them. They were certainly not slaves: they possessed for example a certain freedom of movement and probably a kind of corporative organization. But they were without doubt bondsmen, that is to say, they were bound to their village and to the piece of land that they tilled. They and all their belongings went with the land and village if these were sold (above, pp. 493 ff.). How far their rights were protected by their royal master against the temporary holders of royal fiefs and against the royal administration, we do not know. A stray passage‡ may be interpreted as alluding to a judge who rendered justice to the *βασιλικοί* (sc. *λαοί*) of the Aeolid (*δικαστὴς βασιλικῶν τῶν περὶ τὴν Αἰολίδα*) in the name probably of the Pergamene king. However, if we read with Meineke *δικαστὴν βασιλικόν* instead of *δικαστὴν βασιλικῶν* or supply *πραγμάτων* after *δικαστήν* (as suggested by C. B. Welles), we may interpret the text as referring to one of the royal judges of the Aeolid who, like the royal judges of Dura mentioned above (p. 486), was acting as judge both for the Greeks and for the native population of the Aeolid, especially in cases which involved the interests of the king. In all probability the Parthians at Dura and the Pergamene kings took over this institution from the Seleucids.

* *O.G.I.* 225; Welles, *R.C.*, 36. † *Inschr. v. Magn.* 122 d. 4.

‡ Demetrius of Scepsis *ap.* Athen. xv. 697 D.

Here the same question arises as with regard to the temples: did the Seleucids follow a definite policy in their treatment of the royal territory and the subject-serfs who tilled the soil? The Seleucids never contemplated in respect of the latter—any more than in respect of the temples—any radical reform, such as a wholesale emancipation of the serfs and their transformation into small landowners. How far they improved their condition by legislation, by special orders, and by concessions (φιλάνθρωπα), we are unable to say. Unlike the λαοί of Egypt, the serfs of Asia Minor were passive and silent, and until the time of Aristonicus there were no outbursts of discontent. This may perhaps be interpreted as an indication that the Seleucids showed some consideration for them; but it may on the other hand be accounted for by the fact that circumstances were not the same in Asia Minor, where the λαοί lived in small, almost isolated, groups, as they were in Egypt.

One feature in the treatment of the royal land under the Seleucids requires discussion. I refer to the frequent cases in which such land, after sale or gift, had its status completely altered and became city land. When this occurred, the λαοί may also have changed their official designation, if not their status, and instead of λαοί may have become πάροικοι or κάτοικοι of the city. We know very little of this latter class: we cannot say, for instance, whether there was in Seleucid times any sharp dividing line between them and the λαοί; whether the πάροικοι and κάτοικοι had, as inhabitants of villages, more personal freedom than the λαοί; whether their economic obligations were less heavy; whether they had their own corporative organization; and whether they were subject to the laws of the city to which they were assigned and treated in the same way as the μέτοικοι, πάροικοι, and κάτοικοι who resided in the city. The later destinies of the λαοί will be dealt with in the following chapters.[285]

The social and economic structure of Seleucid Syria, Mesopotamia, and Parapotamia, before the urbanization of these regions by Alexander, Antigonus, Seleucus, and their successors, is less known than that of Asia Minor. But what is known of these regions shows that in many respects they resembled Asia Minor. It must be remembered that in the period with which we are concerned Phoenicia, with its peculiar conditions, and Palestine, including the coast cities and Transjordan, did not form part of the Seleucid Empire (above, pp. 340 ff).

Like the interior of Asia Minor, Seleucid Syria, Mesopotamia, and Parapotamia were a region of temple-states and villages. The few cities that became rich and populous as centres of agriculture, caravan trade, and industry—Damascus, Hamath, Halab, Hemesa, Edessa, Nisibis, and others—are very little known. They had a long history behind them and in the course of this their political status had repeatedly changed. But in none of the phases of their evolution was a sharp dividing line drawn in their organization between State and god, between royal palace and temple. The ruins of the cities clearly show that the principal temple was the dominating feature in their external aspect. In some of them the temple permanently retained the leading role. Hemesa, for example, remained a temple-state and a temple-city in spite of all the vicissitudes undergone by it down to the late Roman Empire. It never received a Greek or Macedonian name. These temple-states, as in Asia Minor, were of different size and of different degrees of fame. The temple of Atargatis at Bambyce recalls the great temple-states of Asia Minor, while the temples and villages of Baetocaece or of Doliche are very similar to the temple villages, of which I have already spoken, in the same region.[286]

The ruins of the Hellenistic and Roman periods that have been excavated in Syria and Mesopotamia are unfortunately few. It is only through systematic excavations that we can hope to acquire information regarding the status of the temple-cities, temple villages, and villages of Syria and Mesopotamia in the pre-Hellenistic, Hellenistic, and Roman periods. As regards the period with which we are dealing, the chief questions that arise relate, firstly, to the attitude of the early Seleucids towards the temples, the temple-cities, the temple villages, and the villages; and, secondly, to the relations between the new Greek cities and the older native cities and villages.

With respect to the temples and the temple-cities, some stray facts may serve as illustrations of the Seleucid policy. I have mentioned above that at Baetocaece one of the early Seleucids transformed the holy village of the god into the fief of one of his officers, and one of the later Seleucids restored it to the god. In all other respects the Seleucids did not interfere with the internal life of the temple and left it in undisturbed possession of its revenues. We hear that the income of the temple was spent as usual by the high priest (who was appointed by the god) for monthly sacrifices and other purposes which would increase the fame of the sanctuary.[287]

As regards the large and ancient temple-cities of Syria, we know that some of them were rebuilt on Greek lines and received Greek names from the Ptolemics and the Seleucids. Thus the venerable temple-state of Bambyce was named Hierapolis, probably in the time of Seleucus I;* Halab received, probably at the same time, the name of Beroea; Damascus, as its plan shows, was rebuilt on Hellenistic lines, perhaps under the Ptolemies, and may have received a Greek name; Hamath probably received its Greek name Epiphaneia at a later date, under Antiochus IV. Does this imply in all cases that a body of Greeks and Macedonians was added to the old population of the temple-city, that the city and the temple were not only rebuilt but also reorganized on Greek patterns, and that the temple villages became dependent on the city instead of the temple? I mention these possibilities to show how little we know and how greatly further knowledge is to be desired.

Similarly with regard to the villages assigned to the cities, that is to say, included in the city 'territory' (as we have seen was done at Europus), we may ask what was the status of the tillers of the soil in the villages before Alexander's conquest; whether they were serfs or bondsmen bound to the villages as in Asia Minor; what their status was after the village had become part of the territory of some city, and what, under the Seleucids, was the status of such villages as were not assigned to the territory of a city and were not parts of temple-states.

We know that in Ptolemaic Syria (above, pp. 340 ff.), as in Egypt and in Asia Minor, the native peasants were called *λαϊκὰ σώματα* or *λαοί*. But the name alone does not illuminate

* Ael. *De nat. an.* xii. 2.

their status. We have seen that there is no indication that in Phoenicia the λαοί were serfs or bondsmen, but neither is there any evidence to show that they were not.

We have copious information about the villages of Syria and Mesopotamia in Roman times. Some of them were included in city-territories, others were not. In none do we find traces of serfdom; the villagers were free men, subjects of the Roman emperors. Nor are there many examples of a theocratic organization. The administration of most of the villages was not theocratic at all, but a sort of combination of tribal organization with that of a Greek city-state. Most of our information, no doubt, relates to the Hauran, which was transformed by the Roman imperial government from a country of shepherds and semi-nomadic tribes into a country of cities and villages. But the little we know of the villages in northern Syria, in the former Seleucid Syria, and in Mesopotamia in the Roman period, shows that they were organized on much the same lines as those of the Hauran. It is a natural suggestion that it was the organization of the former villages that served as a pattern for the organization of the latter.[288]

It is accordingly probable that alongside of the cities of Oriental type, and of the temple-states of various sizes, there were in Syria and Mesopotamia, as in Palestine, thousands of villages with a population of free peasants, each village having a semi-tribal organization. Whether the Seleucids inherited this organization and retained it unchanged we do not know.

Nor is there any evidence for the existence in these parts of the Seleucid kingdom of large royal estates with villages inhabited by royal serfs or bondsmen.

The situation in Babylonia was different from that in Asia Minor and Syria. Babylonia had glorious traditions, a long history, a peculiar and refined civilization, an elaborate religion and cult, a well-established social and economic structure, and an elaborate law. Well aware of this, the Seleucids treated the country with great consideration. I have already referred to their attitude towards the Babylonian temples. It is well known that they showed no less respect for the intellectual life that was closely connected with the temples. Berosus in

Babylonia is a counterpart of Manetho in Egypt, and Babylonists have much to say about the renaissance of Babylonian learning in the Seleucid period.[289]

Many clay tablets with business documents written on them, some clay envelopes for documents on parchment and papyrus with seals impressed on them, several clay seals appended to documents, and a few inscribed bricks—material which has been mentioned and in part used above (p. 424 f. and n. 220)—give us a fair picture of the religious, political, social, and economic life of Babylonia, particularly of Uruk (Ὄρχοι), that venerable centre of Babylonian learning into which the early Seleucids infused new life.

The cuneiform tablets relate mostly to the temples and priests of Babylon and Uruk. Except for some literary texts of high interest, they are business documents concerned with the transfer of property by sale, gift, exchange, division of various pieces of property in land, houses, slaves, 'beneficia' (γέρα in the Ptolemaic terminology); and they record the names and seals of the parties and of the witnesses. They were all written by professional scribes, themselves priests. The 'law' applied in them was the traditional 'cuneiform law', a term used by modern Babylonists to designate the ancient Babylonian law, which was somewhat transformed in the neo-Babylonian and Persian period.[290]

The clay envelopes and seals were used for documents on parchment and papyrus which apparently were deposited in the temple archives for safe custody. The parties which transacted the various kinds of business and the witnesses are represented by their seals only. We do not know their names. Nor do we know exactly the character of the enclosed documents and the legal forms that were in use. But the employment of parchment and papyrus as material, the probable use of Greek and Aramaic, each of them a lingua franca in Syria and Babylonia, familiar to most of the more or less denationalized inhabitants of these regions, and also the style of the impressions and the character of the impressed figures, partly Greek, partly Babylonian, suggest that the parties to the documents and their witnesses belonged to the mixed population of the Babylonian cities in which the Greek element was strongly represented. The same impression is conveyed by the names and seals of the witnesses on the cuneiform tablets.[291] I have mentioned above that the envelopes and the seals bear impressions which attest the payment by the parties of certain royal taxes and which enable us to conjecture the character of some of the business transactions (see pp. 469 ff.).

Finally, the inscriptions on the bricks from Uruk bear witness to the date of the reconstruction of its temples and give the names and titles of those who were responsible for the reconstruction.

A combination of the data supplied by the material described above permits us to form a fair idea of Hellenistic **Uruk**. The inscriptions on the bricks of the temples throw light upon the constitution of the city in early Hellenistic times. They inform us that the temples were built by two members of probably one rich and influential family of Uruk, who held high offices in the administration of the city in the reigns of Antiochus II or Seleucus II and Antiochus III. In 243 B.C. (under Seleucus II) Anu-uballit, 'to whom Antiochus, king of countries [Antiochus Theos], gave as his second name Nikigurgusa [Nicarchus]', was the 'shanu' ('second officer', as translated by A. T. Clay) of Uruk. Later, in 201 B.C. under Antiochus III, a man of the same name, who belonged perhaps to the same family, Anu-uballit 'whose other name is Kephallon', is styled 'the great, the city lord of Uruk' in the inscriptions on the bricks which he used in rebuilding the temple of Anu and Antum. The titles that appear on the bricks are not necessarily translations of Greek titles, as modern scholars are inclined to believe, the second being equivalent to the Greek *epistates* or *strategos*. It is certain, however, that the two officers, if not appointed by the kings (as is probable), at least acted in the capacity of governors of the city with the approval of its overlords. It appears therefore that Uruk in the early Seleucid times was not a Greek *polis*, that is to say, that a Greek or semi-Greek constitution was not imposed on it as the result of the settlement of Greek or hellenized immigrants in the city. Uruk probably retained under the Seleucids its ancestral constitution as it retained its ancestral name.[292]

It is interesting to see how loyal the chief magistrates of

Uruk were to the monarchs of their time and how honoured they felt by their confidence. The earlier of them mentions with pride that the king gave him the privilege of adding a Greek name to his Babylonian one. This probably meant that the favour altered the social, if not the political, status of the recipient. He was now one of the 'Hellenes', whatever the political significance of this term may have been. Subsequently, in the reign of Antiochus III, the second Anu-uballit does not mention any special permission from the king to use an additional name, whether because such permission was no longer required or because the privilege was hereditary.[293]

If Uruk in the early Seleucid period was not a Greek *polis* and if even later in the time of Antiochus III it had not received this privilege, the little we know of the city acquires a double interest, as affording for the first time some glimpses of the life of a native city in the Hellenistic period. The city, as we have seen, was ruled by native magistrates. The temples, as the cuneiform tablets show, maintained their traditional organization and activities, and transacted business according to Babylonian law. No further description is needed: it would merely repeat the familiar picture of life in other Babylonian cities of earlier and later times.

Foreigners, however, more or less numerous, resided in the city and took an active part in its affairs and in those of the temple. The urban population was apparently of a mixed character. It is striking to find, for example, a Greek named Nicanor, son of Democrates, consecrating a slave-girl to Anu and Antum as an offering for the life of the king, his own life, and that of the people and of his family.[294]

With the Greek domination came Greek taxation and Greek financial officials. Royal taxes were paid through them to the *basilikon*, probably by all the inhabitants of the city, Greeks and natives.[295] The temple and the priests may have enjoyed some privileges in this respect. At the same time Greek currency appeared on the market and royal laws regulated certain aspects of business activity.[296]

Towards the native cities in Babylonia the Seleucids were therefore very liberal. They left conditions as they were and certainly showed no hellenizing tendencies. The process of hellenization, that is to say, of penetration of Greeks, took its natural course in the Babylonian city of Uruk.

Yet, liberal as they were in their respect for Babylonian tradition, the Seleucids regarded themselves as successors of the former rulers of Babylonia, as masters and owners of the country. They probably appointed the governors of the cities, both Greek and native; they kept a watchful eye on the economic activities of the temples;[297] they collected from the population the traditional taxes and in addition to them the royal taxes, which may have been, at least partly, new, and for this purpose they employed their own officials. They regarded themselves as owners of the land in Babylonia and, as such, they felt at liberty to assign Babylonian land (even land belonging to temples and cities) to their *poleis*, and to bestow portions of it on members of the royal house and probably on their officials, both higher and lower (above, p. 494).

Regarding the policy of the Seleucids in their Iranian satrapies we have almost no evidence. I have spoken of the cities founded there by Alexander, Seleucus, and Antiochus I, but there are no documents to show the character of these settlements. Nor are we informed about the mode of life of the Iranian nobility and gentry or of the peasants and serfs. In all probability it was the same as we find it to have been subsequently in the Parthian kingdom and under the early Sasanids. The Avroman documents are not typical: they belong to the time of the Parthian domination and probably reflect the life of Iranian hellenized cleruchs of the Seleucid period. More illuminating are some scattered facts relating to the history of such cities as Persepolis and such semi-independent countries as Persis. Much interest attaches to what Herzfeld (*Arch. Hist. of Iran*, 1935, pp. 45 ff.) has to say on the *Fratedara*, the guardians of the sacred fire at Persepolis (cf. above, p. 428).

The many Arab tribes of the Syrian and Mesopotamian deserts, with their tribal sheikhs (φύλαρχοι), were not subjects but only vassals of the early Seleucids. I shall return to them in the following chapters. For the early Seleucid period the evidence relating to them is very slight.[298]

Such are the dim outlines of the conditions that prevailed in the various satrapies of the Seleucid Empire. The principal achievements of Seleucid policy were these: the establishment of a uniform administration, the introduction of a systematic and, so far as possible, uniform taxation, the formation of a well-organized royal army and navy, the construction and maintenance of a network of good roads between the various satrapies, the adoption of measures designed to provide a single abundant and trustworthy currency, a certain control of weights and measures, and, finally, the introduction of a uniform dating (the Seleucid era) and calendar, which were not only valid within the empire but were adopted by many of its neighbours and are still in use in some parts of the Near East. The main object of these measures was to weld the various parts of the empire into one solid body.

(*c*) *The Greeks and the natives; hellenization and orientalization*

An adjunct to this policy of unification, or rather a part of it, was the scheme of building cities and attracting Greek and Macedonian settlers to their dominions. I have already stated my opinion about the general aims of this 'hellenizing' policy of the Seleucids. The result of it and of their attitude towards the native inhabitants was a conspicuous change in the social and economic aspect of their empire.

The most important change was due to the superimposing of a Greco-Macedonian stratum on the natives, a stratum closely connected with the king and certainly enjoying major as well as minor privileges and a higher social position than the old inhabitants. At the head of this class stood the new aristocracy of the kingdom. First of all, the members of the royal 'house' (οἶκος): the king's family and his court, every member of which had in turn his own 'house'. These hundreds of houses included not only families, friends, and clients but also a mass of slaves. Next to them, and, indeed, partly identical with them, came the higher officials. All these men and women were very rich, some of them acquired immense fortunes. Of the wealth of members of the royal family we have an example in the estate of Laodice in the Troad and in the land granted to her and her sons in Babylonia, a gift that she did not care to keep. There were certainly also in early Seleucid times wealthy men who did not belong to the royal family, such as

Aristodicides, Meleager, and Athenaeus, in the time of Antiochus I, their contemporary Larichus of Priene (above, p. 151), the Mnesimachus of the Sardian inscription, the Demetrius of the inscription of Baetocaece. At a later date Hermeias the Carian, the grand vizir of Antiochus III, was rich enough to pay the troops when the king himself, at the time of Molon's insurrection, lacked the means to do so. Dionysius, the *epistolographus* of Antiochus IV, could send a thousand slaves to take part in a procession at Daphne, each with a silver dish in his hand worth a thousand drachmas or more. Besides these high functionaries we may safely include among the new aristocracy the merchants of the great commercial cities, some at least of whom were of Greek and Macedonian origin.

Next to the grandees of the empire stood the permanent army stationed in the capitals of the kingdom, especially at Antioch on the Orontes, Apamea, and the military camp near Seleuceia on the Tigris (later Ctesiphon), and in many military strongholds. Strong garrisons were also placed in some of the more important ancient Greek cities of Asia Minor. The officers and soldiers of the permanent army received regular pay, lived comfortably in barracks or in private houses in cities (σταθμοί), and certainly used their privileged status to improve the conditions of their life at the expense of the cities in which they were stationed.

Much more numerous were the new Macedonian and Greek gentry scattered all over the empire, partly in the recently created Greek and Macedonian cities and villages, partly in the ancient Anatolian, Semitic, and Iranian towns and villages. Among these an important group was composed of royal civil servants, members of the new Seleucid bureaucracy, the majority of them employed as assessors and collectors of taxes. The tax contractors, though they were private business men, occupied, no doubt, a semi-official position. More numerous were the Seleucid colonists, those Macedonians and Greeks, with some Orientals, who were settled in the Seleucid colonies. Most of them received from the king plots of land taken from the natives. These settlers became, therefore, at least from the economic point of view, a privileged body, a class of well-to-do landowners. Lastly, many Oriental and

Greek cities came to have among their residents independent settlers who had emigrated from continental Greece, the islands, Asia Minor, and various parts of the Seleucid Empire—philosophers, scholars, teachers, doctors, lawyers, artists, artisans, merchants, who looked for profitable business in the new world. These immigrants enjoyed no special legal privileges, but they were kinsmen of the privileged Greeks and Macedonians and certainly profited by that fact.

The Greek aristocracy and *bourgeoisie* were new elements added to the corresponding classes of the old population, natives of various degrees of wealth, of whom there were probably many in Babylonia, in the caravan cities of Syria, and in Asia Minor. The Seleucids unquestionably maintained cordial relations with the upper class of the Orientals, their policy in this respect resembling that of the Ptolemies in Syria and Palestine. In this connexion I may recall what I have said above (p. 341) regarding the attitude adopted by Soter and Philadelphus towards their friends and supporters in Phoenicia (especially Sidon) and in Palestine and Transjordan.

Some of these well-to-do natives, members of the upper class of the past, enjoyed the confidence of the rulers of the day and as agents of the government played an important role in the life of their own cities. I may remind the reader of the two men named Anu-uballit—Nicarchus and Kephallon—of Uruk. What degree of cordiality existed between the upper classes of the natives and the foreigners is not known. In later times, for example at Europus (Dura), intermarriages between well-to-do families of Greeks and natives were common. In Phoenicia and in Palestine the upper class in the cities was to a great extent hellenized, as is shown by the instance of Philocles, the king of the Sidonians, and of some Sidonians mentioned in an inscription of Sidon and in the correspondence of Zenon; also later by the tombs of Marissa on the one hand and by the evidence relating to Ptolemaic and Seleucid Palestine on the other.

By spreading over their dominions a network of Greek settlements, whose inhabitants belonged to the same nationality and spoke the same language as themselves, the Seleucids inevitably made Greek the official language of the empire, following in

PLATE LVIII

The hunting scene represented in this plate forms part of the painted decoration of a Hellenistic *hypogaeum* near the city of Marissa, one of the Ptolemaic strongholds in their eparchy or satrapy of Idumaea. An ancient settlement of the Idumaeans, Marissa was refounded and rebuilt (like Beth-Zur) by the Ptolemies. A group of hellenized Sidonians was settled there. This group was organized apparently as a *πολίτευμα* rather than a *πόλις*, with its own, perhaps hereditary (cf. Dura and Uruk), president (*ἄρχων*, cf. this chapter, n. 137). The Sidonians may have been, at least in part, settled soldiers. The city, as shown by several letters of the Zenon correspondence (*P. Cairo Zen.* 59006, 59015 verso, 59537), was in the middle of the third century B.C. an important administrative and business centre. From J. P. Peters and H. Thiersch, *Painted Tombs of the Necropolis of Marissa*, 1905, pl. VI.

The *hypogaeum* is one of the earliest of the vast necropolis of Marissa. It was probably built by Sesmaios, a Phoenician, for himself and his family in the third century B.C. His son Apollophanes (note his Greek name) who was for thirty-three years 'archon of the Sidonians of Marissa' (*O.G.I.* 593) and several members of his family were buried there. Later, as shown by some funeral inscriptions, the *hypogaeum* served as the burial-place for several families of the same ethnical character. The Sidonian colony apparently survived the Ptolemaic domination.

The painted decoration of the central room of the tomb was carried out soon after its construction. It cannot be described here. The scene reproduced forms part of a painted frieze which runs above the loculi on both sides of the central room. The figures of the frieze represent various animals, mostly African, partly real and partly fantastic. Each animal has its name painted above it. The choice of the animals recalls the mosaic of Palestrina (above, pl. XXXVIII) and harks back to Alexandria. The hunting scene painted in the south-western corner of the room serves as a kind of introduction to this zoological catalogue. It shows to the right the figure of a trumpeter, and in the centre the hunter riding a magnificent and spirited white horse, covered with a gorgeous saddle-cloth of Greek style (see pl. XLVI and fig. 2, p. 377). The horseman is represented killing with his long Macedonian lance a leopardess already wounded by a dart (inscription *πάρδαλος*). Two dogs are helping him. For the dress of the horseman see above, pls. XIX, XXXVII, 1, and XLIX, 1. The style of the painting is decidedly Alexandrian (see pl. XLIV, 1). Unfortunately the heads of the two men in the painting have been destroyed by Arabs.

Over the two human figures are remains of painted inscriptions. That over the trumpeter is almost completely lost, that on both sides of the head of the hunter presents a difficult problem. One would expect to find here the name of the horseman, probably the heroized builder of the *hypogaeum*. But the editors give the transcription: *ἵππος Λιβάνου | τοῦ ἱππικοῦ*, which according to them means 'horse from Mt. Libanus of the man on horseback' (I regard this translation as highly improbable). The inscription was probably badly preserved when discovered. The poor remnants of it that still survive (photograph reproduced by Watzinger) show unmistakably *'Ανανου*, not *Λιβανου*. The last word is probably *ἱππ[άρ]χου*, not *ἱππικοῦ*.

On Marissa in Hellenistic times and its *hypogaea* see J. P. Peters and H. Thiersch, *Painted Tombs of the Necropolis of Marissa*, 1905; cf. on Ptolemaic Marissa E. Schürer, *Gesch. d. jüd. Volkes* &c., ii, p. 4, n. 8; V. Tscherikower, 'Palestine under the Ptolemies', *Mizraim*, iv–v (1937), pp. 40 ff., and above, pp. 346 ff. On the plan of the city, C. Watzinger, *Denkmäler Palästinas*, ii, 1935, pp. 12 ff. and fig. 22. On the paintings and the inscriptions J. P. Peters and H. Thiersch, loc. cit.; J. P. Peters, *Art and Archaeology*, vii (1918), p. 187; and C. Watzinger, loc. cit., pp. 18 ff. and pls. 24 and 25. (From photographs of the Pal. Expl. Fund.)

One of the foreign settlers in Ptolemaic Idumaea

Marissa in Idumaea.

1. Munich, Museum antiker Kleinkunst.

2. Chicago, Oriental Institute, Museum.

3. Chicago, Oriental Institute, Museum.

5. London, British Museum.

4. Paris, Louvre.

6. London, British Museum

DAILY LIFE IN HELLENISTIC MESOPOTAMIA AND SYRIA

PLATE LIX

1. Clay seal found probably at Uruk (Orchoi). It was originally appended or affixed to a document on parchment or papyrus. Its official character is demonstrated, as is that of other similar seals, by the portraits of the rulers which it displays. We see on it the jugate heads of Demetrius I and Laodice reproduced no less finely than on the coins (*B.M.C.*, Syria, pl. xv, 1–2). No seal of Demetrius and Laodice has been previously found in Babylonia. I am indebted to Prof. H. Diepolder, Director of the Museum, for knowledge of this seal, a photograph, and permission to publish it. Diam. 0·02. On similar seals see my 'Seleucid Babylonia', *Yale Class. Stud.*, iii (1932), pp. 16 ff. and 44 ff., cf. R. H. McDowell, *Stamped and Inscribed Objects from Seleucia on the Tigris*, 1935, pp. 1 ff. Photograph supplied by the authorities of the Museum antiker Kleinkunst, Munich.

2, 3. Impressions of seals (enlarged) showing portraits of private men, from Orchoi. Second century B.C. One is clean-shaven, the other wears a short beard of the Greek type. My 'Seleucid Babylonia', p. 20, pl. II, 1 and 2, cf. 3 and 4. Photographs supplied by the Oriental Institute, Museum, Chicago.

4. Terracotta statuette of Roman times, found probably in northern Syria, representing two girl musicians on camel-back, seated under a sort of canopy fastened to the richly draped saddle, one playing the drum, the other the double flute. The scene reproduced in the figurine was probably one familiar to the Syrians. The girls are apparently taking part in a religious procession organized by one of the numerous temples of Syria or Mesopotamia. A procession of this kind is, for example, represented in one of the famous painted bas-reliefs of the great temple of Palmyra (H. Seyrig, *Syria*, xv (1934), pp. 159 ff.). Girl musicians were typical figures in the temples of the Oriental gods and goddesses and formed a numerous class of the population of Syria and Mesopotamia. They are frequently represented in terracotta figurines. This group is known in two identical copies, one in the Louvre (here represented), another in the Brit. Mus. (*A Guide to the Exhib. ill. Gr. and Rom. Life*, 3rd ed., 1929, no. 689). Cf. my remarks on the group reproduced here, and on the similar terracottas, in *Dura and the Problem of Parthian Art*, p. 183, figs. 16–23.

5. Terracotta figurine probably from Asia Minor of a half-naked man, perhaps a slave or a peasant, carrying a heavy load. In his right hand he is holding a bottle or dish wrapped in a piece of cloth (rather than a wine-skin—the object is too small to be that); with his left hand he supports a large *diota* or wine amphora on his left shoulder; to his back is fastened a basket, cf. pl. XXXIII, 1. Unpublished(?), mentioned in *Brit. Mus., A Guide to the Exhib. ill. Gr. and Rom. Life*, 3rd ed., 1929, no. 533. Photograph supplied by the authorities of the British Museum, London.

6. Bronze statuette of a donkey with panniers, braying, with head raised and legs firmly planted. An epergne of the same sort is described by Petronius, *Cen.* 31: 'ceterum in promulsidari asellus erat Corinthius cum bisaccio positus, qui habebat olivas in altera parte albas, in altera nigras'. See my *Soc. and Ec. Hist. R. E.*, pl. XXXVII, 2 (with bibliography), and cf. the terracottas reproduced in the same plate (camels loaded with farm produce). Photograph supplied by the authorities of the British Museum, London.

this respect the traditions of Alexander. It became accordingly the language of administration and taxation throughout the empire and also the language of the army and the navy. Since the Greco-Macedonians were mostly well-to-do and certainly took an active part in the business life of the country, Greek naturally began to compete with Aramaic as the language of commerce and tended to become the lingua franca of the empire. It derived an advantage from the fact that trade with the West and North was conducted on the basis of Greek. And finally, business transactions in which one party was Greek and the other native were naturally in most cases regulated by Greek law and recorded in Greek legal documents, and litigation regarding such transactions took place as a rule before Greek royal judges. In this way natives became familiar with Greek law and Greek legal formulas and documents, and certainly adopted them occasionally even in their transactions with their own countrymen.

Thus without pressure and compulsion, and not as the result of a policy of hellenization, a good deal of hellenization was achieved, affecting principally the cities and the upper and middle classes in these. Slaves employed by the Greeks and probably many members of the free working class in the cities also became easily hellenized. But I doubt very much whether Greek made any progress in the temples and the villages. Even in the cities the native *bourgeoisie* did not use Greek exclusively. As late as the first centuries B.C. and A.D. such a city as Palmyra used both Greek and Aramaic (Palmyrene), and at Europus Palmyrene inscriptions of the same period are not uncommon.[299]

Hellenization made conspicuous progress in early Seleucid times, but hand in hand with it went a process of orientalization. The pervasive power of local religions and cults, the splendour and pathos of the ceremonies in the temples, the mystery of foreign cults, the *interpretatio Graeca* of the Oriental dogmas, the charm of Oriental women, all made a strong appeal to the feelings of the Greek population of Syria and Asia Minor. The Greek settlers gradually became worshippers of local gods, whom they called by Greek names. In the first century A.D. there were in Europus (Dura) many temples of local gods who bore Greek names, but not a single purely Greek temple has been discovered during twelve years of systematic excavations. Indeed, two temples of Greek gods were transformed, at about this time, into Oriental temples. One of these, it may be added, was first built (in the Hellenistic period) not on a Greek but on a Greco-Oriental plan, though it was probably dedicated to the great Greek, but orientalized, god Zeus Olympius. The process of orientalization must have started very early in Seleucid Syria and Mesopotamia.

A very strong factor in the orientalization of the Greeks was intermarriage. Our information on this subject is very limited. Double names—Greek and Babylonian—at Uruk do not help us. No direct evidence is available at Europus (Dura). In the earliest document on parchment found there (190 B.C.) the parties concerned and royal officials are Greeks and Macedonians. Then comes a long gap in the evidence until the first century A.D., when the upper class of the inhabitants of Europus appears to be of mixed origin. The women mostly have Semitic names and some of them were probably of Semitic origin. The men mostly keep their ancestral Macedonian and Greek names, but are represented in Oriental dress and as worshipping Oriental gods. At Seleuceia the few names of women that occur are all Greek with but one exception.[300]

To what extent hellenization affected the general trend of economic life in Syria, Mesopotamia, and Asia Minor we are unable to say. I have already discussed the progress made in the use of money as a medium of exchange. I shall say a few words later in this section about industry. But the most important subject—agriculture—remains obscure. We should like to know whether the large estates of the Greeks in Asia Minor and Syria resembled the *dorea* of Apollonius, and whether the owners endeavoured to hellenize the management of them. The inscription of Mnesimachus cited and considered above rather suggests that the estates were cultivated on old-fashioned lines by peasants who tilled the soil, tended the cattle, and looked after the gardens and vineyards from generation to generation in the same way. The change of ownership meant no more to them than a change of overlords, of masters to whom they had to pay rent and for whom they were compelled to work. The inscriptions of Laodice and Aristodicides give the same impression. No one who compares these documents with Zenon's correspondence can fail to be struck by the difference between them.

Other questions arise: whether the above conditions prevailed on the lands of the thousands of cleruchs throughout the Seleucid Empire; whether these Macedonians and Greeks were absentee landlords for whom their estates were tilled by slaves, serfs, and local tenants in the traditional manner; or whether they personally attended to their *cleroi*, if not themselves doing agricultural work, at least actively supervising it and using their own methods of cultivation and management. The answers to these questions may be furnished by further discoveries in Mesopotamia and Babylonia.

5. The Greek City-States other than those founded by the Kings

A considerable part of Seleucid Asia Minor consisted of the Greek city-states with their respective territories, varying in size according to the importance and the history of each. Some of them were newly founded by Alexander, Antigonus, Seleucus, and his descendants, and these I have already discussed. But the more important had a long history behind them when they were incorporated by the Seleucids in their empire. I have referred to the difficulty experienced by Alexander and his successors in settling their relations with these ancient Greek cities, and I have set out the little we know of their policy in this respect. A few words may be said here on the policy of the Seleucids towards them. The question is of great importance for the study of the economic and social life of their empire.

The possession of the ancient Greek cities of Asia Minor, and especially of those on the sea-coast, was of great value to the Seleucids. (1) First and foremost, it enhanced their political international prestige. (2) Secondly, it was all-important from the strategical point of view. (3) Moreover, it served to connect the Seleucid Empire with the Greek world, and prevented a political and cultural isolation which would soon have given it an Oriental character. (4) It put at the disposal of the Seleucids an immense reservoir of men: well-trained specialists of all sorts, good colonists for their new Greek cities in the East, and potential mercenary soldiers. (5) It made trade relations between the Greek world and the Seleucid Empire much easier and much more profitable, for cities like Miletus, Ephesus, and Smyrna were old and well-equipped centres of international commerce, being outlets of the great land routes of Anatolia. (6) Lastly, as the cities of Asia Minor were very rich, it meant a steady revenue for the Seleucids from the regular payments made by them, besides opening up the possibility of drawing on their accumulated capital in cases of emergency.

It was natural that Seleucid policy in regard to these Anatolian cities should be, on the whole, a continuation of that of Alexander and the Successors. The situation was no less difficult for them than it had been for their predecessors. They could not exist without them and they could not live with them.

All the old Greek cities of Asia Minor still regarded themselves, as in the days of Alexander and of the Successors, potentially and theoretically as free (ἐλεύθεραι), that is, as independent states with their own constitution, government, and laws (αὐτόνομοι). They were forced to submit to the overlordship of the kings, but they claimed to be, not their subjects, but independent bodies politic. The Romans, when they interfered in the affairs of Asia Minor, made a sharp distinction, in their diplomatic discussions with Antiochus III and in the reorganization of Asia Minor that followed their victory, between the free and the subject cities of that region.* The Seleucids, however, strictly followed in this respect the traditions of Alexander and of the Successors and never recognized the claims of these ancient cities as valid. They considered them all as their subjects, regardless of the views held by the cities themselves, for they had acquired dominion over them by their victories, 'by their spear'. Antiochus III insisted

* Liv. xxxiv. 57. 10, and Diod. xxviii. 15. 2 on the one hand, and Liv. xxxvii. 56, cf. Polyb. xxi, 24, Liv. xxxvii, 55, Diod. xxix, 11, and App. *Syr.* 39 on the other.

repeatedly on this point, and in this he followed the policy of his predecessors.

The Seleucids sometimes called all the Greek cities of the empire their allies (σύμμαχοι), but they attached their own meaning to 'alliance', viz: that the cities were bound to help them by all means at their disposal. This the cities were supposed to do as a consequence of their good will (εὔνοια) and friendship (φιλία) towards their suzerains and benefactors (εὐεργέται).* Here the Seleucids showed a certain inconsistency, which is reflected in their official terminology. Thus Antiochus I in one of his letters to Meleager† apparently draws a distinction between the cities which belonged to the χώρα, i.e. the territory of the subjects, and those which were in the 'allied' territory or *symmachia*. But in another letter to the same Meleager he speaks of all the cities as being in the *symmachia*.‡ This shows that for Antiochus I the term *symmachoi* was more or less equivalent to the term *socii* used later by the Romans, and did not imply the possession of any special rights by some of the 'allied' cities.

There were certain cities in the Seleucid Empire which possessed 'freedom' (ἐλευθερία). The documentary evidence shows that this freedom (where the term has a more or less precise political meaning and is not used for the purpose of propaganda) was a privilege granted by the kings to particular cities, which each king was at liberty to confirm or to withdraw: we occasionally hear of cities asking for and receiving 'freedom', for example the Ionian κοινόν in the reign of Antiochus I,§ Miletus in that of Antiochus II,|| and Smyrna in that of Seleucus II.¶ What the freedom thus granted really meant we do not precisely know. It certainly did not imply general political independence, nor any right of independent action in international relations, except in some rare cases when the Seleucids were forced to refrain from insisting on their right of suzerainty (as in the case of Smyrna in the reign of Seleucus II). The Seleucids, as has been said, regarded all the

* See, e.g., *O.G.I.* 229, l. 8 ff.

† *O.G.I.* 221, l. 45; Welles, *R.C.* 11, l. 21.

‡ *O.G.I.* 221, ll. 58 and 72; Welles, *R.C.* 12, ll. 8 and 22 f.

§ *O.G.I.* 222, l. 17. || Ibid. 226, l. 5. ¶ Ibid. 228, l. 7.

cities in the empire as being under their dominion (ὑποτασσόμεναι),* and I hardly think that the free cities were any exception in this respect. The king, for example, would not hesitate to place garrisons in the free cities if occasion arose, or to appoint an *epistates* as his own governor of a free city.† 'Freedom' therefore probably meant no more than the recognized autonomy of a city: the term 'autonomy' is often used as synonymous with 'freedom'. It implied the right of self-government and the right of acting as a body politic, as a 'State' in the 'international' relations of the cities, provided that the action was of no importance. It may have signified as a rule (exceptions have been mentioned above) that there was no *epistates* or garrison in the city.

Seleucus and his successors never took from the cities their right of self-government, that is to say, the right of retaining their own constitution and their own laws. They probably even conferred on the cities that they founded constitutions similar to those which prevailed in Asia Minor. But whether a city was free or autonomous or not, the fundamental rule of Seleucid administration, that an order of the king overrode any decision of the people, retained its full force. The frequent exercise of this overriding authority by the king is attested by an interesting observation of Polybius.‡ Speaking of the situation in Asia Minor after the expedition of Manlius Vulso against the Galatians and their pacification, he remarks that the cities of Asia Minor appreciated the benefactions of the Romans even more than the fact that they had been previously freed by them, some from taxes, some from garrisons, and all from the royal orders (βασιλικὰ προστάγματα) of Antiochus III. It is unnecessary to quote all the documents that illustrate the role played by royal orders in the affairs of Greek cities. The inscription at Bargylia, for instance, mentioned above, is typical.§ The grant of autonomy therefore must probably be regarded as a promise by the king not to make any change

* Polyb. xxi. 43; *O.G.I.* 231, I. 25, cf. Welles, *R.C.* 21, l. 15 f. (Ptolemy II).

† e.g. at Priene, *Inschr. v. Pr.*, no. 37, l. 135, and at Bargylia, *S.I.G.*[3] 426, l. 46.

‡ xxi. 41. 2.

§ *S.I.G.*[3] 426, cf. *Inschr. v. Pr.*, no. 24.

in the existing constitution of the city and not to interfere with it in minor matters.

Finally, all the cities of the Seleucid Empire were required to make regular payments to the king (φόρος). It was again only by a special concession that a particular city was granted tax exemption (ἀφορολογησία, immunity). This privilege was granted by the kings rarely and only in special circumstances. I may quote the well-known case of Erythrae in the reign of Antiochus II* and of Smyrna in that of Seleucus II†. We have already seen that the cities greatly resented the obligation of paying a φόρος to the king, which certainly implied a sort of control over their finances.

The normal position therefore of most of the old Greek cities of Asia Minor under the Seleucids was that the city preserved its constitution and its own laws, but had no political independence, and was obliged to obey the king's commands, and to pay tribute and imposts to the king's treasury. There was accordingly very little difference, as regards their relations with the central power, between the new and the old cities of the Seleucid Empire.[301]

Subjection to the king was most plainly revealed in the payment of tribute. This is very clearly brought out in the complaints made by the envoys of Antiochus III to Rome and in the Roman arrangement that after the battle of Magnesia the cities which had formerly paid tribute to Antiochus should be exempt, while those which had paid to Attalus should continue to pay to Eumenes (the texts are quoted above, p. 525).

It is regrettable that we know so little of the mode of assessment and payment of the tribute. A passage in Philo‡ speaks of the payment of a lump sum yearly as the prevailing rule. The payment of a tribute did not, however, exempt the citizens of the cities from the payment of the royal taxes which have been spoken of above. As an illustration of what has there been said I may cite a decree of one of the cities of the Hellespont in honour of Corragus, *strategos* of that region, of which the late M. Holleaux has given a masterly interpreta-

* *O.G.I.* 223; Welles, *R.C.* 15. † *O.G.I.* 228, 7.

‡ *De spec. leg.* 4, 212, and 1, 142.

tion.* It probably dates from the time when the towns of the Hellespont had passed from Antiochus III to Rome and, having been 'conquered by force of arms' and forced to surrender (*deditio*), had lost all their rights and were afterwards handed over by Rome to Eumenes. The position was desperate. The war had ruined both city and citizens, and they were absolutely at the mercy of the conqueror. The king restores to the city what it previously possessed: (1) its laws and its 'ancestral constitution', (2) the temples and sacred plots of land, with funds to meet the cost of worship and of administering the city, (3) oil for the young men, and (4) all (else) that it had formerly enjoyed. He further confirms the citizens' rights to their holdings of land, while those who had none receive grants of land from the king's estate. Finally, immunity from all imposts is guaranteed for three years, which were extended to five at the request of the governor. In addition many grants are made by the king and personal gifts by the governor.

The inscription shows that under Antiochus III and probably earlier the city enjoyed freedom and autonomy, but paid tribute and the royal taxes to the royal treasury. Some of these payments the king returned to the city for the expenses of worship and the like. The treasury also allowed a certain quantity of olive-oil for the needs of the city's *palaestrae* and *gymnasia*. The private property of the citizens in their own plots of land was recognized. The king went even further and granted to landless citizens plots of royal land. This royal land was either included in the territory of the city (as was the case at Priene) or was adjacent to it. The city in its corporate capacity owned the temples and their lands, but apparently had no other landed property.

The same arrangement of imposts may be inferred from the letter of Antiochus II to Erythrae.† The city received immunity from all tributes and imposts, including a special contribution exacted for the defence of the country against the Gauls. But this immunity scarcely included freedom from the payment of royal taxes and of extraordinary imposts as presents to the king, 'crowns' or 'gold for presents'. This

* *S.E.G.* ii. 663; M. Holleaux, *Études d'Épigr. et d'Hist. gr.* ii. pp. 73 ff.
† *O.G.I.* 223; Welles, *R.C.* 15.

probably had to be provided both by cities subject to tribute and by those immune from it.

In an earlier period—a time of distress and adversity during the Galatian invasion and the first Syrian war—another Erythraean inscription in honour of Polycritus, son of Iatrocles, mentions the expense incurred by him in connexion with the garrisoning of the city, other city expenses, and *εἰς τὰ τῶι βασιλεῖ συμφέροντα* that is to say, certain payments which were welcome to the King, which advanced his interests. This may mean extraordinary contributions imposed by the King or even regular tribute.[302]

6. Prosperity of the Seleucid Empire

It is not easy to form an idea of the degree of prosperity that the Seleucid Empire enjoyed under the rule of Seleucus and his successors down to the time of Antiochus III. The little evidence we possess relates only to parts of the empire: Asia Minor, Syria, and Babylonia. And the inferences to be drawn from it are not the same for the various satrapies.

For Asia Minor the rule of Seleucus and of his immediate successors was hardly a blessing. The battle of Corupedion did not put an end to the devastating wars that raged all over that region. The duel between the Ptolemies and the Seleucids was mainly fought not in Syria, but in Asia Minor. It must also be remembered that the first dynastic wars of the Seleucid house affected Asia Minor rather than Syria, and that it was in Asia Minor, devastated by the Galatians (see below), that the minor Anatolian monarchies, especially Pergamon, carried on their struggle for independence.

In this prolonged struggle of the Hellenistic kings the wealthiest and most prominent cities of Asia Minor were the chief sufferers. Such cities as Miletus, Ephesus, and Smyrna passed constantly from hand to hand, underwent troubles and hardships, and were repeatedly besieged and captured. In spite of their sufferings they never remained passive in the struggle between the leading powers of the Hellenistic world, and never gave up the hope of obtaining the full measure of autonomy and liberty which either combatant, when not in possession of them, readily promised, but never granted. While they withheld this liberty, both the Ptolemies and the Seleucids, in order to bribe and pacify the cities, bestowed gifts upon them and helped to adorn them with great and costly buildings. But this did not prevent them from imposing at the same time heavy contributions on the cities in the form of emergency taxes and requisitions.[303]

The invasion of Asia Minor by the Gauls was a real calamity for the cities. The Gauls for a time spread pillage and murder over the whole region. Even when settled in Galatia they never gave up their practice of pillaging and never ceased to be a menace to the prosperous Anatolian cities. The situation of these cities about 270 B.C., when the Gauls were ravaging Asia Minor and Ptolemy and Antiochus were engaged in their bitter struggle, is illustrated by certain inscriptions. Of these two from Erythrae are especially interesting. They show this unfortunate city struggling for existence, obliged at the same time to purchase immunity for itself and its territory from the rapacious Gauls, and to fulfil its obligations towards its overlord, Antiochus I. These included the maintenance of the naval and military forces he had stationed at Erythrae, which in fact were of very little use to it. The city, moreover, suffered heavily from the raids of pirates who were probably in the service of Philadelphus, but may have been acting on their own behalf with very little regard for the Ptolemaic and Syrian navies, which were engaged in operations not very different from their own.

Similar conditions prevailed at Miletus, which suffered heavily from the Galatian hordes, at Priene, at Thyateira in Lydia, and at Celaenae and Themisonium in Phrygia. Tlos and the other cities of Lycia were saved from pillage and devastation by Neoptolemus the Pisidian, general and governor of Lycia in the service of Ptolemy Soter.[304]

When the acute phase of the Galatian terror passed, the situation of the Anatolian cities and of the cities of the Aegean islands showed some improvement, though the raids of the Galatians continued and other raids were carried out by pirates in the Aegean in the middle of the third century B.C. The most difficult years were those in which war raged in the

Aegean, when hostilities provided the pirates with an opportunity of carrying on their depredations in the name of one or other of the combatants.*

Harassed by the wars between the kings, exhausted by the raids of Galatians and pirates, the leading cities of Asia Minor were unable to balance their budgets. The revenue of many of them was no longer increasing as in the preceding period, but decreasing. Ephesus, Smyrna, Miletus, and many cities on the great roads from Syria to the coast of Asia Minor derived a large part of their revenue from the transit trade, as a result of their connexions with the Syrian territory and through it with India, Persia, and Arabia. As long as the cities were in the hands of the Seleucids, their revenue from this trade was certainly large. But most of the time the great seaports of Asia Minor were in the power of the Ptolemies. In these circumstances the Syrian kings would do their best to prevent the caravans from crossing Asia Minor to the Anatolian ports, and make it both attractive and profitable for them to come by secure and well-constructed roads to Antioch and from Antioch to Seleuceia or Laodicea. How far they succeeded in thus diverting the trade to the Syrian ports we do not know. But their rapid growth suggests that they obtained a substantial share in the international traffic of the time.

The losses that Ephesus, Miletus, and Smyrna suffered by becoming subjects of the Ptolemies were only partly compensated by such important gains as they may have derived from the hegemony of the Ptolemies in the Aegean. For the latter the ports of Asia Minor, important as they were politically, were of little value commercially so long as they were not great clearing-houses for Oriental trade in general. Nevertheless Asia Minor, and especially its principal cities, found a certain compensation for the partial loss of the southern caravan trade in the gradual growth of the local Anatolian market, a consequence of the hellenization of the interior of Asia Minor. Perhaps also they benefited by the new foreign markets opened to them by the commercial hegemony of the Ptolemies and by their active commercial relations with the Pontic regions. It is note-

* I have previously referred to the pirates and their activity in the Aegean, pp. 195 ff.

worthy that Asia Minor emancipated itself from the need for imported pottery much earlier and more completely than Egypt and Syria. We have learnt for example from the systematic excavations at Pergamon and Priene how vigorously many Anatolian cities applied themselves to the manufacture of pottery in early and late Hellenistic times; and a similar inference may be drawn from Myrina. We shall certainly be better informed on this subject when a full description of the pottery found in the excavations of Miletus is published. No doubt the more conspicuous development in the field of ceramics dates, for the most part, from a later period than we are here concerned with (I refer to the production of relief vases and *terra sigillata*, perhaps painted pottery on white ground, and the so-called λάγυνοι in general; see below, Ch. VIII). But a good deal of progress, especially in the field of black-glazed pottery, was made in the late fourth and early third centuries B.C. What is true of Asia Minor holds good also for South Russia, which had such intimate commercial relations with Asia Minor. Here, as in Asia Minor, all forms of local industry were rapidly developing, and pottery in particular.[305]

It is unfortunate that Miletus, our barometer of the economic life of Asia Minor, has yielded very little information concerning the period with which we are dealing, and that the list of *aisymnetai* is lacking for the years from 259/8 to 232/1 B.C. It is natural to find Apollo as *aisymnetes* during the four years of struggle between Philadelphus and Antigonus Gonatas (266/5–263/2). It would be interesting to know how often he was *aisymnetes* in the subsequent period, when Antiochus II freed the city from the tyranny of Timarchus, and Euergetes reconquered Miletus and the rest of Ionia. In any case there are no signs of prosperity at Miletus in the period under review, while there are some indications of misery and distress.[306]

Syria, Mesopotamia, and Babylonia, though they suffered less than Asia Minor from the 'Syrian' wars of the Ptolemies, were certainly affected by them. In lower Mesopotamia, for instance, the population complained bitterly of the damage done to Babylonia by the first Syrian war. Certain scholars even speak of an acute economic crisis affecting at that time

PLATE LX

1, 3. Beautiful red-glazed 'Megarian' bowl of Syrian manufacture. On the bottom a rosette. The lower part of the body is adorned with stylized leaves (acanthus and another type of leaf alternating), and between them rich but leafless scrolls. On the upper part of the body, groups of Dionysiac figures divided from each other by scrolls. The central group probably represents Dionysus, Ariadne, and the panther. Diam. 0·16, H. 0·105. Unpublished. Megarian bowls made in Syria are not uncommon. There is, besides the specimen reproduced here, another in Paris, several in Berlin, at least one at Yale. Many are preserved in the museums of Syria, Mesopotamia, and Palestine. Several sherds of Megarian bowls, typical of the Hellenistic layers, were found in the ruins of the cities excavated in Syria, Palestine, and Iraq (see Ch. III, p. 160 f. with notes 33 and 34, and notes 163 and 311 to this ch., cf. Ch. V, p. 615 and n. 17). The group has never been collected and studied. Photograph and drawing supplied by the authorities of the Louvre, Paris.

2. One of the two silver bowls found at Nihavand in Persia forming part of a treasure buried some time during the early Roman Empire. It is adorned with groups of leaves and single leaves separated from each other by scrolls; a dotted Greek inscription is engraved on the rim (ΡΧΑ). I have mentioned the bowl in the text of this chapter, p. 540, with n. 313 (bibliography); cf. Ph. Ackerman in A. U. Pope, *A Survey of Persian Art*, i, 1938, p. 460, pl. 137A (with bibliography). The date of the bowl and its character are disputed. Prof. R. Zahn is disposed to regard it as a purely Greek work of the early third century B.C. probably made in Greece. I have suggested that, while the bowl must be assigned to the third century B.C., it is of eastern, Bactrian, or Syrian workmanship. Other scholars (Herzfeld, Schönebeck, Ph. Ackerman) incline to the second century B.C. or to an even later date, and speak of the bowl as being of Parthian workmanship. I still regard the third century as more probable than the second, and must decidedly reject a still later date. The similarity between the Nihavand bowl and the 'Megarian' bowl reproduced in the same plate is wholly in favour of my date and of the Syrian origin of the bowl. The bowl certainly was made, not by Orientals, but by Greeks residing in the East. Photograph supplied by the authorities of the Staatliche Museen, Berlin.

1. Paris, Louvre.

2. Berlin, Staatliche Museen.

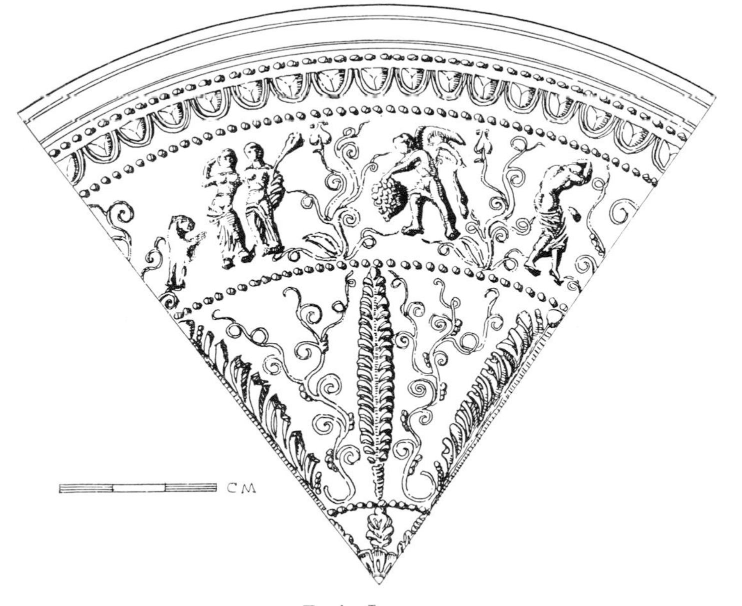

3. Paris, Louvre.

GRECO-SYRIAN INDUSTRY

1. Bagdad, Museum.

2. Bagdad, Museum.

3. Leningrad, Hermitage.

GRECO-SYRIAN INDUSTRY

PLATE LXI

1. Head of a terracotta figurine found in the ruins of Seleuceia on the Tigris during the systematic excavation of the city carried out by Michigan University. Prof. C. Hopkins, director of the excavations, has kindly placed at my disposal a detailed description of this and the second terracotta reproduced on this plate, of which I have made extensive use in my description of them. Helmeted head of a warrior found in the brickwork of a rather late third-level wall, built probably before the middle of the first century A.D. The helmet has three crests, a visor, and cheek-pieces. These last fit close to the face on either side and extend down to the chin, where they are bound together (an early Macedonian fashion which survived at Seleuceia, see above, pl. v, 1, and the coins of Seleucus I; cf. the ivory head in the Museum of Naples, A. Ippel, *J.D.A.I.* liv (1939), Anz., p. 368 f., figs. 16–18). Beneath the helmet was probably a leather lining or cap, perhaps a Parthian trait. Though of late Hellenistic date, the head apparently goes back to an early Hellenistic original. The same is true of the several complete and fragmentary terracotta figurines of soldiers found at Seleuceia (W. van Ingen, *Figurines from Seleucia on the Tigris*, 1939, pls. XXVIII and XXIX). Their equipment is strikingly similar to that of the soldiers of the Sidonian stelae illustrated above (pl. LVII) and to that of the Myrina figurine mentioned in the description of pl. LVII; cf. P. Bienkowski, *Les Celtes dans les arts mineurs gréco-romains*, 1928, fig. 193, and p. 132 f., and my *Dura and Parthian Art*, p. 234, fig. 46. H. 0·057. Photograph supplied by Prof. C. Hopkins.

2. Figurine of a boy with a monkey (lower part of it is missing). Charming statuette found in the mud-brick work of a third-level wall of Seleuceia on the Tigris, probably built after the middle of the second century B.C. It is not entirely clear whether the figure represents a boy or a girl. The first is suggested by the comparison of the head with that of a fine figurine from Seleuceia of a boy supporting a Rhodian jar on his shoulder (W. van Ingen, loc. cit., pl. XLVIII, 341 (no. 720)). The representation of a figure carrying a monkey or ape is very common among the Hellenistic terracottas. The prototype goes back to early Mesopotamian and Egyptian art (W. C. McDermott, *The Ape in Antiquity*, 1938). The commonest type is the ape squatting on the shoulder or hunting for lice in his master's hair (McDermott, loc. cit., p. 174, no. 81, and p. 197, no. 207, both from Egypt); cf. a fragment from Seleuceia (from level Ib; W. van Ingen, loc. cit., pl. LXV, 470). H. 0·09. Photograph supplied by Prof. C. Hopkins.

3. The famous gold cup from Siberia in the form of a Megarian bowl and adorned after the fashion of these bowls with rich scrolls. Aramaic inscription (probably of later date) not yet deciphered. The date and origin are controversial. R. Zahn in a paper soon to be published endeavours to prove that the cup is of Greek make and of an early date (third century B.C.). Smirnov was of opinion that it is Hellenistic but was made in the East, and I am inclined to agree with him. A later date, recently suggested, is in my opinion out of the question. J. Smirnov, *Argenterie Orientale*, pl. VII, no. 20, and Introduction, p. 7; my paper in *Sem. Kond.* vi (1933), pp. 171 ff.; Ph. Ackerman, in A. U. Pope, *A Survey of Persian Art*, i (1938), p. 461 f., pl. 137, B (with bibliography). From J. Smirnov op. cit.

the whole of the Syrian territory. I am inclined to think that such a generalization is not supported by the evidence and that the crisis was local.[307] There is no doubt, however, that the first and second Syrian wars were grievous episodes in the history of the Syrian lands. I may recall the number of Syrian slaves offered on the Egyptian market in the reign of Philadelphus, some of whom, at least, were settled in Egypt (above, p. 203, n. 28).

Nevertheless the reigns of Seleucus and his early successors were without doubt a period of prosperity for Syria and Mesopotamia and probably for Babylonia also. Though we have no direct evidence in support of this conclusion, I may remind the reader of the wealth of Syria in respect of agriculture, horticulture, and pasturage. I have referred to the flourishing state of Coelesyria, Phoenicia, and Palestine during the Ptolemaic domination. There is no reason to suppose that Syria proper, Mesopotamia, and Babylonia, with their great agricultural resources, were less thriving than the Ptolemaic dominions. We shall see later the abundance of Syria's agricultural produce in the troubled times of the second century B.C. We know that this prosperity endured. Very instructive lists of Syrian produce have recently been compiled for Roman times. These lists are based in the main on the data supplied by Pliny and Strabo, who certainly received their information from Hellenistic sources. From them we learn that Syria was certainly an important agricultural, pastoral, and horticultural centre in late Hellenistic times. This position late Hellenistic Syria did not create for itself, but inherited from the past. Its principal products in these later times were the same as those of Coelesyria, Palestine, and Phoenicia in the third century B.C.: grain, grapes, wine, fruit, vegetables, camels, donkeys, sheep, and unguents for which native flowers were used. There can therefore be no doubt that the agricultural wealth of Syria was as abundant in the third century as in the second and first centuries B.C.[308]

The same appears to be true of Mesopotamia. I have referred to the instance of Europus (Dura), which figures in a document of the early second century B.C. as the centre of a prosperous agricultural region planted with trees and gardens.

Finally, a few words about Babylonia, where we find evidence in the Seleucid period of an economic activity as regular and as diversified as it had been in the neo-Babylonian and Persian times. The few published data relating to the prices of the most important commodities, such as grain, sesame oil, and dates, show that the rise of prices which was such a characteristic feature of the Persian régime at Babylon did not continue in the Seleucid period. We have exact data for 274/3 B.C. and again for 233/2 B.C. The prices in these years (under the Seleucids) were a little lower than they had been under the Persians, but in general they seem to have been much lower. The evidence available, however, does not enable us to determine what were the average prices of grain, oil, and dates, and how they fluctuated. For this we must wait until more Babylonian tablets of the Seleucid period are published, translated, and studied.

Alongside of the few data about the prices of the above mentioned commodities, and of slaves, we have several tablets from Uruk which include prices of houses and building-sites (ψιλοὶ τόποι according to Egyptian terminology). Unfortunately the price of a house and even of a building site depends on so many factors besides its dimensions that I hesitate to draw from the scanty evidence any conclusions as regards the rise and fall of prices in Babylonia. In any case a lively market in houses and sites may be taken as an indication of regular business activity in Uruk and of a certain degree of prosperity.[309]

Finally we have some clear evidence regarding the prices of slaves. While the price of foodstuffs apparently fluctuated in the Seleucid period, the price of slaves fell considerably below that prevailing during the Persian domination. It almost reached the very low level of the neo-Babylonian period. It is interesting to note that a woman fetched a higher price than a man. In general, as I remarked before (note 260), we are surprised to find such a large number of slaves in Babylonia in the Seleucid period. There were in Babylon, as has been shown, different types of slaves: temple slaves, slaves in the service of the king and of various branches of administration, and slaves belonging to private persons. It would be highly interesting to study the names of the slaves and to ascertain the proportion that were 'home-born' (οἰκογενεῖς). The same abundance of slaves is a feature of Seleuceia on the Eulaeus in Seleucid times, as is attested by the many extant records of manumissions in the temple of Nanaia. It is worthy of note that all the manumitted slaves of Seleuceia (Susa) were women.[310]

We know very little of the commercial conditions prevailing in the larger cities of Syria, especially in the capitals of the Seleucid kingdom. But there are general grounds for thinking that cities situated on the continuation of the Phoenician coast and intended to be centres of commerce and industry would have in this respect a rapid development similar to that of Alexandria. The circumstances were similar. Behind the large cities lay the areas colonized by the Seleucids, containing an ever growing Macedonian and Greek population, and providing an excellent market for products of Greek industry. We have seen that in the early times of Greek domination in Syria, Phoenicia, and Palestine, conditions remained much the same as they had previously been: Greek merchandise was imported into these areas in large quantities, as is shown by the abundance of imported early black-glazed pottery and of south Italian 'Gnathian' ware found in the ruins of both the Palestinian and the Syrian and Mesopotamian cities (above, Ch. III, n. 33.)

This state of things, however, did not endure very long. Imported pottery was soon replaced by a local pottery of the same and other types. The black-glazed pottery was soon supplemented by large and ever increasing quantities of relief pottery, the earliest being what are known as 'Megarian' bowls. No careful study has been undertaken of the Syrian examples of this type of pottery (of which we have an abundance in the Syrian museums, in the Louvre, in the British Museum, in the Museum of Berlin, and elsewhere) in order to distinguish imported from home-made bowls. My own impression is that the Megarian bowls and the fragments of them hitherto found in Syria are all of local make, and it is probable that some of them belong to the third century B.C. It is evident that the local production of Megarian bowls was begun in Syria as soon as, or little later than, in Alexandria. It was probably undertaken simultaneously in Phoenicia and in Syria by potters who had had the same training. Before this, Palestine and Phoenicia may have imported some ceramic products from Alexandria.[311]

The evolution of the manufacture of glass was similar. Cast glass was produced in the Persian Empire before Alexander. A glass bowl imitating a special type of metal bowls of a form characteristic of the Persian Empire, as is proved by numerous finds made within it and outside it, has been found at Ephesus and was probably manufactured either in one of the great Phoenician centres of glass production or in Egypt. Such glass bowls adorned with gold are mentioned by Aristophanes (*Acharn.* 74) in 425 B.C. An Athenian ambassador to Persia relates how during his journey through Asia Minor he drank wine out of bowls (ἐκπώματα) made of gold and glass. In all probability the production of such glass bowls did not cease under and still less after Alexander. There is reason therefore, for believing that the vessels of cut glass known from archaeological finds, inscriptions, and literary sources (above, p. 370 f., nn. 164, 165) were manufactured in Hellenistic times both in Alexandria and in Syria simultaneously. In Syria they were probably the continuation of a tradition well established in the Phoenician cities in Achaemenid times and thence transferred to Antioch. The same *mutatis mutandis* may be true of the so-called gold-glass (above, p. 371 and below, Ch. VI, n. 198). Though in all probability of Egyptian origin, gold-glass may have been manufactured at the same time in the Ptolemaic dominions of Phoenicia and Palestine, and in Seleucid Syria. It is interesting to note that one of the earliest and most beautiful of these glass bowls, in the Rothschild collection, was found somewhere in Syria, Phoenicia, or Palestine.[312]

We know very little of the activity of the toreutic artists in the early Seleucid kingdom. I shall revert to this subject in the next chapter. But it must be borne in mind that the toreutic artists of the Persian Empire who continued earlier traditions were famous throughout the world and influenced the development of Greek toreutic art. The products of Achaemenid craftsmanship found in South Russia (I may mention for example the early specimens discovered at Kelermes and the numerous finds of the fifth and fourth centuries B.C.) and in Bulgaria (above, Ch. II) and the influence they had on the evolution of Greek toreutic art in South Russia furnish clear evidence of this. They certainly spread far and wide over the Persian Empire, including Egypt (pl. XLVII). The centres of metal work in that empire were probably Syria and Armenia and perhaps Bactria also. There is no reason to suppose that the activity of these centres ceased in the Seleucid period. We may perhaps ascribe to Seleucid manufacture certain products of toreutic art found in the Seleucid Empire and in Russia. In the first place some gold and silver cups found in Siberia and at Nihavand in Persia, and a silver *emblema* found in Syria, which show a striking similarity to the Megarian bowls both in shape and in ornamentation, may be regarded as Syrian work of the late third and early second centuries B.C., since the style of their vegetal ornamentation reminds one of the late Hellenistic ornaments which are typical of the development of decorative art in Palestine. In their Iranian transformation they had a long life in Bactria and in India. I am inclined also to claim for the Syrian artists of the early Hellenistic time the beautiful *emblema* or *phalara* of unknown provenance in the Hermitage in St. Petersburg. The figure of a war elephant with which it is adorned and the style point to Syria rather than to Bactria.[313]

It may be added that discoveries in Palmyra, Dura, Mongolia, and Lu Lan afford evidence (no doubt relating to a much later period, though some textiles of Dura were found in graves of the early first century A.D.) of an extensive Syrian manufacture of woollen stuffs. Since Babylonia, Assyria, and Phoenicia were famous centres of woollen industry from time immemorial, we are justified in suggesting that the Seleucids did not wait until the late Hellenistic period to adapt the local wool manufacture to the needs of the new population of Syria and Mesopotamia.[314]

It was certainly one of the main endeavours of the Seleucids to emancipate the population of their empire from dependence on foreign markets, especially as regards goods of prime necessity, and more particularly those imported from Alexandria and from cities subject to the Ptolemies. A striking illustration is afforded by the history of writing materials in the Seleucid Empire. I have pointed out (p. 423 f.) that the Near East (differing in this from Egypt) was from the earliest times the region where clay was used as the material for writing. With the diffusion, however, of the Aramaic and the Phoenician script and languages, parchment began to compete with clay. In the Hellenistic period clay tablets were gradually disappearing. The question arises whether their place was taken by papyrus rolls or parchment sheets. We hear occasionally of papyrus being grown in Syria, and of papyrus rolls being made in Babylonia from a native plant, perhaps as early as the time of the first Seleucids. From the fact, however, that at Dura-Europus during the whole of the Parthian period it was parchment that was exclusively in use, papyrus appearing at Dura first under the Romans, we may conjecture that the principal writing material used in the Seleucid Empire was parchment. We shall see that the Attalids similarly encouraged the use of parchment in order to reduce the import of papyrus from Egypt.[315]

Our conclusions may be summed up as follows. The little we know of the Seleucid Empire in the period of the balance of power shows many vicissitudes in the history of this vast monarchy, due to foreign wars and to internal troubles. Nevertheless the available evidence, scanty as it is, leaves an impression of a general, steady, and rapid economic advance in almost all parts of it, mainly attributable to its unity, which, despite all difficulties, the first Seleucids preserved. This progress was accompanied by a rapid increase in the Greek population of the empire, involving, at least to some extent, an intensification of economic effort and energy, and the introduction of new and probably more efficient methods in all fields of economic activity: agriculture, industry, and commerce.

We are very poorly informed regarding the general trend of the economic policy of the first Seleucids. But, apart from some attempts to unify taxation and perhaps (but this is very doubtful) to introduce certain monopolies, we see no traces of anything comparable to the vigorous reforms of the Ptolemies, to their efforts to create a planned economy. Even in the parts of their empire where certain features of a planned economy were not unknown, for instance in Babylonia, we cannot detect any sign that the Seleucids systematically pursued this object. The impression left by the meagre fragments of evidence is rather that they refrained from interference with the peculiarities of the constituent parts of the empire and with the economic freedom of their subjects, especially the new settlers, the 'Hellenes'.

7. Bactria

One of the remotest satrapies of the Seleucid Empire, but a flourishing and important one, was hilly Bactria and fertile southern Sogdiana. To relate once more what little is known of the political and dynastic history of Bactria would be out of place here. The last, fullest, and most ingenious treatment of the many problems connected with it has been given by W. W. Tarn. The evidence is slight and scattered, and consequently any reconstruction of the sequence of events is bound to be more or less hypothetical.[316]

For the convenience of the reader it will be enough to say that Bactria began to assert its political independence after the middle of the third century B.C., at the same time as Parthia. Seleucus II was forced to recognize the semi-independence of his remote satrapy by treating Diodotus, its able and ambitious satrap, as his ally rather than his governor, and perhaps by giving him one of his sisters in marriage. When Diodotus died (about 230 B.C.), his son who inherited his power took the decisive step (unless his father had done so before) and assumed the royal title with the support of his contemporary, the Parthian king Tiridates. His rule was short. He was soon displaced by a certain Euthydemus, a Greek from Magnesia, who was supported by the widow of Diodotus I, the Seleucid princess (?), and married her daughter, thereby probably connecting himself with the Seleucid dynasty.

Euthydemus was the real founder of the Bactrian kingdom and of the Bactrian Hellenistic dynasty. The period covered by his reign and that of his son Demetrius was the most brilliant in the history of the country.

So long as the Seleucid Empire was strong, Euthydemus

remained confined within the boundaries of his own former satrapy of Bactria and Sogdiana. His main preoccupation was, naturally, to consolidate his kingdom, exposed as it was to formidable attacks by its nomadic neighbours and by the rising kingdom of Parthia. When Antiochus III carried out his great expedition to the East to assert his supremacy over his Oriental satrapies and to check the advance of the Parthians, Euthydemus offered him staunch resistance. Failing to take Euthydemus' capital Bactra, Antiochus, as is well known, was forced to make peace with Euthydemus, which was concluded (in 206 B.C.) on honourable terms. Tarn has shown that Antiochus yielded to the threat of Euthydemus to ally himself with the powerful nomadic Sacae.

The departure of Antiochus and his subsequent catastrophic struggle with the Romans marked the beginning of the expansion of the Bactrian kingdom at the expense of the Seleucids and the Parthians. Though there is no precise evidence, it appears probable that the rule of Euthydemus and his son was extended in the east over at least a part of Ferghana and perhaps over some tracts of Chinese Turkestan, and in the west over certain Parthian provinces including Margiane (the rich oasis of Merv). In the south Demetrius, after his father's death (about 189 B.C.), annexed some of the Seleucid provinces: certainly Paropamisadae and most probably Aria, Arachosia, and Seistan. Finally he embarked on his ambitious and momentous campaign for the conquest of India, the course of which is comparatively well known: it made him for a short time the successor of the great Mauryan kings and the most powerful monarch of the eastern Hellenistic world.

This sketch of the early political history of Bactria, based on Tarn's research, is of course tentative and hypothetical. Our information is hopelessly scanty, but there is no doubt that in the late third and early second centuries Bactria was a great power which might have exerted some influence on the general development of the Hellenistic world, had it not been for the subsequent events of which I shall speak later.

We should like to know more of the economic and social structure of the immense and rich kingdom of Bactria, but there is practically no evidence about it. Our literary sources contain little of value and archaeological material is almost wholly lacking. The beautiful series of Bactrian coins, one of our main sources for the reconstruction of the dynastic and political history of the country, gives some indication of its commercial importance and its trade connexions, but otherwise yields very little information of an economic kind. The archaeological exploration of both Afghanistan and Russian Turkestan is in its infancy. Bactra, the capital, has never been systematically excavated. The trial excavation of M. A. Foucher did not reach the lower strata. The methodical work done recently by M. Hackin and his associates in Afghanistan has produced excellent results, but these relate mostly to a much later period. Quite recently, however, Hackin has begun the exploration of a very promising site, the ruins of the rich and strong double city Alexandria–Kapisa, capital of the satrapy of Paropamisadae. It looks as if we may soon have a rival to the famous Taxila.[317]

It is needless to speak at length of the brilliant excavations of Sir John Marshall and his collaborators and successors at Taxila, the well-known capital of 'Taxilus', the ally of Alexander. A few words will suffice.

The ruins of the three successive cities of Taxila, built near each other, have yielded abundant and precisely dated material. Unfortunately the city of Demetrius and his successors is the least well-known of the three. It must be borne in mind that after his conquest of Taxila, Demetrius did not care to stay in the conquered city. The finds made in the ruins of this earliest city (under the mound of Bhir), which are in process of excavation, all date from about the seventh to the third century B.C. Demetrius apparently built himself a new city, which lay buried under the mound of Sirkap; it has been thoroughly excavated, but very little has been discovered about it. The excavations have shown that this Hellenistic city, which was in the hands of the Greeks from about 189 to 80 B.C., was completely rebuilt by their successors in Taxila, the Sacae and Pahlavi, in the first century B.C. and the first century A.D. The abundant discoveries made by the excavators all belong to this period and prove that the city of Sirkap, as we know it, was not Greek but Sacian. In the second half of the first century A.D. Sacian Taxila was conquered in its turn by the Kushans, who abandoned it and built a new city for themselves, the third city of Taxila, which is buried under the mound of Sirsukh and has been very little explored.

The exact plan of the Hellenistic city of Taxila and the type of its buildings are consequently unknown. The sole fact that appears to be certain concerns the fortifications and the size of the city. It was in all probability much larger than the Sacian, and was surrounded, not by the existing stone wall, but by a strong earthen wall. Whether the excavated buildings, which are native in character, existed in the same or nearly the same form in the Hellenistic period, it is impossible to say. It is difficult to believe, with Tarn, that Demetrius built for himself a city of the native, not of the Greek, type.[318]

Of the economic and social structure of the Bactrian kingdom very little is known. The following sketch, based on the material collected and explained by Tarn, is therefore no more than tentative. Bactria and Sogdiana, especially the latter, were rich in natural resources. Every one knows the natural wealth of Russian Turkestan, the country around Samarcand: in its agricultural possibilities it rivals Egypt and Babylonia. There is no doubt that developed agriculture flourished here from time immemorial. While Sogdiana was a region of rich fields and beautiful gardens, Bactria proper was a land both of agriculture and of extensive grazing. The Bactrian cavalry was famous, and there is no reason to think that the horses were imported from outside. While rich in grain and cattle, the country was poor in metals: no important silver mines and no gold mines exist in modern Afghanistan and Turkestan, and so it was in ancient times. Some mines of semi-precious stones may have existed in Bactria and Sogdiana, but they would not add very much to the wealth of the country.

Bactria's real source of wealth, apart from its agriculture and grazing, was the transit trade along the caravan roads that crossed the country, connecting India with the Iranian lands and through them with Mesopotamia and Syria. Our information regarding it is poor. We know, however, that Bactra, the capital, was famous for its bazaars and markets, and that Bactria had the reputation of being a country of merchants. Moreover, a recent find of Syrian glass of the finest sort (first century A.D.) and of Indian ivories made in the ruins of Kapisa (above, p. 544), though of much later date, shows that even at the time when Roman trade with India was mostly carried on by sea, the caravan routes by land between India and Syria, which passed through Bactria, were still in active use. They must have been used much more in the early Hellenistic period when the sea route was not yet well developed. I have already mentioned that the early Seleucids had abundance of ivory and spices at their disposal, and I am convinced that a large part of these came to Syria by land and not by sea (that is, by way of the Persian Gulf). I shall return to this point later.

While connected with Syria in the west, Bactria in all probability carried on a lively trade with the north and north-west, with western Siberia and South Russia. The intermediaries between the Bactrians and the Iranian nomads of the north were probably the Sacae. It was from Siberia that Bactria in its early days received its supply of gold. Our evidence on its trade relations with the north and the north-west in the Hellenistic period is slight, but to my mind conclusive. Several beautiful specimens of jewellery and toreutic art in a peculiar style that have been found in Siberia and South Russia, especially in the Kuban region and in the Taman peninsula, were certainly made by Greco-Iranian artists other than those of South Russia, whose style is familiar to us. The most probable assumption is that they were made in Bactria and imported into Siberia and South Russia.

This style has been studied by me in several articles. Its characteristic features are, on the one hand, its predilection for polychromy and on the other its powerful and pathetic naturalism expressed mainly in groups of fighting animals. It had a long life. From the Bactrians it was inherited by the Sacae, with whom it migrated both to northern India and to South Russia. The Sacae transmitted it to the Sarmatians, and with them it came a second time to South Russia. These facts show that the relations between Bactria and the north, once established, continued to exist long after the political death of Hellenistic Bactria.[319]

The beautiful coinage of the early Bactrian kings—a branch as it were of the Seleucid coinage, with its Attic standard and its various Seleucid types—was destined to become and did become the instrument of the caravan trade of Bactria and India. The almost complete absence of Seleucid coins in the Bactrian and Indian hoards (above, n. 243) and the rare occurrence, in stray finds, of coins minted by the Seleucids after the secession of Bactria is an indication of this. It is not improbable that Seleucid gold and silver which reached Bactria directly or through Parthia was reminted by the Bactrian kings. Besides coins of the heavy Attic standard, mostly tetradrachms, they and their successors in India, especially in the later period, minted a good many coins of a lighter weight for local exchange. Though the use of money was not foreign to India in the pre-Greek period, it was Alexander's conquest of the East and the Greek domination in Bactria and in India that made it a prominent feature of economic life in this part of the civilized world, while Parthia, with its abundant coinage and its many mints in the west and in the east, served as the connecting link between Bactria and the Seleucid Empire. It should be noted that the successors of the Greeks in Bactria and India, the Ye-chi (Kushans) and the Sacae, inherited in this as in many other respects the traditions of their predecessors.

The character of the social and economic structure of Bactria and Sogdiana is a matter of guess-work. Both countries possessed some Greek cities, mostly foundations of Alexander and military strongholds. Part at least of their population was Greek. There is no evidence to enable us to form any idea of the constitutions of these cities and of their relations with the king. Besides cities, there were in Bactria, as in other Hellenistic monarchies, rural settlements of a military character, the so-called κατοικίαι.

Bactria, however, was an Iranian country. The bulk of the population consisted of Iranians and some pre-Iranian tribes. The vigour and activity of its Iranian aristocracy, the feudal lords of the many villages scattered over Bactria and Sogdiana, are illustrated by the history of Alexander; but practically nothing is known of its destinies under the rule of Euthydemus and Demetrius. However, the facts that the country maintained

PLATE LXII

1. Gilded silver belt with hook-clasp and scales inlaid with carnelian found near Maikop in the Kuban district. The clasp shows a griffin of the Persian type—with curved wings, the body in profile, the head which forms the hook seen from the back—killing a horse in a forest indicated by stylized trees. The figure of the griffin is full of ferocious force and energy beautifully expressed in the tension of its body; the dying horse, though treated ornamentally with the body distorted, in order to adapt it to the shape of the belt-scales, shows in its head a pathos of agony and death of a realism and vigour which was never attained in ancient art, even in the works of Assyrian animalists. The girdle plates represent stylized birds with outstretched pinions; bodies and heads of the birds are filled up with incrustation and have become geometrical ornaments. The belt cannot be dated with any exactitude. In my opinion it is the earliest product of the so-called Siberian animal style, which was flourishing at the beginning of the Christian era, and may be assigned therefore to the early Hellenistic period. Photograph supplied by the former Archaeological Commission, Hermitage, Leningrad.

2. Belt of the same type and decoration as no. 1, said to have been found in Bulgaria. The hook-clasp is formed by an eagle in front view holding a sheep (?), and a boar biting into the head of the eagle; behind the boar, a stag turned to the left with ornamental horns. The belt from Bulgaria is much more schematic and ornamental than that of Maikop and shows the influence of the 'Pontic' version of the animal style. It may therefore be a little later than the belt from Maikop.

On the belt from Maikop, M. Rostovtzeff, *Iranians and Greeks*, p. 134, pl. XXV, 1; *Arethuse*, 1924, 3, p. 4, pl. XIV, 1; *Animal Style*, p. 47 f., pl. XIII, 1, 2; G. Borovka, *Scythian Art*, p. 58 f., pl. XLVI B. Belt from Bulgaria, M. Rostovtzeff, *Arethuse*, 1924, 3, p. 5 f., pl. XIV, 2; *Animal Style*, p. 48, pl. XIII, 3. Photograph supplied by the authorities of the British Museum, London.

3. Gold plate found in Siberia. A horse crest or a clasp? Heraldic ornamental eagle with tail erect and outspread wings holding an ibex. Cloisons on the neck, breast, and upper wings once filled with carnelians. Persian style, but schematized and adapted to the requirements of the Nomads. Nearer to the true Persian art is the gold torc from Siberia ending in the body of a winged lion-griffin, E. H. Minns, *Scyth. and Gr.*, p. 271 f., fig. 182. Good reproductions of the eagle plate with bibliography in E. H. Minns, loc. cit., p. 273, fig. 112, and A. U. Pope, *A Survey of Persian Art*, i, p. 465, pl. 138 A, B (Ph. Ackerman). Photograph supplied by the authorities of the Victoria and Albert Museum, London.

The problem of the contribution of Bactria to the development of art, and especially of the applied arts, has been touched upon in the text. Our knowledge of Hellenistic Bactria is scanty. But the example of the Panticapaean State which lived in similar conditions, being an intermediary between the Nomads and the Greek world, with its original creations in the field of art designed to meet the demands of the Nomads, leads us to suggest that Bactria, so similar to the Bosporan kingdom, must have played a similar part. A new phenomenon in the history of Nomadic art in the period of the acme of the Bactrian State was the creation of a new version of the Nomadic animal style, a blend of Central Asiatic and Persian elements. The leading features of this neo-'Scythian' animal style were: ornamental use of groups of animals in conflict borrowed chiefly from the art of Persia, with emphasis laid on the pathetic side, and extensive use of polychromy effected by using cloisonné inlaid work, which was well developed in the Iranian world in pre-Hellenistic times and prominent at Taxila in the Sacian period. I may tentatively suggest that Bactria was responsible for these innovations.

1. Leningrad, Hermitage.

2. London, British Museum.

3. Leningrad, Hermitage.

BACTRIA IN THE SERVICE OF THE NOMADS

its reputation for the excellence of its cavalry and that Euthydemus used 10,000 horsemen against Antiochus III show that its feudal aristocracy was numerous, strong, and rich, and lived on peaceful terms with the Greek rulers, which means that the Bactrian rulers made no change in the social and economic structure that they had inherited from the past.

As in other parts of the former Persian Empire, this feudal aristocracy lived in fortified country-houses surrounded by villages. In a country like Bactria, exposed as it was to raids by the nomads, these villages were gradually fortified by their feudal lords in their own interest. The same thing was probably done in the case of the larger town-like villages with their population of artisans and merchants, which may have depended directly on the kings. Such towns are common in the East at the present time. The villages and the towns had their own elders and chiefs and a certain amount of self-administration. This I regard as a natural development in a country where the central power guaranteed its subjects social stability and the feudal lords were no longer afraid of their own bondsmen. It is possible that it was promoted and encouraged by the central government, but I see no signs in our miserably defective evidence of any attempts by the kings to transform the bondsmen into free peasants.

In this way Bactria and Sogdiana became gradually studded with hundreds of cities and fortified villages and towns, and acquired the reputation of being a country of a thousand towns. This expression is used in our Greek sources, and Chang-K'ien, who visited the country soon after it had passed from the Greeks to the Ye-chi, says that the people of Bactria lived in walled towns. Speaking of the transitional period between the collapse of Greek rule and the establishment of a new régime by its new masters, the Kushans, Chang-K'ien describes the country as one which 'has no great king or chief, but everywhere the cities and towns have their own petty chiefs'. There is nothing surprising in this. The feudal lords of the past had been exterminated by the Kushans and for the time being had not been replaced by new ones; and consequently the richer and more prominent members of the community would act as chiefs in the villages and cities. It was necessary that the

Kushans should have some agents on whom they could rely in matters of taxation, and they were not yet able to protect their new subjects from robbers and raiders. How long this 'municipal autonomy' lasted, cannot be said. Nor can we tell whether and to what extent this 'autonomy' had existed under Greek rule.

The relations between the Greek kings and the feudal lords, the obligations of the latter towards the kings, and the Euthydemid system of taxation are completely unknown.

It seems plain, however, that the rulers of Bactria achieved what the Seleucids and their satraps never succeeded in accomplishing: they created a lasting understanding between two nations, the Iranians and the Greeks, and established peace and harmony between men living two utterly different types of life, based on two different social and economic systems, each of them well established and deeply rooted. In this they closely resembled the Parthians, with the important difference, however, that the Arsacids were themselves Iranians and that the leading role in their monarchy was played by the Iranians, not by the Greeks.

The organization of the other parts of the Bactrian Empire was probably very similar to that of its kernel. Tarn has shown that, although it did not differ much in other respects from the Seleucid Empire, it had a peculiar political system. The rulers of its constituent parts were, not satraps, but sub-kings, who belonged to the family of the ruling monarch. Each of them had the title of king and his own revenue. It was a system probably better adapted than the Seleucid to the Iranian character of the empire, inasmuch as it gave greater authority to the subordinate rulers and satisfied the pride of their subjects, the Iranian feudal lords.

It is impossible to enter here into a discussion of the question of the organization which Demetrius established in his Indian sub-kingdoms and handed on to his successors, the Greek kings of India. The slight information that we possess seems to show that no changes fundamentally affecting Indian life were made by the new Greek rulers. If one believes in the historical character and the early date of the kernel of the Arthaśāstra of Kautilya and in the radical centralization of Indian government effected by Chandragupta on 'Hellenistic' lines, one may say that Chandragupta did more to hellenize India than Demetrius and Menander. But the Artaśāsthra seems to be rather a theoretical and speculative work, and very probably has nothing to do with Chandragupta and the Mauryan organization of India.[320]

The splendour of Bactria came to an end when Demetrius perished in his struggle with Eucratides, who was either a rebel against him, or perhaps, as Tarn thinks, one of the relatives of Antiochus IV who acted on his behalf and helped him in his attempt to restore the unity of the Seleucid Empire and to crush Parthia. The results of this struggle were disastrous. The Greek element in Bactria was divided and weakened, and Bactria soon fell an easy prey to the powerful nomads of the north. The remnant of the Greeks retired to India and contributed to the survival and the stability of some of the larger and smaller Greek kingdoms, which, however, rapidly became indianized.

On the destinies of Hellenism in the ancient world Bactria had very little influence, less than Parthia. Its historical importance lies in the fact that it kept alive for three centuries a Greek body politic closely associated with and allied to native—Iranian and Indian—elements, and served as a channel for the penetration of some degree of Greek civilization into Central Asia and India. How strong this Greek influence was, cannot be discussed here. The civilization and art of Bactria itself are very little known.

Part III

THE MINOR MONARCHIES

As I have pointed out, a portion only of Asia Minor was subject to the Seleucids and Ptolemies. Its northern regions were independent and were ruled by their own kings. Bithynia never submitted to Alexander nor recognized the rule of the Seleucids. The nominal dependence of Pontus on Alexander and his successors ended in 302 B.C., when a local dynasty set about the unification of certain parts of Cappadocia under the name of the Pontic kingdom. Cappadocia, for a time a Seleucid satrapy, asserted its liberty about 265 B.C. A little earlier, tribes of Gauls or Galatians settled in part of great Phrygia and Cappadocia. Finally, as early as 283 B.C., the former Mysian satrapy of the Persian kingdom, with Pergamon as its capital, entered on a phase of almost complete independence under the rule of its dynast Philetaerus.

These independent States were not barbarian communities having no part in the political and cultural development of the period we are concerned with, and therefore negligible for our purposes. They had all lived from time immemorial under civilized conditions and had long since come into touch with the Greeks. Early in its history Bithynia was occupied by Thracian tribes, who lived for centuries under the rule of their own dynasts in close relations with the Greek colonies of the Bithynian coast. Pontus and Cappadocia were fragments of the great Hittite Empire and, at a later time, important and strongly Iranized satrapies of Persia. Some Greek colonies were scattered along the Pontic coast, but had little influence on the character of the communities that were subsequently to form the kingdoms of Pontus and Cappadocia. The Gauls or Galatians were new-comers and intruders, possessing a peculiar Central-European civilization. In Anatolia they lived in close touch with the Phrygians, an ancient people, heirs of the great Phrygian traditions of the past. Lastly, the inhabitants of the Pergamene or Mysian region were from an early date in close contact with Greek life and civilization.

In the Hellenistic period all these countries became imbued with a new life. Under the leadership of able and energetic men they all asserted with determination their claim to political independence. Their rulers—most of them hellenized Anatolians—applied themselves vigorously to securing it, by consolidating their power, unifying and organizing their respective countries, developing the natural resources of these, enlarging their territories, and increasing their revenues. The States, when once firmly established in their independence, wished to play their part in the political affairs of the time, and to exert their influence in the Hellenistic balance of power as equals of the great Macedonian monarchies. They all regarded themselves as belonging to the civilized world and promoted

Greek culture in their respective kingdoms. Their social and economic structure therefore merits somewhat closer attention.

A. *PERGAMON*

The best known of them, the Pergamene State, may be dealt with first.[321] The evidence concerning the early history of this kingdom is not abundant. We know the names of the first rulers, their political connexions, their struggle for independence, and their successful wars with their neighbours, the wild Galatians. But we have very little information about the gradual establishment of their *dynasteia* and the measures they took to organize their State and to develop its resources.

The city of Pergamon has, it is true, been carefully and systematically excavated. In three series of campaigns eminent German scholars have revealed the most important monuments of the acropolis, the centre of the city's religious, political, and dynastic life, as well as those of a small part of the remainder of the city. The excavations, which are still in progress, have brought to light a large number of important sculptures and inscriptions. But very few of these relate to the early *dynasteia*. The majority illustrate the kingdom at its zenith and the glorious reigns of its great rulers, in some instances Attalus I, but more frequently Eumenes II and Attalus II. Hardly any of the monuments throw light on the earlier period, when, under the modest dynasts Philetaerus and Eumenes I, the foundations of the future glory of Pergamon were laid.

Yet there are good reasons for endeavouring to reconstruct, if only in mere outline, the history of the Pergamene *dynasteia*. My earlier attempts to do this have led me to the following conclusions.

The history of the Pergamene kingdom must be divided into two main periods—that of the *dynasteia* and that of the *basileia*. The founder of the Pergamene *dynasteia* was Philetaerus, son of Attalus, a half-Greek from Tius. To this man Lysimachus entrusted one of his strongholds in Asia Minor, the fortress of Pergamon, where he kept a part, amounting to 9,000 talents, of his treasure. Philetaerus betrayed his master and handed over the city of Pergamon, but not the treasure, to Seleucus.

In return, he was left in undisturbed possession of the city and the adjacent country and of Lysimachus' treasure, and was probably recognized as 'dynast' of Pergamon. In this capacity Philetaerus ruled over his *dynasteia* until his death, (from 283 to 263 B.C.), and remained faithful to his suzerain.

The little we know of his rule shows that his policy, in its main lines, was the same as that which his immediate successors consistently followed. His dominion was certainly not confined to the city of Pergamon and its territory (if it ever possessed any). We may infer from what is known of his relations with Cyzicus and the other Greek cities of the coast that in fact he was the ruler of what used to be the Mysian satrapy of the Persian Orontes, and controlled the whole of the plain of the Caicus. In his foreign relations he adopted from the outset an active philhellenic policy. He was prepared to help his neighbours, the Greek cities of Mysia, the Aeolis, and the Troad, no doubt with an eye to their ulterior helpfulness to himself, and he initiated the policy of his successors by presenting himself in Greece proper as a worshipper of Greek gods and a benefactor of the great Panhellenic sanctuaries. His gifts to Apollo of Delos and to the Muses of Thespiae are significant.

His principal efforts were directed to building up a strong army, securing for himself the exclusive use of the harbours of the Aeolian coast, especially Elaea, for military and commercial purposes, safeguarding his frontiers,* and organizing his country on sound and efficient lines. It was he finally who began the transformation of the fortress of Pergamon into a permanent home for himself and his gods. It is characteristic of his mentality that the earliest sanctuary of Pergamon was built by him and his brother Eumenes for their mother Boa, a Paphlagonian woman, and that it was dedicated to the great goddess of fertility and procreation, the great mother Demeter, whose mystic cult appealed so strongly to the hellenized Anatolians.[322]

His policy was inherited by his nephew and successor Eumenes (263–241 B.C.) and for a time by the nephew and adopted son of the latter, Attalus I (241–197 B.C.). As a result

* Note the praise of his struggle with the Galatians in the metrical inscription at Delos, Durrbach *Choix*, 31.

of the persistent organizing activity of Philetaerus, Pergamon was now strong enough to assert its complete political independence. This meant a break with the Seleucids and a new orientation of the foreign policy of the liberated State. An alliance with Philadelphus was the natural course for a ruler who challenged Antiochus I (262 B.C.) and wished to have his hands free in the Aegean in order to dispose readily of the surplus products of his wealthy and well-organized country. He did not miscalculate his chances, as the defeat of Antiochus I at Sardis eloquently testifies.

When Attalus I succeeded Eumenes, Pergamon was, in fact, no longer a modest *dynasteia*. Its organization was solid, its revenue considerable, its military forces well ordered. It is not surprising that Attalus I defied the Galatians, refused to pay them tribute, and defeated them repeatedly, thus making his dominion safe on the east. Emboldened by these successes, he regarded himself as the equal of his former suzerains the Seleucids, assumed the title of king, and started to transform the former Mysian *dynasteia* into a Pan-Anatolian *basileia* (228 B.C.).

Here the first period of the history of Pergamon ends, and the second begins; the latter will be dealt with in my next chapter. In this second period the orientation of the policy of the Pergamene kings, its centre of gravity, was no longer the same. The aim of the Pergamene kings was imperialistic and their means were adequate to their aim. The work of organizing the kernel of the state was in the main completed and that of extension begun. The chief concern of the Pergamene kings now lay in their foreign relations and in the organization of the new acquisitions that these relations brought them.

We may conclude that what we know of the organization of the kernel of the Pergamene *basileia* was in the main the work of the *dynasts*. To this the *kings* added very little. It will be appropriate therefore to sum up here our knowledge of this organization, reserving for the next chapter the little we know of the organization of the Pergamene Empire.

The territory of the Pergamene *dynasteia* was not very large. Its extent is not exactly known and it certainly fluctuated, especially in the north. Its nucleus was the valley of the Caicus, a land of villages and temples, of peasants and large landowners engaged in agriculture and cattle-breeding, of arable land, gardens, and meadows. It stretched on the east to the hills and mountains of the Abbaitis, the Abrettene, and the Olympene. On the west it reached the sea. There were only a few Greek settlements in the valley of the Caicus, most of them probably small military and agricultural communities.

On the coast several Greek cities controlled the harbours and the fertile littoral. The natural outlets of the Caicus valley were the Elaean and Adramyttian gulfs, with their respective cities, Elaea and Adramyttium. Elaea, forming part of this valley, was certainly the first to submit to the rule of the Pergamene dynasts. But this could not be the limit of their efforts. Expansion along the coast to the south and north was natural, and was carried on systematically and successfully. To the south the first Pergamene dynasts held probably the coast as far as Myrina, to the north the whole of the Adramyttian plain and the city of Adramyttium and at least part of the coast of the Troad. Further north the Pergamenes could not extend: Ilium, Abydus, Lampsacus, and Cyzicus were too strong for them. But they succeeded in maintaining good relations with them, especially the last three, all of them flourishing and important centres of the trade of the Hellespont and the Sea of Marmora.

Of not less vital concern to the Pergamene dynasts than the coast with its harbours, fisheries, olive-groves, and vineyards, was the control of the southern slope of Mount Ida. They secured it early in their history and never lost it. It was this region that supplied them with timber, pitch, and tar for their ships and buildings and for a profitable export trade in competition with Macedonia. It was here that the best horses for their army were bred. And it was the mines of Mount Ida that provided them with silver and copper and a little gold. Iron they certainly received from the Pontic mines through Cyzicus.[323] The territory of the early Pergamene *dynasteia* consisted therefore of (1) the capital of the kingdom, the city of Pergamon, (2) the few Greek cities of the coast and of the valley of the Caicus, and (3) the rural tract containing the native villages and temples.

Each of these divisions may be briefly described. The city of Pergamon was in the first place the city of Philetaerus and of his successors, their main fortress and stronghold, the centre of the military and civil organization of their *dynasteia*, the abode of the gods who protected the rulers and the State. At the same time it was the most important Greek city of the *dynasteia*, its intellectual and artistic capital, its Greek façade. Pergamon was for the Attalids what Alexandria was for the Ptolemies and it was similarly laid out and organized. In the planning and construction of their capital the Attalids were probably guided by what they knew of the brilliant city of the Nile.

The kernel of the city of Pergamon was its *acra*, the residence of the gods and of the kings. On the slope of this and at its feet extended the city proper, with its temples, public buildings, extensive markets, and private houses. Of this city we know very little.

The imposing group of monuments of the *acra*, rising on terraces one above the other, are known to us in the form that was given to them in the period of the *basileia*, under Eumenes II and Attalus II (see next chapter, and pl. LXIII). But it is more than probable that the plan of the *acra* was the work of the dynasts, not of the kings. The kings enlarged the individual buildings, made them more magnificent, and filled them with thousands of statues, bas-reliefs, and decorative monuments, but they never changed the main lines of their disposition or their general character.

The imposing theatre with its long and spacious terrace, its portico and temples, formed a straight base, from which the two main groups of buildings of the *acra* spread fanwise: the splendid row of temples and religious monuments, and behind it a second row of dynastic and military buildings. The whole was surrounded by strong fortifications.

Two temples, that of Athene and perhaps a temple or *temenos* dedicated to Zeus, were the principal religious buildings of the *acra*. The third great religious monument of Pergamon—the famous altar with its beautiful sculptures, a monument set up by the Attalids to impress on the whole Greek world their greatest service to Hellenism, the crushing of the

PLATE LXIII

1. Model of the restored 'Acra' of Pergamon as seen from the west, made by H. Schleif. See above, p. 557 ff., cf. 661 and W. von Massow, *Führer durch das Pergamon Museum*, 2nd ed., 1936, fig. 31. Photograph supplied by the authorities of the Pergamon Museum, Berlin.

2. The famous statue of the dying Gaul. Copy of one of the votive bronze figures dedicated by Attalus I in the court of the temple of Athena at Pergamon. The date and style of this figure cannot be discussed here. Reference may be made to the latest studies of early Pergamene sculpture enumerated and summarized in *A.J.A.* xliv (1940), pp, 241 ff.; cf. B. Schweitzer, *J.D.A.I.* liv (1939), Anz., pp. 405 ff. I reproduce this well-known statue to illustrate the spirit of the Attalids and their conception of their historical mission. On the Celtic arms carved on the base, P. Couissin, *Inst. mil. et nav.*, 1931, pl. xxxv, 1. Photograph supplied by Alinari.

1. Berlin, Pergamon Museum

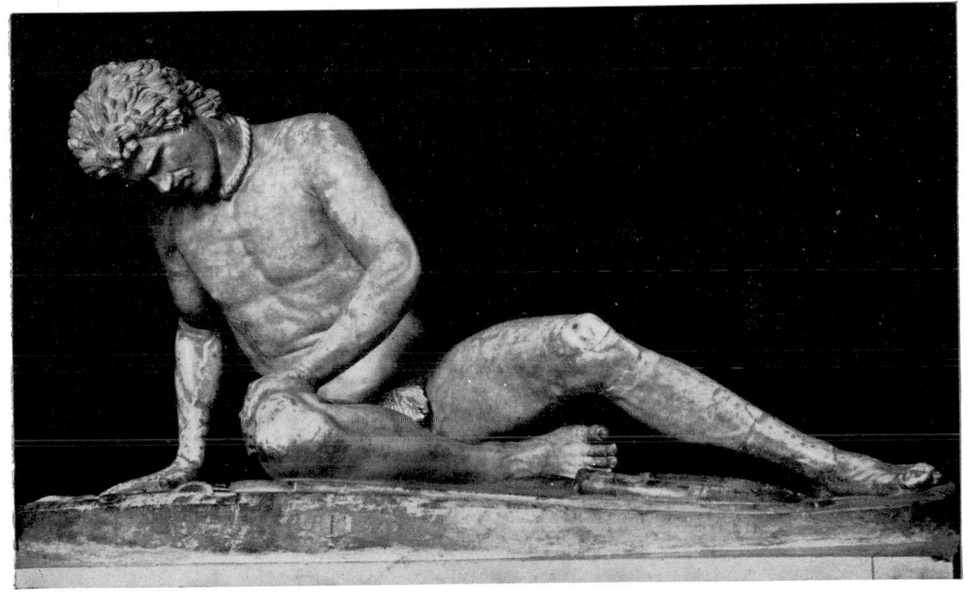

2. Rome, Capitoline Museum

PERGAMON, ITS ARCHITECTURE AND ART

Galatians—was a later addition. The last feature of this group was a fine market-place with a temple, built for the use of the large population of the *acra*.[324]

The second tier of buildings was separated from the first by a street, the main street of the *acra*, which they fronted: they consisted of royal palaces, gardens, barracks, storehouses, and arsenals. Solid and strong, but modest in proportions and in decoration, the royal buildings served as a powerful protection to the sanctuaries, and closely linked the gods with the kings.

This is not the place for a discussion of the plan and the artistic character of the *acra*. The general idea underlying its design was the same as that adopted by the Ptolemies at Alexandria. The royal residence was intended to dominate the city, which lay at its feet as a subordinate annex. This idea was carried out with great skill. The rising tiers of royal buildings towering over the city certainly made as strong an impression on ancient visitors to Pergamon as their imposing ruins make on modern tourists.

Subordinate in its topography to the royal *acra*, the city of Pergamon showed a similar subordination in its constitution and mode of life. It was certainly a Greek city, a *polis*, with its popular assembly, council, and magistrates, its tribes and demes. But, resembling Alexandria in this respect also, this aspect was a mere façade. Behind the screen of its constitution, the life of the city was directed from the *acra*. The chief magistrates—the *strategoi*—were in practice agents of the kings, as were also the other magistrates. Even the minor duties of maintaining order and cleanliness in the streets and houses were regulated by royal decrees and carried out by city magistrates (the *astynomoi*) according to the prescriptions of the law and probably under royal supervision.

The relations between the rulers and the Greek cities of their *dynasteia* are very little known to us. None of these cities have been excavated and no important inscriptions of the Hellenistic period have been found on their sites. There is some evidence that the dynasts may have begun by granting help and protection, loans and gifts, to the Greek cities.[325] How this original relation of friendship and alliance was transformed into subjection we do not know, but the transformation may be accepted as a fact. Attalus I did not hesitate to transfer, for his convenience, after the manner of Antigonus the One-eyed, the population of Gergitha from their old seat north of Mount Ida in the Troad to the source of the Caicus.* The transfer of a part of the population of Miletopolis to Gargara on Mt. Ida is of unknown date. It may have been carried out on the initiative of the people themselves, and in that case there is nothing to prevent us from assigning it to the early days of the *dynasteia*.† We may include in the same class of arbitrary acts the assignment of part of the territory of Priapus to the city of Parium in the Troad‡ and a similar measure affecting Dardanus and Abydus,§ both probably of a later date.

The relations between the rulers and the rural areas, with their temples and villages, are a subject of greater importance. In the official terminology of the Attalids, which was still in use in the reign of Attalus III and in the early days of the Romans, as is shown by the will of Attalus III (see below, Ch. VI), the *dynasteia* consisted of the *polis*, that is, Pergamon, and the *chora*, the rest of the country. The *chora* is not the 'territory' of the city of Pergamon (this did not exist before the Roman period); it is certainly the whole territory, outside the capital, in the possession of the dynasts. The Attalid terminology is strikingly similar to that of the Ptolemies, and different from that of the Seleucids.

From time immemorial the *chora* was divided into villages, with which most of the temples of the Pergamene *dynasteia* were undoubtedly connected. Of these temples none were of any considerable size or importance: those which were not connected with some Greek city were certainly minor village temples of the type that I have described above.[326] None of the villages and temples were transformed by the early Attalids into cities, for these rulers were not city-builders like the Seleucids, but followed in this respect the example of the Ptolemies. There were, however, two exceptions—Philetaeria and Attalia. Both were probably mere military strongholds.

* Strabo, xiii. 1. 70, p. 616.

† Ibid. xiii. 1. 58, p. 611; Mela, 1. 93; Steph. Byz. *s.v.* *Γάργαρα*.

‡ Strabo, xiii. 1. 14, p. 588.

§ Ibid. xiii. 1. 28, p. 595.

Philetaeria apparently did not survive; Attalia later developed into a city.

Villages, therefore, were the predominant element in the Pergamene *dynasteia*. They formed the principal economic and social units and administrative centres, though they were not regarded as the principal administrative units. The lists of ephebes found in the Pergamene gymnasium show that the population of the kernel of the State was divided into three classes: the citizens of Pergamon distributed among the 'tribes' of the city, those who belonged to the *topoi*, and those who were in the eyes of the law foreigners (*xenoi*). The *topoi*, for the most part, either bore geographical names (Lycetta, Masdye, Dascylium, Timnoa, the plain of Midas), probably some of them the names of the administrative centres of the districts (one, for example, bears the significant name Abbukome), or were designated *agroi*, estates, for example 'the estate of Apasion'; some, however, were tracts of grazing land (for example Mandrai), or regions inhabited by soldiers of Anatolian origin—Mysians and Masdyenes—settled on the land.[327]

We may therefore regard the *topoi* as districts. In these districts the greater part of the land either belonged to the peasants and was cultivated by them, or was cultivated by soldiers settled on it, or centred in a large estate, probably a gift-estate of the king (*dorea*). This system of subdivision of the *dynasteia* strikingly resembles that which the Ptolemies established in Egypt and introduced into their province of Palestine. The *nomoi* of Egypt are absent, but we have the *toparchiai* and villages. It is, however, possible that several *topoi* were grouped in a region. We hear occasionally of such a region, the Aeolid, the name being used not as a geographical but as an administrative term. These regions would correspond to the Egyptian *nomoi*.* In later times the same terminology was used for the satrapies of the Attalid *basileia*.†

We are justified therefore in suggesting that the Attalids organized their *dynasteia* on the Ptolemaic model adapted to local conditions. I draw attention again to the friendly relations, amounting in fact to a formal alliance, between the early Attalids and the Ptolemies. The *polis*—Pergamon—had a

* Athen. xv, p. 697 d. † *O.G.I.* 339, 12 f., cf. 330.

separate existence, and so had the Greek 'allied' cities. The rest of the country was *chora*. It was subdivided into regions, districts (τόποι), and villages (κῶμαι), with their respective temples. The land in the *chora* was probably the property of the king. Most of it was cultivated by native peasants, but some parcels were assigned to military settlers, while others were in the hands of Greeks as short-term or long-term leaseholds or perhaps as γῆ ἰδιόκτητος. Large tracts of land (perhaps with the villages included in them) were managed by large landowners, probably as revocable gifts from the king.[328]

We have no information regarding the legal status of the peasants. But since in other parts of Asia Minor they were serfs (λαοὶ βασιλικοί), we may assume that they had the same status in the *dynasteia* of the Attalids, with all that this status implied. Their work in the fields was certainly supervised, probably by agents of the ruler, however these may have been designated.*

The peasants certainly paid rent or a tax to the ruler. We have seen that these payments were not determined by rigid regulations in the Seleucid part of Asia Minor (above, p. 465 f.). They were sometimes made in money, sometimes in kind. It is probable, though far from certain, that the λαοί paid as a rule a *pars quanta*, an *ekphorion*, while the cleruchs paid a tithe, a *dekate* or an *eikoste*.[329]

In the rural districts justice was administered in the name of the king by his judges. They are mentioned incidentally by Athenaeus,† but the reading of the text is uncertain. We may suppose them to have been either royal judges in general—similar to the Ptolemaic *chrematistai* and *laokritai*—or judges who adjudicated in affairs that concerned the interests of the king, or even special judges for the λαοὶ βασιλικοί.

In the *polis* and in the *chora* the rulers showed a remarkable interest in economic matters. We have no direct information regarding their activity in connexion with agriculture and livestock. But we know that they were keenly interested in scientific treatises on agriculture and that one of them, Attalus III,

* τὰ βασιλικὰ πραγματευόμενοι was the usual expression in later times, C. B. Welles, *R.C.* 51, l. 19.

† Athen. xv, p. 697 d, cf. above, p. 508.

himself wrote such a treatise. We know, moreover, that he also devoted the end of his life to experiments in horticulture. Whether this was a personal hobby or an interest traditional in the dynasty, we cannot say. It is noteworthy that the bibliography of Varro includes many natives of Asia Minor among writers on agriculture. It is probable, therefore, that on their own royal territory the Attalids devoted great attention to rational agriculture, and it is certain that they derived their principal revenue from this territory. We may safely assume that their friends and officials, who owned or held large estates,* vied with them in this respect. And it is probable that they were imitated by the military settlers and the holders or owners of 'private' land.

The same keen interest in new devices and improvements was evinced by the Attalids in respect of cattle-breeding. Asia Minor was famous for its sheep and goats, pigs and horses. We have no evidence about Pergamene sheep and goats. But we know that the royal Pergamene horses were prominent at Olympia and the other great racing centres of Greece in the time of Attalus I, and we hear incidentally that Eumenes II bought some famous white boars at Assus. We learn also from casual passages that the kings owned large herds of cattle and studs of horses.[330]

The Pergamene kings were no less zealous in developing industry in the cities of their kingdom, especially in Pergamon. Asia Minor was always famous as one of the greatest centres of woollen manufacture. Phrygia, Sardis, Miletus, and many other of its cities had in this respect a world-wide reputation. Such minor cities of the Pergamene *dynasteia* as Palaiscepsis, Percote, and Gambreon, in the Aeolid and the Troad, were famous for their cloth and carpets. It is natural therefore that the rulers of Pergamon should have made great efforts to apply the skill of their subjects and allies to an extensive production of woollen stuffs in their own capital. Pergamon became known all over the world as the centre of production of special curtains

* They are mentioned in the will of Attalus III (*O.G.I.* 338, l. 25 f.) and we know the names of several of them (at a later period): Craton, the famous flautist of the time of Eumenes II, Diodorus Pasparus, the nabob of Pergamon after the death of Attalus III. Cf. below, p. 805 f.

(*aulaea*), and of a special brocade interwoven with gold threads (*vestes Attalicae*) which in earlier times had been a speciality of Lydia, especially of Sardis. The name may point to the most famous Attalus—Attalus I. We may suppose that the rulers of Pergamon did not neglect the contemporary discoveries of chemistry as applied to the dyeing of textiles. It may be noted that it was about this time that the mining of two mineral dyes, the *rubrica Sinopensis* and *sandarake*, began to be carried out on a comparatively large scale.

It will be remembered that although parchment was not invented by the Attalids, it was they who first brought it into prominence and into competition with the Egyptian papyrus. Here again we may infer that it was the early members of the dynasty who developed the production. Eumenes II, when he established his famous library, had abundance of parchment at his disposal.[331]

I shall return to certain other branches of Pergamene industry in the next chapter. Here I will only add that, although my conclusions as to the economic development of Pergamon are based to a large extent on evidence relating to the later Attalids, it is probable that it was the early dynasts who initiated that development. Confined as they were to a small territory, they were naturally led to make the best of it by a rational exploitation. The later Attalids had other preoccupations and their resources were much larger, but they certainly did not neglect their heritage.

There is no doubt that a large part of the country's agricultural and industrial output was derived from the royal land and the royal factories.* In industry slave labour was certainly employed on a large scale. Royal slaves are mentioned as an important part of the Pergamene population in the decree of Pergamon connected with the will of Attalus III, from which I have already quoted. Some of them were occupied—like the later *Caesaris* or *Augusti servi*—in the various royal offices, in such institutions as his library, in the administration of the *chora*, and in the royal household; but many, especially women, certainly worked in royal factories. The Pergamene artisans

* See *S.I.G.*[3] 1018, a gift to the temple of Asclepius of revenues from certain *ergasteria*.

had an excellent reputation all over the world. About the time when Attalus I built his *pastas* at Delphi,* a certain Dameas resided there (in 197 B.C.), who was 'superintendent of the royal works of King Attalus'; he manumitted a royal girl-slave.† Later in 160/59 Eumenes II sent to Delphi among other gifts,‡ 'slaves for the repair of the theatre and the other dedications'. In 140/39 Attalus II dispatched to Delphi three painters to restore the paintings of an unnamed monument; they were not slaves. It has been observed that the technique of the Pergamene masons was adopted by their fellow craftsmen in various cities of Greece and Asia Minor. Finally, work in the royal mines and forests was chiefly done by slaves, and it was slaves who tended the horses and live stock of the king.[332]

We do not know how work in the royal factories was organized, nor whether certain branches of industry were royal monopolies, and it is idle to speculate on these points.

Trade naturally developed side by side with agriculture and industry. Grain was certainly exported. That there were close commercial relations between the Attalids and Greece is attested by many inscriptions, while their repeated and lavish gifts of grain point to the existence of an extensive export trade in that commodity. Pitch, tar, and timber may have been exported to Egypt. Pergamene textiles and parchment were certainly not produced for home consumption only. Elaea, the harbour of Pergamon, was undoubtedly a very busy seaport.[333]

Taken together, these various signs of economic activity, incomplete and sketchy as they are, suggest that a good deal of thought and care was devoted to this branch of administration by the dynasts of Pergamon. We dimly perceive a well-devised scheme, a certain planned economy, very similar in many respects to that, much better known, of the Ptolemies. The principal aim of the two dynasties was the same: to draw

* *S.I.G.*[3] 523.

† *G.D.I.* 2001; *S.I.G.*[2], 846: *ὁ παρὰ βασιλέως Ἀττάλου ὁ ἐπὶ τῶν ἔργφν τῶν βασιλικῶν*. The slave is styled *βασιλικὰ παιδίσκα*.

‡ *καὶ σώματα εἰς τὰν ἐπισκευὰν τοῦ θεάτρου [καὶ] τῶν ἄλλων ἀναθεμάτων*, *S.I.G.*[3] 671 B 12 f.

as much revenue as possible from the land under their direct control, and to base their general policy on this foundation.

B. *BITHYNIA*

The nearest neighbour and the most dangerous rival of Pergamon was the kingdom of Bithynia in north-western Asia Minor.[334] The kingdom was not large. At the time of its greatest territorial expansion it consisted practically of the valley of the Sangarius and of the adjacent hill and mountain land. On the north and west it extended to the coasts of the Propontis, the Thracian Bosporus, and the Euxine, and on the south to the slopes of Mount Olympus. On the east the frontier was unstable. Here stood the powerful city of Heraclea Pontica, with its large territory, almost a little kingdom, and inland ruled the Paphlagonian and Pontic kings, of whom more presently.

The country was rich. Arrian, a native of Bithynia, who knew the country well, says* that the Sangarius was navigable, that the Bithynians used to be good sailors in the past, and that they possessed a fertile territory, rich in trees and quarries, especially quarries of crystal; in general the country abounded in all sorts of products. So it was in the past, and so we may say it is now. In particular the forests of Bithynia were and still are famous and extensive, furnishing excellent building material. The plain of Brussa and some other plains are still reputed for their fertility, and the hills and mountains provide admirable pasturage.

The country was inhabited by Thracians, who are believed to have come from the Balkan peninsula. They came in large numbers and probably absorbed the native population. They were warlike and brave and much devoted to their country and to their native rulers. They showed more political cohesion than their brethren in Europe. On the sea they were notorious as daring pirates, and had the reputation of being very hostile to foreigners. Xenophon† is explicit on this point. Since, as we shall presently see, all the harbours on the coast were occupied by Greeks, the Bithynians were driven to piracy

* *Bithyn.* frg. 20, Roos.

† *Anab.* vi. 4, 2.

instead of following peaceful avocations as merchants and sailors.

Their coast was at a very early date occupied by Greeks. Calchedon on the Bosporus and Astacus on the gulf of Astacus were early Megarian colonies. Opposite Astacus lay Olbia. Farther to the west lay Cius, a colony of Miletus, and Myrlea, a colony of Colophon. The Bithynian coast of the Euxine is very inhospitable. The first moderately good harbour is that of Heraclea Pontica, which likewise was occupied by Megarians at an early date. Some minor Greek towns near Heraclea depended on that city. Thus the Thracians of Bithynia were almost entirely cut off from the sea, and for the disposal of their produce they were at the mercy of their Greek neighbours, especially the strongest and richest of them—Cyzicus on the Propontis and Heraclea on the Euxine—who controlled the Pontic and the Mediterranean trade.

The Greek historians were well acquainted with the history of the Bithynians. Cyzicus and Heraclea had had their local historians, and the historiographers of the Bithynian kings of the Hellenistic period drew upon them for their information. The work of Nymphis, abridged by Memnon and preserved in excerpts by Photius, recorded the early story of Heraclea Pontica. It shows how well-informed writers of this type were. Arrian's *Bithynica* probably went back to the official historiographers of the Bithynian dynasty. Unfortunately Memnon's sketch is known to us in excerpts only, and the fragments of Arrian's *Bithynica* that survive are very poor and devoid of historical value.

It would be out of place to relate here the history of the Bithynian dynasty. It will suffice to set out the leading features of the policy of the rulers who founded the Hellenistic monarchy of Bithynia. Nominally vassal dynasts for a time of Persia, the Bithynian kings developed a well-defined policy of their own in the days of Alexander. Their principal aims were political independence, increase of territory, and access to the sea. This policy, initiated by Zipoites (327–280 B.C.) and carried on by his capable successors Nicomedes I (280–*c.* 255) and Ziaëlas (255–235), proved very successful. By strenuous fighting and a remarkable display of clever diplomacy, these kings contrived to maintain their independence against Alexander, Lysimachus, Seleucus I, and Antiochus I. They were no doubt responsible for bringing the Galatians into Asia Minor; but though a calamity for the rest of that region, the settlement of these Celts in Phrygia was advantageous to the Bithynians and their Pontic neighbours. The Galatians served as an efficient protection against their chief enemies, the Seleucids.

The Bithynian war of independence was accompanied by efforts to emerge from their political and economic isolation and secure a voice in the world-politics of the time. These efforts began with the provision of a Greek littoral for their Thracian kingdom. In the time of Zipoites Bithynia still had no access to the sea. When he took the title of king in 297 (the initial year of the Bithynian era), he was obliged to build his capital inland. Zipoition was the name given to this short-lived creation, an imitation of the practice of his Macedonian contemporaries. But his successor Nicomedes was able to transfer his residence to the sea. In 264 he founded opposite Astacus, which had been destroyed by Lysimachus, a brand-new Greek city named after himself, with Greek inhabitants drawn from Astacus and perhaps from Calchedon, which was at the same time to be his capital, a counterpart, as it were, of Alexandria in Egypt. This was a decisive act, designed to present Nicomedes to the Greek world as one of the group of rulers who formed the Hellenistic balance of power, a Greek king with a Greek name and a Greek capital. It is significant that Nicomedes about this time, in order to give his new capital an opportunity of developing its commercial activity, made an alliance with Philadelphus, the master of the Aegean. Nor is it less significant that before dying he appointed Philadelphus and Antigonus Gonatas on the one hand and some of the leading commercial cities of the Northern Hanse—Byzantium, Heraclea, and Cius—on the other, to be guardians of his children. Without the support of Ptolemy and Antigonus the Aegean would have been closed to him, and an alliance with Heraclea and Byzantium was a necessary condition of participation in the Pontic trade. His policy towards the Greek cities of Greece proper was naturally the same as that of his contemporaries. He endeavoured to demonstrate his philhellenism by benefactions to the great Panhellenic sanctuaries, as is shown by a statue erected to him at Olympia.*

The policy of his successor Ziaëlas was even more 'Hellenistic'. Ziaëlas did not change his Bithynian name into a Greek one, but his policy in all other respects was exactly the same as that of Nicomedes. A document has been recently discovered which is very illuminating in this connexion. The Coans, not without an understanding with Euergetes, their suzerain, had approached Ziaëlas with a request that he would recognize the *asylia* of their Asclepieion, a mark of their respect for him. The document in question is his reply to this invitation, the letter which he delivered to the Coan ambassadors (*theoroi*). In this reply we read between the lines that he perfectly understood the position of the Coans and the real aim of the embassy. He insists that he will follow the policy of his father and will remain faithful to his friendship and alliance with Euergetes. His friendliness to the Coans was in fact an expression of his feelings towards Euergetes: 'and because King Ptolemy, our friend and ally, is well disposed towards you.'† What the Coans, and behind them Ptolemy, really wanted to obtain from Ziaëlas was an assurance of his friendly and helpful attitude towards Greek merchants, who were ready to trade with him, provided they had this assurance. Ziaëlas replies quite explicitly. He assures the ambassadors that he takes good care of 'all Greeks who repair to us',‡ and in express terms he guarantees complete safety to all sea-going folk who land in Bithynia or are wrecked on its coast.[335] The general purport of his letter is clear. Come to Bithynia, he says, the time is past when Bithynian pirates used to molest merchants. The Bithynians are now friendly to strangers (*φιλόξενοι*) and no longer their enemies (*μισόξενοι*) as they were in the days of Xenophon. Contemporary literary productions inspired by the Bithynian kings undoubtedly sounded the same note. We hear an echo of it in the statement of Nicolaus of Damascus§ in which Bithynians are praised for

* Paus. v. 12. 7.

† *S.I.G.*[3] 456; Welles, *R.C.* 25, l. 22: *καὶ διὰ τὸ | τὸμ βασιλέα Πτολεμαῖον | οἰκείως διακεῖσθαι τὰ πρὸς ὑμᾶς | ὄντα ἡμέτερον φίλον καὶ σύμμαχον.*

‡ Ibid. 11: *πάν|των μὲν ἀφικνουμένω[ν] πρὸς ἡμᾶς Ἑλλήνων.*

§ Frg. 113, *F. Gr. Hist.* ii. 90, p. 389.

their friendliness to all foreigners (it reads like a challenge to Xenophon). We may perhaps see a similar meaning in the emphatic statement of Arrian referred to above* that the Bithynians were traditionally great mariners (ναυτικώτατοι), from the days of their mythical past.

Prusias I, the successor of Ziaëlas, took up the thread of his predecessors' policy. His main achievement was the completion of the Greek littoral, covering the Bithynian kernel of his territory on the seaward side with a line of refounded Greek cities bearing dynastic names. In the latter part of his reign, however, he worked in a different political atmosphere and adapted himself to it. I shall return to him and his proceedings in the next chapter. It is enough to say here that the main lines of his policy were exactly the same as those of his great predecessors.

What were the developments in the interior of Bithynia, behind the Greek screen, we are unable to say. Bithynia is one of the parts of Asia Minor that have been least explored. None of the Bithynian cities have been excavated. Discoveries on and near their sites relate mostly to Roman and Byzantine times, when Bithynia attained great prosperity. Nicaea, the city of Antigonus and Lysimachus, which was incorporated in the Bithynian kingdom some time in the period with which we are concerned, and Nicomedia, as well as some of the cities founded by Prusias I, were in Roman and Byzantine times of enormous size and of great wealth and importance. Under their ruins were buried the comparatively small and modest Hellenistic remains of an earlier age.

It is almost certain, however, that the country, the *chora* of Bithynia, was a land not of cities but of villages. It cannot be said that the Bithynian kings were great urbanizers. They strengthened and developed the Greek cities of their kingdom, but we hear nothing of their having transformed Thracian villages into cities. We hear occasionally of such foundations as Bithynium and Cressa, but we do not know exactly their location and their significance. Nor have we any idea to what extent the Bithynians adopted the Hellenistic military policy of their neighbours, the system of mercenary soldiers and

* *Frg.* 20, Roos.

military *katoikoi*. Their armies appear to have been recruited from their own subjects, reinforced by Galatian mercenaries.

A casual mention by Cicero* of *agri Bithyniae regii* conveys the idea that the land not assigned to the cities, with the exception perhaps of that in the hands of the Thracian aristocracy, was the private property of the kings. But it is useless to speculate whether this royal land was what, in the other Hellenistic kingdoms, was known as *χώρα* or *χώρα βασιλική*, that is to say, the whole of the territory of the kingdom (except the territories of the Greek cities), or merely extensive private estates of the king. Some suggestions on this point will be found in Chapter VII.

Nor do we know anything of the economic policy of the kings: their relations with the cities, their taxation, their development of the natural resources of the country. Their commercial policy shows that it was prosperous and had much to export. Beyond this very general statement we cannot go.

C. *PONTUS AND PAPHLAGONIA*

Bithynia, however peculiar her structure and evolution may appear to us, belonged geographically and culturally to the western section of Asia Minor, which from time immemorial had been connected with western Europe and particularly with Greece. Its eastern neighbours, Paphlagonia and Pontus or Pontic Cappadocia, were in a totally different position. They formed the western sector of the eastern interior of Asia Minor, of that part of Asia Minor which looks to the East, not to the West, and has for its home waters the landlocked Black Sea, once an Iranian, Scytho-Persian lake.[336]

Though closely connected with the rest of the eastern interior of Asia Minor, the Pontic portion of this sector occupies a peculiar position among the territories of eastern Asia Minor. The mountainous land bordering the coast of the Black Sea and the regions north and east of the deep channel of the river Halys have a more varied climate and are more diverse in character than the Anatolian plateau. The mountains that branch off from the Caucasus and run west in a direction parallel to the southern shore of the Black Sea are intersected

* *De leg. agr.* ii. 50.

by rivers which work their way painfully towards the coast. Short and swift in the east, they become longer and less torrential as they lie more towards the west. Three of them—the Thermodon, the famous river of the Amazons, the Iris, and the Halys—form in their lower courses wide fertile deltas, which are the only points where the Pontic coast affords a possibility of harbourage from some of the storms of the inhospitable sea (*Pontos Axeinos*).

Behind the coast the country is a succession of river-valleys, broad lakes, gentle hills, and high mountains. The climate is much milder than that of the Cappadocian table-land, less hot in summer and less cold in winter. The vegetation is luxuriant and the soil is very fertile. Pontus had the reputation of being a rich land: its characteristic products are said to have included cattle, sheep, and horses, agricultural crops, fruits, especially grapes and olives, and the famous Pontic nuts and cherries—a name said to be derived from Cerasus, a Greek city on the coast—and an amazing profusion of flowers and aromatic shrubs.

Even more important was the mineral wealth of the eastern part of Pontus, consisting especially of iron, but comprising also copper and silver. It was the mining district *par excellence* of the Near East; and the almost unanimous tradition of the ancient world ascribed the 'invention' of iron and steel to the clever smiths of the Chalybes. For hundreds of years caravans had carried the metals of Pontus to Assyria, Babylonia, Syria, Phoenicia, and Palestine on the one side, and to the capitals of the Hittites and their successors, to the shores of the Propontis and of the Dardanelles, and to the western coast of Asia Minor on the other. It was not long, however, before the Greeks realized the advantage of the Black Sea route over the land routes for the conveyance of the metals to their country. This was the beginning of the Greek colonization of the south coast of the Black Sea.

Trapezus, the port of the mining districts, and Sinope, the clearing-house for the metal trade, were the earliest foundations, and they kept this trade in their hands for centuries. The next settlement was Amisus, the Piraeus of the Black Sea, a rival of Sinope for the trade with the Crimea, and, last of all Heraclea, above referred to, and the minor towns which later formed the city of Amastris, communities connected closely with the Crimean Chersonesus* and thus rivals both of Amisus and of Sinope.

The Greek cities of the Pontic coast formed a world of their own. Their connexions were all with their sister cities on the Black Sea and with the West. They were little concerned with the land of Pontus, which geographically turned its back on the sea and on the cities of the coast. The Greek cities, therefore, had very little influence on the conditions prevailing among the Pontic valleys, hills, and mountains. Life there remained for centuries exactly what it had been before the Greek colonization of the coast.

Pontus, with Cappadocia, was for a long time the centre of the great Hittite Empire, an empire distinguished for its developed and peculiar civilization and singular social and economic structure. Under Persian domination it became one of the chief strongholds of Anatolian Iranism, which is little known and has been little studied. These traditions never died out in the Pontic territories and retained their influence in Hellenistic and Roman times. We have already come upon them when describing the little we know of the Seleucid dominions in the interior of Asia Minor. But in no part of that region were they so strong as in Pontus and Cappadocia, and none is known to us in its social and economic aspect by so full and trustworthy a description. For Pontus was the native country of Strabo, and his exceptionally detailed account reveals to us the sources of its strength and the causes of its historic role in the Hellenistic period. I shall return to the subject in Chapter VI when dealing with Cappadocia, and will confine myself here to what we know of Pontus.

It is evident that the Pontic kingdom and its political, social, and economic structure, as described by Strabo, were not the creation of the dynasty of the Mithridatids, but a slightly hellenized heritage from the Hittites and the Persians. The country was ruled by the king, and his fortified residences were scattered all over it. The capital city under the early Mithridatids was Amasia, whose citadel was held by a garrison under

* An Ionian city refounded by the Megarians, a Dorian *polis* like Heraclea.

PLATE LXIV

1. Top of a clay askos in the form of a mountain goat, found at Karasamsun (pl. LXV). Brown clay covered with a white slip and painted bright red and dull brown. H. 0·10.

2. Top of a clay askos of the same type as no. 1 in the form of a mountain sheep. The same clay and paint as no. 1. H. 0·10.

3. Clay bowl of brown clay covered originally with red glaze, the greater part of which has scaled off. Found in South Russia but made either in Asia Minor or more probably in Syria. Late Hellenistic or rather early Roman *terra sigillata*. The decoration consists of three zones. In the lowest are represented (in relief) horsemen with lentil-shaped shields facing each other and separated by Egyptian divine crowns standing between ears of corn. The middle zone shows naked warriors running to the right, wearing peculiar helmets and holding in their hands trident-like lances and semi-oval shields. Above them a narrow frieze of dolphins. The warriors may be interpreted as mythological beings (Corybants?), but are more probably fighting natives of Syria, the enemies here of Hellenistic civilization. Unpublished.

I owe the description of the objects on this and the following plate to the kindness of Prof. R. Zahn of Berlin. On the pottery of Amisus represented by nos. 1 and 2 see my remarks and bibliography in n. 355 of this chapter. Vases in the form of crouching animals (somewhat similar to the Greek askoi) and rhyta terminating in the foreparts of animals are typical products of Cappadocia and Pontus. In the Louvre and in the Ottoman Museum, Istanbul, there are several intact vases of this type, found mostly near Karasamsun. According to Genouillac and Prof. R. Zahn the painted vases in the form of animals begin in the seventh century under strong Ionian (and I would add Iranian) influence and last until the early Hellenistic period. In Zahn's opinion the vases here reproduced belong not to class XXIV of Genouillac (VIIth–Vth cent.) but to class XXV (IVth–IIIrd cent.). At Karasamsun they were apparently found together with fragments of Hellenistic pottery. We must await the publication of the results of the excavations of Macridy Bey at Karasamsun to form a final judgement about the evolution of this type of pottery, so typical of the mixed civilization of Cappadocia and Pontus.

Photographs supplied by the authorities of the Staatliche Museen, Berlin.

1.

2.

3.

Anatolian Pottery

Berlin, Staatliche Museen

1. Berlin, Staatliche Museen

2. Paris, Louvre

3. Berlin, Staatliche Museen

Berlin, Staatliche Museen

TERRACOTTAS OF AMISUS

PLATE LXV

1. Mask of a Satyr woman or Satyr girl (some restorations). H. 0·19.

2. Mask of Dionysus. H. about 0·102.

3. Caricature head of a statuette, perhaps of a slave, laughing. H. 0·053.

4. Fragmentary group of a boy and girl kissing each other. The girl holds in her left hand a bird or a purse. Fine work. H. 0·08.

The terracottas reproduced in this plate are specimens of clay figurines found in large quantities at Karasamsun, near Samsun (ancient Amisus) and now in various Museums. With them were found sherds of Pergamene relief pottery. Their style is very similar to that of the terracottas made at Pergamon. But some peculiarities of the style and the character of the clay make it certain that they were all made in one or several Amisene workshops, and not imported from Pergamon. IIIrd–IInd centuries B.C. The Amisene terracottas have never been collected, published, and illustrated, though they fully deserve it.

Photographs for 1, 3, and 4 supplied by the authorities of the Staatliche Museen, Berlin; for 2 by the authorities of the Louvre, Paris.

the command of a military governor. In the citadel were the palace of the king and a large altar dedicated to the divine protector of the dynasty, the Iranian Ahuramazda (whom the Greeks called Zeus Stratios), an indication of the strongly Iranian character of the ruling family. The kings were buried in rock-cut tombs of Anatolian type beneath the citadel. The other royal residences, Gaziura and Cabeira, were probably similar to Amasia.

Pontus was subdivided according to Eastern traditions, which were likewise adopted by the Seleucids and the Parthians, into districts or provinces called eparchies, under governors whose Greek title was *strategos*. Alongside of the fortified strongholds of the kings, the ruling aristocracy had similar strongholds distributed about the country. Strabo mentions several of them. The owners of these castles and of the land around them were feudal barons, most of them of Iranian origin; one of these, known from a Greek inscription, is called Pharnabazus, while his vassal bears a Greek or hellenized name—Meriones.[337] There were no cities of the Greek type in Pontus, other than the Greek cities of the coast. The typical form of settlement was the village. The rich plain near Amasia was called Chiliokomon (the plain of the thousand villages) and we are told that Murena, in one raid, overran four hundred villages.

Temples played a leading part in the life of the country. They were dedicated to gods of various origin—the Cappadocian Ma, the Anatolian Men Pharnaku, the Iranian Anaitis with her two acolytes, the above-mentioned Zeus Stratios—but they were all organized in the Oriental manner. A chief priest was the representative of the god or goddess and the ruler of the temple and its territory. Vast stretches of land were cultivated by peasants who regarded themselves as 'slaves' of the god. In the temple itself dwelt large numbers of similar 'slaves' who attended to it under the direction of various priests. An important part in the life of the temple was played by girl-slaves, the temple prostitutes.

Many temples were centres of industry and trade. Such was that in the large village of Comana in Pontus, the chief emporium of trade with Armenia. It possessed 6,000 sacred slaves or serfs, and the town and temple were noted for their luxury and dissipated life, a paradise for soldiers and merchants. No less famous was the temple of Anaitis at Zela.

In the towns, villages, and temples lived a mixed, heterogeneous population. We hear without surprise that twenty-two languages were spoken in Pontus, for we may recall the number of languages represented in the clay tablets discovered in the various centres of the Hittite Empire.

It is unfortunate that we have no archaeological remains to illustrate the description of Strabo. For Pontus, like Bithynia, has never been thoroughly explored by archaeologists. None of the temple ruins have been excavated. The little information we have comes from the Greek cities of the coast. An occasional document illuminates some aspect of the life of the interior, but does not enable us to visualize it.

Such was the State which, appearing on the political horizon in the period we are considering, was destined to exert a certain influence on the evolution of the Hellenistic world, especially in the last phase of its existence. But if Mithridates VI was able to play so important a part in its later history, this was due not only to his ambition and energy, but also to the resources that had been accumulated for him by his less well-known predecessors.

We have very little knowledge of the early history of the Mithridatids. The founder of the dynasty was an Iranian noble of Pontic Asia Minor, perhaps one of the city tyrants of the late fourth century B.C., a ruler of the city of Cius on the Propontis. He, in his old age, and his son, also named Mithridates, were in the camp of Antigonus in 302 B.C. and were prepared to betray him. The old Mithridates perished, the son survived, and after Ipsus established his residence in Paphlagonian Kimiata, one of the strongholds I have spoken of. From Kimiata as his centre he began to build up his kingdom.

The policy that he and his successors adopted was the same as that of the Bithynian kings. Its main objects were to rule in independence over their kingdom, to extend its territory as far as possible, and to open the country to the outer world by obtaining control of the Greek cities of the Black Sea coast.

Early in their rule they got possession of Amastris, which

was handed over to them by its dynast Eumenes in 279 B.C., when Mithridates II was sharing his rule with his brother Ariobarzanes. They next extended their control to the large, wealthy, and glorious city of Amisus. About 255 B.C. according to Memnon,* when Mithridates III was busy fighting the Galatians, Heraclea sent grain to Amisus for the king's requirements. But although Amisus was dependent on the Pontic kings, it was not subject to them. The early Mithridatids never thought of making it their capital. Sinope, on the other hand, the queen of the trade of the Euxine, defied their attempts to acquire it and maintained its complete independence. It was not until 183 (see below) that, by seizing Sinope, the Mithridatids completed their conquest of the littoral and were able to claim equality with the other Hellenistic monarchies.

It was of no less vital importance to the early Mithridatids to extend their power towards the East, and obtain control of the great mining regions. To what extent they succeeded is unknown. It was reserved for Pharnaces I, the contemporary of Prusias I, to take the decisive steps by which his kingdom was transformed into a wealthy and powerful Hellenistic State.

D. *GALATIA*

I have several times alluded to the effect on the political and economic development of the minor monarchies of Asia Minor produced by the existence in the heart of that region of a body of foreign conquerors and professional robbers who had settled down there and organized a strong State. These were the Galatians. A few words may be said about the social and economic structure of this alien community.

Some time in the early third century B.C. organized bands of Gauls occupied a large part of Great Phrygia on the middle Sangarius and Halys, comprising a stretch of land about 190 miles long and 100 miles broad. They did so either by forcible pressure on, or with the tacit consent of, the nominal overlords of the country, whoever they may have been at the time, whether the Seleucids, the Pontic or Bithynian kings, or Attalus I. In any case, when we first hear about their constitution and their manners and habits, at the time of the expedition of

* Memnon 24.

Cn. Manlius Vulso in 189 B.C.,* they were not newcomers and had adopted a settled mode of life.[338]

The country which they occupied was not very attractive. The greater part of it was rough and inhospitable, hardly convenient for agriculture. Some regions produced satisfactory crops only in years of good rainfall. The people whom the Gaulish hordes found in Galatia were the Phrygians, themselves conquerors superimposed on still older strata of population. They looked back to a long and glorious past. Heirs of the so-called Hittites, they were all-powerful in their own domain for a long series of years until, decimated by the Cimmerians, they were forced to submit first to the Lydians, and then to the Persians. In the Persian Empire they formed part of an important satrapy and later saw their country invaded by Alexander. In Hellenistic times their territory retained its political importance, for through it ran one of the most convenient highways that connected the eastern and western parts of Alexander's empire.

Many cities of venerable antiquity, unaffected by Greek civilization, many famous Oriental temples, and thousands of villages were scattered over the country. The most important cities were Pessinus, the home of the Great Mother Cybele, Gordium, the capital of the ancient Phrygian kingdom, and Ancyra. Like Pessinus, Ancyra and Gordium had undoubtedly their own famous temples. All, but especially Gordium, were centres of local trade and stations at the crossing of important roads. We know practically nothing of the life of these notable cities.

It was certainly under the pressure of hard necessity that the leading powers of the third century agreed to the Galatian occupation of a part of Asia Minor that was of such political and economic consequence. Settled where they were, the Galatians made any sort of unification of eastern Asia Minor impossible and rendered communications between Syria and the western coast of Asia Minor somewhat difficult.

Masters of the country, the Galatians spread all over it. Their three 'tribes' occupied each one part of it, the Tolistoagians (or Tolistobogians) settling in the west, the Tectosages

* The authorities are Polybius xxi, 33–41, and Livy xxxviii, 12–27.

in the centre, the Trocmi in the east. Pessinus and Gordium lay in the section occupied by the first-named.

A peculiar situation was thus created. A small group of foreign conquerors superimposed itself on a native population of alien race, with an entirely different religion, economic and social structure, and civilization. These conquerors were not mere barbarians: they brought with them their own deeply rooted tribal and cantonal organization, their own political, social, and economic institutions, an efficient military system and equipment, a high material civilization and artistic skill. These characteristics are well known from the reports of Greek and Roman writers on the western branches of the Celtic nation in Spain, Italy, France, Britain, and Germany, as well as from methodical and successful excavations of Celtic castles, villages, and cemeteries in both West and East (especially in Czechoslovakia, Rumania, and South Russia). The only Celtic settlements about which information fails are those in the north-eastern part of the Balkan peninsula and in Asia Minor.[339]

The small body of Celtic immigrants found in Phrygia, amid unsettled and perhaps somewhat chaotic political conditions, an old and firmly established social and economic system, a highly organized religion, and a peculiar civilization mirrored alike in monumental and imposing rock tombs and sanctuaries, adorned with elaborate sculptures, and in many inscriptions in native script dating from pre-Greek and from Greek and Hellenistic times. The few excavations that have been carried out in Phrygia have all aimed at the discovery of the earliest remains of civilized life in the country. None has yielded important material relating to the Phrygian, Lydian, and Persian periods of its history. Whatever this life may have been, it was certainly based on deeply rooted tradition.

It is more than probable that in the first two hundred years of their domination in Phrygia, the Galatians made no serious attempt to merge the Phrygian civilization in their own. They were a mere handful, while the Phrygians certainly numbered several hundreds of thousands. On the other hand, in the early period of their rule, they remained wholly unaffected by the Phrygian civilization. The accounts of Polybius and

Livy mentioned above show that they maintained in Asia Minor their hereditary political, social, and economic customs. It is needless to give once more a general account of these. Any good description of the life of the western Celts, such as is given in the chief books devoted to them, will be found to reproduce, one by one, all the features of Celtic life in Galatia as portrayed by Polybius and Livy—tribal organization, tribal kings and cantonal tetrarchs, clans of aristocratic families, military retinues attendant upon kings, tetrarchs, and chiefs of leading families, life in fortified castles forming the centres of large estates, on which agriculture and grazing were carried on for the landlords by native peasants and shepherds. Such were the general features of Celtic life, and they were everywhere the same, in Gaul, Spain, Italy, Britain, on the Danube, in the northern Balkan peninsula, in South Russia, and in Anatolian Galatia.

A question peculiar to Galatia was that of the relations between the Gauls and the cities and temples of the country. On this point we have no information. It appears that in the early period of their domination they avoided the cities and never made them the capitals of their three tribal States. They were probably content to levy a substantial tribute from them. The Celts were a deeply religious and superstitious people and they would hardly dare to encroach unduly on the rights of the temples of the powerful gods of their new country. We may even suppose that the religion of Asia Minor influenced their own. This we may infer from a study of some of the vessels of silver and bronze used in Celtic religious worship, which have been found both in the West and in the East: these seem to me to show unmistakably the influence of Eastern religious ideas and Eastern artistic style.[340]

However, as time went on, the relations between the temples and the Galatian chiefs became more intimate. We hear repeatedly in the late Pergamene period, and subsequently in the time of the Roman protectorate, of Galatians taking an active and prominent part in the life of the great temples, especially that of Pessinus, as chief priests of the sanctuaries.[341]

Isolated in their castles (φρούρια), ruling over many thousands of peasants and shepherds dwelling in open villages, the Galatian

PLATE LXVI

Head of a Galatian warrior. It belongs to the figure of the Galatian of the famous Ludovisi group (a Galatian killing himself after having killed his wife). The group is well known. It is a Roman copy in marble of one of the votive offerings of Attalus I (in bronze) which once stood in the court of the temple of Athena at Pergamon. For a stylistic analysis in the light of other products of the Pergamene school of sculpture see the papers quoted in the description of pl. LXIII. Photograph supplied by Alinari.

A Galatian

Rome, Museo Nazionale delle Terme Diocleziane

1. Berlin, Staatliche Museen

2. Berlin, Staatliche Museen

3. Berlin, Staatliche Museen

4. New York, Coll. E. T. Newell

OBJECTS ILLUSTRATING CELTIC LIFE IN HELLENISTIC TIMES AND LIFE IN ASIA MINOR AND SOUTH RUSSIA

PLATE LXVII

1. Terracotta statuette found in the necropolis of either Myrina or Cyme. Perfect specimen of the realistic sculpture of the early third century B.C. The statuette represents a Galatian standing frontwise wearing long hair and dressed in a heavy cloak (otherwise naked). In his right hand he holds a short sword. The statuette represents one of those Galatians who invaded Asia Minor, not one of the later mercenaries of the Hellenistic kings. H. 0, 14. P. Bienkowski, *Les Celtes dans les arts mineurs gréco-romains*, 1928, p. 126, no. 1; cf. nos. 2 and 3, another statuette of a Galatian of the same type represented in the act of fighting with a dagger in his right hand and an oval shield in his left.

2. Sherd of the Hellenistic period from Karasamsun. Light brown clay, covered on one side with white wash on which the decoration (ivy) is in brownish-yellowish bright and deep brown dull colours. H. 0, 077. Cf. pl. LXIV.

3. An unguentarium of the west slope ware of Athens, found at Panticapaeum. H. 0, 105. Reproduced here owing to lack of room on the next plate. Illustrates the commercial relations between Athens and Panticapaeum in Hellenistic times.

Photographs supplied by the authorities of the Staatliche Museen, Berlin.

4. Celtic Danubian imitations of Hellenistic coins. *a*. Imitation of Alexander. *b*. Imitation of Philip. *c*. Imitation of Thasos. Casts supplied by Dr. E. T. Newell.

Cf. K. Pink, *Die Münzprägung der Ostkelten und ihrer Nachbarn*, 1939, and below, Ch. VI, nn. 11 and 30.

chiefs and their retinues lived in all probability a lazy and sometimes luxurious life. Very few, if any, of them were active tillers of the soil, shepherds, artisans, or merchants. Their leisure was from time to time interrupted by wars and by raids into the countries of their neighbours, both of which usually served to increase substantially their fabulous wealth. Many members of the large and ever increasing retinues of the chiefs, young men greedy of adventure and of gain, enrolled in the armies of the Hellenistic kings as mercenaries. Those who survived and did not settle in the countries ruled by their employers returned to their native country with their belts full of Seleucid, Ptolemaic, Pontic, Bithynian, Macedonian, and perhaps even Bactrian gold and silver.[342]

Some idea of the wealth accumulated in the castles of the nobles may be gathered from the accounts of the first expedition that penetrated into Galatia since the Gauls settled in their new home, that of Cn. Manlius Vulso, and from the reports of the booty that he secured and subsequently brought in part to Rome. No less illuminating in this respect is an isolated literary text little used by modern scholars, which, however, refers probably not to the Anatolian but to the Thracian Galatae. This is a fragment of an ethnographical excursus by the historian Phylarchus, referring to an episode of the year 265/4 B.C. It describes how Ariamnes, one of the Galatian chiefs and a very rich man, organized a mass entertainment (probably in the region under his control) for all the Galatae who might come from the villages and the cities of the country, and also for all *ξένοι* who happened to be travelling on the roads that crossed the territory of the entertainer. The entertainment took place in large tents erected on the roads. It consisted of huge meals of meat, bread, and wine. A curious detail is the mention of large brass kettles for boiling the meat, which Ariamnes ordered from the best craftsmen of the cities. They remind us of the kettle of Gundestrup and of the similar large kettles of the Scythian, Sarmatian, and Mongolian nomads.[343]

E. *THE CITY-STATES OF THE EUXINE AND THE BOSPORAN KINGDOM*

The momentous changes effected by the Ptolemies and the Seleucids and the strenuous exertions of the minor kings of Asia Minor considerably altered the economic aspect of the Aegean world. The improved methods of production, the intensified efforts of the population, the planned economy of the kings, all contributed to this change. The quantity of products offered for sale was now much increased, the exchange of commodities was better organized, and commercial relations were carefully watched by the powerful rulers of the time, each protecting his own trade in various ways.

The supply of commodities was increasing rapidly and so was the demand. I have explained how the number of Greek buyers who had purchased all sorts of merchandise in the past was now enlarged by the settlement of Greeks in the East, and how the native population there gradually became accustomed to Greek products.

The general orientation of economic relations in the Aegean was in consequence changing, and the change affected in some measure all the States that hitherto had been prominent in trade, especially the Greek cities of the mainland, of the Greek islands, and of Asia Minor. I have endeavoured to show in the preceding pages how it influenced the trend of economic development in Athens, Rhodes, Delos, and Miletus.

Alongside of these—the principal marts and the most prosperous communities of the Aegean world—there were a number of other important cities which had played an active, even a leading, part in the Greek economic system of the pre-Hellenistic period. These were the cities that held the keys of the northern trade, especially the trade with the coasts of the Black Sea. There were six groups of these, which took part in the organization and regulation of the trade: (1) the Hellespontine group, especially Sestus, Abydus, and Lampsacus; (2) the Propontid group, of which Cyzicus was the undisputed leader; (3) the group of the Thracian Bosporus, Byzantium and Calchedon; (4) that of the southern or 'right-hand' coast of the Euxine, of which the great commercial cities of Heraclea, Amisus, and Sinope were pre-eminent; (5) that of the western or 'left-hand' coast of the Euxine, including Apollonia, Callatis, Odessus, Tomi, and Istrus; and lastly (6) the group of the northern coast of the Euxine and of the Crimea, including Olbia, Panticapaeum and its dependencies, and Chersonesus.

Each of these groups had its share in the great trade that was carried on between the Pontic and the Aegean worlds. It must be remembered that for about two centuries the countries round the Aegean had drawn from the Euxine their main supplies of foodstuffs (especially fish and grain, and also honey), of metals (particularly iron), of various raw materials (such as flax from the Caucasus, hides, hemp, and wax), and of slaves.* To these may be added certain eastern merchandise brought by caravan trade from Asia to the Euxine by one of the two routes leading thereto: the northern, which ran north of the Caspian Sea and ended at Panticapaeum, and the southern, the Caucasian route, of which the terminals on the Euxine were the Greek cities of its eastern coast—Phasis and Dioscurias.

Olbia, Panticapaeum, and Chersonesus on the one hand and the cities of the 'left-hand' coast of the Black Sea on the other, forwarded the merchandise thus imported as well as that produced in their own territories and in that of their Scythian, Taurian, and Thracian neighbours, to the Greek cities of the Aegean. The cities of the 'right-hand' or southern coast of the Euxine traded not only in the products of that littoral, in particular iron, copper, and silver, but also in goods brought from the Caucasus and Armenia. Byzantium and Calchedon, besides being ports of call for all ships passing through the Thracian Bosporus, possessed productive fisheries. Cyzicus was the great clearing-house for the trade of the Euxine, and a centre of prosperous banking. And finally Lampsacus, Abydus, and Sestus controlled the Dardanelles, Lampsacus moreover playing on a smaller scale the same part as Cyzicus.

The new economic trend of the Hellenistic period, the shift of its centre towards Asia Minor, Syria, and Egypt, profoundly affected the Euxine trade, which ceased to have the same

* Polyb. iv. 38.

importance for Greece as in the past. The volume of this trade inevitably declined. But the extent of the decline must not be exaggerated. Pontic fish had no rival, and the demand for it was in fact increasing rather than decreasing. It was the staple food of the Greeks and there was a large consumption of it wherever they settled. Nor was grain ever produced in the ancient world in quantities sufficient to satisfy requirements. The demand for Pontic grain was probably no longer as keen as it had been; grain in general became cheaper, but it is certain that Pontic grain could easily compete with that of Egypt, Anatolia, and Syria. The same is true of raw materials, particularly metals. The supply of metals on the Greek market was never very abundant, and the Pontic mines were still one of the few sources of this supply. On the other hand, the demand, especially for iron, was urgent; large quantities were needed, above all for military purposes and for the improved methods of agriculture.[344]

We know very little of the economic activities of the leading commercial cities of the north. We possess some evidence relating to political vicissitudes, their struggle for independence, and their interrelations, but our sources are almost silent about what was the principal factor in their lives—their trade. Certain facts, however, are known, and a few words may be devoted to some of the chief cities of the northern Hanse.

Cyzicus. Cyzicus still dominated the commerce of the Propontis.[345] No doubt the famous 'Cyzicenes', pre-eminently the currency of the Euxine trade from the sixth to the fourth century B.C., were no longer minted. Nor do we hear that the 'Cyzicenes' were replaced by other coins minted by the city for the purposes of its foreign trade. This may be explained by its diminishing importance as a clearing-house and centre of banking. We may, on the other hand, attribute the disappearance of the 'Cyzicenes' chiefly to the fact that they had ceased to be of use. There was now an abundance of excellent and reliable coins. First Philip, then Alexander, and finally Lysimachus, had issued such enormous quantities of currency that there was practically no need for Cyzicus to mint her own money for trade purposes. The place of the 'Cyzicenes' was taken by the coinage of Lysimachus, which became the current medium of exchange for the Euxine trade.*[346]

On the other hand, we know that Cyzicus in the Hellenistic period remained as opulent, as beautiful, and as well-ordered a city as in the past. Strabo is explicit on the subject, in his well-known description of Hellenistic Cyzicus, that is to say, of Cyzicus before the time of Mithridates. After a short account of the large island or peninsula of Cyzicus, he proceeds:† 'The city rivals the foremost cities of Asia in size and beauty and in its excellent system of government for peace and war. Its adornment appears to be of a type similar to that of Rhodes, Massalia, and ancient Carthage. Passing over most details, I may mention that it has three architects who take care of the public buildings and the engines of war, and three storehouses, one for arms, another for engines of war, and another for corn, which is prevented from rotting by mixture with Chalcidic earth.' Since the passage that follows relates to the siege of the city by Mithridates, it is certain that he borrowed his description of it from a Hellenistic source. Moreover it is evident that the splendour of Cyzicus was not the creation of late Hellenistic times.

The statement of Strabo is supported by the few facts of the history of the city that are known to us. It appears probable that it never submitted to any of the Hellenistic rulers after Alexander. At least there is nothing which leads us to think that it was a subject city either of Antigonus, Lysimachus, or Seleucus I. It may have been their ally and may have contributed to their expenses, but it probably retained its political independence. This is shown by its successful struggle with Arrhidaeus, and by its relations with its nearest neighbours, Bithynia and Pergamon. These never dared to attack it. I have already referred to an inscription which suggests that

* See ch. III, notes 38, 49, and 52.

† xii. 8. 11, p. 575 f: *ἔστι δ' ἐνάμιλλος ταῖς πρώταις τῶν κατὰ τὴν Ἀσίαν ἡ πόλις μεγέθει τε καὶ κάλλει καὶ εὐνομίᾳ πρός τε εἰρήνην καὶ πόλεμον. ἔοικέ τε τῷ παραπλησίῳ τύπῳ κοσμεῖσθαι ὥσπερ ἡ τῶν Ῥοδίων καὶ Μασσαλιωτῶν καὶ Καρχηδονίων τῶν πάλαι· τὰ μὲν οὖν πολλὰ ἐῶ, τρεῖς δ' ἀρχιτέκτονας τοὺς ἐπιμελουμένους οἰκοδομημάτων τε δημοσίων καὶ ὀργάνων, τρεῖς δὲ καὶ θησαυροὺς κέκτηται, τὸν μὲν ὅπλων, τὸν δ' ὀργάνων, τὸν δὲ σίτου· ποιεῖ δὲ σῖτον ἄσεπτον ἡ Χαλκιδικὴ γῆ μιγνυμένη.*

Cyzicus was in a kind of alliance (*symmachia*) with Philetaerus of Pergamon, and its relations with Bithynia were probably similar.[347]

This is not surprising, for in fact the city was in itself a *dynasteia* of moderate size. Its territory was large and fertile. Strabo describes the ample provision of foodstuffs stored in its granaries. The land belonging to it was in part occupied by its own citizens, in part cultivated by Phrygian serfs (λαοί). We know that this was the position of the neighbouring city of Zeleia and of the adjoining territory, which was royal land (χώρα βασιλική) of the Seleucids. There is good reason to think that Cyzicus had as many serfs as its neighbours.[348] It was therefore able not only to provide for the requirements of its large population and of temporary residents who came from all parts of the world at the time of the famous fair, but also to export part of the produce of its territory, such as wine and fish, and certain industrial products, such as unguents.[349]

Lampsacus. Lampsacus was a minor Cyzicus, as is shown by its abundant coinage, at first of electron and in the fourth century of gold—the 'Lampsacenes'. This coinage shared the fate of that of Cyzicus and for the same reasons. We know less of Lampsacus than of Cyzicus. But Strabo* describes it in terms comparable to those which he applies to Cyzicus: 'Lampsacus, too, lies on the sea, a notable city with a good harbour, and flourishing like Abydus.' We have proof of the importance of Cyzicus and Lampsacus in the trade of the time, for example, in the role played by their citizens at Delos (above, p. 232).[350]

Byzantium. Next to Cyzicus in fame, beauty, importance, and wealth was Byzantium, the queen of the Thracian Bosporus.[351] Polybius describes its situation and importance with lucidity and precision.† 'On the side of the sea,' he says, 'the situation of Byzantium is the most advantageous of any city in our quarter of the world so far as security and prosperity are concerned, while on the land side it is in both respects the most unfavourable of all. For by sea it so completely commands

* xiii. 1. 18, p. 589: καὶ ἡ Λάμψακος δ' ἐπὶ θαλάττῃ πόλις ἐστὶν εὐλίμενος καὶ ἀξιόλογος συμμένουσα καλῶς ὥσπερ καὶ Ἄβυδος.

† iv. 38.

the mouth of the Pontus, that no merchant can sail in or out against its will.' And after having described the character of the Pontic trade in general he proceeds: 'Therefore as common benefactors of all Greeks, the Byzantines might justly expect to receive not only gratitude but also the united assistance of the Greeks when dangers threaten them from the barbarians.'

Polybius is describing Byzantium as it was in 219 B.C. There is nothing in what he says to suggest that its wealth and influence were then less than they had been, or that its trade and importance were declining. His statement is fully supported by what little we know of the city's history in the Hellenistic period. After the time of Alexander it was able to assert its political independence. It came to the rescue of Cyzicus when that city was attacked by Arrhidaeus, the satrap of Hellespontine Phrygia (above, note 347); it must be remembered that Byzantium and Cyzicus were neighbours, for the former owned part of the territory near the Lake of Dascylium of which another part was owned by the latter.* It did not actively participate in the struggles of the stormy times of the Successors and maintained close relations with all the powers that controlled the Pontic trade; Callatis, the Bosporan rulers, and Sinope.† Its main endeavour was to support the interests of the Pontic cities. After Ipsus, though situated in the centre of Lysimachus' empire, it managed to retain its freedom.‡ After Corupedion it took an active part in the war in which the great trading cities of the Euxine (including Heraclea, Calchedon, Cius, and Tius) resisted the threat of Seleucus I to the independence of Heraclea.§ Later it may have remained a member of the Northern League when this league (which included Nicomedes of Bithynia, Antigonus Gonatas, and Heraclea) was fighting Antiochus I (279 B.C.).‖ The city suffered severely in the great Celtic storm. The strong Celtic State of Tylis was formed in its immediate neighbourhood and Byzantium was forced to pay it a yearly tribute. The amount of the tribute was between 10 and 33 talents, rising to 80 talents

* Strabo, xii. 8. 11, p. 576.

† Diod. xx. 25.

‡ Plut. *Moral.* 338 B.

§ Memnon 11.

‖ Ibid. 18, cf. 19.

shortly before 220 B.C. That the city should have been able to pay this is evidence of its great wealth.

The power and influence of Byzantium were recognized by Nicomedes I when he appointed it, together with the rulers who at that time were strongest at sea, Philadelphus and Gonatas, guardian of his children.* It showed its strength, during the domestic war between the members of the Pontic Hanse, by forcing Callatis and Istrus to desist from their ambitious attempt to establish an exclusive control of the waters of the western Euxine, and to break the resistance of Tomi.† Finally, with the help of Philadelphus, the master of the Aegean, and a strong detachment of the fleet of Heraclea, it was able to withstand a siege by Antiochus II.‡ Of its later destinies and the great war for the freedom of the straits of Rhodes I shall speak in the next chapter.

The wealth and importance of some of the Byzantine merchants of the third century B.C. are attested by the decree of Delos in honour of Dionysius of Byzantium, who sold 500 medimni of grain to Delos at a favourable price.§ And Dionysius was no exception.|| The power of Byzantium rested not only on its revenue from trade. Like Cyzicus it owned a large territory¶ and very productive fisheries.** Its territory was strongly fortified and was cultivated by serfs.†† In fact, like the other larger Pontic cities, it was a territorial State of considerable size and inhabited by a large population.

Heraclea. The chief cities of the southern coast of the Euxine present similar features. The best known is Heraclea, a large territorial State owning an extensive 'territory,' settled and cultivated by Mariandynoi. It is a classical example of a State whose prosperity was founded on the labour of serfs (*λαοί*), frequently quoted in the theoretical speculations of the

* Memnon 22. † Ibid. 21. ‡ Ibid. 23.

§ *I.G.* xi. 4. 627; Durrbach, *Choix* 46.

|| See Durrbach ad loc. and above, p. 232.

¶ Polyb. iv. 45. 7, and for a later period Tac. *Ann.* xii, 63; Dio Chrys. xxxv, 25; Herodian iii, 1, 5.

** Aristotle, *Pol.*, p. 1291 b, 23; Archestr. in Athen. vii, 303 e, and Ps.-Hesiod ibid. iii, 116 b, cf. 116 f. and 117 a.

†† Polyb. iv. 52. 7: Prusias I restored to the Byzantines *τάς τε χώρας καὶ τὰ φρούρια καὶ τοὺς λαούς*.

fourth century B.C. on social and economic questions. This is not the place to discuss its history as recorded by Nymphis and Memnon and preserved in the excerpts of Photius. The 'tyranny' which lasted at Heraclea for more than a century is the best known example, apart from those of Bosporus and Syracuse, of the late Greek tyrannies and *dynasteiai* so widely prevalent in Asia Minor, of which I have already spoken. It will be sufficient to observe that although surrounded by dangers and its very existence threatened by the Galatians and by its ambitious neighbours, the kings of Bithynia and Pontus, Heraclea was able to maintain its liberty until the time of the second Mithridatic war.[352]

I have already referred to the active part taken by Heraclea, as an independent power, in the events of the troublous times that followed the death of Alexander, mostly in alliance with other cities of the same type, which were prepared to fight for their independence. It was able repeatedly to help its allies with strong naval squadrons, to send them grain in large quantities and to pay large sums to the Galatians.[353] Its relations with the Crimea, especially with Chersonesus, were as close as in the fourth century, and its commercial links with the Hellenistic world are well known.[354]

Amisus. Less is known about Amisus and Sinope. Amisus was annexed by the Mithridatids at an early date in their history, Sinope almost a century later. Both were large and powerful cities with fertile territories, whose inhabitants had the reputation of being skilful and progressive farmers.

Neither city has been systematically excavated. Some excavations have been recently made in the necropolis of Amisus and at Kara-Samsun by Macridy Bey, and they produced a large number of various objects. Unfortunately the results have not been published. Moreover the necropoleis of both Amisus and Sinope have been for a long time ransacked by native diggers and dealers of antiquities. These 'cities of the dead' are very imposing. Their aspect is very like that of the necropolis of Panticapaeum, with its monumental tumuli, rock-carved tombs, and tombs dug in the soil.

It is worth mentioning that in the Hellenistic period Amisus and probably Sinope were important centres of the ceramic industry. The Sinopic jars have already been referred to (ch. II, p. 108, n. 43). The Amisene pottery, found especially at Kara-Samsun, presents special features. It reflects the mixed character of the civilization of the city and of Pontus in general. On the one hand, we have a local pottery, a particular type of painted vessels of various kinds. Their shapes and ornamentation go back partly to proto-historic Anatolian originals, partly to products of Iranian plastic and ceramic art, with a slight admixture of Hellenistic elements. The terracottas, which are essentially Greek, show a peculiar style fundamentally different from that of the terracottas of Myrina and Cyme. They may be compared to some of the products of contemporary Pergamene plastic art.

Of the trade of the city little is known. Relations with Athens are well attested by the funeral inscriptions of Amisenes who died there. I shall speak in a later chapter of the role played by Amisenes in the life of the Pontic kingdom and in its commerce with the Aegean in the time of Mithridates the Great.[355]

Sinope. Sinope was more important in commerce and wealthier than Amisus. In addition to agricultural resources the Sinopians possessed extensive and profitable fisheries. The range of their trade relations had not contracted: with the Bosporan kingdom, for example, they were as intimate as they had been in the past.* The same is true of the trade between Sinope and the Aegean.

These relations with the Hellenistic world are sufficiently illustrated by the well-known story of the conveyance of the statue of Sarapis to Alexandria at the request of Ptolemy Soter. In the version of the story given by Athenodorus the Tarsian† it was Philadelphus, not Soter, who received the statue from the Sinopians as a present (χαριστήριον) in return for grain sent by him to the city in time of famine. Even if invented, the story testifies to the active relations between Alexandria and Sinope. I have mentioned that the products of Sinope, for instance Pontic nuts, were very popular in

* See, e.g., Diod. xx. 25.

† Clem. Alex. *Protrept.* iv. 48, 2, p. 14 Sylb.; p. 78 Stäh.; *F.H.G.* iii. 487, frg. 4.

Alexandria and the rest of Egypt in the third century B.C. It may also be observed that the route between the Black Sea and Alexandria was well known to Alexandrian and Sinopian sailors.* Not less active were the trade relations between Sinope and Rhodes. We shall see in the next chapter how Rhodes twice—in 220 B.C. and again in 218 B.C.—tried to defend the political freedom of Sinope. This implies that at that time commercial relations between the two cities had already been long established.[356]

Cities of the Thracian coast. Our information regarding the cities of the western coast is even more defective.[357] I may, however, recall the heroic struggle of Callatis, the leading city of this coast, against Lysimachus, in which it had as allies its sister cities on the western coast, and was supported by the Bosporan ruler Eumelus.† I may also mention the conflict of interests that arose between Callatis (supported by Istrus) and Tomi.‡ The period of decay and misery had not yet come for the Greek cities of the Thracian coast of the Euxine, notwithstanding the havoc wrought by the Celts, from which they certainly suffered no less than did the rich city of Olbia at the mouth of the Hypanis (Bug).[358] It is perhaps needless to refer in this connexion to a beautiful and well-known inscription from Olbia, a decree of the city in honour of its benefactor, Protogenes, which gives a vivid picture of the hardships endured by the city during the chaos produced by the Celtic invasion of the steppes of southern Russia.§ The information is supplemented by certain other inscriptions from Olbia. It is perhaps the result of accident that there are no similar documents of the period relating to the cities of the Thracian coast.

Bosporan kingdom. The Celtic wave did not reach the great and remote Bosporan kingdom. I cannot here dwell at length on the peculiar history and the political, social, and economic structure of this powerful Greek State. Situated in the Crimea and the Taman peninsula, it included many Greek cities and a large and ever-increasing territory, and resembled the States of Heraclea, Cyzicus, and Byzantium, but it was on a much

* See note 354.
† Diod. xix. 73, cf. xx. 25.
‡ Memnon 21.
§ *S.I.G.*[3] 495.

larger scale and had much greater stability. It played a memorable part in the history of the South Russian steppes, where the Scythians created a vast and solid empire in the early period of the existence of the Bosporan kingdom.

The period in which the Bosporan State attained its greatest expansion, prosperity, and stability was the late fifth and the early and middle fourth century B.C., when it was ruled by strong and able archons (styled 'tyrants' at Athens), Satyrus I (433–389), Leucon (389–349), Spartocus II (349–344) and Paerisades I (349–310). It was in this period that the foundations of its political, social, and economic system were laid.

At this time the Bosporan kingdom took no active part in the political life of the rest of the Greek world, in its continuous wars. It was satisfied with the assertion of its liberty and independence against Athens. But, while keeping aloof from the politics of the Aegean and confining their interest to the Euxine, the early Spartocids never disregarded the Aegean world, but kept themselves well informed of what was happening there, for on this their prosperity depended to a large extent. Their diplomacy was always active, and they sought by diplomatic means to achieve their own ends. These ends were not of a political nature: it was the Greek economic system, not the political, of which they desired to become established members. And they reached their goal. Their reputation was very high in Greece, especially in Athens, and they became very popular even with the masses of the Greek population. This reputation and popularity were due to the important role that Bosporus played in the economic life of Greece, of which I have already spoken (pp. 105 ff.). The Spartocids were large exporters of various goods, particularly foodstuffs. These foodstuffs (grain, fish, and cattle) were partly the produce of their own territory, the fertile lands in the Crimea and in the Taman peninsula. The estates which they owned in these regions and the landed properties and holdings of the Greek residents in the Bosporan cities were tilled by native *laoi*, bondsmen or serfs, who also tended their cattle and horses. Still more important, however, were their re-exports. These consisted of merchandise received from their powerful neighbours and nominal suzerains, the Scythian kings, in exchange for the agricultural and industrial products of their own country and for goods received by them from the Hellenic world.

As great landholders and even more as active wholesale dealers, the Spartocids became very rich. Their wealth is reflected in the splendid development of their cities and, above all, in the contents of the monumental royal tombs near Panticapaeum and of the more modest graves of their subjects, the citizens of the many cities in the Bosporan State. Their commercial activity and the volume and importance of their trade are proved by the fabulous riches found in the graves of their chief customers, the Scythian kings and nobles, which lie scattered over the whole Scythian Empire and many of which have been excavated by Russian archaeologists. Of these two groups of graves I have spoken in an earlier chapter (Ch. II, pp. 108 and 110), where I have shown that the beautiful and costly objects of gold, silver, and bronze, the pottery, the textiles, and the jars full of wine and olive oil that have been found in them were to a large extent imported from Greece, but came partly from the stores of the Bosporan landlords and from the shops of the skilful artists and artisans of the Bosporan cities.[359]

Such was the position of the Bosporan kingdom in the fifth century B.C. and in the early and middle fourth. At the end of the fourth century and in the first half of the third the political situation changed. At the time of Alexander's conquests in the East large hordes of Iranians began to move from Russian Turkestan northward and westward. The Greek writers call them Sacae and Sarmatae. These hordes began to press on the Scythians of the South Russian steppes and pushed them westward across the great Russian rivers towards the Danube and southward to the Crimea. The Scythian kingdom began to disintegrate. The troubled political conditions in the steppes of South Russia became still more disturbed owing to the great Celtic movement which I have described (pp. 25 ff.). I have shown that this Celtic wave reached the region of the Dnieper and caused distress and bewilderment in Olbia.[360]

The Bosporan kingdom was naturally affected by these events. Paerisades I and his successors Eumelus (310–304) and

Spartocus III (304–284) lived in difficult times: foreign wars, mostly with the Scythians of the Crimea, and dynastic troubles were of frequent occurrence. With Paerisades II (284–250) the troubles apparently came to an end and conditions became more or less stabilized.

It is no wonder therefore that Bosporan prosperity and prestige were not so high as in the previous period. And yet the situation in the kingdom was much better than in Olbia, as is shown by the little we know of its political life. The Spartocids of the late fourth and early third century were able successfully to carry on the policy of their ancestors. They kept their political independence intact and continued to confine their interest to the Black Sea. Paerisades I not only defended his kingdom but probably also enlarged it by successful wars with the Scythians of the Crimea. Eumelus, who figures prominently in the historical tradition of the time, felt strong enough to indulge in ambitious plans for the creation of a vast Pontic empire. He even crossed swords with Lysimachus, but only to safeguard Pontic interests. Finally, Spartocus III renewed the old friendly relations between his kingdom and Athens.*

The policy of the Spartocids of the third century towards the Hellenistic world was the same as that of their ancestors towards the Hellenic States. The Bosporan kingdom continued to be isolated from the rest of the Greek world. The Spartocids of the third century took no part in the ceaseless wars of the Successors and of the later kings, and they never had any intention of doing so. In return the Hellenistic kings made no attempt to add the Bosporan kingdom to their own domains. Even Lysimachus, when forming his Thracian empire, had no thought of including Bosporus and its territory in it. And the same is true of the other Successors and of their descendants—Antigonus Gonatas and the Antigonids, the Seleucids, the Ptolemies and the early Pergamene rulers. We never hear of these rulers even trying to obtain help from this quarter in their long and destructive wars.

In order to place themselves on a footing of equality with their contemporaries, the Spartocids reorganized their State on Hellenistic lines, so far as externals were concerned. They

* *S.I.G.*[3], 370.

assumed, for instance, the title of king: Eumelus was perhaps the first to do so.

Our information regarding the commercial relations of the Spartocids in the third century is very defective, but such knowledge as we have shows that the economic foundations of their kingdom were solid and sound. Bosporus apparently continued to be, though of course on a somewhat reduced scale, what it had been before, a great exporter of corn and other merchandise to the Aegean world. As in the past, it played an important part in the economic life of the Aegean. This may be inferred from some scattered pieces of evidence. The relations between Rhodes and Delos and the Bosporus, especially under Paerisades II, have already been mentioned (p. 232). The commercial and political importance of the Bosporan kingdom is also attested by a document in Zenon's correspondence,* which speaks of envoys of Paerisades II going to Alexandria to see Philadelphus, apparently on a diplomatic mission. We are consequently not astonished to find at Alexandria not only ambassadors of the kings but also some of their subjects, as well as some Greeks from Chersonesus and Olbia.

The archaeological material is in accord with what has been said. I have mentioned the abundance of Rhodian, Thasian, and other stamped jar handles in Panticapaeum. I may add that, although no royal or richly furnished monumental tombs of private persons in Panticapaeum and other Bosporan cities can be assigned with certainty to the first half of the third century B.C., finds of early Hellenistic date are frequent in the ruins and in some graves of the Bosporan cities, for example choice pieces of the various kinds of early Hellenistic pottery. Mention may also be made of notable products of Athenian potters, some beautiful relief vases of Pergamene make, and fine early *lagynoi*. At a very early date the Panticapaeans began to compete with imported foreign pottery by producing large quantities of their own ceramic wares, for example, the above-mentioned water-colour vases and a very fine set of Megarian bowls (above, p. 108 f., and pl. LXVIII, 2).

* H. I. Bell, *Symb. Osl.* v (1927), p. 33, and my article in *J.E.A.* xiv (1928), p. 13.

The unsettled conditions in the steppes of South Russia naturally affected the regularity and stability of the Bosporan trade. The supplies of foodstuffs at the disposal of the Bosporan kings were no longer so abundant and so regular as they had been. But we must avoid exaggeration. Even our meagre historical evidence makes it certain that the Bosporan kingdom experienced no territorial losses in the third century B.C. The Spartocids were able to hold their own in the Crimea against the Scythians, who were retreating before the Sacians and Sarmatians, and also in the Taman peninsula, into which the new invaders of South Russia apparently never intended to penetrate. The produce of this territory, which of course varied in quantity, was therefore still in the hands of the Bosporan kings.

Moreover, the disintegration of the Scythian Empire was a slow and gradual process. It has just been said that one group of Scythians retreated and entrenched themselves in the Crimea, which became their permanent abode. Another group found refuge in the Dobrudja. Nevertheless even in the steppes between the Dnieper and the Bug the Scythians still claimed to be overlords as late as the date of the Protogenes inscription, which cannot be earlier than the time of the great Celtic invasion. The name of king Saitapharnes is well known. The Scythians therefore, especially those in the Crimea, still had much to sell to the Bosporan merchants and made many purchases from them, although the volume of their trade was smaller than before.

These general considerations would find support in archaeological finds, if it were certain that some at least of the royal Scythian tombs of the south Russian steppes belong to the early third century, and are not to be dated earlier. Their date, however, is disputed and cannot be discussed here.[361]

In those parts of the Scythian kingdom that were occupied by the hordes of Sacae and Sarmatae the new overlords naturally inherited the Scythian relations with the native population and the Bosporan kings. They became automatically lords and masters of the natives settled in these regions, who made their living by tilling the soil, fishing, and tending

PLATE LXVIII

1. Triangular gold plaque which adorned the front of a ritual tiara. Found in the queen's grave of the tumulus of Karagodeuashkh in the Kuban region (South Russia). It was probably part of the ritual dress of the queen, as priestess of the Great Goddess. The plaque is adorned with three zones of figures in repoussé work. On the lowest is shown the Great Goddess seated on a throne, clad in a heavy ceremonial garment and wearing a pointed tiara with a gold triangular plaque in front. Behind her are two priestesses with veiled heads. A young man in Iranian (Scythian or Sacian) dress, no doubt a prince, approaches the goddess on the right, and she offers him the holy communion in a rhyton. On the other side a strange figure of a beardless man clad in woman's dress advances towards the goddess with a round vase in his right hand, containing apparently a sacred beverage, probably a eunuch priest of the kind mentioned by Herodotus. Above the communion scene is a figure of a god in a chariot, probably the great Iranian Sun God. Lastly in the uppermost row is a figure of a Greek Tyche, probably the Iranian Hvareno.

On the tumulus of Karagodeuashkh, its date, and the objects found in it see my *Skythien und der Bosporus*, pp. 323 ff. (with bibliography), cf. K. Schefold 'Der skythische Tierstil in Südrussland', *Eur. Sept. Ant.* xii (1938), p. 21; and on the interpretation of the plaque my article 'The idea of Royal Power in Scythia and on the Bosporus', *Bull. Comm. Arch.* xlix (1913), pp. 1 ff., and addenda, ibid.; *Rev. É. G.* xxxii (1919), pp. 462 ff.; *Iranians and Greeks*, pp. 104 f. and 231, n. 10; cf. some other contributions quoted in *Skythien und der Bosporus*, loc. cit.

I reproduce this interesting object because it shows the changed conditions of life in the steppes of South Russia in the early Hellenistic period, the rise under Greek influence of a local art not confined to the animal style, but dealing with religious subjects, perhaps under the influence of a new wave of Iranian tribes which moved into South Russia—the Sacae. Photograph supplied by the former Archaeological Commission, Hermitage, Leningrad.

2. One of the Megarian bowls found in South Russia. It is decorated with figures of divinities (statues and Cupids), garlands, dolphins, etc. A detailed description would take too much space. Its importance in connexion with the subject of this book is that we find on the bottom of this and other similar bowls the factory stamp: ΚΙΡ-ΒΕΙ surrounding the bust of a city Tyche in profile. It has been remarked that since the genitive in -ει of names ending in -εις is typical of South Russia the potter Kirbeis must have been a resident at Olbia or Panticapaeum. This makes it certain that while they imported some Megarian bowls, the Greek cities of South Russia gradually became centres of production of this type of pottery.

R. Zahn, *J.D.A.I.*, xxiii (1908), pp. 45 ff., esp. pp. 55 ff., nos. 8, 9, figs. 14–16; E. H. Minns, *Scythians and Greeks*, pp. 350 and 364; C. W. Lunsingh Scheurleer, *Grieksche Ceramiek*, 1936, p. 165.

Drawing by Prof. E. Mahler.

3. Two fine specimens of cast or cut glass vases reproducing metal vases, mounted in gold inlaid with precious stones and with pendants of precious stones, found in South Russia in the Kuban district. See my *Iranians and Greeks*, p. 127, and this chapter, pp. 370 f. and notes 164 and 312, cf. pl. XLIII, 1. Reproduced from my *Iranians and Greeks in South Russia*, fig. 16, nos. 1 and 2.

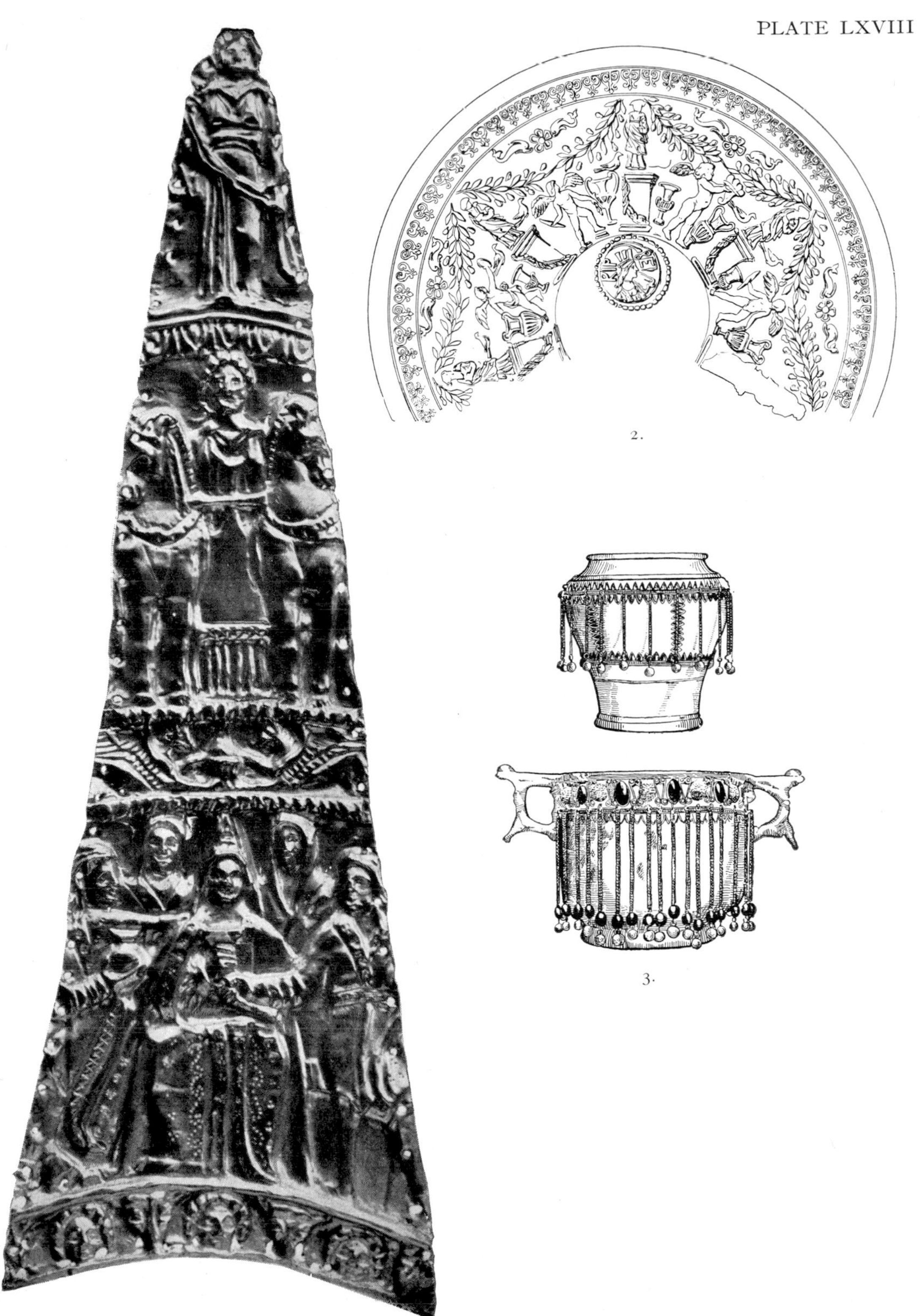

2.

3.

1.

South Russia in Hellenistic Times

Leningrad, Hermitage

cattle, sheep, and horses. Like their Scythian predecessors, they collected their rents and disposed of the surplus produce to the Bosporan merchants.

These new rulers of South Russia were in no way poorer than their Scythian predecessors. Some of their tombs have been excavated, for example those under the tumulus of Alexandropol with their fabulously rich furnishings, probably the graves of a Sacian king and his family. Some scattered finds in the Kuban district and in the neighbourhood of Vorónej show that Alexandropol is no exception. Similar opulence is indicated by the early Sarmatian graves from which probably came the two beautiful belts found, one in Maikop on the Kuban river, the other in Bulgaria. It may perhaps be suggested that the splendid tomb at Karagodeuashkh should be regarded as a connecting link between Scythian and Sarmatian royal graves, being not entirely Scythian nor yet purely Sarmatian, and in this respect resembling those under the tumulus of Alexandropol.[362]

Thus the Bosporan merchants still had large quantities of merchandise to export to the Aegean world. They were therefore still able to import from Greece and the Near East wine and industrial products for themselves and for their old and new customers in the steppes. The artists and artisans of the Bosporan cities continued to work not only for the population of the Bosporan kingdom but also for the rulers of the steppes. They certainly had to adapt themselves to the tastes and fashions of the Sacians and Sarmatians, but they succeeded in this, as is shown by the above-mentioned finds, so little known and so little studied, that have been made in Sacian and Sarmatian graves.

Taken as a whole, the evidence shows that in the third century, despite political vicissitudes, Bosporus remained, on a smaller scale, what it had been in the preceding century. Its prosperity is reflected by its coinage. The beautiful gold and silver coins of the fourth century and the early third, which represent the acme of Panticapaean artistic achievement, continued to be minted. Some time in the third century the gold staters of the old type were gradually replaced by a new royal gold coinage, which was an imitation of that of Lysimachus and bore the name of Paerisades instead of that of Panticapaeum and a portrait head in place of the gods and badges of the city. The style of these coins is much inferior to that of the earlier Bosporan series, and it is hardly possible that it was Paerisades II who first issued them (pl. LXXIX, 2).

PRINTED IN GREAT BRITAIN
AT THE UNIVERSITY PRESS, OXFORD
BY VIVIAN RIDLER
PRINTER TO THE UNIVERSITY